HAROLD PRINCE

A Director's Journey

Harold Prince, 1982
(Photo © Martha Swope)

HAROLD PRINCE

A Director's Journey

BY
CAROL ILSON

WITH A FOREWORD BY
SHELDON HARNICK

Limelight Editions
New York

Harold Prince: A Director's Journey
First Limelight Edition, October 2000

Copyright © 1989, 1992, 2000 Carol Ilson

Harold Prince: From Pajama Game *to* Phantom of the Opera *and Beyond,*
published in 1992.

Cover photo of Harold Prince © Catherine Ashmore

Library of Congress Cataloging-in-Publication Data

Ilson, Carol.
    Harold Prince: A director's journey / by Carol Ilson : with a foreword by
Sheldon Harnick.—2nd Limelight ed.
        p. cm.
    Includes bibliographical references and index.
    ISBN 0-87910-296-9

    1. Prince, Harold, 1928 - . 2. Theatrical producers and
directors—United States—Biography. I. Title

PN2287.P73I47 2000
792'.6'023'092—dc21
[B]   00-032747

This book is for my family

Bernie
David, Elyse
Jimmy, Rhonda
Emily, Jesse, Sadie, and Samuel

with love

CONTENTS

FOREWORD

For anyone interested in the American musical (which for much of its life has been synonymous with the Broadway musical), this book is a treasure trove. I confess that when I began to read it, I was afraid it was going to be no more nor less than a kind of "fact book" of the various productions which Hal Prince had either produced, directed, or both. But through Carol Ilson's carefully researched, step-by-step description of Hal's career in the theatre, gradually a compelling three-dimensional portrait began to emerge of Hal both as a man and as a remarkable theatre artist. All the more remarkable, since Ms. Ilson has scrupulously avoided gossipy (and irrelevant) "show-biz" anecdotes about his personal life.

All too often, when I have read books which touched upon theatrical events in which I have been involved, I have been saddened (or exasperated) to find numerous errors of fact, misquotations and other kinds of inaccuracies which seriously undermined the author's credibility. To Ms. Ilson's credit, in every episode dealing with a show for which I provided the lyrics, her account of what transpired squares with my own recollections. Consequently, as I read about those productions in which I was not a participant, it was reassuring to be able to read, not with a skeptically lifted eyebrow, but with confidence in the integrity of her accounts. Incidentally, unlike those books about the theatre in which the reader has a privileged sense of being taken "backstage," there are moments when Ms. Ilson manages to give us the sense that we are actually onstage with Hal, smack in the middle of a rehearsal, complete with illuminating (and sometimes surprising) descriptions of his directorial rehearsal techniques.

Even though I've worked with Hal and followed his career through the years, I didn't realize until I read this comprehensive account of his theatrical adventures that his career is, in truth, the history of the development of the musical theatre over the past thirty-five years. Among other developments, one watches with fascination and trepidation as the costs of production slowly mount from production to production, with the inevitability of the events in a Greek tragedy (and I use the term advisedly), until they have risen from the manageable costs of a *Pajama Game* to the monumental costs of a *Phantom of the Opera*. (Knowing what the situation is on Broadway today, as I read her objective description of the gradual but seemingly inexorable rise of production costs, I found myself wanting to shout back through time: "Stop! Hold the line now, now before it's too late!")

To accompany Hal Prince through his achievements (and mis-steps) is to experience the tremendous changes which have occurred in this widely popular but genuinely endangered art form. For me the book was deeply disturbing but, ultimately, exhilarating as well. Oddly enough, I feel better equipped to deal with my own difficulties in today's musical theatre for having read it.

Sheldon Harnick

PREFACE

This book was originally published in 1989 as *Harold Prince: from* Pajama Game *to* Phantom of the Opera, then expanded in 1992. Since then, Harold Prince has directed six productions, among them, *Kiss of the Spider Woman* (Tony Award for Best Musical), *Show Boat,* which included many songs written in 1927 but never performed before this revival (Tony Award for Best Musical Revival), and *Parade* (Tonys for Best Book, Lyrics, and Score). This version of the book includes additional chapters that include Prince's work from 1992 through 1999, and was such a substantial expansion on the earlier book, that I felt it warranted a new subtitle: one that more accurately reflects the scope of its coverage.

In addition to the productions cited above, I have included the transcript of a major keynote address delivered by Harold Prince to the League of American Producers and Theatre Owners in New Orleans on 12 November 1999 and the question-and-answer session that followed.

C. I.
January 2000

ACKNOWLEDGMENTS

I would like to express my deepest appreciation to Dr. Stanley Waren, professor emeritus of theatre at the CUNY Graduate Center, Dr. Edwin Wilson of Hunter College and the CUNY Graduate Center and theatre critic for the *Wall Street Journal;* and Dr. Margaret M. Knapp. In addition to their invaluable and astute criticism and patient editorial assistance, they offered an immeasurable degree of personal support for which I will always be grateful.

Much of my research was done at the Billy Rose Theatre Collection, New York Public Library at Lincoln Center, Astor, Lenox and Tilden Foundations, and I am appreciative of the help of Daniel C. Patri and Dr. Roderick Bladel of the library staff. I am particularly indebted to the Theatre on Film and Tape Archives at the Lincoln Center Library, which contains many videotapes of interviews with Harold Prince, Stephen Sondheim and Boris Aronson, as well as videotapes of some of the Prince shows. Richard Ryan and the staff gave appreciated assistance in enabling me to view these valuable tapes. I am also grateful to Donald Madison of the Department of Photographic Services at the Lincoln Center Library for his help.

I want to thank the following authors and their publishers for permission to use portions of their books: Craig Zadan, *Sondheim & Co.* [Harper & Row]; Martin Gottfried, *Broadway Musical* [Harry N. Abrams, Inc.]; Harold Prince, *Contradictions: Notes on Twenty-Six Years in the Theatre* [Dodd, Mead & Co.]; and Richard Altman and Mervyn Kaufman, *The Making of a Musical: "Fiddler on the Roof"* [Curtis Brown, Ltd.]. I also want to express my thanks to the many theatre critics from whose reviews I have quoted. My appreciation goes to Otis L. Guernsey, Jr., editor of *The Dramatists Guild Quarterly,* for permission to use excerpts from various segments of their "Landmark Series." For their assistance with photographs used, I wish to express special thanks to Martha Swope of Martha Swope Photography, Inc., Ron Mandelbaum of Photofest, Clive Barda and Woodfin Camp of Woodfin Camp & Associates, and the Lincoln Center Library.

I wish to extend my gratitude to all my colleagues and friends who offered encouragement, helpful material, clippings and out-of-town reviews of Prince shows to aid me in my work. Their thoughtfulness is appreciated. A special group of close friends have been extraordinary in their support of this project and I wish to extend my deepest appreciation to them. Dr. Frederick Kessler and Joan Kessler suggested I use a computer for my work, and Dr. Kessler spent many hours teaching me the word-processing system, which proved to be invaluable. Additionally, he was always there to help me through the inevitable crisis due to mechanical breakdown. William and Janet Schmitt have also been consistently encouraging of my work from the inception of the project and I am indebted to them for their support.

I want to thank all the people I interviewed for this project. The many librettists, lyricists, composer, designers, actors, actresses, directors and others associated with the theatre gave unstintingly of their time to supply me with valuable first-hand information. They are all listed in the bibliography.

Very special thanks go to George McMillin for his enormous assistance. His intensive and devoted work on typing and helping with editing problems was invaluable and his professional approach, expertise in his work and enthusiasm for this project made my working relationship with him a great pleasure. Noelle Sterne assisted me in the organization of the footnotes and bibliography and I wish to thank her also.

I would also like to give thanks to playwright David Wolf, for his painstaking proofreading of the manuscript.

I wish to also extend my gratitude to Oscar Brockett, general editor of UMI Research Press's series in Theatre and Dramatic Studies, for his supportive and enthusiastic comment on my work, and to Christine Hammes and Marilyn Meeker, for their help, friendship and enthusiasm.

I want to thank Stephen Sondheim for his interest in the book and for his valuable suggestions.

I'd like to acknowledge the kind assistance I received from the staff of the Harold Prince office, particularly the late Howard Haines, who was a key person in helping to get this project started. I'd also like to express my gratitude to Arlene Caruso, secretary to Harold Prince, and to Brad Rouse, for their help.

I am especially grateful to Harold Prince, who was most generous in giving me many hours of his time, talking to me about his work and answering my questions. His kindness to me has been exceptionally encouraging and his interest in the project has been invaluable.

Lastly, I want to express my most heartfelt appreciation to my wonderful family, whose understanding and love have made it all possible.

PROLOGUE

One of the most controversial and creative forces on the Broadway scene is Hal Prince, the producer-director known for being daring, innovative, successful.

In the 1950s, 1960s and into the 1970s, a Prince show meant money in the bank. Backers flocked to invest in his shows, and they were rewarded with a cascade of profits. *Fiddler on the Roof, West Side Story* and *Fiorello!* were hits that made a host of Prince angels sing the praises of his magic touch. In the late 1970s and into the mid-1980s, however, the string of Hal Prince hits was replaced by a series of flops.

After the international success of *Evita,* Prince stumbled by directing *Merrily We Roll Along, A Doll's Life, Play Memory, End of the World, Grind,* and *Roza.* Critics and theatre columnists began to write about Prince's failures as if they were signs of terminal illness. Some wondered aloud if Prince had "lost his golden touch." Investors no longer rushed to back his shows, and the accolades of the press began to go to a new group of successful directors and producers. The parade appeared to be passing by the Prince of Broadway.

But Prince is not one to accept defeat and quietly retire to his mountaintop home in Majorca. Soon after *Grind* had closed, Prince was busily preparing *Phantom of the Opera,* a show that was to have a major impact on the London and New York theatre scenes. He and his *Evita* collaborator, Andrew Lloyd Webber, mounted a new musical production of *The Phantom of the Opera,* which became the hottest new ticket in the West End and on Broadway. It won the Laurence Olivier Award for best musical of

London's 1986–87 theatre season. It opened in New York in February 1988 to the largest advanced sales in the history of the theatre—anywhere. Prince was also directing at the same time a new production of his 1966 hit *Cabaret*, which had a seven-month run in New York. Risen phoenixlike from theatrical limbo, Prince was being widely acclaimed once again for his directing talents and for being able to whip not-very-strong musical and book elements into stunning theatrical spectacle. *Phantom* received grudging praise from New York theatre critics based mainly on Prince's skill at bringing music, story, actors, scenery, movement, lighting and modern stage technology into cohesion. Hal Prince had made a comeback at least as sensational if not more so than the triumphs of his earlier years.

There is little doubt that Prince is an unrepentant "workaholic" who is happiest when he is involved with half a dozen projects. He must have an outlet for the energy and drive that have made him so successful. The pursuit of money for money's sake has never been his main motivation. He could have played it safe and pandered to the public's taste by producing tuneful, tasteless extravaganzas as many other Broadway producers have. Instead, Prince chose the largely untrod road of innovation and dared to be different. He stretched the Broadway form to its limits and is credited with introducing the "concept musical." His productions of *Company, Follies* and *Evita* brought unusual subjects, themes and stage design to Broadway and won the acclaim of critics and playgoers.

His collaborators have been the most creative artists of the late twentieth-century theatre. Jerome Robbins, Stephen Sondheim, Michael Bennett, Boris Aronson, Bock and Harnick, Kander and Ebb and other giants of Broadway were his confreres.

Prince has rarely employed stars to carry his shows. As his mentor George Abbott had done for decades, Prince has cast exciting newcomers and passed-over stars instead of the "safe" box office superstars of the contemporary theatre world. He's never done a show in which the "star" was more important than the book, music and lyrics. He's never sought to star an Ethel Merman or a Mary Martin. Instead, he's used—and brilliantly—talented newcomers such as Barbara Cook, Patti LuPone and Mandy Patinkin. Most of the talented principals in *Company* had never before appeared on Broadway.

The real stars of Prince shows are the elements. It was the great music of Kander and Ebb in *Cabaret* or of Sondheim in *Follies, Company* and *Sweeney Todd* that broke new ground in musical theatre. The visionary talents of set designer Boris Aronson and the whirlwind staging and choreographic energies of Michael Bennett were given full rein in Prince-produced or -directed shows.

But the music, the performers, the stage settings, the choreography of Hal Prince shows are not the only "star" elements, for Hal Prince, himself, is a star—perhaps the first "star" producer-director in Broadway musical history.

1

BROADWAY NOVICE MEETS
BROADWAY LEGEND:
HAROLD PRINCE & GEORGE ABBOTT

Harold Smith Prince was born in New York City on 30 January 1928, "the only child of a privileged upper-middle, lower-rich class, Jewish family, which settled here soon after the Civil War."[1]

> My stepfather raised me and he was a sweet man who was in Wall Street . . . a little shy and austere, but a kind, good man. My own father lived to a ripe old age, but I rarely saw him. . . . I didn't like him. My mother I loved dearly. I had a "mademoiselle" who raised me until I was nine years old. My parents would go to Europe and I to the Catskills, to an all French resort called Chalet Indien. Everyone spoke French and the kids—no matter how young—drank a little red wine with water at every meal. I told the rosary and went to church every Sunday. . . . A nice Jewish family with a nice Catholic boy until I was nine. Then they told the "mademoiselle" to leave. The Depression had come and hit us and we were living not as well as we had been, so I ceased telling the beads and they ceased hanging on the bedpost.[2]

From his stepfather, a Wall Street stockbroker, Prince may have developed his business acumen; from his mother, who was an avid theatregoer, his enthusiasm for the stage. His parents did not attempt to persuade Prince to embark on a career either in finance or in theatre. Prince, however, admits he fantasized about a life in theatre. He wanted to be a playwright. He explains, "I'm a real snob. I think writing is the highest of the arts, but I don't cut it well enough. So I've taken second best."[3] In an interview with *Newsweek* magazine in 1971, Prince recalled, "When I was thirteen I daydreamed that one day I'd have an office in Rockefeller Center in which I wrote and directed plays."⁴ Except for his desire to become a playwright, Prince has realized his ambitions. As for becoming a producer first, he claims he did that to get into directing. "I didn't enjoy producing much; it's frustrating."⁵

Exposed to theatregoing as a young boy, Prince looked forward to attending Saturday matinees and sitting in the top balcony of the Empire Theatre where he watched the great actors and actresses of the day. The first play he saw was a Mercury Theatre production of *Julius Caesar* starring the 21-year-old Orson Welles. Ironically, Prince was not particularly interested in musicals as a child, a lack of interest that prevailed until later in his life. He did, however, like to play with a cardboard theatre model, using toy soldiers as his actors when he was a child. Prince says, "I was addicted early on."⁶ Prince dates his obsessive drive for theatre to an experience he had when he was entering adolescence and which he feels may have influenced his future theatre work:

> When I was fourteen and a half or fifteen, I had a nervous breakdown. It was a bummer and real serious. It lasted (the darkest and most painful part) a summer in New York ... probably three months. I didn't sleep. They tell me you do sleep, but I wasn't aware that I slept. I thought I was going mad (if I hadn't already gone mad). A lot of my earlier behavior filtered through that. In other words, I used to conjure up theatrical events ... collaborations. ... I used to imagine there were people I was going to do a show with ... people I'd seen on the stage. ... I was directing ... we were all friends ... I did it all. Now suddenly when I came to this crunch all that behavior seemed insane, and scared the hell out of me, 'cause you start thinking you're never going to come back from that place. I came back a little bit each day. One night my father, who had seen that I couldn't sleep and knew I was in extreme stasis, said, "Don't try to sleep. Keep your clothes on tonight and sit by that standing lamp and read." And of course I went to sleep for the first time and that was a big breakthrough. Then it just started to go away and one of the things you do (and I've heard artists say this) is out of that you create the person you want to be. It was terrible. I remember it, but I don't live in fear of it ever returning.⁷

In 1944 Prince graduated from Franklin School, a private preparatory school on Manhattan's West Side, where a grandfather had been educated. He attended the University of Pennsylvania and became an active member of the Penn Players. He wrote, acted and directed. In addition, he founded and managed the campus radio station, writing and directing and sometimes acting in weekly play adaptations.

At college he enrolled in a liberal arts program concentrating on English, psychology, philosophy and history. The latter is still his favorite subject. He also enjoyed reading plays. "I went to college when I was barely sixteen and finished when I was still nineteen. Too fast, I think, but to compensate I came to appreciate that I had gotten the beat on my peers. I was working for George Abbott when I was twenty."[8] (He bested his University of Pennsylvania peers in another way, too: the university has named a theatre on campus after him!)

After graduating in 1948, he tried to write plays, sending them to producers in New York. "I was shy and as silent as I am presently loquacious, so I fooled myself into thinking I was 'making the rounds' by writing plays and having them make the rounds instead."[9]

The head of the script department at ABC-TV read one of his plays and sent Prince for an interview to the George Abbott office where Abbott was planning a small experimental TV unit.

At the Abbott office, Prince offered to work "on spec"—for nothing—and the offer was accepted. Within two weeks, however, he was on the payroll, earning $25 a week, remaining at that salary for six months. He did odd jobs as well as writing several television scripts for the company that had been formed by Mary, Abbott's wife at that time. Abbott had backed the project financially and lent the organization his name. The company had an early success, particularly with game shows.

Prince remembers doing a little of everything for the three shows the company produced for television. One was an original musical called *The Hugh Martin Show,* written by Abbott and featuring Hugh Martin, Joan McCracken and Kaye Ballard. It was a modest show, supposedly set in Martin's living room. It appeared on NBC-TV at 7 o'clock on Sunday nights.

> Abbott wrote the first one and directed it, and then he let me write the second and direct it. He simply approved what I was doing and went away and let me do it. Soon I got into a battle with Kaye Ballard, the comedienne on the show. I was a nervous kid in those days, nervous, ambitious, apprehensive. It was irritating to observe how quickly I moved, how intensely I worked. After all, you never know when someone's watching. We clashed, and Hugh Martin, who had brought Kaye into the show and was a great friend of hers, went to Abbott and insisted I be taken off the show . . . and Abbott refused. Martin put it to Abbott: Prince or the show. Abbott chose Prince; the show went off the air. [10]

Abbott soon disbanded the television operation. The projects, which did not make money, had caused too much anxiety and hysteria in the office. Prince was certain, upon hearing the news, that he had lost his job. Robert E. Griffith, however, who was Abbott's production stage manager, had requested Prince as his assistant. Abbott was impressed with Prince's willingness to work and thought that Prince was somebody who would develop. "You couldn't help but notice his enthusiasm, his tremendous vitality," Abbott recalled. "Then I discovered how bright he was. That's a pretty good combination, enthusiasm and intelligence, so I brought him in to work with Bobby [Robert Griffith]."[11] Abbott, in an interview, summed up Prince's ability as the fledgling assistant to Griffith. "Oh, he was a smart fellow—you could tell that!"[12]

Robert E. Griffith, Abbott's stage manager, was born in Methuen, Massachusetts in 1907 and like Abbott began his theatrical career as an actor. He appeared in the original Broadway productions of *Once in a Lifetime, Dinner at Eight* and *Merrily We Roll Along,* the latter a stage play which would eventually become a musical twenty years after Griffith's death, and which would be directed by Prince. Griffith became chief stage manager for Abbott in 1935. He was associated with more than fifty productions, including *Room Service, Three Men On a Horse, Best Foot Forward, Call Me Madam* and *Where's Charley?* Prince, working as Griffith's assistant stage manager, had found a highly qualified teacher to further his training and experience.

Griffith was a shy, easygoing, introverted man, 22 years older than Prince. Despite differences in age and temperament (Prince had a more dynamic, volatile personality), the two men, working out of a small office in Rockefeller Center and backstage, became close collaborators and friends.[13]

When Griffith and Prince eventually formed their producing partnership in 1953, Griffith was called paternal and sagacious, Prince, youthful and irrepressible. Abbott explains about Griffith that "everyone liked Bobby and everyone wished him well for he had qualities of simple goodness that could be appreciated by all."[14] The fact that Griffith was a hands-on worker in the theatre won him the respect of his associates. He encouraged Prince to understand the technical areas of the theatre as well as the economics.

Gwen Verdon developed a great deal of respect for Griffith after working with him on two shows (*Damn Yankees* and *New Girl in Town*). She thought he was a "terrific" person and very calm. Verdon remembered that Griffith was the oil on troubled water. He could take care of what Mr. Abbott wanted plus keep all the actors, the choreographer and the composers content saying "We'll handle it, we'll take care of it." He could run the show at the same time—change all the cues (and every time you change a show—all the cues change), handle all the electricians, the whole crew, change certain cues, all the lights, and deal with the actors, deal with Mr. Abbott and in addition make sure all the changes in the script were typewritten.... I'm sure Hal Prince observed and learned so much from him.[15]

Prince's salary was $85 a week when he began assisting Griffith. He worked nights on the first show, a revue, *Touch and Go,* by Jean and Walter Kerr, which opened on 13 October 1949 at the Broadhurst Theatre. During the day, Prince ran the switchboard, helped with casting, delivered messages. He was the all-around helper at the Abbott office.

A new revue, *Tickets, Please,* with Paul and Grace Hartman, was having trouble in Boston, and the director was fired. Abbott was called in. He needed a stage manager to go with him to Boston. Since Griffith was in Europe at the time, Abbott asked Prince to become his first assistant stage manager. The show opened in New York on 27 April 1950 at the Coronet Theatre and ran until November of that year. During the show's run, Prince worked the show at night. During the day he wrote a play with Ted Luce, who had written most of the material for *Tickets, Please.*

Prince's dream of becoming a playwright seemed about to come true. By Thanksgiving, when *Tickets, Please* ended its run, Ted Luce and Prince had completed the comedy-murder mystery, *A Perfect Scream.* The Hartmans optioned the play and Prince joined the Dramatists Guild. However, the Hartmans soon separated, and the script was never produced.

Prince was next loaned by Abbott to Leland Hayward to cast the Irving Berlin musical *Call Me Madam.* It was understood that he would be Griffith's first assistant on the show. Now Prince began to meet more of the people who would later become important in his future endeavors. Ruth Mitchell, Hayward's stage manager for *Mr. Roberts,* would one day become one of Prince's important associates. He also met Howard Lindsay and Russel Crouse, who later become friends and devoted supporters and investors.

Prince never got to work on *Call Me Madam* as he had hoped to. He was inducted into the Army at 10 Church Street at 5:30 on the morning after the opening of the show, the reviews under his arm.

Stationed near Stuttgart, Germany, with an anti-aircraft artillery battalion, Prince spent many evenings visiting a sleazy nightclub called

Maxim's. It was 1951, and Prince was unaware that in 1966 he would rely on images of that place for *Cabaret,* a musical that he would both produce and direct.

Prince came home in October 1952. George Abbott was producing *In Any Language* with Uta Hagen and Walter Matthau, and Prince went to the opening night at the Cort Theatre where he found Abbott and Griffith a few minutes before curtain time. Abbott asked Prince, "Are you back already?" Prince said, "It's been two years." Abbott then asked him, "And when do you get out?" Prince answered, "Next week." "Well," said Abbott, "if you want to go to work come in next week. We're doing a show with Rosalind Russell based on *My Sister Eileen.*" The following week Prince was working as assistant stage manager to Griffith.[16] (*My Sister Eileen* became the very successful musical *Wonderful Town.*)

Wonderful Town resulted in Prince meeting Betty Comden and Adolph Green. The successful book and lyric writing team would one day write the musicals *On the Twentieth Century* and *A Doll's Life,* with Prince as director. Leonard Bernstein, the composer of *Wonderful Town,* would eventually write the music for *West Side Story,* which Prince would produce. Prince also met Jerome Robbins, who came to help with *Wonderful Town* while it was on the road. Even more important, Prince was busily learning the craft of creating a musical and he was learning it from a master director, George Abbott.

Wonderful Town opened on 15 February 1953 at the Winter Garden Theatre and ran more than 500 performances. During the first half of the run, Griffith and Hal Prince began seriously discussing the possibility of their becoming a producing team. They decided to give the idea a try. This new producing team was to become one of the most successful on Broadway.

Reflecting on the circumstances of Prince's early life, one would have to agree with his own assessment: that he was blessed with good fortune. He grew up in a home that encouraged his enthusiasm for the stage. He had the opportunity to attend the theatre on a regular basis and was eventually allowed to choose a life in theatre.

Prince was fortunate to have gone to work for the George Abbott office soon after his college graduation. There, as assistant stage manager to Griffith, he learned a great deal about theatre from an important "behind-the-scenes" perspective. And Griffith was "a thorough and patient teacher," said Abbott, "as well as a very good stage manager."[17]

George Abbott, as noted earlier, was a level-headed, knowledgeable and successful theatre man. He proved to be a supportive mentor and role model for his young assistant. And, when Griffith and Prince decided to join forces as a producing team, no one gave them more help and encouragement than Abbott. Indeed, Prince correctly assesses that luck and timing in his early life were important factors that led to his later successes.

Abbott is the man who introduced discipline into the creation of musical shows. Prince maintains that he developed his own organized and disciplined way of working from his apprenticeship with Abbott, as well as the concept of being truthful in his work. Prince always plans ahead and is on time for appointments and rehearsals. Prince, like Abbott, is not self-indulgent nor does he engage in histrionics. William Goldman, in *The Season,* his chronicle of a year in the life of the Broadway theatre, said of Abbott, "The man is without ego; he doesn't have it and can't take it in others."[18] Goldman goes on to say that Abbott thinks only of the show: "He never thinks, 'shall I put in a little something flashy so the critics will know I'm around?' It's the show. And you can say anything to him about the show; you can make any suggestion."[19]

Prince has discussed what he feels is the difference between his own style of directing and that of his mentor George Abbott:

> I don't think we work alike at all. I have a darker sensibility. . . . I'm political, he's not. I'm issue-oriented, he's not. He really unabashedly wants people to have a good time, and sometimes I don't give a damn. I want to stimulate them, but I don't care as much. He thinks a good show is one that runs a long time. I couldn't disagree more. . . . However, it's always stimulating to disagree with him and for him to disagree with me.[20]

Like Abbott, Prince has always liked to hire young, gifted talent for his shows—relative unknowns like Liza Minnelli in *Flora, the Red Menace* in 1965, and Patti Lupone, not long out of Juilliard Drama School, as the star of *Evita* in 1979. William Goldman thinks one reason Abbott may like to work with young talent is "so he can dominate."[21] Abbott agrees that being strong is important: "I've got to dominate. If I don't, there's not enough time."[22] Prince's long-time co-producer Ruth Mitchell says that Prince is also a strong director, having the final say in almost every creative decision.[23] Goldman calls Prince "the muscle . . . every member of that [theatre] group sees something in his head [that] he wants . . . translated to the stage . . . only 'the muscle' has a chance to be fulfilled; the others may end up rich, but they'll also end up frustrated. Everyone else's vision dies somewhere along the way."[24]

BROADWAY'S NEW PRODUCING TEAM: GRIFFITH & PRINCE

Although the blame for most of Broadway's disastrous musicals usually falls on poor direction, choreography, libretti, music, lyrics, and performances, invariably it is the producer who is at fault. If the producer does his job, which goes far beyond the raising of production capital, he will see to it that the correct people are hired and every aspect of the show is well conceived and absolutely ready to go into production. If not, he will postpone or even cancel his project. Not that certain producers actually plan to do less than their best, but in many cases their best isn't good enough.
— Craig Zadan, *Sondheim & Co.*

The Pajama Game

Griffith had read the review of a book called *7½ Cents* by Richard Bissell in the *New York Times.* He was busy producing a Ford Motor Company television show so he called Prince and asked him to read the book quickly. Prince liked what he read. By that afternoon, he had obtained the rights from Harold Matson, the author's agent.

When Griffith and Prince told George Abbott about the project, he was not very enthusiastic. "I didn't like the idea at first ... they had to sell it to me. It had a certain novelty in that there had never been a kind of romantic show about a labor union [the story told of a love affair in a factory amidst the problems between capital and labor], the least romantic thing I can think of. We just made a good story out of it.''[1] This was the first sign of Prince's unorthodox taste in his choice of subject matter. Abbott agreed to direct with the proviso that the novel be adapted by a talented playwright. Prince believes that Abbott agreed to direct the show because of his fondness for Griffith.

Every major writer, composer and lyricist they approached turned down the offer to adapt the show. Abbott, in his autobiography, *Mister Abbott,* recalls:

> I did wish to help, and I began to have interviews with several authors in the hope that some good writers would accept the assignment. Others seemed to be even more shy of the material than I was. They felt that a garment factory and a strike was too serious and controversial a subject for a jolly musical. It was after a luncheon with Abe Burrows at the Harvard Club, where I had again failed to enlist an author, that as a result of an argument with Abe I began to see a new plot development.[2]

While walking on Fifth Avenue, Abbott conceived of the title, *The Pajama Game,* and simultaneously thought about a subplot. He hurried back to his office and told Griffith and Prince that if they could get Bissell, he would collaborate with him on the book. Bissell, in the Midwest, quickly made the decision to come East with his family.

Prince has always expressed his gratitude for the support that Abbott gave the new producing team. Prince and Griffith were low on funds and Abbott allowed them to work out of his office without rent. After *The Pajama Game* opened, the producers began contributing their full share.

Abbott's contract for *The Pajama Game,* as well as subsequent Griffith and Prince shows, was more than fair. He worked for a smaller percentage of the profits and a lower royalty than younger successful directors. There was never any squabbling over billing size or position. Abbott had become a model for Prince not only as an ethical businessman but as a disciplined theatre craftsman. Abbott set the example and Prince learned and matured, gaining needed experience with each of his productions. Eventually he would become the steadying influence with collaborators.

The Pajama Game needed a composer and lyricist. Several experienced newcomers were approached but they, too, felt that the pajama factory strike idea was a poor one. Frank Loesser turned them down but he liked the idea of the show and suggested two of his protégés, Richard Adler and Jerry Ross. The young writing team was virtually new to Broadway. They

The New Producing Team of Robert E. Griffith and Harold Prince, 1954

had had a few pop song hits including "Rags to Riches," which they wrote in 1953. *The Pajama Game* would be their first complete Broadway score, although they had contributed most of the pieces to the 1953 edition of John Murray Anderson's *Almanac*. Richard Adler talked about the way he and Jerry Ross were hired for *The Pajama Game*:

> We did four numbers on "spec"—within two days I think. We came back with the four numbers and they loved them all. All of those songs remained in the show and we went on to write the rest of the score in five weeks. Among the songs that were auditioned were "Steam Heat" and "Racing with the Clock," the latter song being chosen to open the show.[3]

Jerome Robbins was the producers' first choice to do the choreography. Robbins had choreographed other Abbott shows and Abbott was anxious to work with him again. Robbins was unable to take the job but recommended Bob Fosse, another newcomer. Fosse had been a dancer in shows and in films and was trying to launch a career as a Broadway choreographer.

For Robbins this arrangement marked the beginning of his move from his usual role of choreographer into the directing arena and ultimately to the status of choreographer-director. Robbins shared co-director billing with Abbott on *The Pajama Game*. Eventually he would direct two famous landmark musicals, *West Side Story* and *Fiddler on the Roof,* both produced by Hal Prince.

With *The Pajama Game,* Fosse proved himself a gifted and imaginative choreographer, utilizing the Jack Cole jazz technique that would become a major form of theatre dance for decades. There were times, however, during rehearsals when Fosse needed help and the more experienced Robbins was called in to lend a hand.

Veteran showman Frederick Brisson became the third co-producer of *The Pajama Game*. The show was capitalized at $250,000, and the producers had a terrible time trying to raise money. There were no big stars in the cast and most of the people with the show (with the exception of Abbott) were unknown to potential backers. Prince remembers an early audition to raise money:

> George Abbott told the story exactly as it was; in other words, strikes and more strikes. In that one night we eliminated every major theatrical investor in the country and were forced to canvass people who didn't normally invest in shows. All told there were eleven auditions which is not really that many. I would tell of Romeo and Juliet in Iowa, eliminating the strike, eliminating

the pajama factory. Adler and Ross would play the score and sing, augmented by four singers from *Wonderful Town,* and Bobby and Freddie would "sell."[4]

Finally the producers managed to raise money (in small amounts) from 164 backers including members of the chorus, backstage employees, family and friends. Griffith and Prince graciously permitted the original investors to invest in later productions. Finally, it was Abbott who advanced the final $28,000 required for the show.

Rehearsals began at the Winter Garden Theatre for an anticipated opening date just one year from the time the producers had obtained the rights to Bissell's novel. Because money was tight, both Prince and Griffith worked as their own stage managers.

Richard Adler remembers that there were very few changes made during the rehearsal period.

> We did write "Hey There" in rehearsal and that was about it. We tried other numbers also. I frankly was so convinced that "Hey There" wouldn't be a hit that I kept writing other songs with which to replace "Hey There" ... because I didn't think it was commercial. That shows what an absolute moron I was. ... I thought it was "too classy" a song to make it. It turned out to be one of the biggest hits of all times. It was recorded over 500 different times and sold countless millions of records.[5]

The other hit numbers in the show were "Hernando's Hideaway" and the show-stopping dance routine "Steam Heat."

Even as a fledgling producer, Prince offered suggestions to the creative people. When Richard Adler was asked what he thought of Prince as a novice producer, he told of a wonderful suggestion Prince gave him for creating the lyrics in the chorus section of the song "7½ Cents." Prince suggested using a time sequence of minutes, hours, days, etc., which Adler then integrated into the lyrics. Adler went on to say:

> [Prince] was very young—but when he came up to me (at rehearsal or somewhere) with that suggestion, I thought, "that was pretty sharp." I sensed something there might go beyond just being another silly producer (if you'll excuse my expression) because most of them are.[6]

The show tried out in New Haven and Boston, receiving wonderful reviews. In New Haven during Holy Week—one of the traditionally bad weeks for show business—it played to full houses. Tickets were at a premium. Bissell had already made his story credible, drawing on his own work experiences in the Dubuque pajama factory owned by his family.

The Pajama Game opened in New York on 13 May 1954 at the St. James Theatre with an advance sale of only $40,000. In 1954 that amount was sufficient to run about one week. The glowing notices, however, drew a line of 400 people to the box office the next morning. Walter Kerr pointed out the wonderful "newcomers" Adler and Ross, Bob Fosse and Carol Haney. "It's a show that takes a whole barrelful of gleaming new talents, and a handful of stimulating ideas as well, and sends them tumbling in happy profusion over the footlights."[7] Brooks Atkinson felt that the tale of factory and labor problems provided an original setting for the show. He called it the "best musical of the season."[8]

The producers inaugurated a policy the day after opening which they continued with subsequent hits. They distributed a check for 20 percent of their investment to their backers along with the reviews. Prince explains this custom:

> It was simply a trick. We deliberately over-capitalized our shows so that if we had a success we could mail a check the following morning. It seemed to our investors a profit distribution, and though they knew the difference they went along happily with the feel of it. Our first shows were capitalized at $250,000, and cost under $170,000. Today, I think what we would have to raise to insure an overage. In fact, costs have so spiraled that I occasionally under-capitalize (the figures appall me) running a personal risk every time I do a new show.[9]

The producers recouped the show's investment and began to distribute profits after fourteen weeks into the run. Griffith and Prince continued their stage managing duties and saw their first production from the wings. Their weekly salaries at the beginning of the show's run were $250 for Griffith and $125 for Prince.

Prince has vivid backstage memories of the opening night of *The Pajama Game,* but because he and Griffith were stage managing, they hardly had a chance to observe the audience's reaction:

> We heard the applause. We shared the show-stoppers over the intercom system, "That went well, God, didn't that go well." And soon, when the curtain came down, we crossed the stage and embraced each other.[10]

The Pajama Game, 1954
Janis Paige confronts John Raitt as Buzz Miller looks on.
(Photo courtesy Photofest)

Within a month, Griffith left stage managing forever and saw his first producing effort from a seat in the theatre. Prince continued to stage manage for another six-and-a-half months.

The Pajama Game launched many careers. Not only did it become a stunning debut for producers Griffith and Prince, but it started Fosse as a choreographer. It established Adler and Ross, in Stanley Green's opinion, as "the brightest new songwriting team to emerge during the decade."[11] It gave Robbins his first chance to move toward directing, and Carol Haney was the "new face" on Broadway. Shirley MacLaine, who understudied Haney, went on in her place one night when the Hollywood producer Hal Wallis happened to be in the audience, which soon led her to movie stardom.

Another Broadway ritual was broken because *The Pajama Game* opened in May, just before summer, generally considered precarious. It was clear that the young Prince and his producing partner were not going to do things routinely. They would take chances on new talent, new opening dates, and most important, on subject matter that many producers rejected out of hand. As Abe Laufe said, "The idea of setting a musical comedy in a factory and developing a story that concerns a feud between labor and management seemed unusual to a great many theatregoers. *Pins and Needles* had dealt with labor problems, but it was primarily a revue emphasizing social consciousness."[12]

The Pajama Game was both risky and unique in the early fifties. It did not contain a libretto made up of the usual conventional musical comedy frippery. A sampling of musicals of the period include *Wish You Were Here,* which pictured life at a Catskills summer camp with a real swimming pool on stage; *Top Banana* with Phil Silvers, which told the story of a TV comic, settling for many old burlesque and vaudeville routines; and *Can-Can,* which concerned the legalization of can-can dancing.

Griffith and Prince in their first producing effort had chosen a show with an unusual story line and it had become a hit. Instead of becoming alienated, audiences and critics enjoyed the fine tuneful score, bright talent, exciting jazz dance numbers and Abbott's staging and dazzling pace.

Prince became the Broadway "Wunderkind" who at the age of 26 had hit the jackpot with his first project. He was at the time the youngest producer on Broadway.

Richard Bissell later wrote a novel, *Say Darling,* based on his experiences with the show. Since Bissell had worked closely with the producers, Prince was one of the characters in the book and was portrayed as a nervous dilettante. Eventually Bissell, his wife Marian, and Abe Burrows dramatized the book with Bobby Morse playing the Prince character on stage. In an interview, Gwen Verdon said, "The way Bobby Morse acted in that show was exactly the way Hal Prince was."[13] Prince was angered at the time. "When I saw it I was furious. But I was like that. I see that now. I was so nervous, so desperate for success. Time was always running out."[14]

The Pajama Game became the eighth musical in Broadway history to run over one thousand performances (1,063 performances). It won the Antoinette Perry and Donaldson Awards as the best musical of the season. Warner Brothers produced a successful movie of the show in 1957, starring Doris Day, and in an unusual move, hired most of the cast of the stage production and brought Abbott on board to co-direct the movie with Stanley Donen, who had danced in Abbott musicals in the forties. The show was revived at the New York City Center on 15 May 1957, less than six months after its long Broadway run.

Damn Yankees

A couple of weeks after *The Pajama Game* had begun its run, Griffith and Prince became involved in their second project. Abbott had agreed to direct a musical based on Douglas Wallop's novel, *The Year the Yankees Lost the Pennant*, which had been brought to his attention by a William Morris agent, Albert Taylor. Abbott would direct the show provided that Brisson, Griffith and Prince produced it. Taylor became an associate producer and Abbott co-authored with Wallop. As they had done in *The Pajama Game*, Adler and Ross wrote the score and Bob Fosse did the choreography.

The subject, baseball, did not easily lend itself to the making of a Broadway musical comedy. George Abbott explained why baseball musicals were considered a jinx: "It's pretty hard to show a baseball game on the stage. You can't show the diamond."[15] Ethan Mordden had the same idea. "Baseball is a definitely unconventional (read suicidal) subject for musical theatre."[16] In the past, producers had had little success doing shows dealing with baseball. Most had been failures.

Despite the poor record of baseball plays, Griffith and Prince moved ahead enthusiastically with their project, titled *Damn Yankees*. Gwen Verdon was cast in the leading role of Lola, a part turned down by Mitzi Gaynor and Zizi Jeanmaire. Verdon had been acclaimed in 1953 for her featured dancing role in *Can-Can*, but she was not considered a star.

With no stars in the cast and two precarious themes (baseball and the Faust legend), there was still no problem in raising money. No backers' auditions were needed after the producing team's success with their first show. As with *The Pajama Game,* 155 people invested in *Damn Yankees* and many of the backers remained loyal to Prince productions for years to come.

Things did not go smoothly in rehearsal or on the road prior to the Broadway opening. Much of the score was discarded and much of the book had to be rewritten. With Abbott as director and co-writer, however, there was no need to panic. He worked steadily and assuredly, as was his habit, and Prince remembers that everything improved except the ending. Richard Adler discussed some of the difficulties:

> There was an awful lot to do in that show—a lot to do! We worked our tails off on that one. It was a very different experience than *The Pajama Game.* We thought we had an immediate smash hit when we were in rehearsal. When we were in New Haven to our great surprise—after "You've Got to Have Heart"—which stopped the show cold from its first performance on—the show went right out the window because the audience was interested in the ballplayers, not in the love story. And that was the problem. And Lola, they were interested in how to bring her in and not detract from the central story of the two middle-aged people [Joe Hardy, who gets turned into a young athlete and his middle-aged wife] and how he misses her and loves her. Ultimately we got there.[17]

Gwen Verdon had little to do when the show first opened out of town. She talked of some of the changes that took place:

> I didn't do "Little Brains." "Lola" was the first thing that I did. And then there was a baseball ballet which I was part of. I did a pas de deux with a gorilla who was supposed to be the New York Yankees. George Marcy was the gorilla wearing the Yankee uniform. Then that was cut out and they wanted another number. Out of the trunk of Adler and Ross came "Who's Got the Pain?" Bob [Fosse] and I put the number together in about two hours.[18]

Verdon is sorry the original number was cut because it was, in her opinion, "a fabulous ballet."[19] Everyone was in the number and they were dressed as different baseball teams—e.g., the Orioles dressed as birds. Originally, the ballet was placed at the end of act 1. Verdon was not sure

Damn Yankees, 1955
Producers Robert Griffith and Harold Prince (*standing*) with director
George Abbott.

who made the decision to alter the placement or cut numbers out of the show:

> You never really knew who wore the hat or who was the ax man. I have a hunch it was George Abbott. But Griffith and Prince did all the work saying, "that's cut—this is what we're going to do." But I'm pretty sure decisions to cut things came from Abbott. He was the boss.[20]

One of Verdon's favorite numbers in the show was "Two Lost Souls." The original music for the song was one of the first pieces of rock music; very early rock. Abbott was against it. Verdon talked about that song:

> Adler and Ross were kids, and they knew everything that was going on in the music scene. And rock was just beginning. . . . However, when Abbott heard it he said, "What's that?" and they said, "that's the new music." And Abbott answered, "I hate it, change it." And they changed it almost to a cowboy sound similar to "There Once Was a Man" from *Pajama Game* where they sort of yodel while singing it. They changed the orchestration and it was less rock and roll and more swing. I thought the original version was fun and when we did a revival of the show in Chicago and Westbury (almost 10 years later) we got the notation of the original orchestration, had it redone, and although it sounds old-fashioned now—it went back to rock and roll.[21]

Another number Verdon was fond of was "Lola." It was the first time she had done anything quite like it. The song, dance and scene were all blended "like a mini little show right in the middle of everything."[22]

Damn Yankees opened in New York on 5 May 1955 at the 46th Street Theatre. Walter Kerr, in the *New York Herald Tribune,* wrote that "one of the neatest tricks of anybody's season would be to bring off a fantasy about Hell and baseball. . . . The funny thing about this show is that it does the toughest things best."[23] John Chapman loved the show, saying, "It breaks the jinx, for there has been a legend that the topic of baseball is murder in the theatre, on account of some mysterious whammy."[24] Although the reviews were generally favorable, the show had two problems. First, it was too long, and second, the audience, having become enamored of Gwen Verdon as Lola during the show, resented her turning into an ugly old crone at the end.

The day after opening, Griffith, Prince and Abbott, along with Adler and Ross, called a rehearsal. A major number, "Not Meg," was deleted from the show and a second-act number was moved into the first act. The ending was changed also. The Devil now changed Lola back into a beautiful seductress again.

With the changes Abbott made, *Damn Yankees* played better and ran twenty minutes less at its second performance. In an unusual move, the producers asked Walter Kerr to return and re-review the show. He did, and he liked it more than he had on first viewing.

In spite of the changes and the good reviews, the audiences resisted coming. During the first four weeks, not more than $250 worth of tickets were sold daily. Prince, who had an instinct for what would sell tickets, decided to remove the picture of Gwen Verdon in a baseball uniform from the ads and to replace it with a picture of her in a more revealing costume. He deleted references to the baseball theme of the show. Gwen Verdon recalls that "People didn't originally know what the show was about. They either thought it had something to do with the South or only baseball, because on the posters everyone including me was in a baseball uniform. So [Prince] changed the record album cover, all the photographs out front, the *Playbill.* Everything was changed."[25] Within a month there were long lines at the box office. Abe Laufe said, "*Damn Yankees* might have been unsuccessful if the producers had emphasized the sport angle. Instead of concentrating on baseball, however, they capitalized on two popular themes: regained youth, as symbolized by *Faust,* and sex."[26]

Although Prince believes that a show doesn't require a star to be successful, he did hire Bobby Clark to play the Devil in the *Damn Yankees* national company. He played the role that had been played so successfully by Ray Walston on Broadway. For the touring company, Prince believed that he needed a star as box office attraction. He had worshipped Bobby Clark from childhood and the idea of using the renowned comic in one of his productions was irresistible. Prince feels, however, that Clark did not work out. With Clark in the role, the show became a vehicle for the comic. In New York, the show had won many awards with Ray Walston, a fine actor rather than a star personality.

Richard Adler agreed with Prince about Clark, and felt that he didn't really fit into the "tapestry" of the show:

> [Clark] was a different kind of an Applegate. He was hamming it up all over the place, as I recall. The audience loved it and it didn't matter much as far as the box office went. But artistically—he wasn't near the performer Ray Walston was.[27]

Prince learned his lesson well. He would remain firm in his philosophy of doing shows with virtual unknowns in leading roles if he thought they were best for the show.

Later, working as a director, Prince said that *good* actors can add greatly to a production, and are indeed collaborators. Prince felt that the actors in *Sweeney Todd* (1979), for example, including the ensemble, were very creative and helped him with some imaginative ideas. "It is not unusual for material to get short shrift, for otherwise good material to seem inferior, in the hands of a dazzling personality. Stars have a way of saving themselves at the cost of the material."[28] On the other hand, if a star is the best person around for a particular role, Prince won't hesitate to hire him.

Damn Yankees played over a thousand performances (1,012) and won the Antoinette Perry Award for best musical. The collaborators of the show had triumphed for a second time, but Prince was uncertain about a third project. He felt that *Damn Yankees* wasn't as good a show as *The Pajama Game* and that the next show probably wouldn't have been any good at all. The decision about whether to continue with songwriters Adler and Ross for that next show was resolved in a tragic way: Jerry Ross died suddenly in 1955 from a chronic respiratory illness.

Damn Yankees was bought for the movies and produced in 1958 by Warner Brothers. Gwen Verdon again played Lola, and Tab Hunter played Joe. Abbott did the movie and once again, as with *The Pajama Game,* he hired most of the original Broadway cast.

The "Wunderkind" Hal Prince, with his second big Broadway musical hit, was establishing himself in the commercial theatre. Prince, at this time, was assertive, impatient and outspoken. However, he was not considered abusive or caustic. He was an extrovert whose emotions surfaced easily. He would erupt in anger, but then quickly revert to his usual happy, pleasant self. He was known for his nervous energy and vitality, his activities continuing from early morning until late at night. Adler remembers the youthful Prince as being much like a "hyperactive child, in his kinetic energy. He was jumping up all over the place. It was definitely nervous energy. He's still very energetic, but it's more tempered now . . . well, he's much older."[29] When talking on the telephone, Prince would pace anxiously, neither sitting nor stopping for a moment. His speech was rapid as was his walk and many could not keep up with him. He walked quickly to appointments and to rehearsals, arriving faster than by taxi. To some he appeared to be a restless listener.

As a producer, Prince involved himself in nearly every creative phase of the work—from the writing to the selection of the props:

> He generally chooses all the scenery for his shows and he has been known to make vital last-minute cast changes, to recommend specific revisions in a script, to suggest a way of disentangling a ponderous muddle in a second act, and to advise a composer and lyricist that a certain kind of number is needed to fill a hole in a third act—all matters that normally fall to the director.[30]

Such total involvement might have posed a problem for others. The producer is the "boss" and everyone must pay attention to his opinions. If his ideas are poor (or good, for that matter), the cast and crew might resent him. Prince, however, was not only a creative man, but a man of taste and was most often perceived as an asset to his productions.

New Girl in Town

Prince waited almost a year to do his third show, *New Girl in Town,* and it was an important show in his development as a major producer and director since it revealed to him the possibility of using serious dramatic material as the basis for a musical. It paved the way for his later work with more substantial subject matter in shows such as *Sweeney Todd, Evita* and *The Phantom of the Opera.*

Additionally, a conflict over a dance number between Prince, Griffith and Abbott on one side of the argument, and actress Gwen Verdon and choreographer Bob Fosse on the other, taught Prince the importance of holding firm to an original concept. The decision over whether to change or eventually cut an entire ballet sequence was an important lesson in Prince's growth as a truly creative producer.

In 1956, a conversation in Hollywood between Doris Day and George Abbott set an idea in motion for the third Griffith-Prince-Abbott musical. Day liked some Bob Merrill songs written for a new screen version of Eugene O'Neill's Pulitzer Prize-winning play *Anna Christie* (1921). The MGM movie studio had planned to do the film, but later decided against it. Abbott called Griffith and Prince in New York, asking them to get in touch with Merrill (who was in Manhattan at the time) about the songs. The producing team met with Merrill, a composer of popular song hits including "How Much Is That Doggie in the Window?" and "If I Knew You Were Coming, I'd

Have Baked a Cake.'' They liked the score and Abbott later agreed with them. Griffith and Prince decided to produce a musical stage version of *Anna Christie* called *New Girl in Town* and asked Merrill to write additional material. Abbott would write the book and direct, and Fosse choreograph.

They made a deal with MGM for the release of the score and the screen rights to *Anna Christie*. Abbott also called on Mrs. Carlotta Monterey O'Neill, the playwright's widow, to explain his conception of a musical of the play and secure the stage rights from her at a reasonable fee. As a producer, Prince felt that a play must be able to exist at 60 percent of capacity. Negotiations with MGM were prolonged until, in the final settlement, the 2 percent originally required by MGM was split between the O'Neill estate and the movie studio.

George Abbott told Don Ross of the *New York Herald Tribune* that he thought *New Girl in Town* was the first O'Neill play to be set to music. He said, "There have been plans to make musicals of *Desire Under the Elms* and *Ah, Wilderness!* but nothing much seems to have come of them."[31] Abbott liked the idea of making a musical of the O'Neill play.

> Why not? There's lots of serious material on the musical stage today. *Pal Joey* is serious material. *Carousel* is. American musicals have progressed far beyond the musical comedy stage; a musical comedy implies a kind of *Follies* atmosphere. The trend of our musicals is to try to give honest characters and an honest story and have the musical development come out of that story. There can be added pleasure at a musical from the feeling that the people are real and their situations are those which you have empathy for. *New Girl in Town* is a love story between a woman who seemed to have a shattered life and a man whose whole life was bare. It's the story of courage, of the triumph over environment and I think courage is always interesting, whether in life or on the stage, whether in a drama or a musical.[32]

With *New Girl in Town,* director George Abbott, acknowledged master of fast-paced musicals and zany farces, turned to serious subject matter—undoubtedly strengthening Prince's contention that the Broadway musical could deal with serious, challenging ideas, and leading him on to the ever-more-unorthodox subjects he would tackle in later years.

New York had rediscovered O'Neill at that time. When *New Girl in Town* opened in 1957, three of the playwright's works were on the New York stage. There were revivals of *A Moon for the Misbegotten,* which had started its run in May at the Bijou Theatre, and the 1957 Pulitzer

Prize-winning *Long Day's Journey into Night* playing on Broadway. *The Iceman Cometh* was an Off-Broadway revival which had started two years earlier at Circle-in-the-Square. Perhaps this revived interest in O'Neill gave Griffith and Prince additional motivation to proceed with the musical adaptation of *Anna Christie*.

Abbott took six weeks to write the book, which he kept as close as possible to the original play. He did, however, move Anna's story to the turn of the century instead of the 1920s. He explained, "The clothes were prettier in 1900. . . . They had the ugliest clothes in the world in 1921. In 1900, too, woman's place was a more inferior one, making her problem greater. Women could vote by 1921, there was considerable emancipation by then."[33] Merrill's songs, which had inspired the project, seemed too contemporary (MGM had planned to do the movie in a modern setting), and he was asked to do "a new score suitable to the rhythms and language of 1900."[34] Merrill wrote sixteen new songs for *New Girl in Town* before it went into rehearsal and three more during rehearsals. Only two of the original songs written for the shelved movie version were used. One of them is "It's Good to Be Alive."

The search for an actress to play Anna was extensive and many actresses were auditioned. Gwen Verdon was eager to play the part in order to demonstrate her ability as an actress, since her previous shows had been vehicles for her singing and dancing talents. Verdon recalls:

> I did an audition with Mr. Abbott—he read with me—and afterwards he said, "Well, that's in miniature but that's right." Then, I did a musical audition. I sang "Good to Be Alive" and broke right in the middle of it. I just couldn't sing it. It looked bad but there's something about defeat that does something to me. "Give me three weeks," I said, "and let me audition again."[35]

After three weeks of daily singing lessons, Verdon won the role. Prince was happy with the choice but Abbott was uncertain. He had planned a show without dance and was concerned about audience reaction to a nondancing Verdon. The collaborators had agreed previously that Anna shouldn't and wouldn't be choreographed. However, once the show was in rehearsal, Verdon was given dancing moments. Dialogue was cut as dancing chores increased. Prince admits this hurt the show. "*New Girl in Town* was far better when we stuck with a concept conscious of risking the wrath of our audience."[36] Prince had come to believe that it was better to stick with an idea, a concept, approach to a show, no matter the audience risk, than to try to please everybody by making modifications.

Verdon claims she fought with Abbott throughout, feeling that he was commercializing it too much. She agrees with Prince that they should have stayed with the original concept. Brooks Atkinson noted the problem: "Mr. Abbott's effort to make a bigtime festival out of a somber theme is not altogether successful. The two substances do not blend easily."[37] Walter Kerr, however, had the opposite opinion: "Mr. Abbott, in reworking the tooth-and-nail love story, has minded his business and played the whole thing straight (perhaps too straight—there was some sound robust comedy in the original that is missing here)."[38]

There was a major conflict out of town between Fosse and Verdon on the one hand, and the director and producers on the other hand, over a dream ballet which Fosse had created for the second act, called "The Red Light Ballet." George Abbott, in his autobiography, *Mister Abbott*, explained that the "cold, shocked reaction of the viewers made us realize that the sequence was just plain dirty."[39] Abbott and the producers cut out the number after the New Haven tryout and destroyed the $40,000 staircase used in the scene. They objected to the ballet as "pornographic, an artistic mess."[40]

Prince said, "The movement, possibly, was lovely (Gwen and Fosse thought so). Erotic, yes. But it had been imposed on the play. We had entered a musical brothel, our prostitutes became dancers, our Anna Christie, Gwen Verdon."[41] Gwen Verdon discussed the conflict:

> I didn't know that the number was out until we went into Boston. When I asked to talk to Abbott about it Hal Prince told me, "He's too busy to talk to you." I said, "I'm too busy to go on" and I left. But I did the show because Bob Fosse said you'll be blackballed forever if you don't and he convinced me to go on.... Fosse tried several versions of the ballet and George Abbott hated them all. It was his decision and he was the boss so you go along with it.[42]

Abbott didn't like the new versions any better than he had the original. For the opening in New York, the ballet was taken out. Verdon said, "They finally did put the number back into the show a few months later (June 23rd ... I remember because it was Bob's birthday). They didn't therefore have the staircase and they weren't going to build another one. And there was much more musical accompaniment now. Originally it was done in silence, which made people very nervous. About 80 percent of the choreography was the same as the original. They put it back in because I wanted it. If I decide I want something, I'll go off a cliff to get it. I knew it was good."[43]

George Abbott called the ballet "a very depressing experience, both in its effect on us and its effect on the audience."[44] As a result of this artistic donnybrook, the professional association of Fosse, Verdon and Prince was so damaged that they never again worked together.

Verdon, who during their two shows together perceived producer Prince as "very young," said that she spent a day with Prince and his family in Majorca in 1972 (fifteen years after *New Girl in Town*) and that he amazed her. "I guess I never expected Hal to mature but he really grew up a lot. He'd become quite a figure in the theatre and in humanitarian things. And thank goodness, I matured enough to recognize that he, too, had really evolved as a human being."[45]

New Girl in Town, which was capitalized at $300,000, opened on Broadway on 14 May 1957 at the 46th Street Theatre and ran almost thirteen months (439 performances), generally playing below capacity. It not only returned the investors' money but even realized a substantial profit. On 11 November 1957, a letter was sent to investors with the final 10 percent of their investment. The letter stated they were in the black and doing capacity business.[46] The show set a new high for Broadway tickets with the top price at $9.20 for an orchestra divan seat and $8.60 for the regular orchestra seats (on weekends). The cast album was recorded by RCA Victor.

Variety's Hobe Morrison said that

> Abbott's adaptation of the O'Neill classic can't entirely remove the bitter quality of the story . . . so it lacks much of the romantic aura likely to bring mass popularity but it's solid and propulsive. . . . Verdon easily surpasses her previous performances. . . . It's vigorous and graphic, if possibly limited in range.[47]

John McClain in the *New York Journal American* said,

> Devout O'Neill fans will not find much of the atmosphere of the original in this book by George Abbott, but they will be treated to a thoroughly zestful and engaging musical period piece, a show with style, humor and a rollicking score.[48]

Prince later came to believe that the subject of prostitution was not a romantic one, and rarely was it comical. Additionally, he felt that the

O'Neill material as remolded for *New Girl in Town* came out looking conventional and that the vision of the creative people had been superficial. For Prince, the main reason for doing the show had been his need to get back to work. There'd been over a year's layoff since *Damn Yankees* had opened, and Prince had been eager to start a new project. He now says that *Anna Christie* should have been done as an American opera. He admits it might have had a shorter life span but it would have remained faithful to the original O'Neill, which was serious, not comedic.

Although *New Girl in Town* was profitable, Prince still considers it an aesthetic failure. Soon after the show closed, Frederick Brisson moved back to California, breaking up the producing trio of Griffith, Prince and Brisson, which had been responsible for the successful three-hit streak.

BROADWAY INNOVATION:
West Side Story

*I get bored with the same thing. . . . I like theatre when it's
not like what you get in other media.*
—Harold Prince, Interview with Dick Cavett, 19–20 February 1980

Hal Prince and Stephen Sondheim had become good friends in the early
fifties after meeting for the first time at the opening of *South Pacific* in
April 1949. Sondheim's reputation as a theatre renaissance man had reached
Prince while Sondheim was still a student at Williams College—the triple-
threat composer-lyricist-librettist of *Climb High,* a musical that told the
story of a young man who aspired to become a Broadway actor.

According to Prince, he and Sondheim would discuss the future of
the American theatre over sandwiches in Walgreen's drugstore, a theatrical
hangout of the time. They talked also of their rightful places in the American
musical theatre, not knowing then that their first collaboration in that
American musical theatre would be *West Side Story*—a groundbreaker
in the musical history of Broadway, and a first step in the forging of a
producer-composer alliance and later a producer-director-composer alliance
that would change forever the way the American musical theatre looked,
sounded and felt to an audience raised on the mindless librettos of pre-
Oklahoma! musicals and the carefully wrought, artfully integrated story
musicals pioneered by Rodgers and Hammerstein and Lerner and Loewe.

West Side Story was the first musical that Hal Prince produced without
George Abbott as his director and spiritual guide. "At that time," recalled

Stephen Sondheim, "Hal was completely under Abbott's wing."[1] According to writer Gary Paul Gates in a *Holiday* magazine article, Prince's career was reshaped when he and Griffith rejected the counsel of their collaborator and mentor, George Abbott, and took over the production of *West Side Story*. Sondheim maintains that, if Prince hadn't had the confidence to reject Abbott's advice, he would have continued to produce only "George Abbott musicals." "Instead," says Sondheim, "he trusted his own instincts and became very much his own man. After *West Side Story* he never stood quite as much in awe of Abbott. Not that there was ever any trouble. But now they're colleagues, associates. Up until *West Side Story,* the relationship was definitely that of teacher and pupil."[2]

Prince recalls that time. "It was difficult to come out from under Abbott's protective arm. On the other hand, he gave us [Griffith and Prince] his blessing easily. George Abbott is a secure man."[3]

West Side Story is a contemporary treatment of the Romeo and Juliet theme. Set on New York's West Side, it contains violence, poverty and ethnic hostility. It is a musical tragedy and expresses itself poetically and through the use of dance. The show is an innovative departure from the integrated musicals of the period. Other musicals repeated the successful formulas of the past, but *West Side Story* was hailed as a new kind of musical theatre.

The idea for the show began to evolve with Jerome Robbins in 1949. Arthur Laurents, who had never written the book for a musical before, but whose produced plays included *Home of the Brave, The Time of the Cuckoo* and *A Clearing in the Woods,* worked on Robbins' idea of the story of a Jewish girl and a gentile boy on the East Side of New York. Various changing titles for the project were *East Side Story* and *Gangway!* Leonard Bernstein, represented on Broadway by *On the Town, Wonderful Town* and *Candide,* soon joined the show as composer. The collaborators could not decide on the direction or focus of the piece and the project was soon abandoned. It remained in limbo but over the years Laurents altered the libretto to relate to the demographic changes that had occurred in the city, changing the story to deal with the conflict of Puerto Ricans and "whites" who lived on the West Side of Manhattan—a concept eagerly accepted by Jerome Robbins.

In 1954 Bernstein, dissatisfied with his own lyrics, asked Stephen Sondheim to help him. Sondheim complained to his mentor, Oscar Hammerstein II, that he was reluctant to accept the job because he wanted to compose. Hammerstein convinced him to do it. He said, "To work with men of the professional caliber of Bernstein and Laurents and Robbins is invaluable experience. And I think also it'll be a foot in the theatre for you. You can always do music on your next show."[4] Sondheim agreed to do the show.

Bernstein felt that Sondheim's contribution was enormous. He said, "It far exceeded even *my* expectations. What made him so valuable was that he was also a composer and I could explain musical problems to him and he'd understand immediately, which made the collaboration a joy."[5] The manner in which they collaborated varied. Sometimes they worked together, sometimes apart. Two songs in which the tune came first were "Cool" and "Gee, Officer Krupke!" "Cool" was a new tune, but the latter was originally written for *Candide*. With "A Boy like That," the lyrics were written first.[6] When the show opened in New York, Bernstein, in a gracious gesture, removed his name as co-lyricist, thus giving newcomer Sondheim deserved recognition.

George Abbott had decided not to produce the original musical and Griffith and Prince also declined the early script. The show was then owned by Cheryl Crawford, in association with Roger Stevens, who had financed the project since its inception. Eventually, Crawford dropped out.

The collaborators were desperate. Every major New York producer had turned the show down, and they feared that the project would again fall apart. Bernstein remembers,

> We thought at that point that it would not get on. Everybody told us to stop. They all said it was suicidal. I don't know how many people begged me not to waste my time on something that could not possibly succeed. After all, how could we do a musical where there are two bodies lying on the stage at the end of the first act and everybody eventually dies? . . . A show that's so filled with hatefulness and ugliness?[7]

Prince was in Boston with his production of *New Girl in Town*. In those days, he remained on the road while the production was trying out. His New York office was run by Carl Fisher, his very capable general manager. One day, Prince and Sondheim, by then very close friends, compared notes on how badly things were going for each of them. Sondheim's depressing news about *West Side Story* affected Prince. He talked to his partner Griffith and called Sondheim back—a fateful telephone call, as it turned out, for it would take the career of Hal Prince in an entirely new direction.

I knew the show backwards and forwards, though Bobby had not heard it, for Steve had played all the music for me unbeknownst to Lenny, since he didn't want anybody to hear it. So when I called Steve back I told him that Bobby and I could come to New York on Sunday to hear the score while George Abbott rehearsed *New Girl,* but if they wanted us and if we wanted to do it, we would go right back to Boston because we had a show in trouble and we would not talk about their show, would do nothing about getting a theatre, would do nothing about raising money, and they would have to just leave us alone.[8]

Griffith and Prince came down to New York from Boston, heard the material together and decided they would, indeed, become the producers of *West Side Story,* putting it into rehearsal as soon after the Broadway opening of *New Girl in Town* as possible.

The day after *New Girl in Town* opened on Broadway, Griffith and Prince began work on *West Side Story.* Within a week they had raised the $300,000 needed for the show and it soon went into rehearsal. Prince was again tackling a show whose subject matter was perceived as controversial. In fact, the show was considered by those close to it as revolutionary. It did not compromise with a happy ending. In fact, the ending was tragic. With the exception of two songs, "America" and "Gee, Officer Krupke!," it was humorless. Richard Watts, Jr., would write later, "To start with a sweeping understatement, *West Side Story* is far from being a regulation Broadway musical play."[9]

The director and authors were determined to search out new young talent for the cast of *West Side Story,* performers who could dance, move well, act, and who could sing the difficult Bernstein score. The arduous job of casting took six months, but it was the show that was to be the star, not the performers. Larry Kert, who was signed to play the role of Tony, felt that the creators of the show did not want anyone to overshadow the production.[10]

In addition to Kert as Tony, leading roles were assigned to Carol Lawrence as Maria and Chita Rivera as Anita. Others in the company were professionals, many who had never played roles before; mainly, they were young dancers who had done some chorus work.

Prince claims that watching Jerome Robbins at work during the creation of *West Side Story* helped shape his theatrical vision. Although it would be some years before Prince would begin directing (and although he has said that Robbins' method of putting a show together is quite different from his own), he credits Robbins for much of the directorial know-how which he absorbed during the rehearsals of the show. Prince said, "I learned from Robbins how to prepare a concept musical—although I hate the term—but Jerry had an aesthetic view—a vision of the visual elements of production."[11]

Prince and Abbott, Prince and Robbins—a visionary producer having the good fortune—more likely the good sense—to align himself with two of the theatre's best directors as he eyed the director's seat for himself! And the theatrical lives of the three men are oddly entwined, Robbins having gotten his baptism as a Broadway choreographer in *On the Town,* directed by the old pro Abbott. During the next thirteen years Robbins staged the dances for such other Abbott-directed shows as *High Button Shoes* (1947), *Look Ma, I'm Dancin'* (1948), and *Call Me Madam* in 1950. The three— Abbott, Prince and Robbins—came into convergence with *The Pajama Game,* which Robbins co-directed with Abbott for producer Prince.

Critic Martin Gottfried sees the Abbott-Robbins liaison as one in which the older man was grooming the younger as a successor.[12] Not much of the Abbott style of working with his collaborators, however, rubbed off on Robbins, who is by no means "beloved" in theatre circles. According to Gottfried, Robbins is an "uncompromising perfectionist, and has no time for niceties and no inclination for tact in making demands on those with whom he worked. His sharp tongue regularly reduced performers to tears."[13]

Prince says that Robbins's "abrasive" approach to co-workers is not uncommon among choreographers who are also directors, but this is one area in which Prince does not emulate the otherwise influential Robbins. Prince needs fun and laughter no matter how emotional things may get. He shies away from contention, feeling that the show is not the most important thing in the world.

Jerome Robbins has been called a "method director." He used this systematic approach on *West Side Story,* and later, *Fiddler on the Roof. West Side Story* has no chorus and each gang member was given a name and a fleshed-out history and background. The cast cut out items about gang wars from the papers and covered the theatre's walls with them. After the show's first run-through, the consensus was that the show was too slow and a bit self-conscious. Robbins was persuaded to modify his "method" technique and to stress "line readings" and the show began to come together in less than a week's time. The hours that Robbins spent early on probing in method style Prince credited as having given the show its "legs."[14] Prince did not emulate Robbins's "method" technique when he began directing. Prince works quickly and doesn't spend much time working out inner motivations in rehearsal. As Lonny Price, who starred in an early eighties Prince musical, *Merrily We Roll Along*, said, "Prince expects the actor to do all that as part of his homework."[15]

Bernstein's score was well received. Richard Watts, Jr., said that the mood of the music

> lies somewhere between the sardonic bite of his score for *Candide* and his considerably more popular songs for *Wonderful Town*. If it leans more in the direction of the former, it is because of what seemed to me a certain chilliness that didn't altogether capture the hot-bloodedness of grimly embattled youth in *West Side Story*. But the vitality and the harshness of the musical tragedy's mood are there, and there can be little dispute about the vigor of the music.[16]

Other musical highlights were "Maria," "I Feel Pretty," and "Somewhere," a lyrical dream ballet accompanied by off-stage voices singing the lyrics, which expressed the young people's hope for a better life. Again, dance was used to both explain and, even more important, to help set mood.

The comedy numbers are "America," in which the Puerto Rican girls sing of their "happy" life in this country, and "Gee, Officer Krupke!," a satire on the "problem of juvenile delinquency."[17]

Sondheim has reservations about some of the numbers in the show. He dislikes "I Feel Pretty" and "One Hand, One Heart," although Bernstein loved them. Bernstein had originally written the latter for *Candide* and revised it for *West Side Story*. Sondheim believes "I Feel Pretty" goes against character. He had wanted to show that he could do inner rhymes. "So I had this uneducated Puerto Rican girl singing 'It's alarming how charming I feel.' . . . So there it is to this day embarrassing me every time it's sung, because it's full of mistakes like that."[18]

Before the show went into rehearsal, Sondheim played seven songs for Dorothy and Oscar Hammerstein. They especially liked "Maria." Sondheim felt that it was like a "Hammerstein lyric in that it had the one quality Oscar valued above all others: . . . Absolute honesty about a character and what he is saying."[19] Sondheim says he still tries for this quality in his lyrics, regardless of style.

A special run-through was staged for Hammerstein prior to *West Side Story*'s Philadelphia tryout. Hammerstein was thrilled, but had one major criticism, and that was his feeling that "Tonight" was not a sufficiently

West Side Story, 1957
Chita Rivera (*center*) in the dance number "America."
(Photo © Martha Swope)

"soaring" song for the balcony scene. Hammerstein said, "It's a nice song, but it doesn't seem to me to take off enough."[20] "His instinct was unerring," said Sondheim, "because the truth was that the song had not been written for that scene but was used there as a last resort."[21] Even though Sondheim and the other collaborators knew he was right, the song remained in.

There were not many changes made during the out-of-town tryouts (exceptional for a musical). Sondheim said the show was changed least of any musical he has heard of.[22] (This was true until *Sweeney Todd.*) Robbins had prepared thoroughly and attempted to fix things at an early stage. The show rehearsed an unprecedented eight weeks, with Robbins doing much work both before and during rehearsals. When he later became a director, Prince would emulate this style of preparation, which entails a good deal of pre-rehearsal work.

Minor revisions made out of town included the rewriting of the release for "Jet Song" and the adding of a few notes to "One Hand, One Heart." Robbins also made some changes in the second act ballet. In Washington, a new number for the characters Anybodys, Arab and Baby John called "Kids Ain't" was written and then rejected. Laurents and Sondheim feared that the audiences would love this typical musical number for its commercial elements and it would detract from the show as a whole.[23]

Bernstein and Sondheim also thought of changing the opening to "This Turf Is Ours," thinking that heightening the violence would improve the number. It proved to be "too" violent and they went back to "Jet Song."

Robbins had worked a great deal with dance projects and dance theatre which depend more on lighting than scenery. *West Side Story,* therefore, became the first show for which Prince hired a lighting designer. In earlier shows, the company electrician, George Gebhardt, and Griffith had done the lighting. Prince recalls, "It was a matter of lights up for the scene, and lights down for the song. Lights up again after the song with George Abbott shouting from the orchestra, 'more light on those faces—this is a funny scene.' "[24] Jean Rosenthal did the lighting for *West Side Story.* As a result of her good work, she would do many future shows with Prince.

The reviews in Washington were raves. In Philadelphia, the reception was not nearly as good, but the collaborators remained calm, since, in Sondheim's words, "Philly is an antitheatrical town."[25] *West Side Story* opened at the Winter Garden Theatre in New York on 16 September 1957. The show received generally favorable reviews and a few raves from the critics. John Chapman wrote:

The American theatre took a venturesome forward step when the firm of Griffith and Prince presented *West Side Story* at the Winter Garden last evening. This is a bold new kind of musical theatre—a jukebox Manhattan opera. It is, to me, extraordinarily exciting. In it, the various fine skills of show business are put to new tests, and as a result a different kind of musical has emerged.[26]

Brooks Atkinson said:

Everything in *West Side Story* is of a piece. Everything contributes to the total impression of wildness, ecstasy and anguish. The astringent score has moments of tranquility and rapture, and occasionally a touch of sardonic humor. And the ballets convey the things that Mr. Laurents is inhibited from saying because the characters are so inarticulate. The hostility and suspicion between the gangs, the glory of the nuptials, the terror of the rumble, the devastating climax—Mr. Robbins has found the patterns of movement that express these parts of the story.[27]

Robert Coleman said, "Robert E. Griffith and Harold S. Prince, the hit boys, have another sensational smash on their hands. They've come to bat four times—with *Pajama Game, Damn Yankees, New Girl in Town* and *West Side Story*—and whacked out grand slammers for a perfect record."[28]

The show played a year and a half on Broadway (734 performances). Prince admits he then made a poor decision. The producers had finally lowered the ticket prices and initiated a two-for-the-price-of-one policy. Audiences flocked to the theatre, but Griffith and Prince had already booked the show for a national tour. Craig Zadan writes:

It was one of the few business mistakes of Hal's career. Hal didn't realize what a large audience there would be once ticket prices were reduced, so he made the mistake of booking a tour too early and the last couple of months you couldn't get into the theatre. To make up for that he brought it back to New York after the tour for a run of about six months—also on reduced prices—and it did quite well.[29]

Prince agrees that *West Side Story* left New York about six months too soon. "It takes a peculiar talent to know when to close a show and this office is short on that talent."[30] He agrees that the show is an important one but also that important shows are not always smash hits. All the awards that year were won by *The Music Man,* which ran years longer than

West Side Story. However, Jerome Robbins won a Tony as best choreographer.

While the Broadway production of *West Side Story* recouped its costs, actual profits were minimal. Royalties from record sales, however, put the show firmly in the black, and United Artists paid $315,000 for the film rights plus a piece of the profits (in those days a high price), eventually putting over $3 million into the pockets of the producers and original investors.

The road tour of *West Side Story* finished before the year was out. The show did well on the West Coast but not in Chicago. When it reopened in New York, Bernstein conducted the overture on the first night. The critics re-reviewed the show and decided that the book was special, that Sondheim was an important new lyricist, and that the show had a place in musical theatre history. The show played another six months in New York this time around, and could have run longer had it not been for a dispute between Prince and the musicians' union.

Because another musical was booked into the Alvin Theatre at the time, Prince wanted to move *West Side Story* into the Broadway. The show had begun to lose money and he thought a bigger theatre would let him drop ticket prices and enlarge his audience, giving *West Side Story* perhaps another six months of Broadway life. The move would mean several days' layoff, however, requiring concessions from the unions which the musicians refused to give, forcing Prince to close the show.

Among many others, its composer Leonard Bernstein thinks *West Side Story* is a genuine landmark in the journey of the American musical theatre from showgirls and pratfall comedians to a respectable art form:

> So much was conveyed in music, including the enormous reliance upon dance to tell plot—not just songs stuck into a book. . . . I thought, Oh well, now I've really done my bit for the Broadway theatre and I can become a conductor and seriously think about Beethoven and Wagner [Bernstein was so sure that the show was a unique contribution to the American musical that he accepted the directorship of the New York Philharmonic the same month as *West Side Story* opened]. . . . I was perfectly confident that there would be dozens of kids who would take the next step and pick up on the hints of *West Side Story* that I was convinced would lead to some form of American opera.[31]

Bernstein could not know at that time that two of the collaborators on *West Side Story*—Prince and Sondheim—would be two of the "kids" who would continue to move the American musical play on to other forms and subject matter. Prince, having learned his trade well through his working experiences with Abbott, Robbins, Bernstein, Laurents and Sondheim, would emerge with a unique vision of his own for the American musical theatre. Although Prince had been raised with an American musical theatre that might be labeled conventional, it had moved through various steps. Shows such as *Lady in the Dark, Pal Joey, Oklahoma!* and *Allegro* were all landmark musicals. Now, *West Side Story* was hailed as a breakthrough but, in Prince's opinion, *West Side Story* was a product of what had come before, and turned out to be the pinnacle of a tradition rather than a complete new vision.

That opinion aside, it was clear that Prince and Griffith left the "conventional" Broadway musical behind when he did *West Side Story,* just as the show's director Jerome Robbins had left it behind when he finished the staging of *Bells Are Ringing,* an archetypal "old-time" Broadway musical of 1956, on which he followed the rules he'd learned from George Abbott—"compartmentalizing the play, the songs and the dances."[32] The following year, finally realizing his old dream of staging a Romeo and Juliet story in the streets of New York, Robbins, under Prince's watchful and creative producer's eye, and with the exciting writing of Bernstein, Sondheim and Laurents, catapulted the American musical light years ahead of anything that had gone before. This was perhaps the first "concept" musical, a genre that Harold Prince would later embrace and fine tune. With *West Side Story,* Jerome Robbins proved "that the conventions of musical comedy were much more flexible and expressive than the public, producers and most critics had thought—that a musical tragedy derived from musical comedy was possible."[33] It was a lesson that Hal Prince, producer of *West Side Story,* would never forget as his own directing star began its ascendancy. From *West Side Story* on, Prince followed a different path from other American producer-directors—a path that led him both down into the thicket of failure and up to the pinnacle of success, but always in pursuit of the untested talent, the unusual story, the challenging idea that other creative forces in the American musical theatre had avoided as "death at the box office." Prince was determined to show that musical theatre—the popular offerings of Broadway—could touch, stir, even inspire and shock audiences and still draw long lines to the ticket window.

THE FIFTIES END

A Swim in the Sea

In 1957, Prince decided to present a straight play, *A Swim in the Sea,* by Jess Gregg, which had originally been titled *The Sea Shell.* The play dealt with incest in a Southern family and featured a sixty-year-old woman as its central character. It had previously been the property of the Theatre Guild. When Joshua Logan was unable to stage the drama, the Guild dropped the option and it was picked up by Griffith and Prince.

This was Gregg's first play. He had worked five years on the script, polishing it for production. Both Shirley Booth and Helen Hayes had turned down the opportunity to play the central role, and Elia Kazan, Harold Clurman and Joshua Logan had all rejected the job of directing it. Prince and Griffith, however, were determined to get the play into production and would not allow themselves to be discouraged by the rejections of others. Prince said later that he had let himself fall in love with the play, the kind of self-deception that often leads otherwise reasonable, talented theatre folk to failure.

They arranged for a two-week winter stock production to open at the Royal Poinciana Playhouse in Palm Beach, Florida on 28 April 1958, following six days of previews at the Annie Russell Theatre in Winter Park, Florida. Palm Beach, they believed, would prove a good place for a tryout.

Peggy Wood, who had played the role of Mama for eight years in the television series *I Remember Mama,* was persuaded to appear in the Florida production, even though Prince felt she was miscast. Others in the cast were Inga Swenson and George Peppard.

Elliot Silverstein was chosen to direct on the recommendation of literary agent Audrey Wood. Silverstein had done graduate work at the Yale Drama School (as had Gregg) and had been a stage director for television's *Omnibus*. Prince had never seen his work before and was not very happy with the results.

Shirley Ayers, a former Broadway actress and the widow of the late and noted scenic designer Lemuel Ayers, was associated with Griffith and Prince in the production of *A Swim in the Sea*. She had picked up the option on the script after the Theatre Guild dropped it but she turned it over to the producers in return for associate producer billing.

After ten days of rehearsals, they opened in Florida to fairly good reviews. Although the producers realized that local papers often encourage local theatrical offerings and may not give a true reflection, they decided to bring the show to New York. At this time, *New Girl in Town* was in its 48th week and *West Side Story* was in its 29th week. The producers planned an opening at the Lyceum Theatre on 30 September 1958 with a capitalization of about $100,000. There would be a pre-Broadway tryout in Philadelphia.

Peggy Wood and George Peppard dropped out of the show, Inga Swenson and Silverstein staying with it. A young, inexperienced actor replaced Peppard and Fay Bainter replaced Wood.

The show opened in Philadelphia. It didn't work and the reviews were terrible. Waters, reviewing for *Variety*, said:

> It has the benefit of an impressive cast and numerous impressive scenes, some excellent characterizations and considerable effective dialogue, although some of the last-named is on the declamatory side. . . . Elliot Silverstein's direction seems sometimes a trifle vague and obtuse. . . . The actors are good. . . . It has some soap opera overtones . . . but it has considerable to recommend it too, and the good may eventually out-balance the flaws. But it's still not too promising a Broadway entry.[1]

Prince was so upset by the reviews that he and Griffith decided to close the show in Philadelphia, thereby saving the investors at least 52 percent of the money they'd put up.

Prince has always believed that it is possible to learn from failure. He doesn't allow a failed production to diminish his enthusiasm for the next project. It is this resiliency that has sustained his career as a producer, and later as a director.

Fiorello!

The idea of doing a musical based on the former New York City mayor, Fiorello LaGuardia, originated over lunch at the Coffee House Club. Arthur Penn suggested the project to Prince. Penn had already researched the former mayor's public and private life. Small in stature, LaGuardia was a bundle of dramatic paradoxes. He had a volatile personality but was warm-hearted. He was ruthless but also sentimental. At times he was petty but he was also generous. Prince had always had an interest in historical subjects, especially the private lives of historical figures; and so he was taken with the idea.

Griffith also loved the idea for the show and suggested Jerome Weidman, an old friend and neighbor in Connecticut, and the author of *I Can Get It for You Wholesale,* as a possible choice for librettist. Weidman agreed to write the book. Penn wanted to guide the writing and to direct. The producers met with LaGuardia's widow, Marie, at the LaGuardia home in Riverdale, New York, and promised to give her an outline of the show as soon as possible.

Penn suggested that the leading lady might double playing (in act 1) the mayor's first wife, who died while giving birth in the 1920s. In the second act, years later, the same actress would play Marie, LaGuardia's secretary and assistant. At the final curtain, Marie and LaGuardia would be married.

The producers called Mrs. LaGuardia when the outline was ready and the next day she phoned her agreement for them to do the show.

Arthur Penn was disappointed with Weidman's script. He wanted more of the internal conflict and psychological foundations of his *The Miracle Worker* and *Two for the Seesaw.* However, Weidman's version was highly nostalgic and that pleased Griffith and Prince. Prince had a clear vision of the future show. He felt that Penn's vision wouldn't leave room for music and dance and that Fiorello LaGuardia wasn't the right subject for an intense treatment.

Penn left the show, retaining an author's interest. Griffith and Prince then asked George Abbott to direct. Abbott hated the idea of Fiorello LaGuardia as a subject for a musical. Abbott disliked most of the ideas the producing team had had for musicals and didn't hesitate to tell them so, but he also had no difficulty changing his mind.

Abbott became co-author with Weidman as well as the director of the show. He and Weidman worked well together. In an article in *Theatre Arts,*

Weidman talked about working with Prince, Griffith and Abbott: "I found they were articulate, personable, witty, strong-minded people. . . . There were no fights."[2]

Now the collaborators began looking for a composer-lyricist for the show. George Abbott favored a team who could write satire but who could also give the score a period flavor. A new songwriting team, Jerry Bock and Sheldon Harnick, was eventually contracted to do the show. Bock had written *Mr. Wonderful* for Sammy Davis, Jr., the previous year and Sheldon Harnick was a composer and lyricist known for his special material and for some fine numbers he had contributed to small revues. Prince had already attended the opening of the songwriting team's *The Body Beautiful.* The show was not a success, but he was impressed by the gifted composer and lyricist.

Harnick recalls his first meeting with Prince on the opening night of *The Body Beautiful* at Sardi's. When the reviews came out (the show was a flop), most everyone at the table deserted him. Harnick remembers either Bill or Jean Eckart (the show's sets and lighting designers) coming over to his table to say that Prince wanted to meet him. He says that Prince was honest in his appraisal of *The Body Beautiful,* not particularly liking it, but enjoying the score very much and finding a lot of it very fresh. Harnick appreciated Prince's gesture of support.

Within a year Bock was hired by Prince and Griffith to do the music for *Fiorello!* Although Bock and Harnick were anxious to work together, they were not hired as a team at first. Harnick was told that the book writer, Jerome Weidman, wanted to do his own lyrics. Weidman did write some songs but the producers were not happy with them. Stephen Sondheim was then asked to do the lyrics but he did not want to. Harnick said, "I'll be forever grateful to Stephen Sondheim because they asked Steve to do the show and Steve had just decided that he wouldn't do a show in which he could only do lyrics. He wanted to do both his own music and lyrics."[3]

Other lyricists were considered but Griffith and Prince decided not to use them for various reasons. The producers believed that Harnick's songs were clever and sophisticated but they weren't certain that he could write songs that were earthy and warm. Finally, however, they asked him to write some songs on speculation. They outlined the show and suggested spots where they wanted him to write some songs. Harnick remembers what happened when he and Bock came in with the numbers:

When we played "Till Tomorrow," Bobby loved it. For me it was an unusual song because it was a highly sentimental song that was meant to reflect what I figured was the tone of an Irving Berlin waltz from about 1917 . . . so one of the lyrics in it was "parting is such sweet sorrow" (the quote from Shakespeare). . . . I happened to be looking right at Hal Prince when I sang that and because it was uncharacteristic of me I couldn't help but grin as I sang that line. At the end of the song Hal said, "That song is a put-on . . . you're mocking it, nobody will take you seriously" . . . and the grin disappeared from my face. I said, no, no, no . . . I really believe this is what that song should sound like, and Bobby Griffith, bless him, said, "No, Hal, I'm older than you and this is what those songs sounded like." Hal said, "Nobody will take that seriously. . . . I don't think Sheldon can write that kind of song." They were arguing and my heart was sinking. The doorbell rang. It was our choreographer, Peter Gennaro. Before Pete came in, Hal said, "Everybody shut up—don't say anything—just play it." So we played and sang "Till Tomorrow." Peter grinned and said, "Oh! That's 1917—it's perfect!" And Hal grinned and he looked at me and said, "You've got the job." And that's the way it started.[4]

It is interesting that Stanley Green called "Till Tomorrow" one of the most memorable moments in the score.[5]

Bock and Harnick began working as a team on the show, musicalizing most of Weidman's clubhouse scene and producing the satirical and critically acclaimed number, "Politics and Poker." Harnick is quoted in an article for *Playwrights, Lyricists, Composers on Theatre*, edited by Otis L. Guernsey, that the latter song exhibited Weidman's generosity. It is difficult for librettists to have their ideas, jokes, lines of dialogue (perhaps even whole scenes) appropriated by the composer and lyricist (a common occurrence in the creation of a musical), but Weidman was most gracious:

One of Jerome Weidman's early drafts of *Fiorello!* contained a scene in which a number of ward-heelers were playing poker when they should have been attending to the business of choosing a candidate to run for Congress from their district. As written, it was an amusing scene which seemed certain to play well. Now, I had long had a desire to write a lyric involving poker terms which had struck me as especially colorful and tangy ever since I had played a lot of it in the army. When I read Mr. Weidman's scene, I had an instant vision of an effective song which could incorporate much of the scene and to which I felt I could contribute a great deal. I asked him if he would mind if Jerry and I tried to "musicalize" his scene. Generously, he told us to go ahead and to feel free to use anything in the scene which we felt would be valuable. I then proceeded to construct the lyric for "Politics and Poker," rephrasing what I felt were the most valuable aspects of the scene, and adding to them my own notions. When we played the song for Mr. Weidman, he was genuinely delighted, which must have taken great generosity of spirit indeed, for he must have seen that he would get no credit for a number of funny notions in the song, including the notion for the punch line ("You idiot, that's me!").[6]

Bock and Harnick soon wrote "On the Side of the Angels" as the opening number. Prince says that it is the major songs in a score that are usually the first to be written.

> This was true of "Wilkommen" in *Cabaret,* of "Company," of "Racing with the Clock" in *The Pajama Game.* Probably it's a very good idea, as they establish (or should) the ground rules for what is to follow ... the tone, style, concept, and often the point of the evening. Oscar Hammerstein said most musicals are made in the first five minutes.[7]

Fiorello! opens with a prologue based on an actual moment in history. LaGuardia, as mayor, is reading the Sunday "funnies" over the radio to the children of New York City during a newspaper strike. "In this one instant, Bosley establishes himself in his role; it's as though we are all listening again to the meanest, cussedest and sweetest chief executive this town ever had."[8]

Prince had no trouble raising the $300,000 for *Fiorello!* Most of his investors had been with him since *The Pajama Game.* Prince wrote them all once a month, but did not want to do backers' auditions. Prince claims that he doesn't understand the workings of his car and never asks the mechanic to show him the engine. Using similar reasoning, he sees no need to show investors how a show looks or sounds before they give him the money.[9]

Prince continued to learn from Abbott about how to structure a book for a musical and how to make a show "work." Sheldon Harnick recalls Prince's attitude towards his mentor:

> As a producer, Prince had great respect for Abbott as the director. Abbott was still at the peak of his powers although he was in his seventies. ... Abbott was very important in the theatre. He didn't like to feel that any point was

being labored. Get it done—do it—get on with the show. That was his style. So . . . there was always a great deal of editing in the shows. I think Hal carried on in that tradition—find out what the show is about and say it as succinctly and as entertainingly as you can and get on with it! Just make it move—make it move along. That's my recollection of the similarity between them.[10]

Harnick remembers that Prince was very encouraging during the creation of the show."One felt his buoyance, ebullience, his confidence and energy."[11] He gave young talent opportunities in his shows and he was very supportive of them. Harnick recalls one incident while rehearsing *Fiorello!*

> Hal did something that was wonderfully reassuring. One night on the way home from someplace in a taxi he said to me, "You're going to be one of the great lyricists." I felt so far from that because although I'd had a couple of songs in revues, I'd never had a hit song (I still don't have many hit songs). But I'd never had hit songs then and I'd written one Broadway show that was a flop. So I had very little to base feelings of confidence on and Hal was just very quiet and said you're going to be one of the great lyricists. And that was a wonderfully reassuring thing to hear.[12]

As he had done before and would again in the future, Prince gave the leading role in *Fiorello!* to an unknown—a 32-year-old Off-Broadway actor, Tom Bosley. The more experienced Eli Wallach was the one that they all had wanted for the leading role. Wallach was anxious to do it, but he lacked the vocal range required by the score. No other actor impressed them and so they went with the unknown Bosley, who had the look of LaGuardia.

Many changes were made during the out-of-town tryout of *Fiorello!* Numbers were taken out of the show and new ones added. "Little Tin Box," which was written on the road two weeks before the Broadway opening, became the much needed "eleven o'clock" show-stopper. Prince commented,"I remember hearing about eleven o'clock numbers all my life. Though I don't care much for formulas, I would settle for an eleven o'clock show-stopper every time. Those don't even hurt operas."[13]

Prince may have accepted the idea of an eleven o'clock show-stopper but he was not as positive about the inclusion of the subordinate story of the flapper and the policeman. The use of secondary characters was a common device in musicals of the forties and fifties. It enabled the writer to move away from the major story line and add diversion and supply comic relief. Subplots and secondary characters often provided the opportunity to use dance in the show. This was true of the Eddie Foy, Jr.,-Carol Haney duo in *The Pajama Game*. Prince felt that the use of secondary characters was a major flaw in *Fiorello!*. He was beginning to think that the American Musical Theatre needed restructuring to move it away from tried and tested formulas.

The out-of-town tryouts took place in New Haven and Philadelphia. Prince felt that the critics in Philadelphia were dangerous, "that audiences there were encouraged by criticism to go to the wrong shows, not to be discerning. . . . When *Fiorello!* was there *Saratoga* was doing the business."[14] In later years, Prince changed his mind. "Now, I think it's worth the try. Philadelphia is O.K. We need the cities."[15] In the case of the little city of New Haven, Prince was right—the reviews there were encouraging.

News film was used in the show to depict the years of World War I when LaGuardia went off to battle. Aram Boyajian was at the time a film editor working on *20th Century,* a CBS-TV program hosted by Walter Cronkite. Prince asked Mel Stewart, a researcher at CBS, to put together some footage. Stewart found the film and asked Boyajian to edit the section together for the show. Boyajian remembers that Prince and his people were very genial, allowing him the freedom to follow their instructions as he saw it. He remembers it as "very nice":[16]

> After many years in the business I realize how rare that quality is of allowing creative people to do their bit. And I had a feeling that this must work all along the line . . . [Prince allows] people to do their best. [Prince and his people] commented on it [Boyajian's work], but they gave [me] that freedom. I've worked on networks, cable, etc. and this is practically impossible to find.[17]

Fiorello! opened on 23 November 1959 at the Broadhurst Theatre in New York. The reviews were very good. Brooks Atkinson, in the *New York Times,* said, "The Little Flower is the most dynamic figure in the musical arcades this season. Again, everyone feels happier because his enkindling spirit is with us again."[18] Robert Coleman, in the *Daily Mirror,* said, "Robert Griffith and Harold Prince are still batting 1,000. They put their hit streak on the line last night with *Fiorello!* and whacked out another four-bagger. As usual, they are managing a team of talented newcomers, with old pro George Abbott in the clean-up spot."[19] Richard Watts, Jr., in the *New York Post,* liked the fact that the title role was well-rounded and not a cartoon character.[20]

The show won awards, including the New York Drama Critics Award and a Pulitzer Prize, the third musical comedy to win that honor. The first musical awarded a Pulitzer Prize was *Of Thee I Sing* in 1932, and Gerald Bordman compares the two shows. Bordman admits that "George Abbott and Jerome Weidman's book, Jerry Bock's score and Sheldon Harnick's lyrics were no mean achievement."[21] (The second musical to have won the Pulitzer Prize was *South Pacific* in 1949.) *Fiorello!* also won the Tony Award for Best Musical, tying with *The Sound of Music*.

Abbott was asked why he thought *Fiorello!* became such a critical success: "It happened to be about a political matter . . . an honest mayor. But basically it was just a good show and the lyrics worked and everything worked."[22]

Fiorello! ran 795 performances, not a great run after such a wonderful reception. Prince claims that he may have been responsible for the disappointing run. After a year at the Broadhurst, the show was moved to the larger 1800-seat Broadway Theatre. The producers then lowered the prices to $5, $4, and $3 (from the $7 top ticket price). They advertised the new price range but unfortunately the number of tickets sold did not increase. They were filling the same number of seats at a lower price. Prince says, "I simply assume the price of tickets wasn't the problem in 1960 after all."[23]

Prince gives another reason for the foreshortened run of *Fiorello!* In the spring of 1960, a strike ensued after weeks of negotiations between Actor's Equity and the League of New York Theatres, the latter representing producers and theatre owners. This was the first strike since 1919 (right after Actor's Equity was formed). The producers, rather than allowing a strike of a different show at each performance as Equity had planned (sensing that this method would confuse the public and keep them away), decided to black out all the shows. The strike lasted eight days. Due to the extended media coverage about "A Blacked-Out Broadway," audiences continued to stay away, destroying Broadway's momentum. "I believe," says Prince, "that the 1960 strike cost *Fiorello!* six months on Broadway."[24]

Fiorello!'s run and critical success insured Prince's place as one of the leading Broadway musical producers. The decade of the fifties was over and Prince and Griffith had had five major hits and only one failure. It was a fantastic six-year record and one that seemed destined to continue in much the same vein in the decade to come.

After *Fiorello!* Prince evinced an interest in becoming a director. In 1960, Roger Stevens offered him the opportunity to direct a musical version of *Juno and the Paycock,* but it never worked out. Prince asked Griffith how he felt about the idea of his partner becoming a director. Griffith suggested they co-direct their own shows. Prince felt that this is the one area in which Griffith treated him unfairly.

> It was the one thing in the world he didn't want me to be, and he didn't face it. . . . He had always said he was going to direct, even before I knew him. But he hadn't. I do not believe he would have been a particularly good director. It had become his curious, quiet failure, something which really didn't bother him—not until I became interested. . . . He had a true and unerring sense of what was honest acting. I had a stronger sense of what was good material. He had a better facility for working, dealing with people. I had the edge on him with respect to text and the physical aspects of a production, the scenery, costumes. We collaborated well, but when it came to direction, we could hardly have been co-directors.[25]

Abbott realized that Prince had a strong urge to direct and that Griffith did not wish to go along with it. Abbott said,

> I used to send the boys on the road to fix up shows and performances that were getting a bit shoddy—from being played too long. I always found that Prince could get good results. But Bobby didn't want to let go of him. He wanted to share in the thing. Once I said, "I'll send you separately!" But Bobby said, "No, we want to be together." Bobby wanted to direct also, but he didn't have the ability."[26]

Prince says that the most important thing that Abbott did for him was to encourage him in his desire to become a director. "Besides my family, he's the only person who, when I was anxious to direct, said, 'You can direct and go ahead and do it.' "[27]

THE SIXTIES BEGIN

Tenderloin

The creators of *Fiorello!* enjoyed their experience working together. Even before *Fiorello!* had opened, Abbott, Weidman, Bock, Harnick, Griffith and Prince began talking about their next show. Prince had been sent the galleys of the novel *Tenderloin* by a friend at Random House. The book was written by Samuel Hopkins Adams who died in 1958 at the age of 87 just as his book was going to press. Prince felt that the Gay Nineties period would lend itself to becoming a popular musical. They decided to adapt the work into a new musical entitled *Tenderloin.* They obtained the rights and proceeded at full speed. The subject of the novel was based on the attempts of the Reverend Charles H. Parkhurst to clean up the Tenderloin district of New York around West 23rd Street.

Abbott and Weidman as co-librettists hoped to give a feeling that debauchery was fun during the Gay Nineties in one of New York's most popular red-light districts. Prince's faithful backers, as usual, came up with the money, and the new show, capitalized at $350,000, went into production.

Sheldon Harnick discussed what he felt were problems. He thought they organized *Tenderloin* too quickly, and that they didn't follow the original source material closely enough.[1] He suggested where things may have gone wrong:

> We made a conceptual mistake that was everybody's mistake. If you read the novel you find out that the minister is a vital role but a relatively small

role. The main character is the boy. We made the mistake of making the roles equal in importance and then casting a star in the role as the minister. The reality of the Tenderloin situation was that it was an ugly place with disease and corruption. But in musical comedy you don't talk about disease and in a musical comedy corruption is a subject for comedy, not for social cure. So the minister who wanted to close the Tenderloin was a bore because the Tenderloin was what provided the excitement of the show.[2]

Prince agrees that the book of *Tenderloin* had many problems, but feels the major trouble with the show was that it did not establish a particular tone. When the creators became aware that they were unable to solve the problems with the libretto, they secretly asked help from two brothers, James and William Goldman, who would later go on to write, respectively, *The Lion in Winter* and *Butch Cassidy and the Sundance Kid*. Unfortunately, their help came too late. Prince now concludes that it was a mistake from the beginning to adapt that particular novel as a musical.

Prince also believes that they erred in casting Maurice Evans in the role of Rev. Brock. Abbott had favored Hugh Griffith for the part, who would have given the character an eccentric, even lunatic, sensibility. Prince, however, insisted on the Shakespearean star because it was offbeat casting.[3]

Richard Altman, who later became Jerome Robbins's assistant director on *Fiddler on the Roof*, had received a Ford Foundation grant to observe the creation of *Tenderloin*. In Altman's opinion, neither Abbott nor Evans had ever been clear as to who or what Brock was. Evans, however, was very pleased with his association with Abbott. An item in the *New York Daily News* said that he was awed at the Abbott pace, and at the speed with which the show was being whipped together.[4] Altman also commended Abbott on his staging ability and the way he blocked a huge crowd scene, juggling groups of 25 people extemporaneously. "After twenty minutes," said Altman, "everything was working, with much detail. Incredible!"[5]

As for Altman's impressions of Prince, he felt he was the epitome of the buoyant, effusive, always enthusiastic producer in action and was very much like the Robert Morse character in *Say, Darling*.

For Bock and Harnick, creating the score did not prove as easy as it had for *Fiorello!* Jerry Bock explained that "*Fiorello!* was easier in the sense that LaGuardia's life provided a more rigid historical framework to work within. With *Tenderloin*, one had to be more inventive. We wrote about three times more music than the show required."[6]

Harold Prince in the 1960s
(Photo courtesy Photofest)

The show opened with a hymn sung in a Park Avenue church, followed by the rousing "Little Old New York," a production number sung by the low-lifes who inhabited the Tenderloin. Prince says it is one of the best opening numbers he has ever seen. He also felt that the Bock and Harnick score for the show was a very good one. Ethan Mordden, in his book *Better Foot Forward,* agrees with Prince about the score, claiming that the songwriting team was "summa cum laude in the writing of integrated theatre scores" and that the "opening number was especially effective, an exponential proof positive that musicals weren't going to limit themselves to 'fourth-wall' literalism any more."[7]

Tenderloin opened in New Haven to mild reaction. Everyone was buoyed, however, by the fact that Stephen Sondheim saw the show and was positive and enthusiastic. At the meeting held after the New Haven opening, Prince was the only one of the collaborators disturbed by the show. No one else seemed concerned.

They opened in Boston with the same basic problems, except for the fine new opening number. The reviews in Boston were mixed. Three were favorable and three were not.

Altman offers a possible reason for Abbott's reluctance to make any changes out of town. Evans couldn't (or wouldn't) learn his lyrics and Abbott in desperation told him to carry the lyrics, pretending that they were letters from his parishioners. An entry in Altman's diary says, "Prince says Abbott is afraid to make changes now because Evans is such a slow study."[8] However, a new song, "Dear Friend," was added to the show and helped a great deal.

Cecil Beaton did both sets and costumes. His work, Prince felt, was tasteful and chic when it should have been vulgar. He did the right job for the wrong show.

Tenderloin opened in New York on 17 October 1960 at the 46th Street Theatre with an enormous advance sale of more than $750,000. It seemed that the public wanted to see the show. Prince does not agree, and feels that audiences rarely know in advance what they want to see. The opening night audience applauded almost all the musical numbers but was quiet during the book scenes. There were four curtain calls. John McClain, in the next morning's *Journal American,* wrote, "Sad to say, I believe *Tenderloin* is a clinker."[9] On the positive side, John Chapman, in the *News,* said:

> If I stopped to analyze the libretto of *Tenderloin* I could find some flaws, but last evening I didn't want to stop. I was having too good a time listening

to the Bock-Harnick songs, including many fetching choral numbers . . . and watching Joe Layton's frisky dancers doing modern tricks with old-fashioned dances like the schottische. It's a grand show, and I don't think my morals have been damaged much.[10]

Although the creators of *Tenderloin* were the same as those who had successfully shaped *Fiorello!,* and although many of the elements in this show were excellent and were admired by critics, the show failed. It was a definite disappointment. Afterwards, Prince said that he would never again do a show just because he thought it might be popular.

Tenderloin closed in New York after 214 performances. After the closing, Prince was, as always, eager to get back to work immediately. Throughout the years Prince—a self-confessed workaholic—has admitted that he is most happy when he is involved in a production. While rehearsing one show, he is usually busy planning his next. He schedules a meeting of his entire office on the morning after one of his productions opens. This meeting is meant to demonstrate that the office will actively start work on his next project (plans of which have usually been in the works for some time). This need to always have a project in the works has led Prince on occasion to do pieces that might better have been left undone. Prince has admitted to this. He suggests that, because of his need to start something new after *Tenderloin* closed, he rushed too quickly into his next project, *A Call on Kuprin,* his second attempt at producing a straight play.

A Call on Kuprin

A Call on Kuprin is an adaptation of a science-fiction novel published in 1959 and written by a British writer, Maurice Edelman, a member of Britain's Parliament. Edelman had written five novels and a half-dozen television plays for the British Broadcasting Company. The story is based on Russia's efforts to put a man in space. Prince believed that because most of the book was written in dialogue form, there would be little difficulty in preparing the script.

Jerome Lawrence and Robert E. Lee, who had written *Inherit the Wind* and *Auntie Mame,* were chosen to do the adaptation. Prince had wanted to call the play *An Adventure* and hoped, along with the writers, that it would not be a cartoon-like view of Moscow filled with gloomy Czarists or comic Communists. When they began shaping the play, the event which provides the fictional thrust of the story—the sending of a Cosmonaut into space—had not as yet taken place in the real world.

George Abbott was engaged to direct *Kuprin,* his 77th show on Broadway. Prince decided to risk a late season opening. Instead of waiting until fall, he went into production immediately with *A Call on Kuprin* and opened the play May 25, a week before the season expired. Prince felt he had too good a play to wait till fall.

After failing to sign Henry Fonda as star, the producers hired Jeffrey Lynn to play the role of Jonathan Smith, an American science writer determined to persuade his former astronomy professor, V. V. Kuprin, now Russia's most brilliant space scientist, to defect to the West. George Voskovec was set for the role of the scientist, Leon Janney to play a Soviet professor, and Lydia Bruce was cast as the romantic interest. Eugenie Leontovich, who played Kuprin's mother, was a Russian expatriate actress and a member of the Moscow Art Theatre before the Russian Revolution. In a cast of over 30, there were 19 speaking parts, of which 13 or 14 were played by Russian-speaking actors. Authenticity was pursued relentlessly.

The *Kuprin* physical production was mammoth. George Abbott, overheard at an out-of-town run-through, exclaimed, "Oh! For one of those one-set plays!"[11] Jack Gaver, in his syndicated UPI column, tended to agree with Abbott's sentiments, and said:

> Griffith and Prince specialized in musicals and one of their claims to fame was that, in these days of astronomical costs, they were able to bring in such productions for astonishingly moderate sums and make them pay off. Yet all of a sudden they brought in a basically simple melodrama—at the wrong time of the season—and spent enough money on the unnecessarily heavy physical production to finance at least two nonmusical shows. You got the impression that they thought they were presenting a combination of *Ben-Hur* and *Gone With the Wind.*[12]

Rehearsals for *Kuprin* began in New York on 10 April 1961 and the show opened a two-week pre-Broadway engagement at the Forrest Theatre in Philadelphia on May 8. The budget of $150,000 was high for a straight play. The cast was huge and the backstage crew equaled that of a musical comedy. Henry T. Murdock of the *Philadelphia Inquirer* liked the timeliness of the show as well as its melodramatic elements. He concluded, "If the theatre is ripe for melodrama, particularly a timely melodrama about space exploration and the U.S.-Soviet rivalry therein, then the prospects look bright for *A Call on Kuprin.*"[13]

Around the time the show was rehearsing and previewing in Philadelphia, first the Russians and then the Americans sent men into space.

Now the play, more than any of the collaborators had imagined, truly paralleled the current news. Prince believes that timing is very important in doing a project. Sometimes what starts as a unique idea loses its uniqueness in the time it takes to develop the idea into a play. Prince feels that this is what happened with *Kuprin.* The sense of awe and mystery disappeared when the real-life event took place.

Gaver reiterated the problem of dealing with shows based on current events. "Theatre through the ages has never been noted for successes about things of the moment, except possibly, in the case of topical revues."[14]

A Call on Kuprin opened on 25 May 1961 at the Broadhurst Theatre in New York. Taubman, in the *New York Times,* said that the play "is not only contemporary and tautly suspenseful but also says something of vast importance. . . . After a slow start, it holds and then grips the attention. But there need be no secret about the underlying truth it affirms that knowledge has no national borders."[15]

Prince had chosen to present a theatre piece that would challenge the audience. Although the *Times* review was excellent, the public didn't come to see the play. Prince remembers, "We sold one ticket (not even a pair) between 10 A.M., when the box office opened, and noon."[16] He kept the show open for a second week, thereby losing another $20,000. *A Call on Kuprin* closed on 3 June 1961 after fourteen performances. It was the second nonmusical that Griffith and Prince had produced and both had been failures. Prince was not deterred, however, from doing another straight play. Shortly he was involved with the comedy *Take Her, She's Mine,* and this play would be successful.

They Might Be Giants

It was around this time that Prince became excited about the work of an English director, Joan Littlewood. He had seen her production of *The Hostage* and was fascinated with her fresh approach and innovative staging. He liked the way she brought in fragments of songs which often seemed to erupt from the production rather than growing naturally out of the plot.

Littlewood influenced Prince after he began to direct. He claims that, after seeing *The Hostage* and for a decade afterwards, he and Sondheim discussed her technique. The manner in which songs were introduced in Prince's 1970 production *Company* owed a conscious debt to the work done by Littlewood in *The Hostage.*[17]

Littlewood also directed *Fings Ain't What They Used to Be* (the first

Lionel Bart musical) and *A Taste of Honey,* both of which Prince liked. However, when he first saw her work he was unaware of her working methods. She usually depends more on improvisation than on the existing script. *The Hostage* had less than one act on paper when she started work on it. *A Taste of Honey* had no real structure and was merely a collection of scenes. Littlewood also improvised *Fings Ain't What They Used to Be* with Lionel Bart in a free style that Prince suggests may have been the precursor of Tom O'Horgan's *Hair.* What Prince liked was Littlewood's irreverence and looseness.

Littlewood's 1964 production of *Oh, What a Lovely War,* which was created at her Stratford Theatre Workshop in England from improvisations and ideas and bits of dialogue from a group of writers, utilized scenes which were unrelated to plot but held together by the time (1914–18) and by theme (the folly of war). Bare, unlocalized sets stressed the universality of the show's theme and its disturbing ironies. An electrical sign, hung upstage, periodically spelled out statistics about World War I. In addition, giant projections of battlefield photos made bitterly ironic comments about the patriotic songs and slogans and comic routines. In the years that followed, as Hal Prince began to direct his own musicals, his theatrical vision paralleled that of Joan Littlewood's. Glenn Litton noted:

> One of the greatest admirers of *Oh, What a Lovely War* was Harold Prince, who believed it had "fractured the musical (comedy) form into something resembling a revue, discarding central characters, a story line." Here was a form that freed the musical from the rigid prescriptions of the integrated book, particularly the rule that all songs in a musical must grow out of its dialogue, that they must help tell its story. The countless alternatives suggested by *Oh, What a Lovely War* were especially inspiring to a producer/director who, since *West Side Story,* had been trying to renovate rather than replace the book musical but who had become increasingly frustrated by his efforts.[18]

In the fall of 1960, while the out-of-town tryouts of *Tenderloin* were in progress, Prince acquired the rights to the play *They Might Be Giants,* written by James Goldman, one of the two Goldman brothers who had come to Boston to help the troubled musical. Goldman, a native of Chicago, had spent two years writing *They Might Be Giants.* The script, his first play, was "about a wealthy American with a Sherlock Holmes fixation, about his family who sent him to a psychoanalyst to have him declared insane so they could get their hands on his money."[19]

Prince was most anxious to collaborate with Joan Littlewood on some project, and sent a note to her in England introducing himself and sending her a copy of the Goldman play. She replied quickly that she would like to do it. Rehearsals were scheduled for June with a projected opening on 28 June at the Theatre Royale, Stratford (Littlewood's Theatre Workshop), which was in the East End of London. This was to be the first time in its fifteen-year history that another theatrical management would be associated with a Theatre Workshop production at the Theatre Royale, Stratford. It was even more unusual in that it was to be an American management (Griffith and Prince). Littlewood would direct the play and the plan was to move it to the West End and then to Broadway the following season. In New York in April 1961 the run of *Tenderloin* ended. *A Call on Kuprin* had had a quick opening and closing. Prince, therefore, did not get to London to meet with Littlewood until three days before the scheduled opening of *Giants*.

When he arrived, Prince was startled to see that the actors were still improvising and doing exercises to better inform themselves about their roles. It was very close to opening night, and the situation appeared chaotic, but Prince decided that they open on schedule. Littlewood wanted an additional week to rehearse, but Prince ruled against it. Littlewood was known to do her best work after a show had opened.

The show, which featured Harry H. Corbett as Holmes and Avis Bunnage as an American spinster (both of whom had also been in *The Hostage*), opened on schedule and was a failure. One report of the production in the English press said:

> The script is often funny . . . but the casting is drably inept. Neither Harry H. Corbett nor Avis Bunnage comes within miles of the Robert Morley-Katharine Hepburn partnership that the author seems to have envisaged; and Joan Littlewood is the last director I would choose to send the more whimsical nuances of New York wit winging across to a paying audience.[20]

British theatre critic Milton Shulman suggested that Goldman's theme may have been about the wickedness of materialism, the need of togetherness and the sanity of the insane. He said that Goldman's philosophical approach to life is about as significant as the cards collected in your nearest weighing machine. Shulman went on: "Even more disturbing than the juvenilia of the symbolism is the gauche and awkward manner in which Joan Littlewood has directed this odd offering."[21]

Littlewood took full responsibility for the chaos. It was clear that her previous experiences had not been with scripts like Goldman's, which had tightly structured scenes and dialogue that was carefully thought out, even providing stage directions. With the wisdom of hindsight, Prince realized that Littlewood's lack of a disciplined style of rehearsing made the carefully structured Goldman play the wrong vehicle for her. Littlewood, upset at the play's failure, closed her theatre and went to Nigeria. It was the last production of the Theatre Royale for many years.

Prince returned to New York and Goldman suggested that Prince direct the play on Broadway himself. Prince, anxious for a directing career, agreed. Knowing there was something wrong with the script, however, and anxious to discover what it was, he arranged a reading of the piece with George C. Scott and Colleen Dewhurst. Prince says that as good as the reading was, the play didn't work and he couldn't zero in on the flaw.

Prince was reluctant to give up on *They Might Be Giants* but eventually he did. The play never reached Broadway. However, the motion picture rights to the piece were retained and in 1968 Universal made a film of it starring George C. Scott and Joanne Woodward and directed by Anthony Harvey. With a percentage arranged for the producers, they eventually and most unusually got back all the money they had lost in 1961.

With the closing of *Kuprin* on 3 June 1961 and the Littlewood production of *They Might Be Giants* being readied in London, Griffith and Prince had no show on Broadway for the first time in seven years. Griffith felt badly about the failures of *Kuprin* and *Tenderloin* and decided to slow down. He suggested that Prince produce some shows without him. He did not want to discontinue their partnership, but wished to function only as an adviser, retaining minimal interest in Prince's solo projects. He seemed anxious to devote more time to his private life.

Prince didn't feel that their partnership would end. The partners had been together for eight years, often working closely from nine in the morning until eleven at night, six days a week. He did feel, however, the conflict involving his own desire to direct and Griffith's inability to support that desire. Then, early in June 1961, Griffith, while playing golf with Abbott at the Westchester Country Club, collapsed. He died early the next morning, 7 June, in Parkchester Hospital.

Abbott recalls the unique partnership of Griffith and Prince:

It was a very strong emotional relationship. Obviously, as time progressed, Hal must have felt held back by Bobby who was not as smart as he and who objected to his wish to direct. Bobby was a good enough theatre man but he wasn't in Hal's class as far as theatre knowledge went. However, I think had he lived, Hal would never have deserted him. They were very strong friends.[22]

Prince found it difficult to analyze the relationship he had had with Griffith.

A brother, maybe, and certainly, in the area of stage managing, a teacher, a patient one, for I was emotionally ill-suited to that job. But he covered for me during those years, and I got out and into producing before anybody caught on. A friend. We loved each other. Ironically, he helped me in very real ways to calm down, to enjoy life, more, in fact, than he was able to enjoy his own. He was generous, the delight of the panhandlers in front of the Lambs Club.[23]

Sheldon Harnick also discussed the relationship between the two partners:

Bobby and Hal complemented each other wonderfully. Hal was ebullient and outgoing. Bobby was quiet, thoughtful. What their method of working together was like, I don't know. I only saw the public side of it and from the public side of it it always looked like Hal was the moving force, because he seemed to dominate the conversations, take the lead. In private it may not have been like that at all. But that was the impression one had.[24]

After Griffith's death, which Prince has called the loneliest period of his life, he found himself having to make independent decisions and to reassess many things. He decided to produce himself and mainly without partners, except in very special cases. Some people questioned Prince's ability to manage successfully on his own. He had depended on Griffith's considerable knowledge and experience in the theatre. During his years with Griffith, Prince the mercurial and nervous one, gave the impression that he would be lost without his steady balance wheel. Ironically, as the years progressed, and as Prince matured both personally and professionally, he became the balance wheel to many of the people working with him.[25]

He restructured his production company, making Ruth Mitchell an associate and Carl Fisher, who had been general manager, a partner, taking on the many business chores that Griffith had attended to and which Prince disliked doing. Prince was capable of delegating responsibilities to staff members without feeling threatened. This allowed him to turn his energies towards his major ambition at the time: becoming a director.

A CHANCE TO DIRECT

People in general become closed to life, and that's very bad for people in the arts, particularly successful people. You find most successful people repeating themselves; because it's safe. To do anything, particularly in the theatre, is really walking out on a gangplank and diving out into a sea of shark.
—Arthur Laurents, Quoted in the *New York Times,* 21 August 1983

Take Her, She's Mine

Judy Abbott had given Prince a script of a light comedy to read, *Age of Consent,* by screenwriters Phoebe and Henry Ephron, later retitled *Take Her, She's Mine.* Based on the Ephrons' family life and two daughters, the play focused on Nora Ephron, the eldest child (called Mollie Michaelson in the play) and the pain a father feels when he hands his daughter over to another man. Prince liked the play and decided to produce it.

Abbott agreed to direct, his 80th directorial assignment on Broadway. Art Carney, a television star on the *Jackie Gleason Show* and familiar to audiences for his portrayal of Gleason's sidekick Ed Norton, was given the role of the father; Phyllis Thaxter, a motion picture actress, was cast as the mother. Elizabeth Ashley, a 21-year-old Baton Rouge, Louisiana ingenue, who had been understudy to Barbara Bel Geddes in *Mary, Mary,* was set for the role of the elder daughter.

The show was capitalized at $150,000 and, in a most unusual arrangement, Prince sold the rights to 20th Century-Fox shortly before the production opened its pre-Broadway tryout tour in New Haven. The picture deal, said *Variety,* "is understood to involve a down payment of $150,000 plus a percentage of the gross on profitable weeks up to an undisclosed ceiling."[1]

William and Jean Eckart, who had designed *Damn Yankees* and *Fiorello!,* were hired to design the multiple settings required for the play: the family's California home, the college and surrounding spots in New England.

The Ephrons gave a witty interview to Stuart W. Little in the *Herald Tribune,* saying more humorously than bitingly that they were disturbed about New Haven, where the play opened on 25 November. They said they had asked Prince not to take the play to either New Haven or Boston since those were two places written about in the play. Ephron said, "We talk about Harvard and Yale and all the women's colleges around them, the so-called 'Heavenly Seven.' So naturally he's sending us right to New Haven and then to Boston."[2] However, Prince was right in his judgment because the reviews in both cities were very good.

In Boston, Elinor Hughes of the *Boston Herald* said that the huge audience that filled the Shubert Theatre initially came prepared to enjoy Carney. They remained to enjoy not only Carney but also the play. "They enjoyed it so much they are probably still laughing. . . . It is a clean, funny and attractively presented comedy about the difficulties parents have in understanding their growing children."[3] Hughes concludes that "Harold S. Prince in his first solo venture as a producer has come up with a winner."[4]

Take Her, She's Mine was ready for its 21 December 1961 opening on Broadway. The comedy was the first legitimate show to play the completely redecorated Biltmore Theatre in ten years. Not since the fall of 1951 and *The Number* had the Biltmore housed legitimate shows; it had been host to television, originating shows for CBS, for eight years.

In Prince's opinion, the only good reviews were those from out of town.

Take Her, She's Mine played the Shubert in Boston, with a seating capacity of 1700. The size of the theatre made for a bigger, broader performance. That, plus the greater decibels of laughter, created a perfect relationship between the stage and the audience for the easy, good-natured superficiality of the material. In New York we played the Biltmore, seating 948. The actors were forced to modulate their performances. Laughter was cut by half, and the play begged for more serious scrutiny.[5]

John Chapman in the *Daily News* said:

> As a piece of theatre, it lacks pace, but it almost makes up for this shortcoming with charm. . . . It was not designed to kill you with laughter; all it wants to do is warm your heart. Maybe it will, if your heart is warmer than mine to begin with.[6]

The show played for a little less than a year and then toured an additional season. It made a decent profit and was a "surefire" commercial venture. This made it unnecessary for Prince to accept Abbott's gracious offer, for the second time in his producing career, of free office space until his new producing setup became secure. Producing "solo" had started off for Prince quite successfully.

Up until now, Prince had not lacked the courage to present shows containing subject matter that his fellow producers often avoided. However, at the same time, he had been involved in projects that could be described as "run-of-the-mill" commercial ventures. Perhaps he had not yet formulated a clear picture of what he wished to accomplish or change in the musical theatre. That part of his career was still ahead of him. He said, "*Take Her, She's Mine* could have been produced by anyone. A number of shows that preceded it fit that category. Others, the best of them, the Abbott shows, had a texture which was his, but even he wasn't so much concerned with content as I was going to be."[7] However, a new phase in Prince's career was about to begin.

A Family Affair

Prince began his long-sought-after directing career on Broadway by attempting to rescue the musical *A Family Affair* early in 1962. He had not been involved with the project from its inception, but replaced the original director, Word Baker, near the completion of the show's out-of-town tryout. As Gary Paul Gates said in his *Holiday* magazine article, "The show, a mindless trifle, was being quietly put to sleep in Philadelphia, when Prince was called in for last minute resuscitation and he managed to breathe enough life into it to give it at least a brief Broadway run."[8]

Prince had been made aware of the property about the time he was working on *Tenderloin*. Sondheim had suggested that he look into *A Family*

Affair, an original musical. Prince felt that the book by James and William Goldman was humorous and that the score by John Kander was superior. Kander had started his theatrical career as a conductor for stock company orchestras and then arranged the dance music for *Gypsy* and *Irma La Douce.* *A Family Affair* was his first original score. The story dealt with the actions of a young Jewish couple planning their wedding from the time of their engagement to the ceremony itself. The only thing standing in their way is the cold war that develops between the girl's guardian and the boy's parents as they make their plans for the big event. *Variety* in Philadelphia called it a "kosher version of *Father of the Bride.*"[9]

Prince had earlier decided against doing the show as its original director. He had not been happy with the predictability of the story. Later, however, he was so anxious to direct a Broadway production that he took over the assignment from Word Baker when it was offered.

In early 1961 Leland Hayward had bought the rights to the show and planned to present it in association with Jerome Robbins, who was expected to both stage and choreograph the production. Eventually they decided against doing it and the play was optioned by a lawyer, Andrew Siff. It was to be his first show. Siff hired Word Baker, a director of two prominent Off-Broadway productions, *The Fantasticks* and *The Crucible.*

Baker cast Shelley Berman, who had made a name for himself as a nightclub stand-up comedian, as Alfie Nathan, the bride's guardian and bachelor uncle. Berman had a brittle, desperate style of delivery.

With John Butler as choreographer, sets and lights by David Hays, and costumes by Robert Fletcher, the show went to Philadelphia for its pre-Broadway run scheduled from 23 December 1961 until 1 January 1962 at the Erlanger Theatre. It was due to return to New York for a week of previews and an opening on 27 January 1962. The show was capitalized at $350,000 and United Artists Records was a substantial investor. They also put out the cast album.

The reviews were not good in Philadelphia. *Variety* said that the show needed momentum and wrote, "The production was rough . . . and in the second act virtually all the ensembles failed to jell."[10]

The producer, Siff, was about to close the show and cancel the New York opening, but first he sent out a call to Robbins, Abbott and Gower Champion to see if they were interested and/or available to come to Philadelphia to help the show. None of them was. It was at this point that the collaborators, who all knew Prince, turned to him although they knew he had never directed before. Prince said, "Failing with every musical director in New York, they invited me."[11] Prince remembers what happened:

I visited the show in Philadelphia. It was a mess. The material that I liked so much on paper was impossible to see for the production that was imposed on it, a unit set that looked like a tiered wedding cake, with doughnut turntables that moved at a snail's pace, and a cyclorama of wedding lace in front of which they played the entire show. . . . Instead of a realistic old-fashioned musical with walls, and doors, and corners, they had gone chic with yards and yards of China silk and surrealistic costumes. It had a big chorus it didn't need. It was a disaster. . . . Still, I remembered the material and if you could simply put back on the stage what I'd read, in focus so we could *see* it, that alone would have to make an enormous difference.[12]

Prince sized up the situation quickly. He believed that he could fix the show or at least make it respectable. He was given the assurance of full authority. However, there was no audience for the show in Philadelphia and they were unable to meet expenses. To make matters worse, they were scheduled to open in New York in a little over two weeks.

Prince didn't think the show would be a hit, even if he fixed everything that was wrong with it. When he called Abbott for advice, Abbott told him to keep that thought in mind so that he would not be disappointed if it failed. Abbott encouraged and supported his desire to work on it.

Prince replaced director Baker on 5 January in Philadelphia. Baker was said to have resigned because of artistic differences with the management but would receive program credit. Bob Herget was also called in to help John Butler with the choreography. Knowing they would need extra time to get the show into shape, the New York opening was changed from 23 to 27 January. Prince made it clear to everyone involved in the show that there was no time left for "collaboration." They would have to do exactly what he said if he were to whip the show into shape for its opening in New York. This was a big demand from a novice director, yet everyone agreed.

Prince worked closely with the authors. In order to establish the confidence of the company, he worked on the least successful scene of the play first. The sequence entailed a passage of time, a type of scene common in musicals of the day, which used mime, music or people rushing about the stage to denote that it was now "later." The Goldmans wrote in Prince's idea for the scene involving new dialogue for Berman, who became incensed and refused to play. Prince remained tough, offering to return to New York and leave them with their troubled play. Berman relented. When the scene was played, it worked and the cast congratulated their new director. Berman apologized. After that, Prince felt he was in command.

In New York on 18 January, Prince added three new scenes and re-staged one whole number. *A Family Affair* continued with a long string of paid previews before its 27 January premiere. Berman, who eventually was most enthusiastic about Prince's work on the show, said about his new director in an interview with Joseph Morgenstern of the *Herald Tribune* a week before the show opened:

> He's a murderer, a marvelous murderer . . . a benevolent killer. Anything cute goes out. Is he ruthless? Of course he's ruthless. Of course you've gotta be a murderer with your own stuff. That's why Prince is so marvelous for us. Otherwise, everything is a jewel. Everything is gospel.[13]

Prince told a newspaperman, in relation to Berman's labeling him as ruthless, that he didn't think he was so at all. "I want to be liked too much. But coming from Berman, who can be pretty ruthless himself, it's my favorite compliment."[14]

Prince handed the principals as many as five new pages of script to learn at each preview performance. However, not all the material was new. A good deal of the earlier work done by Baker had been retained but changed. Prince said:

> I know now we could not have accomplished what we had in ten days were it not for Baker's initial direction. The performers knew who they were. There has to be that solid a foundation for you to be able to tumult it to the degree I did in such a short time without destroying it.[15]

Prince ordered new lyrics, and the set was simplified. Carpenters were ordered to obliterate with black paint as much as they could of the many elements in the set. Although Prince had initially refused billing as director, after working so diligently to make it work, he changed his mind. He said, "it seemed to me sheer cowardice to hide behind someone else's credit."[16]

A Family Affair opened on 27 January 1962 at the Billy Rose Theatre. Although the show wasn't a success, it was not totally dismissed by the critics. Howard Taubman of the *New York Times* felt that

> the writing of *A Family Affair* is not strong on taste; it resorts to the clichés of Jewish domestic attitudes. Nor is it fresh in style; it often has the air of a busy, good-humored borrower from various musical-comedy sources. Since some of these sources are first-rate, some numbers are lively.[17]

John Chapman in the *Daily News* liked the first-act finale quartet sung by Bibi Osterwald, Jack De Leon, Gino Conforti and Linda Lavin. He also felt that "Harold Prince has directed the show with an eye to humorous effect."[18] The *Herald Tribune*'s Walter Kerr liked much of the show, mainly because of what he thought composer-librettists John Kander and William and James Goldman had contributed to it. But he also pointed out where the show had failed:

> It falls off in the vacuousness of some of its blackouts, falls off in the repetitiousness of quarrels that don't progress, falls off most notoriously in its second-act reaching for incidental numbers (such as a bachelor party) that are far enough afield to be arrested for vagrancy. . . . A most appealing "almost."[19]

Richard Adler, who did the lyrics for *The Pajama Game* and *Damn Yankees,* felt *A Family Affair* was not a very good play. He said:

> Hal and I were friendly in those days. He was given an opportunity to direct his first show. I didn't think he did much of a job on it. I thought—just like all orchestrators want to be composers, all producers want to be directors. I thought he'd never succeed after seeing *A Family Affair.* But, I was being intolerant and not remembering that it was a first effort. And look what he's gone and done! I think that the staging in later years of *Candide* and *Evita* are two of the most brilliant pieces of musical stagecraft I've ever seen.[20]

Although *A Family Affair* lasted only 65 performances, Prince felt that it "gave me a chance to feel my own strength, my influence over people."[21] His lifelong dream of becoming a Broadway director had finally been realized.

A Funny Thing Happened on the Way to the Forum

Prior to Griffith's death, Prince had read a script called *A Funny Thing Happened on the Way to the Forum,* written by Burt Shevelove and Larry Gelbart. The piece had had a long history before it was a product for the American Musical Theatre. Earlier, before World War II, while he was in his freshman year in the Department of Drama at Yale University, Shevelove had written the lyrics for a musical version of Plautus' *Mostellaria.* Richard O'Connell (who would later become the authorized translator of Lorca's plays) had directed a production of the play as a partial requirement for his master's degree. O'Connell had "conceived it as a Broadway musical comedy," wrote Shevelove many years later.[22] "I remember one of the songs was called 'A Couple of Greeks on a Roman Holiday.' It was that sort of show. The faculty and students adored it."[23]

Later, when Shevelove was the resident director of the Yale Dramat, the club did a musical called *When in Rome,* loosely based on Plautus' *Miles Gloriosus* and *Pseudolus.* After the war, Shevelove became a successful theatre and television writer and director. One evening he and a group of friends were sitting around complaining about the lack of low comedy on Broadway. Shevelove recalls the sentiments they all shared: "There were plenty of touching, even tragic, lovers, plenty of dream ballets, and plenty of important truths, stated and restated, but no fun."[24] Stephen Sondheim was excited by Shevelove's idea to do something farcical on Broadway using Plautus' plays. He encouraged Shevelove who then got hold of Larry Gelbart, another witty television writer, to do a book based on the plays, for which he—Sondheim—would do the score. It was about the time that *West Side Story* had begun its initial Broadway run, and Sondheim was undoubtedly eager to write both music and lyrics for a show.

Shevelove explained the restrictions that he and Gelbart had imposed on themselves:

> We would preserve the classic unities of time, place, and action. We would use the classic characters of Plautus. We would have no anachronisms or sly references to today. But we realized we would have to invent a plot (the original plots are negligible) to accommodate all the characters we wanted to use.[25]

By early 1958, the first draft of *Forum* was nearing completion. It would go through fifteen rewrites, three producers and three directors before opening on Broadway.

Sondheim called Jerome Robbins, who was looking for a farce. Robbins was excited by the project and a tentative agreement was reached to do what Shevelove referred to as *A Scenario for Vaudevillians.*[26] The authors referred to their show as a "play for vaudevillians."[27]

Leland Hayward evinced interest in the project but soon dropped out. There was a delay while Sondheim worked on the lyrics of *Gypsy,* with Robbins directing. Sondheim offered what was to become *Forum* to Prince but he and Griffith turned it down. By then, David Merrick had optioned the show. Robbins dropped out because "Robbins and Merrick didn't get along well."[28] Eventually, the creators returned Merrick's $4,000 option and Robbins, who had now renewed his involvement with the project, suggested that Prince and Griffith be asked to produce. Prince remembers that his partner was not anxious to do the project. "Bobby [Griffith] wasn't enthused. I was. They went about arranging a release from Merrick, and I sent the script to Phil Silvers, for whom it had been written."[29] Silvers turned the project down because it was "old schtick, not realizing that that was precisely the show's intention."[30] Others also turned down the project because they weren't excited by the script. It was offered to the American Theatre Society, a board of producers and theatre owners in Washington, D.C. They wouldn't even consider it for a Theatre Guild subscription. They didn't think it was funny, and in addition said it was confusing. Prince said, "Somehow at the piano and on paper it was a show that, to put it mildly, was attractive to a minimal number of people."[31] Shevelove said:

> People are oriented by the shows they've seen before. They said, "There's only room for one or two dances in it and you don't care anything about the kids." And we said, "You're not supposed to care anything about the kids." Also, one set of costumes didn't strike them as a musical. Our reason for putting it on was an affectionate one. Low comedy and farce in America are rarely done and are rarely successful.[32]

Prince, however, was eager to do *Forum,* having the same kind of conviction and excitement about it as he had had with *West Side Story.* Griffith finally but unenthusiastically agreed to co-produce it. His sudden death, however, left Prince as the sole producer.

Take Her, She's Mine went into production, and Prince shelved *Forum,* deciding to wait until the spring of 1962 to go into rehearsals with it.

When Prince returned to *Forum,* he released the news that Milton Berle would be playing the role written for Silvers. Craig Zadan said that Berle, afraid that many of his best lines might be cut during the numerous revisions of the libretto, insisted that script approval be included in his contract. He also wanted a say on casting, choice of choreographer, scene and costume designers, as well as the theatre to be rented. Prince refused and Berle withdrew.[33]

Zero Mostel was finally signed to play the role of Pseudolus, the slave who wanted to be free, in a show that Martin Gottfried called in his book *Broadway Musicals,* "the most intellectual of our musical books ... the least likely book of musicals to date. ... [I]ts brains are applied to showmanship."[34] Gottfried noted that the show had been written for Silvers, announced with Berle, and opened with Mostel which, "as its title suggests, was a tribute to comics."[35] Prince wanted Zero Mostel because he loved his work in clubs and his performance in *Rhinoceros,* which had earned him a Tony Award for the best acting of the 1960–61 season. Mostel had become known in theatre circles for his work on that show as well as for *Ulysses in Nighttown.* He had also appeared in *Beggar's Holiday* in 1946 under George Abbott's direction. Initially, Mostel refused the part in *Forum* but he later noted that it was his wife who convinced him to accept the role.

The authors of the show were very unhappy with Prince's decision to cast Mostel as Pseudolus. They had wanted him to play Lycus, the pimp. According to Prince, the atmosphere became unpleasant. It was now December of 1961 and the aim had been for a February rehearsal period and a spring opening. Prince remained firm, and the deal with Mostel was made.[36]

Abbott, who had been asked to direct after Robbins left the production, supported Prince, saying that if Mostel wasn't accepted he would withdraw from the show. Shevelove and Gelbart, unhappy as they were, decided to go ahead with Mostel.[37]

The authors of *Forum* were never completely satisfied with Mostel. They recognized his talent, but felt that he lacked stage discipline. He would improvise lines and business rather than do what had been set in rehearsals. The authors and Prince himself felt that Mostel's ad libs often detracted from the material and the smooth running of the production. However, Prince contends that Mostel was brilliant in the role.[38]

Forum director George Abbott recalls that the show's authors, too, had to be reined in:

> I never had anything to do with the show until it was in its last stages. Hal came to me and said, "We want you to take it over." I said I would cut it so drastically that the writers would hate me. Hal said, "No, they won't. . . . They now need a strong hand to go to work on it." So I took it to my country home, and I cut it a lot. And [the writers] said. "Dandy!" The script, you see, had been very verbose.[39]

Sondheim contends that the writers had a hand in cutting the script also, accepting some Abbott cuts and rejecting others.[40]

The show was a mixture of vaudeville, musical comedy, farce, and burlesque. "Not all the gags that turn up at the Alvin appear in the Roman originals," noted Walter Kerr.[41] There were all kinds of crossed eyes, dropped pants, crossed spears and curtains that fell down when they were

A Funny Thing Happened on the Way to the Forum, 1962
John Carradine, Jack Gilford, David Burns, and Zero Mostel perform the
musical number, "Everybody Ought to Have a Maid."
(Photo courtesy Photofest)

supposed to go up, and unexpectedly opened doors. In addition to Mostel, the cast included an array of such clowns as Jack Gilford and David Burns. Stephen Sondheim, in an interview with Brendan Gill, said "*Forum* tells a story, but not in terms of characters. It's a show without characters. It basically uses vaudeville techniques. And Shevelove originally wanted it in front of an olio."[42]

Sondheim is a great fan of the libretto of *Forum*. He thinks that people don't give sufficient credit to it.

> We worked on the show over a period of four years. It took Larry and Burt eleven complete and distinct separate drafts, and everybody thinks that it was whipped up over a weekend because it plays so easily. The plotting is intricate, the dialogue is never anachronistic, and there are only two or three jokes—the rest is comic situation.[43]

The action of *Forum* takes place in a single setting of a street in ancient Rome containing a brothel and the houses of two patricians. There is a small cast of stock comic characters out of Roman farces: the cunning slave, the painfully honest young virgin, the lovesick young man, the lecherous old man, the domineering wife, the hysterical slave, the befuddled old man, the avaricious pimp, and the braggart warrior.

Sondheim's first complete score for a Broadway show won approval. He claims that, while writing the score, he was rebelling against the kind of writing he had learned from Oscar Hammerstein II. "There were other ways to write shows outside the Rodgers and Hammerstein tradition."[44] He found it most difficult, since he had been trained to use songs solely for dramatic purposes, unlike other songwriters who received their training in revue or nightclub work in which a song must be its own entity without having to relate to anything around it.[45] *Forum*, said Sondheim, "is about 'let's sing about this moment'—an old-fashioned concept but a highly sophisticated form."[46] Sondheim feels that the show was experimental. Shevelove, however, convinced Sondheim that the show would become tedious without the songs. He said:

> Without the songs, the show would become relentless. It would exhaust you and you wouldn't get any breathers, any savoring of certain moments. . . . When Steve [Sondheim] first started, he only wanted to write songs integrated into the show that would advance the plot and increase your knowledge of the characters. I tried to tell him that the songs don't have to do that. Plays have breathers, too, and in *Forum* the songs can be respites.[47]

The reaction of the critics to Sondheim's score was generally not very good, with some dissent. His music was not as highly praised as his lyrics, the notices suggesting that he didn't write "hummable" tunes. *Variety* said that Sondheim's score contained "overly clever words" and "music which seems not so melodic as serviceable in terms of comic situation."[48] Leonard Hoffman in the *Hollywood Reporter* felt that Sondheim's score was "not of top calibre."[49] *Newsday*'s George Oppenheimer, however, praised him highly, saying that he had made a happy debut as composer-lyricist.

Forum opened at the Shubert Theatre in New Haven on 31 March 1962 to unenthusiastic reviews. Much of the material that Abbott had suggested be cut was put back into the show because the writers felt a good deal of the fun had been lost. The complications of all the various plots and subplots were reinstated. The ingenue and juvenile were recast, Preshy Marker and Brian Davies replacing Karen Black and Pat Fox, but Prince was still not happy with the casting of these two parts:

> Somewhere earlier I had brought in a girl and boy, namely Barbara Harris and Joel Grey, and I was laughed out of that audition. The point that I was trying to make was that the two young people should have been terribly comic. I still think I was right and if I was doing the show today, that's the way I'd do it. They would probably still fight me, but I'd win. Let's put it this way, in those days they were happy with me just as a producer. And I think I was a good one.[50]

In Washington, D.C., the show opened at the National Theatre with a benefit performance for government officials, which Prince believes was not a good idea.

> They began to walk out on us soon after the curtain went up. By the bows we'd lost over 50 percent of them. The reviews reflected it. Richard Coe, of the *Washington Post,* perhaps the most influential and respected of the critics, suggested closing it.[51]

Coe wrote, "It's not a bad idea to have an intimate little musical from an old Roman farce, but a good deal more steam will be needed to reassure you that you haven't wandered into amateur night."[52]

The collaborators thought that the audience did not know how to react to the show, but they did not know the remedy. Although audiences remained small and the press had advised them to close the show, Prince remained firm in his determination.

I think my biggest contribution to the show was that I was very sure about it. When the whole world's falling apart, you should have *somebody* who's sure. I never doubted for one minute that the show would be a smash in New York. The problems were all with the authors—they weren't getting along very well at that point. Steve [Sondheim] needed somebody else to tell him what to do.[53]

It was at this point that Sondheim suggested they bring in Jerome Robbins to look at the show and Prince agreed.

Prince believes that in a situation like this one he has to move decisively and without fear. He felt he knew what to do and he didn't waver. Many of his collaborators agree, saying that Prince, once he decides what must be done, has the courage of his convictions. Robbins, who had originally been scheduled to direct the show, now went down to Washington as "play doctor." The problem for him was the opening number. "Love Is in the Air" did not tell the audience what the show would be about. "Up until now, we'd thought *A Funny Thing* was about love being in the air, but of course it wasn't," said Prince.[54] Robbins felt that the audience did not realize that they were about to see a low comedy and were not prepared to laugh. At Robbins' suggestion, Sondheim was asked to write another opening number. "So one weekend in Washington I wrote 'Comedy Tonight.' Jerry staged it over the next week (along with restaging several other musical numbers in the show and reblocking the end chase scene)," said Sondheim.[55] On the first night of the first preview in New York with the new opening, the audience reaction changed. Sondheim says there was more to it than that. He had originally written an opening number called "Invocation" which was turned down by Abbott and Prince in favor of "Love Is in the Air." When Robbins suggested that they change the opening number Sondheim went back to the feeling of "Invocation" and wrote "Comedy Tonight" in the same vein.[56] As is customary with "play doctors," Robbins was not credited in the program. It is common knowledge, however, that his ideas had a most important impact on the production. And happily, he and Abbott got along together compatibly.

Jack Cole created the few dances in *Forum*. There was no dance chorus. As Howard Taubman said in the *New York Times,* "There is choreography by Jack Cole—it says here—but not much."[57] One of the scenes Cole staged was an amusing funeral sequence and dance.

Zero Mostel and George Abbott, 1962
Star and director talk backstage in Mostel's dressing room during the run of *A Funny Thing Happened on the Way to the Forum.*
(Photo courtesy Photofest)

Forum was capitalized at $300,000 and opened at a cost of $240,000 at the Alvin Theatre in New York on 8 May 1962 after eight previews. The New York reviews were mostly good except for John Chapman in the *Daily News*. It was a late season opening and there was an advance of only $40,000. However, within two months it began selling out. Richard Watts, Jr., in the *New York Post* said:

> The new musical comedy which opened last night at the Alvin Theatre makes no pretenses of subtlety, delicacy or lavishness, and it can lay no claim to distinction of story, song or choreography. It is simply a burlesque show with a pseudoclassic Roman setting and a firm conviction that pace and simple basic humor are important to farce. But the fact remains that, in its shameless fashion, it is downright hilarious.[58]

Forum won the Tony Award as best musical in 1963, and it was recorded by Capitol Records. A revival of the show was presented in 1972 with Phil Silvers playing the role that had been written for him, with co-author Burt Shevelove directing. Although the reviews were even better the second time around, Prince believes that the production was not as good as the original.

A film version of *Forum* had Silvers playing Lycus rather than Pseudolus. The writers of the Broadway show disliked the film because the story wasn't told well.

Forum is regularly performed professionally all over the world and is a staple of stock and amateur groups in the U.S. Prince had contributed a great deal toward making the show a success in the guise of producer. But he was now more interested than ever in directing.

She Loves Me

Prince received an assignment to direct a New York State touring production of *The Matchmaker* in the fall of 1962 for the Phoenix Repertory. The project helped to hone his directing skills and to develop further his credibility as a director. When Abbott saw it, he told Prince, "it's time you directed for Broadway. Your apprentice days are over."[59]

David Merrick agreed with Abbott and asked Prince to direct the musical which would later become known as *Hello, Dolly!* (at first called *Dolly: A Damned Exasperating Woman*). His experience with *The Matchmaker* might have been perfect preparation for this show, which was based on the Thornton Wilder play, but Prince decided against doing it. "I didn't care for the score, particularly the song 'Hello, Dolly!' I couldn't for the life of me see why those waiters were singing how glad they were to have her back where she belonged, when she'd never been there in the first place."⁶⁰ Instead of directing *Hello, Dolly!*, a big, lavish-style musical, Prince chose to direct and co-produce in association with Lawrence N. Kasha and silent partner Philip C. McKenna, *She Loves Me*, a charming, romantic show which songwriter Jerry Bock called "one of the smallest musical shows on Broadway . . . featuring a small cast of actor-singers [7 principal characters, 20 lesser roles, and 12 other persons], an orchestra consisting mainly of strings as opposed to brass. There would be no lavish production numbers and only a small smattering of dance."⁶¹

Kasha had initiated the idea of adapting this Broadway musical from Ernst Lubitsch's film *The Shop around the Corner*, which had starred Margaret Sullavan and James Stewart and which had been based on the Hungarian play *Parfumerie* by Miklos Laszlo. In 1949 MGM had also made *The Shop Around the Corner* into a musical, *In the Good Old Summertime*, starring Judy Garland and Van Johnson. Kasha thought he had obtained the rights from MGM and brought Bock, Harnick and writer Joe Masteroff together. As the project got underway, MGM reneged. Masteroff believes that the movie company thought the score and book writers weren't important enough to do the adaptation. Once Prince was asked to help, however, he was able to get MGM to release the rights.

The songwriting team of Bock and Harnick attempted to keep the intimacy of the original 1940s Lubitsch movie in their score. They wrote fewer songs but more music than is contained in the usual twelve- to fifteen-song musical. Harnick felt that this was part of a trend. Bock explained, "It's a way of getting more closely involved in the show's book . . . taking up the briefest possible moment if there's a part of a song idea in it . . . instead of just looking for the rounded song."⁶² Harnick summed up their intent to keep the show small by comparing it (without directly saying so) to the score of *Hello, Dolly!* "We have ignored any temptation to take it out of the store and go to downtown Budapest where a parade might be passing by."⁶³ In their contemporary treatment of this period piece, they wrote 30 or 35 songs, of which 24 remained in the show.

Masteroff wrote the libretto or script as a straight play. Then he, Bock and Harnick worked out the spots for the songs. Masteroff said, "I happen to feel the music is more important than the book. If you don't feel that way you can't possibly work on a musical. . . . The songs came so naturally, there was only a little adjustment needed. I never did a major rewrite job."⁶⁴

Originally, producers Kasha and McKenna wanted Gower Champion to direct *She Loves Me*. Champion, however, had another show to do and asked them to wait for him. Harnick recalls:

> None of us wanted to wait. So, roughly we said no. Then when we started to think who we did want, we thought of Hal. We had worked with Hal on two shows as the producer, and we liked him, and we also had seen his production of the straight play *The Matchmaker*. And we had also seen the remarkable job he had done when he was called in to help a show that was in trouble—the Kander-Ebb-Goldman *A Family Affair*. We were very impressed with what Hal had accomplished in those things. And we knew that Hal wanted to do it. We said, "let's take a chance on it . . . let's gamble." And Hal was delighted. Just before we signed the contract, Gower Champion called and said the other show he had planned to do had fallen through and he was now available and would like to do *She Loves Me*.[65]

Prince offered to step aside feeling he, as a novice director, was not recognized as being in the same league as Champion, who had successfully staged *Bye Bye Birdie* and *Carnival*. The writers called a hasty meeting.

> We thought, "let's go with Hal . . . we can't take it away from him." And also, suddenly there was something very exciting about the idea of working with this very gifted man, even though it was an unknown quantity. I now believe that if Champion had done it it wouldn't have worked at all. Or, to put it another way, it would have changed direction so totally that I probably would have been fired. I don't think I could have worked with him because watching his shows subsequently, I grew less and less enamored with Champion in terms of the kind of musicals I like. I felt that Champion was cold and technical and funny. Omitting *42nd Street* which I loved, I didn't like a lot of the work he did and I don't think I could have worked with him.[66]

Prince has always appreciated the loyalty of his collaborators on *She Loves Me* for providing him his first opportunity to direct a Broadway musical from scratch.

When Prince started working on the project, the writing was basically completed. He thought it was wonderful and asked for relatively minor changes.[67] What he asked for, according to Masteroff, "was a good deal of trivial dialogue to be written for the shop scenes. He felt more comfortable having that to use so that people coming into the shop had their own lines."[68] Masteroff noted that Prince already had strong ideas. One was his feeling about not using stars as box office insurance. Masteroff said:

It was the first time I ran into Hal's feelings about stars. Julie Andrews was quite anxious to do *She Loves Me*. We were going to do it in the spring of 1963 and she said if we could wait until the fall of 1963 she would do it. Hal didn't think it was that important to wait for her and so went with Barbara Cook. Part of his feeling was that stars were really not very vital— that if you have a good show to start with, it didn't matter. This is one case where perhaps it might have mattered commercially. I don't know.[69]

Prince wrote honestly about his decision not to wait for Julie Andrews until she completed the film *The Americanization of Emily*. He was in a hurry to work, but says, "Julie Andrews would have overridden the sugary reviews. Had I waited six months, the show might have run three years."[70]

Most of the action in *She Loves Me* takes place in a perfume and cosmetics shop in a Middle European city which closely resembles Budapest in the 1930s. The major plot deals with a pair of young lovers who correspond and fall in love without meeting, only to find out later that they work in the same shop and are not exactly friendly in that milieu.

Prince cast the show with the idea of using people who were equally gifted as actors and singers. He was rewarded with excellent notices for all of them. Barbara Cook, a familiar face in musicals but not yet a star, had last been seen in *The Gay Life* a season earlier. Her brilliant voice, looks and talent won her raves in the role of Amalia. Richard Watts, Jr. in the *New York Post* said, "Miss Cook is a constant joy. She makes the shopgirl wonderfully appealing, playing her scenes of humor and emotion delightfully and singing charmingly, and, when she goes into a moment of exultance in a number called 'Ice Cream' she is what can only be described as terrific."[71]

The producers had some trouble casting the male lead in *She Loves Me*, auditioning just about every young male singing lead in the country. The problem was the shyness of Georg, a boy who had written for months and months to a "dear friend" without ever having the courage to meet her. They could not get an American who they felt could convince an audience that he was shy. At the last moment they thought of Daniel Massey (the son of Raymond Massey), who lives in England. They paid his fare, took a chance, and he turned out to be just what they wanted.[72]

Massey, one of England's most popular stars, was well received in the role. Howard Taubman in the *New York Times* said he was a perfect fit for this type of show, "awkward and shy and disarming as the hero."[73] Cast in other important roles, Barbara Baxley and Ludwig Donath also received positive comments from the critics. Jack Cassidy was commended for his portrayal of the shop cad and ladies' man who makes his big mistake by dallying with the boss's wife. Masteroff said that they wrote a part that *was* the late Jack Cassidy. "He played himself, and played beautifully."[74]

Prince had difficulties with the actors, however. He has said that they made his life miserable by continuously challenging and questioning him. He was naturally insecure in this, his first full-fledged Broadway directorial effort, not having established his credibility with the actors as a director. He had not had the same problem with *A Family Affair* because the actors in that show were so desperate for help. Prince said:

> I am trusted now. I can be as scared on the first day of rehearsal as I was then, but it is different. My record gives them the confidence they need. Actors test directors, much as children do parents, to see how far they can go (often they don't know where they want to go), to see how protected they are. . . . Today I can go dry, waste a day working in the wrong direction. All I have to do is admit it. Invariably it works to my advantage, giving the relationship the mutuality rehearsing requires. . . . In 1963 I didn't know that. I knew only to stay strong.[75]

The only actor that Masteroff remembers as being difficult was Barbara Baxley. "She was famously difficult with every director. Prince handled her in the right way and she proved to be not too troublesome. As far as I could ever see, she seemed to be quite happy—to like Hal a lot and I think they had a good relationship."[76] Harnick remembers some of the problems with Baxley. "Barbara was not used to working the way Hal worked. She was an Actors Studio actress . . . a method actress. At first she said it was difficult, but she learned how to work with Hal. Ultimately, she loved the working relationship with him."[77]

Masteroff said that his relationship with Prince while working on *She Loves Me* was a good one. If this was a frightening time for Prince it did not get in the way of the director's working relationship with his collaborators. Masteroff recalled:

> I think we all got along wonderfully. He didn't want me to come to rehearsals as he was staging the book. I could understand it . . . he was feeling insecure and preferred for me to stay away. When he had something to show, I would come in and he would show it to me. I thought in every case what he was doing was terrific. I don't recall that we had any disagreements about any aspect of the show . . . and I thought that finally, when the show was put together, it was glorious! That what he was doing was terrific. I just loved the look of it, the feel of it, everything about it.[78]

She Loves Me, 1963
Daniel Massey and Barbara Cook meet in front of Maraczek's perfume and cosmetic shop.
(Photo courtesy Photofest)

Prince, in his first major directing assignment, was discovering there was much to learn about putting a show together. He said, "I knew the effect I wanted in *She Loves Me* but I didn't know how to achieve it."[79] One of the things he attempted was to keep a fresh eye on the total play. He had learned from both Abbott and Robbins that a director can direct good scenes but that is not the whole story. It is important for a director to have an overview. Prince said, "Abbott and Robbins know from beginning to end what the evening is going to be. They may not know details along the way, but they see the total."[80] Harnick didn't watch Prince's staging very often. He does remember, however, that in many ways he was a lot like Abbott.

> Abbott had a way of telling you he didn't like something but in the most flattering terms. Hal had his own way of injecting a director-writer relationship with *excitement.* And with a wonderful feeling that you're going to come up with something absolutely wonderful and that when you do he is the best audience that you will have because he understands every nuance and he is wonderfully appreciative because he himself is so talented, so sensitive. You feel when you've done a song that he likes that you can do anything! He does create an ambiance in which there's excitement and it's fun to explore and work.[81]

Carol Haney, who had played in *The Pajama Game,* choreographed *She Loves Me.* Prince liked her imagination and wit as well as her ability to keep seeing the entire production. Prince felt the show needed a modest approach and Haney's ego did not get in the way of her creating the right movement in response to her director's vision. As George Oppenheimer said, "There are no ballets, not even a chorus in this intimate musical and they are not missed. Carol Haney has staged the numbers with humor and grace."[82] The numbers she did stage were a great asset to the show. These included the staging of Christmas Eve with last-minute shoppers fully clothed in their hats and coats, and a "fast, funny" fandango in the romantic cafe.[83] The latter was a triumph not only for Haney but for Prince in its satirizing of the romantic cafe so familiar in Viennese operettas. Henry Hewes wrote that this scene in the cafe is an example of the way Prince, through the disciplined use of several techniques, managed to both spoof the clichéd locale and situation and still fill the show "with all the rich Mittel-European pastry-stuffing of a bygone day."[84] Hewes added,

The most obvious of these techniques is a spoofing of conventionally romantic clichés, best exemplified near the end of the first act in a number titled, "A Romantic Atmosphere," which is sung by a restaurant manager as he tries to preserve his ridiculously ersatz combination of candlelight and gypsy fiddles. . . . Every time he is on the verge of achieving his goal, the magic mood is shattered by an awkward busboy, or by a pair of customers whose romantic progress is not proceeding with prescribed fairy-tale smoothness.[85]

She Loves Me played its out-of-town tryouts at the Forrest Theatre in Philadelphia and the Shubert in New Haven, opening in the latter city on 18 March 1963. Harold Bone of *Variety* said, "There is much to commend in this effort as pleasant musical fare."[86] He went on to write that

a thread of charm runs throughout the show as a group of personable characters weave in and out of the action. *She Loves Me* could well be a welcome change of pace from the brassy, rapid-fire musicals of recent vintage. . . . Harold Prince's staging has set a happy pace.[87]

Bone also commented on the fact that there was no standard overture, the play proceeding into vocal action after only a few orchestral bars.

Prince commented on the William and Jean Eckart sets. "There is more scenery than in any other musical I've ever done. You don't notice it, watching the performance. But it's there. . . . It's a heavy show."[88]

There were six public previews in New York before opening night on 23 April 1963 at the 1046-seat Eugene O'Neill Theatre. With a pre-opening capitalization of $300,000, Prince had considered doing the show at the Ziegfeld Theatre, where weekly receipts might have reached $75,000 if the show was a hit. He decided, however, that his romantic love story would be lost in so vast an auditorium as the Ziegfeld, so he reluctantly booked the smaller O'Neill where the weekly potential gross was only $57,000. Later he admitted that he "overestimated the importance of the size of the theatre on the play's effectiveness."[89]

There's no question but that there is a kind of play that needs an intimate theatre, but that intimacy exists only off-Broadway or in the Booth Theatre and is common to England and the Continent. Excepting the D. H. Lawrence plays at the Royal Court, I know of nothing that could not be transferred painlessly from a six hundred seat house to a twelve hundred seat house.

She Loves Me played wonderfully at the O'Neill, but it would have played equally well in a theatre half again as large, and we would have made up on Wednesday matinees, on Friday and Saturday nights, what we lost on Mondays and Tuesdays, and doubled our run on Broadway.[90]

Prince followed Abbott's practice of requesting modest billing in the ads and in *Playbill*. When he was asked if his billing, which was only half the size of the supporting players, was unusually modest, Prince replied: "If the show is a success people will know who produced and directed it. If it isn't, you look silly. Anyhow, I'm not going to have my name bigger than George Abbott has his when he's directing."[91]

She Loves Me received excellent reviews from the New York critics with the exception of Walter Kerr, writing for the *Herald Tribune*. Kerr said of the show, "It will have no truck with dancing girls, production numbers, extra scenery, or—for that matter—jokes."[92] He did not care for the Masteroff book either. Taubman, in the *New York Times*, was quite taken with the show.

> The humors of *She Loves Me* are gentle rather than robust. The characters are the familiar figures of happily bittersweet fairy tales; yet they have individuality and charm. You keep thinking that you cannot digest an array of desserts, no matter how attractive and tasty they are, but you find yourself relishing nearly all of them in *She Loves Me*. . . . The secret is this: Everyone concerned with *She Loves Me* has played fair with the basic ingredients.[93]

Martin Gottfried, in *Women's Wear Daily*, described the show as a "musical that takes a little while to get used to, especially after a long and steady diet of up-and-at-em, razzle-dazzle shows. It grows steadily and blossoms forth in its second act as a rare and lovely thing."[94] Almost every critic complimented Prince, the director, on his "unfailing good taste,"[95] and for presenting a show that is "expert and professional."[96]

Henry Hewes, writing for the *Saturday Review*, explained that the musical was not really a spoof as some writers had suggested. He pointed out that Prince managed the difficult feat of both poking gentle fun at the conventional romantic clichés that inhabited the musical theatre ("the falling in love of two appealing innocents is an outmoded and not essentially truthful representation of life"[97]) and yet kept the romantic aura of a "bygone day." Hewes concluded that the show "manages to have its strudel and eat it, too."[98]

Howard Taubman did a follow-up story in the *New York Times* a week after the show opened and praised the people who made *She Loves Me* for their courage in remaining faithful to its fragile structure.

> It's a rare musical that denies itself the luxury of a blockbusting production number merely because it does not belong. Such self-restraint requires the discipline of good taste as well as confidence in the integrity of one's work. In the end it is also good business, for the public, less complicated and wiser than the calculating merchandisers of entertainment realize, has an instinct for what fits and what does not.[99]

Taubman went on to suggest that the show was bound to thrive because it did not pretend to be what it was not, and because the creators refused to violate the essential nature of their subject. But Taubman was wrong. The public didn't come to see the show in spite of the wonderful reviews. Prince was confused as to why it didn't draw audiences. "I have given it more thought than I like to give projects after the fact."[100] He finally decided that the main reason it did not run more than nine and a half months and was never made into a movie was because "it was a style piece, an unsentimental love story. It had irony and edge to it. It was funny, but not hilarious. It was melodic, but not soaring. There were only two dances, and they were small. No one came to the edge of the footlights and gave it to you. It was soft-sell."[101] Prince still believes that *She Loves Me* is one of the best things his office has done, and "as far as I'm concerned, it's as well directed as anything I've ever done."[102]

After 302 performances, *She Loves Me* closed. It had been well received by critics and selected by most of them as the year's best Broadway musical. This led to some of the reviewers wondering about why a show that had been so well received didn't last. Edward Sothern Hipp in the *Newark Evening News* addressed himself to this.

> I do not often note at length the passing of a Broadway attraction but in the death of *She Loves Me* there was something to prompt anyone charmed by its delights to sit up straight and shake his head. After all those fine reviews, there was a swarming at the box office and Harold Prince's entry was accepted as one of the season's few authentic hits. It was, too—for a time. But after those 302 performances did the investors gather to cut up their profits on a $300,000 production? Hardly. *She Loves Me* has gotten back less than $50,000 of the $300,000. . . . What is there about the economics of Broadway that seems to make it impossible for a tuneful, wholesome and unpretentious offering to compete with the blockbusters?[103]

Hipp went on to answer his own question. He felt that the show had failed because there were reminders in it of yesteryear's operettas, which, however faint they may be, carry the message of "death" at the box office. In addition, the show's unaffected story and lack of production dance numbers probably figured into its demise. Hipp concluded that tourists were also a big part of the Broadway economic scene.

> They have their little list of shows to be seen but it has been selected with emphasis on guffaws or surface stirring. The girly-girly musical, the comedy saturated with belly-laughs, the so-called serious play in which some facet of sex is the serious problem—these are Broadway's "musts" for most out-of-towners.[104]

In recent years, Prince has become philosophical about *She Loves Me*. Until recently he felt that because the show lost money, it was a flop. Now, he says:

> A work is not necessarily measured in its own time properly. Success is not measured at the box office. The chances are, if you work often enough, consistently enough, some of your best work will be underestimated, some of your poorer work will get by. If you work consistently enough, it balances out.[105]

In 1963 Prince had yet to direct a big smash hit, and investors would not continue to back him as a director unless he did. He also needed more personal reviews about his directing ability. He explained: "It has been said that in the best direction you do not see the director's hand. That isn't necessarily true. Brecht was hardly unobtrusive. I was always aware of Kazan. There are projects that should not be co-authored by the director, but I felt I must find a project that begged for such authority my next time out."[106]

MGM recorded the cast album of *She Loves Me* on 28 April 1963 and released it in May. One of the few two-record original cast recordings, it contained every note of music of the show, perhaps a testimonial to the production's true worth.

A London company of the show opened on 29 April 1964 at the Lyric Theatre and, beginning in the late 1970s, it gathered an ever-growing but relatively select circle of devotees. It was called a "cult musical" and there were various attempts to revive it. An all-star concert version took place in Manhattan's Town Hall and a shortened British telecast was shown repeatedly, to much acclaim, on U.S. public television. A revival was mounted at Connecticut's Goodspeed Opera House and a Playwright's Horizons production was seen in the theatre at Flushing Meadow Park in Queens.

Prince's first "from scratch" directorial effort on Broadway, then, was not a major box office smash. And he did not garner many personal reviews for his work. However, *She Loves Me* did establish him as a gifted director of taste, humor and imagination.

BROADWAY HISTORY:
Fiddler on the Roof

Abbott influenced all of us by making us organized . . . but Jerry [Robbins] influenced me by being more cautious than Abbott. . . . Jerry is cautious to a fault. I mean he just never goes into rehearsals—he's so damn cautious. I think that possibly a sense of pictures—stage pictures—is something I might have begun to trust in myself from watching Jerry . . . because those pictures of his are so choreographic . . . and I do like to move people that way. . . . I feel very comfortable—I never know quite why. I mean why do you say to an actor—"a foot over that way"—you know— it's about space. . . . It's a sense of relationships.
　　　　—Harold Prince, Interview with the author, 14 March 1983

I try not to dope out what [audiences] want. My theory is to do what you want and hope they go along with it. Unless you're extremely avant-garde in your approach, they're likely to fall into step with you frequently enough.
　　　　—Harold Prince, Interview with Dick Cavett, 19–20 February 1980

Instead of directing another show after *She Loves Me,* Prince decided to produce *Fiddler on the Roof,* which, in the words of John Chapman, became "one of the great works of the American musical theater . . . darling, touching, beautiful, warm, funny and inspiring . . . a work of art."[1]

Fiddler's genesis dates back to 1960, according to the show's three creators, Jerry Bock, Sheldon Harnick and Joseph Stein. They had worked together on *The Body Beautiful,* and were looking for a new project. A friend of Harnick's suggested he look into *Wandering Star,* a novel by Sholem Aleichem, thinking there might be a musical in it. The story concerned a Yiddish theatrical troupe touring Russia, and the three writers loved it. Stein, however, felt the story was too big and sprawling for the stage, and they decided to look into other material by Sholem Aleichem.[2]

They read Aleichem's Tevye stories and felt that "within the character of Tevye, there was the basis of an intriguing musical."[3] Monologues by milkman Tevye, the seven stories are about his seven daughters (for *Fiddler* the number of daughters was eventually reduced to five). There were further Aleichem stories about Tevye beyond the "daughter" stories. Stein said, "Out of all this material, we selected three (and some of a fourth) stories around which we felt a total overall story could be written."[4] David Ewen quotes Stein as saying, "The structure of the play required the creation of new scenes and new dialogue. Practically none of the dialogue from the original stories was usable, since the original material was not written for the stage, and the dialogue within it had a very special appeal."[5] Tevye in the original stories was a simple, passive man but Stein felt it was necessary to give the role sufficient strength to make him the moving force while still keeping character shadings of the original. The world of the stories was the

> esoteric world formerly completely ignored by the popular musical stage. It was the world of the East European Jew, bound to century-old traditions, whose customs, beliefs, superstitions, way of life and thought, ideals, habits, and dress were all as exotic to non-Jews (and even to a great many Jews of American birth) as might be those of a remote African tribe or those of characters in a Kabuki theater.[6]

A rough outline was sketched by the middle of 1961 and Bock, Harnick and Stein began negotiating for the stage rights to the musical. The story line constructed at that time is basically the one used for the production. "It's never changed," said Stein.[7] It tells of a poor Jewish milkman, Tevye, from the Russian village of Anatevka around the turn of the century. One daughter, Tzeitel, wants to marry the poor tailor, Motel, whom she loves, rather than a well-to-do butcher. Another daughter, Hodel, falls in love with a penniless student who is sent to Siberia for revolutionary activities. Chava, a third daughter, runs off with a gentile, pushing her father and tradition too far. All the marital difficulties are played out against a pogrom which banishes the Russian Jews from their homes and leads, by the end of the production, to the great exodus of Russian Jews to the new world.

A unique aspect of *Fiddler* was that this was the first show of Bock and Harnick's that was conceived by *them*. Till *Fiddler,* they had always written scores on assignment or commission from producers.

Harnick and Stein differ in their recollections about one matter concerning the creation of *Fiddler.* Harnick thinks that the realization that the stories added up to the changing of a way of life came later. "In the early stages of creating the show we concentrated on the romances of the various daughters and Tevye's relation to them and not so much on the dissolution of the culture."[8] Stein believes that at an early stage, in order to change the original material into a stage piece, "we decided to make it the story of this community—the story of the breakdown of this community with the stories of the three daughters illustrating that breakdown."[9] Whether the concept was incorporated into the script at an early or late stage, the rupture of a community became the spine of the piece.

Excepting the number "Tradition," written later, the show from the beginning started with the house scene, and continued in much the same way as it would on opening night, including the wedding scene and the pogrom. The first act has always ended with the pogrom and the second act with the exodus to America.[10]

About the time they were completing their first draft of the play, Bock, Harnick and Stein approached Prince about producing, because "we were closest to Hal."[11] Prince read the script and had two immediate concerns. He remembers thinking:

> One, ethnically, I have no background; I don't understand it so I can't direct it, and originally I was looking for a show to direct as well as produce, after all the years of being a straight producer, which I was beginning not to like. Two, I don't think it's universal in its present shape. I suggested that they either get Jerry Robbins to direct it, because only he could give it the universality it needed, through the expression of movement, or else put it away and forget it. As far as I'm concerned, Jerry remains the only person who should have directed that show. And I still say, "Put it away if you can't get him." There are not many projects you'd feel that way about, but I absolutely do about this one.[12]

Robbins, however, was working on *Funny Girl* and was unavailable, resulting in the temporary shelving of the project.

Writing the score for *She Loves Me* filled the void for Bock and Harnick, once again working on assignment for Hal Prince, who says, "I understood that one [*She Loves Me*] because I'm an old Hungarian so we went ahead with it."[13] Work stopped on *Fiddler* while *She Loves Me* was in production, and Joseph Stein turned to writing his hit play *Enter Laughing*. The three creators of *Fiddler*, however, continued to search for a producer for that show.

Fiddler was turned down by many producers. Arnold Saint Subber became interested in producing it, as did Fred Coe. Both loved the script of what was then entitled *Tevye and His Daughters* (other titles considered were *The Old Country* and *Tevye*). Neither producer, however, could raise the money needed within a reasonable time, backers feeling the show was too special and "ethnic" for general audiences. David Ewen notes: "*Fiddler on the Roof* was a bold undertaking rooted in and based solely on the textual subject. Bolder still was the way in which little effort was made to commercialize the product by offering a recognizable American musical with some Jewish trimmings."[14] It was shortly before rehearsals began that the title chosen was *Fiddler on the Roof*, the idea coming from the painting by Marc Chagall of an oval-eyed violinist dangling over the roofs of a peasant village. Prince said, "The title was absolutely suggested by the Chagall picture. I think Chagall hovered over the look of the show for a long time. I remember being asked if I would try and get Chagall to do the ad so I wrote him a letter but he never replied."[15] Harnick recalls that Prince liked the *Fiddler on the Roof* title because "the word 'fiddler' connected the show with music."[16]

When Robbins re-entered the picture as director and choreographer, he had reservations. As Harnick recalled:

> [Robbins] found there was much wanting in what he heard. He loved the source material. Somewhere along the line he told us that when he was six he had been taken to Poland. He said he never forgot the experience because his forebears came from there. Robbins said what he wanted to do was put the shtetl life onstage—to give another twenty-five years of life to that shtetl culture which had been devastated during World War II. That was his vision ... he kept asking and hammering at us for months:"What is this show about?" If we gave him an answer like, "Well, it's about this dairy man, and he has three daughters," he would reply, "No, if that's what the show is about, then it's the previous adventures of the Goldberg family, and it's not enough." He said, "We have to find out what it is that gives these stories their power." And he kept asking that same question: "What's it about?" I don't know which one of us finally said it. Maybe it was Jerry in one of

those endless pre-production meetings. But *somebody* said, "Do you know what this play is about? It's about the dissolution of a way of life." Robbins got very excited. "If that's what it's about," he said, "then we have to show our audience more of the way of life that is about to dissolve. We have to have an opening number about the traditions that are going to change." This number had to be like a tapestry against which the entire show will play. And that was the beginning of "Tradition."[17]

Robbins had found a concept or theme on which to base the musical. Working so closely with Robbins on *Fiddler* no doubt helped Prince to eventually incorporate this specific defining of a theme in a production into his own method of directing.

Before Prince came on as producer of the show, Robbins was wrestling with the frustrations of being unable to sign contracts with certain creative people he wanted, such as set designer Boris Aronson. Fred Coe, still listed as the producer, hadn't as yet raised the needed money. All this made Robbins extremely nervous and he requested Prince as co-producer. It was explained to Robbins that Prince hadn't wanted to do the show when it was offered to him earlier. "However," says Harnick, "Jerry [Bock] talked to him, and maybe it was because this time we had more of a show, or maybe it was because of Robbins, but Hal finally said yes."[18]

Prince and Coe did not work out as co-producers. Coe was doing the movie of *A Thousand Clowns* and was unavailable a good deal of the time. Prince recalled:

> I was doing the work and I didn't want to have a co-production with somebody who wasn't available. Also, I had a feeling I'd be spending all my time on the phone being nice, and he wouldn't know how to deal with me either and would probably feel he'd have to be nice in return. He wanted to make a movie and I wanted to do the show, so why should we waste time patronizing each other? I put it to him just as straight as that, and he agreed to let me buy him out, which I did. He has a substantial interest in the show, of course, and has made a great deal of money out of it.[19]

The prerehearsal time of about six months was filled with endless probing and questioning. Harnick said of Robbins, "Before he set foot on that stage he did as much work as possible, so that it would be right and he wouldn't be panicky in rehearsal or on the road."[20] (This method of a long prerehearsal working period would eventually be adopted by Prince.) Finally, rehearsals were scheduled to begin in June 1964 after many delays

due to Robbins's constant fear that the show was not ready. He also asked
Prince for an 8-week rehearsal period. When the June rehearsal date arrived,
Robbins again procrastinated. At this point, Prince sent Robbins a telegram
telling him he would have to pay the $55,000 that another delay would
cost. Prince told Robbins that if he did not pay the additional costs, he
would be sued. Robbins was very upset but he was forced to start rehearsals.
Prince said:

> I understand it all much better now than I did at the time, and I'd probably
> be more compassionate about it—because the day before *Follies* [the trail-
> blazing show Prince would direct in 1971] went into rehearsal, I thought
> I had hepatitis, and I went to the doctor for a checkup. The next day I realized
> it was not an illness, just naked fear. That's all it was. I suddenly didn't
> know what I was going to do with that stage or those fifty people. I didn't
> think I knew what the style of the show was, after all that time, or what I
> was actually going to do. [21]

Fiddler was capitalized at $375,000, not high in 1964 for the size and scope
of the production. As Richard Altman (Robbins's assistant) said, "Hal was
a savvy producer; he knew when to spend money and when and how to
cut corners. Even with new numbers added out of town and old ones
dropped, there was very little waste."[22]

Robbins had a total vision for *Fiddler* that extended to every aspect
of the production. He was indispensable. He helped clarify what the musical
was about: the struggle of parents to preserve traditions in changing times.
This theme gave the show a universality which was communicated to people
of all races and nationalities. As with *West Side Story,* each person in the
cast, from Tevye and his family down to the townspeople of Anatevka, all
were given backgrounds and became individuals. Opening the show with
the entire company singing and dancing "Tradition" set the style, tone
and theme of the evening.

Staging and choreographing the entire production, Robbins worked
tirelessly for authenticity. He studied life in the shtetl (or "little Jewish
town") as it was lived by Middle European Jews. "One of his basic sources
was a sociological study called *Life Is with People.*"[23] As he had done in
West Side Story, Robbins used improvisations to help with the acting scenes.
He did not pre-block and there did not appear to be an order or plan for
the day. Prince remembers two improvisations Robbins used in particular
and how they influenced his—Prince's—own work:

One took place in a white-owned bookstore in the South and involved the attempts of blacks to purchase books. A lesson in minority relations. The other took place in a concentration camp after the time covered by *Fiddler.* Again Robbins created respect in the actor for himself and for what the play was about. I borrowed liberally from the experience with *Fiddler* when I did *Cabaret.*[24]

Boris Aronson was eventually signed to design the sets for *Fiddler,* as Robbins had wanted. Aronson would become one of Prince's most important collaborators in later years. As Prince said, "I consider the day I met Boris second only to the day I met Abbott."[25] Russian-born Aronson was in his sixties when he worked on *Fiddler.* He had been designing shows for Broadway since Abbott's *Three Men on a Horse* in 1935, having spent his first twelve years in the U.S. working in the Yiddish theatre in New York. A gifted and versatile painter and sculptor, Aronson was equally happy designing operas, plays or musicals. He wasn't completely satisfied with his work on *Fiddler* and Prince agrees that the show didn't utilize the designer's gifts to the fullest. Aronson said that, because of Robbins's vision, he let himself be too influenced by Chagall. Given another opportunity to design the show, he would have done it differently. Aronson and Prince, unaware that they would become close collaborators on such shows as *Cabaret, Zorba, Company, Follies, A Little Night Music* and *Pacific Overtures,* did not foresee that not only would they initiate changes in the specific style of Aronson's set designs, but would also change the way all American musicals looked in future years. Prince explained, "Over the years Boris and I, mutually encouraging, moved further and further from naturalism, from props and doors and tables and units, wagons with rooms on them, until with *Follies* there were no tables, no chairs, no doors, no windows."[26]

Aronson found working with Robbins somewhat exasperating. Robbins was tireless in his trial-and-error tactics and the designer found this hard to deal with. More an artistic designer than a technician, Aronson was annoyed with Robbins's constant demands that things be made bigger or smaller. Aronson was not particularly concerned about how things worked or how they got on or off stage. He was lucky to have as his assistant his wife, Lisa Jalowetz, a very gifted craftswoman knowledgeable about theatre mechanics. Aronson found Robbins's prodding annoying and Robbins was impatient with Aronson's slow articulation of his intentions and feelings. Richard Altman said, "Apparently, no such gaps have separated Boris and

Hal.''[27] Prince, addressing his debt to Aronson, said, ''I thank Jerry Robbins for Boris Aronson every day of my life.''[28]

Zero Mostel was Prince's choice for Tevye. Robbins wanted Tom Bosley. Among others discussed were Danny Kaye, Alan King, Howard da Silva, Danny Thomas, and Julius LaRosa. Prince wanted a strong presence and eventually signed Mostel even though Mostel agreed only to a nine-month contract. Prince liked the short contract, as Mostel was known to ''cut up'' as soon as he got bored in a part. In addition, ''If an actor is signed to a long-term contract in a starring role and becomes identified with the show, it's very possible and even likely he will be encouraged to make greater and greater demands on the management because he feels indispensable.''[29]

Bock created musical numbers with an Eastern European Jewish flavor ''without resorting to quotation or direct imitation of Yiddish folk songs.''[30] The costumes were designed by Patricia Zipprodt, who had done the costumes for *She Loves Me*. She had to dip and dye the peasants' clothes until they looked sufficiently worn and aged. Some of the clothes (specifically Chava's orange blouse) were worn inside-out because Robbins thought they looked better that way. Jean Rosenthal, a dynamic yet gentle woman, did the lighting. She would go on to light other Prince shows such as *Baker Street, Poor Bitos* and *Cabaret*. Although Robbins was easily upset, Rosenthal handled the temperamental director well. Robbins dedicated a ballet, *Dances at a Gathering,* to her after her death.

Prince trusted Robbins implicitly and rarely felt the need to intervene artistically. Altman said, ''Prince never attempted to compete directorially with Robbins.''[31] They respected each other and worked well together as producer and director. Prince did make creative contributions to the show, however. Robbins was preparing a big second-act production number (an ''11 o'clock number'') to be inserted just before the conclusion of the piece. *Fiddler* ends with the dark but hopeful mood of people forced to abandon their homes, and there was no reason for a big splashy number.

> Robbins had come up with a fantasy number to enliven things. Prince realized this was not a formula show and the fantasy was extraneous. He suggested that they drop the fancy production number and concentrate on the story. Thus, ''Anatevka'' was born, a simple number in which the Jews sing wistfully, ironically of the shabby, dangerous ''home'' they are leaving as they set out for America.[32]

Fiddler on the Roof, 1964
Zero Mostel and Michael Granger in the song, "To Life!"
(Photo courtesy Photofest)

Here is Harnick's version of what happened:

> We were working on a song for that moment called "A Little Bit of This." Robbins had very inventively created a band out of items that these people who had been forced out of their homes carried onstage—their pots, their pans. Suddenly, all these sound effects made a percussive and rhythmic beat. He did some absolutely beautiful things for the girl dancers. But he wasn't sure about the number. He showed it to Hal—as much as there was to show—and Hal very objectively said, "You can't do that. It's not that kind of a show. This is, in effect, the villagers gamboling on the green, and they wouldn't do that." He said, "Let's be brave and do what the moment *really* is. It's a serious moment." At that point, Robbins agreed and decided we should take that piece of music we were talking about before—which was originally a Russian dance—and slow it down and put a new lyric to it. That, introduced by some of the music from "A Little Bit of This," became "Anatevka." Out of these pieces was developed a moment which was right for the show and which the audience accepted.[33]

In Washington, Prince became concerned about the length of the show.

> He felt strongly that judicious trimming was necessary to sustain audience interest and fend off somnolence, particularly during that book-heavy second act. He continually prodded the creative staff to go through the script as though with a microscope, and to cut anything superfluous. "We don't want a shred of fat," he insisted, and he pushed the point relentlessly.[34]

The result, according to Altman, was that every excision, no matter how small, helped to make *Fiddler* tighter and more economical. It also sharpened audience response. Prince's input with the script in Washington, according to Altman, helped it to function like "a precision instrument—consistently and predictably."[35]

Fiddler opened in Detroit for its pre-Broadway tryout during the summer of 1964. There was a newspaper strike and thus no reviews, but business was very good. The show was a success at the box office. *Variety* did print a review and it was "devastating," according to Joseph Stein. "I don't remember the exact words, but it said something like 'an ordinary, run-of-the-mill show, looks like all of the other shows, amateur time, etc.' We were all very depressed."[36]

After four weeks in Detroit, where extensive repairs were made on the second act, the production opened in Washington, D.C. The second-act opening, a song for the revolutionary Perchik called "As Much as That," was cut. The number "Letters from America" was changed. This was one of the versions of "Anatevka" containing much that ends up in the final version. Another number cut was the tailor's song, "Dear, Sweet Sewing Machine," which had never worked.

The show was very well received in Washington and was just about sold out. Harnick remembers that the reviews were very good. Word filtered into New York that there was a good show in Washington. Then came previews in New York. "Anatevka" was listed in the program in New York for the first time, although it had been seen in Washington.

Fiddler on the Roof opened in New York at the Imperial Theatre on 22 September 1964 after an eight-week rehearsal period and an entire summer spent in Detroit and Washington. "In retrospect, that may have been too long," said Harnick.[37] Most of the out-of-town work was on the second act. The first act remained pretty much the same. The long ballet in the second act, which occurs when Tevye learns that his daughter has married a gentile, was originally a ten- or twelve-minute number. Feeling that the show died at that point, the creators urged Robbins to cut it, which he did. "Finally," said Stein, "it was down to that tiny little crossover called 'Chavaleh.' That helped the show."[38]

The reviews in New York were very favorable and singled out the star, Zero Mostel, for praise. One or two critics expressed some minor reservations. Walter Kerr's review in the *Herald Tribune* had some negative observations. His lead: "*Fiddler on the Roof* takes place in Anatevka, a village in Russia, and I think it might be an altogether charming musical if only the people of Anatevka did not pause every now and again to give their regards to Broadway, with remembrances to Herald Square."[39] Finally, he wrote:

> Emotion does reach out and claim us before the evening is thoroughly done. A leavetaking scene in which all of Anatevka—particularly a daughter who had married a Gentile—lift hands in silent farewell, blown leaves in the cold wind of a pogrom, is directly affecting. Character is there to be touched. But *Fiddler on the Roof* dips below its own best possible level by touching character too casually and sometimes soiling it with the lesser energies of easy quips, lyrics that stray too far from the land, and occasional high-pressure outbursts that are merely marketable. The result is a very-near-miss, and I very much miss what might have been.[40]

Prince was not upset by the Kerr review. Richard Altman said that the reviews were read aloud at the Rainbow Room after the opening. Prince recalls:

The thing I remember about that evening was I wasn't interested in reading any reviews. This was because of my total confidence that the project was off and running. I never doubted it for one second. The minute I saw the show on the stage in Detroit, the minute the sets and costumes were there and it was all of a piece I knew that this was to be a very special theatrical experience.[41]

Howard Taubman in the *New York Times* said that

the new musical which opened last night at the Imperial Theater is filled with laughter and tenderness. It catches the essence of a moment in history with sentiment and radiance. Compounded of the familiar materials of musical theater—popular song, vivid dance movement, comedy and emotion—it combines and transcends them to arrive at an integrated achievement of uncommon quality.[42]

Although Richard Watts, Jr., of the *New York Post* said that the fact that the show "works out as effectively as it does is due partly to the taste and imagination of the production,"[43] he also felt that the show was successful chiefly because of the brilliant performance of Mostel.

Fiddler won the Critics' Circle Award as the best musical of the New York season and nine Tony Awards in 1965—Mostel (musical star), Maria Karnilova (featured actress in a musical), Pat Zipprodt (costumer), Prince (producer), Stein (author), Bock and Harnick (composer and lyricist), and Robbins (director and choreographer). Since its opening in 1964, *Fiddler on the Roof* has grossed over $20 million at the box office worldwide.

It became clear to Prince after the opening of the show that Robbins would not return to check the production as is the custom of some directors. According to contract, a director is supposed to keep an eye on the show during the run to help the staging remain clean and fresh and to tighten any staging that has somehow drifted. Robbins was very displeased with Mostel's "fooling around." When Mostel's 9-month contract came up for renewal, Prince didn't want to meet the actor's terms and asked his collaborators how they felt. They agreed with him to let Mostel go and see what was drawing people to the box office—the star or the show. *Fiddler*'s continued success without Mostel gave them the answer. Luther Adler, Herschel Bernardi, Harry Goz, Jerry Jarrett, Jan Peerce and Paul Lipson took on the role of Tevye on Broadway—all to the applause of packed houses.

Fiddler eventually toured with a national company and played in 32 foreign countries. It was performed in 16 languages and 18 original cast albums were produced. The show was sold to United Artists for $2 million which, according to Prince, is "less than was paid [by Hollywood] for *Man of La Mancha, My Fair Lady, Mame;* but the 25 percent of the distributor's gross after recoupment of cost will more than compensate for the discrepancy."[44]

Fiddler ran 3,242 performances on Broadway, becoming at the time the longest-running Broadway musical when it closed on 21 July 1971.

Fiddler on the Roof was an important show in the history of the American musical theatre and made an important contribution to Harold Prince's career. For the next dozen years or more backers supported anything he chose to do. "In effect, his experiments in musical theatre until the mid-seventies were subsidized by the loyal, grateful backers of *Fiddler,*" explained Howard Kissel.[45] And *Fiddler* and Robbins exposed Prince to the idea of basing a musical on a "concept." "Plainly," said Martin Gottfried, "after *Fiddler,* Prince saw himself as Robbins's successor."[46] Prince would one day use Robbins' ideas, expanding them to create his own form of the American musical theatre.

Prince had gradually become more and more interested in the possibilities of musical theatre as a serious medium. He felt it was impossible to live in the modern world and not recognize the "awful disillusionment of people."[47] Although he had to make money to stay in the theatre, he was not in the theatre to make money. Years later, after he directed two of his groundbreaking shows, *Company* and *Follies,* he compared them to *Fiddler* and pointed out where they differed:

> *Fiddler* is no girlie show. But it views its world through rose-colored glass, especially when compared with the harsh complexities of *Company* which examines the ambiguities of marriage (and of bachelorhood), and, even more so of *Follies* which is a study of disenchantment on several levels.[48]

In the years following the great triumph of *Fiddler on the Roof,* Harold Prince continued to expand his vision of the American musical theatre as a reflection of reality and a comment on the human condition—a vision he knew he could share with his audiences only as a director—not as producer—and since that time, he has indeed become more and more noted as a director, producing only two or three shows which he did not also direct.

A MUSICAL HOLMES
&
A BLACK COMEDY

Baker Street

Baker Street is a musical adapted from several of Conan Doyle's Sherlock Holmes stories. Long before Hal Prince became involved in the project, Jerome Coopersmith, who had done a great deal of writing for television, had been shaping the book for a musical about Holmes. Alexander Cohen had liked the work and agreed to produce it, bringing in Marian Grudeff and Ray Jessel to write the score. The producer knew the team from his days in Canada when he was chief booking agent for the O'Keefe Centre in Toronto. Coopersmith recalled that "[Cohen] apparently showed Marian and Ray the script and asked them to spec on some songs. I didn't know about this until one day Alex called me and said, 'I want you to hear something.' That was when I met these people for the first time."[1] Coopersmith says he was pleased with the Grudeff and Jessel songs.

Among the Holmes stories Coopersmith used in fashioning his libretto was "A Scandal in Bohemia" because, he says, "It was the only one that had a dramatically viable woman [Irene Adler] in it."[2] He also used "The Adventure of the Empty House," in which Holmes pretends to be dead but returns to life, as well as "The Final Problem" and "A Study in Scarlet." Coopersmith's libretto for *Baker Street* was hailed as a superior book which wisely followed the spirit, not the letter, of the Sherlock Holmes adventures, and preserved the Conan Doyle wit. Norman Nadel said, "[Coopersmith] has used this material exceptionally well, so that *Baker Street* has the flavor, the purposeful pace, and the piquant surprises of a Conan Doyle original."[3] The libretto was not changed very much in the process of creating the piece as a musical. "I was lucky," said Coopersmith, "because the construction of the book was pretty solid."[4]

After choosing the various Holmes stories on which to base his material, Coopersmith felt he needed something to tie all the stories together, some element that would unify the show. He said:

> I went to the public library and studied [Victorian England] for a long time. . . . Something did leap out at me and that was the Diamond Jubilee parade and festivity which they had in 1897 (exactly the period when Holmes was a private detective) and it was the biggest event in Europe, let alone England. It was the 60th Anniversary of Queen Victoria's reign.[5]

The story line of *Baker Street,* then, deals with Holmes's attempt to retrieve some letters sent to the actress-singer Irene Adler. Holmes quickly turns her into his ally, and they're off in pursuit of Moriarty, who is planning to steal Queen Victoria's jewels during the celebration of her Diamond Jubilee.

Michael Langham, who later became artistic director of the Tyrone Guthrie Theatre in Minneapolis, was then directing at the Stratford Shakespeare Festival in Canada. An Englishman who had never done a musical, he was asked by Cohen to direct *Baker Street.* He did not, however, stay with the show for long. Coopersmith remembers that "Langham was a very nice man, but he really had no experience with musicals. Whether that was the reason for his leaving the show or not I don't know. They never tell you. One day you just find out they've left."[6] The second director was Joshua Logan, and Coopersmith was very pleased to be working with such a gifted and successful man of the theatre. The songwriters and Coopersmith spent many months collaborating on the production with Logan in his New York apartment. Logan, however, decided not to continue with the project.

Logan's departure more or less converged with Hal Prince's highly praised direction of *She Loves Me,* and Cohen approached Prince with the idea of his taking over the helm of *Baker Street.* Prince was amenable. "I had always figured that some day I would give up producing and direct exclusively for other managements. I would put behind me advertising campaigns and theatre terms and actors' agents and union negotiations; that would be my nirvana."[7]

After an audition at which Prince heard the score, he decided that he liked only two of the songs. His agreement stated that if the new numbers that Grudeff and Jessel would write by Labor Day of 1963 were unacceptable, they would be replaced by Bock and Harnick. Prince worked closely with the composers on the score.

Labor Day arrived and Prince asked that Bock and Harnick be brought into the show.

> I was told that Alex Cohen was committed to Grudeff and Jessel and that if I backed out now, it was too late to replace me and the rights would revert to the Conan Doyle Estate, forfeiting four years of work and massive out-of-pocket preproduction costs.[8]

Prince decided that it was not worth giving up the show. He now feels that he was easier to work with in those days, not making excessive demands, holding back his anger until it was too late. He has since said, "It is calamitous to accept inferior material. And arrogant. There are so many surprises in the making of a show, unanticipated disappointments, problems, you cannot afford to make compromises up front."[9]

One major compromise Prince made was in regard to the size of the show. Prince had planned a much more intimate production than was ultimately presented but, since he was not the producer, he did not have final say. He wanted the 1,100-seat Broadhurst Theatre but instead Cohen arranged for the 1,800-seat Broadway Theatre. Consequently, Prince had to make adjustments such as a larger chorus and more elaborate sets. Coopersmith remembers that as soon as they were booked into the Broadway, Prince said, "We're defeated. This show needs some intimacy between the audience and the performers and that is such a huge barn we'll never get it. The audience will be separated from the show by a huge gulf."[10] Elliot Norton, writing for the Boston *Record American,* agreed: "*Baker Street* is also handicapped at the present time by the size of its physical production, which is vast and cumbersome."[11] Near the end of its Broadway run, *Baker Street* was moved to the Martin Beck Theatre. There, according to Coopersmith, "it played much better. Hal was obviously right about that. There were too many chorus girls, too big a spectacle. But I think Alex liked it that way."[12]

Eventually, there were 34 people in the show, which was capitalized at $600,000. Cohen is known for his tremendous public relations campaigns and the one for *Baker Street* was no exception. As Norton Mockridge in the *New York World-Telegram and Sun* said, "Alexander Cohen spent four years to acquire the rights to Conan Doyle's material, get the thing written, cast it and produce it and launch one of the most powerful publicity campaigns I've ever seen."[13]

During the show's pre-production period, Prince was still busy with *Fiddler on the Roof* and he and Coopersmith exchanged many letters. Prince was also in London part of the time, with Coopersmith working in Hollywood and at his home on Long Island. Much of the correspondence deals with Prince's ideas for the show and for changes he wanted made. "Prince had input into every single department," said Coopersmith, "script, score, costumes, design."[14] There is a Prince letter to Oliver Smith, the set designer on *Baker Street*, which shows quite vividly how Prince the director involves himself in all details of a production.

> Probably not important, but as you are making your ground plans I would like in the Moriarty Yacht scene, when the Buddha upstage swivels revealing Moriarty, that he be on a rather high pedestal in front of his blackboard. It should not be obvious to the audience except that when he steps off it we see how short he is. This whole aspect of the Moriarty-Holmes encounter will be heightened by the fact that the ceilings are low enough to cause Holmes discomfort and to intimidate him. If he is hunched over and Moriarty is able to stand up straight, the audience will see that he has taken the psychological advantage.[15]

An American actor, Fritz Weaver, was cast in the leading role of Sherlock Holmes. Aware of the many distinguished actors who had preceded him as Holmes, Weaver spent over a year in preparation. He visited London and the famous 221B Baker Street address (nonexistent in the 1890s) where Holmes and his faithful Dr. Watson had their "digs." He toured the familiar landmarks and immersed himself in Holmesian atmosphere.

Cohen tried to convince Prince that George Rose should play the role of Dr. Watson. Prince, however, preferred Peter Sallis and in a letter to Coopersmith, expressed his feelings on the subject:

> Alex, having failed at convincing me that George Rose would be good as Dr. Watson, called the composers and put some pressure there just before he left. I don't know what his objections are to Sallis except that Sallis is too young. Bosh. And humbug. (I always speak in the language of my plays. It's a great relief giving up mazeltov [here Prince's Yiddish allusion is to *Fiddler on the Roof*].) Sallis is the same age as George Rose and quite settled.[16]

Martin Gabel was cast as Professor Moriarty and his voice, said Richard Watts, Jr. in the *Post*, "had the perfect quality of menace for the sinister genius of crime."[17]

In mid-August, Prince hired a choreographer for *Baker Street*. Various contenders were Onna White, Donald Saddler and Danny Daniels. Prince had also asked Bob Fosse to do the choreography and musical numbers but Fosse was interested only if he could also be co-director. Prince said, "I didn't see how I could share the job [of directing] effectively."[18]

Once again Prince proved, as he had in the past and would in the future, that he is willing to hire a young and untried talent. Prince admired Lee Becker (later Lee Theodore). She had played the role of Anybody's in *West Side Story* and had gone on to do some choreography. Prince wrote:

> There is a ground swell of excitement about her work, and I have been getting unsolicited advice from Steve Sondheim, Jerry Bock, and Jerry Robbins' dance composer and dance assistant on *Fiddler*, both of whom worked with her last year. The feeling is that she has fresh talent and inventiveness. . . . I think she promises more than the others and I would prefer taking the chance. The point being, I don't know what we would get with the others. Let me point out, this is not the first time I have made this decision. I did it in 1954 when Bob Fosse choreographed *Pajama Game*, and in 1959 when Pete Gennaro did *Fiorello!*[19]

Thus, Lee Becker Theodore, who later founded the American Dance Machine to preserve the work of Broadway choreographers, was given her first Broadway choreography assignment. In an interview with Theodore, she explained that she had originally met Prince when she was hired as a chorus replacement in *Damn Yankees*. She had gone to the audition and they asked her to sing. She angrily spoke up and explained that her mother had not spent all that money for her daughter's dancing lessons for her to come to what she thought was a dance audition and be asked to sing. Prince raced down to the stage, obviously moved by her outburst, and said, "Just sing a few lines of 'Happy Birthday' for everybody and I'm sure you'll be all right." She did just that and got the job. She then went on to do the part of Anybody's in *West Side Story*. Although Theodore was an untried Broadway choreographer when Prince hired her for *Baker Street*, he was again willing to take a chance on ability and talent.[20]

Theodore said that after she read the script of *Baker Street* she began

Baker Street, 1965
Fritz Weaver and Inga Swenson.
(Photo courtesy Photofest)

preparing madly. Then Prince, rather than asking her to come up to his office to discuss her ideas for the show, took her for a walk in Central Park.

> He was as adorable as always. And I told him all my ideas. And he said they sounded good. . . . That was the first time I really had a chance to get to know Hal. He was like a child. Childlike in his enthusiasm and in his approach to things. . . . He was never blasé. I just liked his enthusiasm. He knows how to behave with choreographers . . . he knows we're not the most articulate people (choreographers don't have to be—we deal in dance images and impulses and we invent during rehearsals).[21]

Theodore turned out to be a good choice and many of the reviews of *Baker Street* praised her work, describing it as "spirited," "unusual," and "graphic."

Prince, as mentioned earlier, had input into all phases of the show. In a letter to Coopersmith, he made suggestions about choreography as well as the score: "If our song is going to be based on timing and precision, cannot a sizable chunk of the dance be done in silence with no accompaniment from the orchestra or possibly just the ticking of a clock? It could be very exciting."[22]

Although Prince was full of ideas, he was always willing to defer to a collaborator if the idea was a good one. In another letter to Coopersmith he said, "Apropos the book, you've won me over. I have come to think the hijinx in Irene's parlor is too much and could be very damaging. Catch me up every time you see that temptation."[23]

Song writers Grudeff and Jessel were Prince's major problem while working on *Baker Street*. In the pre-rehearsal period he told Coopersmith, "my biggest worry on this show is the amount of time it takes them to write numbers. I think we should have at least three or four songs over what we need when we go into rehearsal."[24] Later, in an article in *Holiday* magazine by Gary Paul Gates, Prince was said to have blamed the score for ruining *Baker Street*. Gates said:

> I became aware of Prince's disenchantment with the musical portion of *Baker Street* when I flew up to Toronto to catch a glimpse of the show in the final stages of the pre-Broadway run. By then the situation had so deteriorated that reinforcements had arrived and were busily at work writing new songs for the show. The reinforcements were composer Jerry Bock and lyricist Sheldon Harnick, as formidable a pair of rescue workers as one can find.[25]

Although paid for their work, Bock and Harnick knew that what they wrote would be credited to Grudeff and Jessel. Producer Cohen did not share Prince's pessimism about the music. Even after *Baker Street* had been running for six weeks, Prince was arranging for new Bock and Harnick numbers to be inserted in the show—as always, never tiring in an effort to "fix" a show he thinks needs it. Bock and Harnick's "I'm in London Again" appears in the *Baker Street* cast album but was taken out after the Broadway opening. Their "I Shall Miss You Holmes" and "The Cold Clear World of the Intellect" stayed in. Prince's feeling about the score was upheld by most of the New York critics: Richard Watts, Jr. thought Grudeff and Jessel's handiwork didn't help the show and Norman Nadel did not list the score among *Baker Street*'s strengths.

Prince was particularly proud of one of his staging ideas:

> The second act called for Queen Victoria's jubilee procession along The Mall to Buckingham Palace. I asked Bil Baird to build a parade of animated wooden soldiers, followed by a tiny gold coach with Victoria inside, waving a lace handkerchief. Although we had added thirty-six dancers and singers, we retained our puppets in Act II, and they walked off with the show. They showed the multimillion-dollar musical, "with a cast of thousands," on the biggest stage on Broadway, what it might have been.[26]

Author Coopersmith loved the idea of the puppets.

> Oh, it was wonderful, it was a showstopper every time . . . wonderful. Bil Baird was a terrific talent to work with also. It wasn't a lot of people pulling strings. Bil had a puppet device that one person cranked offstage . . . and everything worked with that one person cranking and little carriages with horses came by and Coldstream Guards. . . . Then finally came the Queen's carriage. . . . You don't see the Queen . . . but a lady's hand comes out of the carriage and waves a handkerchief to the crowd. It was enchanting.[27]

The critics were also enchanted with this scene. The *Saturday Review* called it a "theatrically effective moment."[28] Walter Kerr wrote, "the attitude is fundamentally promising and the special effects are more than that, they deliver, particularly when Bil Baird is arranging a military procession with right-angled puppets."[29]

The sets by Oliver Smith were thought effective. Howard Taubman in the *Times* praised Smith's use of fog and clanging Big Ben in a scene where Holmes and Irene Adler wander through the haunts of the underworld. He said, "*Baker Street* has atmosphere and illusion."[30]

Prince never changed his original view and felt that the show would have been better had it kept to more intimate production values. He would have preferred one small atmospheric set, no chorus, and he thought the antiseptic love affair between Holmes and Adler was a bad idea. Inga Swenson, however, had been set for the role when Prince took over and she and the love story were part of the package. Since Prince wasn't the producer, he could not always make the final decision.

Jerome Coopersmith enjoyed the collaboration with Prince, and said:

> Hal is a dynamo. He's a very energized kind of person. There's a motor working inside him at all times. There's always a little smile on his face. He had a kind of elfin, boyish, mischievous quality. That boyish quality is one reason why he sometimes goes into farce a bit. He knows that. He says, "I have this tendency, so please watch me and catch me on it every time I do this."[31]

The show received mixed notices when it opened in New York at the Broadway Theatre on 16 February 1965. John Chapman of the *Daily News* called it "an absolutely captivating entertainment,"[32] and Howard Taubman in the *Times* felt *Baker Street* overcame some of its problems early on: "Before the end of the first half it has caught the master detective's mood and style, and the second half is capital fun."[33] Richard Watts, Jr. in the *Post* was not complimentary and felt the show a distinct disappointment.[34] Walter Kerr of the *Tribune* felt the show had a potentially jolly attitude that it didn't maintain.[35]

Although Prince received some good notices as director (Chapman: "Prince has kept the show in steady motion," adding that the Jubilee Parade was the most imaginative touch in the show),[36] he was taken to task by Kerr: "There's a certain fuzziness about the staging, which has been attended to by Harold Prince, that fails to say exactly *when* a particular joke is being made. The tongue-in-cheek point is there, somehow, but in a very generalized, lazy unfocused way."[37]

Prince had hoped to give up producing and just direct for other managements, but *Baker Street* taught him that if he wanted to truly direct a show his own way with full artistic control, he would have to keep his production office open. In order to be free of the many business aspects of producing which he disliked doing, he would have to begin delegating these responsibilities to his staff. Ruth Mitchell would eventually become his associate producer, and Howard Haines would succeed Carl Fisher as general manager. He realized that, by arranging things this way, he could be more in control of the projects he directed. Another motivation which made him decide to retain his production office was his fear of being replaced on a show. Knowing that even the most successful musicals are in some trouble during their out-of-town tryout period, Prince worried that another producer could fire him. And, too, if he gave up producing, he would be at the mercy of job offers. There simply is not enough work on Broadway to keep most directors busy. As a producer, Prince felt that he could continue to create new directing opportunities for himself.

Baker Street ran for 313 performances in New York, closing on 14 November 1965. It was until then the longest-running play about Sherlock Holmes ever staged. It received three Tony Award nominations—for best leading actress in a musical, best set design, and best musical book. It was, however, the year Prince's *Fiddler on the Roof* won virtually all the awards. However, Oliver Smith's *Baker Street* sets won the Tony Award, over Aronson's work on *Fiddler.*

As he feared, Prince received no offers to direct from other managements after *Baker Street* was on the boards. In fact, three years would pass before another producer came to him with a directing project. Ever eager to be at work again, Prince geared up his production office to get two of its own projects on stage—ironically, neither to be directed by him.

Poor Bitos

A production of *Poor Bitos* by the French playwright Jean Anouilh was playing in a small theatre club in London at the time Hal Prince was directing the London production of *She Loves Me.* He liked the production and decided to present it in New York, even though he knew it had limited commercial appeal—another sign of Prince's strengthening philosophy that artistic merit sometimes takes precedence over monetary gain.

Poor Bitos is a black comedy in which Anouilh juxtaposes the political upheavals of France in 1955 with a searing flashback to the Reign of Terror following the French Revolution, striking at the heart of political extremism. The play was first produced in France in 1956 when the country was hopelessly entangled in Vietnam and after Dien Bien Phu had fallen. Algeria was in revolt and the old Empire was crumbling.

To bring the three-act play to New York, Prince gathered a capitalization of $90,000, all of which was lost in this failed production.[38] Prince presented the Lucienne Hill translation in association with Michael Codron and Pledon Ltd. The play rehearsed in New York with an American cast supporting Donald Pleasance and Charles Gray of the London company. Shirley Butler, who had staged the play in the West End, was an American and restaged the production in New York, which she duplicated physically except for the costumes, designed here by Donald Brooks. Prince felt that there was no fun in doing the production because it finally became an exercise in repeating what had already been done on the London stage.

Poor Bitos opened in New York on 14 November 1964 at the Cort Theatre after two weeks of sold-out preview performances. The critics did not like the play but they found it arresting. John McClain, in the *Journal American,* said:

> Like *The Rehearsal,* this is an enlightened experience—perhaps a little aimless at times—but certainly performed brilliantly and produced to perfection. . . . It is a magnificent commentary on the frayed fabric of the human make-up, the inflexible blindness of the dedicated, but it is doubtful that it will have general appeal as a theatrical attraction. . . . There aren't enough people that want to be disturbed.[39]

Norman Nadel, in the *New York World-Telegram and Sun,* praised Prince for bringing the play with Pleasance and Gray to New York.

Business at the Cort box office slumped immediately. Prince reduced prices to keep the show running on a week-to-week basis, but no one came, and *Poor Bitos* closed after two weeks. It had been Prince's second producing effort—and first failure—of the season. The earlier *Fiddler on the Roof* was keeping his office financially secure, and his well-received direction of *Baker Street* for producer Alexander Cohen had made him more creatively secure. And true to form, at the time *Poor Bitos* was being readied for a quick burial, the Prince office was at work on pre-production plans for another musical, *Flora, the Red Menace.* To add to his already busy schedule, Prince was serving as president of the League of New York Theatres. Indeed, there was scarcely time to mourn the passing of *Poor Bitos.*

A Parting with One Superman— A Meeting with Another

Flora, the Red Menace—Prince's Last Show with Abbott

With the later exception of *Side by Side by Sondheim* in 1977, the last Prince-produced show that he didn't also direct was *Flora, the Red Menace.* Based on the book *Love Is Just around the Corner* by Lester Atwell, the story is about a spunky young girl, Flora, looking for a job as a commercial artist in the thirties, and her involvement with the Young Communist League. The show aimed to be a nostalgic satire of the idealistic American communists of the Depression era. *Flora, the Red Menace* was the fourth show brought to Broadway by the Prince office in the 1964–65 season, and the third Prince-produced or -directed musical of that season.

John Kander, who had written the music for *A Family Affair,* and the lyricist Fred Ebb were asked to compose some songs for *Flora.* Prince had known both men individually but he now teamed the two songwriters for their first show together (although they had worked together on the non-Broadway ballad "My Coloring Book"). Ebb had come to musical theatre in 1963 with the show *Morning Sun* (produced by the Phoenix Theatre), for which he did both book and lyrics. He had also written lyrics for various revues and for the television show *That Was the Week That Was.*

Garson Kanin was asked by Prince to do the adaptation but Kanin suggested Robert Russell, with whom he had written a Tracy-Hepburn film. Russell had also co-authored the Jackie Gleason musical *Take Me Along.* It was Russell who gave the show its title, which Prince believed hit the tone of the show perfectly.[1] However, it did not take long for Prince to realize that Russell was not adept at writing a musical libretto. He recalled that "there was an obduracy, an unwillingness to bend, an impracticality, difficult to analyze. I came to think he had an uneasy compact with failure on this one. . . . Eager to work on the one hand but pessimistic about the outcome."[2]

Prince asked George Abbott to co-author with Russell and to direct. Prince hoped that the more experienced Abbott would be able to use Russell's good work while adding his own professional touch. Abbott liked the original source material and some of Russell's dialogue. However, the first draft Abbott sent to Prince contained very little of Russell's original material. Now the best song numbers did not fit the libretto, and the show somehow lacked emotion. Prince sent Kander and Ebb to Abbott in Florida to work on integrating the script and score, and to try to put the missing emotion back into the show.

"Although Prince didn't direct *Flora*," said choreographer Lee Becker Theodore, "Hal was already becoming the director as we know him today. He would not sit back any longer and say 'Let the creative people do what they want.' He'd go right in there. I think probably in the early days Hal was in the shadow of Abbott. But now he was growing up creatively and artistically. And he now had opinions and insights of his own, that were his own personal perspective."[3]

Abbott, who enjoys the warm Florida climate during the winter months, was not willing to come north for any extended period of time to work on the show. Instead, he tried his hand from a distance and it just didn't work. Russell was very angry about the way the project was going but was at a loss as to how it could be fixed. And Prince admits that, "because [Russell] didn't and he was the outsider, we closed ranks around Abbott. Sometimes protecting Abbott took precedence over protecting the play."[4] Prince admits that he was wrong not to insist that Abbott come to New York to work on the show or at the very least, he now feels, he should have postponed the project until the following season. They moved ahead, however, and even the supervision of the scenery and costumes was left to the producer because of the absentee director. Prince feels that they were not ready when they went into rehearsal since the script was not complete.

Russell had written his first draft of *Flora* with Barbra Streisand in mind, but she was unavailable and 19-year-old Liza Minnelli was cast as Flora. She had auditioned for Prince two years earlier and at that time he felt she was too young for the role. She then appeared in an Off-Broadway production of *Best Foot Forward,* which provided her with a perfect showcase. Subsequently, she toured with *The Fantasticks* and *Carnival.* She also appeared frequently on television and at the London Palladium. When she auditioned again for *Flora,* she wanted the part badly but the audition was somewhat less than successful. This time, however, she was not considered too raw or too youthful a performer "with nothing but her parents' names to recommend her."[5] Called back for a second reading, Prince told her exactly what he wanted in the role. She pleased him and was hired. Minnelli claimed that to prepare for the role she took her first formal vocal lessons. She also observed acting classes conducted by Uta Hagen and Herbert Berghof.[6]

In an interview with Stuart W. Little of the *Herald Tribune,* George Abbott, at the time rehearsals were about to begin, suggested that this may well have been the first musical to take a kidding view of the radical movement of the 1930s and Union Square communists. At least Abbott couldn't remember any other. "I wouldn't want to do this one if I could think of any others," said Abbott.[7]

Abbott and Prince once again turned to largely unknown performers. *Flora* was Minnelli's first Broadway show as it was for five of the fifteen principals. Bob Dishy as Harry, who wins Flora's love while luring her into communism, had received national exposure on TV's *That Was the Week That Was,* and was a veteran of "Second City." Cathryn Damon, who played Comrade Charlotte, had been Shelley Berman's girlfriend in *A Family Affair,* and had done some Off-Broadway shows. Mary Louise Wilson had last been seen in a comedy role in *Hot Spot,* as well as the Julius Monk revues. Abbott claims that he does not ask what experience actors have had when they audition for him. He is interested only in their talent and how well they will please an audience.[8]

Flora was capitalized at $400,000. Abbott, involved with his 105th show at the age of 77, was to share with Prince in 55 percent of any net profits earned by the musical, backers sharing the other 45 percent.

Lee Theodore was hired to do the choreography. Prince was happy with her work as choreographer on *Baker Street* and before that show had even opened, he asked her to choreograph *Flora.*

Hal liked a "serious approach." . . . He didn't like a lot of fluff and nonsense and I felt that influence very strongly in *Flora. Flora* was pitted against the backdrop of communism and Hal was not content to ignore that. . . . He wanted a head-on confrontation really—and a facing-up to the theme of that show. And Abbott didn't have the same viewpoint. Abbott was doing *Meet the People.* He was doing an entertainment and I think that they were in conflict on that show. . . . I was privy to a lot of the production meetings out of town when the show opened. Hal was very generous that way. He wanted me to learn and felt that he had been given many, many opportunities and apparently I was lucky enough to be chosen by Hal to sit in on almost every possible production meeting whether with the designer, the backer, a tech person or the lighting person.[9]

Flora completed its first out-of-town stand in New Haven on 10 April 1965. Prince considered the New Haven reviews much better than he had hoped, but was nevertheless worried that the show still "didn't have the right tone . . . and it's been very sluggish. There's still an awful lot of work to be done."[10] In the midst of the run in New Haven, Prince had to return to New York to attend a meeting of the League of New York Theatres, the organization of Broadway producers and theatre owners of which Prince was president at the time. Gary Paul Gates quotes Prince as saying that he was quite confident he would win that season's Tony Award for producing *Fiddler,* but spoke with guarded optimism about *Flora.* He praised Minnelli and the score, but said there were things in the show he was not happy with but hoped they would be resolved before the Broadway opening.

On 15 April 1965 *Flora* opened in Boston's Colonial Theatre and played there for two and a half weeks. As in New Haven, it was well received by the critics. Kevin Kelly in the *Boston Globe* felt that Abbott had some work to do on the book. However, he thought that the show was a good bet.[11]

Abbott and the other collaborators continued to work on the show and it showed signs of improvement. Prince didn't bother much with it at this point, although he felt it needed to be reworked. The improvements were so striking, however, that even Prince's hopes were raised during the New York preview performances.

Flora, the Red Menace opened at the Alvin Theatre in New York on 11 May 1965. The reviews were generally poor and the show ran only 87 performances. Taubman in the *New York Times* said of the show, "It has the appearance of being pasted together with bits and pieces. A promising idea has not been enlivened by a creative spark."[12]

Walter Kerr questioned whether there was really so little "bubble" to those days during the Depression. He asked, "Wasn't there—even in the worrying—more heart and more fun?"[13] He summed up the show's problems:

Flora, the Red Menace, 1965
Bob Dishy and Liza Minnelli.

The comedy is matter-of-fact and the party-line romance highly tentative. Perhaps nobody wanted to get our heroine in too deep. Is that why "Flora, the Red Menace" pulls its punches? And why it so often chooses to wander afield? Having decided to look at an era fairly, the show hedges, can't quite cut loose. In spite of competence everywhere, some heart is hesitant.[14]

Prince was disappointed at *Flora*'s short run. He had been very eager to direct the show himself and felt that had he directed it things might have turned out differently. However, he lacked the courage at that point in his directing career to tell Abbott what he wanted to do. Now Prince feels, had he approached Abbott with the idea that he direct, Abbott might have been surprised but characteristically, after the surprise wore off, Abbott might have agreed. Prince feels that had they worked together, he might have been able to create a consistent attitude toward the material. One of the problems Prince saw with the show was that Abbott did not have enough sympathy for the subject matter. Prince said, "Abbott brought to *Flora* no clear attitude about the Party. His communists were cartoon characters, some of them farcical, others evil."[15] He went on to suggest that Abbott's inability to identify with the theme was due to the fact that Abbott had been "secure financially for over sixty years. He is essentially an apolitical man."[16] Fred Ebb, when asked how *Flora* might have differed had Prince directed it instead of Abbott, said:

I don't know what might have happened to that show if Hal had directed it. I think it might have been a little tougher in fact. Tough shows seem to be what Hal always (at least at that stage in his career) was attracted to most, personally. He wasn't producing them, but I think that down deep that's what he wanted to do. Out of which came *Cabaret*. I think he may have taken a harder view of the *Flora* material. I know he was disappointed with what the show eventually looked and sounded like.[17]

Although *Flora, the Red Menace* was not successful for Prince, it did have, as with many of his shows, important consequences in the world of the American Musical Theatre. He had teamed two songwriters, Kander and Ebb, who had never done a show together before, and he introduced young Liza Minnelli to Broadway. After their collaboration on *Flora*, Kander, Ebb and Minnelli would work together on many important projects and the Kander-Ebb-Prince alliance would flower shortly in *Cabaret*.

Almost immediately after his busy 1964–65 season ended, Prince took some time off from the theatre and spent much of that summer and fall working for his friend John V. Lindsay in the campaign that resulted in New York gaining its first Republican mayor in twenty years. When the election was over, Prince had planned to take a well-deserved vacation. But, as usual, idleness tended to unnerve him and he soon jumped headlong into his next project: producing (in association with Ruth Mitchell) and directing *It's a Bird . . . It's a Plane . . . It's Superman.* Since another project he had been working on—the musical to be titled *Cabaret*—had been put on hold for awhile, he found doing *Superman* a timely opportunity.

It's a Bird . . . It's a Plane . . . It's Superman

Charles Strouse and Lee Adams, the successful songwriting team of *Bye Bye Birdie* fame, did not originate the concept of doing a show about Superman. They did, however, want *Esquire* writers Robert Benton and David Newman (who also scripted the film *Bonnie and Clyde*) to write something for the theatre on which they could all collaborate, since they felt Benton and Newman were "very funny satirical writers."[18] Benton and Newman had invented the "Dubious Distinction Award" for *Esquire*. Adams and Strouse had met them and felt that they were talented young men. "We asked them to come up with an idea for a show and they came up with the idea for *Superman*. So the four of us got the rights and wrote it."[19]

At first, David Merrick showed interest in producing it but later dropped his sponsorship. The four writers then began looking for a new producer and a director. When the show was partially written, they asked Prince to read it. He liked the material and decided to produce and direct it. Prince was not deterred by the fact that shows based on comic strips usually failed; only *Li'l Abner* of some years before had delighted Broadway audiences with its bizarre citizens of the mountain town of Dogpatch. (This was, of course, years before *Annie* was a tremendous hit.) As usual, Prince was undaunted by unfavorable statistics, and went ahead with *Superman.*

Ruth Mitchell had been Prince's production stage manager since *West Side Story.* For the first time, she became his co-producer. Indeed, she was virtually his assistant director, taking charge of the technical elements of the production and leaving Prince free to concentrate on the creative aspects.

Original musicals are not as common as adaptations and successful originals are rarer still. The script of *Superman* deals with the Superman legend and parodies the hero in a kind of pop art fashion. The show was written in 1964, anticipating the pop art craze. Prince expected that their show would be the first theatre piece incorporating that style. However, the show which opened in 1965 after taking thirteen months to write actually followed on the heels of the pop art fad, which had flourished in the intervening months. A *Batman* series was being presented on television and pop art and camp were seen everywhere. Prince said, "This show was another case where the show lost its uniqueness in the time it took to put it together. *Superman* was planned long before *Batman* appeared on the TV tube, but it seemed old hat by the time we presented it."[20]

Casting just the right actor-singer as Superman was not an easy task. Shirley Rich, who was then Prince's casting director, put out a call for a 6'4"-tall, 190-lb. actor who had a facial and physical resemblance to the comic strip character. There were additional physical expectations which eliminated most of the competitors. Prince specified he wanted someone who had a 17" neck, 50" chest, 32" waist, 37½" hips, 18½" biceps, and 26½" thighs. However, he was looking for more than physique. Those who *looked* promising and sounded musical were given a Clark Kent scene to read. If that test was passed, the candidate got to read a few lines of a Superman scene. The man finally chosen was Bob Holiday, who had played the law clerk in *Fiorello!*, and the critics praised him in the role. Richard Watts, Jr. in the *New York Post* said that he "has the physique and stalwart good looks just right for the title role, and acts with likeable and appropriate modesty."[21]

Michael O'Sullivan was hired to play a villainous nuclear scientist against whom Superman is pitted and he, too, received excellent notices, capturing the right mixture of comedy and seriousness written into his role. Patricia Marand played Lois Lane and Linda Lavin was Sydney, a secretary on the staff of the *Daily Planet*. Television viewers later came to know Lavin as the star of the successful series *Alice*.

The one cast member who was clearly a favorite of all the reviewers was Jack Cassidy, cast in the role of Max Mencken. Norman Nadel said that Cassidy "blends oily smoothness, unshatterable conceit, staunch singing and all the vaudeville razzmatazz in the book into his part as a *Daily Planet* columnist."[22] "The Woman for the Man," delivered by Cassidy, was lyricist Adams's favorite in the show, along with "You've Got What I Need," a duet between O'Sullivan and Cassidy. Adams said it "was kind of funny, odd—not love song, but these two enemies of Superman were getting together. I like that number a lot. That was a big raucous number."[23] Lee Adams talked about Cassidy's performance: "I can't describe what he did but it was funny and very effective. . . . Walter Winchell was an ex-hoofer . . . an ex-dancer, so Cassidy did a lot of fake balletic stuff and a little funny step at the end of the stanza.''[24]

Superman was not an enjoyable experience for Prince. Challenged by certain performers in the cast, he felt he wasn't yet being granted respect as a director. During rehearsals, Prince found it necessary to expand the subordinate role played by Jack Cassidy. After the show opened in Philadelphia to bad reviews, Prince realized that the show needed to be shortened. Cassidy, unhappy with Prince's decision, continued to suggest additional lines and business for himself. Lee Adams discussed the rough time that Cassidy gave Prince:

> [Cassidy] was a very strange guy. He was a funny, wonderful man but he had his own problems. He would come in with scenes he had rewritten, rewritten lyrics, suggestions for music. Jack was full of ideas, that's all. When you're trying to get a show together, it's a very complicated process. . . . You've got too much else to worry about without having the actors telling you how to write it. But Jack was superb in the show . . . a funny man![25]

Prince dealt with the Cassidy situation as best he could. He said of the conflict:

> I won, or I think I did, but I realized how castrating an actor can be if he chooses. We are all familiar with the occasions in which a director can bully an actor into confusion, but there are just as many times when actors run off with the play. Stars do it all the time.[26]

This was one more incident in Prince's many years of experience producing and directing musicals that may have influenced him against using stars in his shows.

Superman was capitalized at $400,000. This was a big physical show which gave Prince plenty of opportunity to exercise his remarkable sense of stage pictures. A scene hailed by almost all the reviewers was one in which the director made the stage appear as if it were a page in a comic book, with a progression of boxes set up in which the actors appeared. It was not an easy visualization to accomplish on stage. *Variety*'s Philadelphia critic, Jerry Gaghan, said, ''There is one standout multi-sectioned set in which the whole company appears as though on a comic book cover.''[27]

Other staging ideas which received plaudits were the telephone booth which bowed and danced away when Superman changed into his newspaper reporter costume; Superman striking an "Atlas-supporting-the-world" pose as he lifted a platform loaded with orators; a documentary film tracing Superman's background, in which the narrator asks, "How much do we really know about Superman?"; and Superman flying up and away across the Alvin stage on a wire, with the wire in full view of the audience. After a graceful landing, Superman would consciously back up to a spot where a colleague would unhook him. The fact that Superman is held up by a wire that gleamed in plain view was, in critic Walter Kerr's opinion, "a comment that all our dreams were nonsense."[28]

Prince's adept direction was noted by Richard Watts, Jr., in the *Post*: "Most of [*Superman*'s] invention has gone into the mechanics of the staging. It is essentially an achievement of the electronic age in the theatre."[29] Lee Adams remembers that the use of so many technical things gave them problems. He said of *Superman*, "That show had to have those effects because [Superman] had to fly. The show is done, however, in amateur productions and summer stock and he doesn't fly. He just points his hands and runs offstage . . . but there they can't fly people, it's too expensive."[30]

Ernest Flatt, known for his work in television, staged the dances for the show. As he had done with *She Loves Me,* Prince kept dance in *Superman* to a minimum. He wanted to pare away the customary reliance of musicals on big dance numbers. The *Variety* reviewer in Philadelphia noted that whatever dance there was,

> because of the actional storyline[,] tends to acrobatics and calisthenics in simulated brawls. . . . The format of *Superman* is on the spectacular side, but the production has no big dance number as such nor any chorine terping displays. Dependence on performances and gimmicks make it seem more like a play with music added.[31]

Superman opened at the Shubert Theatre in Philadelphia on 15 February 1966, and its future didn't look bright. Prince felt that the reviews were humiliating. The engagement had to be curtailed for intensive repairs, and Joan Hotchkiss, playing the role of Lois Lane, was replaced by Pat Marand. Lee Adams feels that *Superman* had problems similar to most musicals. His own recollection is that it was a happy work experience and the show eventually came out well. Discussing the work that is done on a show while out of town, Adams said:

> There are very few shows that haven't had big problems out of town. A musical is such a complicated animal to get together—so much to do. A play has

a few sets, a few costumes, a few light cues. In a musical, you may have 400 light cues. Everything is to the 10th power in a musical. . . . You change a number and everything shifts, so there are always problems. . . . The actors begin to know what they're doing, finally. . . . And audiences tell you some but not everything. Most opening nights are terrific. Everyone screams and yells, the backers are all there and you think you have a hit. It's a horrible business, it's just terrible.[32]

Superman opened in New York at the Alvin Theatre on 29 March 1966 to generally good to glowing reviews, with some critical resistance dampening the enthusiasm. One of the more glowing reports was Stanley Kauffmann's for the *New York Times,* who called it

easily the best musical so far this season, but, because that is so damp a compliment, I add at once that it would be enjoyable in any season. It has some tunes that are at least recognizable as tunes, brisk lyrics, some clever staging and some very engaging performers. What's best, the whole show has been based on a witty point of view.[33]

This point of view, which Kauffmann as well as others referred to, and which they felt made the production special, lay "between doing it straight—in comic-strip or TV-serial fashion—and doing a broad burlesque, which would have run dry."[34]

Walter Kerr felt that Prince's direction was "unusually tidy" but that the self-conscious camp which he felt at the core of the show's concept did not hold up for more than the first part of the production.[35] George Oppenheimer liked the show and felt Prince produced and directed with "his customary taste and flair."[36] *Cue* magazine felt grateful that the collaborators on *Superman* did not camp up the show.

Instead, the writers and director Harold Prince give us a gentle, affectionate satire which never descends to vulgarity. The satire touches lightly and brightly on a number of subjects—self-righteousness, male ego, Fourth of July pomposity. Mr. Prince et al. take it for granted you are intelligent and don't need your entertainment heavily underlined.[37]

Superman had built up a modest $100,000 advance but despite the many good reviews and the Kauffmann rave, the show did not sell well. Prince tested a new ticket price system with this show, offering lower-priced tickets in the orchestra as well as the balcony: the 437 balcony seats at the Alvin ranged from $2 to $5, with the mezzanine at $8 and the orchestra at $9, $10 and $12. The higher price for the first eight rows made it possible to charge only $9 for not-as-choice locations—a low orchestra price for Broadway musicals at that time. Despite this ticket-price range, the show did not sell out. Although the show was not designed for children, Prince soon realized that it appealed to them and introduced extra matinees in hopes of boosting ticket sales, but the show still failed and closed in four months. Prince feels the pop art craze had peaked, and he couldn't compete with *Batman* five nights a week on television.

At the time Prince was directing *Superman,* he was still unsure of himself as a director.

> As in *Flora,* there was another show in *Superman,* but I had neither the self-confidence nor the *comprehension* of what I might bring to the work of other people. The trouble is, everything the show might have been became clear after I'd done it. A concept, a point of view emerged after the work. That was because I had not yet begun to think of myself as a director. It was a costly way to learn.[38]

When asked what he thought of working with Prince, Lee Adams said that he enjoyed him very much as a director. He said, "I respected him." Adams went on to describe Prince:

> Hal is a very kind man. He's also very convincing. He can be very seductive in getting what he wants, both from writers and actors. His best quality for a writer is his enthusiasm. He makes you feel you're onto something terrific and he appreciates your good stuff. . . . If he doesn't like something he tells you right out front—"That isn't good enough," or "that doesn't work." He's very straightforward. He's not devious. Some directors are. I enjoyed working with him.[39]

Years later Prince said that he felt *Superman* might have had a better chance if it had been done realistically. Boris Aronson, in a conversation with the director long after the musical had closed, said that *Superman* was the one show that he wished he'd been asked to design because it could have been the definitive contemporary musical. Adams felt the show worked very well and doesn't know why it didn't run.

> Audiences liked it, critics liked it and yet people just didn't come. At one time there was a theory that it didn't succeed because they were showing *Batman* on television free and people weren't going to come to see a comic

strip for whatever the tickets cost. I don't know if that's true or not but it just didn't catch on with a large audience.[40]

Soon after the closing of *Superman*, Prince was off to California for the San Diego opening of the national company of *Fiddler on the Roof* with Luther Adler. He was also planning to go into rehearsal by the fall of that year (1966) with *Cabaret*. Once again, Prince didn't leave himself much time to brood about a project that hadn't turned out as successfully as he had hoped.

A Major Hit
&
A Near Miss

I really do not think that a successful play is the reason for living. . . . I don't think that each play is the most important thing. . . . You can destroy your personal life—lose your friends. . . . It seems silly to me. . . . It's just a play and there will be another play after it. I dedicate a lot of my time and love and emotions to the success of a play—but there'll be another play. It seems silly to think of it differently.
   —Harold Prince, Interview with Dick Cavett, 19-20 February 1983

The Taganka Theatre was traumatizing (in a good sense). It totally changed my life—there's no question about that! That one performance in the theatre totally altered my vision of the stage and what I would want to do with that space. . . . It's very simple—it's saying look at the stage and put there what cannot be done by films and television. Take stage machinery and identify what is unique and exciting about a stage . . . in the vernacular of today: what turns you on! It's all instinctive obviously.
   —Harold Prince, Interview with the author, 14 March 1983

By 1965 the American Musical Theatre appeared to be beginning a period of decreasing creativity. The war in Southeast Asia had been escalating daily. There were riots in cities across the country and on campuses. The government for a long time was insensitive to the growing unrest and negative feeling about the unpopular war.

The streets adjacent to the New York theatre district were becoming sleazier and there were perceived possible dangers to the theatregoing crowd because of the porno shops and derelicts in the Times Square area. Inflation didn't help theatre either. After holding the line pretty much through the sixties, ticket prices kept rising steadily and by 1970 were hovering around a $12 top. To compensate for the increasing costs of producing a show and to deal with the smaller audiences, producers began to reduce the number of performers hired for chorus jobs and to cut budgets of costumes and sets, with basic unit sets becoming prevalent.

In addition, with the lucrative rewards of films and television beckoning, the best young talents in New York were leaving for the West Coast. As a result, there were few exciting musicals offered during this late sixties period. Some were repeats of past shows and forms.

The most notable influence on the musical at this time was the music of the Beatles who, in 1964, came from England to appear on the *Ed Sullivan Show*. They helped propagate a new musical sound across the country. In the American Musical Theatre the tradition of the melodic show tune was being severed. Gerald Bordman has said, "As far as memorable melodies went, the American Musical Theatre had suddenly become not very musical. With rare exceptions audiences rarely left new musicals singing their music."[1] The role of importance usually reserved for the songwriters of musicals was now shifting toward directors and librettists. Gower Champion, Bob Fosse and soon Harold Prince and Michael Bennett became the names more closely identified with a work instead of a Rodgers or a Gershwin. In addition, said Bordman, "the director sometimes assumed dictatorial creative control—originating the very ideas for their musicals and shaping their entire development."[2] The stage was being set for directors with strong personalities and imaginative and artistic visions.

Prince was ready for the challenge. His next project was the production and staging of the musical *Cabaret*—a musical that broke new ground. Its unusual content and form, as well as its use of stagecraft, influenced the shape of the American Musical Theatre for decades afterward.

Cabaret

In the opinion of critic Martin Gottfried, Hal Prince's major work began with *Cabaret*. Gottfried wrote, "Since the concept musical was still in a formative stage this was a schizophrenic show. One-half of it was an ortho-dox musical play whose story unfolded in dramatic scenes with duly integrated book songs. The other half, however, startled and changed Broadway."[3] Prince effectively applied different levels of realism: the expressionistic and the conventional.[4]

"The idea for *Cabaret*," said librettist Joe Masteroff, "came from Hal Prince."[5] The two had just finished working together on *She Loves Me* when Prince suggested doing *I Am a Camera* (the John van Druten play based on the *Berlin Stories* of Christopher Isherwood) as a musical. Once the collaborators for *Cabaret* were set, it took a while to establish the form of the project. Eventually the show used the Isherwood stories rather than *I Am a Camera* as a jumping-off point. Prince and his col-laborators saw a parallel between this material, which dealt with anti-Semitism and the spiritual decline of Germany in the 1920s, and the racial hatred in the United States which led to assassinations, violence in the streets and the march on Selma in the summer of 1965. Prince recalled, "I went so far in one draft of the show to end it with a film of the march on Selma and the Little Rock riots, but that was a godawful idea, and I came to my senses."[6]

Musicalizing *I Am a Camera* had occurred to a number of people. At first it didn't appeal to Prince, probably because all the drafts he had seen were motivated by the desire to find a star vehicle for Gwen Verdon or Tammy Grimes. Prince explained the kind of approach for the show which turned him off:

> [Sally Bowles] works in a club, see, and she dances and sings, sings all night long, and it's racy. . . . No point. It was only after we'd come by a reason for telling that story parallel to contemporary problems in our country, that the project interested me.[7]

One version, with book as well as music and lyrics by Sandy Wilson of *The Boy Friend* fame, was to star Julie Andrews. Masteroff said:

> Hal came to me telling me about the Sandy Wilson project and explained that Julie Andrews was anxious to do the show but that she thought the book needed some work. She thought that the songs were great, however, and she wanted Hal to direct or produce it. Prince then suggested I might be able to do something with the book. As I recall, we went to somebody's apart-ment to hear Sandy Wilson play the score. I realized there was really nothing

wrong with the songs except they all sounded like *The Boy Friend.* The fact that it was 1920s Berlin had led Wilson to do the same thing as he had for 1920s Brighton (or wherever it was). When we left the meeting I said to Hal and Hal quite agreed that it isn't the way I would hear that show at all. If you were going to do *that* show then it should sound like Kurt Weill and Lotte Lenya. That's the sound this musical had for me. . . . So we let it go at that. Then there were lots of negotiations and dealings and somehow Hal Prince turned out to be the producer of that show and Sandy Wilson was no longer involved in it. However, I was never privy to everything that went on. All I know is that suddenly we were free to do it. And a producer named David Black who had been the original producer was somehow no longer involved but was getting some share of the property. What Sandy Wilson got, or what the deal was with him, I really don't know. But he was out and we were in.[8]

Wilson expressed his side of the story in a letter to the *Dramatists Guild Quarterly:*

At no time did Julie [Andrews] read my script, so there was no question of her being "not too happy" with it. Her manager refused to consider letting her play such a part, and shortly after that she was cast in *The Sound of Music.* . . . In the late fall of that year I went to New York, taking my script and about two-thirds of the score (I shall never forget the date of my arrival: Nov. 22, 1963). Mr. Black [who had commissioned Wilson to write the show] suggested that another author should be called in on the book—to which I gladly agreed, particularly as his first choice was Hugh Wheeler. But he was having problems with the rights, as they were all tied up in the estate of John van Druten. . . . One evening Hal Prince, whom I knew well at the time, invited me out to dinner. He asked me what I was working on, and when I told him, he was astonished. "But that's what *I'm* working on," he said, "and I think I'm going to get the rights." In view of Hal's status as a producer, this seemed more than likely. He then told me that he had engaged Joe Masteroff to write the book but had not decided on a composer and lyricist. Would I be prepared to play the score to him and Masteroff? I naturally agreed. Hal gave me tickets for *She Loves Me* at a matinee, after which I went and performed my score. At the end Mr. Masteroff told me that he liked my work, but it did not fit in with his conception of Sally Bowles. And that was that. A few months later, Hal wrote and told me that he had indeed secured the rights and was going ahead with the show. The rest, as they say, is history.[9]

When Prince was ready to hire a composer and lyricist he suggested composer John Kander and lyricist Fred Ebb to Masteroff. Since Masteroff

was a great admirer of Kander and Ebb's score for *Flora, the Red Menace,*
he was warm to the idea and the project got underway. Fred Ebb remembers
Prince approaching him to do the show:

> Sometime during the Boston run [of *Flora*], Hal said, "Would you like to
> do *I Am a Camera*?" He said, "No matter what happens to *Flora,* the day
> after it opens we'll go to work." That seemed like a good deal to me. So
> we agreed to do it. I didn't have a clue how to do it, I must say. The fact
> is, *Flora* was not a success; and the fact is, at four o'clock the next afternoon
> we did meet.[10]

Cabaret distanced itself from *I Am a Camera*. In order to develop the
concept, Prince arranged, as Masteroff recalls, for "thousands of
meetings."[11] The show had a slow metamorphosis. Masteroff wrote the
first outline in the summer of 1963. Until the show opened in November
1966, there were many drafts, based on many notes from Prince to Masteroff
and from Masteroff to Prince.

The collaborators worked very closely on the project. Ronald Field
was eventually hired as choreographer. He had been doing nightclub work
all over the world at the time. Previously, he had done a couple of unsuccessful shows on Broadway, but his staging of Liza Minnelli's nightclub
act was an enormous success. Kander and Ebb used their persuasive power
to convince Prince to hire Field. After Prince signed the choreographer,
he saw a production of *Show Boat* that Field had staged at Lincoln Center,
a production that the choreographer himself felt was terrible. Field said,
"I was told [Prince] was having great trouble with the decision he had
made and that he was very nervous about me. So it was under that cloud
I went into rehearsal for *Cabaret*."[12] Field had not been hired in time to
attend all the preliminary meetings on *Cabaret* but he did spend a summer with Prince discussing the show. Prince chose Field because he liked
his enthusiasm for the project. The choreographer proved to have a wealth
of ideas to contribute to the many numbers he was responsible for staging. Field said in reference to his collaboration with Prince, "Let me say
that in the mature age I have gotten to, I now realize I paid no attention
to the things I should have paid attention to working with that man."[13]

The idea of the cabaret as the central metaphor of the show evolved
gradually. Prince wanted to establish the show's atmosphere at the opening. He asked Kander and Ebb for a melange of songs set all over Berlin
to show what was happening there at the time. The composers wrote five
short songs as a kind of prologue. One was about Herman the German.

One took place in a radio station, and one was a Chinese song sung by a Chinese girl to show the decadence of the period. One of these five songs was called "Wilkommen" and was the first song written for the show. It was decided during early production meetings that at the end of these five songs (or prologue), the story of Sally Bowles and writer Cliff would begin and that this "story" part of the show would have its own score.

Prince recalled his experiences when he was stationed with the army near Stuttgart in 1951. He had vivid recollections of the shows presented at Maxim's, a nightclub situated in an old church basement:

> There was a dwarf MC, hair parted in the middle, and lacquered down with brilliantine, his mouth made into a bright red cupid's bow, who wore heavy false eyelashes and sang, danced, goosed, tickled, and pawed four lumpen Valkyres [*sic*] waving diaphanous butterfly wings.[14]

These images helped formulate the ideas for *Cabaret*. Soon the little man was the master of ceremonies and the thread for the entire musical. They decided to insert the five prologue songs between the book scenes in random fashion instead of at the beginning of the show. The songs intruded on the book scenes, however, and "Wilkommen" was the only one retained. The MC's first numbers reflected his and Germany's low self-esteem. As the show progressed, the MC changed. He found his strength through National Socialism, although it corrupted him morally. The MC, through the eight numbers he eventually did, became the metaphor for Germany "in an ascending curve energetically and descending curve morally."[15] The cabaret's mindless gaiety is played out against the menace of the inflation-gutted pre-Nazi Berlin of 1929–30. By turns funny and chilling, the production was ultimately "a challenge to audiences conditioned to the jolly predictability of our musical stage."[16] John Chapman of the *Daily News* said after the show opened that the collaborators, in an unusual move in musical theatre, ended the show "on a down beat—out of necessity."[17]

Masteroff created Clifford Bradshaw, the Isherwood character of the *Berlin Stories*, as an American instead of the Englishman he was in the original. Sally remained very much the same as she had been written in *I Am a Camera*. However, Masteroff never felt her character worked successfully in *Cabaret*. He said, "This worried me a lot until it was pointed out to me that there just isn't time in a musical to develop characters very thoroughly. If I'd had more stage time, I think Sally could have been a much more interesting character."[18] Because he believes he had not fleshed out the role, Masteroff feels that none of the actresses who have played the role of Sally have ever been very successful. Masteroff said in an interview, "It had seemed to be a star part but it kept getting smaller and smaller as other things kept poking their way into the show and eventually it turned out to be not that crucial a role. The whole show had swung around and Sally Bowles was still in it but she was no longer the sine qua non of it."[19] Although *I Am a Camera*, which starred Julie Harris on Broadway, was a play about Sally Bowles, with *Cabaret* it didn't really matter. Prince made the point to his collaborators while they were in Boston that the show would not live or die because of the Bowles character. He felt that even if her character didn't work, the show could still succeed. Ultimately, Bowles was given only two and a half songs to do. "In many ways," said Masteroff, "Prince turned out to be right."[20]

There were some critics who were disappointed with Prince's choice of Jill Haworth in the Bowles role. Walter Kerr was the most emphatic, calling the casting of Haworth the show's "one wild wrong note."[21] Kerr felt that Bowles, according to the narrative, is a "fey, fetching, far-out lassie with a head full of driftwood and heart she'd rather break than shackle. She is a temperament, and she needs a temperament to play her."[22] Kerr stated that this miscasting of "a pretty but essentially flavorless ingenue in the role was for Harold Prince a totally uncharacteristic lapse of judgment."[23] Other reviewers were less critical of Jill Haworth. In Richard Watts, Jr.'s opinion, "Sally may be a blind, wayward, somewhat soiled heroine, but as played by the talented and attractive Jill Haworth, she is a charming one."[24]

Kander and Ebb wrote about 47 songs for the show; eventually, only 15 were used. Ebb said, "The narrative kept shifting, and there were many more scenes that were seriously considered that never were done. Also, characters were being added. The whole Lenya-Gilford relationship came later, I think."[25] As was the case with Bock and Harnick in *She Loves Me*, Joe Masteroff gave Kander and Ebb an outline with no moments for songs marked. He left it to his composers to select spots for songs. Masteroff said, "I wrote the scenes and Fred and John plucked the songs out of them in every case. I'm talking about the book songs, of course. We never talked about it in advance. They just took the scenes and found what turned them on."[26] The pineapple exchange was originally dialogue in which Fraulein Schneider is touched by the gift of a pineapple from Herr Schultz, the fruit store owner. Kander and Ebb turned the scene into the song "It Couldn't Please Me More," which John Chapman called "an affectionate, endearing song number."[27]

The scene of the show, then, is Berlin and the time, just before New Year's Eve in the year 1930. The Master of Ceremonies welcomes us with "Wilkommen." We meet the cabaret girls and the Kit Kat Klub Kittens, the members of the all-female band, who help set the Germanic jazz tone.

Prince had very specific actors in mind for most of the roles in the show. Ebb said, "One of the miracles of *Cabaret* was that we got them. I mean, the people we had in mind were the people we got."[28] They were really writing for Lenya and Gilford as Fraulein Schneider and Herr Schultz and for Joel Grey as the Master of Ceremonies. But they did have a lot of trouble with the other two leads, Sally and Cliff. "I don't think we ever found exactly what we wanted for those parts," said Masteroff.[29] Kander and Ebb wanted Liza Minnelli in the Bowles role. Prince was strong in his decision not to use her. He said, "[Minnelli] wasn't British—I'm not sure why that was important to me—and she sang too well. I still think that was a flaw in the film."[30]

At a point in the creation of the show (1965), the collaborators became stymied. Prince had no idea of how the show should look and how it all would work. Rather than do the show with only "half a concept," he postponed it and did *Superman* instead. Prince maintains that if an audience can predict what it's going to see on the stage, it's more than likely going to be disappointed. Since *Cabaret* would be dealing with popular, familiar material, he felt that it was important to locate surprise in his concept. After *Superman* had opened and closed, Prince took a trip to Russia. The trip proved to be critical in his thinking as a director.

While in Moscow, he saw a performance of the Taganka Theatre. He had arranged well in advance to attend the theatre, perhaps at the suggestion of Boris Aronson, his set designer for *Cabaret*. Aronson was born in Kiev in 1900. He came to this country in 1922 just five years after the Russian Revolution. He had worked in theatre in Kiev after the Revolution and was informed about the innovations in theatre craft in both Russia and Germany. After arriving in the United States, Aronson worked as an artist, sculptor and set designer, at first for the Yiddish Art Theatre in Manhattan and the Unser in the East Bronx, going on to become one of our most gifted Broadway theatrical designers. During his career he designed about 140 theatrical productions, including *I Am a Camera*. Aronson felt in the latter years of his career that "naturalism is deadly in theatre today."[31] Expressing his ideas about stage design in an interview with Garson Kanin, he explains that he especially liked working with Hal Prince since, by the time *Cabaret* was done, he had decided "only to take on projects that would not compromise his experimenting.''[32] Aronson was compatible with Prince since he felt that the greatest achievement on a show was when all the people collaborating on it "have the same approach. . . . There has to be a common language.''[33] This is also an important goal for Prince and why he spends so much time meeting with collaborators for years prior to a show's going into rehearsal. Aronson explained, "I have no interest in symmetrical scenery. I design from inside of the people who inhabit the play, not architecturally. . . . Basically I'm more concerned with the nature of the script. . . . The tendency is to do beautiful sets. Some shows and their themes and characters don't call for this.''[34]

Prince was most impressed with the Taganka Theatre techniques, which borrowed heavily from Vsevolod Meyerhold, a Soviet director who had become prominent during the years following the Russian Revolution. He differed from Stanislavsky and realism, fostering symbolism, mechanization and the de-emphasis of emotion. Meyerhold and Alexander Tairov were advocates of constructivism. Simple cubes replaced cumbersome chairs so as not to provide the audience with a literal, realistic presentation. At this time in Russia, the theatrical world was innovative.

At the Taganka, Prince began to rethink his ideas about stagecraft. Until this point he had believed that the book was the most important element of a musical, and the score, the secondary. Prince felt that the text he saw that night in a political revue suggested by John Reed's *Ten Days That Shook the World* was absurd. However, "the techniques, the vitality, the imagination to make every minute surprising, involving, yet consistent with a concept''[35] were primary at the Taganka Theatre, and the mounting would influence Prince's future work.

The Taganka was conventional in that there was the stage, the proscenium, the orchestra pit, the auditorium: nothing environmental about it. However, there were technical devices which knocked me out. An apron built over the orchestra pit into which searchlights were sunk. These lights, slanted over the heads of the audience to the last row of the balcony, when lighted, instead of blinding, became a curtain of light behind which the scenery was changed. Paintings on the wall spoke, inanimate objects animated, disembodied hands, feet, and faces washed across the stage. There were puppets and projections, front and rear, and the source and colors of light were always a surprise. All of it made possible by the use of black velour drapes instead of painted canvas. I date my love affair with black velours from that performance. . . . Each of these ideas capitalized on the special relationships of live actors and live observers. It is that relationship which is exclusively ours in the theatre. Film and television cannot touch it. And properly appreciated, it gives us the chance to make connections, to string unseen emotional bands between actor and audience. The business of physical contact is the least of it.[36]

Prince admitted that these techniques were not necessarily new, but that he had never seen them used so effectively. A few seasons later he saw the Taganka production of *Hamlet* and noted the use of fabric strung from guy wires which, when moved in various directions, could suggest walls, furniture or a door. Prince also saw a production of *Hedda Gabler* directed by Ingmar Bergman, and was impressed with the way the actors effortlessly "moved a blood-red screen, about the size of a door and mounted on casters, to divide rooms, to construct unseen walls, to isolate the interior workings of a character's mind from his external behavior."[37] Later, as Prince became more and more respected for his directing work, critics compared his innovative techniques to those of Brecht. Prince feels, however, that his major influences came from the Taganka Theatre and their Meyerhold-like staging and from working with Aronson, who was well-versed in the innovative Russian and European theatre techniques of the 1920s.

> I'm tired to death of reading about how influenced by Brecht I am. I am not influenced by Brecht. I don't like Brecht all that much. That whole alienation thing. Alienation by definition is alienating. And I want to be enveloped, engaged in the theatre. Now that does not mean I don't have respect for some of the Brecht I've seen. I'm very, very fond of *The Caucasian Chalk Circle*. There have been along the way, Brechtian experiences that have thrilled me. But I do not feel remotely—or at least not consciously—influenced by Brecht. No, I'm influenced by Meyerhold, that's who I'm influenced by, and I'm influenced by Piscator. I know where my influences come from.[38]

After his trip to Moscow, Prince was ready to get to work on *Cabaret*. He and Aronson now had a vision for his show. Kissel, of *Horizon* magazine, felt that Prince created a concept musical with *Cabaret*; it was created around a key metaphor rather than a conventional plot.[39] Prince describes his first directorial collaboration with Aronson:

> We talked for three months, rarely of things visual, mostly of the characters, false motivations, interpersonal behavior, people in different countries, ethnic

peculiarities, emotional expression as affected by national or ethnic consideration. Of course, he collected thousands of photographs, but he never observed
the predictable; never the leg of a table, the shape of a lamp post, the iron-
work on the hotel balcony rail. Rather he would call my attention to the quality
of light in a room, the emotional content in the architecture of a section
of the city. . . . [W]hen Boris talks, I hear and see things I neither heard nor
saw before.[40]

Aronson had a penetrating vision of people, time and places. During
his long sessions with Prince, he would be working on the set designs. When
the meetings seemed to have come to an end, Aronson would produce his
beautifully rendered (in watercolor and gouache) set designs. He would
also offer a quarter-inch scale model. Usually nothing major had to changed.
After the small details were corrected, Aronson would construct a half-inch
scale model. This would be utilized by the builders of the set, the stage
managers and by Prince to help him and the actors become familiar with
his set. The pieces of the model were large enough to remove and hold
in your hand. It was very detailed and finely realized down to the texture
of the wallpaper, or the design of a stained-glass window.[41]

For *Cabaret,* black velours were used to surround the rear and sides
of the stage, and side panels could be flown quickly to enable the scenery
to be rolled in on winch-operated trucks. An iron staircase was designed
by Aronson although it was not asked for by Prince, who was, however,
delighted with this "surprise" from his designer. It enabled him for the
first time to experiment with the idea of using observers on the stage. He
placed chorus members on the staircase, lighting cigarettes, observing the
realistic scenes indifferently. This image made a comment on the theme.
Prince felt the people on the stair became a symbol of the surrogate German
population.

In another surprise, Aronson presented Prince with a mirror, a
trapezoid that hung above center stage, to reflect the audience and involve them in the play. Aronson said, "I asked Hal, 'Why are you making
this musical?' His answer was, 'My main reason is to show that what happened then in Berlin could happen here now.' I felt the only way to get
this was the mirror tilted to show the audience. Since then I have seen
more mirrors in shows where it has no reason. There it meant a lot."[42]

Walter Kerr commented on Aronson's design:

The first thing you see as you enter the Broadhurst is yourself. Designer
Boris Aronson, whose scenery is so imaginative that even a gray green fruit

store comes up like a warm summer dawn, has sent converging strings of frosted lamps swinging toward a vanishing point at upstage center. Occupying the vanishing point is a great geometric mirror, and in the mirror the gathering audience is reflected. We have come for the floor show, we are all at tables tonight, and anything we learn of life during the evening is going to be learned through the tipsy, tinkling, angular vision of sleek rouged-up clowns, who inhabit a world that rains silver.[43]

Prince was happy with the unexpected design elements. He likes to be surprised by his collaborators and is therefore thrilled when they come in with something more than he could conceive of at the time.

Remembering the lighting at the Taganka Theatre, Prince asked Jean Rosenthal, his lighting designer, for a curtain of light so that scenery could be changed behind it. She felt this was impossible because of the size of the Broadhurst Theatre. The throw from the source of light to the top of the balcony wouldn't be intense enough to accomplish Prince's aims. They had to devise some other way to deal with the material. Prince came up with the idea of splitting the stage into two areas—one representing the "real world" which would encompass scenes taking place in Sally's boarding house, the train, or the cabaret. The other area would represent "the mind." The MC would do some of his numbers in the area representing the cabaret and other numbers in the area which became known as "Limbo," to suggest changes in the German psyche. Responding to this idea, Rosenthal produced a light trough which was placed six feet upstage of the edge of the apron. It was covered with a wooden shield and rose electronically at a 45-degree angle upstage to the rear wall. Downstage at 45 degrees, the audience was momentarily blinded and at 90 degrees straight up into the flies, it produced a curtain of dust. Prince was able to send his chorus across the stage with only their legs lit. The light trough also became the MC's footlights. The lighting enabled communication with the audience. It explained and clarified without the use of words or music.

A major problem arose in regard to a song that Joel Grey sang, entitled "If You Could See Her through My Eyes." The Master of Ceremonies sang it as a love song to a gorilla dressed in a pink tutu. They hugged each other and danced together. It all seemed harmless and silly until the final line of the song when Grey looked at the gorilla and sang as if in a whispered confidence to the audience, "If you could see her through my eyes she wouldn't look Jewish at all."

Ebb claims to have dreamed the idea for this number:

What happened on this runway was that Joel Grey came out, and there was a gorilla in a tutu. . . . No words, no music, but that was the image. And then I told Hal I had dreamed it. I said that I dreamed about a number in which Joel would come out with a gorilla in a tutu, and he thought that was kind of baroque. Which it was. And then I tried to get a song—I know it is silly—to fit that image. It was clear to me that it would look wonderful. Eventually the song came. It was him, of course, loving this gorilla. . . . So the song could serve to show how anti-Semitism was creeping in. I thought it had a dramatic validity.[44]

Prince loved the song and used it in the show. Audiences laughed and then when they realized what they were laughing at, they would stop laughing. It made them very nervous which, Ebb said, "was exactly what Prince wanted."[45] The collaborators felt that everybody knew the ending of the story, and knew that the Nazis were going to come to power. However, toward the end of the Boston run, they started to get letters, including one from a rabbi who was terribly upset. Near the end of the previews in New York, a woman accosted Ebb in the lobby and told him that if the lyric weren't changed, pressure groups would be after them.

Prince was deeply worried about the issue. Ebb remembered:

There was a visit to his office where there was a real threat of cancelling theatre parties over *one* lyric line. There was a meeting at the bottom of the Broadhurst Theatre, which I remember vividly, where I was asked to take that line out. Hal (who is noted for his courage and his daring) could not at that moment of his life—with as much as *Cabaret* meant to him and to all of us—take the chance of bucking an enormous group.[46]

There were many others who made it clear to Prince that he had to change the song's ending. Finally, Ebb changed the line to "She isn't a *meeskite* at all." Prince felt that he had made the right decision since it would have been foolish to allow the show to close over one line in a song.

Ebb was angry with Prince for what he felt was his pandering to the public.

I wasn't doing it [changing the lyric] with a full heart. I wasn't doing it for what I thought was the good of the show. I was doing it for what I felt were the wrong reasons. But I knew it had to be done anyway. . . . I wish Prince had held firm. But it was his first big chance at having a successful show as a director and I can now understand and have great compassion for his not wanting to blow it for something as seemingly mild as one line in a song.[47]

The original line was sometimes put back into the show. Ebb asked for the line when Walter Kerr came. He also wanted it used for the Actors' Fund performance. "And Joel would literally go out and say it as if he had just forgotten that he was forbidden to say it."[48] But the new line stayed in the show for the three years of *Cabaret*'s run in New York. Bob Fosse, when he did the movie, was willing to put the original line back. But, said Ebb, "If you listen very carefully, it is totally tacit in the movie. Joel turns to the camera and says (whispering): 'She wouldn't look Jewish at all.' There is no music. And that is because, had *he* [the movie's director, Bob Fosse] had any flack, he could have gone in and rerecorded it."[49]

Kander, discussing the incident, explains it as a miscalculation that they made which he cannot understand to this day.

> The song was to end that way, to have you laughing and then catch your breath, to make you the audience realize how easily you could fall into a trap of prejudice. And the Jewish members of the audience, my family included, all insisted that the song was really saying that Jews looked like gorillas. It's a puzzle that has never been solved.[50]

Another miscalculation was the original idea to do the show in three acts. They thought it would be fun to open in three acts because musicals were generally done in two. It didn't work very well and so they immediately returned to the two-act form. It was an improvement.

To achieve the style of music they wanted, Kander and Ebb obtained records of German jazz and German cabaret songs of the twenties, and tried to incorporate the flavor of these songs. Some critics, however, felt that Kander and Ebb had written watered-down Kurt Weill. Kander told Lotte Lenya, a cast member and widow of Weill, that he never intended to imitate Weill. According to Kander, Lenya "took my face in her hands and said, 'No, no, darling. It is not Weill. It is not Kurt. When I walk on stage and sing those songs, it is [the city of] *Berlin*.'"[51]

Prince was generally firm in his decisions about which songs of Kander and Ebb would be used and which would not. Ironically, the hit title song, "Cabaret," had originally been turned down by Prince. He hadn't wanted to use two title songs and he felt "Wilkommen" already contained the "welcome to the cabaret." According to choreographer Ron Field, Prince didn't want another song with the word "cabaret" in the second act.[52]

Cabaret, 1966
Joel Grey in his Tony-winning role as the MC.

Field loved the number and persuaded Prince to reconsider it. Prince gave the song another hearing and they decided to use it after all.

Ebb compared working with directors Abbott and Prince, since he had done so with Abbott on *Flora* and with Prince on *Cabaret*. He didn't think they were very similar in their directing methods, although

> they do have some similar terrific traits such as their professionalism, never coming late, etc. And they're clear, sure and authoritative. . . . They're both good captains, and are never wishy-washy. In Prince's long association with Abbott, Prince must have learned a great deal about just how to manage a show. It's a very difficult, complicated thing to do and they both do it extraordinarily well. They make it look easy.[53]

Jerome Robbins attended the run-through before *Cabaret* went to Boston. He thought the show was wonderful, but suggested that any dancing that didn't take place as part of the performance at the Kit Kat Klub be cut from the show. He recommended cutting the telephone number, as well as the engagement party dance that Lenya did with some sailors. To Field's relief, Prince, in spite of his respect and affection for Robbins, did not take his advice and the numbers stayed in the show and played successfully.

Another suggestion came from Goddard Lieberson, the record producer, and from others who knew the director was still fixing the show. The song "Cabaret" was to be removed from the end of the show and used to replace Sally's first song, "Don't Tell Mama," which introduces her to the audience. In place of "Cabaret," Prince was advised to use "I Don't Care Much," a song that Kander and Ebb had not written for the show, but which Prince liked. Lieberson, who was producing the original cast album, felt that "Cabaret"—which was by that time a hit song— would be stronger in the first act. Although Prince was against it, he decided to try it mainly because so many people were advising the same thing. Three days before the New York opening, they put the new song in and, as Kander recalls, "it was a disaster."[54] Prince described the situation:

> It went in that night and destroyed the show. The climactic moment of *Cabaret* was half as effective with the new song. The song, coming at the top of the show, went by unnoticed; the giddiness of "Don't Tell Mama" was missing. It was as though we had leveled the emotions of the show across the board.[55]

Prince put the songs back in their original spots.

Joe Masteroff remembers that the show did not do well during its Boston tryout. He said, "People just kept streaming out of the theatre. Ten minutes after the curtain went up, people started departing."[56] The reason for this, Masteroff feels, is that the title of the show did not prepare the audience for what they would see. They expected a normal kind of Broadway musical and within ten minutes, they had seen these not-so-great-looking chorus girls, and the show seemed to be on the grim side. The librettist remembers Boston as a depressing time for the collaborators.

Cabaret was capitalized at $500,000 and because of Prince's track record and his good fortune with *Fiddler*, it was not necessary to hold backers' auditions to raise the money.

Cabaret opened in New York on 20 November 1966 at the Broadhurst Theatre to excellent reviews. Walter Kerr gave the most favorable notice, saying that other than the fact that he felt Jill Haworth was a poor choice of casting, he liked the show and that its "marionette's-eye view of a time and place in our lives that was brassy, wanton, carefree and doomed to crumble is brilliantly conceived."[57] Richard Watts, Jr., in the *New York Post*, called the show

> brilliant and remarkable. . . . It is all wild, hysterical fun and sex, but from the first there is that rising undercurrent of decadence and vulgarity that was preparing the way for the ease with which a brutal racial insanity was able to take over a country. . . . It is the glory of *Cabaret* that it can upset you while it gives theatrical satisfaction.[58]

Some reviewers felt that it was the cabaret scenes rather than the realistic book scenes that made the show a success. Norman Nadel, in the *New York World Journal Tribune,* said, "One thing that never lapses is director Prince's sense of theatre. Even to the final ensemble scene, which is anticlimactic and a trifle mawkish, he sets a commanding stage. He makes the decadence of 1930 Berlin as memorable as Rome's."[59]

In addition to Prince's positive personal reviews for direction, the show was an enormous box office success which created a new public awareness of Hal Prince. With *Cabaret,* Prince established himself as both a showman and a director. Richard P. Cooke in the *Wall Street Journal* said, "That able showman, Harold Prince, has done it again. *Cabaret* is one of the most exciting, imaginative and effective musicals to come to Broadway this year or any other."[60] Whitney Bolton, in the *New York Morning Telegraph,* said:

Harold Prince has directed a show [set] in a period when he could not have been more than a gurgling infant. How he got the feel, unless Miss Lenya imparted it to him, defies answer. But he has it down pat, follies, naughtiness, audacity, sadness, despair, all of it the air of Berlin as the Nazis found it and fouled it.[61]

Joel Grey became an overnight sensation. He had been a successful and talented performer for 24 years in almost every medium of show business but had never received the kind of recognition that this project provided him. Writing of *Cabaret,* Martin Gottfried observed: "With Joel Grey as the androgynous master of ceremonies in the Kit Kat Klub, Broadway has never seen anything like the visual metaphors of decadence that Harold Prince daringly presented on a stage accustomed to pretty pictures."[62]

Grey, when asked how he was able to make the master of ceremonies character real and full without dialogue, said it was Prince who helped him achieve his outstanding performance. Grey said, "[Prince] knows what he wants and has tremendous taste."[63]

According to David Ewen, *Cabaret* was the "hottest ticket" on Broadway in 1966.[64] It won the New York Drama Critics' and the Antoinette Perry Awards as the best musical of the year. Little more than a year after opening on Broadway, a national company began a tour, opening in New Haven on 16 December 1967 and lasting for several years. Other successful productions were presented in London, Iceland, Holland, Switzerland, Germany, Denmark, Austria, Finland and Sweden. The New York company played 1,166 performances and finally closed on 6 September 1969.

Although Prince achieved success with *Cabaret* and was soon being offered plays to direct by other managements, he has often stated that if he were to do the show again, he would do it differently. He and his collaborators had persuaded themselves in 1966 that the musical comedy audience expected a heterosexual love story as well as a subordinate story line such as Hinesie and Gladys in *The Pajama Game.* He feels they were wrong to pander to audience expectations and that they should have made the audacious choices for *Cabaret.* He would have that opportunity more than twenty years later, when a revamped *Cabaret* would be offered to 1987 audiences.

Zorba

The idea to turn the Nikos Kazantzakis novel *Zorba the Greek* into a musical was Herschel Bernardi's. He and librettist Joseph Stein approached Prince and asked him if he would produce and direct. Since Prince liked the philosophical ideas and the exciting moments of music and dance as presented in the Michael Cacoyannis film of the novel, he agreed to take on the project. Kander and Ebb were equally enthusiastic and were signed to write the score, making the team of collaborators on *Zorba* basically the same as had created *Cabaret,* except for librettist and lighting designer.

The concept fell into place easily. Prince used a facsimile of a Greek chorus to comment on the action. It was led by a girl dressed in black, supported by several bouzouki musicians. Prince had observed a similar group of musicians in a bouzouki restaurant near Piraeus. He remembers

> thirty-eight men and women sitting in a semicircle, each holding a musical instrument, dressed in the gaudiest of makeshift costumes with spangles, smoking, talking, singing solos or in unison, interrupting each other with horseplay and laughter.[65]

The musical is set in a similar bouzouki café in modern Greece. Clive Barnes said, ''The concept of placing the entire action within the framework of a café works very well, giving the piece a shape it would otherwise have lacked.''[66] The song that is performed here is ''Life Is.'' It focuses our attention at the start on the philosophical theme of the show. ''Life is what you do while you're waiting to die,'' say the lyrics of the song.

> More important is the way this number and designer Boris Aronson's seemingly simple scenic arrangement set a style that director Harold Prince consistently follows throughout the production. This style employs a device wherein some of the people in the opening number change costumes to enact roles in the story, and others become a chorus, which both evokes action and makes comment on it.[67]

The story of the play deals with Zorba, a happy, earthy, free soul, who attempts to teach a guileless young man about the mysteries of sex, masculinity and running a coal mine, as well as one's attitude toward life. He teaches the young man, Nikos, the secret of living in the moment, as if whatever he is doing he's doing for the first time, as if each moment might also be his last.

This was not a light musical comedy. Richard Watts, Jr., of the *New York Post* said that it was "decidedly a musical drama, and a grim one at that, despite its interludes of humor."[68] Clive Barnes said of Prince, "He is trying—even more than in his previous *West Side Story* and *Fiddler on the Roof*—to demonstrate, admittedly with only uncertain success, that the musical can be a reflection of life. Indeed life and its meaning is the essential theme of *Zorba*. ... Mr. Prince possibly makes the most commanding attempt yet at a truly serious musical."[69] By the final curtain, Zorba, who represents the joy of life—wine, women and song—has converted his young friend Nikos, who realizes that in living only a life of the mind he has missed much.

Prince decided to team Maria Karnilova with Bernardi, since they had had such success playing together as Tevye and Golde in *Fiddler*. He thought that audiences would want to see them together again. Instead, their playing together created unnecessary comparisons with *Fiddler* and worked against the show. Eventually, Bernardi and Karnilova began fighting. Bernardi's personal problems turned into physical problems and he began to miss performances. Karnilova also missed many performances, and soon both stars were out. The reviewers, however, loved Bernardi and Karnilova. John Chapman called their performances "star-spangled, throat-catching."[70] There were other comments, however, that suggested that Bernardi had patterned his performance after Anthony Quinn's in the film. Barnes suggested that "the result is far from disaster, but it remains a pity."[71]

Boris Aronson's sets for *Zorba* were basically blacks, greys and whites. Prince describes Aronson's work:

> Boris' basic unit was the classic Greek amphitheatre with levels in a semicircle. Onto these levels he introduced fragments of scenery, an olive tree, the entrance to a church, a restaurant, a store, a balcony, and by the third scene in the play we'd constructed a realistic village in Crete, made of molded styrofoam, and climbing the side of a hill. By then the entire company was realistically costumed.[72]

The director and designer did more thinking about space than they had done in their other shows. Give and take led to experimentation with people standing around, observing and commenting, as had been done in *Cabaret*. Prince was still experimenting with his ideas, his visions emerging, but at this stage in his career he was not yet adept at carrying out those ideas and visions:

There was a ballad in the second act of *Zorba* in which a young man sings to the woman he loves, and it becomes a trio as a lady representing the Greek chorus observes the scene and joins in. I never got it to work. . . . In *Follies* several years later I had a man sing to an apparition of a young girl he'd been in love with thirty years earlier, while her counterpart, the woman she'd grown up to be, stood by and mistook his song as being sung to her. Two women and a man, essentially the staging quite the same. In *Follies* I knew how to make it work. . . . So you learn. Boris said *Follies* would not have happened had it not been for *Cabaret, Zorba,* and *Company.*[73]

Prince was disappointed at the staging of the mine disaster in the second act. In the film, tons of explosives on a real mountain with hundreds of extras helped to achieve the desired effect. On stage, Prince used two smoke pots, a taped explosion and 38 people running about the stage in terror. Prince said, "Had we acknowledged the limitations of the stage, we might have made capital of the mine disaster. Dance might have worked, though I'm tired of it. There had to be something imaginative, but we were stuck with realism, and what was worse, we couldn't keep the events offstage."[74]

Ronald Field choreographed *Zorba.* The major dances were Greek celebrations, the most notable being one at the opening of Nikos's mine. The critics made unflattering comparisons of Field's work with Jerome Robbins's dances in *Fiddler.* In one scene, a dancer in the foreground is echoed by a spotlighted figure on a rear platform. This image of a spotlighted dancer or dancers would become a kind of trademark in many of Prince's shows. He had begun to use it in *She Loves Me,* with a pair doing a tango at the Café Imperiale, and continued to use similar couples gliding across the stage.

Reviewers either liked the Kander and Ebb score for *Zorba* or were indifferent to it. Clive Barnes liked it.

The music by Mr. Kander and lyrics by Mr. Ebb have much of the deft facility that characterized their work for *Cabaret* and *The Happy Time,* but here the ethnic Greek element to the music and the cheerfully philosophical note struck by lyrics—often Mr. Ebb is both witty and true—endow *Zorba* with much more fire and spirit. This is far more stylish than the other two.[75]

Zorba had its out-of-town tryouts at the Shubert Theatre in New Haven beginning 7 October 1968, followed by a three-week engagement at the Shubert in Boston. The reviews were good in New Haven and the collaborators thought they had a success. Harold Bone, the *Variety* critic, said:

Zorba has the ingredients—and the people who know what to do with them. It should end up as a highly satisfying musical embodying, as it does, an absorbing book, a good score, fine cast, lively choreography, smart staging, and an interesting physical production. . . . [Zorba] is stirring entertainment and a welcome contrast to much of the "protest" and "message" fare that has been occupying the stage currently.[76]

The show was capitalized at $500,000 and had a $2 million advance sale. It opened at the Imperial Theatre on 17 November 1968 after a series of New York previews. It appeared to be a "smash hit," opening to favorable notices and strong box office business. Barnes in the *New York Times,* who liked the show, called Prince "one of the very few creative producers on Broadway—a man who can put his own imprint on a show, and that imprint is planted all over Zorba like a sterling silver mark."[77] Richard P. Cooke, in the *Wall Street Journal,* said that "Mr. Prince has again come up with a musical whose every detail has been carefully thought out."[78]

In spite of good reviews, the advance sale gradually faded and by the early summer of 1969, there was a drastic slump in business. The stars' fighting and their subsequent absences did not help. Prince didn't have the motivation to replace the two leads. He said of the show, "it hung on without either joy or relief."[79] On 9 August 1969 Prince closed the Broadway Zorba after 305 performances and began putting together two touring companies, one for the Civic Light Opera in Los Angeles with John Raitt and Barbara Baxley, and Chita Rivera as the chorus leader, and the other company to tour the country with Michael Kermoyan and Vivian Blaine. Boris Aronson won a Tony Award for his settings for Zorba.

The failure of Zorba was disappointing to its creators. Prince said, "I think Zorba was a first-rate, if depressing, show. What exhilarated me evidently depressed others. The opening number was called 'Life is What You Do While You're Waiting to Die.' Arthur Laurents said that sank us."[80] Fred Ebb feels that the show left audiences with a "down" feeling.

There were a lot of deaths in it and it was Greek and there was philosophy. I wondered if they were as entertained as they thought they'd be when they walked into the theatre and getting Herschel and Maria. . . . Maybe you think you're going to get *Fiddler* and then when you don't maybe you're disappointed, and maybe that's why [the show failed].[81]

Zorba ran for over a year on the road and it continues to be revived. Prince said,

It's interesting that *Zorba* has had rather more life in Europe than in this country, and that has to do with the prevailing blackness of its mood, its European acceptance of mortality. I loved it at the Theatre an der Wien in Vienna. It was also a success in the Scandinavian countries, particularly Finland, where there were four companies playing simultaneously.[82]

A major revival of *Zorba* was mounted at the Broadway Theatre in New York on 16 October 1983. It ran almost a year, receiving mixed reviews for the show, but rave notices for the performance of Anthony Quinn, who had earlier played the role of Zorba in the film version. Frank Rich in the *New York Times* suggests that Michael Cacoyannis, who directed the revival as well as the earlier film version starring Quinn, had lightened the show and eliminated "the studied bleakness that Harold Prince originally gave to the musical."[83] The show's opening lyric was softened: life was no longer "what you do while you're waiting to die" but "what you do till the moment you die." However, Rich favorably recalled Prince's use of a "fierce female narrator (or, if you will, Greek chorus) to establish his production's dark mood."[84]

Whitney Bolton in the *Morning Telegraph* had expressed sorrow when Prince closed the original version of *Zorba.* "I count it as a great pity. I loved *Zorba* from the moment I first saw it. I thought then and think now it is and was a much better musical than it ever received credit for—and nothing can shake me from that opinion."[85]

It was about this time (1969) that Prince became involved with the Off-Broadway Phoenix Theatre (it was noted earlier that he had been asked by their artistic director, T. Edward Hambleton, in 1961 to direct a production of *The Matchmaker*). As the company was beginning to crumble, a triumvirate of artistic directors—Stephen Porter, Harold Prince and Michael Montel took over. Later, Prince directed O'Neill's *The Great God Brown* for the company (during the 1972–73 season). Reviews were good but business wasn't. The following season (1973–74) Prince directed Duerrenmatt's *The Visit*—expressionistically. He had visited Duerrenmatt in Switzerland, where the playwright encouraged the director to do an audacious, primitive version of his play. The production was spare and the sets used panels and periactoids that could be moved around the stage to represent trees or to enclose a room. Prince also directed *Love for Love,* the Restoration comedy by William Congreve, for the Phoenix Repertory Company in the fall of 1974. The bawdy farce featured Mary Beth Hurt, John McMartin, Charlotte Moore and Glenn Close. Prince's directorial experience with the Phoenix Repertory Company gave him the opportunity to experiment and try out new staging ideas away from the commercial arena.

PRINCE & SONDHEIM
AND THE
"MODERN MUSICAL"

The man most responsible for the musical book's most dramatic change after Hammerstein's development of the musical play was not a writer but a director. Harold Prince created the musical theatre's first production-oriented scripts—the scripts for concept musicals correlating text with performance. These made no attempt to be ordinary plays. They became drastically shorter as more book weight was shouldered by music, lyrics and dance. Prince's name has never appeared on a program as an author. Yet he has been the dominating collaborator on every musical he has directed.
— Martin Gottfried, *Broadway Musicals* (1979)

Innovation is one of those words I don't think means anything. . . . The two shows I've done that had the most impact on the theatre were West Side Story, *because it was a new way of blending song, story and dance, and* Company *because it was the first show on Broadway that I know of that had a story but no plot; that is to say it was the first plotless musical that wasn't a revue and that ushered in the whole era of shows such as* A Chorus Line, *for an example, that depend on vignettes and not on plot. So those two shows have had the most impact. One can say there are innovations in all other shows—but those two shows, it seems to me, have*

> *had a lasting effect on other writers, etc., and other*
> *shows. . . . The only thing that really matters in that area is*
> *whether a show influences other shows or not.*
>
> —Stephen Sondheim, Interview with the author, 20 July 1984

> Company. *That was me making my decision to marry Judy.*
>
> —Harold Prince, Quoted in the *New York Sunday News,* 20 June 1976

Company

Harold Prince and Stephen Sondheim had last worked together on *A Funny Thing Happened on the Way to the Forum.* Since then, Sondheim as composer and/or lyricist had had two failures on Broadway, *Anyone Can Whistle* (April 1964) and *Do I Hear a Waltz?* (March 1965). He had also been involved in various other projects that did not reach fruition. Prince, on the other hand, had had a good deal of success as producer-director, and was at the time represented on Broadway by *Fiddler, Zorba* and *Cabaret.* Now they were about to collaborate on a musical entitled *Company* that would ultimately be hailed as one of the most innovative in the modern American Musical Theatre, and which would influence future Broadway musicals. Martin Gottfried would call the show "revolutionary."[1] In addition, this show would establish Sondheim as a most gifted composer-lyricist and would usher in a series of Prince-Sondheim shows, which, though not all commercially successful, would be considered courageous departures from the usual Broadway musical theatre offerings.

George Furth, a West Coast actor and friend of Sondheim's, had written eleven one-act plays titled *Company.* A few of the plays were about some of the marriages he had known in Southern California. A Broadway production was planned for the fall of 1968 and a stage manager, Philip Mandelker, and Porter Van Zandt, who had been a production supervisor on various shows including *The Goodbye People,* owned the rights. Kim Stanley was expected to play all the wives and George Morrison was set to direct. However, they could not raise the money for the production and so, in January of 1969, Furth called Sondheim in despair and asked his advice. Sondheim suggested that they send the plays to Prince, who recalled his reaction:

> I read them and told Steve that although I felt that Kim Stanley was one
> of the best actresses in the country, I thought it wasn't viable to have her

running around having eleven makeup jobs and eleven wigs and being eleven different people.[2]

Prince did, however, like Furth's writing and it suddenly occurred to him that the plays contained a wonderful idea for a musical. For the past few years Prince had had a notion of doing a musical about contemporary marriage.

> I was knocked out about [the Furth plays], seeing a potential musical which would examine attitudes toward marriage, the influence upon it of life in the cities, and collateral problems of especial interest to those of us in our forties.[3]

Sondheim was excited about this new approach and brought Furth to meet Prince. They discussed Prince's idea of doing an unconventional musical using a type of revue form. The three agreed to begin work on this modern musical comedy called *Company* in which a central male character, 35 years old and unmarried, finds himself unable to make a commitment to anyone. He would be perceived as observing his married friends' lives. Sondheim named the character Robert "so that he could be referred to differently by each of his friends. In other words, 'Bobby,' 'Bubby,' 'Baby,' 'Robbie,' 'Rob,' and so on."[4]

Sondheim was working at the time on another musical, *The Girls Upstairs*, with James Goldman, and rehearsals for that show were scheduled to begin in the fall of 1970. The plan, therefore, was for *Company* to follow in the spring of 1971.

The major difficulty the collaborators faced was finding an effective form for *Company*. They knew that the kind of songs Rodgers and Hammerstein wrote, in which the characters express their feelings, wouldn't work with Furth's script since he writes, explains Sondheim, "the kind of people who do not sing."[5] Sondheim felt that exploring the characters wouldn't work because they were primarily presented in vignettes and to try to expand them by means of song would be a mistake. The composer suggested the Brechtian approach of comment and counterpoint, although he doesn't really like Brecht. He felt this would be a difficult task since the style of writing that would emerge was not common in American musicals. He had never worked on a show before which didn't have a clear story line. This show seemed to work best in an episodic form. Having been geared to integrate his songs, the fact that now half of the songs would happen unexpectedly made *Company* a unique experience for him. You can't always tell when the dialogue is building to a music cue. Sondheim explained, "In *Forum* the songs were respites from the relentlessness of the comedy. In *Anyone Can Whistle* there were comment songs. [*Company*] is a combination—respites that are comments."⁶ Introducing songs in this unexpected manner was not an altogether new technique. Prince and Sondheim, after seeing Joan Littlewood's production of *The Hostage* some years earlier, were "both struck by the way Littlewood propelled those fragmented songs at you unexpectedly and by their force and theatricality. Suddenly somebody burst into song."⁷ They had always felt that someday they would want to do something like that; *Company* would be the result.

Sondheim composed a score for the members of the company not involved in a particular vignette—"the observers," said Prince. Those observers' songs interrupted the story and commented on the action taking place in much the same way as a Greek chorus. *Company* is not sentimental and needed a structure to suit its cooler, drier attitude.

Only two of Furth's original short plays were adapted for the musical; he wrote three more. The original scenes retained are of the karate couple and the pot-smoking couple. The show has five married couples, plus Robert and three single girls, Robert's inamoratas—fourteen characters in all, a small cast for a Broadway musical. Some of Furth's material not used for *Company* was used by the playwright in a later project, a play called *Twigs*.

From May until July of 1969, Prince worked on the show with Sondheim and Furth and, although no songs were written as yet (Sondheim never begins a score until a script has been started), the director's work with the writers went well. Boris Aronson, who was hired to do the sets, was busily involved in designing this show. Prince had already booked theatres in Boston and New York for the following spring, and planned to go into rehearsals by February. Elaine Stritch was cast as Joanne, a role that was basically written for her. Prince left for Germany that summer to direct the film *Something for Everyone*.

At the beginning of July, Prince received a call from Sondheim explaining the troubles they were having getting *The Girls Upstairs* produced. Sondheim and Goldman had reached an artistic impasse with their producer, Stuart Ostrow, and director Joseph Hardy. Ostrow dropped the show, Hardy then wanted rewrites, and Sondheim asked Prince to postpone *Company* to give him some extra time. Prince, upset at the idea of postponing *Company* because of all he had already done on the show and because he did not want to be without a show himself the following season, refused.

Sondheim was now depressed by the fact that *The Girls Upstairs*, a show he had worked on for so long, would be dropped. He said he could not work on the score of *Company* in this state of mind. Prince, as a friend, had originally read *The Girls Upstairs* five years earlier (at the time he had been working on a final draft of *Cabaret*) and didn't like it very much. It was then to be produced by David Merrick and Leland Hayward. However, because of Sondheim's present situation, Prince once again thought about *The Girls Upstairs*. After getting some new ideas about how the show might be improved, he told Sondheim to get to work on *Company* and, as soon as it opened, he would produce the other show. Sondheim went right to work and shortly flew to Germany to deliver three songs to Prince. One was "Company," which became the show's opening number. Sondheim wrote this song after seeing a picture of the model of Aronson's set; he likes to know the way the stage will look before he begins writing. "These things free me," said Sondheim.[8] He recalls saying at the time, "Now I see why [Prince] thinks this ought to be a musical, and this was after talking for four months."[9] Aronson explained that his set was very complex, and yet Prince did something that "no other producer would do. He had a wooden replica built of it—very expensive—so the cast could rehearse on it and get the feel of the levels and stairs."[10]

Company shows us a bachelor, Robert, in his mid-thirties, going from one apartment to the next observing married life among his friends. It deals with the loneliness of people in big cities, individuals seeking to change their solitary and independent existence by linking up with another lonely person to achieve fulfillment—or risk losing themselves. As the action begins, Robert's best friends, five married couples, all dote on him. He's attractive, witty and bright. He's also guarded and distant. His friends give him advice, mother him, criticize, are jealous of him, and try to find him "a nice girl" whom they know will never be good enough for him. At the finale, Robert seems to be ready to move on to become involved and make his own life instead of clinging to his married friends. At least he "seems" ready to begin.

Prince has always insisted that *Company* is intended to be pro-marriage and a plea for interpersonal relationships. However, there are those who insist the creators of *Company* had the opposite in mind. Sondheim was quoted in an article in *Time* magazine on the subject of whether the show is anti-marriage or not, and said, "[*Company*] says very clearly that to be emotionally committed to somebody is very difficult, but to be alone is impossible."[11]

The collaborators set their show in New York City because, said Sondheim, "We want to make a metaphor about Manhattan and marriage."[12] Prince and Sondheim like to use secret metaphors that nobody knows ex-

Company, 1970
Susan Browning, Donna McKechnie, and Pamela Myers sing the Stephen Sondheim song,
"You Could Drive a Person Crazy."
(Photo courtesy Photofest)

cept the authors and some of the other collaborators; it helps to hold the entity together. In *Company,* the authors are making a comparison between contemporary marriage and the island of Manhattan. "We made a vaudeville joke about it in the middle of 'Side by Side by Side,' and then took it out because we decided never to let anybody know that that's what we were about. But it justified my writing a song about Manhattan, 'Another Hundred People,' which is the only song that doesn't deal with one-to-one relationships."[13] There were times, however, when the two collaborators thought differently about the show. To Prince, it dealt with marriage and relating to people. Sondheim said *Company* was about the increasing difficulty of people relating to one another in a mechanized society. But they never had fights or disagreements about their slightly different viewpoints.[14]

Prince discussed the scenes representing Robert's birthday party. It is not always clear whether it is the same (35th) birthday party or different years of birthday parties.

> We constructed a framework of gatherings for Robert's thirty-fifth birthday, each appearing to be the same, but dynamically different from the others. Pinteresque in feeling, the first was giddy, somewhat hysterical; the second (at the end of Act I), an abbreviated version of the first; the third, hostile and staccato; and the final one at the end of the show, warm, loving, mature. Since Robert never arrives for the final celebration, there was some question whether they represented one birthday or a succession of them. I am certain they were one.[15]

The script reads like a movie. There are close-ups, cross fades, dissolves—all film techniques. When Elaine Stritch stood looking down, saying, "It's the little things," it was as if a camera were brought in for a quick cut to her face. Prince would use similar techniques in his later shows.

Boris Aronson felt that *Company* was his most successful work with Prince, that on this show he had done his personal best. He felt that on this show, as all true theatre men wish to do, he had added something that went along with all the elements. Mrs. Aronson explained that her husband did not wish to produce a set that would be acclaimed for itself. He was interested only in what it did for the show.[16] Prince, in answer to the question of how he picks a set designer for a particular project, says:

> You pick a set designer just as you cast any other creative person. Certain set designers have a gift for the primitive abrasive . . . those are complimen-

tary words. That's the stuff I like, just in case anybody is misunderstanding me. Other designers have an incredible gift for props; others enormous structural facility and no patience whatsoever with props. You just have to pick the right person for the material.[17]

In an interview with Lisa Jalowetz Aronson, Aronson's widow and long-time assistant, she explained that Prince never typecast her husband as any particular style of set designer as producers often do. "[Prince] didn't pigeon-hole Boris into the idea of being good at only one mode of design. Instead, Prince challenged him on each show they did together. And each one was obviously in a style unique and fitting the project."[18]

At first Prince and Aronson worked toward a spare production for *Company*, with a minimum of tables, chairs, a bench, a bed and a few pots and pans. They agreed that the set had to be a structure which would make possible the change of five separate bedrooms into a kitchen, a nursery or a library. Prince explained,

> The couples would move from room to room in the course of living even the mundane moments of their lives. And the decor in each room would identify its married couple. To focus our attention on a particular couple, we would reproduce their room—center and stage level. As if that weren't enough, company numbers ("What Would We do Without You?") would be performed on the entire unit without any scenery.[19]

This idea proved too difficult to carry out and was discarded.

Aronson studied how many buttons he pushed from morning to night in order to find the characteristic picture of movement in New York. He said:

> New York is like a gold mine. I could never have done the set for *Company* years ago when I first came here. It took me fifty years to know New York and to know it isn't only Times Square and Coca-Cola signs. New York is becoming one enormous cubist painting. . . . We live in a button-pushing world. So I made notes on how many buttons I pushed from morning to night. I was all over the place . . . in a modern city . . . get the hospital quality. . . . My whole inspiration was the lobby of Lincoln Center. . . . Get the essence of a place and what the city does to you. In New York you keep moving from place to place to keep from getting run over.[20]

Garson Kanin, in an essay on Aronson for the brochure of an exhibition of the designer's theatre work at the Vincent Astor Gallery in 1981, said:

In *Company,* Boris put New York City on the stage for the first time. Before beginning so much as a sketch, he walked and walked the streets of the city, with his beloved and invaluable Lisa at his side; circumnavigated Manhattan Island on the Circle Line; studied hotels and apartment houses and restaurants; and, finally, discovered the key: cubism. . . . "You know what is New York?" he exultantly asked me at lunch one day. "Cubist!" It took them fifty years to catch on. But the cubists influenced the architects and the architects the builders—all of them, van der Rohe and Johnson and Stone and Saarinen and so now we got here a cubist city on account of because a bunch of French painters who got sick from painting the same, the same as always.[21]

Aronson discovered his design concept for *Company* while sitting in the reading room of the New York Public Library at Lincoln Center. He looked out at the multi-level buildings that make up the Lincoln Center complex and realized what he wanted to do. The result was a breathtaking set of metal and glass, using projected backgrounds behind louvered walls. Six hundred slides were projected in the Broadway show and forty in the national company. The shiny rectangular frames of the massive construct became the various rooms needed in the show and they were "as cold and sterile as the shadowy people caught in their metallic embrace."[22] There is no paint on the set of *Company,* only steel, projections and plastic. Prince, always delighted when a collaborator surprises him, was very excited by the two elevators Aronson had included in the design. The reviewers were enthusiastic about Aronson's work. Stanley Kauffmann's review in the *New Republic* epitomizes the response:

Boris Aronson is seventy—probably the oldest scenic designer now active in the American theatre. This is much more than a moist-eyed Grand Old Man note because his setting for *Company* is marvelous. Aronson's styles have ranged through his career, from the naturalism of *Awake and Sing* to the abstraction of *J. B.,* but for *Company* he has made a setting quite unlike any of his work that I know. It is a skeletonized structure of (seeming) plexiglass and steel with two open elevators in it and a huge cyclorama behind it on which rear projections flow past to supplement or specify the action. Yet this is no mere stack of boxes like Robin Wagner's set for the recent feeble production of *Mahagonny;* Aronson's setting *dramatizes* the cellular, scarily clean feeling of a modern Manhattan apartment house including a touch of wit and a lot of good, varied playing spaces. Like so much that is new, the basic concept is a fresh use of the not-new. The mode is Constructivist and suggests the influence of two Russians, the sculptor Tatlin and the director-designer Meyerhold (Aronson was born in Russia and lived there until he was twenty-three, so possibly knew their work first-hand). . . . I dwell on the setting because first, it is excellent, and second, it is the best element in *Company,* and third, I'm convinced that, in a decisive way, it "makes" the show. The ultra-hip tone of *Company* rests on the work of this seventy-year-old designer.[23]

Lisa Aronson explains that Prince made it possible for her husband to function at his best. Prince created a fertile climate in which his collaborators were able to do creative work. She says that Aronson believed that working with Prince freed him to accomplish his best work. Prince encouraged his collaborators to "dig as deep" as they could and "stretch" their creative specialties into their best. Mrs. Aronson suggests that Prince was always there as a kind of editor—taking what he liked from his collaborators and rejecting what he felt would not "work." However, she said, "He challenged people in a big way and helped them to come up with unexpected ideas."[24] Prince was as demanding of Aronson as he was with all his collaborators, but Lisa Aronson felt that his tendency to be demanding was a very good quality. Prince is not an insecure man, she suggests, and does not expect his creative staff to come up with precisely what he has asked for. He prefers inspiring them to come back with surprises, his position as captain of the ship secure.[25]

Ironically, the set which Aronson designed to give the illusion of spareness was heavy and difficult to assemble. It required six tons of steel, two electric SCR motorized elevators, and 28 carousel projectors.

Tony Perkins, whose only previous musical was *Greenwillow* in 1960, and known for his role in the Hitchcock thriller *Psycho,* was slated to play Robert in *Company.* However, he was anxious to begin a career as a director and Dean Jones was hired to play the central character. The agent Flora Roberts felt that Jones was an inspired choice. "Dean broke your heart . . . he looked so dopey and innocent."[26]

Since there was no singing or dancing chorus in the show, each cast member doubled as character and company. Although most of the cast were actors who could sing, they were also required to dance. Some moved quite gracefully. Others, according to Prince, appeared ungainly and that is what Michael Bennett wanted. The one professional dancer, Donna McKechnie, had the only dance solo. Bennett felt the company should seem like real people (i.e., a group of PTA members) and not a singing or dancing chorus.

Michael Bennett was hired to choreograph and stage the musical numbers for *Company*. He had staged the dances for four previous Broadway musicals, the most recent being *Promises, Promises* and *Coco*. The pairing of Prince and Bennett proved to be an exceptionally inspired move. As Lisa Aronson said, "Bennett was a wonderful balance artistically for Prince."[27] However, they would do only two shows together, since Bennett wanted and had the ability to direct on his own. He had a very successful career on Broadway, with his major hits being *A Chorus Line* and *Dreamgirls*, before his life was cut tragically short by AIDS in 1987.

Company proved to be a difficult show and took six weeks to rehearse. With most musicals, the director rehearses the principals while the choreographer works with the chorus in another area. Here, with the principals and the chorus one and the same, Prince had to wait while Bennett set the musical numbers, which proved frustrating to the director. Librettist Furth was also eager to get on with the dialogue rehearsals so that he could see what needed to be done on the book.

Prince, although he loved the form of the show, found it to be a most difficult directing experience. In many ways, the show's theme affected him personally and made him uncomfortable. "It was painful from the beginning to end," said Prince. "Because it took *me* until I was thirty-five to get married and Bobby was thirty-five in the play."[28]

Although the rehearsal period was difficult for Prince and Bennett, they were genuinely aided by Sondheim. Bennett said that working with him was different than working with anyone else. When Sondheim's material arrives it is not only fine work but truly written for the stage. Sondheim explained that, when he worked on *West Side Story,* Jerome Robbins taught him how to write for a show and he never forgot the lesson.

I always stage every number within an inch of its life when I'm writing. As I write a number, I always explain in great detail what I intend. The director is free to change it or not but he has a blueprint. He never has to turn to me and ask, "What am I going to do here?" I always give him more than enough. One of the things Hal has complained to me about on a number of occasions is that the songs are overstaged when I give them to him because I stage everything. I time things, I time beats out. If you want the character to cross from here to there, or has to pick up a coffee cup and drink it or whatever it is, I time those things here in my studio. Then I say OK now, during these beats or in between, he empties the coffee cup. The director may say, I don't want a coffee cup in the number and that's all right. But that's the idea and almost no other composers do this. When I first worked

Company, 1970
Donna McKechnie and Dean Jones.
(Photo © Martha Swope)

with Michael Bennett and I did the opening number for *Company* he couldn't believe it. He said that he never had anybody give him stuff like this before. He'd always had to invent out of nowhere. I explained that I learned it from Jerome Robbins and you can take what I give you or throw out what you don't want but at least there's a blueprint for you to work from. I saw Boris' design for the set of the show, and that allowed me to write the opening. I staged that entire number in my head around that elevator. I asked Boris how long it would take the elevator to get from the top to the bottom so that I knew that I could get the people off the stairs and onto the stage level and that's what that climax is about. That's why I built that number of bars over the word "love" to allow the elevator to move and allow all those people to get down onto the stage. . . . So then Michael could take what he wanted to take.[29]

Bennett also appreciated Sondheim writing for character and specifically for the show. He doesn't write show tunes in the Rodgers and Hammerstein mode. You have to live with his music awhile and get familiar with it. "Steve, of all the composers I've worked with, understands more about the musical theatre than anyone," said Bennett.[30]

Although Sondheim's score received positive reactions from reviewers, with descriptions such as care, imagination, freshness, vitality, wit and intelligence, there were those who felt his lyrics were more entertaining than the music. Douglas Watt suggested that Sondheim does not necessarily create new forms but enriches old ones. "It takes several hearings for one's awareness to grow," said Watt.[31]

During the show's out-of-town tryouts in Boston, everything went smoothly. There were no cast changes (Prince was very pleased with the casting), no major revisions and no delay in the Broadway opening date. One minor conflict occurred between Prince and librettist George Furth. Before one performance, Furth gave Beth Howland a staging suggestion which messed up one of her exits that evening. Fritz Holt recalled the incident:

Hal was furious and I don't blame him. You just can't do that. And George realized that, he's an actor. He apologized for it and that was that. But it was never evident that there was anything the matter between George and Hal until way after we opened. And that's essential . . . regardless of what's happening there's a place to determine where your feuds are and where you appear united.[32]

Sondheim wrote "Being Alive" to replace "Happily Ever After" during the last week in Boston. Prince felt that the latter imposed an unhappy ending on a play which he wanted to remain ambiguous. Additionally, "Happily Ever After" seemed to frighten audiences. Prince said, "It was the bitterest, most unhappy song ever written, and we didn't know how devastating it would be until we saw it in front of an audience. . . . Stephen was writing an affirmative song, but he put *everything* in it and that *everything* overrode the affirmation."[33] Sondheim, because his collaborators kept using the word "negative" about "Happily Ever After," wrote the replacement number. He loves "Being Alive," but he feels that the "ending of the show is a cop-out. When Bobby suddenly realizes that he shouldn't be alone at the end of the scene, it's too small a moment and you don't believe it."[34] Prince agreed. The director asserts that the last minutes of *Company* are *not* a cop-out but are not as skillfully done as the rest of the show. He adds that they just "never got it quite right. The marriages in the show are not bad marriages—they're just marriages that are holding together because people either live little lies or look the other way. It's called human. What happens to Robert in the end is what we wanted to have happen to him. We didn't ease into it properly and that's what's wrong with the show . . . there'll always be something."[35]

At first the show in Boston played far too seriously. Prince felt that the cast, who were all well-trained actors, were playing motivations, subtext, and concentrating on the neurotic, dark side of their characters. The comedy of the piece was lost. Prince suggested that the cast let the comedy rise to the surface and at subsequent performances everything was lighter and played the way the director felt it should.

Prince also utilized a technique he had learned from Abbott. "No amount of light is enough on an actor to get laughs."[36] He filled the stage with light and had the actors play as many scenes as possible in a shallow area downstage to involve the audience sufficiently to make them laugh.[37]

The reviews in Boston were mixed, but Kevin Kelly in the *Boston Evening Globe* called the show, "brilliant, just brilliant!" continuing, "not only is it the most original musical I've seen in a very long time but, unless I miss my guess, it's destined to become a classic in the American musical theatre. . . . On its own hard-headed, straightforward, uncompromising merits, *Company* is in a triumphant class by itself."[38] He could imagine people complaining about the production being cold and stubborn (which they did). "So it is," said Kelly. "So, my friends, is life."[39]

Although some comments in Boston papers pointed up the bleakness and bitterness of the show, the most damaging review was *Variety*'s. Guy

Company, 1970
Larry Kert, who replaced Dean Jones in the role of Robert, is seen along with his married friends in a musical number which features Boris Aronson's multilevel set.
(Photo © Martha Swope)

Livingston accused Furth of being a woman hater and said that his show was "for ladies' matinees, homos and misogynists."[40] Prince's comment about the *Variety* review to a reporter from *Look* magazine who asked him about it was that it was "interesting."[41]

Capitalized at $550,000, *Company* opened in New York on 26 April 1970 at the Alvin Theatre. Clive Barnes, who at the time was the powerful first-string critic on the *New York Times,* found the characters unlikable and said:

> The conception has two difficulties. In the first place these people are just the kind of people you expend hours each day trying to escape from. They are, virtually without exception—perhaps the airline stewardess wasn't too bad—trivial, shallow, worthless and horrid. . . . Creatively, Mr. Sondheim's lyrics are way above the rest of the show; they have a lyric suppleness, sparse, elegant wit, and range from the virtuosity of a patter song to a kind of sweetly laconic cynicism in a modern love song. The music is academically very interesting. Mr. Sondheim must be one of the most sophisticated composers ever to write Broadway musicals, yet the result is slick, clever and eclectic rather than exciting.[42]

Walter Kerr praised but disliked the show. He thought that Sondheim had never written a more sophisticated score, and that Bennett had applied endless inventive high-pressure patterns. "Often [Bennett] uses entirely traditional devices, say straw hats and canes, in provocative new ways, letting the hats slash the air and the canes slap the floor to stress the harshness of what is being stomped out in 'Side by Side by Side.'"[43] Kerr also liked Prince's staging.

> Mr. Prince's own work is immaculate; jog-trotting waiters spin past tables without colliding, or without taking orders, like jagged metal figures of a children's game board; the entire company dissolves and reassembles at will in the heavens, malicious gods and goddesses changing shapes as cumulus clouds do.[44]

In spite of all this praise, Kerr suggests that if he were asked if he "liked" the show he would have to say that he didn't. And yet he said, "I admired it, or admired vast portions of it. . . . I left *Company* feeling rather cool and queasy, whatever splendors my head may have been reminding me of, and there is a plain reason for that. At root, I didn't take to Mr. Jones' married friends any more than he did. . . . On the whole I had difficulty—what do you call it?—empathizing."[45]

John J. O'Connor of the *Wall Street Journal* felt that the credit for the show's vitality had to go to director Hal Prince. "Mr. Prince makes such clever and imaginative use of his small cast that, on leaving, the spectator is bound to start recounting those names in the program to make sure he hasn't overlooked a couple dozen performers."[46]

Jack Kroll of *Newsweek* and Ted Kalem of *Time* loved the new musical and called it "a landmark." Richard Watts, Jr., in the *Post,* felt it was "surprisingly uningratiating,"[47] and Henry Hewes in the *Saturday Review* said that as a work of art the show "has remarkably distilled the essence of today's middle-generation New York life."[48] John Lahr summed up his feelings: "Whatever the limitations of *Company,* it is attempting to advance the musical form. . . . Thanks to the energy of Stephen Sondheim and Harold Prince, the genre is not yet a fossil."[49]

Bennett said that this was the only time in his career that he didn't care about the reviews. "It was a show that I loved, it was a show that I was proud of, and there wasn't a review in the world that could damage that."[50]

One of the problems pointed out was that Robert, playing an observer, was basically portrayed as an unpleasant cipher, an antihero. Prince replied: "Of course. He is a cipher, an empty vessel—but who says you can't do plays about empty vessels? The world is filled with walking empty vessels."[51]

Sondheim felt that *Company* was controversial because it didn't have a plot. He discussed the fact that the show deals with the increasing difficulty of making one-to-one relationships in an increasingly dehumanized society. "One of the reasons we had it take place in front of chrome and glass and steel was that it took place in an urban society in which individuality and individual feeling become more and more difficult to maintain."[52]

The star of the show, Dean Jones (Robert), became despondent soon after the show opened in Boston. Although he appeared to be physically ill, Prince suspected that his problem was psychosomatic. Jones was going through his own divorce at the time and felt that the show was anti-marriage, "perhaps because," said Jones, "at the time I was anti-marriage."[53] To insure a performance from him on opening night on Broadway, Prince offered to replace him after the opening. Grateful, Jones gave a fine performance for the critics and two weeks later left the show. The news release claimed that he had contracted hepatitis. Larry Kert stepped into the role.

Prince felt that with Kert the show became more of a musical comedy. It wasn't the show he had intended, nor did he think it was as good as the one on opening night. It was softer and the laughs were more indulgent. However, audiences enjoyed Kert more than they had liked Jones.

Prince said, "Had Dean stayed, there's no telling whether the show would have been successful."[54]

According to Prince, except for the show's final moments, *Company* represented the first time he had worked without conscious compromise. "It represents as total a collaboration of authors, director, choreographer, and actors as I can remember. *Cabaret* established me as commercially successful. *Company* established me in my own eyes."[55]

Although the musical received enough favorable reviews to produce a long run, *Company* had only limited audience response. It played to sixty percent of capacity and never had a sold-out week. However, it did pay back its investors and it did show a profit.

Company won the New York Drama Critics' Award as best musical of the season and won six Tony Awards, including one for best musical. Thomas Z. Shepard produced the original cast recording for Columbia Records.

The show ran for only twenty months; Prince blames the Barnes review in the *Times*. "Audiences are influenced by reviews."[56] Sondheim disagreed, suggesting that even if Barnes had raved about the show it would not have turned out differently. In Sondheim's opinion, many of the Prince-Sondheim collaborative efforts are shows that tell the audience what it doesn't want to hear. Sondheim said, "Shows that run a long time tell the audience what they want to hear."[57]

Both Prince and Sondheim were probably right about the audience response. There were, however, other elements that may have detracted from *Company*'s commercial success. The show had no plot, no singing or dancing chorus, no real costume changes, no lovable characters and no stars. George Abbott, whom Prince likes to invite to run-throughs or tryouts because he values Abbott's opinions, said that he went back to see *Company* twice because he wasn't sure about the ending. He told Prince that he had received different messages. Prince responded: "Good, that's what I wanted."[58]

A small but growing audience, however, appeared to be looking forward to the new and adventurous concepts that Prince and Sondheim seemed ready to deliver. Martin Gottfried summed it up:

Harold Prince's direction of *Company* blended music with dialogue and dance and even scenery as had never before been done in the musical theater. Boris Aronson's chromium and glass structures and skeleton elevators gave Prince a picture through which to set the style, mood and point of the show. No musical had ever looked like this one before, so abstract and self-contained and cool. Sets have moved vertically before, but only in the sense of scenery being flown down from above the stage. Here, Prince also set his human traffic moving vertically on the elevators giving the feel of life in New York's chilly skyscrapers. Doubtless, few directors could have conceived of a musical made from George Furth's related playlets about marriage. Prince's literary imagination gave him the edge.[59]

Company opened in London with most of its original cast intact. It received outstanding reviews, but it ran in London for only six months with Kert and Elaine Stritch and only a little more than two months with British replacements.

Richard Pilbrow, co-producer of the London production as well as London's foremost lighting designer, is quoted in Craig Zadan's book as saying, "The investors wrote in to say that they were sorry the show was closing but that they were glad they were involved in it. They'd lost their money happily. *Company* advanced the musical theatre in this country . . . we'd never seen anything like it before."[60]

Company remains a landmark show. Although it was not a huge commercial hit, it affected future Broadway musicals. It contained an innovative book and structure, extended the use of music, and broke down the old rules for dancing and singing choruses. Prince and Sondheim had become a creative musical team to watch.

Follies

> · *John McMartin, approaching 50—realizing his youthful*
> *dreams and ideals were lost forever—that was me getting*
> *scared about getting older.*
> —Harold Prince, Quoted in the *New York Sunday News,*
> 20 June 1976

As *Follies,* Prince's next show after *Company,* was being readied for production, Prince turned 43. At this point in his career (with *Company* running and receiving many major awards), he was considered by critics and collaborators a director of original, offbeat, even revolutionary musicals. Some reviewers feared, however, that his shows were calculated to send musical comedy audiences scurrying up the aisles to the exits. Prince agreed. "I'll never do a show that some people won't walk out on."[61]

During the 1970–71 season, only 46 productions opened on Broadway, which at that time was "the puniest record in the history of the American Theatre."[62] Of the season's seventeen new musicals only *No, No, Nanette,* a revival, and *Godspell,* produced Off-Broadway, returned their investments. Litton said, "Only one of the season's offerings, *Follies,* affirmed unequivocally that the American Musical Theatre still had creative energy."[63]

During the summer of 1970, the problems of *Follies* were being thrashed out among Prince, Sondheim, Bennett and James Goldman at Prince's summer residence in Majorca. The show, however, had been conceived at least five years earlier.

Sondheim and Goldman had discussed the possibility of doing an original musical together in 1965. Goldman, who had wanted to do a show about reunions, thought the subject of unfinished business in people's lives was one that stirs up the emotions. He then read an item in the *New York Times* about a Ziegfeld Girls Club and thought they might try to work on something related to that. Goldman and Sondheim called their new project *The Girls Upstairs* and by the end of 1965, the first draft of the libretto and five songs were finished. David Merrick and Leland Hayward were scheduled to produce. They had asked John Dexter to direct the musical, since Sondheim had worked with Dexter on *Do I Hear a Waltz?* Eventually Merrick, who didn't want to work with a partner, and Hayward, who couldn't raise all the money himself, dropped the project.

Sondheim next sent the script to Prince to read as a friend. Prince said:

> I found the script to be awful and I didn't know how to cushion how bad I thought it was. It was about two men who took out two girls who were in the dressing room upstairs, and it was a personal story and they were four people self-pitying and, as far as I was concerned, pitying themselves sufficiently that I didn't have to involve myself in their problem. I then heard some music and, well with Steve, that's devastating because he's *just* that good. Jim Goldman is a very good writer. He'd written *Lion in Winter,* but this had none of the strength and vitality, none of the self-consciousness, and the best of his writing has an edge of self-consciousness which I like, a literary quality, but these mundane people were speaking down so I didn't feel there was any style in this work.[64]

Prince also felt that the play didn't work in its realistic form. He envisioned something more abstract and "audacious" (a word he often uses). The show should have a "gauzy feeling," he said.[65]

Stuart Ostrow picked up the option on the show and a new draft was written. Prince read the new draft and still didn't like it, but as a friend, he wrote a long, 3,000-word summary of what he thought was wrong with the script and what they could do about it. Joseph Hardy was hired to direct *The Girls Upstairs* and the plan was to go into rehearsal by the end of 1969.

Prince turned his attention toward doing *Company.* Sondheim was still absorbed with *The Girls Upstairs.* While Prince took time out to make the film *Something for Everyone* in Germany, things fell apart on *The Girls Upstairs.* Sondheim was despondent. He said, "I feel like a father with a kid and I've been over this kid for five years and I cannot write *Company* until I've done *The Girls Upstairs.*"[66]

Prince then recalled what he had written in his critique of *The Girls Upstairs* three years earlier. He felt that Jim Goldman had to see the play in a new light.

> He's got to be able to write these people big and if they're small, really small, he's got to be able to use of himself what was so remarkable in his previous plays. I mean Ben and Phyllis [one of the two couples in *The Girls Upstairs*] are the Kennedy fellow and the Kennedy wife. They're a king and a queen. Well, if he could write that king and queen in *Lion in Winter,* he could write these characters for me. This show is not *The Girls Upstairs,* this show is *Follies.*[67]

After *Company,* Prince was ready to concentrate on a concept for the show that was now to be re-titled *Follies.* The new title was meant to be a triple play on the word: it could suggest the *Ziegfeld Follies,* the French word *folie,* meaning "madness," or it could be interpreted as a folly in the British sense.

Prince used a photograph of Gloria Swanson which had originally been published in *Life* magazine as his visual metaphor. The aging star was captured on film while standing in the rubble on the site of what had once been the Roxy Theatre. The photographer Eliot Elisofon had photographed her standing glamorously in the rubble. Prince felt that Elisofon had captured the metaphor of *Follies.*

Years before, Prince had been asked by an agent of the Italian director Federico Fellini whether he would be interested in creating a musical of the film *8½.* Prince said, "The movie is a masterpiece, and I was flattered and tempted but came to realize soon that it represented Fellini's autobiography and not mine."[68] He then arranged a screening for Michael Bennett and Ruth Mitchell, his associate producer. Prince claims he was reminded of *8½* because *The Girls Upstairs* had as its hero a character, Ben Stone, who is "the perfect 1970s monolith approaching menopause on the cusp of a nervous breakdown."[69] Prince's idea was for *Follies* to become surrealistic, as inspired by *8½*, using rubble as a key word. Prince said,

> Metaphoric rubble becomes visual rubble. A theatre is being torn down. On its stage a party in celebration of that. The celebrants for whom the theatre represents youth, dreams lost, a golden time, are to be orphaned. . . . Is the theatre torn down? Will it be torn down tomorrow? Or was it torn down yesterday? Keep it ambiguous, a setting for the sort of introspection that reunions precipitate, a mood in which to lose sight of the present, to look back on the past.[70]

Sondheim and Goldman approved of Prince's scheme for the show and went to work on yet another draft, at least the thirteenth since 1965. Prince asked choreographer Michael Bennett to work on the show, since he felt their collaboration on *Company* had been very creative and stimulating. However, Bennett turned down Prince's offer, feeling he was now ready to begin directing himself. Prince then offered to share the directorial duties and Bennett agreed, with Prince directing the dialogue scenes and Bennett staging the musical numbers. Although they worked well together, there were disagreements. Prince recalled the partnership: "A difficult arrangement for two giant egos . . . there were conflicts, but never with respect to what we want the evening to be, to say nor the quality of its theatricality."[71]

The new musical took a year to get ready. The realistic and naturalistic *The Girls Upstairs* became the surrealistic *Follies*. Originally, Sondheim and Goldman wanted the show to be a backstage murder mystery with an attempted murder being planned. The idea was dropped. Prince, working with his collaborators, decided to use only the two couples that had been written to be the major characters, and to use the theatre locale. He encouraged the authors to utilize the younger selves of the leading characters, an idea that Sondheim and Goldman had resisted throughout eleven drafts. Four new cast members would represent the leading characters as they had been thirty years earlier. "They were to wander as silent memories across the paths of their present selves."[72] As this idea took hold, the "memories" intruded more and more into the script. Goldman gave them lines to speak. They confused time, in a Proustian manner, confronting the past as well as the present. "Ultimately," said Prince, "in a sort of collective nervous breakdown, they took over."[73] Sondheim remembers that they had thought Prince's idea about the "ghosts" or "shadows" corny. Prince, however, had insisted that they would be corny only if they were staged cornily. Sondheim said:

> Before Hal became involved we never had the past embodied on the stage. We had the principals falling into the past and talking and behaving as though they were twenty years old—they were middle-aged people sort of playing a charade. Hal said that he thought we were assiduously avoiding the use of flashbacks. . . . Through a series of discussions, Jim got an idea of how to utilize the flashback images. So during the summer of 1970, the book changed drastically with the addition of the young people, the shadows, the ghosts.[74]

After floundering for five years, Prince became the new collaborator who influenced the final shape of the piece. Sondheim now described the show as "a dream play, a memory piece."[75] It was Bennett's idea to dress these figures of the past in black and white with light makeup in contrast to the older members of the cast, of the present, in full color. Prince felt it was a brilliant concept.

The final draft of *Follies* tells the story of two unhappily married middle-aged couples, Ben and Phyllis and Buddy and Sally, who had met during their youth when the women were showgirls in the then-popular Weismann (read Ziegfeld) *Follies* and the men, typical of the era's "stagedoor johnnies," were courting them. They now meet after about thirty years. The scene is the crumbling stage of the old Weismann Theatre, on the eve of its demolition. Weismann has invited the old stars and performers to a farewell party. During the course of the evening, Ben and Sally, now married to others, try to recapture the lost love of their youth. All the principals in the cast encounter their youth in one way or another, bewailing their failures, remembering triumphs, and in the end, vowing to somehow adjust to their lives as they are now.

During *Follies'* final twenty minutes, it transforms itself into a metaphorical *Follies,* in a segment called "Loveland." Tall, lovely girls descend the traditional staircase. At first the creators of the show thought that the "Follies-Loveland" section should be realistic. Prince and Bennett, however, felt that a literal use of "Follies" was a mistake. During this episode, each of the four principals does a song and/or dance number denoting his or her folly. T. E. Kalem says, "Buddy's is self-hatred; Sally's, being in love with love; Phyllis', a blurred identity; Ben's, self-proving quests,

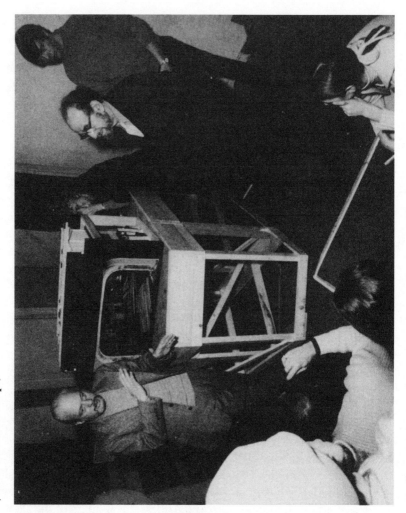

Follies, 1971
At a production meeting, producer/co-director Harold Prince, lighting designer Tharon Musser, set designer Boris Aronson, and stage manager Fritz Holt gather around as Prince introduces a model of the set.
(Photo © Martha Swope)

no satisfying goals. . . . Rarely have such searching, unsentimental questions and answers been put to a Broadway audience with such elegance and expertise.''[76] Harold Prince says of the characters:

> They were able to make an adjustment to each other. I think we have a terrible tendency in life, when things are going wrong, to look into the past and moon over it. The point of the show was that you should *use* the past to look into the future.[77]

Prince was very interested in the ''memory'' aspect of the show. He did not want the musical to be about failing marriages. Sondheim explained what Goldman wanted the show to express:

> The reason Jim chose the *Follies* as a metaphor was that the *Follies* represented a state of mind in America between the two world wars. Up until 1945, America was the good guy, everything was idealistic and hopeful and America was going to lead the world. Now you see the country is a riot of national guilt, the dream has collapsed, everything has turned to rubble underfoot, and *that's* what the show was about also—the collapse of the dream. It's not about how difficult it is to stay married over a period of thirty years. . . . It's how all your hopes tarnish and how if you live on regret and despair you might as well pack up, for to live in the past is foolish.[78]

Casting for *Follies* began in 1970. The principal roles were filled by veteran actors, singers and dancers who had not been superstars in their day, but well known ''names'' in various media. Because of the somewhat plotless nature of the libretto, the collaborators could insert roles when outstanding auditions were delivered by these performers. Actresses Ethel Shutta and Fifi d'Orsay, both well-known performers in musicals during the 1920s, were given numbers in *Follies* after ''wowing'' them at the tryouts. Yvonne De Carlo, who was well known to movie audiences of the 1940s, seemed wrong for the role of Phyllis but ''fit perfectly the rebuilt part of Carlotta, the mantrap.''[79] Prince was the one who decided that Alexis Smith, another movie name of the 1940s, ''would lend the show a permanent radiance in the role of Phyllis.''[80] She was not taken the first time she auditioned. However, she spent months taking singing and dancing lessons and then satisfied Prince. She proved to be the one that the critics unanimously adored. John Simon, not generally known for handing verbal bouquets to Broadway ladies, had this to say about Smith, and it parallels what almost every other reviewer said:

But there is Alexis Smith, whom I used to like in the movies, but never suspected of harboring such a cache of dazzlement. Miss Smith sings decently, dances infectiously, and delivers her lines with the most supple finesse. She acts out her songs with exemplary conviction, and stays pungently in character even doing a standard dance step. She is also irresistible, with a cosmopolitan elegance that travels well through time, a polyglot beauty that speaks to all eyes.[81]

Dorothy Collins, cast as Sally, was well known from television's *Your Hit Parade,* but had settled down to being a homebody and bringing up her family. Gene Nelson was a popular song-and-dance man in films and Prince felt he was right for Buddy. Prince insists he did not cast these stars of yesteryear in order to be campy or produce a nostalgic effect, but because these particular actors were the best ones for their roles. Martin Gottfried is quoted as saying that he felt the casting could be looked on as cruel since the above-mentioned stars, along with Mary McCarty, were chosen to embody the point of *Follies* by their very presence. Craig Zadan echoed Gottfried's opinion:

The audience knows these people from its own past, remembers their faces from a performing youth. Now they are aging and we see them aged, and *Follies* is about aging and age. In a sense these actors are being used as people rather than performers. . . . And since John McMartin [Ben] is the catalyst in the story, he is the one major cast member who is not a shadow from the past.[82]

Gottfried said of McMartin: "He is the one lead with no roots in our youth but, having always had something oddly of the past in his presence and being one of the few singing actors in the theatre, he is impeccably cast."[83]

Bennett and Prince went to Las Vegas to cast the tall, beautiful showgirls who would portray the "shadows" or "ghosts."

The script of *Follies,* at Prince's request, was more like a screenplay than a stage play. As was done in *Company,* Prince utilized equivalents of pans, wipes, tracking shots and dissolves. It seemed as if the action never stopped. He created the effect of a close-up by isolating an actor. With lighting and movement, Prince created a movie-like appearance on stage. With such effects Prince also created a cinematic simultaneity of action. This was necessary since he was unable to use the film technique of flashbacks. Prince would find these techniques useful in his future productions. In *Follies,* Michael Bennett said, "there was a place for your eye to go every minute."[84] Goldman felt that the way the scenes bled in and out in the show was very similar to the movies.

Follies, 1971
Dorothy Collins and Alexis Smith.
(*Photo © Martha Swope*)

One of the best numbers I've ever seen was "Who's That Woman?" The physical impression you got from that was anguishing. To see the decay of the flesh—all those bright young beautiful girls and their lovely bodies with all the sense of youth and the promise of what's to come contrasted against what *actually* became of it. That's devastating . . . very disturbing and very movielike. The theatre rarely utilizes visuals to make important statements, but films do. It's putting the picture in front of you and there was a lot of that in *Follies*.[85]

Prince capitalized *Follies* at close to $800,000, which was the highest budget he had ever contemplated. There was no problem raising the money; ever since *The Pajama Game*, his backers had remained loyal and new "angels" were always eager to risk their funds. In fact, $60,000 was returned to the investors because it was not needed. There was a cast of fifty and a large orchestra. Aronson designed a complicated setting. By anyone's standards, this was an enormous show. Prince, however, felt that the high production budget was necessary, that the show could not have been done on a smaller scale.

Although Prince had proven himself a knowledgeable and gifted director, he was not super-human. The day before rehearsals for *Follies* were scheduled to begin, he appeared to have all the symptoms of hepatitis—fatigue, nausea and yellowed eyes. After all tests proved negative, Bennett asked him what he had. Prince finally realized what the problem was. "Fear. . . . It was panic. I always panic. It usually lasts 24 hours."[86]

Rehearsals were hectic. Prince said, "We were busy every living, breathing moment from the time we went into rehearsal. It was like trying to get eighty-five shows on at the same time."[87] Prince and his collaborators discussed the motivations of the characters in the musical. As Prince explained,

> During these sessions, it became clear that Buddy [Gene Nelson] was a masochist, rejecting love, courting rejection. So Steve wrote "Buddy's Blues" and Michael Bennett staged it. . . . Dorothy Collins' Sally learned nothing from the evening. Stripped of her life, she went mad. Inadvertently, Steve had written her song. "Losing My Mind" gave her the chance, in *Follies* terms, to be Helen Morgan.[88]

Sondheim had written it to be sung by both Sally and Phyllis, but Alexis Smith suggested that he might write a number which she would utilize her dancing abilities and leave "Losing My Mind" as a solo for Dorothy

Collins. Bennett had difficulties because some of the principal players had problems keeping to a steady beat. The number "Waiting Around for the Girls Upstairs" was one of the most difficult to stage. The actors were unsure and performed it tentatively—and, said Bennett, "that number cannot be done tentatively."[89]

There was much pressure because of the limitations of time during the rehearsal period. One of Sondheim's numbers was taken out of the show, just before going to Boston. Costumes had to be ordered for new numbers that hadn't been seen or heard as yet. While waiting for the new numbers to be written, Bennett had the showgirls walking in slow motion for hours. Bennett said, "We had the show staged so that the girls changed with each scene, almost like a new drop coming in."[90]

They didn't decide on the entire "Follies-Loveland" sequence until they were in the third week of rehearsal. John McMartin recalls reading his first script and when it came to that section, the script said "to be written."[91] This is why certain musical numbers were written during the rehearsal period.

Several unconventional methods were used in staging the musical numbers. In the tap dancing sequences, Bennett had chorus boys stationed in the theatre basement under the stage. It was a technique he had used in *Company*—it was the sound of their taps the audience heard rather than the performers on stage. "In fact," said Bennett, "no one on stage wore tap shoes."[92] Bennett liked this effect; the tapping had a ghostlike quality. Various other numbers were prerecorded and the tape was used along with live singing on stage.

Boris Aronson said that *Follies* was about "American women picketing their own ages and about [the fact that] in this country, cities have no time to develop a patina. As soon as a building goes up, they make plans to tear it down. They're right!"[93] With this view of *Follies* and America in mind, the designer created a multi-level set: culs de sac and planked paths connected by metal stairways. With the rubble that he used to frame the stage, he achieved the effect of a building which had been torn down and was crumbling away. The set had three motorized sections which could move upstage, downstage, and then diagonally offstage. Prince said, "From the start we had to decide where we would put every scene and number though most were yet to be written."[94] There was nothing on stage that would help indicate who people were, where they were, or the chronology of their actions. It helped to achieve the abstract effect of the production. Hubert Saal in *Newsweek* said:

Prince went with the spirit of the set and staged the work abstractly, by implication, using the proscenium much as Peter Brook used it in his *A Midsummer Night's Dream,* as a place, space, the air, the universe. Characters enter and exit on different levels in the middle of sentences; scenes change with the lifting of an eyebrow, and the focus of a spotlight provides a precinct of privacy on a crowded stage.[95]

Rehearsals during the first four weeks were held at the American Theatre Lab, Jerry Robbins's dance studio. They worked on a mock-up, of the set with indicated elevations (one foot to every five). During the final two weeks of the six-week rehearsal period, they moved to the Feller Scenic Studio in the Bronx and worked on the finished set. The stage was raked and the company was shocked to learn that they would have to sing, walk and tap dance at such a steep angle. Prince, who budgets carefully, said, "It saved a great deal of money adjusting there [at the scenic studio] (instead of in Boston with stagehands and orchestra hanging around)."[96]

For the "Follies-Loveland" sequence, Aronson used mirrors and tinsel and lace. Critic Harold Clurman summed up the brilliant effects created by the designer:

> Boris Aronson once again demonstrates the multiplicity of forms his imagination can assume. His decayed and gutted "backstage," in which a constructivist design is not only evocative but theatrically furnished—a machine for movement—together with the airy frivolity which gays up the "Folly" numbers at the end, create a masterpiece in decor.[97]

Sondheim's 23-song score, at least seven of which he had written for the original *The Girls Upstairs* project, was acclaimed for its dramatic intensity and stylistic diversity. It is not unusual for Sondheim's songs to seem custom-made for a performer. He writes songs for both the performer's abilities and limitations. He also writes more quickly when he knows for whom he is writing. Sondheim explains:

> You look at the stage and you know exactly who you're writing for—you know what the performer's capabilities are so you can write for him. You can write for that spot in the show—you know exactly what the tone of the number should be because of where it occurs—you see it! It's not in your head anymore—it's on the stage. It's much easier to write.[98]

A favorite number was Yvonne De Carlo's "I'm Still Here." In Boston, this number had replaced "Can That Boy Fox Trot," which everyone soon realized would not work. "I'm Still Here" contained idiomatic expressions and internal rhymes for which Sondheim is noted. "Waiting for the Girls Upstairs" is a tender number in which the two couples reminisce affectionately about their courtship days. Gene Nelson sang the comic "God-Why-Don't-You-Love-Me Blues." Among the songwriters Sondheim tried to echo during the course of the evening are Kern, Berlin, Rodgers, Porter, DeSylva-Brown-Henderson, Victor Herbert, Rudolf Friml, Arlen, Gershwin and Coward. Mel Gussow quotes Sondheim as saying, "The score is not satirical . . . it's a *pastiche*. . . . I was looking at the past with affection, respect and delight. In no way am I pointing out how silly the songs were because I don't think they're silly. What they are is innocent."[99] Sondheim said that he was aware that these numbers would evoke other periods for the audience. However, rather than outright parody, they were done with great affection. "In *Follies* I imitate people. But in each of the songs, there's always something of me added to the imitation of Kern or Arlen or whoever it is. That's something I couldn't avoid—my own comment on the style."[100] Brendan Gill in the *New Yorker* said:

> I admire Mr. Sondheim for not hesitating to explore again the wastelands of aloneness and self-repugnance that he opened up for us in *Company,* and I hope it is clear to him that what has proved unworkable in *Follies* is the subject matter and not his great themes.[101]

The review that Clive Barnes gave Sondheim's score was ambivalent:

> Mr. Sondheim's music comes in two flavors—nostalgic and cinematic. The nostalgic kind is for the pseudo-oldie numbers, and I must say that most of them sound like numbers that you have almost only just forgotten, but with good reason. This non-hit parade of pastiche trades on camp, but fundamentally gives little in return. It has all the twists and turns of yesteryear, but none of the heart—and eventually the fun it makes of the past seems to lack something in affection. The cinematic music is a mixture of this and that, chiefly that. I doubt whether anyone will be parodying it in thirty or forty years' time. . . . The lyrics are as fresh as a daisy. I know of no better lyricist in show business than Mr. Sondheim—his words are a joy to listen to, even when his music is sending shivers of indifference up your spine. The man is a Hart in search of a Rodgers, or even a Boito in search of a Verdi.[102]

Gottfried answered the negative statements about Sondheim in a Sunday *New York Times* article, saying "Sondheim's qualities as a theater composer can hardly be overstated. He is constantly extending his vision, a composer applying a trained imagination to a stage he intimately understands."[103]

McMartin's number "Live, Laugh, Love" was finally written during the last week of rehearsals. Bennett had to choreograph the dancers and complete the staging with McMartin in the Bradford Hotel ballroom in Boston and on the stage of the Colonial Theatre as the stagehands hung the set and focused lights.

Follies was barely ready to open for its out-of-town tryout in Boston. Prince recalled:

> Coming out of McMartin's number, we planned a Felliniesque kaleidoscope of impressions of the events of the evening. Jim Goldman improvised a scene, I staged it, ending in chaos, using the fifty members of the company all over the set. Again, in Boston, at dress rehearsal, with Tharon Musser still lighting, the cast in costume, and the orchestra in the pit for the first time, the chaos was choreographed, adapted to the moving scenery, and something acceptable achieved to open with.[104]

Prince always tries to schedule his openings out of town on a Saturday so that he can polish on Sunday. On Monday he schedules a full technical rehearsal, and by Monday night "the show is beginning to look like something."[105] However, in the case of *Follies,* he did not open in Boston until Wednesday, which allowed him six full technical rehearsals before the critics would arrive.

A disagreement between Prince and Bennett involved the placement of the intermission. Bennett wanted to do the show in two acts and Prince didn't want an intermission. The show had been written in one act. During the New York previews Prince decided to try out the intermission idea, and so the two-hour-and-twenty-minute show was interrupted during the show-stopping number "Who's That Woman?" The curtain came down on a stage full of beautiful women tap dancing in unison and was raised for the second act at the same place in the number. It was effective but tended to cut applause. Prince explained: "I'm not concerned with creating show-stoppers. I sometimes think that in the name of perversity (integrity?) I frustrate an audience's desire to applaud, which is contradictory in view of how I feel about involvement."[106]

Prince felt that no matter where they put a break, it would take the show five minutes to regain its momentum. Three days before the show was due to open, there was still no agreement. Ultimately, the show played without any intermission. McMartin felt that Prince and Bennett generally did not get in each other's way. They did their own staging separately. When the show came together, if they had any suggestions, they were made privately. "They'd go into a huddle and then a movement would be changed."[107]

Florence Klotz, who designed the costumes for *Follies*, had to do 140 designs. The job was enormous and the showgirl outfits were lavish. Some were based on originals that the designer found during her research into the *Ziegfeld Follies*. She exaggerated some of them, such as the three-foot-high headdress of black and white willow ostrich for a backless sheath of bugle beads that spread into a peacock train. It was worn by a 6'2"-tall Las Vegas showgirl whose platform shoes made her look even taller. The costumes were so laden with beads that many had to be folded into cardboard cartons instead of being hung on racks at the end of each performance. Some were hung backstage. They couldn't fit into the dressing rooms and were lowered on to the girls when they were ready to put them on. The memory costumes for yesterday's people were all black and white. Worn with alabaster makeup and sometimes two sets of sheer white nylon tights to give a marble shimmer, the result was a bit ghostly. All the black fabrics were "reflective," according to Klotz. "They were shiny satin or velvet and the beads and embroideries aren't really black at all but deep purple or Burgundy red."[108]

The reviews in Boston were mixed, the nice things said overshadowed by the negative. *Variety*'s critic said that the production "had too many characters, too many leading players, too many scenes, and the most bewildering plotline in years."[109] Sondheim agreed. In Boston he said, "Our main problem is that there is too much of everything. It's the biggest, most complicated musical ever, and we're just going to have to cut it down to size. It's an embarrassment of riches."[110]

A major problem was the restaging of the opening before moving to Broadway. It was staged about six times and in three different versions: one during rehearsals and two in Boston. Finally, *Follies* was ready to begin previews in New York.

During the final week of previews in New York, Gene Nelson's nine-year-old son was hit by a truck in Los Angeles and was in a coma from which he eventually emerged. Prince had to make a quick decision about when to open the show officially. As was Prince's custom, the critics were given a choice of four opening performances, but this time he invited them all for the Wednesday night preview while Nelson would still be in New

York. Prince said, "I suggested to the authors and Michael Bennett that we open Wednesday and not run the risk of waiting till the end of the week. Nelson might not be there by then, and even if he were, the pressure of these days would surely affect his performance. Meanwhile, we put his understudy into rehearsal."[111]

In spite of the fact that the reviewers were about to come to see the production, the authors put in a new last scene for McMartin and Smith and Prince staged it. They were perfect that evening and Prince was thrilled. McMartin explained why he and others can "come through" with these last-minute changes and pressures: "I truly believe people 'do' it for Hal ... they just 'do' it. Because he's so inspiring, so wonderful you do things for him that you wouldn't be able to do for other people ... and you envy people who get into any Hal Prince show."[112]

Gene Nelson had an additional crisis at the Friday night performance when, during his dance number, he tore a leg muscle and began to hemorrhage. He was not allowed to dance during the next three weeks but managed to walk through his numbers.

Follies opened at the Winter Garden Theatre on 4 April 1971. Although most of the reviews were quite good, the show's reception was controversial both critically and with audiences. McMartin said that he had never been in a production where so many either loved it and saw it over and over again, or absolutely loathed it. "It was a real love or hate thing," he said.[113] The spectacle and extravaganza elements of the show were lauded, but the book was panned across the board. The critics were confused and bored by the libretto and found the characters either not thoroughly fleshed out or not particularly interesting. T. E. Kalem in *Time* magazine said of Goldman's book that it "lacks the dry brilliance called for by Prince's direction."[114]

Douglas Watt was one of those who admired the show and didn't hesitate to say so. His review said that *Follies* is "so stunning in conception and execution that it adds an extra dimension to a Broadway musical theatre that has been, except for such exceptional triumphs as *Promises, Promises, Fiddler on the Roof* and *Company,* in danger of stagnating."[115]

George Oppenheimer of *Newsday* felt the show went downhill after a promising beginning, never fulfilling its initial promise or premise. However, he summed up saying that the show is "so much better than any musical we have had this season. It is, in truth, more a revue than a musical play, but it is a cornucopia out of which pour scores of rewards in the form of superior entertainment by superior entertainers."[116]

Follies, 1971
Former "Weismann Girls" Alexis Smith, Dorothy Collins and Mary McCarty (*center*)
relive the past in the musical number "Who's That Woman?"
(*Photo © Martha Swope*)

Barnes wrote a mostly negative review of the show. He felt the story was shallow and narrow and raised expectations that were never filled. "It carries nostalgia to where sentiment finally engulfs it in its sickly maw. And yet—in part—it is stylish, innovative, it has some of the best lyrics I have ever encountered and above all it is a serious attempt to deal with the musical form."[117] Kerr was among those upset by the lack of an intermission. He felt it was an exhausting performance to view, that the plot was meager and that the production moved too slowly.

> No one likes to dismiss the ingenuity that producer-director Harold Prince has splattered all over the Winter Garden stage—platforms bearing jazz bands gliding in and out of the dark, curtains made of candy-box lace raining down from the skies, the ghosts of showgirls past stalking in black-and-white butterfly wings through the ruins of a once-festive playhouse—but ingenuity without inspiration can quickly become wearing and we are not too long in our seats before we realize that no one on the creative staff has had an idea for the evening capable of sustaining its weight in silvered feathers. . . . Mr. Prince is willing to make his musicals dark, or at least caustic, with liveliness worked in only where it is legitimate; and that is courageous. Unfortunately, the liveliness here is all left-field, and the legitimacy in the love-stories that ought to give the evening its solid foothold is skimpy and sadly routine.[118]

Jack Kroll in *Newsweek* compared Prince to England's Peter Brook and asked, "How many theatre people in this country have the talent, taste, inventiveness, resourcefulness and high professional standards of Prince? And perhaps it is fitting that this superb director-producer specializes in the musical, where America by popular legend is supposed to have made its greatest theatrical contribution."[119] Kroll goes on to say that *Follies* is a brilliant show, "wonderfully entertaining, extraordinarily intelligent, and having both a stunning direct appeal and a rare complexity of feeling and structure. . . . With *Cabaret, Company,* and *Follies,* Harold Prince has created a generation of musicals which captures much of our time in a form that in his hands refuses to die ."[120]

Martin Gottfried, in his *New York Times* response to Barnes and Kerr, called *Follies* "monumental theatre . . . moreover, its importance as a *kind* of theatre transcends its interest as an example of a musical."[121] Gottfried admitted the book of the show was weak and that the ending which shows the couples accepting their lost youth with a sense of wisdom was "pure baloney."[122] However, he was most flattering about Prince. Gottfried coined the phrase "concept musical" about *Follies* because it is a show whose music, lyrics, dance, stage movement and dialogue are woven through each other in the creation of a tapestry-like theme. He said, "Mr. Prince, who is heading toward the inevitable elimination of musical books, has stripped the story down, making the production itself the main event."[123] According to Sondheim, however, some concept musicals do have plots, and in an interview he noted that "*West Side Story* and musicals such as *A Little Night Music* and *Sweeney Todd* [which Prince would direct later] have a lot of plot."[124]

Prince's concepts and techniques were startling audiences, critics and performers alike. Gene Nelson said, "I couldn't make head or tails of it. . . . It was all in Hal's mind. This was a whole new kind of theatre, multiple scenes and overlapping lines, a story in reverse. . . . Hal Prince seemed from the looks of this show to be finished with winches, sets with doors, chairs and tables."[125]

Sondheim said that the phrase "concept musical" is just for critics. He doesn't feel that he and Prince should be labeled founders of "the concept musical." Sondheim explained: "Moss Hart did a concept musical. His *Thousands Cheer* was a concept musical in 1933. Concept musicals have existed forever."[126]

The original cast album of *Follies* was recorded by Capitol Records and Prince admitted that he erred when he signed the contract. He did not stipulate that the entire score be recorded, and Capitol refused to do the four sides the 22 songs would have required, saying the album wouldn't sell.

Follies lost $685,000. It cost $80,000 a week to operate, and needed to play to about 70 percent of capacity to break even. If the show had been completely sold out, it would have repaid its investment in about forty weeks. However, *Follies* did not sell out. It ran for 522 performances (65 weeks) and grosses ranged from over $100,000 to about $32,000.[127] The show closed on 1 July 1972, with the unfortunate effect of eroding the confidence of Prince's long-loyal investors.

Follies won the Drama Critics' Circle Award as best musical of the year and won seven Tony Awards, including a best director award to Prince and Bennett. Prince sent the show on the road for what was supposed to be a tour of some major cities with the original Broadway cast. The first opening was in Los Angeles, where the show was the premiere presentation at the new Shubert Theatre in Century City. The theatre had no subscription audience and, although the reviews were excellent, business was poor. The show closed and the remainder of the tour was cancelled.

Looking back, the collaborators tried to understand what went wrong and why there was no business in spite of a generally good critical reception. Goldman theorized that older people were made uncomfortable by the subject matter since they identified with the characters who were too old to change the errors of their lives. He says that if he had the chance to write the book over again he would probably change the ending and not have Ben and Phyllis accept their fate and stay together. [Ironically, when the show was revived in London in 1987, Goldman has them stay together.]

Bennett didn't like the book. It was over this that he and Prince began fighting. Bennett wanted to call in Neil Simon to fix the book and Prince said, "That's where we had our standoff battle."[128] Bennett was bitter about the failure of *Follies* and felt that eighty percent of it was the greatest musical ever produced. He said, "So much of that show was better than anything I've ever seen or anything I've ever done."[129] Goldman felt that Bennett was very ambitious for success:

> He was not at the time in his life when he was interested in the kind of feelings that the show had to have or the risks that we simply had to take. I think if we had gone Michael's way the show might still be running. That's perfectly possible. But at the same time we would have disemboweled it, and I think Michael was perfectly willing to do just that and of course I wouldn't have wanted that to happen. You want something to succeed for being as close to what you wanted it to be, not something else.[130]

Looking back on *Follies* years later, Prince said,

> Bob Fosse and Michael Bennett shared a quality in common. The play was the thing, beyond reality for them as far as I'm concerned. I remember saying to Michael Bennett when he had suggested we get Neil Simon to help with the book [of *Follies*], I said, "Neil Simon couldn't help with this book the way this book should be, Michael." But what he was saying was, "let's not have a flop." And the truth of the matter is I didn't care that much. I wanted *that Follies*. And I think you can be true to your work and still make mistakes which destroy it but you come out resilient, you go on, not to compromise the next time, you hope. But one thing is for sure, what dominates that personality—that says, "this show is everything to me," does not always make a hit. . . . I'm not just sitting here smugly saying I am a happy man, I am not. I am as happy as you can be doing what I do, and I'm happier than most people I know. But I can be lonely in my work, and

I can be dark, and my mood swings can be dramatic, and I have succumbed to melancholia—all that stuff, no question. Nevertheless, no show, no one show is that important. There's another show where that one came from.[131]

After *Follies* closed, Prince admitted that it cost too much and that he didn't produce it as well as some of his other shows. On the other hand, he doesn't see how it could have been done for much less money since it needed a lavish look. Sondheim felt that there were too many *pastiche* numbers in the show which hurt both the book and production in general. He wonders whether the show would have been more successful with fewer songs. In the long run, Prince was pragmatic about *Follies*. He said, "I am happy I did *Follies*. I could not do it again because I could not in all conscience raise the money for it.[132]

In 1987 a successful revival of *Follies* was presented at the Shaftesbury Theatre in London with a revised book and some new numbers. It starred Diana Rigg, Julia McKenzie, Daniel Massey and Dolores Gray, but Harold Prince was not involved with the production.

A MUSICAL IN 3/4 TIME
&
AN ENVIRONMENTAL RESTAGING

*Sondheim remembered how he and Prince pondered the
future of Broadway years ago. "I remember walking down
the street and his saying, 'It's going to be terrific. We're going
to be able to do anything we want to do.' And I'm thinking,
'Oh, God, he's crazy. What a fool! We're going to be starv-
ing or dead in the gutter in two years.' You see, he was always
the positive one. I was the pessimist," says Sondheim with
an amused pause, "and he turned out to be right."*
—Linda Winer, *USA Today*, 29 October 1984

Follies may have been a box office flop, but with its positive critical reception and following as it did on the heels of such Prince hits as *Cabaret*
and *Company*, it put him in a special category of "star" directors. Fosse,
Champion, Bennett and Prince were reshaping scripts, songs and initiating
their own projects. Martin Gottfried explained, "There was a recognizable
stamp to their shows. Directors were being accepted as those most responsible for what finally takes place onstage."[1] The difference between Prince
and the other major musical directors of the period was that they had started
as choreographers. Prince's one advantage over his choreographer-director
colleagues was his book-sense. "He was better equipped to deal with book
problems," said Gottfried, "and book problems are the musical theater's
main problem."[2]

A Little Night Music

Within a day of closing *Follies* (1 July 1972), Prince also closed his long-run hit *Fiddler on the Roof* (2 July 1972). The producer-director now found himself in an uncomfortable position. *Fiddler* had long supported his production office, but now Prince needed a show that would make money. In other words, he needed a hit. Nevertheless, he wanted to accomplish this in his uncompromising, artistic and adventurous style. *A Little Night Music* proved to be the show he was looking for.

The project had its genesis in 1957 when Sondheim and Prince had discussed the possibility of doing a "court masque, a chamber opera, elegant, probably about sex, a gavotte in which couples interchange suffering mightily in elegant country homes, wearing elegant clothes."[3] They considered adapting Jean Anouilh's *Ring Round the Moon* but Anouilh was unresponsive to Prince's request for the rights and Prince dropped the idea until 1971. After *Follies* opened, the producer-director again tried to secure the rights to the Anouilh play but was informed by the author's agent that Anouilh did not want the play turned into a musical.

Prince and Sondheim were still determined to do a romantic musical, but found it difficult to find source material with sufficient crises, love and foolishness. Prince then brought the writer Hugh Wheeler in for discussions. Wheeler, in Prince's estimation, was one of the few "serious playwrights who can handle the stresses of musical collaboration. His peers shy away from writing libretti on the basis that the composer and director get all the credit. Hugh's experience with *Night Music* and later *Candide* and *Sweeney Todd* surely has given the lie to that," said Prince.[4] Wheeler had also recently adapted the screenplay for Prince's film *Something for Everyone,* and for twenty years or more had written mysteries in England under the pseudonyms of Patrick Quentin and Q. Patrick.

Of the many possible sources they tossed around, the two most promising were Sondheim's suggestion of Jean Renoir's film *The Rules of the Game* and Ingmar Bergman's *Smiles of a Summer Night.* They therefore arranged a screening of the films. Prince said:

> There are interesting similarities in *Rules of the Game, Smiles of a Summer Night,* and *Ring Round the Moon.* Each takes place in a summerhouse on a weekend. Each contains a party, each a play within a play. The characters are similar. There is an old lady in the wheelchair who is adjusted to death. There are the young people on the threshold of life. And there are the lovers in varying degrees of frustration.[5]

They felt that the Renoir piece was not right and decided on *Smiles of a Summer Night* because of its darkness, human qualities and its well-constructed screenplay. In a letter to Bergman, Prince assured the film-maker that he did not intend to do a literal translation of the screenplay. Prince explained that the musical was to be "suggested by" rather than "adapted from." A wire arrived from Bergman on 7 December 1971 with permission for the rights to the property and wishing them all good luck on the project.

Sondheim was wary of the project, feeling he didn't know much about Sweden at the turn of the century. What he and Prince decided to do was to "lyricize the various aspects of love."[6] Prince, too, found it a difficult show to discuss. None of the collaborators had ancestors in Sweden nor did they relate specifically to the characters in the book.

Nevertheless, Prince began to visualize his new show. The piece suggested a Magritte painting. It was like "figures . . . anomalies in a landscape. A gentle greensward on which to play scenes in bedrooms, dressing rooms, dining rooms. I wanted the figures in the landscape out of context, for no more reason than Magritte puts them there."[7]

The original Bergman film, set in Sweden at the turn of the century, deals with the problems of an actress who is retiring and wants to marry the father of her daughter—a child he doesn't know is his. The actress's plans, however, are complicated by a current love affair with a jealous dragoon. In addition, the father of her child is now married to an 18-year-old girl who is still a virgin after eleven months of marriage. Finally, the child bride is falling in love with her husband's 21-year-old son by a previous marriage.

During six weeks' work in adapting the film to the stage, Wheeler completed several drafts. When working with Prince, Wheeler said, they always started with the play first. "It's always been 'here is this play and then we will use it.' "[8] Among the revisions he made was to change the actress's child, who is a 4-year-old boy in the film, to a 13-year-old girl, and to expand the role of the actress's mother, a retired courtesan. "Basically his book became a straightforward telling of Bergman's story, although Prince and Sondheim planned to treat the show as an operetta instead of a musical comedy."[9] Wheeler, when asked if there was much discussion with him during the creation of the show about a metaphor or concept, said, "Well, the metaphor figures slightly larger in their [Sondheim's and Prince's] minds than in mine. We do have metaphors and in the case of *Night Music* it was 'The Follies of Love' if that's a metaphor. I don't quite know what a metaphor is! It's a concept, if you want to call it that."[10] In point of fact, Prince suggested to Wheeler that he forget all the discussions about concept and think of the libretto as a screenplay. Wheeler then finished the script in two weeks.

Prince found raising the money for the show's $650,000 budget difficult. Despite the director's excellent record of Broadway hits, he found that many of his older and richer investors had died and that some potential backers were now wary because *Follies,* in spite of its critical acclaim, had been such a commercial failure. Prince was upset at the idea that he might have to go back to auditioning his show, which he had not had to do since *The Pajama Game.* To his great relief, the financing for *A Little Night Music* was finally accomplished without resort to auditioning, although they did audition the show for record companies for extra money.

Sondheim used the literal translation of Mozart's "Eine Kleine Nachtmusik" to arrive at the show's title, *A Little Night Music.* He had long before decided that the score should be composed entirely of waltzes, numbers in three-quarter time or multiples of that time. There were fughettas, canons, contrapuntal duets, trios, a quintet, and a quartet and a double quartet. Sondheim explained that "the score was made up mostly of inner monologue songs in which the characters described their deepest thoughts, almost never singing to one another."[11] Prince said that they were not actually all waltzes, but in some "ingenious musical way that I don't understand, everything is indeed in some form of triple time."[12] Besides the waltzes, Sondheim wrote scherzos, minuets, barcaroles, and polonaises. After completing six songs that were dark and bleak and, according to Sondheim, "almost out of Strindberg,"[13] he had Prince listen to them. The composer had written the songs as if the project were dark and Bergman-like, as in the film. Prince felt that Sondheim's first numbers were too dark. Sondheim admits that Prince was correct.

> I usually love to write in dark colors about basic gut feelings, but Hal has a sense of audience that I sometimes lose when I'm writing. He wanted the darkness to peep through a whipped-cream surface. And, quite simply, I was writing for Bergman's film, not Hugh Wheeler's play.[14]

Sondheim's final score, much lighter in feeling, was in the styles of Brahms, Rachmaninoff and Ravel and much more to Prince's liking. When he discussed orchestrations with Jonathan Tunick, Sondheim said he wanted the show to have a perfume-like quality, not just to bubble like champagne. Prince wanted *Night Music* to have a series of reprises of all the songs at the finale; only five, however, were used and Sondheim felt this was very effective.

Sondheim wanted a Liebeslieder group in the show in place of a conventional chorus. He wasn't sure how they would function but he included them throughout the score. Prince decided after three months of pondering on the idea that the singers would do a singing overture and act throughout as a "frame" for the proceedings.

> Everyone in *Night Music* is frustrated, humiliated by sexual role-playing. The five Liebeslieder people are secure. Perhaps they are operetta singers, optimistic, extroverted observers. Each is a personality, each has a response to the events of the evening. No two are alike. They make the piece accessible because they lead the audience into it.[15]

Casting for *A Little Night Music* began with Hermione Gingold wanting the role of Madame Armfeldt, the most difficult role to cast. Prince felt she was wrong for the role. He wanted the humor to flow from the character, and he thought of Gingold as a comic. She, however, was determined to prove the director wrong and, turning up unannounced at one audition, asked if she could do a reading. " 'As it turned out,' Mr. Prince says, 'she was magnificent.' "[16] Gingold discussed what she went through to gain the part:

> I rang and rang Hal's office and I told them the *least* they could do was allow me to audition. And *I* haven't auditioned in forty years! They finally said it would be all right and I went down and sang a song I remembered vaguely that I'd done on TV two or three times. I sang it and Steve [Sondheim] said, "now would you sing something else . . . and don't speak it quite so much, sing it more." And I said, "I'm sorry, but I only know one song. I'll sing it again if you'd like." And I did . . . and about ten days later I was told I had the part. I'd never been so nervous in years. I'd played for royalty, but Steve Sondheim and Hal Prince were too much for me.[17]

Glynis Johns, a very successful English actress, was cast in the principal role of Desiree. Prince felt Johns had a vulnerable quality which he liked for the part. Len Cariou auditioned for the role of Carl-Magnus, Desiree's lover, but was cast instead by Prince as Fredrik. Laurence Guittard played the Count, and Patricia Elliott played the Countess Charlotte.

A week before rehearsals began, Actors Equity ruled that the people in the Liebeslieder roles be considered "chorus"—that since they had no dialogue, they must sign chorus contracts. By taking this position, the union was threatening the future of the show, because the difficult-to-cast singers refused to sign chorus contracts. Prince would not agree to Equity's ruling and he and the singers went ahead with rehearsals while the union harassed them and threatened arbitration proceedings. Equity eventually backed down when Prince gave the quintet names in the show and then listed them in the program.

Boris Aronson was again asked by Prince to do the set designs for the show. The designer, too, was hesitant about working on *Night Music,* since he felt his Russian heritage made him unfamiliar with Swedish sensibilities. Prince reassured him that there was very little difference between the landscape around Leningrad and that in Sweden, arguing that "It's all birch trees as far as I am concerned."[18] Realizing that there would be a number of scenery changes, Aronson devised a set consisting of six sliding panels hung from three parallel bars over the stage. Made of transparent plastic and painted over in part by a forest of birch trees, the panels could be slid across the stage and arranged in ways that would suggest a variety of settings to the audience. The panels, when completed, were 24 feet tall. A miniature model was constructed for Prince's approval and then the model was sent off to the Feller Scenery Studios in the Bronx, where the actual sets were built at a cost of $150,000. Prince said the effect of the trees on the plastic was like Faberge enamel on crystal. The stage was carpeted to create the effect of a gently rolling green lawn. Again, as in *Follies* and *Company,* the scenery was designed by Aronson before the show was fully written.

Patricia Birch was asked to do the choreography for the show. A former dancer who had performed with the Martha Graham Company as well as on Broadway, Birch had first worked with Prince as a performer in *West Side Story,* going on to do the choreography for the hit Broadway musical *Grease* and the Off-Broadway *You're a Good Man, Charlie Brown.*

Birch remembers that she was called in quite early on all the shows she did with Prince. With *Night Music,* she did some preliminary work at Prince's home in Majorca. The song "A Weekend in the Country" had not been written as yet, and one of the discussions concerned "what would take place here and who would come in with suitcases there, and we'd do this and then do that. . . . It was just major blocking. But we had to wait for the music to *really* do it."[19] When rehearsals began, Birch said, "There was a lot of discussion and then on purpose he'd leave me alone, quite alone. Then I'd show him something when it was ready. Very often he'd

A Little Night Music, 1973
Laurence Guittard and Glynis Johns in the bedroom scene.
(Photo © Martha Suope)

feed me the objective or we'd find the objective together. The thing I do best is moving from the book into the music and back into the book again, making it seamless."[20] Birch had difficulty staging the number "The Glamorous Life" and Prince kept instructing her to have the number "swirl, swirl, swirl."[21] However, Birch couldn't get the number to "swirl." She feels that Sondheim's numbers are generally difficult to stage. She also had to figure out how to stage numbers for Gingold, who would be sitting in a wheelchair all night. Birch and Prince also spent a good deal of time trying to figure out how to stage the lieder singers.

Birch said that she did a lot of research for the show and consulted with an expert in Swedish dance forms. "Dance-wise, you have to have a certain amount of vocabulary ready. For this show the Swedish waltz is quite different from other waltzes."[22] Birch said that she and Prince worked well together. She learned a good deal of what was expected of her from discussions with Prince and from watching and "hanging out." She said:

> Hal picks his collaborators carefully, and he and I connect without a lot of words. We worked very closely. Sometimes we'd just look at each other and know something was going wrong or something was going right. We had a kind of mutual respect. There were times he'd ask me if something was working that had nothing to do with dance. And we have a good time working together.[23]

Rehearsals for *Night Music* began on Sunday, 10 December 1972 in the American Theatre Laboratory, a rehearsal studio on West 19th Street. During the first few days of rehearsal, three of Sondheim's thirteen numbers which were ready were cut, including "Two Fairy Tales" and "My Husband, the Pig." Prince suffered through staging the show with almost half the score missing. He said, "It was maddening and I'll never allow it to happen again with anyone."[24] Sondheim admits that he is very slow and neurotic about getting his scores finished on time for rehearsals. One of the few songs that Sondheim wrote for *Night Music* that has become a popular hit is "Send in the Clowns." It wasn't ready until two weeks before the production left for Boston. "One day," Sondheim said, "after seeing Glynis [Johns] perform her second act scene with Len [Cariou] in a different way, I got an idea, went home, and that night wrote "Send in the Clowns."[25] Prince, although hindered greatly by Sondheim's incomplete score for which six more songs were needed, admitted that it also had its advantages. As an example, "A Weekend in the Country," the climax of the first act, was written after Sondheim had watched the scene performed in rehearsal. Prince said, "That enabled Steve to blend the song in perfectly with the mood and feeling of the scene."[26]

Prince finished staging the book and, with Birch, set Sondheim's eight completed numbers during the first two weeks of rehearsal. The director became restless waiting for the additional songs to arrive and decided to play around with the staging of the final scene in Act I with the actors. It was a sequence that included the entire company, and Wheeler offered some ad libs to facilitate things. As Prince recalls:

> I began to move the actors around . . . you go here and you hand this person an invitation and you say, "Look what happened, we've been invited to a weekend at the Armfeldts' in the country," and you say, "Well, I don't want to go," and you say, "Oh, please," and you say, "Well, I'll reconsider," and so on.[27]

The scene emerged as a mock operetta. When Sondheim saw what was happening he went home that night, altered a great deal of the order of events, yet wrote the sequence so that Birch didn't have to reset the musical blocking. Prince said, " 'A Weekend in the Country' is such an accomplishment that Steve was prompted to suggest that next time we should stage our libretto without any music, show it to him, then let him go away for six months to write the score."[28]

Prince was very proud of the staging of the dinner table scene and the final scene on the lawn. They were extensions of technical work that had begun in *Cabaret* and *Company*. The last scene, which takes place in various areas of the estate, appears to be happening only on the lawn. There is one scene that shows the young wife and her stepson running in a hall and off to the country. Another shows Desiree with her lover in the bedroom. Additionally, the Countess and Fredrik are having a conversation on the lawn. Prince knew that these situations could not be done on a stage and therefore had suggested the screenplay idea to Wheeler.

> What I did was put it all on the landscape and I don't think the audience quarreled with it . . . or even asked where they were. I think people sense some things. I think people sense that *you* know where they are so they leave it alone. I think if they ever sense that you're unsure of what you're doing, that insecurity filters through the work.[29]

Glynis Johns worked well with Prince. She was quoted as saying about her director, "He has eyes in the back of his head and a real driving force, a life force. And with it goes a great deal of love. He calls us 'crew' and himself 'captain,' and he's heartbroken when the opening night is over, simply because he doesn't want to be away from us. I think he falls in love with his company."[30]

The show moved from the rehearsal studio to the stage of the Shubert Theatre on 8 January 1973 for additional rehearsals and a "gypsy" run-through, in which makeshift sets were used and the actors performed to piano accompaniment and some on-stage explanations by Prince. The audience, consisting of friends of the audience and dancers, singers, actors, and others from the broad spectrum of the New York theatre, gave the show a standing ovation. The run-through was performed with only fifteen of the show's eventual sixteen songs.

On Monday, 15 February, the cast boarded a chartered Greyhound bus and headed for Boston for the pre-Broadway tryout. Hal Hastings, the music director, had gone to Boston earlier and was busy hiring local musicians, since expenses involved in transporting and housing New York musicians out-of-town are prohibitive.

Things went comparatively well in Boston. There were technical problems, however, with spotlights. With close to 400 spots operating from the balcony alone, the six lighting technicians had difficulty picking up the right actor at the precise moment he or she stepped forward to sing or speak. In addition to the lighting problems, the sets made "groaning" noises. During one performance the wagon on which the dining table rolled made such a sudden halt that silverware and china flew in all directions. However, night after night things got better.

Not all parts of the show captured the audience's interest. The show's biggest problem was the slowness of the first fifteen minutes. Prince wanted the piece kept as simple and quiet as possible. He knew that the show would take time to get started. "I said it's Chekhov in style," said Prince; "let's stick to Chekhov and they've got to go with us. The only reason for doing it was we wanted to do this kind of musical. If we gave them a wham-bam opening number so that they felt comfortable, we would in the long run, fail. And we stuck to our guns and we *were* popular."[31]

The authors then began to make cuts. Every night's performance revealed to the director changes he would have to make at rehearsal the following day. He decided at one point that a prop invitation was too small to designate a summons to a great manor house. At that evening's performance, larger paper invitations were substituted.

In addition, Prince worried that his capital would run out, hoping that reviews would be good enough to bring in audiences large enough to help meet operating expenses. Prince said, "There's a sinking fund of $35,000 in each show. It has been that figure for twenty years; $35,000 doesn't last long if you're in trouble."[32]

A Little Night Music received good but not overly enthusiastic reviews in Boston. Kevin Kelly of the *Boston Globe* is quoted as saying it stirred admiration but "not much feeling."[33] He believed it was a musical for a special and limited audience. Elliott Norton in the *Boston Herald* felt it slowed down at the end, thereby losing some of its brightness and irony, but he did feel it was a lovely, amusing show.[34] Bonnie Jacobs, in *Boston after Dark,* called it "simply the most breathtaking musical I've seen in a very long time. . . . Prince has once again shown himself to be a theatrical innovator and polisher of the first degree—his shows are never 'easy,' and with what he has to work with, this one is going to be brilliant."[35]

After the fifth preview in New York, and just three days before opening night, Glynis Johns fell ill and was hospitalized. Barbara Lang, Johns's understudy, went on for her and Prince postponed the opening indefinitely. Tammy Grimes was the one possible replacement Prince considered. He recalled:

> [Grimes] came to see [the show] and we talked about getting her up in the part and opening a week late. She agreed, but she also raised a number of questions respecting interpretation, attitudes, and most specifically, the costumes. It was too late to make the kind of changes she was suggesting. For the show to open with a substitute star in seven days it would have to be the one I had rehearsed, and any alterations, including to the costumes, would have to be just that—alterations.[36]

Prince then considered flying to London to find a replacement for Johns. However, the following day his leading lady was ready to return to the show, having missed only three performances.

A Little Night Music opened in New York on 23 February 1973 at the Shubert Theatre to excellent reviews. Clive Barnes of the *New York Times,* who had panned *Company* and *Follies,* gave an absolute rave to this show.

> At last! A new operetta! *A Little Night Music* is heady, civilized, sophisticated, and enchanting. It is Dom Perignon. It is supper at Laserre. And it is more fun than any tango in a Parisian suburb. . . . People have long been talking about Mr. Prince's conceptual musicals; now I feel I have actually seen one of the actual concepts. . . . Good God!—an Adult musical![37]

Edwin Wilson of the *Wall Street Journal* found it refreshing that two such innovators as Prince and Sondheim had created a musical with the charms of yesteryear.

> Ironically, the very men who brought us *Company* and *Follies,* Harold Prince, the director and producer, and Stephen Sondheim, the composer and lyricist, are the ones pushing the pendulum back again in *A Little Night Music.* Sociologists can make of it what they will, but romance and the finer things have made their way back to Broadway.[38]

While most of the reviewers were enthusiastic about the new Prince production, some found it cold and lacking in emotion. This was to become a fairly common complaint about the Prince and Sondheim shows. Some described it as a lack of feeling and others complained that they didn't care about the characters in their shows. Of *A Little Night Music,* Douglas Watt of the *Daily News* said:

> Exquisiteness is so much the concern of *A Little Night Music,* a beautifully designed and staged operetta of intimate proportions that opened last night at the Shubert, that there is little room for the breath of life. . . . It reveals the work of superior craftsmanship. But stunning as it is to gaze upon and as clever as its score is, with its use of trio and ensemble singing, it remains too literary and precious a work to stir the emotions.[39]

Martin Gottfried, one of Prince's greatest champions, said the show was "a great disappointment to me."[40] He felt the major problem was in the script, which he felt dominated the show in spite of its flaccid and un-dynamic tone. He said, "The story simply goes along, developing plot without much humor or charm, and certainly no dramatic peaks."[41] Gottfried did like the score but not the cast, with the exception of Len Cariou. He concluded:

> There are moments that suggest frustrated intentions: as if Prince had had a first vision that either didn't work out or is not as clear as he thinks it is. There is an operetta quintet of singing commentators—a Chorus—and several songs begin with a singer practicing the piano or the cello. It is as if the idea of performing music might have been a production theme. . . . Given Prince's tremendous, proved and important talent, it is a letdown.[42]

A Little Night Music, 1973
Barbara Long, Glynis Johns and Beth Fowler.
(Photo © Martha Swope)

A Little Night Music won both the Drama Critics and Tony awards as the year's best musical. Additionally, Tonys were awarded for best music and lyrics (Sondheim), best book (Wheeler), best costumes (Florence Klotz), best actress in a musical (Johns) and best supporting actress in a musical (Patricia Elliott). Within six months the show had returned its investment and Prince began receiving offers for European productions of the show. It ran 600 performances on Broadway and its touring companies did well.

Sondheim felt that the show was more successful than *Company* and *Follies* because it was less tense and made audiences feel more relaxed. He said, "What I really think is that *whatever* the last show would have been, they would have liked it more than the first two. They're just getting used to our stuff. . . . I suppose I'm finally wearing them down."[43]

Prince could not understand the critics who wrote that there was a natural progression from *Company* to *Follies* to *Night Music.* This was especially bewildering to him since after *Follies* they noted that he was moving in the direction of the plotless musical, whereas *Night Music,* he felt, had more than enough plot for one musical. Prince has said that he didn't enjoy doing *Night Music* because he didn't dig as deeply or extend himself as far as he likes to. He called *A Little Night Music* a stylish and intellectual musical but felt it was too pale and romantic and not bloody or emotional enough. "And it was not very controversial."[44] However, he appreciated the fact that *Night Music* was the "hit" that he needed so badly. Lisa Aronson, however, remembers that her husband felt differently: "Boris did not agree when Hal put off the show as just looking for a hit or being easy. . . . He felt it was Hal's best work."[45]

Ingmar Bergman, after seeing *A Little Night Music* in November, 1973, said to Prince, "I was surprised that it was possible to eliminate the shadows of desperation, eroticism, and caprice without the whole story collapsing. At the moment I forgot that this entertaining and witty musical had anything to do with my picture. I enjoyed it tremendously and I loved your actors."[46]

Candide

> *There was not really a successful staged version until Hal Prince came along, with his idea of a brief, racy, stripped-down version.*
>
> — Leonard Bernstein, Quoted in the *New York Times,*
> 10 October 1982

> *There's something going on that's fresh almost every second*
> *in* Candide. *It's just opening up Pandora's Box and letting*
> *out all of those wonderful tricks—including the idea of using*
> *quadraphonic sound. I was fascinated with it.*
>   —Richard Adler, Interview with the author, 30 June 1983

Although *A Little Night Music* was the success that Prince needed at the time, he did not entertain thoughts of doing something in the same vein for his next project. Instead he headed toward a production whose theatrical style—environmental theatre—was one with which he had no experience. *Candide* presented quite a different challenge to Prince. When it was over, he had another hit.

Prince had lent his name to the Advisory Board of the Chelsea Theatre Center for about ten years. He had been impressed with several of their productions, particularly Edward Bond's *Saved.* Robert Kalfin, the artistic director of the Chelsea, asked Prince if he would like to work on a project with them, and Prince agreed. Kalfin suggested a revival of the musical *Candide,* which had been done originally on Broadway in 1956. Lillian Hellman had written the libretto, an adaptation of the Voltaire novel. Leonard Bernstein had written the music, with lyrics by Richard Wilbur, John LaTouche and Dorothy Parker.

Prince didn't think a revival would work:

I'd seen the original version on Broadway and hated it. It was a heavy, pretentious, labored production that bored me. It had Leonard Bernstein's great score, but it had a bad book, a bad mix of production values and it had been badly directed by a great director, Tyrone Guthrie. It was a "classic" instead of a theatre piece.[47]

In addition, Prince felt that

half the show was politically and socially oriented and the other half was oriented to the satirization of musical operetta, Bernstein's musical-theatre joke. I think it's unfair to say, as some people have, that the book was the villain. Tyrone Guthrie takes second place to no one in recent history, but he made his mistakes and *Candide* was one of them. The book, music, lyrics, and physical production were inappropriate to one another.[48]

Kalfin, however, persisted in his attempt to revive *Candide,* and had the Hellman libretto reshaped. Six months later, Prince, after reading the new treatment, still didn't think it right and he abandoned the idea of doing the piece.

After *A Little Night Music* opened, however, the producer-director, on the lookout for a project for the 1973-74 season, decided to give some more thought to *Candide* and read the original Voltaire novel. He said, "I was surprised at how light and impulsive and *unimportant* it is. Apparently, [Voltaire] wrote it quickly and denied having written it, putting it down as a schoolboy's prank. And that's the spirit of it."[49] Prince felt that *Candide* needed a fresh concept, one that would be "as outrageous in contemporary terms and, curiously, as naive."[50] Voltaire's novel was a classic but Prince felt that the original collaborators on the musical had treated the piece too reverently, not catching the fun and outrageous quality inherent in the work. Prince had to decide on the appropriate structure for a work that contained many high and low moments and no real crises.

Prince felt the piece could easily become boring. In the director's own words, "The hero beginning his odyssey, runs into negative forces and overcomes them or subverts them, and then runs into more negative forces and more negative forces, and then after a while, a pattern is achieved and the audience loses interest."[51] Prince decided on a relatively short show, only about an hour and three-quarters long, with the second act seeming like a reprise of the first. In fact, the 1974 revival of *Candide* runs about an hour and fifty-seven minutes and has no intermission.

Prince, as usual, tried to synthesize the project for himself with a visual image. *Candide* became a cartoon for him, a triptych.[52] How could he animate a triptych? He came up with something akin to the mansions of medieval theatrical staging, where he would use small sets one after another to illustrate Candide's odyssey.

Prince asked Hellman to write the revised production of *Candide.* She loved Prince's ideas, saying that his approach was similar to what she had wanted to do originally, but she remained unwilling to work on the new show. She did not object, however, to his hiring a new librettist, with the condition that none of her original dialogue be retained in the revival. Prince agreed. He then received permission from Bernstein and Wilbur to do an updated version of the show. Bernstein, too, said that Prince's concept was what he had always wanted. Getting the contracts negotiated was a complicated business because of the many original collaborators.

Hugh Wheeler was hired to do the new libretto. He and Prince listened to all the music on the original cast album, and underlined favorite parts in the Voltaire work. Wheeler took two weeks to present a first draft and Prince thought it was "hilarious."[53] Prince helped Wheeler to shape the libretto by keeping the work down to a manageable length and making certain the songs were effectively placed. The author and director brought in two Voltaire episodes, including the Constantinople interlude, that had not been used in the original production. Prince also wanted a new opening number, feeling that "The Best of All Possible Worlds" was a statement of philosophy which didn't properly introduce the character and emotion of the show. The director sought a number which would set the tone of the production and orient the audience to the production's time and place. Sondheim, therefore, wrote a lyric to incorporate four little vignettes, set to Bernstein's music from "The Venice Gavotte" and called "Life Is Happiness Indeed."

Prince's new concept for *Candide* imposed a new look and sound on many of the Bernstein songs. His idea for "Glitter and Be Gay," the heroine Cunegonde's big aria and one of the score's most popular songs, was to have a pianist, in eighteenth-century French dress and white powdered wig containing shining diamonds, appear from a trapdoor. During the song, Prince said, "Cunegonde would denude the powdered wig of its diamonds, covering herself with them."[54] Raymond Ericson in the *New York Times* was convinced that "Glitter and Be Gay" was a "satiric masterpiece."[55] Prince also decided that Candide and Cunegonde would undress each other during the song "Oh, Happy We." Prince explained that this would play "against the materialism in the lyrics."[56]

Prince hired Eugene Lee to design *Candide*. He had seen the environmental set Lee had done for LeRoi Jones's *Slave Ship* at the Chelsea a few seasons earlier, and also knew of Lee's work with Peter Brook. Prince discussed with Lee his sideshow concept for the production, and Lee suggested varying the levels and sizes of the stages, using curtains on only several. Prince then thought of playing scenes simultaneously on stages at opposite ends of the theatre. Prince remembered seeing the Italian production of *Orlando Furioso* in Bryant Park in 1970 which used this concept, and which he had liked very much.

Lee was back in a few weeks with drawings and elevations. Prince, who can't read drawings, asked Lee to construct a model. The designer created a model for the show in a shoebox as it would look in the Chelsea Theatre. Prince studied the shoebox, taking it to Majorca in the summer. The original set contained seven playing areas. In the six-month period before rehearsals started, entrances, exits, trapdoors and stairways were continually changing. However, the final set retained seven stages, two of which were proscenium, a connecting ramp, and two bridges. Prince was shocked when he eventually saw the space for the show in Brooklyn. He had been visualizing it in a theatre such as the Broadhurst, not in a 180-seat house. He had been told that they would be using a converted ballroom space at the Brooklyn Academy of Music which held 500 people, and he had imagined the show with this room in mind. Peter Brook, however, had booked that space and it was necessary for Prince to make both mental and physical adjustments. The tiny fourth-floor 180-seat house at the Academy of Music was ramped and a modified circus midway created with runways, booths and mini-stages that could be changed instantly from a corpse-filled battlefield to the city of Constantinople. Bleachers were placed around three-quarters of the playing space. Some of the audience sat on stools in the two pits that flanked a small central platform, others between ramps, drawbridges, and along runways. The actors, making their way through the audience, could sing and dance either on platforms or the bridges connecting them. Litton explained, "On the fourth side of the Chelsea loft was a small, shallow proscenium stage, where scenes requiring backdrops could be played."[57] Litton indicated that Prince was "impressed with the idea of environmental theatre and *Candide* was his opportunity to stage a musical in an environmental setting including a bit of 'madcap farce.' "[58]

One thing that particularly bothered Prince about the Brooklyn production of *Candide* was that there were so few people in the audience watching the show. He felt that

> the relationship of the people with the people, the audience with the audience, is what makes *Candide* exceptional. The relationship of audience with actor is fairly standard. . . . People are self-conscious about responding when they're alone, and 180 people in the Chelsea were, except in a few areas, very much alone. If they wanted to laugh, they were aware that they might just be laughing by themselves. In Brooklyn we found that sometimes we had celebrations with our audiences, but more often we had silence. Smiling, grinning, nudging each other, but self-consciously editing audibility out of their responses.[59]

Prince doesn't like the actors coming close to and touching the audience, a possibility that was kept to a minimum. He advised actors that, even though they might be only a foot away from the audience in any given scene, they should respect the audience's privacy. He instructed his actors to say "please" and "excuse me" when they were crossing in front of a member of the audience.

Groups of the show's small orchestra sat wherever there was room, "its members cheerfully tootling along amidst the crowd like spectators who had suddenly been inspired to play along for the fun of it."[60] Bernstein wanted to reorchestrate the show to emphasize the smaller groups and Prince left this chore to him, John Mauceri (the musical director) and Hershy Kay, who had orchestrated the original 1956 version. This trio designed what is now called a quadraphonic concept—thirteen musicians parcelled out in four separate areas of the theatre and surrounding the audience. Richard Adler, who thinks *Candide* and the later *Evita* are the two shows on which Prince did his best work, said he "loved the quadraphonic sound in *Candide*."[61]

The roles of Candide and Cunegonde in the original version had been cast with an emphasis on operatic abilities. For the new version, Prince wanted wide-eyed, innocent-looking young performers between the ages of sixteen and twenty. Even the musicians were to be recently graduated Juilliard students. Eventually, Maureen Brennan and Mark Baker were signed for the roles of Cunegonde and Candide.

Prince wanted Jerry Orbach for the role of Voltaire-Pangloss because of his ability as a farceur, but he was not available. Lewis J. Stadlen, whom Prince had admired as Groucho Marx in *Minnie's Boys,* was finally hired for the role. Prince asked Nancy Walker to play the Old Lady but she wasn't interested, and the role was given to June Gable.

Prince lunched with Pat Birch in a Chinese restaurant and told her about *Candide,* assuming that, with her many offers to stage dances, she wouldn't want to involve herself in this Brooklyn production. Birch remembers his saying that there was nothing for her in the show.

> But I told him, "Yes there is—there's plenty for me to do in it and I want to do it." ... The fun I had working with Hal was that he'd let me go a little wild. I do a lot of humorous, slightly off-beat stuff, and he's the first one to love all that. On *Candide* we were lucky out there—the main physical part of the set was built, so we did the staging right on the set. It was a lot of fun.[62]

Dance critic Deborah Jowitt discussed the use of movement in *Candide*:

> There is an immense amount of motion, but nothing that the eye is supposed to light on as "choreography"—no people who stand out as trained dancers.... Prince and Birch have made the action move so fast that you can hardly take it in. They've staged Candide's travels rather like a frantic board game along the perilous ramps that festoon the Broadway Theatre [where *Candide* moved after its Brooklyn run].[63]

Prince hired Franne Lee, Eugene's wife, to do the costumes. She had designed the André Gregory production of *Alice in Wonderland* and Prince felt that her sketches were sophisticated, detailed and witty. The designer showed Prince a suitcase filled with bits of fabric, remnants of old clothes and costumes. She explained that everything in the show would be made out of some used item, which would give the feeling, Prince said, that

> we had emptied a closet, unlocked an attic trunk, a multiplicity of events, time, places. . . . [Franne Lee] put three or four of these pieces on my desk and told me that they looked like the character of the Old Lady. Another collage, Cunegonde. If I put one next to another, against a third, I began to see the characters emerging. Something meshed, something seemed right about that kind of thinking. . . . Had I been doing a show for $600,000, I wouldn't have had the guts to go along with it. And therein lies one of the problems of the commercial theatre.[64]

Rehearsals began on 21 October 1973 in Brooklyn. There were to be six-and-a-half weeks of rehearsals before the first preview. It was a rewarding rehearsal period, one in which there was no pressure—time or otherwise—to produce the "big commercial blockbuster for Broadway." It was fun for Prince because he wasn't worrying about investors. He said, "I was doing a show for five weeks in Brooklyn."[65]

Birch and Prince staged the entire production in eight days. Prince said,

> If we had a sluggish day, we let it go. If things were going well, we worked a full five hours and quit. We rarely bothered to break for lunch—avoided coming back loggy and distracted. If someone's voice was bothering him, he saved it. . . . I began to appreciate the privileges of socialized theatre. Also, we had the luxury of four weeks to try it on small groups of friends. Based on their responses, we kept filling and building. *Candide* evolved.[66]

They opened over a ten-day period at the end of December 1973 with critics at almost every performance. The Brooklyn run was extended for two weeks because the show was sold out before the opening. The reviews were generally good. Geoffrey Holder on NBC-TV said, "*Candide* is just pure fun . . . and I'm glad I saw it after waiting 17 years for the revival."[67] Jack Kroll said of the director,

> Prince seems to have been influenced in his staging by the astonishing Italian production of *Orlando Furioso* that came to New York some seasons ago,

Candide, 1974
The company is featured within the environmental set designed by Eugene and Franne Lee.
(Photo © Martha Swope)

in which a stadium-size playing space was overrun by performers pell-melling through the audience. . . . The unflagging motion of the show may be *too* labyrinthine, but it does capture the winds-of-fortune movement of Voltaire's moral tale.[68]

George Oppenheimer of *Newsday* called the score of *Candide* an unadulterated delight. He said, "Harold Prince, the proficient, prolific and productive director-producer, has staged with magical effects."[69] Douglas Watt, who called this show an "out-and-out burlesque" and an "excessively campy production," felt that although reading about Candide's adventures may be entertaining in book form, they "are merely repetitious on stage."[70]

Prince's long-time champion Martin Gottfried noted that Prince revealed knowledge of the avant-garde in his use of the environmental setting. He said,

The main problem is the story itself, still going from one place to another with the same joke in hand; still going with not a character to enjoy; still going on the literary and definitely untheatrical wheels of satire. . . . Wheeler's book is no better than Ms. Hellman's. . . . What Prince seemed to do was finally give up on the book altogether and stage a theater work of music and movement, which is a great idea but not when meant as camouflage.[71]

Although some of the positive reviews suggested moving to Broadway, the *New York Times* felt that something might be lost in the transition. The Chelsea Theatre Center, however, had a hit on its hands and plans were made to move *Candide* across the river. For Prince, the show's success vindicated his belief that a revival needed a fresh concept.

The decision to run the show on Broadway raised the costs considerably. *Candide* had been produced in Brooklyn for $100,000; the Broadway capitalization was $450,000. Operating costs were $65,000 a week, the break-even point. These high costs proved a dilemma. The theatre had to be large enough to accommodate the needed paying audience, but not so large that the intimacy, the close contact between audience and actors, so much a part of *Candide*'s success, would be lost. The Prince office began its search for the right theatre. Hotels and ballrooms examined were either too small or unavailable. Howard Haines of the Prince staff checked the City Center basement, an abandoned bowling alley, and the Sert Room at the Waldorf-Astoria. Prince, however, liked the idea of the Winter Garden or Broadway Theatres. He envisioned removing the seats and placing some of the audience on portions of their huge stages. Both theatres were available. The huge Broadway was selected, which "meant a total revamping of the theatre's innards to limit the audience to no more than 900."[72]

To begin making a profit from the move, the period between the closing on 20 January 1974 in Brooklyn and the opening in Manhattan had to be minimal. They met with architects on the restructuring to keep it within the Fire and Building Departments' regulations. The Broadway playing area became twenty feet longer than in Brooklyn, but the stages were identical. An audience of 900 could be accommodated, as against 180 in the Chelsea space. Some bleacher seats would be sold on a first-come, first-served basis, and Prince moved the show into a bleacher area as often as possible. To retain the feeling of intimacy, most of the Broadway's endlessly receding balcony was closed and a lighting grid was hung overhead to give the effect of a lowered ceiling. Everything was the same, just a little bigger.

Howard Haines assumed most of the responsibility for the move to Broadway during the seven weeks that it took to get the production on. He worked with the architect, Leslie Armstrong of Armstrong, Childs and Associates, who had supervised the reconstruction for the musical *Dude* in the same theatre a year earlier. Others, such as the consulting engineer Henry M. Garsson and the builder Peter Feller, attempted to stay within the specifications of the city agencies. Prince remained apprehensive during the seven-week period while the interior of the Broadway Theatre was being altered.

> No sooner had we accommodated [the city agencies'] rules, but I would come into the theatre and eliminate seats. One day I took out 121 in the bleacher section because of sight-lines. The point is, with *Candide,* no one in the audience sees everything, but everyone must see almost everything.[73]

There were problems, too, with the audience. The re-built theatre structure frightened them and some reacted by refusing their seat locations, complaining that they couldn't see. There were also those who complained about sitting on the hard wooden bleacher seats. As Prince explained, "An environment which would have been acceptable to them in a ball park offended them in a theatre."[74]

The theatre lobby was redecorated and the marble floors covered with unfinished plywood. Hot dog and beer stands were set up, balloons and streamers hung, along with the canvas drops from the Chelsea production to hide the crystal chandeliers and the gold leaf of the Broadway Theatre. At a central booth, t-shirts, buttons and cast record albums were sold. At curtain, a costumed actor entered to announce the location of the ten stages and two drawbridges and to caution the audience against leaving programs, peanut shells, and feet on the ramps and stairs to help safeguard the actors. The orchestra was divided into four sections and was coordinated by means of closed-circuit television. The playing areas had to be electronically amplified, although Prince prefers a nonamplified show. Lewis J. Stadlen, playing Voltaire, wore a Vega microphone strapped to his leg for three-quarters of the performance.

One thing that disturbed Prince about the move from Brooklyn to Broadway was his unhappy negotiations with the musicians union. Prince blamed the rigidity of the union for the eventual closing of the show. The Broadway Theatre, like all standard musical houses, is supposed to carry 25 musicians under terms of the union contract. As an intimate musical, *Candide* was scored for 13 musicians. The director asked the union for special dispensation and the union compromised, saying that Prince need hire only 15 musicians. Then, in the *Times,* Mel Gussow quoted Prince as saying "the union went back on its word,"[75] causing members of the union to object to the compromise and the union to finally demand that Prince hire the full 25-musician complement. It was too late for Prince to turn back since he had already signed contracts for the theatre and the architects. Prince said if he had known in the beginning that he would be forced to accept 25 musicians, he would not have done the show.[76]

Prince increased the size of the orchestra from 13 to 18 and had difficulty fitting them on the small mini-stages. He said, "There were five absolutely unnecessary musicians. But I couldn't bear the idea of twelve musicians playing pinochle."[77] For the run of the show the seven extra musicians were each paid $290 a week for not playing. They were listed as "understudies," known on Broadway as "walkers," meaning they walk to and from the show, but don't actually work the show. For *Candide* they showed up only on Wednesdays to collect their paychecks. Prince said, "The streets are full of such musicians . . . there are 12 nonplaying musicians in *Chicago,* five in *A Chorus Line,* none in *The Wiz.*"[78] Mel Gussow in the *Times* explained that Prince felt that the

increased payments that he had to pay the musicians that he didn't need made it extremely difficult for the show to turn a weekly profit for 24 weeks, but only in nine of those weeks was the profit equal to the $4,000 he was paying the unwanted musicians. For 19 other weeks, with author, producer and other creative personnel taking cuts in royalties, the show broke even; the other nine, it showed a loss.[79]

Candide re-opened at the Broadway Theatre on 5 March 1974 with the same cast that had appeared at the Chelsea in Brooklyn. The critics praised the show. Richard Watts, Jr., liked the idea of an actor handing his shirt to a member of the audience and then asking him to hold it while he did a scene. After the scene was over, he thanked the audience member and recovered his garment. Another thing Watts enjoyed was the delight on a young boy's face in the front row when Candide looked at him wistfully and asked, "Will my trouble never cease?" Watts called the show

> wonderful. Much of its brilliance is due to Hugh Wheeler's adaptation, Leonard Bernstein's score and the lyrics of Richard Wilbur, but what makes it all the more delightful is Harold Prince's imaginative direction which, among other things, has torn the playhouse apart and transformed it into an intimate gathering place where you are part of the show.[80]

Martin Gottfried in *Women's Wear Daily* felt that in spite of the fact that the show still had book problems the move from Brooklyn was a good one, the show becoming just a little bigger. He said that

> the whole business, the way it moves, behaves and feels—has been made tighter, stronger and smoother . . . is definitely better at the Broadway Theatre than it was at Chelsea. . . . Prince's ability to work unitedly with a choreographer—Patricia Birch—is unique and tremendous. Since so much of this production is pure musical theater—virtually a choreographed concert—[Prince's] concern with choreographer, the musical director, the physical company and the voices is as admirable as it is uncommon.[81]

Clive Barnes wrote that the show was even

> sharper, funnier, wittier and, if possible, more musically elegant than it was in Brooklyn. . . . Mr. Prince has, in the past, given Broadway innumerable gifts, but nothing so gaudy, glittering and endearing as this. It is one of those shows that take off like a rocket and never come down. . . . The cast is perfect. . . . This is a doll of a show. I loved it and loved it. I think Voltaire would have loved it too.[82]

Douglas Watt, like some other critics, found fault with the book. The libretto was

> still something of a drag and even confusing at times. . . . But Prince's inventive staging, like an imaginatively prepared party with bright surprises

scattered all over the place, helps compensate for the story's repetitiousness, as evidenced by all the smiling faces in the house.[83]

At the end of its run, *Candide* still had a deficit of about $310,000 on its $450,000 investment. The production recouped about $15,000 during its seventeen months at the Broadway Theatre. The accounting reveals that only four weeks showed an operating profit. Costs were kept down through royalty waivers by most of the creative team. *Variety* felt that *Candide* was robbed of profits by the limited seating capacity of the theatre due to the extensive alterations. Moreover, since *Candide* was such a difficult show to mount, its touring prospects were limited and it didn't have the prospect of post-New York engagements to recover its deficit.[84]

Candide closed after 741 performances. Prince said,

> It occurs to me that I loved working on *Candide* in Brooklyn and I hated bringing it to Broadway. . . . I must conclude from this that I am growing older, the wear and tear on the nerves is more difficult to take. Is it possible that explains why so many theatre artists seem to retire in their forties or move away from directing or writing for the theatre into a more solitary creative experience? Or, and this is just as likely, maybe I simply don't enjoy producing.[85]

Prince was soon busily planning his next show, *Pacific Overtures,* and wasn't seriously entertaining the thought of moving away from either producing or directing. Since Prince enjoys the musical theatre because of its collaborative effort, there wasn't much danger that he would soon retire to some solitary creative experience. *Candide* had been a critical success and Prince had liked mastering the environmental theatre form. But now it was time to try something new.

In the fall of 1982, the New York City Opera decided to produce *Candide.* People questioned whether it could hold its own on an opera stage. For the new production, the Bernstein score was revised further by the composer with the aid of Hershy Kay and John Mauceri. Hugh Wheeler revised the book once again and Prince re-staged the operatic version for the huge proscenium stage at the New York State Theatre. It was done in two acts for the New York City Opera production in spite of the fact that earlier it had been done in one act. Donal Henahan in the *New York Times* titled his review "Bernstein's *Candide* Is Back as a Winner."[86] It proved to be a great success critically and with audiences. On 17 October 1983 a critic for the *Times* said of a performance of the opera, "Harold Prince's direction is full of fine little funny details, and its smart-alec wit has a wonderful instinct for knowing just when to draw back."[87] After seeing a performance of the production two years after its opening at the City Opera, Donal Henahan said,

> Since the premiere, the cast have tightened their ensemble work considerably. However, the whole cast still seems to be having a grand, uninhibited romp, which gives special gusto to such hilarious moments as the ballroom scene in which silhouetted males toss their partners like the limp dummies they obviously are. The Harold Prince staging is pretty much as it was, a crafty mix of Broadway clichés and vaudeville turns that serves as a counterpoint to the work's black comedy.[88]

Candide is now a successful fixture of the New York City Opera's repertory.

A DARING VENTURE:
Pacific Overtures

John Weidman, while still a student at the Yale Law School, wrote an outline for a play about Commodore Perry's expedition to Japan. Having majored in East Asian history during his undergraduate days at Harvard, he felt that the subject would make good material for a play. Although Weidman had never written a play before, he had done a good deal of writing for the *National Lampoon* as well as other magazines. He had written a letter about his ideas for the play to Hal Prince, and remembered how their relationship developed:

> I had met Hal once or twice when I was a kid and when my father [Jerome Weidman, who wrote *Fiorello!*] was working with him around 1959–60. . . . I sent him a letter saying that I doubted if he would remember me, but I had an idea for a play about the opening of Japan and I just wanted to get a reaction from him. I really did not expect to hear back from him but I did and very quickly, saying he thought it was an interesting idea and if I was in New York I should make an appointment and come in and talk with him. I was in New Haven which isn't far from New York and so I went in to see him. He obviously sparked to the material. There was something about Perry's expedition to Japan which turned him on. He and I talked about it a bit. We had a bunch of meetings at the beginning. It was either during the first, second or third meeting that he suggested that the way to approach the material that was of interest to him was from the Japanese point of view and to make use of Japanese theatrical techniques in telling the story. That idea came from him at the outset.[1]

Prince remembers that Weidman's first idea was to do a realistic play in the style of *The Caine Mutiny Court Martial.* This isn't the kind of theatre that interests Prince and he suggested to Weidman that he rewrite the script in Kabuki style with the Americans in the story presented as traditional Kabuki villains.

Prince took an option on what was as yet nothing but an idea for a play. During the following summer and fall, Weidman wrote his play, experimenting with alternative ideas as he progressed. Prince liked the first draft, but it was too long, and he asked for many rewrites. As Weidman went to work again, contracts were signed and the *New York Times* announced the work as Prince's next project. Prince began casting the play, expecting to open it on Broadway the following season. Weidman came to New York regularly for auditions. They decided that all the Asian parts would be cast with Asians and that Caucasians would play the American roles. Boris Aronson was hired to do the sets.

There was a reading in the basement of the Shubert Theatre with George Irving reading the part of Commodore Perry, which resulted in a major change of plan. Weidman explains:

> I came in from New Haven for what was going to be the last set of auditions. I went up to meet Hal and he said he wasn't sure any longer about the project. He wanted to rethink the material and think of it as a musical instead. . . . I was a little bewildered by the decision, not because I didn't think it was a good idea, but because it was so unexpected.[2]

Prince felt the project needed more "size." Music would give it "size." Prince said of the original Weidman draft:

> I thought of it as terrific musical theatre material. . . . I'd had in my mind for awhile the notion of doing a play about a serious subject in every theatre style conceivable—French farce, melodrama, opera, musical comedy, vaudeville, burlesque, non-music, blank verse and so on. In other words, treating one subject in the full spectrum of theatre styles and that's what I initially wanted to do with this. Then the idea of doing it in Kabuki style really took hold. The final version of the play did have elements of all kinds of theatre. But the Kabuki was so strong that it dominated everything.[3]

Prince explained all this to Weidman. He was going to his home in Majorca for the summer. Before he left he gave the script to Sondheim, whom he hoped to interest in the project. Weidman went away half thinking that

that was the end of the project—that he had come close to getting his first play produced but that it just hadn't worked out.

Sondheim was not receptive at first to the idea of the project. However, Prince said that in a recent conversation, Sondheim had said it was his favorite work. In an interview with Sondheim for this book, he did say, "I love that show a lot."[4]

They returned from Majorca in the fall and began adapting Weidman's play into a musical. Weidman was anxious, but work with both Sondheim and Prince went smoothly. Prince said, "I thought Steve and John worked extraordinarily well together. Steve was inspired."[5] Weidman felt that it was very much a collaborative process, with

> Hal sort of in the driver's seat. Hal had a stronger vision than anyone else in the room of what he wanted—how he thought the piece should work. He would sit with me and Steve and talk about it. Eventually we reached a point where I went away and did the first half of the first act and everybody was happy with that. Then I went away and did the second half of the first act. Hal didn't like that at all and so I did a rewrite which he was much happier with.[6]

By the time Weidman had written a second act they were well into the process of producing the musical. Although Sondheim had been at all the initial meetings, he waited until some of the libretto was completed before he went to work on the score, which was his usual custom. For Sondheim, the most important and most difficult thing in creating a musical is for the collaborators to find a mutual tone. In the case of *Pacific Overtures,* there was a struggle to find the exact tone. Sondheim wanted to avoid "cute Japanese," vulgarity, and straight, authentic Kabuki. He said, "I'm not going for the impression that one is listening to Japanese music."[7] Finally, all the collaborators began to locate the tone they wanted for the piece. Sondheim called the show a documentary vaudeville, a show of ideas about America and the world. He felt that musicals don't usually deal with ideas. Prince's major aim was to make *Pacific Overtures* a musical about the clash of two cultures without too much emphasis on the human aspects of the story.

Prince and Sondheim went to Japan to explore Kabuki and Noh theatre. Their Japanese hosts expected them to be bored with the productions, which could last eight hours. Both Prince and Sondheim, however, enjoyed the shows. Prince said,

Just that one walk across the stage which takes an hour, we found hypnotizing, and mesmerizing so we very reluctantly left each theatre and always late. . . . The only frustration was that we were never allowed to see anything in toto. We went from Tokyo to Kyoto seeing Kabuki twice and Noh theatre once. Of course what they really wanted to show us were showgirls in top hats, tails, and sequins, but we avoided it. . . . The rhythm of Kabuki theatre— the fact that there's such incredible energy all harnessed in this dignified way—probably made me reconsider energy in Western terms for the rest of my life. American theatre often confuses energy with running around.[8]

Weidman did not go to Japan. However, he did do a tremendous amount of research and reading. He saw films, immersed himself in Kabuki, receiving much help from the Japan Society in New York. Eventually, Prince asked Hugh Wheeler near the end of the pre-production period to provide additional material for the book. Patricia Birch was set to do the choreography and, along with Aronson's set designs, Florence Klotz and Tharon Musser, respectively, were hired to do the costumes and lighting. Jonathan Tunick again did orchestrations and Paul Gemignani became musical director after the death of Hal Hastings (during the run of *A Little Night Music*). Prince once again had surrounded himself with his talented collaborative team.

There were problems casting the show because there wasn't enough of a work pool in the Asian community. The simple decision to try to gather an all-Asian cast for the show turned out to be, in Prince's words, "the hardest show I've cast."[9] Joanna Merlin, who heads Prince's casting department, contacted the Asian community and theatre groups, Asian newspapers and the State Department. "She followed one dancer through Europe by mail and chased a singer on tour with *Hair* across country by telephone."[10]

Eventually Prince and Merlin went to California and selected some of the actors there. Prince said:

There were probably more actors available on the West Coast than on the East Coast because there's a large Asian community there and because there are movies being made and a lot of television and they get to play the "yellow peril" every week, to make a living that way. We still were not able to find all the rest of the Asians we needed. Now, mind you, we found good actors— but we were looking for good actors who could sing and dance and that was hell. We did the best we could. We did pretty damn well, in fact. There were a number of paradoxes. We finally ran out of Asians and cast a Greek boy who pretended to be one-eighth Asian. We grabbed him.[11]

Most of the cast were Americans (American-born or naturalized Japanese). There were also Chinese, Hawaiians, Filipinos, Burmese and Koreans in the cast. Only one boy, Isao Sato, was actually from Japan. He had tried to audition for Prince and Sondheim when they were in Japan but could not get to them at their hotel. So he came to America and auditioned for the chorus call (also known as the open or non-Equity call) and got one of the leads in the show. Prince said, "We probably ruined his theatrical life because there simply is not that much employment."[12] There were finally 19 actors cast to play the 61 solo roles. Had there been more actors to choose among, the director would not have doubled up as much on the roles.

Mako, one of the leads, was born in the Orient but moved with his parents to this country a long time ago, spending most of his life in California. He had many theatre and television credits and was nominated for an Academy Award as best supporting actor in *The Sand Pebbles*. A third of the cast, however, were not experienced actors. Alvin Ing, an actor in *Pacific Overtures* who played a merchant, an American admiral, a delicately homicidal royal mother, and who was also president of Theatre for Asian-American Performing Artists, Inc., said:

> The Harold Prince office made a concerted effort to audition any Asian actors who wanted to audition, which is very fortunate for us. . . . It's so heartbreaking when they cast non-Asians in Asian roles . . . so when we have that kind of sincere effort I feel we should commend the producer, for it's been so seldom done.[13]

Prince recalled that, although much of the cast was Oriental, they were *totally* American in attitude, right down to their Adidas and blue jeans. He said:

> Most of our Asian actors were so American that they had little interest in learning about Asian traditions. However, as we rehearsed, they became fascinated with their theatrical antecedents, with the political history of their country as affected by ours. They began to prepare themselves for performance in the traditional Japanese way. You'd come in backstage a half hour before the show and there'd be thirty or forty "islands," each actor meditating. By the time *Pacific Overtures* closed a year later in California, they were enthusiastic Asian-Americans.[14]

There were some authentic Kabuki techniques utilized in *Pacific Overtures*. Easily recognizable upon entering the theatre was the long polished wood ramp or runway called the *hanamichi*, which allowed performers to make entrances and exits through the house. Actors glided back and forth across the stage—representing journeys. The brightly colored Kabuki-style stage curtain (*hikimaku*) replaced the customary Broadway brocade. The musical begins with the sharp percussive sounds from the trio of musicians onstage (*degatari*). The exaggerated wigs and the make-up—white foundation and penciled eyebrows and lips—project characters from heroic samurai to villainous lion. Female roles were played by males in keeping with Kabuki tradition, excepting the final scene, which depicts contemporary life. Still another Kabuki convention was the black-clad stagehands. Black symbolizes nonexistence; the stagehands, therefore, are invisible to a Japanese audience. The trio of onstage musicians used wood clappers and other percussive sound effects to underline the action. Finally, the use of a reciter in kneeling position with prompt book resting on a stand (*tayu*) follows Kabuki tradition.

According to the program notes in the *Playbill* for *Pacific Overtures,* the show, with some dramatic license, depicts historic incidents and characters accurately. The United States did dispatch Commodore Perry to Japan in 1853 to reopen commerce with that isolated country. The first act deals primarily with the old Japanese Empire, isolated and frightened by Perry's attempt at "pacific overtures." The title is a political euphemism coined by Perry in 1853. His diary recounts the historic display of American naval power that President Fillmore sent to forcibly persuade Japan to commence trade relations after 250 years of complete isolation. The threatening presence of our American warships gave Japan a shock which quickly propelled the feudal kingdom into the nineteenth century. The transformation is what *Pacific Overtures* is all about. The final scene of the play jumps to 1976 and the entire company, in modern dress, performs "Next" against a backdrop of neon and ads that might pass for Times Square. They sing and dance in a frenetic manner in celebration of Japan's progress. The Reciter closes the show with his comment, "There was a time when foreigners were not welcome here. But that was long ago. A hundred and twenty years. Welcome to Japan."

Boris Aronson, who was a gifted painter as well as designer, collected Japanese prints and toys. His passion for Eastern prints benefitted him in his work on *Pacific Overtures,* basing much of his set design on prints by Sharaku. "Designing the movable screen, the stylized trees, the brushstroke clouds," Aronson said, "was a coming together of all my personal interests."[15] The designer also collected Japanese kites (a large black kite is used on the opening curtain) and studied the way Japanese wrap things. Bamboo structures, for example, are held together by rattan or reeds. Aronson also studied Japanese fans and prints of Perry's warships. He said:

> The Japanese artist has a peculiar way of seeing things. For instance, the white backdrops in *Pacific Overtures* are the way in which the Japanese depict clouds. Since this is a play about issues and not about people and moods, Hal and I decided on white lighting. The white shows everything on stage. It has a crispness, a simplicity, a directness about it.[16]

The whiteness of the set presented Prince with a major problem, however. Lights bounded off the very light wooden traditional floor on the stage. He could never obtain a real blackout or a dark enough stage. "Generally," said Prince, "the shows I do are in a black box. This was in a whitish box. The minute it's in a white box it's impossible to get a decent blackout. And that frustrated the hell out of me."[17]

Although Aronson achieved the rice paper "look" in his sets, he was prohibited from using real rice paper because of New York City fire laws. He did, however, find a viable substitute. The keynote of his design was "space." A large playing area was usually made available to the actors, and screens were carried delicately on and off stage by company members during songs. Aronson never allowed the stage to become cluttered. The house was on platforms and elevated slightly above the general playing area, providing a multilevel set of visual interest, a Kabuki technique.

Aronson had devoted well over a year of thought and research to the development and execution of the design. He worked closely with Prince and was complimentary of the constant experimenting and looking for new concepts. He said, "Hal knows how to challenge me. He also challenges himself with each new production."[18]

The show was enhanced by Florence Klotz's 140 opulent and colorful costumes for ceremonial and everyday use. Klotz said, "It's the most complicated and challenging production with which I've been involved."[19] The costume designer made a trip to Japan to observe as much Kabuki and Noh as possible.

Sondheim finally found the musical style he wanted for *Pacific Overtures*. He wanted a style of both lyrics and music that didn't violate the spirit of Japanese theatre and at the same time was not pretentious or coy; he believes that is what ritualized theatre tends to promulgate. He spent a month researching Japanese music, discovering that the Japanese pen-

Pacific Overtures, 1976
The "Chrysanthemum Tea" scene.
(Photo © Martha Swope)

tatonic scale had a minor modal feeling and reminded him of the composer de Falla, whose work he likes very much. He began to imitate de Falla's music, taking the pentatonic scale and bunching the chords together until they resembled the Spanish guitar sound. He was then able to relate to it. It has a Western feeling and at the same time a feeling of the East. Having seldom written in minor keys, he was quite excited to try.

Finding the lyric style was less difficult than Sondheim thought it would be. He described it as

> a kind of translator-ese, parable sentences, very simple language with very simple subject-predicate structures, and very little in the way of rhyme. The only heavily rhymed song in the show is the admiral's song, which is all about foreign powers. . . . The show starts in the middle of the nineteenth century, when the Americans came in, and then it's about the Americanization of Japan. I decided that as the score went on it would get a little closer to Broadway, until finally it would become an industrial show. We were very heavily criticized for this. In fact *Variety* which didn't like it, said, "the last number looks like nothing so much as an industrial show." I took it as a high compliment.[20]

Since Japanese music doesn't have any chords, Sondheim had to invent a way to make a "Japanese" chord which would retain the Eastern sound. The composer also blended Japanese *haiku* poetry into his lyrics, which was "a lot of fun for the puzzle-nut and amateur mathematician who communicates with equal facility in the three principal languages, words, music, and numbers."[21]

Patricia Birch spent her hours preparing for the musical by looking at film, working with Kabuki people and Haruki Fujimoto, her Kabuki assistant on the show, and learning to use her fan. She spent hours learning symbolic hand language, learning folk dances and rhythm technique. She also realized that her early training with Martha Graham had taught her much of the basics of Japanese dance movement. It was Prince's idea to have the Lion Dance at the end of act 1 and Birch at first felt it was a rough assignment. However, her Japanese assistant helped her. She created the image for the number, which was General MacArthur's slogan "I will return." Birch said:

> I stuck everything in there from cakewalks, etc. It was half Americanized and half Lion Dance and half bravura and half cocky American, you know. I took the vernacular of the Japanese dance and turned it in my own direction. In that case Prince was continually supportive. He loved where I was

going. And the thing Hal always does with me is stop me from ripping up everything I do. I'll get something to a point where it's really working and then at that stage, I rework maybe a little too much. . . . And he was wonderful about that—telling me to go home, or stop, quit, stop![22]

Prince remembers that he had great "fun directing the show. . . . I don't remember being troubled by anything much. All of it was joyful. And then it opened in Boston (on 11 November 1975) and almost none of it worked. Two percent off here, off for clarity, off, off, off. But none of it totally. And none of it so that it was dangerous. Nevertheless, we woke up the day after the opening of the show, which we were very proud of, and read a fistful of terrible reviews."[23] Weidman remembered that Kevin Kelly disliked the show intensely. He said it was too long and needed a great deal of work. In fact, he hated it.[24] Prince continued:

It played to empty houses. We fixed everything piece by piece by piece. It was an act of professionalism. We never lost the inspiration we had. Each element was repeated in some detail, so that by the time that we got to New York, it was the same blamed show we always thought we had, but this time it worked.[25]

They next took the show to Washington, where it opened on 4 December 1975 to very good critical reception. A series of thirteen previews began in New York on 12 December. Prince related what happened during the early New York preview performances:

On the first or second preview of the show in New York, a mouse, believe it or not, dislodged plaster over the standing room section of the theatre in a light fixture (a chandelier). You heard the mouse, but you didn't know what it was. Suddenly you heard rumbling and then plaster started to tumble down on the people who were standing in the back, very little bits of plaster, but enough to suggest that something was going to happen. And somebody screamed BOMB. And the audience emptied the theatre. At another performance somebody actually phoned in a bomb threat. It was very nervous making. . . . But the show itself was in shape for New York.[26]

Pacific Overtures opened on Broadway at the Winter Garden Theatre on 11 January 1976 to mixed notices. The critics who were negative about the show cited narrative structure and balance and the jolting effect of the finale. They claimed that the play was more of a lecture than entertainment. Those who raved about the show called it a significant achievement in the evolution of the Broadway musical and a thought-provoking production for the serious theatregoer. Michael Feingold in the *Village Voice* said, "The result is far from being a fully consistent, fully satisfactory musical theatre piece—but I would hate to have missed it."[27]

Douglas Watt didn't like the show at all. He called it a "mish-mash" and "a sluggish musical."[28] He went on to say that the musical was "as thin and insubstantial as the painted screen used for scenery. Indeed, the frills are everything in a prevailingly dull, semi-documentary entertainment about the corrupting influence of Western civilization on Asian culture."[29]

Walter Kerr raised questions about the lack of excitement and the plausibility of doing the story from the point of view of the Japanese.

> No amount of performing, or incidental charm, can salvage *Pacific Overtures*. The occasion is essentially dull and immobile because we are never properly placed in it, drawn neither East nor West, given no specific emotional or cultural bearings. The evening is a Japanese artifact with a stamp on the back of it that says "Made in America." And perhaps turnabout is fair play. But it does raise a basic question, for us if not for the Japanese. Why tell their story their way, when they'd do it better?[30]

Hobe Morrison in *Variety* felt that the finale, which attempts to show modernized Japan, looked like an annual Milliken industrial show.[31] Weidman said that the ending had been tried a number of ways. One idea they had was to use puppets and other Japanese theatre devices to depict what had happened to Japan during the past 100 years instead of jump-cutting to the present. However, the idea was abandoned during rehearsals. It was felt by the collaborators that it wasn't necessary to build up to the end result as the audience would be ahead of them. Because it was like an epilogue it was possible to change it and not have it affect what preceded it. It was not an accident, however, that the finale seemed like an industrial show or something out of *Grease*. Weidman said, "It really was our intention. . . . We wanted to show the elegance of this culture which we had all tried to indicate all evening turned into something very different. And if it felt like it had turned into a number from *Grease,* Amen!"[32]

Prince agreed that the end of the show was a problem:

> We didn't have the money to destroy the traditional Kabuki environment and replace it with the Ginza, with neon signs and transluxes. For the last number to have really worked, some coup de theatre (as in *Follies*) was required. But with *Follies* we knew beforehand what the last segment would

be and Boris was able to design the total production keeping that in mind. *Pacific Overtures*'s last number was written too late and though I liked it, it wasn't helped by a bare Kabuki-like stage. We should have gone Western— tastelessly Western.[33]

Positive reviews cited the show for its beauty, and the creators for attempting such a serious and ambitious production. Clive Barnes, however, put a damper on things when he wrote in the *New York Times*:

There are generic and stylistic discrepancies in the musical that are not easily overlooked—but the attempt is so bold and the achievement so fascinating, that its obvious faults demand to be overlooked. It tries to soar—sometimes it only floats, sometimes it actually sinks—but it tries to soar. And the music and lyrics are as pretty and as well-formed as a bonsai tree. *Pacific Overtures* is very, very different.[34]

Prince's reaction to the Barnes review was:

The most seriously damaging review was Clive Barnes'. He didn't get the show, but he never gets anything. He didn't get *Follies*. He didn't get *Company*. When his review of *Pacific Overtures* came out I wrote him a letter. I'd never done it before and I've never done it since. I said, "You've just closed the show and you will regret it someday," and I sent it over by messenger. Well, of course, they never regret these things. But my heart was in this show. It's not the kind of show you do to make money.[35]

Edwin Wilson in the *Wall Street Journal* felt that "some sections of *Pacific Overtures* are hauntingly beautiful, both visually and vocally."[36] Martin Gottfried agreed that the show was physically gorgeous, and said,

At its core is an amazing parallel between Boris Aronson's gorgeous settings and Prince's staging. . . . Prince presented an exquisite, enchanting, touching, intelligent and altogether remarkable work of theatre art. Prince is not merely the most important man in the modern American musical theatre. He is a man who refuses to repeat himself. He will move, almost contrarily, from the chilly brilliance of *Company* to the bitter grandeur of *Follies*. If there is anything that can be expected of him, it is the unexpected.[37]

Howard Kissel called the show "the most original, the most profound, the most theatrically ambitious of the Prince-Sondheim collaborations. It is also, for this viewer, the production in which the team that sets Broadway's highest standards most fully meets the astonishing objectives they set themselves."[38]

Pacific Overtures was a commercial failure. It ran six months in New York, closing on 27 June 1976 after 193 performances, and lost a great deal of money (its entire $650,000 investment). Prince, who does not invest in his own shows as a rule, did so with *Pacific Overtures* when it ran out of capital. When it failed, Prince felt that he would not produce again for a while because he would now have to look for investors and this is something he does not enjoy. Prince felt that a basic problem with the production was that it was too much to ask of an audience, explaining, "the show was a case of a lot of elements which were too exotic for the audience to assimilate. The style was very unfamiliar. But this didn't occur to me until we closed. We ran six months here and six months in California where there is an Asian population. . . . But it was all worth it."[39]

Prince, speaking about the project in 1984, said *Overtures* was more difficult to do than any he had done other than *Merrily We Roll Along*, which he produced and directed in 1981. He felt that the storyteller's sequence was too long and that some of his pauses were too long. Although the director thought he demanded too much of an audience which hadn't been exposed to Asian theatre, he loved the show and felt it worked very well for the most part. He said, "Certain things were extraordinary, like the 'Bowler Hat' number and 'Someone in a Tree.' It was full of good stuff."[40]

Weidman, also looking back on the show, said that he was very satisfied with the final production.

> I think we tried to do something unique and it was that if nothing else. . . . It seemed to me that if there was any problem at the center of the show it was that we had not been totally successful in integrating two different approaches to the storytelling process. One was the story of two particular Japanese men and what happened to them as a result of the arrival of the Americans. Around that, surrounding that and intertwined with that was a great deal of material which was not extraneous to that story, because it all dealt with the process which was affecting these two men but which was not related to their story in any direct plot sense. I was satisfied with the balance that we struck between those two elements but I have sometimes asked myself if a decision to tip more in one direction or the other might not have made the show accessible to more people.[41]

RCA Victor put out the original cast album soon after the show opened. A videotape was made of a performance from the stage of the Winter Garden Theatre for TV presentation in Japan. It was the first telecast of an American stage musical in that country.

Although the musical was not a commercial success, it was considered by many to be an artistic one. It was awarded two Tonys for scenic and costume design, and named best musical of the 1975–76 season by the New York Drama Critics' Circle. In 1982, Prince attempted to do the show at the Mermaid Theatre in London, streamlining everything, but was unable to get it financed and the project was dropped.

Martin Gottfried summed up Prince's role in the creation of *Pacific Overtures*:

> The writing of its book marked the most advanced use of libretto the Broadway musical had yet achieved. There had never been so theatrically conceived a musical script. It may seem unfair to credit it to Prince rather than Wheeler or Weidman, as it may seem unfair to credit him with the books of *Cabaret* or *Company,* but even if Prince never wrote a word in shaping and dominating these scripts he was most responsible for them. Inherent in the scripts of Prince's shows are their movement and their textual content, their entire mode of presentation.[42]

On 25 October 1984 the Shubert Organization in association with Elizabeth McCann and Nelle Nugent presented a revival of *Pacific Overtures* at the Off-Broadway Promenade Theatre on Manhattan's Upper West Side. Directed by Fran Soeder, who had worked as a production assistant on Prince's 1979 musical *Sweeney Todd,* the revival did not involve Hal Prince. Director Soeder is quoted by Craig Zadan as saying, "There were theories that the size of the original production overwhelmed the material. I only remember seeing the original show that Hal created and being in a state of wonderment. I think it was a breathtaking show on every level."[43]

Critics tended to compare the revival with the original, generally feeling that the smaller-scaled production worked better for the piece although it was agreed that *Pacific Overtures* was still not the general musical theatre audience's "cup of tea." Prince was very upset when the Off-Broadway production was praised for its modesty, saying,

> That's not what Kabuki is. The idea was to do Kabuki. It's bold painting— it's not subtle theater. I conscientiously didn't see the other production. I knew that it was very much influenced by my direction . . . the whole way

it was directed was mine. A popular thing to say is that the original show was overproduced by Boris and me. That's not true.[44]

Choreographer Pat Birch tended to agree with Prince. She said, "It was our show. I saw it and I thought, well, the structure was exactly the same but it was on a smaller stage. I got very angry about it. . . . Hal was livid. I took a look at it and I said, wait a second. Nobody has taken this and reconceptualized it. It was Hal's concept and my concept."[45] The revised *Pacific Overtures* lost its entire investment of nearly half a million dollars and closed on 27 January 1985 after 109 performances—84 performances fewer than the original.

AN EBB OF THE TIDE

Side by Side by Sondheim

Having carried the responsibility of being both director and producer or simply director during the past few years, Hal Prince returned to the role of producer for his next project, the American production of *Side by Side by Sondheim.*

The genesis of the original London production began when David Kernan, who played Count Carl-Magnus Malcolm in the London production of *A Little Night Music,* decided to produce a Sunday concert of Sondheim songs. He enlisted Ned Sherrin, who had once produced the BBC television show *That Was the Week That Was,* to put the piece together. There had been in London for a few years prior to Kernan's idea a kind of small hybrid musical revue built around a theatrical composer, with lots of songs and a little patter. The shows were created at the Mermaid Theatre and then moved to larger West End houses. The series began in 1972 with a Noel Coward show (*Cowardy Custard*), and continued in 1974 with a Cole Porter evening.

Kernan and Sherrin were joined by Millicent Martin, who was well known to English audiences for her starring roles in musicals and for the impact she had had as a regular on the aforementioned *That Was the Week That Was,* and by Julia McKenzie, who had appeared in the London production of *Company.*

The concert led to a production at the 200-seat Mermaid Theatre at a cost of £6,000 or about $10,000. Opening on 4 May 1976 the show quickly became one of the most popular entertainments in London and was narrowly beaten by *A Chorus Line* in a critics' poll for best musical. About two months after the opening, the show moved to the 400-seat Wyndham Theatre, where it again became a sell-out.

Although the response was almost all favorable in London for this cabaret-style musical, Benedict Nightingale, writing in the *New Statesman,* felt that Sondheim was a far better lyricist than composer, a complaint that has been lodged against Sondheim's work from time to time during his career.[1]

Prince, who had not produced the show in London, decided to bring *Side by Side* to Broadway as his first musical import. "The only reason why I did that was it was a natural. It was our material ... that we worked on together ... so it seemed I should have something to do with it," said Prince.[2] He capitalized the show at $250,000 and presented it by arrangement with the Incomes Company, which is the name the original group of creator-performers gave themselves. The name is taken from a line in the title song of *Company* ("Phone rings, door chimes, in comes company!"). The Incomes Company shared in the profits and an item in the *New York Post* said it was "very rare in the theatre that performers share in the profits."[3]

A protest from the Actors Equity membership ensued over the scheduled appearance of four English performers. American performers felt that the English singer-actors were not unique talents or personalities and, since all the songs were American, the material might be performed as well or better by Americans. The union's Alien Committee, however, was persuaded by Prince to okay a waiver of the rules, their decision based on the fact that the show had been conceived and arranged by the performers themselves.[4]

Side by Side by Sondheim opened in New York at the Music Box Theatre on 18 April 1977 after five preview performances. There were 29 songs presented in the show, plus a medley of perhaps a dozen more, including numbers dropped from Sondheim shows during either rehearsals or out-of-town tryouts. The stage was bare except for two pianos and four stools for the singers, who "go at their work with a sense of love and style that positively glows," according to Alan Rich in *New York* magazine.[5] At the end of the show, vertical rows of lightbulbs were used in a spectacular light show. Sherrin, an articulate, Oxford-educated lawyer, used topical jokes that seemed to be plucked from the news of the day as he introduced the various Sondheim songs and narrated the production. Sherrin said, "What I try to do is read the newspapers daily and add something different every night."[6]

Martin Gottfried, a great Prince and Sondheim fan, was unhappy about the show. He found it difficult to understand the use of an English cast for the American composer. He additionally was unhappy with Sherrin's role as narrator. He felt that the narrator's stories were trivial, familiar and obsequious. Gottfried felt that Sherrin's "supercilious manner and campy attitude turn the whole performance slantwise."[7] Gottfried went on to say in a follow-up story that "Sherrin, who also directed the production, is so sycophantic toward Sondheim that he appears to be the glib priest for a cult and I hate to see Sondheim or the musical theatre subverted that way."[8]

The show was billed as "a musical entertainment" and received generally favorable reviews from the New York critics. Douglas Watt said that Sondheim's "cleverness, skill and daring have never been accorded the warmth of expression given them by these smiling strangers [the opening night audience]."[9]

Edwin Wilson in the *Wall Street Journal* felt that *Side by Side* had established the right format for a showcase of Sondheim's work. He said, "They have the right sensibility and have found just the right key to presenting his material."[10] Wilson also liked the grouping of songs to point up themes which run through Sondheim's work, such as "an ironic, questioning view of marriage, a fondness for reworking older musical forms, etc."[11]

RCA Records repackaged the British cast album and sold it in the United States. After many months, on 11 November 1977 a new and American cast replaced the English performers. Hermione Gingold took on the narrator's role, and Nancy Dussault, Larry Kert and Georgia Brown sang the Sondheim songs. On 22 February 1978 *Side by Side* moved to the Morosco Theatre. Near the end of the run, the narrator's role was taken over by Burr Tillstrom and his puppets, Kukla and Ollie, who had played the show successfully in their native Chicago. The show had a Broadway run of 384 performances. Prince said, "It turned out to pay off—but not make any money for anybody to speak of."[12]

Some of My Best Friends

Producers Arthur Whitelaw, Jack Schlissel and Leonard Soloway were about to produce a new comedy called *Some of My Best Friends* by Stanley Hart, who had co-written *The Mad Show* with Larry Siegel, a show which had run for two years Off-Broadway in 1966 and 1967. The producers sent the script to Hal Prince, inviting him to direct. Prince agreed, finding the play "ingenious and hilarious."[13]

Prince worked with the author on rewriting the comedy about a former business executive who, several years prior to the time of the play, had suffered a nervous breakdown and who has mellowed and talks only to creatures other than adult humans: a baby, an Afghan hound, a tree. He lives with these unlikely friends in a garret where he enjoys painting. Prince said that working with the author was "fun to do, to work up to rehearsal."[14]

Rehearsals were scheduled for 12 September 1977, with an out-of-town tryout planned for the first two weeks of October in Philadelphia. A week of previews in New York were to begin on 18 October and the Broadway premiere was set for the week of 24 October.

Prince had no problems casting the comedy, hiring Ted Knight for the leading role of Andrew Mumford. Prince feels Knight's performance in the play was "wonderful."[15] Knight had played the egomaniacal news anchorman on the *Mary Tyler Moore Show* on television for seven years and was anxious to become successful on Broadway. He said:

> You could say Broadway is a tonic. I know I'm gambling. But playing Ted Baxter finally bored me. I was the pompous ass, the butt of all jokes. And I couldn't betray the character by making jokes about the others. I'm a man as well as an actor. That image was rough on my ego, on my emotions. . . . Broadway is still the bastion of real prestige for an actor. The Big Apple really counts.[16]

Others in the cast included Alice Drummond as Dorothy, the hero's wife, and Bob Balaban as Lawrence, his son. Trish Hawkins and Gavin Reed were cast in secondary roles and a tree named Irving Buxbaum was played by Lee Wallace.

Prince discussed the rehearsal period and the aftermath.

> I found the rehearsal period more fun than anything. I just went into rehearsal every day and laughed myself silly. I never had so much fun. I started casting the touring company productions. I was so sure it would be the biggest and most popular success . . . I showed it to people in a rehearsal hall (we worked at the Minskoff). I'd go home at the end of a workday with Ruth Mitchell, who is my assistant, and say, "This is the surest thing, isn't it? I mean we're not crazy are we? This is just hilarious." . . . And then we put it in front of an audience in a theatre and it didn't work for one minute. . . . We were in shock.[17]

Before leaving for Philadelphia, Prince did a performance for a group of invited actors without scenery and costumes and he felt it also worked then. He said, "It was only once it got into a theatre with proper scenery and costumes and a set that we lost it. But we *totally* lost it.... It didn't remotely work."[18]

The comedy opened in Philadelphia on 11 October 1977 at the Walnut Theatre, and was blasted by all the critics. Jonathan Takiff for the *Philadelphia Daily News* said that "most fantasy yarns come off seeming pat, superficial and hodgepodgey, fine for youngsters but not worth an adult's attention and serious consideration. And that is the regrettable reality of Stanley Hart's new comedy, *Some of My Best Friends*."[19] *Variety,* in its out-of-town review, said of the show, "Ted Knight is believable as the supernaturally endowed hero.... Harold Prince's staging appears to be inventive."[20] Bob Sokolsky, the entertainment editor of the *Philadelphia Evening Bulletin,* felt both Knight and Prince did commendable jobs coping with the major problem, a poor script.[21]

Prince found it difficult to visualize a dog and a plant as played by actors.

> I don't know what I did wrong, but it didn't work and I didn't know why it didn't work. *Harvey* worked. *Harvey* originally had a rabbit on stage. But they eliminated the rabbit, you didn't see him. On the other hand, I could not have eliminated the plant and the dog, because they worked ... they were hallucinations. But they had so much dialogue. Harvey had no dialogue you see.[22]

Some of My Best Friends opened at the Longacre Theatre on Broadway on 25 October 1977 and the reviews were as negative as those in Philadelphia. Richard Eder in the *New York Times* described the plot and said, "All this may sound better than it is. *Friends* seems to be a notion that struggled to become a play and failed, lacking as it does, density, characters, conflict or one single line that is either witty or graceful."[23]

Martin Gottfried wondered what Prince was doing at the helm of this vehicle. He said, "I don't doubt that Prince is wondering himself.... A director of not inconsiderable talent, responsible for many great musicals and several earnest engagements with classic plays, Prince has now lent himself to somewhat less than a professional play."[24] The show closed on 29 October 1977 after seven performances and eight previews.

Prince has said that they made a mistake with the set—too serious and dour.

> The designer, Eugene Lee, with whom I'd had terrific success, thought it was about a crazy man and so the set should look like a hospital room. He

was wrong. It shouldn't have, but that was an additional depressant. But I went along with it and insofar as I'm the editor, I'm at fault.[25]

Prince, however, learned an important lesson from his experience with *Some of My Best Friends*: "I learned that there is no correlation between the pleasure I get doing what I do and my creativity. I mean, I had not a hell of a lot of fun doing *Sweeney Todd* [a musical Prince would do in 1979] and I know I did first-rate work. I had a ball doing *Some of My Best Friends* and obviously my work wasn't first-rate."[26]

Although the failure of the comedy was a disappointment for Prince, he was soon busy on a new project, directing a musical called *On the Twentieth Century*. A little over three months later, he would be opening this major musical. And again, he would direct, not produce. True to form, there would be little time or inclination to ponder a failure.

BACK ON BOARD:
On the Twentieth Century

The musical *On the Twentieth Century* is based on the 1932 Ben Hecht-Charles MacArthur play *Twentieth Century*. Set on the famous 1930s train which covered the distance between New York and Chicago in sixteen hours, the 20th Century Limited, the musical project began when writers Betty Comden and Adolph Green and composer Cy Coleman decided they wanted to do a show together. In the mid-seventies they had written a few numbers for an Off-Broadway workshop revue directed by Green's wife, Phyllis Newman, at the American Place Theatre. They had resolved to do a full-length show as soon as they finished the revue. Green remembered their search for a project:

> After some months of digging for an original story and coming up with nothing but frustration and blank paper, we decided to turn a silk purse into what we hoped would be another kind of silk purse. We decided to make a musical of the classic 1932 American stage comedy, *Twentieth Century*, by Ben Hecht and Charles MacArthur (which in turn had been derived from an earlier play by Bruce Mulholland).[1]

It was a struggle to obtain the rights, but once they were acquired, the writers and composer reread the play. They were convinced that, although it was quite funny, it would be very difficult to make into a musical. It was verbose and contained many subsidiary characters. In addition, Green said, "The frame of association was that of 1930s Chicago newspapermen steeped in the then all-pervasive imagery and cynicism of H. L. Mencken. Also, for God's sake, we were stuck on a train. All around us, people were exclaiming, 'What a great idea! Making *Twentieth Century* into a musical!!!' Inside us, we heard the constantly nagging query that asked simply, 'How?' "[2] In addition, they were not permitted by Columbia Pictures to adapt anything from the famous 1934 movie version of the play which had starred John Barrymore and Carole Lombard. The creators then decided to create their own fourth entity.

They streamlined the story of the glamorous and famous stage and screen star, Lily Garland, who is at odds with a once-big-time Broadway director, Oscar Jaffee, during the overnight train ride from Chicago to New York. Jaffee, a theatrical has-been, is desperate to make a comeback by winning over Lily, his former star and mistress. What stands in his way is her new lover, the young and handsome Bruce Granit. The plot is fraught with farcical situations and the possibility of a renewed romance between the protagonists.

In their attempts to tighten the book, the writers completely eliminated two Oberammergau actors from the original play. They were refugees from a lost company of the *Passion Play*. Comden and Green recall:

> We eliminated them completely, but we still needed something of a religious nature to provide Oscar with the inspiration for the project he hopes Lily will agree to star in—the Passion of Mary Magdalene. We did that by building up the character of another passenger on the train, a religious fanatic who goes around putting up stickers that say, "Repent, for the time is at hand." We also decided to make the character a woman—it's a man in the play— because there are so few women in the original story. It became the role Imogene Coca plays.[3]

Although the writers cut much, they also added a few things, including a new character: the young, dashing and good-looking leading man named Bruce Granit, who is Lily's current love interest.

With two larger-than-life leading characters—Lily Garland and Oscar Jaffee, extravagant, egomaniacal giants of the theatre—the writers searched for the right musical style. They did not want to write a thirties musical, nor did they wish to use rock or any other contemporary sound. They began thinking of the show as an overblown bravura musical. Comden and Green explained:

> One day, working with Cy [Coleman], we improvised a musical sequence that was highly flamboyant, verging on the operatic. We laughed, dismissed it

as "too much," and then suddenly realized that it was really the way Oscar and Lily should sound. In fact, it was the way the entire show should sound. We felt we had the key.[4]

The authors do not suggest that they wrote *On the Twentieth Century* as an opera. However, they did use certain operatic elements to create what they hoped would be an "irreverent, extravagant musical comedy."[5] When Coleman experimented with the overture in the style of Rossini, they left it that way. The creators of the show worked on the musical for over a year, taking time out for Coleman to write *I Love My Wife* and Comden and Green to perform in their own one-woman, one-man show, *A Party*.

About this time, Prince entered the planning stage. It was much later than usual for him to begin work on a show, but Prince had had some bad years. He had been terribly dismayed that *Pacific Overtures* had not had a longer run. He had also lost some of his own money needed for it to open on Broadway because of the poor reception in Boston. The bad reviews there created losses on the show. Prince explained:

> We ran out of money so I had to use my own in order to get it to Broadway. When it did, the show represented not only something we were very proud of, but something that lost me my shirt. I was worried about being able to keep my office open. I had not saved a great deal of money over the years. I was reputed to have a lot more than I did have. And so I shopped around for assignments. And the first thing that came up was the movie of *A Little Night Music*. I took that to make money. I should have known better. Every time I take something to make money, it double-crosses me. A year and a half later *On the Twentieth Century* was offered.[6]

The producers of the musical, Cy Feuer and Ernie Martin, as well as writers Comden, Green and Coleman, approached Prince to direct. He listened, thinking the idea of doing all the numbers in a kind of chamber opera fashion a good one. Prince recalled, "In fact, they were *not* all chamber opera pieces. I think that was its flaw. But I thought the work was ingenious. I thought it was intelligent fun and I needed a job. So I accepted."[7]

The style of the show represented a change for the director. Known for his sophisticated, sardonic collaborations with Sondheim, Prince was taking an excursion into something different. It was an up-beat show (with farcical scenes) intended to make people feel good. The director said, "It's

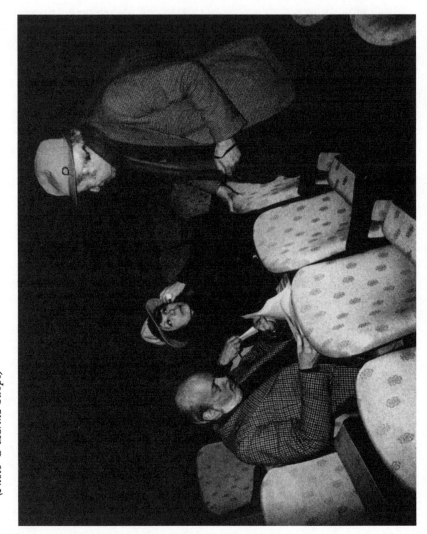

On the Twentieth Century, 1978
Harold Prince confers with collaborators Betty Comden and Adolph Green during rehearsals
for the musical.
(Photo © Martha Swope)

nice to work on something that's up!''[8] Prince did, however, insist on some rewrites after he began directing the musical. But basically, the material was in hand. He had to get it designed properly, cast properly, and staged. Comden and Green remembered that Prince made important contributions to the creation of the piece.

> Hal sharpened and focused the shape of our book and censored any lyric that might be considered filler. Hal also has a marvelous visual sense. Often, when we wrote scenes, we were never quite sure of how they could be made to happen onstage. We would just write them down in the blind faith that somebody would see how they could be done. Hal worked closely with our scenic designer, Robin Wagner, on the visual effects involving the train, which are quite spectacular. It was also his idea to use train personnel as a kind of connective tissue between scenes.[9]

Feuer and Martin very much wanted Alfred Drake to play the lead. Prince felt he was wrong for the part. Instead, he cast John Cullum, who had won the 1975 Tony Award as best musical actor for his performance in *Shenandoah*. Cullum had also starred in *On a Clear Day You Can See Forever* and *Man of La Mancha*. Because of the tensions that resulted from cast changes, Feuer and Martin left the show and another group of producers came in: Producer's Circle 2, Inc., Robert Fryer, Mary Lea Johnson, James Cresson, Martin Richards, in association with Joseph Harris, and Ira Bernstein.

Comden and Green said that they agreed on John Cullum for the Oscar Jaffee role because there was ''big'' singing in the show. Cullum played the role as a John Barrymore-type ''ham.'' In an interview, Cullum said he wanted a cross between Adolph Menjou, George Brent, Clark Gable and Gilbert Roland. The character Jaffee was an extravagant person in every way. Cullum said,

> I think the character lends itself to zaniness, and I love zany, crazy characters. Hal Prince, the director, and I talked over the role often, and we both felt I could go even further than the script. I don't think it would be very interesting if I played it straight. After all, his lines are not that inherently witty, so you've got to get across that beneath all that drive of his, he's covering up something, and that something is his vulnerability.[10]

Madeline Kahn, who was cast as Lily, ''in addition to being a comedienne, is a trained opera singer.''[11] Kahn, best known for her roles in such films as *What's Up, Doc?, Blazing Saddles* and *Paper Moon,* had also appeared on Broadway in *New Faces of 1968.*

Prince was very pleased with finding Kevin Kline for the role of Bruce Granit. Kline was a founding member of John Houseman's Acting Company, and had appeared on Broadway and on tour in many of the company's productions. He had played Jamie Lockhart in the original Broadway production of *The Robber Bridegroom.* Kline auditioned for *Twentieth Century* in costume. He had never done that before but he wanted the role so badly that he slicked down his hair 1930s-style, and wore an ascot, baggy pants and a white jacket. After his first audition, he was told to come back dressed exactly the same way to audition for Prince, and the next day he was offered the part. Prince said of Kline's work in *Twentieth Century,* "He was very contributive. We built up that part in rehearsal and I thought it was a very strong point."[12]

Kline credited Prince with having shaped his performance into something notable: "Hal created a wonderful climate to work in. . . . He always gave the actors a chance to explore their impulses, so that in a very real way the style of the show evolved organically from all of us. He would tell us what was good and what was bad, and helped to give form to the good things."[13] As an example, Kline cited a bit of business for which he invariably got a tremendous hand from the audience—the scene in which Bruce Granit is literally swept off his feet when Lily bursts into her Pullman compartment. "Mr. Kline manages to ricochet from wall to wall like a rag doll in a slow-motion ballet," said Robert Berkvist in the *New York Times.*[14] The idea to stage it in this way came about one day at rehearsal when Lily burst into the compartment and Kline decided on the spur of the moment to throw himself around. Prince liked it and told the actor to keep bouncing, and then helped him to refine the scene. "That's what I mean about him," said Kline. "He let us be silly. Nothing was too outrageous and so we tried anything. He'd either say 'Great, keep it!' or he'd turn thumbs down. He'd never intimidate you."[15]

Judy Kaye, who played the role of Agnes, was a singer-actress whom Prince had seen in California when he was auditioning for the national company of *Company.* He didn't use her then, but remembered her. When he got ready to do *On the Twentieth Century,* he asked his office to "get hold of that girl, she's so talented." The only mistake, said Prince, "is that I should have gotten hold of her to do the lead originally and the show would have been a success. I mean more than it was. It ran a year and a half or something. It would have run on and made a lot of money and all the rest of it, if we hadn't got into the Madeline Kahn 'thing.'"[16]

On the Twentieth Century, 1978
George Lee Andrews, Kevin Kline, and Madeline Kahn.
(Photo © Martha Swope)

The Kahn "thing" was the conflict that arose between Prince and the other collaborators and the leading lady, and which eventually led to Kahn being replaced by Kaye. Kahn played the role less than eleven weeks and she often missed performances. When Kaye took over in April of 1978, the official reason given for the replacement was that Kahn wanted to play six performances a week and that this was not agreeable to the management. Unofficially, the word was that Kahn had personal problems that kept her off the stage more than she was on.[17] Prince describes the episode as destructive.

> She's [Kahn] a talented girl. She was inventive surely, but her effects were small, not big enough for the theatre. Kline and Cullum were big performers and it's a bold farce. One of the reasons I undertook the show was that it was new territory for me. Years before I had directed *The Matchmaker* which has farcical elements, but I'd done nothing like it since. I wanted to know whether I had the necessary invention. I did. I greatly enjoyed creating slapstick comic business with Kevin and John. Madeline, though detailed and intelligent, resisted commanding the energy you need to play physical comedy eight performances a week. On Broadway opening night she finally gave the performance we'd been working towards. I ran backstage after the curtain call, "You see, you can do it!" I assumed that the reason she hadn't done it up to then was fear. "You see you can do it. You did it." And she looked into her makeup mirror at me and replied, "I hope you don't think I'm going to be able to do that every night." My heart sank. We were dead. I waited for the day (or night) when she didn't show up for a performance. When that happened, Judy Kaye went on and knocked the audience out. But then Madeline Kahn returned . . . and left . . . and returned . . . and left. And it got extremely confusing for people. It took some time before she could be persuaded to leave. It was too late. It hurt the show. If that show had opened with Judy Kaye, I believe it would have run a few seasons. I have read quite a bit about my resistance to stars and truthfully I don't feel the way I'm reputed to feel about them—not if they're Angela Lansbury. In the old days Ethel Merman and Mary Martin didn't miss a performance. The *New York Times* had thousands of words to say on that subject just a few weeks ago.[18]

For many of the reviewers, the hit of the musical was set designer Robin Wagner's enormously effective re-creation of the famous Twentieth Century train. Wagner claimed to have worked closely with Prince, utilizing the director's suggestion that the set take the place of choreography. The gleaming Art Deco full-scale mock-up of the famous train cost $196,500. It excited audiences as it surged onto the stage at each performance and then zoomed away again. It could assemble and disassemble into various configurations and the audience was shown its silvery exteriors and its posh interiors. In a *New York Times* article entitled "On Broadway, the Spectacle's the Thing," Geoffrey Holder suggested that the theatre needed spectacle.[19] If that was the case, *On the Twentieth Century* was probably the most lavish spectacle on Broadway at the time. Richard Eder of the *Times* said:

> The train itself, with its art deco fittings, all silver and cream-color, and its constant movement, is one of the more spectacular achievements of the production. Mr. Wagner manages all kinds of extraordinary things; he produces compartments, aisles, and a sense of the night passing by outside.... Mostly we are inside the train, but at a moment's notice we are on the platform looking in, or the engine is bearing down on us. Mr. Wagner even manages a motion-picture-like effect of seeming to alternate closeups of the train with medium and long shots in quick succession. It is a matter of sliding flats in and out and swiveling things, but it looks like plain magic.[20]

Prince had not stepped out of character. It was clear that he felt that content dictates form and that this show demanded glamour and spectacle. The furs, satin negligees and train sets cost a fortune (the show was capitalized at $1,064,000), but Prince felt that the script and its concept warranted that type of treatment. Prince disapproves of spectacle for its own sake, but if the show calls for it there is reason to do it as spectacularly as can be afforded. (Many years later, he would employ spectacular effects in *The Phantom of the Opera*, a show that clearly demands this approach. Michael Billington, theatre critic for Britain's *Guardian*, said, "*Phantom* is intelligent spectacle and necessary spectacle.")[21]

In spite of the fact that *Twentieth Century* offered Prince the opportunity to direct farce, he continued to pursue a more serious theatre. He said,

> During the Nixon years, I couldn't muster the joy to do a musical like *Twentieth Century*. I'm not one who says, "Life is so hard that when I go to the theater, I go to be entertained." When life is hard, I go to the theater to be pricked or to engage in controversy or to talk back. Theater, I think, is probably still headed right where it has been headed for years, and that is toward simpler, more imaginative forms. Black velour is still the most effective thing in the theatre—it gives free rein to the audience to use its imagination. Theatre is about a black box and some shafts of light and the audience using its imagination in collaboration with the director and the actors and the writers and I think that's what it will continue being.[22]

On the Twentieth Century began its four-week out-of-town tryout at Boston's Colonial Theatre on 7 January 1978. The *Variety* critic F. Snyder felt that the show had all the ingredients of a Broadway hit. He suggested, however, that some revisions and cuts were needed in addition to simplifying the elaborate physical production. Snyder liked the cast and noted that Imogene Coca was a "standout" in the role of the religious eccentric and with her number "Repent." Prince's direction, he said, "seems well-paced without being hurried amid the elaborate scenic and technical effects."[23]

The musical opened on Broadway on 20 February 1978 at the St. James Theatre. The critics cited the sets and the train itself as the star of the show. Richard Eder of the *Times* said the show was a welcome return to musical "comedy." He called it

> funny, elegant and totally cheerful. Its elegance is not that of a perfectly integrated and organized piece of musical theatre. It has rough spots, flat spots and an energy that occasionally ebbs, leaving the cast and the director to re-group their energies for the next assault. . . . But the elegance is there, nevertheless; the kind that allows itself to be unpredictable, playful and even careless. The musical has an exuberance, a bubbly confidence in its own life.[24]

Douglas Watt said that Prince directed the show "cleverly, pacing it well," adding that although Larry Fuller had staged the musical numbers "deftly," there was no dancing to speak of in the show."[25] This was certainly not an unusual occurrence in a Prince musical.

The reviews were somewhat confusing. The critics seemed to like the show a good deal while, at the same time, faulting certain elements. Prince, it was generally felt, brought a great deal of style, pace and farcical humor to the piece. Howard Kissel said that with the sumptuousness of the sets and the glamour of the costumes, the show might seem cold if it were not "complemented by the broadly stylized movement director Hal Prince has given the large cast. . . . Prince has provided a veritable encyclopedia of artifice—the mannerisms he has given the actors seem to have a vitality of their own, as if they had been in mothballs for the last fifty years and were exhilarated to be back out in the open air."[26]

If Prince needed a boost after the unhappy experience of *Pacific Overtures* followed by the failure of *Some of My Best Friends,* the praise of *On the Twentieth Century* helped some. He was happy to learn that he could work successfully in a farcical, heightened style. Said Clive Barnes, on Britain's televised *South Bank Show,* "You can see the way Prince has imposed a style on *On the Twentieth Century.* It's all done (even the acting) in a 1930s movie style. In my opinion the overall style of the show is absolutely brilliant . . . all slightly stilted and larger than life."[27]

The original cast album was recorded by Columbia. *Variety* called the album "splendid," with the exception of the one weak spot, Madeline Kahn.[28]

Prince commented on his experiences working on the musical: "I had a nice time. It was laughter; we laughed a lot. *Twentieth Century* was like an exercise for me. I'd never done physical farce. I wondered what it would be like. Could I make people laugh at Marx Brothers routines in trains?— And I did. But I didn't know that I could do that, so I thought, you have to try that and see."[29]

On the Twentieth Century won five Tony Awards and closed on 19 March 1979 prior to a national tour that included San Francisco, Los Angeles and other major cities.

THE CONQUERING MUSICAL:
Evita

In Evita, *the things Hal uses!! For instance, the way he goes through Peron's ascendency; his rise—with musical chairs— where the other generals are eliminated. That's one of the most brilliant things I've ever seen.*
— Richard Adler, Interview with the author, 30 June 1983

We were thinking after seeing the sets of Evita, *that "[Prince]'ll never get this one done the way he wants!"*
— John McMartin, Interview with the author, 10 June 1982

Hal took this LP of Evita *and made it into a religious experience!*
— Judy Prince, Quoted in the McMartin interview, 10 June 1982

Soon after *On the Twentieth Century* opened, Prince began to ready his next project, directing the London production of an original musical entitled *Evita*. It would be the first time that a Broadway production of his would begin life in London, and it would be the first show he had directed which had been produced first as a recording—an unconventional practice begun some years earlier by Britons Tim Rice and Andrew Lloyd Webber. The team had used this approach with *Joseph and the Amazing Technicolor Dreamcoat* and *Jesus Christ Superstar*. They brought Prince the demonstration tape of their new record called *Evita*.

The concept for this musical recording about Eva Peron came to Rice in the early 1970s when, on his car radio, he heard the end of a play about the controversial first lady of Argentina. Gerald McKnight, Andrew Lloyd Webber's biographer, said of Eva Peron, "She was glamorous, sexy, beautiful, adored and had swayed the fortunes of an entire nation. All right, she was a superbitch, but who had that ever robbed of interest? Her cruelties, hypocrisy, even the use she had made of men and her own body, had never been seen as vile enough to quench the mesmeric ardour of her subjects."[1] The radio dramatization made Rice wonder how the theatre world would receive a musical version of Eva Peron's life, and he approached Lloyd Webber with the idea. His partner agreed that it was potentially exciting, "involving as it did the fiery Latin music of Argentina which such composers as de Falla and Ravel had captured. The passion and glamour of the project were undeniable. But first, [Lloyd Webber] insisted, they ought to complete another work which he and to a lesser degree Tim had been toying with haphazardly for some time: a musical to be based on the Bertie Wooster novels of P. G. Wodehouse, one of [Lloyd Webber's] favorite authors."[2] (This turned out to be *Jeeves* and was a flop.) With regard to the Eva Peron musical, Lloyd Webber didn't really want to do "another piece about an unknown who rises to fame at thirty-three and then dies . . . we've just done that with Jesus Christ!"[3]

Rice, although unwilling to be discouraged about his idea for a musical about Eva Peron, valued Lloyd Webber's judgment. He also knew that the composer would not work well unless his enthusiasm was complete on a project. After "much lengthy and sometimes acrimonious discussion and debate, he grudgingly agreed to try his hand at the Wodehouse idea first . . . provided that Andrew would also agree to put in some spare time on his *Evita* notion, composing whatever he could for the words Tim had already written."[4] (Ironically, the book and lyrics for *Jeeves* were finally written by Alan Ayckbourn.)

Rice's obsession with the *Evita* project can be seen in the fact that when his first child was born, a daughter, he and his wife christened her Eva-Jane. When *Jeeves* failed, Lloyd Webber turned to the Peron musical, but he still was not excited about the idea. He was worried about how to handle the piece politically. Lloyd Webber is quoted as saying, "I suppose many composers wouldn't have worried about politics in the slightest . . . I mean, the violence and so on. But *Evita* from this point of view did worry me. On the other hand it also intrigued me, partly I suppose because of what was going on in Britain at that time."[5] (The composer was referring to the rising tide of violence which, in 1975, was revealed in vandalism, hooliganism and the plummeting decline of wealth in England.)

Rice, meanwhile, probed deeply into Eva Peron's background. He read the books available in England about her but there was no work which he could call reliable. He went to Argentina to get the feeling of the country and he experienced the semi-mystical legend which, combined with her early death, had made Eva Peron a cult idol. It was this charismatic allure from the grave which excited him and which he passed on to his partner. Lloyd Webber finally admitted,

> She was easily the most unpleasant character I've written about, yet I found her story fascinating. Dying when she did—which must have infuriated her!—there had to be something about her which made people admire her. . . . The hostility of the military and the aristocracy to this jumped-up actress from the sticks, combining effectively with her illness to create a feeling of inevitable doom, was very exciting to compose for.[6]

Rice and Lloyd Webber went to see Prince before the record of the *Evita* score had been issued. They had produced a rather elegant demonstration tape using the London Symphony Orchestra and a group of wonderful singers. Prince heard it at his summer home in Majorca. He didn't know what to make of it but he was impressed. He was especially excited by the concept of Eva Peron's funeral, which took place within the first five minutes of the tape. The director recalls that day:

> The opera began with a funeral in the streets of Buenos Aires. Thrilling! Now, how do you stage a funeral with 200,000 people? Daunting! I played this portion of the tape for my wife and we both caught the fever. There was some material I didn't care for—the exploration of Che Guevara as an insecticide salesman—but mostly I loved it and always it was challenging. I agreed to direct it and offered to put my thoughts in a lengthy memorandum.[7]

Rice and Lloyd Webber left for London and Prince sent them 3,000 words about the project. He received a cursory thank-you note pointing out that they were making a concept album and it would be dangerous to open themselves to such specific recommendations. Prince recalls, "I told Judy Prince, 'I guess that's it for me. They didn't like my comments.'"[8]

About a year or year-and-a-half later, however, Princed was in his office when his receptionist told him that there were two gentlemen in the reception room and they had something they wanted to hand him. They were brought into Prince's office and it was Rice and Lloyd Webber. They handed Prince their record and explained that it was now not only published but it was the number one record all over Europe (but not in the States). The composers were here to release it in this country and they had brought Prince his own copy. Prince thanked them and said he had thought he was never going to hear from them again. He remembers their reply:

> They said, "No, not at all. Your notes so frightened us—because they had to do with a show and not the recording—and we thought . . . let's get our record out and then go back and talk to him. So here we are now. *Now*, do you want to do it as a show?" And I said, "Yes, I do, but I can't because I have many commitments and would not be available for about a year and a half. Will you wait?" They said they'd have to think about it. Stigwood [their producer, Robert Stigwood] apparently independently said to them, "Wait! Even though the record is #1 now, if you wait a year and a half the record will no longer be #1 and perhaps because it's a show it will get a whole second life, which it wouldn't get if you do the show immediately." So they waited.[9]

When Tim Rice was asked if *Evita* was a rock musical, he replied that all three of his and Lloyd Webber's shows including *Evita* could have been written only in the rock era. "I suppose you could say they are 'rock-culture musicals.' "[10] In any event, the musicals these men wrote may not be considered "rock" by everyone but they do relate to rock in many ways. Eventually the show was called the "new rock opera."

By late 1977, Prince had completed his other commitments, but had also thought about *Evita* for more than two years, and was ready to go to London to begin rehearsals. The piece had almost no story line or dialogue. The first script was just some "slippery pages in a two-record long-play album. I took them and made a script out of them. This takes place in this scene, this in that, etc. Each scene needed a conflict—almost none of them had one—so they had to write a conflict in."[11]

The notes for the original cast album say that "*Evita* is an opera based on the life story of Eva Peron, the second wife of the Argentine president Juan Peron. Eva Duarte was born in 1919, illegitimate, poor, without privilege. She became the most powerful woman her country had ever seen, the First Lady of Argentina at the age of 27. She died in 1952 of cancer, aged 33."[12]

The character called Che—based on the Cuban revolutionary Che Guevara—acts as narrator of *Evita,* and as an observer of the action in the manner of a Greek chorus. His role has also been compared to that of the Master of Ceremonies in *Cabaret.* He gives a sense of unity and continuity to the piece. In addition, he is the device that enables Eva Peron to receive personal criticism. Che may also be viewed as the conscience that Eva does not seem to have had and his "omnipotent manner reveals the truth beneath the surface. These two polarized revolutionaries, who have similar goals but entirely different methods of achieving them, created an interesting juxtaposition throughout the play."[13] Che's role has been described as a *raisonneur,* ironic antagonist, satiric commentator and enemy and victim of Eva's ruthlessness. Although there is no evidence to prove that the real-life Che Guevara had ever met Eva Peron, Prince felt his presence on the scene of the musical was valid.

> With historical figures, you have to try to be responsible with facts at the same time you're being theatrical in their presentation. . . . In regard to Che Guevara, they never met [but] historically, there is a connection, indeed. Che, an Argentinian, was deeply influenced by the fight for social justice in his country, and by Peronism. He was a mature 23-year-old college student when she died, so the tie-in is there. . . . Eva Peron was a fascinating woman. She did many good things—working to give women the vote in Argentina—she also was a megalomaniac.[14]

The real Che Guevara was strongly opposed to the Peron regime during Eva's time. It is not unreasonable, therefore, to conjecture that his revolutionary activity was in part a reaction to the government that was in power in his youth.

While the London production of *Evita* was being put together, the set designers, Timothy O'Brien and Tazeena Firth, called Prince and said that something indefinable was missing from the set. Shortly thereafter, Prince visited Mexico City and, while wandering through Chapultapec Park, saw murals by Diego Rivera and David Alfaro Siqueiros. Immediately he knew that this was the answer to the problem. He had great murals prepared to flank the proscenium. They depicted a range of Argentinian peasant types. In *Evita*'s cast of 48, only five actors have solos. To add character to the people who did not have solos, Prince suggested that they identify with the people in the murals.[15]

When Prince was ready to cast the London production, he hired a young musical actress named Elaine Paige for the title role. Paige had been in the chorus of the Lloyd Webber-Ayckbourn failure *Jeeves.* Joss Ackland was signed to play Peron and David Essex was set as Che. The Irish actress Siobhan McCarthy was to play the small role of Peron's ex-mistress.

Prince was at the height of his talent as he went into rehearsals with *Evita* in London. He had confidence in his ability to stage a show deftly, authoritatively and artistically. His many years of producing and/or directing both hits and flops had left him with many rich experiences that he might call upon. He said, "*Evita* is the beneficiary of *Pacific Overtures*. They're both documentary revues; incidents; highlights. Neither is lineally constructed. I found out where I was boring in *Pacific Overtures* with *Evita* I knew how to stop and move on at the right place and get the rhythm right. . . . Things last too long in *Pacific Overtures*."[16]

Prince explained what *Evita* was about.

> [Eva Peron] was corrupted by all that power. We try to show both sides. It's less about Eva Peron than about the media—what people see on a screen or hear on the radio—We're living in a horribly media-oriented era, and I'm always fascinated with what happens—on a stage and in real life—when real people are imposed against their media images. . . . On the politics of *Evita,* both the right and the left adopted Eva Peron (people want simplicity in the theatre). My personal view is: she was a villain, corrupted by all that power. But there's also a sympathetic part that draws me to her . . . Evita, illegitimate and a woman . . . a 10th class citizen in Argentina. And she made it sexually. It's grim and grimy stuff . . . the rage of ambition at work.[17]

For Prince, *Evita* is political theatre. The people in the story are symbols which warn about

> the perniciousness, the dangers, of media hype, of what packaging and selling can do and how you can sell the public anything if the bands make the right noises and the banners are the right colors and everything's set up well. But she's not a heroine remotely, by anyone's standards, but [Evita] is a figure. Now it seems to me the form of opera makes these figures, Sweeney [*Sweeney Todd*] and Evita work better on the musical stage. If you had a lot of book spoken, I tend to think it might trivialize them because, remember, the marriage of music and spoken text is a strange one, and the more spoken text there is, the more artificial the moment is when the character opens his mouth to sing. But if they sing all the way through then the convention is consistent and it's easier to live with the emotions and truth of the piece.[18]

Prince's concept for *Evita* was based on the movie *Citizen Kane*. He looked at the material and thought that he'd always wanted to do on the stage something similar to what he saw in the Orson Welles film. He said, "It was so particularly about movies; I felt *Evita* can be particularly about the stage. But *Citizen Kane,* that strange juxtaposition of myth and reality, people and people-as-objects . . . you can either deal with those things, those resonances, those aftertastes, those problems if you want to, or you don't have to.[19] Prince feels that if audiences are unable to see what he wants them to see in *Evita,* they can still see *Evita* as a pageant.

The more Prince looked at the material, the more he saw it as "a kind of mystery story. How did Eva Duarte become Eva Peron, arguably one of the half-dozen most powerful women in history? How did she get from Junín (a little dirt-road village) to the Casa Rosada? Each episode would unravel the mystery."[20]

Prince is fond of reprising all the songs at the end of a show, similar to what was done in *A Little Night Music.* When he worked on *Evita,* he was impressed by certain leitmotifs, and by the audience's recognition of them, how, as with movie music, the same emotional underscoring occurs.

Only minor changes had to be made on the show from its life as a recording. Very little of the textual substance was changed for the show. One song was removed and replaced by a new one. One subplot was dropped (Che's hope of becoming an entrepreneur) and the lines of a few songs were changed. Additional narration was written for Che. Lloyd Webber continued to have agonizing doubts about *Evita* and was sure it wouldn't work. He said at the time of rehearsals, "It looked to me as if it was staggering slowly, blindly towards completion."[21]

Prince rehearsed in London for only three-and-a-half weeks before the nine preview performances. Some critics and newspaper people came to the first preview although they were not invited by Prince, the writers or producers. Prince recalled how it all happened:

> The newspapers all came and they reviewed it. In other words the accredited critics may not have come but the newspapers did. So the day after the first public performance the newspaper headlines on the front page were "Don't Cry for Eva—Argentina's a Hit!" and so on. The show was a smash after its first public performance. Then we waited nine more performances until we were properly reviewed and it didn't matter. It was almost anti-climactic. There were lines at the theatre from the first day the box office opened. They got longer. For at least two years there was a return ticket holder's

Evita, 1979
During rehearsals for the New York production, Prince supervises costume
fitting for Patti LuPone. Seated in the rear is hair stylist for the show,
Richard Allen.
(Photo © Martha Swope)

line probably 150 to 200 people every night hoping that a bus would break down allowing them all to get in.[22]

Evita opened officially in London on 21 June 1978 at the Prince Edward Theatre. The critics almost ran out of superlatives. Elaine Paige starring as Eva Peron scored a great personal triumph. The reviewers felt she sang with power and feeling, dancing well and acting superbly. David Essex also received excellent notices. The score was well received and Gerald McKnight quotes Derek Jewell of the *Sunday Times* as saying that "the score is an unparalleled fusion of twentieth-century musical experience. Echoes of the past, Tchaikovsky, Puccini, and church choral music, shimmer hauntingly through. But it is the interweaving of pop, rock, jazz, Broadway, Latin and other elements which make the brew so astonishingly potent."[23] The whole production, said Jewell, was "breathtaking."[24]

Evita played to capacity business. Scalpers outside the Prince Edward Theatre received two and three times the price of tickets for seats which were being booked three months in advance. Although Lloyd Webber could forget his early fears about the show, his anxieties about the political nature of the show lingered. Lloyd Webber is quoted as saying that he was forced in *Evita* to take a position about a woman regarded by many as a poisonous, indeed murderous, dictator in her own right. He said, "I had to accept the fact that there would be people who would charge us with glorifying fascism. Of course I worried about it."[25] Rice did not have such qualms. He has since explained, "People tended to have extreme views about Eva Peron . . . they either loved or hated her. I was somewhere in the middle."[26]

The London production of *Evita* cost £400,000 which to British producers seemed an enormous sum, although the Broadway production would be much more expensive. Producer Robert Stigwood, because of his confidence in the show based on its London success, would back the entire Broadway production himself.

Andrew Lloyd Webber has said that he feels *Evita* was enormously aided by the recording of "Don't Cry for Me, Argentina," made more than eighteen months before the show opened on stage.

Anthony Bowles, who conducted the orchestra for the record, was asked by producer Stigwood to stay and direct the music for the stage adaptation as well. However, Bowles was fired during the early run of *Evita,* creating a great deal of ill feeling in Bowles toward Prince. Lloyd Webber offered his explanation of why Prince fired Bowles: "For some reason Anthony, from the word go, didn't seem to get on with Hal. A great pity.

I'm very, very fond of Anthony, but Hal is a strong-willed man and Anthony is equally so. Hal is an emotional man too, but in a *great* way. He's so talented that you can't—I mean, it's just one of those things, really."[27] Prince eventually phoned Bowles to clear the air, expressing his hopes that there would be no ill feeling but that he had a need for someone who "doesn't just come in and throw his weight about while just doing one show a week," which was, Bowles said, agreed to in his contract.[28]

Bringing *Evita* to the United States did not create any major problems. Prince had to put a clause into his original contract that the producers and writers of the show could not do this version of the show in America without his permission. He explained that when he made his original agreement with them,

> I thought the show might work in Europe [and] would probably be a great success there. . . . I was very anxious to work on it—but . . . I did not think it was for American audiences and . . . I did not want it seen in America without my permission. So they very unwisely (from their point of view) gave me a contract which would have made it possible for me to embargo the production. What happened was that, of course, it turned out to be *Evita* and I was delighted that it should be seen everywhere. It is also, obviously, the show that has given me the financial independence that everyone thought I always had![29]

Prince made many changes in order to prepare the show for American audiences. The opening at the initial performances in London was five or ten minutes longer than the version which eventually had a long run in London and the version which played in the United States. The original ending of the play was also much longer. Prince explained:

> It's on the recording that way. It goes on rather too long for my money. The same thing is true of the bedroom scene that immediately precedes the finale . . . a kind of reliving of her life in her head. That bedroom scene with Peron is longer. Longer on the record and longer in London, longer originally. We made those cuts after it was such a success in London. Then the performance of Che in London was much more genteel, much more laid back and charming. I would say that he was not the driving force in the English production. He was really charming, but he was more the observer than the driver. When it came to be done in this country, I determined that it should be more political here and that Che would have to be the force that drove the story along . . . that American audiences would not respond to it—not to the same degree as the British had (I found parenthetically that the British prefer their production and the Americans, when it opened here said, "Well

of course, it's a much better show here than it was in London." And I assumed
that would happen.) I also thought it would cushion some of the disappointment that people might feel because, except for *Fiddler*, I've never been
involved with a show where from the moment it was announced in London
there were lines. In order to counter that disappointment, it seemed to me
that they had to decide proprietarily that this production was theirs and that
they liked it better than they had in London and that's why we calculated
to do it the way we did. And that's why we made the changes and they were
mostly in *emphasis*. It's also why we went to California and played for four
months out of town, so that there would be a build up from out of town
of this show . . . this show . . . this show . . . which would start to confuse
things. It wasn't just this London show, it was now this California show that
was making its way to New York. And it happened precisely that way.[30]

Prince made the show "tougher" for this country. He did everything
"tougher."[31] He took the show to Los Angeles and San Francisco before
going to Broadway. He felt that with this advantage of time he might work
out some of the things he had wanted to do in London and couldn't. The
show did become more abrasive and more political. As for *Evita* being called
an opera, Prince agrees that it is in spite of the many critics who disagree.

Opera is and always has been, musical theatre of its time, presented in a
form using limited dialogue. Puccini and Verdi—who are the musical heroes
of Andrew Lloyd Webber, incidentally—were pop composers of their era. . . .
There are certain elitist lines of rigidity drawn around opera. The word tends
to carry with it a type of awed reverence that has been a barrier to acceptance of the contemporary opera works. But those operas by Verdi and Puccini
were the show-biz musicals of their time.[32]

Prince considers *Pacific Overtures, Sweeney Todd* and *Evita* modern operas.
He anticipated that they would one day join major opera repertoires and,
indeed, *Sweeney Todd* as well as the Prince-directed *Candide* are now performed in repertory by the New York City Opera Company. And *Pacific
Overtures* has been performed (and recorded) by a British opera company.

For the Broadway production of *Evita*, Prince cast Patti LuPone as
Eva. A graduate of the Juilliard School, she had appeared on Broadway
in *The Robber Bridegroom* some seasons earlier. Mandy Patinkin was hired
to play the role of Che and Bob Gunton played the role of Peron. Jane
Ohringer was set as Peron's ex-mistress. Firth and O'Brien continued as
costume and set designers as they had done in London, and Larry Fuller
was hired to do the limited amount of choreography.

From an interview with Kenneth W. Urmston, who was assistant stage manager and dance captain for *Evita*, we obtain valuable insight into the way Prince works. Urmston was impressed with the way Prince worked with large groups of people, in fact, with his whole manner. He said that Prince loves stage pictures, and discussed his perceptions of the director in action.

> Prince had a concept that he brought to rehearsal, but he would change it if he felt it wasn't working. But it seemed he had everything worked out in his mind. He worked fast and he just moved . . . moved . . . moved. I was impressed. Hal came the first day and gave a whole talk on the history of it, and he goes on and on, he can talk for four hours, and then [Prince and Fuller] show slides of the set and slides of Eva and they have a tape of Eva's last speech when she was 33, and it sounds like a 60-year-old woman with an old voice with cancer. Prince does this with each cast. He tells different stories about her. Prince researches for years—the history, even the whole story of the murals and how that came about. He closely supervises all the technical stagecraft. He likes instant results. If he has an idea, he doesn't have patience to go through "method" techniques. He throws out ideas and wants you to give it to him. In five minutes he can sharpen up something by the tone of his voice or his whole manner. I would have taken a week to get it like that . . . just the way he works. I learned from him. . . . He "hollers" a lot. He calls, "STOP, now do this, let's take it again," rather than having a number going all the way to the end and then giving notes, etc. He's not polite. He'll just stop, saying, "You're not doing it! THAT'S IT!" Then everyone's on their toes. Then he gets mad if they don't do that. He tells the actors when they hit it. He works very fast. Some actors can't deal with it. They can only do it if it's "truth within," you know, and that sort of thing. If you do a fake thing for him, you go off on your own and work on it and come back and give it to him. He'll take a lot of suggestions from the people also. He'll listen—mainly according to *who* it is . . . from someone like a John McMartin, he'll take almost everything. McMartin *gives* a great deal. Prince knows he basically doesn't have to do much with him, he only has to direct him in traffic and he'll fill in the rest. Even with his collaborators, Prince wants what he wants and fast (from the stage crew also). I'd say he is the last word on his productions. When he comes back to check a show, everyone's on their toes. He'll have notes, but he really gets involved even after a show is running one and a half years, and he'll have a real good rehearsal. He'll help a new actor a lot. It's exciting to watch it. If they don't respond, he'll fight to a degree, but then he'll tell Ruth [Mitchell], "You fix it."[33]

Evita, 1979
Bob Gunton as Juan Peron and Patti LuPone as Evita in the New York production.
(Photo courtesy Photofest)

The New York production of *Evita* opened at the Broadway Theatre on 25 September 1979. The reviews were not outstanding but they were generally quite good. Prince said:

> It's popular to say that the reviews in America were not good. It's not true. If you look in the lobby, you can see that the reviews were fine. What is true is that they were not *all* good and they were nowhere near as excitingly good as the reviews had been in Europe.[34]

Martin Gottfried suggested that with *Evita* Prince had finally become one of the most important directors in the American theatre. He felt that because Prince had achieved this success with *Evita*, a show done without Sondheim, he would now be looked upon as one of the most important creative figures in the modern musical theatre. *Evita*, said Gottfried, astounded almost everyone and credit for that has gone to Prince rather than the authors of the piece. "For the show's power is in its production concept, its fabulous imagery, and these visions were Prince's."[35] Prince's visualizations were compared by Gottfried to the visual lines used by such artist-directors as America's Robert Wilson and Germany's Peter Stein. They built their shows on visual elements. Unlike them, however, Prince "introduces such innovation to mass audiences; he subjects his shows to the practical, professionalizing demands of commercial theatre."[36] By breaking away from Sondheim as he did in *On the Twentieth Century* and *Evita*, Gottfried felt, Prince "more successfully straddled Broadway's twin realms of art and commerce. These shows were not above laughs and thrills."[37]

Indeed, *Evita* did contain a grand array of stage pictures. Prince utilized dynamic lighting (he set dozens of lights flush into the stage floor to create vertical patterns and walls of light). His constructs and black velours produced exciting effects. His use of film clips made strong comments and accented scenes. The murals, projections and exciting stylization which he had mastered since visiting the Taganka Theatre in the Soviet Union years earlier, his work with Boris Aronson, and his study of Joan Littlewood's and the new visual artists' work, all coalesced in *Evita* to assure audiences of a rich theatrical experience. For example, at the end of the first act, a vast political rally, with banners dropping from above and the entire company waving flags and holding torches, shows how Prince's brilliant technique and his use of abstract and constructivist sets creates a thrilling theatrical effect. The scaffolding-like stage design and lighting is dynamically used to heighten the excitement of the huge rally. It is also "dramatically effective in its simplicity incorporating the use of still photographs and motion pictures, to create great depth and height."[38] The danger, cautioned Gottfried, is that since Prince could now make anything into a fabulous show, he would have to be wary that "the materials must always come first."[39]

Walter Kerr felt that vital scenes were missing from *Evita* for a clear understanding about how this "remote heroine managed to get close enough to Peron to work her will on him, what it was she did to endear herself to a gullible population."[40] Because of these missing scenes, Kerr felt that there was no conclusion, no judgment, which could be arrived at. He felt, however, that the evening was not boring. As for Prince's direction, he said, "Prince has put his customary firm mark on the staging, making economical, highly efficient use of placards, banners, torches and bodies as he conducts the Perons through their open-air rallies and ostentatiously glittering inaugurations."[41]

Edwin Wilson of the *Wall Street Journal* pointed out what he felt were the show's weaknesses. In spite of the fact that Che is used to show us Eva's shortcomings, and that this was accented even more here than it was in London, "it is not enough."[42] Wilson's major complaint was the authors' "confusion toward the subject."[43] He said, "If the authors do not wish to glamorize Eva and have not succeeded in denouncing her, it is difficult to know what they do want."[44] Wilson also felt there was no clear line of development in the way the authors concentrated on Eva's death. On the other hand, Wilson was most complimentary about the physical production.

> In the theatre, *mise-en-scène* is a French term that means more than the staging and choreographing of a play and more than the visual aspects of the scenery, lighting and costumes. It means all of these together. For *Evita*, the new musical that opened last night at the Broadway Theatre, it is appropriate to speak of the *mise-en-scène* because the play's physical production is dazzling . . . one is forced to conclude that where its artistic viewpoint is concerned—not to mention its politics—*Evita* is hopelessly muddled. This is all the more regrettable because the *mise-en-scène* is so superb.[45]

The score was only mildly praised. Lloyd Webber's music was considered eclectic but not noteworthy. The favorite number was "Don't Cry for Me, Argentina." Howard Kissel said:

> Lloyd Webber's music frequently sounds like mis-hummed fragments of familiar tunes. The best known song in the score, "Don't Cry for Me, Argen-

tina," starts with a paraphrase of the opening line of an old Latin standard, "Yours," veers off into the first line of "Rose Marie," then quotes a few consecutive phrases from Brahms' Violin Concerto before going off on its own. Another song blatantly recalls the Beatles' "Yesterday." Most of the music is characterless, often singsong—perhaps it was kept deliberately simple to guarantee we would be able to grasp Rice's banal lyrics.[46]

Clive Barnes thought the show was stunning but he had reservations.

Make no mistake about it, Harold Prince's latest venture at Broadway opera, *Evita*, is a stunning, exhilarating theatrical experience, especially if you don't think about it too much. . . . I have rarely if ever seen a more excitingly staged Broadway musical. Its director, Harold Prince, helped by the choreographer Larry Fuller, has designed and developed a virtually faultless piece of Broadway fantasy that has shadow exultantly victorious over substance, and form virtually laughing at content . . . it is a definite marker point in the ongoing story of the Broadway musical.[47]

The cast of the show was mostly praised, with an occasional reservation. Patinkin, said Kissel, "has one of the purest, most beautiful tenor voices ever to hit Broadway, projects genuine passion—but the strength of his emotions only emphasizes the hollowness of the material."[48] Patti LuPone, said Kroll in *Newsweek,* "can act, sing and dance, and she'll get stronger in the role. But right now she doesn't transmit the driving force, the astonishing charisma that made an ambitious trollop into a tremendous political force and a folk saint for millions of people."[49]

The staging of a few scenes was singled out by many of the critics as being most imaginatively realized on stage. One was the scene in which a group of Argentinian colonels who are in line for the presidency sing about "The Art of the Possible" as they smoke cigars and play the game of musical chairs on a group of rocking chairs. On a screen over their heads we can see tanks and street warfare as the military men look each other over warily and scramble for the remaining seats. Dark, ironic overtones are present in the scene in which Peron wins the game.

Another powerful scene shows Eva using men to help her achieve success. The mirrored door to her bedroom, explains Edwin Wilson, "literally becomes a revolving door. In a song called 'Goodnight and Thank You,' she escorts one man out, only to have the door turn as another man enters."[50]

The set by O'Brien and Firth, consisting largely of girders and a moving bridge, has been echoed in other Prince shows in varying sizes and shapes

Evita, 1979
Patti LuPone in a scene from the hit musical.
(Photo © Martha Swope)

(e.g., *Sweeney Todd,* 1979; *A Doll's Life,* 1982). It provides an impression of coldness and mechanization. Howard Kissel said:

> Flanks of spotlights in both wings make the acting space seem like a sports arena, a place for momentous contests. The starkness and austerity of the basic set are modified by an enormous, mobile movie screen, which, sometimes dominating the forestage, sometimes hovering almost subliminally at the back, projecting images of the real Eva, gives one the sense of watching an epic.[51]

After the show had been running a while, there were various cast changes, including new actresses playing the role of Eva. Prince was often asked whom he liked best in the role. He said,

> They're all very different. Paige created it and she was wonderful. The girl who just left it in London, Stephanie Lawrence, was wonderful. Patti [LuPone] I thought was extraordinary. I love Loni [Ackerman] and Florence Lacy, both of whom are playing it now. No two ladies have been alike....
>
> For me the most interesting element in *Evita* is its abstraction. Because it's all sung, it's not realistic. It was necessary in working with the actors that they know in considerable detail where they physically were even though what the audience was looking at was a bed or a door on a bare stage. They also had to know where they'd been immediately before the audience encountered them. To some extent this is true in every theatre piece, but even more so when there's so little text and so little detail. The audience can look at a bed with two people in it. They're sharing a cigarette and arguing. They have just made love. No reference is made to that, but the audience senses something like that has just happened. When someone walks across an empty stage, if he's walking down a hallway and that hallway is in his head, the audience may not specifically know where he is, but it will know he knows. I had that task with *Follies* and again with *Evita,* and in both instances I found it exhilarating.[52]

Evita ran on Broadway for almost four years, closing in June of 1983. It won seven Tony Awards for the 1979–80 season, one for the best musical (Robert Stigwood in association with David Land), best actress in a musical (LuPone), best featured actor in a musical (Patinkin), best direction of a musical (Prince), best score (Rice and Lloyd Webber), best book of a musical (Rice), and best lighting design (David Hersey). It also won six Drama Desk Awards, including one for best director of a musical, and the New York Drama Critics' Circle Award for best musical.

Evita has had three touring companies in the United States and another eighteen productions worldwide. Prince was delighted with the economic and professional success this show brought him. He had proved that he could succeed without Sondheim, but Prince scoffed at this:

> That's just nonsense. One of the things I cannot do, though I sure as hell would like to do anything Steve ever writes, is that I can't just wait for Steve, because then I'll work too rarely. I need to work—all the time. And there's nothing wrong with that. I used to think there was something wrong with that. I used to think, you're a workaholic, or there's a neurotic drive here. I don't think there's anything remotely neurotic about it; I get pleasure and I'm a hell of a lot more fun to live with when I'm working, so why not continue to work?[53]

Prince felt that with *Evita* he had finally directed a show that would chasten those critics who had called the Prince-Sondheim shows cold and cynical. He said of audiences watching *Evita*, "People were moved. It is an unabashedly emotional piece."[54] There was some agreement with him, yet there were those who argued that again they had not been made to care terribly much about the protagonist, in this case, Eva Peron. Prince, however, was not too concerned; he was already busy readying his next project, *Sweeney Todd.*

BROADWAY MEETS GRAND GUIGNOL: *Sweeney Todd*

Hal's interests have led him to a different kind of theatre.
Evita and Sweeney Todd *were cold but thrilling as theatre.*
That excitement compensated for what was missing in human
values—just sheer theatrical excitement and verve and
imagination and invention.
—Sheldon Harnick, Interview with the author, 4 February 1982

The story of Sweeney Todd, the Fleet Street barber, was a legend in London dating back to the early nineteenth century and had been the subject of popular plays in England for 150 years. It told of a barber who slit his customers' throats, shuttling their bodies through a trapdoor to the cellar of his shop where they were made into meat pies with the help of Mrs. Lovett, a neighborhood woman. The crimes are eventually discovered because of a telltale thumbnail.

Daniel Gerould, in his book *Melodrama,* supplies "A Toddography" which traces the many varied forms in which the story has been told in literature and the performing and visual arts. The plays dealing with the legendary barber include George Dibdin Pitt's *The String of Pearls* (1847) and Wilham Latimer's *Sweeney Todd* (ca. 1900), each presented over the years in various adaptations. There was a British film in 1936 titled *The Demon Barber of Fleet Street* and a ballet, *Sweeney Todd,* choreographed in 1959 by John Cranko, with music by Malcolm Arnold and presented by the Royal Ballet Company.

On 17 April 1970 a new dramatic version of the story called *Sweeney Todd (The Demon Barber of Fleet Street)* by Christopher Bond, a Liverpool playwright, opened at the Victoria Theatre, Stoke-on-Trent, England, with the playwright playing the role of Tobias Ragg. Gerould says, "Incorporating elements of Dumas père's *The Count of Monte Cristo* and Cyril Tourneur's *The Revenger's Tragedy,* Bond's play makes Sweeney Todd a victim of injustice and gives motivation for his actions."[1] Bond's play was then produced at the Theatre Workshop, Theatre Royal, Stratford (Joan Littlewood's theatre) in 1973 and was published by Samuel French in London in 1974.

Stephen Sondheim was in London in 1974 helping to prepare the West End production of *Gypsy.* He had always been interested in Grand Guignol and in melodrama. The *Sweeney Todd*s that existed before the Christopher Bond version had been clunky, simple-minded, unmotivated and contained few bloody scenes. In these earlier versions, Todd was primarily a villain and Mrs. Lovett an accomplice. "There was no attitude or tone. It was simply a matter of seeing the villain get caught in the end."[2]

Sondheim heard about the Bond play, went to see it and thought it was wonderful, since "it had a combination of charm and creepiness. I don't remember being particularly frightened."[3] He bought all the published versions of the story even though he thought they were terrible. He considered Bond's version richer than the others.

Sondheim thought the play would make an opera. After speaking to John Dexter about his idea, Dexter encouraged the composer to try to get the rights. Sondheim says,

> That's how it all started. It was seeing the play at the Stratford East that sparked my desire to write a melodramatic piece—I certainly wasn't thinking about melodrama. I had written melodramas before although I didn't do the music in the case of *West Side Story;* after all, *Romeo and Juliet* is a classic melodrama. So I wasn't looking for a melodrama; it was just there.[4]

Sondheim was attracted to Bond's version of the legend because it remained true to the melodramatic tradition of the piece, and yet the playwright managed to humanize the characters, giving them more motivation for their actions than had existed in earlier versions. Sondheim said,

> Everyone in Bond's version is larger than life; the characters are not real people. The events are extraordinary, melodramatic in the sense that they

are larger than life; in real life there may have been mass murderers and even ones who used razors—but their stories were not compressed and heightened this way. *Sweeney Todd* is larger than life as a story and larger than life in technique.[5]

Producers Richard Barr and Charles Woodward were also bidding for the American rights to Bond's *Sweeney Todd,* wanting it as a straight play. When Sondheim, who had just committed himself to Prince to write the score for *Pacific Overtures,* approached them with the idea of the three of them doing a musical instead, they agreed to wait until he had finished his other commitment. Sondheim said, "I didn't get around to starting work on *Sweeney Todd* until the summer of 1977, so Barr and Woodward have been very patient for five years."[6]

Sondheim approached Prince with the idea of their collaborating on this project, but Prince was not sure he understood how it could work as a musical. Finally, however, he decided to try. He elaborated:

Sweeney was one of the rare instances in my relationship with Steve where I backed in and he was the driving force. He gave me Christopher Bond's play, which he had seen in London, to read. I thought it was a little on the campy side, about serving meat pies at intermission and hissing the villain and applauding the hero. He said, "No, no, this is very serious. It's about revenge. This is tragedy in the Greek sense." Accepted. And certainly Todd, whose wife had been raped, driven crazy and possibly murdered, had cause for revenge. But Mrs. Lovett, his vis-a-vis, and the rest of the cast seemed also driven by revenge. What do they all have in common? Expecially in the case of the chorus we face the problem of motivating its presence onstage. In the old days in the chorus of a musical you called someone "The Butcher," someone else "The Baker," and the "Candlestick Maker." You gave "The Butcher" an apron and one line of dialogue about butchering. Today your ensemble must populate the piece with a shared experience. This is where metaphor becomes so valuable in modern musicals. Our way to shared revenge became the incursion of the industrial age on the human spirit. For that Eugene Lee designed a factory to house our musical, and our cast—*all* our cast—became victims of the class system. It wasn't written into the script. We simply told our story inside that factory, dirty window panes blocking out the sun.[7]

Although Prince had not been taken at first with *Sweeney,* Sondheim recalled that "as he started to work on it, he fell in love with it too. That's the way it should be in a collaboration. I think if we ever worked on something for any length of time and one of us wasn't enthusiastic, we would certainly stop. It hasn't happened yet."[8]

A major aim was to retain the spirit that had attracted Sondheim to the play originally. Since it would be necessary to give the book greater depth than the usual shallow melodrama, it was decided to treat the material seriously and not as camp. Sondheim explained:

> I wanted to make a melodrama but with a twentieth-century sensibility. Perhaps in a hundred years, or even in fifty years, audiences would hiss the villain and make fun of the play. I wouldn't mind if it acquired that patina, but I wanted it taken seriously by an audience today, the way the original *Sweeney Todd* was taken seriously in the nineteenth century.[9]

Wanting to establish a serious mood from the beginning, Sondheim called the play a musical thriller, so that the audience would know in advance what they were coming to see. It didn't seem right to call it a musical comedy, since there were no chorus girls. To call it a musical melodrama might have suggested that they were making fun of the genre, "with villains galloping across the stage, the heroine tied to the railroad tracks, and the audience cheering and clapping. Starting with the subtitle 'A Musical Thriller' and going on to the set and the music, we have made sure that by the end of the opening number the audience will know what they are in for."[10]

A second help in establishing a serious mood was the set. Sondheim said:

> One of the miracles of the set is that when the spectators first come into the theatre and see it, they know that we're not kidding. Right away there is nothing about the set to suggest that a curtain is going to drop from the flies, plop on the floor, and disclose bats painted on it. Because of the solidity and scruffiness of the set, even if you wanted to do a spoof of melodrama, it would be impossible to get a laugh, except for the kind of laughs we get, which are character laughs. But for the make-fun-of-it laugh, the set is far too brooding a presence.[11]

Sondheim wanted to frighten the audience but not only by means of stage effects. He said, "The true terror of melodrama comes from its revelations about the frightening power of what is inside human beings. And if you write about kings and queens and are a great poet, you end up with a first-class tragedy; if you write about ordinary people and are an ordinary writer, you end up with a melodrama. That's exactly what this show is."[12]

When Sondheim and Prince first began to develop the show, they decided not to "soap-box" it. They both like didactic theatre but don't like "soap-boxing." Sondheim said,

> I try to do it by just inserting here and there throughout the lyrics words like "engine," basic images, not just inserting the words but using them as little motivating forces to make a slightly wispy connection with the industrial revolution. I was afraid if we made too much of a connection it would put too heavy a weight on the image or on the metaphor. I don't think it did.[13]

Sweeney Todd took four years of preparatory work before it was seen by audiences. Prince said,

> The first three years were about *how* in hell do you tell that story and how large do you want it to be? I worried to death for the longest time that, first of all, I was the wrong director for it, inasmuch as I couldn't see beyond Sherlock Holmes. I saw structure, real bricks and some turntables, and that's it. I kept protesting—not out of modesty, I assure you, but out of my real sense that I didn't feel comfortable here. Finally we were able to determine what the show was going to be, what its "motor" was going to be. That's how I always think of it, as the motor—it has a lot to do with the way the scenery is going to look, and how the people are going to move around in telling the story.[14]

Prince, however, confessed that he really didn't understand the Bond play until he was within a week of previewing. He had read it years earlier when Sondheim had brought it to his attention but, except for Sondheim's assurances about the way it played, it seemed too terse. He couldn't visualize it for a very long time.

> I couldn't imagine how those scenes were played. Then we got the libretto and went to work, and occasionally went back to Bond, and he was very helpful. But originally, I did not understand that play. . . . I was very frightened of *Sweeney Todd,* I will have to tell you. I think that's a good sign now, a kind of key word. I shouldn't give this away, but whenever I say to myself, "Oh, God, is this pretentious," I am usually on pretty good grounds. It's when I am not frightened that I have to watch out, because maybe it's too easy.[15]

Sondheim began to work on *Sweeney* as an opera. Bond's text, however, was so filled with materials that he realized it might turn out to be a nine-and-a-half-hour Ring cycle. Sondheim explained:

> It didn't seem worth that kind of time and attention. . . . So, I thought, I will do a little cutting and snipping—but it is plotted so well and so intricately that I got frightened. I bogged down, and at that point Hal came to my rescue. He suggested that it would help move it along if Hugh Wheeler would be willing to adapt it. . . . As we got to work on it, much of the second half of the piece started to change in shape and in tone and style. That was the result of the three of us sitting in a room and pounding away at what it should and shouldn't be.[16]

Prince had always felt that exchanging ideas is one of the most important things collaborators can do while putting together a musical. He said, "It's accurate to report that at the core of so many creations of musicals, people do *not* sit in a room together. They do not talk, they operate independently and bring each other finished work."[17] When the show was about to open, Prince called *Sweeney* a "romance," a play of passion.

> It's not Grand Guignol and it's not a pastiche or period piece or camping for laughs. It's the most melodic and romantic score that Steve has ever written. The music is soaring, with a rich melodic line. *A Little Night Music* was slightly removed and contained. This is allowed to spill over. I hope that it will engulf the audience. . . . The show calls for big classical bravura acting. . . . The musical is not just about revenge, but about the incursion of the industrial age and its influence on souls, poetry and people.[18]

Prince moved the show more and more toward the romantic, partly as a balance for the gory material.

Hugh Wheeler worked on the adaptation of Christopher Bond's play. Prince finds it crucial to read through and play through a show he is working on a number of times before he goes into rehearsal (a method that Robbins used years earlier in *Forum*). Therefore, in May 1978, he arranged for the first of these readings on *Sweeney*. Sondheim had completed over seven songs and Wheeler had a first draft of the first act. They arranged for the actors to read it. At first, Prince wanted to center the action on the young lovers, feeling that the audience would not be able to root for Sweeney Todd. He admitted that he was wrong about this, however, during the first previews and then cut a climactic scene involving the young couple trapped in a cellar. The play picks up Todd on his return to London after fifteen years in an Australian prison, where he had been sent on a trumped-up charge by the evil Judge Turpin, who desired Todd's wife. Bent on revenge, Todd comes back to London hoping to find the Judge and his equally evil Beadle. He then finds that his wife has died, and he joins forces with Mrs. Lovett, a vendor of meat pies. Together, they set out to wreak revenge on London's authority figures, Todd cutting the throats of victims as they sit in his barber's chair, their bodies falling through a trapdoor into the pie store below, where Lovett turns them into meat pies. The secondary story involves the plight of Johanna, Todd's 16-year-old daughter who has become a ward of the evil Judge Turpin, and is about to be forced into an unwanted marriage to her lecherous benefactor. In addition, a young sailor who had saved Todd's life on the trip back from Australia falls in love with Johanna.

Prince felt after this first reading that the piece was "a very serious, heavy, relentless, misanthropic business with *no* humor, none anywhere."[19] In Prince's opinion, the reading warned them about a lack of variety in a thoroughly relentless show. The original seven songs were, with the exception of one for Mrs. Lovett ("The Worst Pies in London"), very grim. By the time the summer of 1978 arrived, Sondheim had written more of the scene, however, and they were all encouraged. By the fall of 1978, they had a third reading. Sondheim said:

> With these pre-rehearsal tryouts, by the time we went into rehearsal the show was in much better shape than most shows are because they don't take the trouble in advance to read it aloud. . . . That's why the shows we have done, whether they were successful or not, have had a minimal amount of changes between opening out of town and opening in New York.[20]

They used a good deal of time trying to establish the style of the show. Prince said, "It then takes about a year to create a show."[21] At Prince's insistence, *Sweeney Todd* became his first collaboration with Sondheim in which the score was virtually complete (except for the last twenty minutes of the show) before the show went into rehearsals. Sondheim explains that he likes to complete his work close to rehearsal time. However, he says that Hal doesn't feel this is early enough since he likes to have more time to "digest" the numbers before beginning to stage them.[22]

Prince and Sondheim differ in their personal metaphors about what the show means. To Sondheim, the story of *Sweeney Todd* deals with personal obsession; to Prince, it is about impotence, quite a different matter. Prince said,

> The reason that the ensemble is used the way it is, the unifying emotion for the entire company, is shared impotence. Now, obviously Sweeney's is the most dramatic, to justify all those murders. Obviously all those other people who don't see the sky except through filthy soot-covered glass would not justify mass murder, but in fact they all suffer from the same kind of impotence, which then creates rage, and rage is what is expressed most by Sweeney's behavior.[23]

Prince refers here to the Eugene Lee set in which the sky is never seen, making the show also about a hemmed-in feeling, a rage. Sondheim said, "Christopher Bond emphasized the whole class structure and how Sweeney came out of that, which of course was never in any of the other versions. So Hal and I are not contradicting each other as much as it may seem. Shows *are* about different things. I think that in *Company* and *Follies* we did hit on a common metaphor."[24] Sondheim discussed his and Prince's differing views of *Sweeney*:

> I really did not relate it very much to the milieu. I did a little bit, perhaps, when I referred to the class structure, because Christopher Bond does that. But the sense of the city, which is in fact, a sense of the industrial revolution, machinery, steel, and all that, is very much Hal's approach to the material.[25]

Prince, as we have noted, in such previous shows as *Cabaret, Company* and *Evita,* tried to relate his work to the society from which the work springs. These productions and, at this point in his career, *Sweeney Todd,* reflected this interest strongly.

Sondheim felt that Prince and librettist Wheeler stimulated and encouraged him during the creation of *Sweeney,* providing him with needed responses, for him an absolute necessity. If Prince did not understand a line or if he thought something was clumsy, he did not hesitate to tell his composer. Sondheim explains that Prince never says, "That isn't pretty; he always asks, 'Is that pretty?' Sometimes I say no, and sometimes I say yes. I don't think I could *not* talk to people about my work. I need too much encouragement."[26]

Sondheim wanted the *Sweeney Todd* orchestra to frighten people. He asked his arranger, Jonathan Tunick, to use an electronic instrument and an organ. He felt that the loud crashing organ sound would be both scary and have a Gothic quality. In addition, electronic sounds can unsettle a person. Sondheim said, "I kept saying, I want it to be unsettling, and I want it to be scary, and above all I want it to be very romantic, because it is a very romantic show."[27]

Howard Kissel pointed out in his review of the show that the loud piercing whistle which interrupts the organ and cuts the air from time to time sounds like a shrill factory whistle. This sound has "the hard, pervasive sound of authority, of oppressive economic power. Apart from its metaphoric aptness, the whistle is a shrewd theatrical device, a way of jolting and chilling the audience."[28]

Len Cariou was cast very early for the role of Sweeney, as was Angela Lansbury for Mrs. Lovett. Sondheim was very happy to write for actor-singers whose capabilities he knew. He said, "*Sweeney Todd* was easy to write the minute we had cast Angela Lansbury—it wasn't a matter of writing for Angela Lansbury, it was a matter of writing for Angela Lansbury as Mrs. Lovett. . . . With Cariou it was a matter of writing for Len as Sweeney, not just Sweeney and not just Len. That's the best kind of collaboration."[29]

Len Cariou discussed his character's obsessive single-mindedness. "Sweeney is a man possessed by the fact of revenge. Once he gets the taste of blood, he rather likes it. He becomes his own victim."[30] Lansbury called her character, Mrs. Lovett, an amoral bawd. "It's like a good old-fashioned bawdy Restoration comedy, or Feydeau. It's almost Gilbert and Sullivan. There's a musical give and take on stage and every possible kind of song. A lot of colorful people roar around. I never stop running upstairs and downstairs. We're playing the lowest comedy you can imagine in the highest comedy manner."[31] Lansbury had some revealing thoughts on her collaboration with Harold Prince on *Sweeney*.

Hal is a very organized person. You can rely on him, which is terrific on the one hand. He certainly had a great job to do, to place this huge canvas on that stage, and I think he did an extraordinary job. But it took me a while to get used to his style of working. I was always looking for a director who was going to help me with my actual performance. And Hal does not want to do that. He wants to leave that to the individual actor. He doesn't want to talk about character motivations. Nothing is ever said. You learn your lines, you come out, you deliver your lines. And to me that's just the very beginning . . . then the work begins. But the work never began and I realized I had to do it myself.[32]

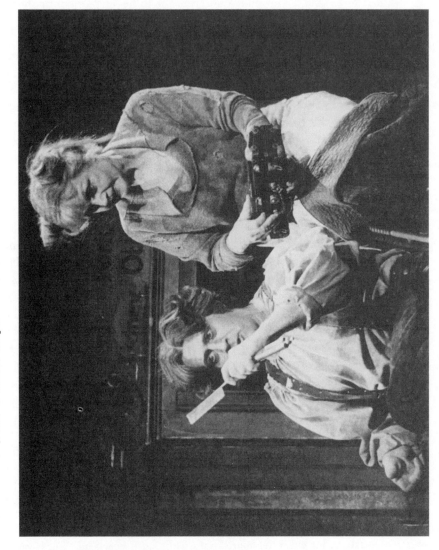

Sweeney Todd, 1979
Len Cariou as the mad barber and Angela Lansbury as Mrs. Lovett.
(Photo © Martha Swope)

Prince conceived the urban setting of a foundry for *Sweeney Todd* and hired designer Eugene Lee to transform his concept into the show's settings. Lee purchased $7,000 worth of parts from old foundries in Rhode Island, and spent $100,000 to have them shipped to New York. It took three weeks to erect the set on the stage of the Uris (now the Gershwin) Theatre. Because the production was so technically complicated, with the cast of thirty swirling through trapdoors and down secret chutes, the show was not taken out of town for a tryout period.

Designer Eugene Lee had hoped passionately that *Sweeney Todd* might be staged in an environmental, rather than a proscenium theatre. When he and Prince had collaborated on *Candide,* the director had approached the Lincoln Center board with a proposal for turning the derelict Beaumont Theatre into a permanent environmental performing space in which *Candide* might be done. He and Lee had worked out a tentative plan for a changeable space that would accommodate 700–800 spectators. Nothing came of that proposal and so Lee's dream of doing *Sweeney Todd* in that or a similar environmental space did not materialize. Arnold Aronson, in an article in *American Theatre,* said:

> The mechanical barber's chair in which the victims' throats were graphically slit before they slid down a chute beneath the chair, was to be on a central stage in the midst of an audience. *Sweeney Todd* was eventually done at the Uris Theatre ... the biggest house on Broadway. The setting, which filled the entire stage and spilled out beyond the proscenium, was a Victorian foundry created in part from scrap metal and mechanical devices from old factories in Rhode Island. There was a peaked roof of grimy glass panes supported on steel trusses and rusted iron beams. Stairways and platforms filled the sides of the stage. The back wall was made of corrugated tin and rose to reveal a painted drop of 19th-century London. There was also a catwalkbridge suspended from a traveling girder and there were all sorts of moving parts that did little but create an atmosphere. Specific locales were delineated by scenic units on rolling wagons. Prince points out that while the superstructure of the set was huge, the show itself was very small and intimate—"the whole play took place in a module and a few stairs."[33]

Prince and Lee's vision of the *Sweeney Todd* setting as a Victorian factory was the link between the title character and all the others on stage, "what the industrial age had done," said Prince, "not only to the quality of life of so many people in the ghetto just in practical terms, but to the peacefulness and harmony in people's lives—in the environment, the atmosphere. With the industrial age, people could not see the sky for the puke that was flying in the air above them. That's what we tried to do. The whole thing is encased in glass. No one sees the sun except through glass."[34]

The gigantic foundry to some extent overcame the cavernous atmosphere of the Uris Theatre as well as creating a sense of overwhelming and "assaulting" the audience. However, it remained a frontal and proscenium-enclosed production. Some critics felt that the suspension bridge moving in and out on the set was distracting. Rex Reed said, "A damned suspension bridge keeps clanging into place above the singers' heads in the middle of important songs. I prayed that the thing would disappear from the show completely. It never did."[35]

Another complaint voiced by several critics concerned the central wagon unit which housed both Lovett's pie shop and the barber shop. Harold Clurman felt that, since the wagon was the site of most of the action in the piece, the large foundry elements only confused and distracted from the major scenes played in the shops.[36] Jack Kroll felt differently, saying, "Rolling free within this structure is an ingenious shanty on wheels in which most of the action takes place. The effect of this monstrously beautiful setting is to body forth the Industrial Revolution as a portentous, ambiguous edifice—part cathedral, part factory, part prison—that dwarfs and degrades the swarming denizens of the lower orders."[37] Prince put the huge factory set there because the theatre was enormous and he didn't want to look at it. He wanted to obliterate some of the theatre so he could focus on what was happening in the middle of it. Prince explained, "It's a very small production if you analyze it carefully. . . . And what was around it [the factory] was like a curtain would be or a false proscenium . . . something to confine your eyes to the story."[38]

Prince was never really comfortable or secure while directing *Sweeney Todd.* He worried that his contribution was not up to what Sondheim needed from his director. Throughout the rehearsal period, Prince kept asking Sondheim to come in and look at what he had staged. When Sondheim and Wheeler did watch what he had done and told him that they liked it, he still didn't know quite why.[39] Prince recalled:

> Finally one day very near the end of the rehearsal period (we were working at the ANTA Theatre which is now the Virginia Theatre), I invited some guests: Angela Lansbury's husband, my wife and so on, and we put the show together for them. At the end of it they were sobbing. Good enough for me![40]

Prince usually senses, particularly during the early stages of rehearsals, songs that are eventually going to be cut. But, Sondheim says, "he always gives them a chance, which is one of the reasons I admire him."[41] Prince was aware that the first act of *Sweeney Todd* seemed too long, but he didn't want to make any cuts until it was playing correctly and was set on stage. He wanted to let the actors play the show for a few performances. Still, ten minutes of the first act had to be cut. About eighty percent of the act is sung and so it was unlikely that the dialogue could be cut. Prince wanted to take out a large chunk of the Pirelli scene, and in fact they did cut part of the song. Sondheim said,

> The other place was the Judge's song (a flagellation song), which is a song that Hal had sensed from the beginning wasn't going to belong in the show; and indeed, the Judge's song is one of the two songs in the first act that isn't in the straight line of the story. . . . The other is Mrs. Lovett's song "Wait" in the middle of the act, but if she didn't have that it would be a great musical gap for her—and I am not talking about Angela Lansbury. I am talking about the character Mrs. Lovett. Also, it sets up Sweeney's hesitation in killing the Judge.[42]

They found they could learn enough about the Judge with a couple of lines of dialogue interspersed throughout the rest of the act and that the song wasn't needed. Sondheim, however, missed the song even though he did not think the decision was wrong because the Judge is now the only character not established musically. The act now had a more appropriate length, playing smoothly and intelligently. Prince and Sondheim sympathized with the actor Ed Lyndeck, who played the Judge and sang the number very well. Sondheim decided to include it when the show was recorded just to please Lyndeck.

The collaborators argued for quite a while about the conclusion of *Sweeney Todd.* It had to do with tone. Once they had decided on the tone, Prince wanted to have a last-minute rescue, a melodramatic moment for Anthony and Johanna. It didn't quite work and it was cut. Sondheim planned for all the themes—the musical themes—to collide in the end. He determined to start each character out with a specific musical theme and to develop that character's music out of the theme. Sondheim said, "It's a handy compositional principle, and it seemed to me that it would pay off nicely at the end."[43]

Prince's love of reprising songs at the conclusion of his musicals was utilized in *Sweeney Todd.* Sondheim had been working toward that end with all the little modules of music throughout the piece. He said, "And so I wrote the last twenty minutes of *Sweeney Todd* while we were in rehearsal. Even Hal wasn't upset that I lacked the last twenty minutes because it seemed inevitable, all the homework and all the groundwork had been done."[44]

The company performed two weeks of previews at the Uris. Prince said, "By and large, the show was secure. . . . People came in, I remember vividly, and apparently they stayed clear of me and Steve, because they were so dismayed for us. We thought the show was terrific. . . . Right from the first preview on, we thought, well we have to do this and this and this and this . . . and we did those things and it opened. And that's the end of that."[45]

Sondheim believes that this show may be the first musical ever that never had an orchestra call between the first preview and opening night. There was never enough new material going into the show to warrant any changes that they weren't able to dictate. Sondheim said, "I don't think that's ever happened in a musical. What that means is that the show—in spite of its being overlong and in spite of some clumsiness that we wanted to fix up—was the show that we were going to open with, so it opened in excellent shape, with less change, musically, than any other show."[46]

This way of working on a show, without taking it out of town for tryouts, was introduced to Prince from his work in opera where there is no time for tryouts. Prince said, "I dearly believe in Parkinson's Law. I think the more time we give ourselves, the more time we waste."[47]

Capitalization for *Sweeney* was set at $900,000, with 271 investors supplying the funds, a very large number at a time when institutional investors were common. One hundred thousand dollars came from RCA Records— the largest single investor—presumably in return for the cast album rights. It wasn't the largest budget for a Prince show, but there was still a lot of money riding on *Sweeney Todd* as it commenced previews at the Uris Theatre in New York in mid-February, 1979, and sailed relatively smoothly toward its opening night of March 1.

Most of the reviews were ecstatic. Some critics compared it to Brecht's *Threepenny Opera.* Others pointed out similarities with Dickens, and some called it Breughelesque. Howard Kissel called it "not just a musical—it is total theatre, a brilliant conception and a shattering experience."[48] Edwin Wilson in the *Wall Street Journal* said that "portions of the musical hover between art and grand Guignol, but other parts cross into the realm of a striking artistic achievement."⁴⁹ Later Wilson said, "Whether for the controversy of its subject matter or the artistry of its presentation, *Sweeney Todd* will be talked about for a long time to come."⁵⁰

Richard Eder in the *New York Times* agreed that *Sweeney* was a "display of extraordinary talent." He felt, however, that there was "a kind of confusion of purpose."⁵¹ Eder thought there was an excessive amount of throat cuttings, which he felt were too bloody and seemed to be used to beat the audience. He went on to say,

> Mr. Sondheim's and Mr. Prince's artistic force makes the Grand Guignol subject matter work excessively well. That is, what needs a certain disbelief to be tolerable—we have to be able to laugh at the crudity of the characters and their actions—is given too much artistic power. The music, beautiful as it is, succeeds, in a sense, in making an intensity that is unacceptable. . . . Furthermore, the effort to fuse this Grand Guignol with a Brechtian style of sardonic social commentary doesn't work. There is, in fact, no serious social message in *Sweeney;* and at the end, when the cast lines up on the stage and points to us, singing that there are Sweeneys all about, the point is unproven. . . . These are defects; vital ones; but they are the failures of an extraordinary, fascinating, and even ravishingly lovely effort."⁵²

In regard to the cast pointing their fingers out to the audience at the end of the show, Prince said,

> That was Steve. He wrote it with them doing that. I staged it, but I always thought it inaccurate. I don't think he [Sweeney] is sitting next to me in the theatre. I wouldn't like to sit next to him in the theatre—and I didn't feel legitimately that everywhere I looked there was a Sweeney.⁵³

Michael Feingold in the *Village Voice* cited the grandness and ingenuity of Prince's visual staging and called this "his most brilliant directing to date."⁵⁴ In the same paper, Feingold's colleague Julius Novick felt that the show is about nihilism although it doesn't espouse it. He said, "Its emotionalism of operatic boldness is just what our theatre needs."⁵⁵

Jack Kroll in *Newsweek* admired the show for its sheer ambition and size and for its tremendous achievements. He did, however, have reservations and said that the show "lashes at the jugular instead of touching the heart."⁵⁶ In addition, he was unhappy about the way the character Johanna was presented. He felt there was something equivocal about the way the role was written. He said, "Johanna is treated both tenderly as the endangered innocent and satirically as the Victorian virgin, her head positively infested with Shirley Temple curls."[57] Kroll did go on, however, to compliment the director's intelligent eclecticism and the power of his work. "*Sweeney Todd* must be seen by anyone who cares about the gifts and risks of Broadway at its best. In his staging, Harold Prince exhibits the broad tactics of a field marshal and the intimate strokes of a genre painter."[58]

Sondheim's score was considered closer to opera than anything he had done in the past, since the show's texture is almost all musical. Sondheim felt that the show had a creepy atmosphere, as in a thriller. When the show is comic, however, the music tends to be in the music hall tradition and in the case of ballads, it is romantic. He explained about the show:

> It is highly plotted. You can't spend a lot of time saying "it's a lovely day today." I've used simple choral devices, trios and extended musical development. It has a feeling of a score as opposed to a collection of songs. The music is almost continuous, about 80 percent of the show.[59]

John Simon in *New York* magazine said, "Harold Prince has evolved into an extremely able director of musicals, and any past reservations I may have had no longer apply."[60] But he also listed what he felt were the show's problems. How to make the numerous throat slittings, if not less gory, at least less repetitious, remained a problem for him, as did the staging of the Bedlam scene where "the silhouette technique, not exploited imaginatively enough, ends up looking like a gratuitous intrusion. . . . All else is cogent and sturdily managed."[61]

The cast received fine notices, with Lansbury and Cariou singled out for their outstanding performances. It was Sondheim's score and Prince's staging, however, that were especially complimented.

Prince was delighted that the show had turned out so well. His surprise was that it did well at the box office. He said in an interview with Dick Cavett:

> I said at one point to Sondheim that this show is going to be wonderful but no one is going to come to it. It's a miracle what's happened . . . and the thing that worried me in those days was that I thought that our collaboration which I treasure would be endangered. There is going to be a point where people are going to cease to finance shows that we do together, because we're bad for each other—or they will *think* that. *Sweeney* has saved the day.[62]

Sweeney Todd won eight Tony Awards including one for the best musical of the season. It also received the Drama Critics' Circle Award for best musical. It opened in London the first week of July 1980 to mixed reviews, not achieving the success that it had had in New York. British theatre critic Michael Billington feels that Prince often tries to compensate for something that he feels may be lacking in a story by overcrowding or filling the stage with too much activity. He cited *Sweeney Todd* as an example of this:

> I think [Prince] puts these shows in big theatres, like the Drury Lane here in London, and there is so much going on on the stage in terms of people being wheeled on, balconies, being trucked in, etc., etc., that you don't have time to digest what the songs are saying, what the lyrics are or what the characters are about. I thought in *Sweeney* it was a classic case of just too much production.[63]

In 1983, Prince discussed *Sweeney* and its subject matter:

> The show worked. It turned a lot of people off . . . because of the nature of the material. Too bad, that's the way it is. The trouble is that I just don't think there's any room on Broadway for that sort of show anymore. I think if Steve and I were doing *Sweeney Todd* now, we could not do it on Broadway. We couldn't raise the money, there's no way. You see, for years we've been experimenting right on Broadway.[64]

Prince didn't mind if audiences were unable to perceive *Sweeney Todd* as one outcome of the Industrial Revolution, the loss to people of soul and spirit and poetry. However, he could not have directed the show if that hadn't entered into his own perception of it. He is aware that many viewers see the show only as a "thriller." Sondheim feels that Prince changed the tone of *Sweeney* from what he had originally intended. Sondheim said that he wrote an intimate horror show and "Hal made it into an Epic, a social story. It was the only way he could interest himself in the piece. It wasn't what I intended but he had a whole other way of looking at it."[65]

In the fall of 1982, *Sweeney Todd* was presented in a televised version by the Entertainment Channel on local cable outlets and later on stations of the Public Broadcasting Service to great acclaim and audience response.

In October 1984, Harold Prince's restaged "operatic" version of *Sweeney Todd* opened as part of the repertory of the New York City Opera

Company, following the success there over several seasons of the Prince-directed *Candide.* It was an immediate hit on the opera stage. Prince had doubled the chorus singers to 32 for this production and the orchestra was expanded from 25 to 50 pieces. On Broadway the director had worked with actors who also sang; at the City Opera, he dealt with people who were singers first—principals like Rosalind Elias, Leigh Munro, Adair Lewis, Timothy Nolen and Chris Groenendaal. Bernard Holland, writing in the *New York Times,* said, "We are told, in other words, to expect a show in which music will take precedence."[66]

The success of *Evita* and *Sweeney Todd* on Broadway had re-established Prince as one of the American musical theatre's foremost directors. Soon, he was busily preparing his next production, *Merrily We Roll Along,* which he felt would once and for all prove that he and Sondheim could do something that was warm and likeable. He was unaware that he was about to take on what would prove to be one of the most troublesome shows he had ever directed.

A STRING OF VALIANT ATTEMPTS

Merrily We Roll Along

> *There are particular things I need to hang on to. One is the visual. I never had a visual sense of what* Merrily *should look like, never could root it anywhere . . . and, of course, there was nothing larger than life about it. The show's realism confined me. Once we started previews, I tried to get rid of all that stuff, make it abstract. Too late.*
> —Harold Prince, Quoted in the *Los Angeles Times*, 13 June 1982

The idea to do a musical about young people first came from Prince's wife Judy, who said to him, "Why don't you do a show about kids that reflects the two kids you have in your home, and what you see around you, because they're real smart, and they're curious and they have a vision of the world, and they have a vision of what we're doing wrong."[1] Judy Prince was referring to their two teenagers, Charley and Daisy, who were 18 and 16 years old at the time. Prince thought his wife's idea was a good one, and he began thinking of what he might use as a vehicle for a musical about young people. His idea of combining his wife's suggestion of a show about kids with an early play by George S. Kaufman and Moss Hart called *Merrily We Roll Along* came to him one day while shaving. Prince felt here was a proper framework for a cast of young people and for what he wanted to say about American life during the past, often disillusioning, 25 years. The musicalized *Merrily We Roll Along,* a show about youth and their ideals, did in fact become Prince's next musical and ironically, his daughter Daisy, who had appeared in musicals at the Dalton School, would eventually be given the small role of the sexy starlet who becomes the third Mrs. Franklin Shepard.

The original *Merrily We Roll Along* was the 1934–35 drama by Kaufman and Hart about disillusionment among a group of theatrical artists. It told of a misguided playwright. Kaufman and Hart's theme is that youth should not surrender its idealism. At the beginning of his career, the playwright, Richard Niles, is determined to write "truly fine plays." Little by little he yields to the pressure of circumstance until he becomes an agreeable but corrupt man who writes successful sex fables for Broadway. The structure of the play moves backward in time, covering the years 1934 back to 1916. Each succeeding scene takes place at an earlier time than the preceding one, starting at the present and moving backward to the idealistic days of the protagonist's youth. The Kaufman and Hart play opened on 29 September 1934 and was their second collaboration (the first play they did together had been *Once in a Lifetime*). *Merrily* received good notices and was named one of the season's ten best plays. It had, however, a modest run of only 155 performances.

Prince had never seen the Kaufman and Hart version when it was on Broadway. However, he was familiar with the play (his late producing partner Robert E. Griffith had appeared in the original version). Prince remembered that the original piece ends with Polonius' advice in *Hamlet*: "This, above all, to thine own self be true," which, Prince said, "is putting it very clearly what I wanted to say."[2]

Prince called Stephen Sondheim to see if he was interested in doing the project with him. The composer agreed to do it right away, which was unusual since, as Prince explained, "He has rarely ever agreed to do anything so quickly."[3] *Merrily* would reunite Prince and Sondheim as collaborators for the first time since *Sweeney Todd*.

George Furth was asked to do the book. From the time Prince thought of doing the show until it went into rehearsal took almost two years. Many of the regular Prince collaborators were hired, such as Eugene Lee as set designer and Paul Gemignani as musical director. Ron Field, who had done such a fine job on *Cabaret,* was set as choreographer, and Jonathan Tunick as orchestrator.

Prince collaborated with librettist Furth and composer-lyricist Sond-heim "on the structuring of the play."[4] He retained the structure of the original *Merrily* for his musical. The theme was broadened to include the subject of friendship as well as the frustration of youthful ideals. He changed the time frame, going backward 25 years from 1980, rather than from 1934.

The musical version tells the story of Franklin Shepard, an attractive young man who wants to write music. Other young people are drawn to him: his talented high-school classmate and good friend Charley Kringas, a lyricist, with whom he composes the graduation song and collaborates on three Broadway shows; the promising writer Mary Flynn, who falls in love with him, but becomes an alcoholic when she can't cope with her suc-cess; and an aspiring singer, Beth Spencer, whom he marries. One by one he loses them.

The show takes place from 1980 to 1955, a period during which America became fragmented, "me-centered," and enamored of instant celebrity. Almost every scene unfolds in a public place. The cocktail parties; the court-house steps with the omnipresent newscasters; the nightclub wedding; and, most dramatically, the studio where Frank and Charley's collaboration is torn asunder on national television: all are symbolic of our loss of privacy. An invitation to the 43-year-old Franklin Shepard to be the speaker at his high school's 1980 commencement—the 25th anniversary of his own graduation—triggers the action.

Prince, known for "concept" musicals, was asked about the concept of this one.

It's more like, What is success? . . . I wanted to show that success is not necessarily measured in bank deposits. It can be measured as well in per-sonal satisfaction and in feeding internal things. Charley's O.K. He's lost his good friend, Franklin, so out of the three, one is fine, and he happens to be the one who's the most idealistic. I like Franklin a lot, but I'm sorry for him, because success is very seductive, particularly today, when there's no privacy. It's so difficult for people to be private. The show concerns itself very much with that. There's his instant celebrity and instant temptation and "Oh, I'll go to that party, what the hell" or I'll succumb to that once and then twice and then a third time, and eventually you lose track of the pleasure you got from doing the work. And I think that's very much what happened to Franklin. He starts to incorporate, instead of write music. . . . Mary's another case. There have been Marys forever. These are people so Simon pure, so really idealistic, that they can't cope with the real world, and they become alcoholic, or they become embittered, and nothing ever comes up to their standards.[5]

Prince assured everybody who cared to ask that, although the leading character, Franklin Shepard, is a composer who becomes very successful at an early age, and both Prince and Sondheim also became successful at an early age, the characters were not modeled after the two collaborators. Prince explained:

> At no point did we say it's going to be about us. . . . But it certainly would have been about our times, because these are our times, these 25 years are our 25 years. But I don't think for one minute either one of us is in jeopardy of giving up what we want to do to be incorporated, and I think we have a long enough record to prove that.[6]

Between his commitments to the many productions of *Evita* being presented all over the world, Prince flew into New York to cast *Merrily*. Lonny Price, Jim Weissenbach and Ann Morrison were hired for the leading roles of Charley Kringas, Frank Shepard and Mary Flynn respectively. Price had done office work in Prince's production office while he was an acting student at Performing Arts High School. He had since received outstanding notices as well as winning a Theatre World Award for his role in the Off-Broadway play *Class Enemy*, and had appeared in *4 Jews in a Room Bitching* (later known as *March of the Falsettos*) by William Finn. Prince called in some young actors to his office to audition them for a reading of the *Merrily* script to see if "kids" could pull off that sort of sophisticated "bitchy" New York banter. At his audition for this reading, Price had read only the first half of the first scene when Prince told him it was "terrific" and to come to the Broadway Theatre (where *Evita* was playing) to take part in the reading. Price read the role of Charley. The next week they asked him to sing. That same night he was notified that he had won the role. Price said, "It was really a dream. . . . It was the best thing that ever happened to me. It was incredible."[7] Prince said of the actor who would play Charley, "Lonny is extraordinary—a quirky, wonderful, eccentric person."[8]

Weissenbach, a newcomer to New York, is the son of a former classmate of Prince from the University of Pennsylvania. He had moved to New York from the midwest wanting a career as an actor. Prince said, "Jim's father wrote to me and asked me to meet him, so I invited him to the office one

Merrily We Roll Along, 1981
Ann Morrison, Lonny Price, and Jim Walton are pictured in the rooftop
scene from the show.
(Photo © Martha Swope)

day.''[9] Weissenbach was soon cast in the role of Franklin Shepard, his only previous credit being Barnaby in a summer theatre production of *Hello, Dolly!*

Ann Morrison as Mary was also making her Broadway debut after appearing in a few regional shows and in an Off-Off-Broadway production of *Dreamtime*. Morrison was chosen because of her big voice, which reminded Prince of Judy Garland. Additional featured roles in the musical went to basically untried, though talented, teenage youngsters.

The casting was completed by May 1980, with rehearsals set to start in December 1980. Sondheim, however, had not finished the score by December. Prince, too, had prior opera-directing commitments. *Merrily* was postponed until almost a year later: September 1, 1981.

Rehearsals began in a studio on lower Broadway. On the first day, as usual, Prince spoke to his cast of 26 young people about the show. He showed them sketches of the costumes and a model of the set. He told them that *Merrily* was about "corruption, the anti-hero, friendship and the years between 1980 and 1955."[10] He explained why the original version of the story had had a relatively short run, that it didn't really work. The protagonist was an anti-hero who sold out for riches. In the 1930s, an anti-hero was not a sympathetic figure. In 1981, however, the anti-hero is "one of the boys."[11] Prince reassured his young cast that anyone who did not already smoke would not be asked to smoke onstage. He then asked them to read the script aloud for a run-through and said, "Move for speed. You think with speed. . . . Don't be cautious. . . . Don't let us slow you down. Audacity—I want to see that. No one here is even remotely in trouble with job security."[12]

Cast member Lonny Price discussed his perceptions of Prince as a director:

> He's not a method director. Prince is not as concerned with *how* you get there as long as you get there. There's just not the time frankly to do a lot of the kind of work you would do in a play in terms of exploring this and that. He stages very quickly and very well, immediately. I think we blocked the entire show in a week. We had the first reading on the first day or rehearsal and that was the last time we read it. The next day you start blocking from the first scene. And he's very quick and a lot of fun to work with because he's very energetic. The best thing about Hal Prince—and it's the most charming thing about him, and I'm very fond of what it is—is that he has this sort of 12-year-old enthusiasm—of a 12-year-old little boy—who has this big toy—and he's thrilled and excited and he can't wait to build

it and put it on its feet and show it to people. I mean, he's just like a little boy with the best Christmas present in the world . . . and the energy and enthusiasm is so positive and so strong! It's an amazing force and it's totally infectious and it's swell, it's terrific. And very important, I think for doing anything. I think it kept our spirits up during a lot of the bad times on *Merrily*. You'd see his face and he'd be smiling and jumping around and you just said, "Well, *he's* happy, so *I'm* just not going to worry about it." He lets you do pretty much what you want with your character. Hal knows what he wants, he has a very specific idea of what's right and what's not right. When you're doing it wrong he'll try to explain what he wants from the scene. I had a lot of problems with my character and he would arrange meetings in which he would tell me what he thought I was doing wrong. He hardly ever did this in front of the cast which the actors appreciated. He was usually quiet about criticism. He's not the kind of a person who yells at you from the back of the theatre. He yells at the sets and he yells at the technical people a lot, but he doesn't much yell at the actors to embarrass them. He's not a "humiliating" kind of director, I don't think, and the nicest thing about it is that when he's telling you to do something (I mean, I can see it in other people, not so much in myself), he'll stop you and say, "No, what I want is so and so," and then you do it. His face would light up. You'd know exactly when you had pleased him and when you had not. There was no question about it. But pleasing him was like getting 100 on a math paper or something, 'cause he's real important and he gets excited. It's that boyish enthusiasm! After all these years it's just amazing that he hasn't lost it![13]

Prince decided not to take this show to Boston or New Haven to try out. He arranged instead for preview performances beginning 8 October 1981 at the Alvin Theatre in New York. This was becoming the practice for Broadway musical producers and directors; Prince had done it before with *Sweeney Todd*. Unfortunately, the creators of the show found themselves working out problems in the public eye. With *Merrily*, "every firing became a headline; every misstep prowled the street."[14] Prince justified the psychological risks with the economic realities. He said, "It's all economic. Even in the old days, we could lose $300,000 in a [try-out] city. We were more isolated from rumor mongering, but we don't have to pay transportation and per diem here. . . . Here we can play five weeks of previews and actually have a tiny profit. And shows get reviewed in the dailies and *Variety* on the road. So what's so isolated about that?"[15] Linda Winer in her *Daily News* article said, "Still, there is something courageous and naked about two of Broadway's most intelligent, uncompromising heavyweights exposing their creative agony in public."[16]

Hal Prince and Stephen Sondheim, 1981
The long-time collaborators are shown here during a rehearsal for
Merrily We Roll Along.
(Photo © Martha Swope)

Prince admitted that there were many more problems with *Merrily* than he had had since producing *A Funny Thing Happened on the Way to the Forum*. Ironically, before the previews, word around town was that the creators of the show were thrilled with it, and thought they had a big hit on their hands. Lonny Price said, "They all thought that *Merrily* was fine and spectacular. They had enormous faith in it, and it meant more than any show personally to Hal."[17]

What went wrong? When the musical began to preview, it became clear that it was not working. Audiences were confused and hostile during the first two weeks of the preview engagement. They would often walk out after the first act. As the collaborators made changes, the audiences began to stay for the entire show. Prince was constantly asking Furth and Sondheim for new scenes and numbers, mainly to clarify the show's intent. Lonny Price said, "I have a box of rewrites on *Merrily* that—for each scene we did there were at least five or six versions of it."[18] It was not unusual for the cast to rehearse four new scenes all day to be put into the show the same night. The opening number was revised by the composer at the director's request. There had been last-minute changes in other Prince-Sondheim shows but nothing like this. Before the first preview performance, Prince requested an entirely new set of costumes. The original costumes had been designed surrealistically to depict the many characters in the story and it didn't work. Many were beautiful, lavish and dramatic to fit the lifestyles of the people. However, with teenagers playing the roles, most of the costumes looked foolish and out of place. Sweatshirts for the cast were produced with names or titles such as "Charley," "Ex-wife," "Producer" and "Best Friend." Now, the addition of a feather boa or a headpiece would be sufficient to indicate how the character might have dressed.

Many of the original sets were discarded. Lonny Price said, "The original idea was for the whole set to look as if the kids had built a big tinker toy. That's why we had all those bleachers. Initially, the bleachers were the whole set. They were able to change into various configurations. They never worked right and they were ugly to boot. So little by little they kept throwing them out and they brought in the projections. They tried to pretty it up."[19] At first, a large collage of *Life* magazine cover photos depicting people and events of the 25 years covered in the show was used as a front curtain. Within a day or two after the first preview, the curtain was struck.

Two weeks before the first scheduled opening date (there were several postponements), one of the three leads, Jim Weissenbach, was replaced by Jim Walton, another member of the cast, because Walton was more extroverted. A few days later, Larry Fuller replaced Ron Field as choreographer because of "artistic differences." Lonny Price believes Field was wrong for what they were working for in *Merrily*. Field's movements didn't look as if kids were doing them. In addition, Price feels that with a Sondheim score, the intricate lyrics must be understood. Movement should be minimal during the songs (notwithstanding dance breaks, of course) because you want to hear those lyrics. "They're brilliant and they should be heard," said Price, "and Ron just wasn't right for the piece, as it worked out."[20] With Fuller, there continued to be much restaging of the dances and musical numbers.

Lonny Price lost a small part of the "Old Friends" number in the Polo Lounge scene which was reassigned to Mary. He was sorry to lose it since it had become Charley's theme song. He said, "It was very warm and sunny and open and very lovely."[21] Many of the speaking roles were cut, as characters were eliminated, with many of the cast who originally had featured roles ending up as chorus. Yet the entire cast had a feeling of camaraderie and continued to be friends.

Prince admitted that this show had more changes of material (book, costumes and lines) than any he had done:

> This is more than I'm used to, I'll tell you, and it hasn't been easy. . . . One of the biggest problems was that we were charmed by the "rawness" of the 26 youthful actors in the musical, all of whom are in their late teens or early 20's. I was charmed by the beginnings of their artistry, the roughness of their craft, their inexperience. I was charmed as hell by that, but we realized that other people were not as charmed, and that they wanted more polish. They were also very confused by 26 characters, and so much information . . . so we decided to take away some of the things that the 26 actors were contributing as a group and settle pretty much on the six major characters, for clarity. We did this after we realized that the audience was getting confused in the previews, and when an audience gets confused, it gets hostile.[22]

Prince eventually realized that *Merrily* was forty minutes too long, and that its dramatic structure, moving backward in time, made it difficult for the audience to follow. The collaborators cut the show but he did not change the structure. A few years later, Prince discussed this unhappy period:

We were not in good shape. There was so much to be done. But even that we could cope with, and did a great deal in three weeks, professionally. I think we turned it around from chaos to a show. The trouble is that the newspapers snapped at our heels. From the first moment, Liz Smith wrote a hundred million words (well, she did the better part of a column) about people walking out on us, hating it, saying it was tacky, vulgar looking and ugly, and play, blah, blah, blah. [Here Prince refers to the Liz Smith article in the *New York Daily News,* October 18, 1981, p. 12, "Not So Merrily They Roll Out of the Theater."] And that became a sort of signpost because she did it soon after we had our first public performance. She was picked up and you read everywhere what trouble we were in. Audiences began to storm out of the theatre (they were storming out anyway, it wasn't Liz Smith's fault they were storming out). But then they read that they were storming out so they had to oblige. Yet we kept working. And the poor kids on the stage kept working. Daisy [Prince's daughter] came home from the show one evening and reported, "The first eight rows were empty by the time we took our bows." We postponed the opening of the show another three weeks. By the last two weeks, they were not leaving the theatre. They were not storming out. We took out most of the scenery, all of the costumes (it began to look a little like the bare-stage production I'd originally proposed). We behaved professionally. We did the most we could do. For me what was missing was clarity in the script and, of course, a "look." The show has played elsewhere and often, and it works as well as it does because Steve's score is extraordinary. He didn't know it at the time. When we first went into rehearsal, he thought he was going to be the one who let us down. You never know.[23]

Sondheim's score contained more popular songs in it than the composer ordinarily writes. Frank Sinatra recorded "Good Thing Going" as a single before the show opened and Carly Simon recorded an album containing "Not a Day Goes By." Although the show failed, Stephen Holden in the *New York Times* wrote about the RCA Red Seal original cast album, saying,

> With its plethora of brash show tunes, *Merrily We Roll Along* is Mr. Sondheim's most conventional score since *A Funny Thing Happened on the Way to the Forum.* . . . On record, however, *Merrily We Roll Along* holds up so well that one is inclined to speculate that the judgment against it will eventually be reversed. . . . With its show business setting and the blaring orchestrations, *Merrily* might strike the casual listener as Mr. Sondheim's bow

to the Broadway mainstream of *A Chorus Line, 42nd Street,* and *Woman of the Year,* etc. But on closer inspection, it is hardly a formula musical . . . the recurrent choral refrain, "How Did You Get There from Here, Mr. Shepard?," spurs a real moral and artistic quest for the self's truest ideals. Is it possible to be a rich and famous songwriter and not lose one's youthful dreams? By taking us backward, instead of forward, Mr. Sondheim suggests that underneath all the trappings of success, the pure idealist in us is always there, waiting to be uncovered. Nobody, after all, begins life cynical and money-grubbing. One of the reasons that modern musical comedy has lost its artistic footing, Mr. Sondheim implies, is that it has become too concerned with show business razzmatazz and not enough with music of real quality.[24]

Sondheim explained that because the show is about friendship, the score focuses on the friendship of Frank, Mary and Charley, all their songs interconnecting through chunks of melody, rhythm and accompaniment.

And since the story moves backwards in time, it presented an opportunity to invent verbal and musical motifs which could be modified over the course of the years, extended and developed, reprised, fragmented, and then presented to the audience in reverse; extensions first, reprises first, fragments first. For example, a release in one song would turn up later—as a refrain in another (e.g., "Rich and Happy"/"Our Time"), a melody would become an accompaniment ("Like It Was"/"Old Friends"), and so on, according to the relative importance of the characters' feelings at each point in their lives. Along with this would be the transformation of Frank's hit song from "The Hills of Tomorrow" through his development of it during "Opening Doors," which we actually witness, to its emergence as "Good Thing Going." In fact, if the score is listened to in reverse order—although it wasn't written that way—it develops traditionally.[25]

By the time the musical was ready to open, the cast's morale had improved considerably. Sondheim said, "It didn't become what it was until the last five previews. It turned out to be very good. We changed a lot.[26] Although the Prince-Sondheim musicals had often been labeled cold and cynical, with this show Prince was sure those adjectives would change to "heartfelt."[27] Prince said before the show opened, "I think it will be received in the spirit that is intended, with at least some people crying. I don't mean sobbing wildly. I just mean feeling—feeling for the kids and feeling for yourself and wanting to say to yourself, 'I did the best I can.' "[28]

Merrily We Roll Along opened on Broadway on 16 November 1981 to terrible reviews. Lonny Price called them "hateful, nasty and angry."[29] In the actor's opinion, the critics saw a vulnerable show, with no stars and

Casting Director Joanna Merlin and Prince, 1981
Collaborators meet during rehearsals for *Merrily We Roll Along*.
(Photo © Martha Swope)

no advance sale. It was an easy show to kill. "They went after Sondheim and Prince with an ax."[30]

Frank Rich in the *Times* wrote, "Sondheim has given this evening a half-dozen songs that are crushing and beautiful—that soar and linger and hurt. But the show that contains them is a shambles."[31] Rich went on to say that this new version of *Merrily We Roll Along*, although rewritten and updated, repeated the mistakes of the original drama, adding a few of its own. Rich said:

> Mr. Furth blunts the shock effect of the original play's structure by enclosing it within a conventional flashback, and, even so, he fails to solve its major dramatic failure. We never do learn why the characters reached the sad state they're in at the outset. While a busy story—often built around unconvincing, melodramatic twists—does tell us how the three friends fell apart, that's not enough.[32]

Rich called the principal players "appealing" and said that "Mr. Price, in the most sympathetic role, is a charming, Woody Allen-esque fellow who brings fire to the show's angriest song ("Franklin Shepard, Inc.") and a plaintive undersell to its most conventional ballad ("Good Thing Going")."[33]

John Simon's review of Sondheim's score in *New York* magazine was as always negative, and he was almost alone among the critics in his dislike of it, writing, "If Sondheim has been erratic as a composer before, this is the first time that his lyrics, too, seem to drag their feet."[34] Simon was not enchanted with the large cast of young unknowns in the show.[35] His major complaint, however, was with the creators:

> Back in 1934 Kaufman and Hart thought at first of calling their play *All Our Yesterdays* and that is pretty much what Sondheim, Furth, and Harold Prince, the director, have given us. There are plot, staging, design, music, and dance concepts from just about all their previous shows cluttering up the stage; rehashed, warmed-over, or half-baked. Thus we get the interweaving of two song numbers, progression by alternating fits and starts in book and score, present and former selves interacting (*Follies*), movable platforms of different levels (*Company*), closely packed human blocs dancing as viscous mass (from Prince's *Evita*, likewise choreographed by Larry Fuller), and reams of music and lyric writing that broken-wingedly take off from, or are takeoffs on, former Sondheim songs. No wonder audiences applaud bits of the overture as they ordinarily do only at revivals. They are welcoming back old Sondheim melodies even if they sound older and leaner after a long absence of invention.[36]

T. E. Kalem in *Time* magazine wanted to understand why the protagonist, Franklin, an unappealing hero, was false to his wife, his best friend
and his creative gift. Kalem said, "Outside of the cliché lure of Hollywood's
big bucks, George Furth's brittle, bitchy book never offers a plausible
clue."[37] Of Fuller's choreography, Kalem said it was mostly of the "hop,
skip and jump variety."[38] Sondheim's score didn't impress him, since he,
like Simon, heard repeated "fragmented strains from *Pacific Overtures,
A Little Night Music, Company* and *Follies.* On the other hand, he thought
the ballad "Not a Day Goes By" "beautifully captures the bittersweet
mystery of love, and the single smash number of the musical, 'Good Thing
Going,' has the stamp of permanence about it."[39] Kalem summed up what
for him was the major problem:

> Harold Prince and Stephen Sondheim seem to have been born middle-aged.
> Rue, disenchantment, a kind of middle-aged *tristesse* recur in their collabora-
> tions. In the most brilliant of them, *Company* and *Follies,* melancholia about
> marriage and success was imminent but airborne; in *Merrily We Roll Along*
> it falls with the thud of a foregone conclusion.[40]

Although Douglas Watt in the *Daily News* dismissed the musical, he said,
"Harold Prince has directed the book as inventively as possible."[41]

The one qualified positive review was written by Clive Barnes in the
New York Post, who suggested that his readers forget the negative things
they had heard about the musical and see it for themselves. He said, "The
word of mouth on the latest Stephen Sondheim musical, *Merrily We Roll
Along,* was so bad that all the words seemed dirty and the mouth was twisted
in a permanent sneer. Unquestionably the show was beset with trouble,
but in my opinion it has equally unquestionably triumphed—at least it
should as long as people distinguish between what they are actually seeing on stage and what they heard about the show during previews."[42] Barnes
said that "irony is very much the name of the game for the book and the
score."[43] The one problem for Barnes was that the cast, as they receded
25 years in time, never aged. He said, "If Prince was to blame for this—
and presumably he was—the rest of his work is credit all the way. . . . Prince
keeps the show whirling like confetti in the wind, stopping only for dramatic
points and major songs which are punched in with authoritative zest."[44]

Prince was devastated by the failure of the show. It closed two weeks
and sixteen performances after its long delayed opening. Prince talked
of his deep feelings abut *Merrily* and the youngsters in the cast:

> I suppose there is no play that I wanted more to succeed—no more traumatic failure. There were all those kids. I know it was better for them to have worked with us, better for them to have had a Broadway play dedicated to them. But it failed them.[45]

Sondheim believed that *Merrily* had turned out to be a very good show even though it had come together only during the last five previews. He talked about all the changes that had been made during the tryout period. "We made an attempt to simplify the production which turned out to be impossible because the production was just too heavy and complex and unattractive. The production was unattractive—visually. Hal kept trying to simplify it—but we couldn't simplify it enough. The writing was fine, the show is fine, there is very little in it that I would rewrite. I think the show is swell."[46] Lyricist Lee Adams said that "Sondheim told me that *Merrily* should have been done small."[47]

Ten hours after *Merrily* closed, the cast album was recorded. Although the show was a "flop" in Broadway jargon, Prince had claimed even before this show that "flop" is an expression he doesn't mind using. He explained that one-third of everything he'd done had been a flop and that if *Merrily* proved to be a failure he would do what he always does the morning after an opening night. "I call a meeting in my office to talk about my next show. It's something George Abbott taught me. The meeting is already set, and I've found it's the very best thing you can do."[48]

A Doll's Life

The day after *Merrily We Roll Along* closed, Prince had his usual "morning after" meeting. The next show on his agenda was the musical *A Doll's Life*. The idea for this show began with Betty Comden and Adolph Green, who wrote the book and lyrics. The story was to be about Nora Helmer, the heroine of Henrik Ibsen's *A Doll's House*, and begin after she leaves her husband Torvald and their three children. The writers would examine the next four years of Nora's life, observing her working for pay, attaining power, having love affairs and concluding with her next major decision about her life.

The musical reflected both Comden and Green's experiences, including their four-decade working partnership. Each had been married and had children. Comden's husband had been a very enlightened man who was interested in his wife's career and encouraged her collaboration with Green. Comden was aware, however, that not all women have this kind of healthy relationship with their mates. This concern and sympathetic interest in the subject led to the idea of continuing Nora's story.

Comden and Green presented Prince with the proposed project about two years before it reached the stage. Prince liked the premise and encouraged them to start writing. Prince explained why he was stimulated by the idea. "I like shows that are about something. I particularly like them if they are political and yet, at the same time entertaining. *A Doll's Life* touches on an important issue; it was an important issue 100 years ago and it's still an issue. Can you really imagine what it was like for Nora to walk out of that door in Norway in 1897?"[49] Prince felt there was a danger that the piece could easily become a theoretical lesson in "knee-jerk feminism."[50] The last thing he wanted was a staged lecture.

> It isn't about a woman's rights any more than *A Doll's House* was. . . . Ibsen didn't intend that. He intended it to be about people standing on their own feet—in this case, not only Nora but her husband as well. Nora's story forces you to examine the issues. You hear that she can't operate her own business, that she can't have her own bank account, that she has no legal rights. Some of these things have changed, others not at all. What I like about *A Doll's Life* is that *we* don't have to force those issues on the audience—the mere fact that the story is being told causes those issues to be raised.[51]

A Doll's Life meant a return to the Scandinavian setting of *A Little Night Music*—and to romance, but not empty romance. Prince warned Comden and Green that "good ideas tend, in the theatre, to be great disappointments."[52] Realistic musicals do not generally excite Prince. On the contrary, he is more interested in nonrealistic materials.

After working on the script of *A Doll's Life* for two years with the writers, Prince felt that the idea remained compelling, but the "show lacked the poetry that abstraction brings."[53] The script was finally completed under Prince's editorship, with the director helping to release it from its realistic constraints. Much of what happens in *A Doll's Life,* therefore, is the product of Prince's imagination. He conceived the idea of setting the story within the context of a modern-day rehearsal of an Ibsen play.

Prince's visual concept for the piece followed a trip to Norway. He found Norway hard, masculine and exciting. He visited several museums to see the work of Edvard Munch. Prince felt Munch's colors were severe and swirling, "the colors of crisis."[54] The painter Munch and Ibsen shared obsessive relationships with women. Prince said, "The thing about Munch and Ibsen is there's that incredible love of women, but it has a dark side, as in Munch's *Vampires,* in which a woman sucks at her husband's neck, or *The Dance of Life,* in which the stages of a woman's life are dramatically depicted. The Munch figures inform Tim O'Brien's and Tazeena Firth's lavish settings and provide another, more severe level from which the audience is able to look in on Nora's 'education.' "[55] The symbolic use in *A Doll's Life* of a group of women shown at different stages of life was patterned after Munch's *The Dance of Life.*

Prince also wanted this musical to reflect the problems of men as well as women. Prince said, "I do think it's very key to the piece, from my own point of view, that it is about men as well, how we are forced to be good little soldiers, protectors, father figures. Yet it carries with it the need for a whole lot of accuracy about what women think, which I would not be aware of. So my wife's been a sort of sounding board."[56]

Prince suggested Larry Grossman to do the score for *A Doll's Life.* The composer's previously produced shows were *Goodtime Charley, Snoopy!!!* and the best known of the three, the 1970 *Minnie's Boys,* which lasted only 76 performances, but had a score greatly admired by Prince. He said, "I like Grossman's work very much, very much."[57] Grossman's work, however, was not familiar to Comden and Green, and teaming the three creative people required Prince's "time and diplomacy," said Jeremy Gerard in a *New York Times* article.[58] Grossman is quoted as saying, "Hal said something really helpful that I kept in the back of my mind. . . . He told me, 'Just remember, there are no rules.' "[59] The result was a score that the composer described as having "a certain unorthodox quality. I had to use a whole different set of tools for this, it stretched me."[60]

Prince was to direct the musical as well as co-produce. The Shubert Organization declined to invest in *A Doll's Life,* and James Nederlander, president of the Nederlander Theatrical Corporation, became the show's major investor, contributing $1 million of the $3 million capitalization. Nederlander said, "With Hal Prince, you're talking about one of the theatre's greatest talents—it's like going with Babe Ruth on the baseball field. I never read the script—I went with him and Comden and Green."[61] The show's other producers were Sidney L. Shenker, Warner Theatre Productions, Joseph Harris, Robert Fryer of the Ahmanson Theatre in Los Angeles, Mary Lea Johnson, and Martin Richards of the Producer Circle Company.

Once again, Larry Fuller was asked to choreograph; Timothy O'Brien and Tazeena Firth were hired to do set designs, Florence Klotz to do costumes, and Ken Billington to do the lighting.

Prince signed the 29-year-old Betsy Joslyn to star. She had first been in the chorus of *Sweeney Todd* on Broadway, eventually taking over the role of the ingenue Johanna early in 1980, and continuing the role on tour. Joslyn was chosen by Prince after hearing some 200 singer-actresses audition for the part of Nora in Los Angeles, Chicago and New York. The call was for someone in her late twenties with a fine soprano voice plus the ability to ''belt'' a song. Joslyn said after getting the role, ''It's a gigantic role. I think I leave the stage just once to change costume. It's the first really big thing I've done and it's very exciting for me.''[62] Prince did not wish his Nora to be a sophisticated woman. He had seen the two movie versions of the play, one with Jane Fonda and the other with Claire Bloom. He thought they played the role

> with the knowledge that in 100 years' time, there would be a woman's movement which would embrace the character of Nora as an early champion. They play Nora as a modern woman, the product of a century of change. You cannot play it that way and set the action in 1879. . . . Nora's decision (to begin life anew) was a frightening and anxiety-ridden one, and I think a little crazy. She's having a mini-nervous breakdown when she slams that door. It's not ''Kramer vs. Kramer.''[63]

George Hearn was signed to play Nora's husband Torvald and the lawyer Johan Blecker. He had last been on Broadway and in the national tour of *Sweeney Todd*. He had many Broadway and Off-Broadway credits and has since won a Tony Award for his role in *La Cage aux Folles*. Giorgio Tozzi, who had last been seen on Broadway as the star of the revival of *The Most Happy Fella* in 1979, was signed to play the role of Eric Didrickson.

After two years of preparation, the production began rehearsing in a compound of studios on lower Broadway on 19 April 1982. As is usual with Prince, more than half the work of mounting *A Doll's Life* had occurred before the company came together for the first time. They rehearsed eight hours a day, six days a week.

During rehearsals, Giorgio Tozzi was replaced with Edmund Lyndeck. Prince explained, ''Oh! He couldn't handle it. He's the nicest man alive, but he couldn't sing it and he couldn't act it. I thought he was wonderful in *The Most Happy Fella* but it was a different ball game. That's another case in point—you hire stars sort of blindly, you don't audition them, if you'd auditioned him you wouldn't have hired him. It's as simple as that and too bad.''[64]

Descriptions of Prince, how he looks, acts and rehearses, are often the subject of articles about him. He is described, for this show, as directing on his feet, pacing the bare wood floor of the rehearsal studio, while massaging his forehead as if looking for inspiration, a veritable perpetual-motion machine, never at rest. His typical outfit might be a tan pullover sweater in lieu of a jacket, matching slacks and a dark blue shirt and, sometimes, no socks. He is noted as slender, gray-bearded, balding, with his glasses perched on his head. Though in his mid-50s at the time of *A Doll's Life,* he had—and has—slightly protruding front teeth that give him a youthful look. Hal Linson of the *Los Angeles Herald Examiner* felt that Prince, during rehearsals, "moves gracefully, without agitation or haste, and though he is clearly winging it, his reactions are sharp and instinctive, evincing little indecision. If one approach doesn't play well, the next one—or the one after that—will."[65] His eyes dart constantly, missing little. Jeremy Gerard, writing in the *Los Angeles Times,* said, "He can be openly affectionate with the people he's working with, and equally brusque, expecting egos to be as sturdy as his when often they are not. A Prince rehearsal looks a lot like film work, the way scenes are repeated over and over until they're right and then 'set.' "[66] George Hearn admitted during rehearsals of *A Doll's Life* that he had previously done very little acting the way Prince directs. He said, "It's sort of choreographed. Hal has, it seems to me, an inner film of what he wants to see. It's not my favorite way to work as an actor, because it doesn't start from within and work out. . . . The gratification with Prince is working with someone so bright, so fast, and so generous. He's going like wildfire all the time. It's exciting to be around that mind."[67]

There are times during rehearsals, however, when Prince may feel that he is not working well. At such moments, he says "I'm sorry," and turns the rehearsal over to associates Ruth Mitchell and Paul Gemignani. Most times, however, he clearly conveys to his cast what he is aiming for. Jeremy Gerard goes on to say,

> The rehearsal process is one of synthesizing, from live actors and real objects, a replication of the picture of the show Hal Prince has in his head. . . . At the run-throughs, Prince watches intently. He is, at times, his actors' greatest fan, laughing at the jokes, impatient when outside noise breaks their concentration. . . . Reflecting on nearly six weeks of rehearsal, he proudly notes: "I have not wasted five minutes of rehearsal time on something I didn't believe in."[68]

There are recognizable directorial elements in *A Doll's Life*: the constantly busy background action, a "continuing legacy of his mentor George Abbott—and the use of distinct actors in lieu of a bland chorus."[69] Additionally, the movement appears less like formal dance, but flows naturally. Prince explained, "I don't believe in choruses. I don't gravitate toward shows with a lot of choreography. It puts the control out of my hands, and I mean, I might as well be responsible."[70] It was noted during rehearsals of *A Doll's Life* how Prince maintains control. Jeremy Gerard reported that Fuller was working on some movement comprising graceful swirling and sweeping gestures in accord with the romantic theme. After several hours, Prince came in to watch and it was "obvious to an observer," said Gerard, "that the movement didn't work for him. Mr. Prince then described to Fuller what he wanted. Returning to work after the break, Fuller told the dancers, 'We'll just keep doing it till we get what he's got in his head.' "[71]

Audiences invited to the final New York run-throughs were enthusiastic, and the company prepared to go to Los Angeles where the show was to try out for ten weeks. Much rehearsal time was spent with Paul Gemignani, sharpening the choral work to the point where its "tonalities are characteristically those of a Hal Prince musical."[72] In Los Angeles, on 15 June 1982, after a week of technical rehearsals and four previews, the musical opened at the Ahmanson Theatre. The local reviews were mostly negative. Dan Sullivan in the *Los Angeles Times* said that the musical was in keeping with Comden and Green's view of things and was "a mild-mannered satire in an operetta framework."[73] He went on to say that the show proves how wise Ibsen was not to pursue Nora out into the world after she slammed that famous door. '

> The question mark at the end of *A Doll's House* may be one of the reasons the play still intrigues us. What actually happened to Nora isn't as interesting to contemplate as the myriad of things that might have happened. In general, Prince's staging gives signals of importance that the text keeps revoking. One instance is the cannery sequence, which looks as dark and baleful as a scene from *Sweeney Todd,* with a clank-your-chains chant from composer Larry Grossman. Then Nora's co-workers start bitching, and it's as harmless as *The Pajama Game.* The depth of the writing won't support the show's visual superstructure.[74]

Reviewing the show for the *Los Angeles Daily News,* Rick Talcove discussed Prince in his role as director. He said that even the dullest musicals have been known to be saved by an inventive director, and there is "no director more inventive than Harold Prince. As always, Prince's work is efficient, graceful and pleasing to the eye."[75] In spite of these compliments, Talcove went on to say that he thought this show was the most unoriginal work of Prince's career.

> You might say that *A Doll's Life* is, directorially speaking, Prince's "Remembrance of Things Past." The show abounds in staging techniques that have been used earlier—and to greater advantage—in previous Prince musicals. From *A Little Night Music* we have scenery with peering nude figures, an impromptu banquet and no choreography. From *Sweeney Todd,* there is the imposing bridge, a disruptive chorus, slamming door finale and no choreography. From *Evita,* we see two dancers dancing a tango in counterpoint to the main action and a heroine who sleeps around to attain success. Obviously, all directors have basic tricks they use to propel a show into action. But *A Doll's Life* which rehearsed seven weeks in New York, has somehow been refined to the point where it exists as being pretty but utterly passionless. On this occasion, Prince's staging technique cannot overcome the basic lackluster material he is working with.[76]

Although the local reviews in Los Angeles were negative, the company was bolstered by a favorable one in *Daily Variety:* "The show as it now stands is a breathtaking visual treat with a sensible book and score. With improvements it might become one of the great tuners of all time."[77]

There was plenty of time to make changes, since the musical was booked into the Ahmanson for ten weeks. For the next five, Prince and his company worked on relatively minor changes. They clarified ambiguities, condensed a prologue-like opening, moved a song and generally tightened the musical. This done, they decided that the cast members now needed time to settle into their roles. Dan Sullivan returned to see what had been done three weeks into the run. "It's a clearer, quicker, lighter show now than it was opening night, more like its frothy TV commercial," he said.[78] Still, he felt many problems remained.

Business was poor in Los Angeles in spite of the fact that tickets had been presold as part of the Civic Light Opera subscription series. The weekly box office revenues were far short of potential, resulting in a loss of some $100,000 a week. Prince felt that a vacation would give him a fresh perspective and left for his home in Majorca. Everyone asked how he could leave a show in trouble but the director said, "The truth is I think we did our work in those first five weeks."[79]

By the end of the 10-week run in Los Angeles, the show had incurred an additional $1 million in costs. The money was raised by the producers without much difficulty. Nederlander advanced $300,000 more, noting that if "Hal had enough faith to put a lot of extra money in himself, and if he had enough faith to back the show, I had to back him, too."[80] (Prince had reportedly pledged $350,000 of the needed million and also made certain guarantees against future losses.)

When the director returned from Majorca along with the show's writers, they felt that things looked fine. Eager to avoid extra expenses, Prince cut the California run by two weeks and on 8 September, began previews in New York. The reaction of preview audiences was sympathetic but when *A Doll's Life* opened on Broadway on 23 September 1982 at the Mark Hellinger Theatre, the reviews were terrible.

Frank Rich in the *New York Times* described the musical as a well-intentioned show "that collapses in its prologue and then skids into a toboggan slide from which there is no return."[81] Douglas Watt in the *Daily News* found the effect of the sets too ominous. He thought Joslyn a poor choice for Nora. She could handle her songs well, but was devoid of charm. Hearn, he felt, was somewhat better in a thankless role. Watt continued:

> Nothing is right about this show; not the capriciously unwinding Comden-Green book, not the Larry Grossman score, not even Harold Prince's staging, which seems obtrusive and heavy-handed. Of course, the whole thing was obviously a lost cause to begin with, and it's no wonder that all these people, as well as the cast, appear hopelessly adrift all the long evening.[82]

To Clive Barnes in the *Post, A Doll's Life* remained the dream of a musical unfulfilled. He said:

> The show itself lacks involvement. The book and lyrics miss the weight of Ibsen. The music sounds written to order. It invites comparison with Stephen Sondheim's *A Little Night Music* and falls short. . . . Except in its look and performance, the show itself never flies with the concept. And even the performances waver dangerously in some no man's land between the Broadway musical and the classic theater.[83]

John Simon didn't like the show but he credited Prince in his *New York* magazine review with "one clever idea (again involving doors!)."[84] He described the scene where "an opera is seen from the vestibule of a set of boxes, and whenever a loge door opens for a few seconds, the ludicrous operatic dumb play becomes, yet more ludicrously, audible."[85]

The almost unanimously poor reviews shocked the company. A closing notice was immediately posted: they would close following the Sunday matinee after a total of five performances. It left the collaborators dazed and unable to perceive what went wrong. Was it poor judgment, a poor idea, unwarranted optimism or just bad luck? Some felt that a workshop production might have been of help, others argued that more effort in California might have turned the show around. There were questions about the quality of the book and music. A few insisted that the staging and the casting of an unknown Nora were at fault. "Still others contended," said Michiko Kakutani in her *New York Times* article,

> that no one could have saved the show, that the idea was simply a bad one from the start. How, they asked, could one hope to base a musical on Ibsen and the issue of feminism? And yet, similar questions might have been asked of earlier Prince efforts: certainly shows based on an Argentine dictator and a murderous barber must have seemed equally incongruous—that is until *Evita* and *Sweeney Todd* went on to become hits.[86]

Prince, himself, was asked to consider what he felt happened with *A Doll's Life.*

> I know there are things wrong with *A Doll's Life.* Maybe we should have scratched deeper. But we scratched deeper than people acknowledged. I was accused of repeating myself (as a critic said to another critic who said to a friend, off the record, "I guess everybody was just tired of him doing his 'thing' "). Well, I tried to analyze what my "thing" was and I think I was caught between two "things": expressing myself and repeating myself. A lot of people out there are not expressing themselves. They're expressing their craft—smoothly and slickly and professionally—but not themselves. Still, I don't want to rip myself off, any more than I particularly want people to rip me off. Ironically, what probably bothered people more than anything else was that bloody structure upstage that looked like the bridge in *Evita.* You know, I didn't realize it until we were in the theatre and I suddenly saw the similarity. But I wasn't using it the same way. Had I known it was going to come up in so many of the criticisms, I would have excised it. Still, I'm proud of *A Doll's Life.* I know what's wrong with it. I hope it's going to have a life of its own. It deserves one. I believe that people resented it because it was a play about women—the inequity of being one. These are

conservative times. The ERA is as far from acceptance as it ever was, and our musical was pointing out that not enough had changed in a hundred years. Oddly enough, I think the Europeans would accept it. I hope that when we change horses—*if* we change horses—someone will undertake a fresh production of this material.

There's another aspect to the quick failure of that show which is worth mentioning. If you open a show in the Fall, as we did *A Doll's Life,* the entire season stretches ahead of you and the critics tend to be harsher. *West Side Story* opened in the Fall and the reviews were equivocal. *Evita* opened in the Fall and they were mixed (by the Spring it won the Drama Critics' Circle Award). Memories are short and maybe the season is a disappointment. I believe had *Doll's Life* opened at the end of a Broadway season— that Broadway season—it would have been gratefully received.[87]

Prince didn't dwell for long on the fact that he had just had his second consecutive failure. He took a day off and then began to work with Hugh Wheeler on a new version of *Candide* to be added to the repertoire of the New York City Opera. George Hearn, when asked how he felt about the quick closing of *A Doll's Life,* seemed to echo Prince's own credo, observing, "All of us in the theatre live with that rhythm and danger of failing. It's tiring but it's also worth a gamble because it's exciting, and it's not just about having a job or a career, but it's about ideas and values. In the end, it's what we live for."[88]

Operatic Ventures

I think there's a real relationship between courage and fear. It certainly figures in my life. . . . I can't speak for everybody—but I'm certainly aware of that when somebody says "I don't know how you do it" . . . maybe the simple fact of going to opening nights of your own more than once every five years, having to do it three and four times a year. It saved my neck because I was so depressed by what happened with A Doll's Life *and two weeks later* Candide *opened [at the New York City Opera]. That was very helpful and a month after that* Madama Butterfly *opened in Chicago and I was as proud of that as anything I've ever done. So that was very important. Now I've got* Turandot *this spring. So in a fiscal year I will have done four things. I think there's a real rela-*

> *tionship between the fear I have of flying and the amount*
> *of flying I do. It's called "get on the horse again" and*
> *"courage." Some of that I learned from George [Abbott].*
> *No question.*
> —Harold Prince, Interview with the author, 14 March 1983

After *A Doll's Life* closed, Prince was terribly depressed, but he soon found himself busy with other commitments, beginning with the direction of *Turandot* at the Vienna Staatsoper. Following on the heels of his *Candide* and *Sweeney Todd* for the New York City Opera, he staged *Madama Butterfly, Ashmedai* and *Silverlake* for that company. He also staged *Fanciulla del West* for the Lyric Opera of Chicago and the San Francisco Opera, and *Willie Stark* and *Candide* for the Houston Grand Opera. Prince's approach to staging operas is basically the same as in the theatre. The process doesn't change much, including the way in which he casts the performers. Since he can't read music, he directs from a script. He listens carefully to the score, relying somewhat on instinct. *Willie Stark* could have been staged realistically, but he wanted to make things larger than life, and treated it like a Greek drama with stairs and pillars on the set. Prince, who attended many operas as a child, sitting with his grandmother in a box at the old Metropolitan Opera House, talked to Beverly Sills about why he appears to be fascinated by opera:

> I'm fascinated with musical theatre and I love to work there. I equate it with opera. The quality of the acting, people doing the ensemble work is just as demanding. There should be no compromises. Operas are directed the same way as Broadway shows.[89]

The only problem Prince has in directing operas is how to deal with the multitudes of chorus members. "How do you make stage pictures with all those people?"[90] Instead of keeping them all on the stage, Prince often has some singers offstage. He compares this to the nineteen chorus members he used in *Sweeney Todd.* He broke the chorus into small groups and yet the stage seemed to be filled with people.[91]

Play Memory

In 1983, after Prince returned to New York from his opera assignments in Europe, he went into rehearsal with Joanna Glass's *Play Memory.* Glass had had two of her plays appear Off-Broadway: *Artichoke* and *American Gothic*. She had been represented on Broadway with *To Grandmother's House We Go*. *Play Memory* is a slice-of-life drama about a family man's alcoholic self-destruction. Set in the wintry outpost of Saskatoon, Saskatchewan in the period from 1939 to 1968, the play deals with the man's betrayal by his employee-friends and his deteriorating relationship with his wife and daughter. Starring Donald Moffat, Jo Henderson and Valerie Mahaffey, the play opened at Princeton's McCarter Theatre in October 1983, running for three weeks. It was presented in association with the Annenberg Center, University of Pennsylvania. The local Princeton critic, Phil Cornell, in the *Courier-News*, said, "As for noted Broadway director Hal Prince, his work on *Play Memory* is a remarkable reflection of a consummate talent. Prince unfolds these scenes with blocking and a natural flow and power that are wonders to behold."[92] On the other hand, Cornell thought that the play had serious structural problems, only blunt exposition, and ambiguous characterizations.[93] Mel Gussow reviewed the show in Princeton for the *New York Times*:

> The production has been skillfully directed by Mr. Prince. . . . The evening is shadowed by its antecedents, especially *Death of a Salesman* and *Da*, both of which centered on strong-willed fathers with far richer dramatic results. In *Play Memory* the potential exists for an evocative play about a daughter coming to terms with her childhood, but the memory would benefit from further distillation.[94]

In spite of the mixed reviews, Alexander H. Cohen and Hildy Parks (Mrs. Cohen) decided to present *Play Memory* on Broadway. It opened at the Longacre Theatre on 26 April 1984 with the same actors in the leading roles. Frank Rich didn't like the piece, writing in the *Times* that "*Play Memory* is full of memories, but it can scarcely be called a play. . . . Miss Glass can't transform her sincerely felt material into drama. Though tragic events unfold with clocklike regularity in *Play Memory*, we feel nothing."[95] Rich also found fault with Prince's work: "Though Mr. Prince almost always imparts a high gloss to his productions, this one is raggedly paced on a rickety set."[96] *Play Memory* closed quickly.

Prince, called by Carol Lawson in the *New York Times* "the Henry Kissinger of theatrical directors"[97] because of his shuttling from one big project to another, was about to open yet another play less than two weeks after *Play Memory* opened.

End of the World

Arthur Kopit's new play *End of the World* was scheduled to have a four-week out-of-town tryout in Washington, D.C., and open in New York on 6 May 1984 at the Music Box Theatre. Starring Linda Hunt, Barnard Hughes and John Shea, the play is an autobiographical story of a playwright's attempt to write a drama about the nuclear arms debate. Kopit's play was the first new serious American play of the 1983–84 season, one of the very few in recent years produced directly for Broadway instead of originating Off-Broadway or at a not-for-profit regional theatre. This kind of serious play was a risky Broadway project. It posed the question: Could a play that searches out the moral and spiritual underpinnings of the nuclear arms debate engage a Broadway audience? The more cautious approach called for holding off the Broadway production until the play had proven itself under less pressured circumstances. Yet author Kopit, director Prince and the producers, the Kennedy Center and Michael Frazier, were willing to take a chance. Kopit's feelings about his play and about theatre in general seem to parallel Prince's own philosophy and may have been why Prince willingly took on this assignment. Kopit said:

> When you ask an audience to pay money and sit in a theater, you've got to do more than just delight them. Television can do that. Movies and musicals can get by just with glitz, dancing, entertainment, sheer technical excellence. In the theater, you must feel and think also. It has to do with why theater has always existed in civilization. Theater *matters.*[98]

Frank Rich of the *Times* didn't like the play.

> Mr. Kopit alights on a red-hot subject—the specter of nuclear holocaust—and bungles it so completely that he might as well be writing about toadstools instead of mushroom clouds. . . . One must assume that *End of the World* is merely an aberration in the career of a talented writer whose distinguished credits include *Indians* and *Wings.* One might also say that Mr. Kopit deserves brownie points simply for thinking about the unthinkable at a time when many playwrights look obsessively inward. . . . The director is Harold Prince, who keeps things moving as sleekly as possible on a stage decorated with atmospheric projections by Clarke Dunham and Lisa Podgur.[99]

End of the World closed after a short run, and Prince was soon preparing *Diamonds,* which opened in December of 1984. Presented by Stephen

G. Martin, Harold Defelice, Louis W. Scheeder and Kenneth John Productions in association with Frank Basile, this project, a revue, opened at the Off-Broadway Circle in the Square Downtown Theatre. The unifying theme of the revue was baseball, with sketches by such heavyweight writers as John Lahr, Ralph Allen, John Weidman, Roy Blount, Jr., Richard Camp, Sean Kelly and Alan Zweibel. The show's composers included Cy Coleman, Larry Grossman, John Kander and Gerard Alessandrini and among the lyricists were Betty Comden, Adolph Green and Fred Ebb. Here was Harold Prince, directing a show about baseball—the same Prince who, early in his career, had co-produced *Damn Yankees*, "the all-time champ of baseball musicals."[100]

The show received mixed reviews. Frank Rich liked only the setting, saying, "A more impressive move is Mr. Prince's choice of Mr. Straige's environmental set. Although neither the staging nor lighting fully capitalizes on the designer's work, the arena-shaped house has been transformed into a happy jumble of verisimilitude and whimsy—complete with a playing field, floating clouds and vintage Coca-Cola billboards."[101] With very few exceptions, Rich was not impressed with either the songs or the sketches. Clive Barnes was completely negative about the show. He begged Prince to "say it ain't so, say you had nothing to do with that director named Harold Prince associated with a show called *Diamonds*."[102] There were, however, some positive reviews, Douglas Watt of the *Daily News* calling the show a "winning affair," and writing, "Let's call *Diamonds* a Little League homer and let it go at that."[103] The modest Off-Broadway revue—certainly the "littlest" show Hal Prince had been associated with since his debut thirty years earlier—survived for a few months before audiences stopped coming.

Grind

Hal Prince had not had a successful show on Broadway since *Evita* and *Sweeney Todd*. The series of failures beginning with *Merrily We Roll Along* appeared to be never ending and must certainly have taken a toll on his confidence and what was widely recognized as his positive personality and endless supply of enthusiasm. Years later he talked of receiving a great deal of support at home from his family during the lower periods in his career. "I've got no reason to go and sulk somewhere. It's not in my nature, but it also isn't in my home. At home there's a lot of anger when I'm mistreated, there's a lot of fury, my wife is the most wonderfully intelligent and interesting (and often volatile) human being that ever lived—and supportive."[104] Given this support, it was not long before Prince threw himself into preparing his next project, a musical called *Grind.* While he was working on this show, he was also beginning to formulate plans for his own personal career goals and for his production office. He had been increasingly concerned about the soaring costs of mounting a Broadway musical, and whether or not he should even try to continue as a producer with the attendant and mounting problems of that job as the economics of Broadway became more and more complex. The offer to produce and direct *Grind,* however, forced him to set aside any thought of making major decisions about closing his office and establishing new priorities.

Grind had begun its long journey toward a life on Broadway in 1975 when writer Fay Kanin was approached by a pair of producers from Universal Studios to prepare a screenplay about a bi-racial burlesque house in 1930s Chicago. Kanin prepared the script but the project never materialized. Toward the end of 1982, Kanin approached Prince, an old friend, and suggested that the screenplay might make a good musical. Prince read the script and soon called Kanin back to say that he loved it and would start preparing it as a stage musical. In his later *Newsweek* review of the show, Jack Kroll said, "You can see why Fay Kanin's book appealed to Prince; it's reminiscent of such Prince shows as *Cabaret* and *Follies* in its attempt to use showbiz as a metaphor for the dislocations of reality."[105]

Larry Grossman was again called on by Prince to supply the music, with Ellen Fitzhugh writing the lyrics and Lester Wilson devising the choreography. Kanin spent the next two years rewriting and simplifying the complex love story, and working with her collaborators.

Prince was to produce *Grind* in association with Kenneth D. Greenblatt, John J. Pomerantz, Mary Lea Johnson, Martin Richards, James M. Nederlander, Michael Frazier, Susan Madden Samsons and Jonathan Farkas. Raising the money for the show was not a happy task for Prince. Never enthusiastic about having to do this part of a producer's job, *Grind*'s $5 million budget forced Prince to seek backers far afield of his usual Broadway haunts. He recalled that

> it started right at the beginning with my being asked to go down to Houston, Texas to do a backer's audition for a bunch of oil people. I didn't want to, but I did. No one told me that all they wanted to do was shake my hand and have many, many drinks and chat. Instead, we played fourteen songs and sang them . . . and no one listened. That was the beginning, and from

then on it became an experience of auditioning here and there with producers (nice enough) and their wives and families in attendance. I have never been professionally that unhappy in my life.[106]

The director felt that *Grind* was different in some ways from other shows he had done except for *Cabaret*, referring to the fact that there were elements in both shows (chorus girls in sexy stockings and garters, for example) which had overt commercial appeal. *Grind* gave Prince the opportunity to mix "commercially" humorous and erotic elements, as he had in *Cabaret*, with a serious depiction of the kind of violence inherent not only in Chicago of the 1930s, but today. The story takes place during the Depression and tells of interracial love and conflict against the backdrop of a burlesque house that features two casts, one black, one white, "each group rigidly separated both on- and offstage."[107] Jack Kroll in *Newsweek* said, "Metaphorically, the place is also the world, with all its problems of division between people. The tension is embodied in an interracial triangle."[108] Prince admitted, "Of course, it would have to have had serious underpinnings or I probably wouldn't have become interested in doing it."[109]

For his cast, Prince turned to such seasoned professionals as Ben Vereen and Stubby Kaye and, with his usual enthusiasm for young and largely untried talent, chose Leilani Jones and Timothy Nolen for other leading roles.

Clarke Dunham was signed to create the set, which rotated to reveal the burlesque theatre's marquee and facade at one point, its stage, wings and the lights of stairs leading to a dingy, cluttered dressing room at another. Reginald Marsh paintings were consulted to inspire the feel of the Depression-era burlesque palace.

Lester Wilson's choreography was described by Jack Kroll in *Newsweek* as "a jagged blend of urban elegance, vulgarity and pathos . . . the best in a Prince show since Michael Bennett struck out on his own;"[110] he went on to say that the dances were "the cumbersome musical's best assets."[111] Douglas Watt in the *Daily News* singled out Ben Vereen's "spiffy second act solo dance,"[112] and went on to say that

it has been no secret along Broadway that *Grind*, in serious trouble out of town, gained the assistance of Bob Fosse (uncredited in the program) in touching up a few dance numbers, among them that dandy Vereen solo. Just as the controlled sensuality that is his trademark coils and uncoils in the star's happy dance, there is no mistaking the Fosse hand in the imaginative second-act opening in which strippers are seen langorously dressing for their act, or in the opening female ensemble.[113]

Subsequently Prince commented:

Apparently Mr. Watt knows more about the show than I do. Bob Fosse had no hand in the "imaginative second act opening" and didn't touch up any of the other dance numbers. That was all the excellent work of Lester Wilson.[114]

Several years later, Prince discussed Fosse's participation in *Grind*:

It was the beginning of our resolving some of the old problems we'd had in past years and it gave me pleasure. When Ben Vereen asked Bobby to choreograph a number for him, he agreed providing that I agree. I said, "Sure, I don't care, certainly if it's going to make Ben behave and feel more secure." So Bobby did it. Cruelly, Ben let Bobby down. He kept him (Fosse) waiting for an hour and 45 minutes at rehearsal—and Bobby was doing *him* the favor. One afternoon Bobby auditioned that number for me and Gwen [Verdon, Fosse's former wife] who was there for moral support. It was one of the dearest things because he was so nervous worrying what I would make of it. I liked it and I thanked him. I suppose he was afraid people would say Bob Fosse was taking over Hal Prince's direction. For that reason, he never came near the theatre. He'd worked punishing hours in a rehearsal studio and took nothing for it.[115]

Prince talked of how, not long after Bob Fosse died, the trajectory of their lives came full circle.

We had absolutely some kind of nice bridge to each other. . . . It was on the first day of rehearsal of *Phantom* [*The Phantom of the Opera,* a musical Prince would direct some two years after *Grind*]. There I was on 19th Street at the Michael Bennett rehearsal studios introducing the show to the cast and looking down and seeing Nicole [the daughter of Bob Fosse and Gwen Verdon who was in the show], and I found that very moving, extraordinary. And then at the first dress rehearsal of the show when I was in the theatre, Gwen had sneaked in and was sitting way in back of the theatre. I looked around into the house and saw that red hair. I went back to find her and I had great warm feelings about her sitting there watching her daughter. And then on opening night, she sat in the box near where Judy and I sat . . . and I saw her there. So I felt . . . family about everything.[116]

Grind was capitalized at $4,750,000 and was scheduled to open 16 April 1985 at the Mark Hellinger Theatre in New York after a Baltimore try-out and local previews which were prolonged by a last-minute postponement. It arrived at the close of a Broadway season which many had judged to be, in the words of *Time* critic William A. Henry III, "among the worst in a decade or more. . . . The prime barometer of trouble has been the lack of even one new musical hit."[117] Of the seven musicals that had made it to Broadway in the 1984–85 season, four closed after runs of three weeks or less.

Reviews for *Grind* were mostly negative, the major focus of criticism being leveled at the book and music. Clive Barnes in the *Post* felt that the book was confused and muddled in its dramatic purpose, although it was an "ambitious and in some ways innovative, almost despairingly innovative, new musical."[118] He went on to say that there was "too much book chasing too little music—or, at best, too little noticeable music."[119] Barnes felt that Prince had done a "great job. He has always appreciated a directorial challenge, and he grabs up this show's heavy gauntlet with gallant alacrity."[120] Frank Rich in the *New York Times* agreed with Barnes and suggested that the creators' intentions remained cloudy. He said, "We don't really know what's happening, but, for a while there's so much to watch that we don't really care."[121] Rich felt that Prince had knit the arresting incidents of the show together "with more assurance than he's mustered in any of his musicals since *Sweeney Todd*."[122] He felt, however, that the undertow of anger and rage which rippled throughout the songs and scenes and performances of the first act were not justified by what the book offered. Rich concluded his review with, "For all that's gone wrong with *Grind*, one never stops admiring the valor with which Mr. Prince and company get themselves out there and give it all they've got."[123]

Grind closed within a few weeks. Some years afterward, Prince expressed his feelings about the show.

I should have known better. I loved a lot of the material in that show. I knew it was good. I loved a lot of the score. I think it has one of the most beautiful ballads, "All Things to One Man." I think Larry Grossman and Ellen Fitzhugh are enormously talented. We started with something simple, but because of considerable external pressure, most of it imposed by the conditions of Broadway financing, we compromised. What Fay Kanin and the rest of us had in mind was a show about violence—every conceivable kind of violence which, sadly, we come to accept as a part of our everyday lives. That would have worked on Broadway fifteen years earlier; it would have had a run. It was never "commercial," but neither was *Pacific Overtures.* I loved the idea of that show, but when you're raising $5 million, the first question is, "Who's starring?" Instead of walking away then and doing it in a little theatre somewhere else on the globe (most obviously I was the leader) I'm to blame for taking them down the garden path. Back to the original question: "Who's starring?" According to Bernie Jacobs of the Shubert Organization, Ben Vereen at that time was the only financeable black performer in the country (there would be others today). So we interested Ben Vereen. But understandably, he wasn't going to play a small role, a cameo. So we started to twist the material to accommodate him, and gradually the show became about a black and white confrontation. Just as gradually we began to smooth down its hard edges to make it "entertaining." It became for me the most painful working experience of my life. I hadn't been true to myself or my collaborators.[124]

Prince's career as well as his spirits were at a record low, and he decided to go ahead with his plan to close his production office. He would take a year off to think through how and where he would want to do shows in the future. He spoke of his feelings after the failure of *Grind* and about the state of producing for Broadway at that time: the vast amounts of money were just too much for him to deal with.

> I had patronage all those years. That's what it really amounts to. I raised $250,000 via a one-letter-offering sent to 175 people, most of whom invested $1,000. They were undoubtedly as proud of the adventurous failure as they were of the success. For $1,000 they had a piece of *Follies*. When a show made money, of course they were thrilled. When it lost, they seemed genuinely interested in what we had attempted. Nobody interfered. There were so many of them. Nobody asked to read a script. Nobody wanted a drink at Gallagher's after a preview to express how he'd fix the show. Today the same show costs $8 million and anybody who is going to put up that kind of money feels he has a right to that drink at Gallagher's. Maybe so. All of this clearly compromises the quality of the art. You can't experiment. You can't *lose.* Experimenting is for elsewhere. But where? I am lucky to have been born when I was, but times have changed. Let's just say it's had 50 to 70 years to be done in a certain way, and now it will have to find a new way.[125]

It was a sad commentary on the state of the musical theatre that a man of Prince's talents and artistic integrity, who had brought so much to Broadway, was now feeling forced to do his shows elsewhere. He wasn't the only one, however. Other artists of the musical theatre were also planning projects to be done in workshops and Off-Off-Broadway (Stephen Sondheim and James Lapine would soon do *Sunday in the Park with George* as a showcase Off-Broadway). The fact that Prince, who had influenced so strongly the course of the Broadway musical, was thinking of turning elsewhere to work was also a signal that he intended to remain true to his own principles. He hoped he would not have to compromise his goal of a substantive and innovative musical theatre. It was assumed by those close to him that his artistic voice would no doubt remain strong wherever he chose to do his work.

Prince closed the producing end of his office totally, and decided to hire himself out as a director. He and his staff moved into offices in Rockefeller Center half as large as the space he had had for over thirty years while functioning as a producer. Prince made public his unhappiness about the state of Broadway and its economics by quitting its trade group, the League of New York Theatres and Producers. Angered by soaring ticket prices and labor costs, his letter of resignation stated that "for some absurd reason, no one is willing to admit that the interests of the producers and the theatre owners are not the same."[126]

When Hal Prince got back into action in August of 1986, it was the beginning of a very fertile period in his artistic life, one in which he would direct *The Phantom of the Opera,* the most financially successful musical ever to be presented on Broadway, while at the same time shepherding an unsuccessful musical called *Roza* and his long-anticipated revival of a revamped *Cabaret* in the fall of 1987. Prince had shaken off much of the unhappiness he suffered after the failure of seven of his shows in a row. He has often stated, however, that his main objective in doing these three new shows in rapid succession was not just to have something of his on Broadway. In his inimitably enthusiastic manner, Prince said,

> I think everything has turned out for the best in my life. I think one needs an abrasive and traumatic period and then, with some luck and perseverance, maybe a *Phantom of the Opera* will come along.[127]

Roza

With *Roza, Cabaret,* and *The Phantom of the Opera,* Hal Prince took on only the role of director—not of producer. But limiting himself to just directing was a trade-off. In a 1987 interview with *New York Newsday* he said, "You relinquish the final work when you give up being producer.... It was simpler being a producer in one way. The only element that is better about being a director and not producing as well is the burden of raising money. But, in return for working with producers, there's another voice, there are other options. Things are a little bit more complicated."[128] Prince went on to explain that, just as he doesn't like raising vast amounts of money for a show, he doesn't like spending it. "It's dangerous artistically," he said.[129] Because he has so much experience producing, however, he ends up handling some of the production matters even if he doesn't carry that title. He says, "I know quite a bit about how to do it, so people are not unwilling to seek my advice when I'm working with them."[130]

The director's 1987 musical *Roza* may, it has been observed, represent Hal Prince thinking small. The musical is based on the 1975 book *Le Vie devant soi* by Romain Gary, which became the source material for the French film *Madame Rosa* starring Simone Signoret and which won the Oscar for best foreign film of 1977. The book, movie and play tell the story of an aging Jewish Parisian prostitute who makes her living raising the children of her colleagues, and of her close relationship with one of her charges, a young Arab boy named Momo. Prince said, "I did not care for it at all. . . . Too grim and self-pitying."[131]

French composer Gilbert Becaud, known for such songs as "What Now My Love," had wanted to write a musical version of the film soon after seeing it, but there were many problems in clearing the rights. Romain Gary, who had died before plans were made for the stage musical, had written the novel under a pseudonym. Because the name he had used happened to be the name of a real person, lawyers spent a great deal of time in resolving the issue, and it would be a couple of years before Becaud could approach Prince to direct his now-completed musical version of *Madame Rosa*. Becaud had seen several shows directed by Prince over the years and was a great fan of the director's—very impressed with Prince's approach to musical theatre. Some years earlier, Becaud had written to Prince, saying he would like to work with him and Prince had told the composer that he would be interested in such a collaboration. Prince recalls that in 1961, after the sudden death of his friend and producing partner Robert E. Griffith, he had gone off to Europe feeling very low. There, he met Judy Chaplin, who played a recording of a song for him in Paris which had been written by Becaud and sung by the composer—a song about losing a friend. Judy Chaplin became Prince's wife and, now, more than two decades later, he and Gilbert Becaud became collaborators on *Roza*.

It took almost seven years and several abortive attempts before *Roza* would see the stage. It was originally due to open in Paris. Prince said at the time that he wouldn't do it in America. "I insisted it be done in Paris and they said fine. I thought it would be fun to live in Paris for six weeks and work."[132] When Paris didn't happen, plans were made to stage *Roza* in London's West End in 1981. Prince, in fact, was against doing the show in the West End but that problem was resolved when the producers lost their money the day before going into rehearsal for the London production. Prince then called in two Broadway producers, Martin Richards and Mary Lea Johnson of the Producers Circle and through their combined efforts with Center Stage, a Baltimore nonprofit regional theatre, they were willing to take on the project with the knowledge that the musical might never become a commercial success. Prince had been impressed with another production he had seen at Baltimore's Center Stage, and suggested the theatre for the premiere presentation of *Roza.*

The relationship between commercial legitimate theatre producers and nonprofit resident theatres was taking on a new twist at this time. The resident theatres had previously confined themselves to presenting mainly straight plays; however, during the late 1986 and early 1987 season, musicals were being given full productions at such nonprofit League of Resident Theatre companies as San Diego's Old Globe Theatre and the Center Stage in Baltimore. The built-in audiences at regional theatres allow the production of a musical at one-third the cost of a commercial undertaking. *Roza* was able to benefit from this new and more flexible attitude at regional theatres.

With a cast headed by Georgia Brown of *Oliver!* fame and Bob Gunton, who had played Juan Peron in *Evita, Roza* opened at the Center Stage in Baltimore in December 1986 and ran through January. The show was very well received by critics and audiences alike, who obviously thought well of the Becaud score and the book and lyrics by Julian More, an Englishman living in France. The show set a box office record at the Center Stage in January.

It was at the nonprofit theatres that Prince, until the phenomenal success in London of *The Phantom of the Opera,* was greatly accepted. Here, working outside the commercial Broadway situation, he found he had more time to work and with less pressure. He said, "I don't think I would want to go into rehearsal, perhaps ever again, when we were going to preview in five weeks and open on Broadway in eight. The economic burden, the whole thing just takes over."[133] Another advantage, Prince feels, of working away from New York, is the chance to flop with a show (as in London) and still get a year's run. "Even if a show doesn't work out at the box office, emotionally an investor feels better if it's been allowed to run. It feels as if it's been worth the trouble."[134] Prince feels this is the way writers and directors are nurtured. "One of the nice things about doing opera," he says, having done many both in the United States and Europe, "is knowing that I'm not going to kill *Madama Butterfly.* I'm either going to do a swell production or I'm not. But the opera will last beyond my statement."[135]

From Baltimore, *Roza* moved on to the Mark Taper Forum in Los Angeles, another prominent resident theatre. It still needed a lot of work and Prince added a new opening number, some new scenes and some new lyrics. Additionally, one character's role was extended and there were changes in the costumes and sets. The Los Angeles critics were mostly favorable and cited the physical production designed by Alexander Okun, whom Prince feels has a great talent and with who he hopes to work again. The critics also liked the vitality of Prince's staging. "Director Hal Prince has struck gold with *Roza,* a heartfelt musical employing not only a story with universal appeal, but also grouping together the talents of composer Gilbert Becaud and Georgia Brown to create a memorable experience."[136] Tom Jacobs, writing in the *Los Angeles Daily News,* was not so admiring: "*Roza* is the sort of show for people who like their sentiment among other things—laid on thick."[137] Audiences, however, loved the show. It was a sellout and the producers began plans to take it to Broadway.

Roza had been a hit at two regional theatres, breaking box office records in Baltimore and enjoying an extended run in Los Angeles. Producers Mary Lea Johnson and Sam Crothers representing Producers Circle convinced the Shubert Organization to join the producer lineup, and an opening on Broadway at the Royale Theatre was tentatively set for 27 August 1987. During this time, Prince was as busy as at any time in his career— readying his London smash *The Phantom of the Opera* for its Broadway debut, rehearsing his revival of *Cabaret* and, of course, whipping *Roza* into final shape for its New York opening. The three shows were to open on Broadway within three months of each other.

A firm opening date for *Roza* was announced for 1 October 1987 with previews scheduled to begin 14 September. During previews, audiences seemed to love the show. When it opened, however, critics did not share the audience enthusiasm, some reviewers feeling the characters were mere caricatures and not fully fleshed-out. Howard Kissel in the *Daily News* said "*Roza* gives vulgarity a bad name."[138]

Clive Barnes of the *New York Post* noted that Prince, who had been chiefly associated in the past with spectacle, was attempting a more intimate chamber-like piece: "Here [Prince] shows his mettle no less effectively in smaller measure."[139] Barnes went on to praise Georgia Brown's performance as Roza, and said she "is more than sweet, she is fantastic."[140] Howard Kissel felt the transsexual character, Lola, was "played with great finesse by Bob Gunton."[141] TV reviewer Joel Siegel agreed, feeling that Bob Gunton was "extraordinary."[142]

Evita and *Roza* co-star Bob Gunton said that Prince isn't usually around when the reviews come in. "He goes somewhere and when he gets [the reviews], he digests them. He's also very direct about how he feels about them. He doesn't say, 'Oh, they don't affect me' or 'I don't care what they say.' He does care what they say, and he gets angry. Then he lets it go."[143]

Having had two major roles in Prince musicals, Bob Gunton has some valuable insights into the director's methods:

> He's tremendously articulate in kind of an abstract way . . . but in a moment-to-moment human interaction that actors have to stumble through, he certainly knows when it's right, when it's truthful. Then he gets this wonderful kind of grin and he sits still . . . and when he's grinning and sitting still (and maybe his eyes are moistening a little bit), then he can give you even better feedback and of course can frame all of this within the piece. . . . The added motivation on my part is to keep him from getting bored because he has a very low threshold of boredom. . . . He makes it known when you're not "banging the gong," so it's fun to surprise him, if possible, with something different or surprising, or try a new take.[144]

Gunton talked of Prince maturing and gaining more wisdom in recent years. He said that Prince had been more volatile while working on past shows, but by the time of *Roza,* said Gunton, "he had reached that stage in his life where he wants to do things as kindly as possible, and has discovered that that's also the most efficient."[145] Gunton admires Prince for having the courage to bring in a show like *Roza* and "allowing it to be what it was . . . not fiddling around too much with it."[146] Gunton said that "the most thrilling thing was [Prince's] generosity in allowing us, particularly Georgia [Brown] and I to explore all kinds of ways of doing these things. He would normally have his suggestions but he was very, very open to our input. It was the best collaborative effort on a character in a musical that I've ever had."[147]

Prince, himself, talked about the experience of directing *Roza.*

> I loved the *Roza* experience on the stages in Baltimore and Los Angeles where it broke house records. It should never have come to Broadway. I knew that

from the first and I told the authors and producers, "Just don't make Broadway the end of the line." *Roza*'s copyright would have been worth something because of its success in Baltimore and Los Angeles and there would have been productions all over the U.S. There were productions being negotiated for Scandinavia and Paris and Germany. All of these fell threw when the show failed on Broadway. Today there are more ways to skin a cat. Sam Shepard has never had a success on Broadway and he's a Pulitzer Prize-winning playwright.[148]

A Re-Vision:
Cabaret

A plan to revive the 1966 Hal Prince hit musical *Cabaret* was set in motion twenty years later by producers Barry and Fran Weissler. They hoped to go into rehearsal in early 1987 and begin a national tour with the show on 26 February 1987 in Wilmington, Delaware, commencing then to such cities as Miami, Chicago, Los Angeles and San Francisco, before opening in New York seven months later.

The producers asked Prince to restage their revival and he agreed to do it. Prince said, "No one else was going to touch *Cabaret*."[1] Prince had always wanted to remount *Cabaret* and felt some helpful improvements could be made the second time around. He felt the revival accomplished just that. "Joel's [Grey, repeating his role as the Master of Ceremonies] performance is better . . . we all know that. He's grown into it . . . there's a disillusionment and a kind of pathos in it."[2] Although Prince feels that the rewriting of the book wasn't meant to make it an in-depth or flagrant examination of a homosexual writer, the collaborators were eager to show that the character Clifford was not relating to the Sally Bowles character because he has homosexual problems. Prince explains, "We didn't deal with it originally. . . . We did this time."[3] The director went on to discuss changes made in the score.

I never thought "Why Should I Wake Up" was up to the rest of the score. I think "Sally, Stay" is a beautiful song. "I Don't Care" had been written for the original production for Lotte Lenya to sing, but we couldn't use it. This time around Joel Grey sings it in the second act Kit Kat Klub scene.

"Meeskite" was written pure and simply for Jack Gilford. Without Jack Gilford, it didn't seem to belong in the show. I feel the changes were appropriate.[4]

The one thing that Prince feels may have "gone wrong" involved the design of the opening set for this new production. He asked that the first set as well as all the others in the show be based on Boris Aronson's 1966 designs, understanding that the audience must be given the initial, original image that Aronson created. Prince recalls:

I asked for Boris's initial stage picture. At the time it was innovative. People remember it, or *some* of it. They remember a mirror and a neon sign. But there were also trolley-car cables and globe street lamps which went upstage diminishing in size to give a sense of distance. It was strong and abstract and definitely Berlin pre-war. It was sacrificed on the grounds that it was too difficult to tour. All the rest of the scenery in the show was extraordinarily faithful to Boris' original design. Lisa Aronson, his widow, consulted on the new production and saw to that. But sacrificing the original image had a devastating affect on the *New York Times* critic. Mr. Rich, who had just co-authored (with Lisa Aronson) a definitive and excellent book on Aronson's career, criticized the tacky scenery, accusing the producers of saving money. Overkill on the part of Mr. Rich.[5]

The revival of *Cabaret* opened in New York at the Imperial Theatre on 22 October 1987. Although Joel Grey was repeating his role of the Master of Ceremonies, Prince had set an all new cast headed by Alyson Reed as Sally, Gregg Edelman as Clifford, Regina Resnik as the landlady Fraulein Schneider, and Werner Klemperer as Herr Schultz.

The critics were generally positive about the revival. Clive Barnes in the *Post* said,

Prince now takes the slightly harsher tone that the movie (six years, note, after Broadway) adopted. Thus Cliff is now accepted as a bisexual with no very strong heterosexual bent, and the Nazis' anti-Semitism is more pointed, particularly in the savage punchline of Grey's duet with a gorilla, as in the movie but earlier omitted on Broadway.[6]

Howard Kissel of the *Daily News* loved the show and felt that "Prince has recreated a brilliant show brilliantly."[7] Frank Rich in the *Times* pointed out that, in the original production, Joel Grey had received fifth, not first, billing, which was commensurate with the master of ceremonies role. Rich noted that "this time the performer must carry the entire show as if it were a star vehicle."[8] Kissel further commented on Werner Klemperer's characterization of Herr Schultz and said it was "refined, stressing the *German* rather than the Jew in his character, an important, deeply moving choice."[9] Klemperer himself discussed his feelings about working for Prince in *Cabaret:*

> Harold Prince is a super director. He gives the actors a lot of freedom in suggesting new ways to do things. When you show him three approaches to a scene, he will instinctively say, "This one is right, that one is wrong, and so is that one wrong." He has a wonderful eye for what will work.[10]

The revival of *Cabaret* ran on Broadway until June of 1988 and then continued on its national tour. Both Regina Resnik and Werner Klemperer were nominated for Tony Awards.

This was the first time that Harold Prince had directed a revival of one of his own shows. He was pleased with the reception, but he was soon very busy readying his London hit *The Phantom of the Opera* for its Broadway opening in January of 1988.

HIS "GREATEST PERSONAL SUCCESS"
—SO FAR:
The Phantom of the Opera

The Phantom of the Opera was first presented for public consumption in 1911 when French author Gaston Leroux published his novel *Le Fantome de l'Opéra.* It did not sell very well as a novel, but caused some interest when serialized in newspapers. Over the decades it gained greater popularity as a performance piece, becoming the source for no less than seven motion pictures, including a glossy Technicolor epic with Claude Rains in the title role in 1943, a British version in 1962 with Herbert Lom, a TV film in 1983 with Maximilian Schell, not to speak of a satirical rock adaptation called *The Phantom of the Paradise,* directed by Brian De Palma in 1983. The earliest screen incarnation, however, is perhaps the definitive *Phantom,* with Lon Chaney scaring the daylights out of worldwide audiences in the 1925 silent version. Additionally, there were British stage adaptations of *Phantom* in 1975 and 1984 (the latter a musical), as well as an American stage production in 1978. Coincidentally, another stage musical of *Phantom,* composed by David Bishop, was being performed Off-Broadway in New York at the time Andrew Lloyd Webber and Hal Prince were opening their musical version in London in 1986.

Lloyd Webber had seen the 1984 East London musical version of *Phantom.* The producers of this show had asked Sarah Brightman to play Christine, the object of the Phantom's affections, but she had been unavailable at the time. She would later get together with the Phantom, however, when her husband, Andrew Lloyd Webber, tailored the role to her talents in his own musical version.

Lloyd Webber had at first thought that *Phantom* would make a great camp-style musical in the vein of *The Rocky Horror Picture Show.* Feeling that it would be a good bet for a West End run, he called his producer Cameron Mackintosh with the idea and Mackintosh agreed that it was a good one.

Setting out on a search for a copy of the Leroux book, which had been out of print for years, Lloyd Webber found one in a second-hand book shop in New York and Mackintosh discovered one in his aunt's garage. Reading the book convinced Lloyd Webber and Mackintosh that the camp approach was wrong and that *Phantom* would be much more effective as a romantic musical—the kind of musical Lloyd Webber had wanted to write for years. Though Mackintosh assumed the composer intended to write a full original score, Lloyd Webber's first plan was to use mainly famous classical themes for the score, writing new incidental music as necessary as connective material.[1] This idea, however, was eventually discarded at the urging of a friend, Australian director Jim Sharman, who had directed *The Rocky Horror Picture Show,* and Lloyd Webber decided to compose the whole score himself.

The Leroux story of *The Phantom of the Opera* is about Erik, born severely deformed, and one of the architects of the Paris Opera House. During the building's design, Erik had built a secret hideaway far beneath the theatre, where he could escape from a world that derided his deformity, and where he could pursue his desire to write music. The story takes form as Erik falls obsessively in love with Christine Daae, a dancer in the corps de ballet. Christine, however, is in love with the handsome Viscount Raoul de Chagny. Ultimately, she must choose between the young and wealthy blond aristocrat and the deformed man who lives isolated in his basement hideaway.

In June of 1985 Lloyd Webber and his wife, Sarah Brightman, and Prince had dinner in London. *Grind* had closed and Prince was in the middle of what he calls "a famously over-publicized year off to nurse my wounds."[2] Lloyd Webber told Prince that he was beginning to work on *Phantom* and asked whether he would be interested. Prince had been thinking that the next thing he wanted to direct—to *see* on a stage—was a romantic musical. Harkening back to *South Pacific,* which is one of his fondest memories (and coincidentally is Lloyd Webber's favorite musical), without hesitation he agreed to direct the show.

After the Prince-Lloyd Webber *Phantom* opened, critics noted that its visual impact was refreshingly different from the high-tech extravaganzas that were threatening to re-define the musical theatre. Prince said, "It was this very difference that first attracted me back in 1985. . . . I was tired of what spectacle had become: high-tech, multi-media. If our *Phantom* was spectacular it would be through the use of Victorian stage techniques, signalling a return to an earlier sense of theatrical occasion."³ Michael Billington, theatre critic for the *Guardian* in Britain, agrees that *Phantom* is intelligent—or necessary—spectacle. He said,

> It is not laser beams. In a funny way, I think it goes against the trend of recent musicals just to give you mechanization, obvious dehumanization, enormous, scientifically-created spectacle, high tech. I thought *The Phantom of the Opera* a romantic musical and basically I thought Prince got that across—that it is actually about passion and thwarted love and all those other things and that's partly why it works. . . . I think the production, again, is spectacular and it's beautiful to look at. But the effects seem to me . . . they're certainly not dependent on visible technology . . . you're not bombarded in the way you are by *Time, Starlight Express* and those other idiot shows. I suppose Prince is helping to take the musical backwards. But that's just the way the musical has to go, because the way forward seems to me to be a terrible cul de sac. It's more and more expensive making spectacles but they just drain audiences and cost too much to stage . . . so the musical is bound to go backwards, it seems to me, towards characterization, stories and people . . . and that seems to be what *Phantom* is about and why it worked. . . . I think the musical has to be taken back some years to where it was when it was good with books and characters and things you identify with and passionate music and that's why people like *Phantom of the Opera.* . . . So if Lloyd Webber thinks Prince understands his work . . . it may be that Trevor Nunn was taking his work in the direction of spectacle and Hal Prince has sort of taken it back towards what I call "necessary spectacle." . . . I mean Nunn took it in the direction of jazzed-up technology.⁴

During July 1985, a first-act draft of *The Phantom of the Opera* was presented as a work-in-progress at Lloyd Webber's English country house at Sydmonton. The lyrics were written by Richard Stilgoe, a writer and musician who had also done the lyrics for *Starlight Express.* Maria Bjornson designed the presentation, even dropping a chandelier for the occasion. (The menacing chandelier above the heads of the Paris Opéra audience had been a major feature of the Leroux story and various of its theatrical and film incarnations, and would become a much-discussed stage effect in the Prince-Lloyd Webber *Phantom.*) The collaborators were all encouraged by the presentation's enthusiastic reception and decided to move ahead with plans for a major production in London's West End.

Prince felt that the Leroux novel had offered readers much more than had been expressed in the film adaptations. He noted the book's deeply rooted psychological overtones and an attention to detail that the films lacked. He felt that the Lon Chaney screen version was the one adaptation that "came closest to respecting the honesty with which Leroux had charted the emotional course of the characters. Perhaps, he said, "it follows that only music, operating primarily, could add to the power of silence."[5]

From June 1985 until the show went into rehearsal on 18 August 1986 in London at Her Majesty's Theatre, Prince met in both London and New York with the authors and stage designer Maria Bjornson. He also visited Paris to study the opera house where the action of *Phantom* takes place. The theatre, built between 1861 and 1875 by architect Charles Garnier, is a marvel of construction. Occupying three acres, it is the largest such theatre in the world, with the auditorium and stage areas taking up only a fifth of the total space. It is seven stories high, and once housed a stable of horses and a massive lake whose water was used to operate the hydraulic stage machinery. Prince visited the site of the famous lake five stories below the stage in the depths of the opera house, and climbed to the rooftop where the final scene of act 1 of *Phantom* takes place. Prince recalled,

> There is no path up there, there are no handrails to hang on to, you simply scramble behind a nimble-footed Paris Opera engineer. The wind is blowing, you don't look down, and when you get to the top, one foot perched on either side, you look across to the people on top of the Eiffel Tower.[6]

Prince and Bjornson knew that they wanted to do the musical in a "simple black box, capable of displaying the Phantom's bag of tricks—an area in which selectively we could recreate the perfumy aroma of our story ... a dangerous place. Aside from examining and exploiting the wonders of Victorian theatrical machinery (we are blessed with Her Majesty's Theatre which contains the oldest still operating stage in the world), our job was to find a visual metaphor for the psychological underpinning of the play.'"[7]

Then what Prince has described as a breakthrough occurred. The director found the metaphor and the psychological underpinnings he was seeking in a BBC-TV documentary called *The Skin Horses* which he watched quite by chance. He said:

> It is a 45-minute series of interviews with handicapped people, among them a quadraplegic, a victim of multiple sclerosis whose speech is so distorted

that her intelligent commentary had to be translated in subtitles across the bottom of the screen, and a beautiful girl deprived of arms by thalidomide. These interviews were interspersed with segments from the 1930s classic film *Freaks,* and the famous scene from *The Elephant Man* in which the actress kisses "Merrick." Some of those interviewed spoke willingly, eagerly of their sexuality; it was an element which had been missing in the design [of *Phantom*] and which, indeed, informed the subsequent rewritten drafts of the libretto.[8]

Watching the documentary, Prince found the subtext he wanted and which led him to "the undercurrent of tension and eroticism in the Phantom's attempt, however distorted, to reach for love."[9] Prince remembers, "A particular quality that came leaping through the television screen was these people's healthy, uncomplicated assertion of their own sexuality and their own needs. . . . I showed the program to Maria and I could see from her eyes that it meant the same thing to her as it did to me. We realized that the real emotional pull of *The Phantom* is erotic. It's not so far beneath the surface in Leroux's book, and it's in our show, including the scenery."[10] Michael Crawford, much praised for his performance of the Phantom, said, "Prince saw the character as a very sexual thing between myself and the Christine character . . . but it's very hard . . . you actually can't think sexual . . . what you have to think is great passion and love for her and then hopefully it will look sensual to the audience. . . . I think that's what has happened . . . so it was a great journey."[11] Prince's favorite piece of staging in the show is "Music of the Night," which he feels is "very erotic . . . not explicit, but erotic . . . and audiences respond to that."[12]

In addition to the BBC documentary, other visual inspirations which gave the show its unique look were the paintings of Edgar Degas, Venice at night, the Victorian theatre with its dim lighting and opulent spectacle, the drapes and candles in a Greek Orthodox church, shadows, silent movies, the half-masks worn by some disfigured veterans of World War I, darkness and the Paris Opera House with its "gilded statuary and stately rehearsal rooms and strange subterranean lake."[13] Critic Michael Billington suggested that Prince's directing often gives the stage a sense of constant motion and animation. Although Billington says this can often work against a production, "I think it works for [*Phantom*] because [Prince] is very good at creating a sense of an opera house as a working theater and you feel there's a lot going on in this place in terms of rehearsals, performances and backstage life and that is what he's so brilliant at, I think. Just using people on the stage to suggest a whole world."[14]

As Lloyd Webber worked on the score for *Phantom,* it became less a book show and more operatic in tone. The composer said he was consciously modeling the role of Christine for his wife, Sarah Brightman, who has a wide vocal range. Feeling that the lyrics and book needed work, the authors approached Alan Jay Lerner and he agreed to work on the show. Producer Cameron Mackintosh felt that Lerner was "encouraging but perceptively critical."[15] The *Phantom* creators had several meetings with Lerner who helped with some major structural problems, but Lerner soon became too ill to continue on the project and, in fact, died some months later. Tim Rice, Lloyd Webber's former partner, was also approached, but he was involved with his own project, the musical *Chess.* Richard Stilgoe was eventually replaced by 25-year-old Charles Hart, whose major experience had been writing for university musicals. Asked to set lyrics to a melody at an audition, Hart impressed Lloyd Webber as a promising young lyricist and he was asked to join the team.

Maria Bjornson, the show's scenery and costume designer, had made her reputation as a designer for nearly eighty opera productions. Lighting designer Andrew Bridge had worked extensively in theatre throughout the world, and for ten years had been singer Shirley Bassey's personal lighting designer.

A good deal of restoration was done on Her Majesty's Theatre, where *Phantom* was to open. It is one of the last theatres which still contains a subterranean machine room and it was restored to full operation for the show. In the machine room, according to Bjornson, "men actually crank up some of the scenery by hand, as they did a century ago."[16] This ancient technology reinforced the attempts of Prince and the design team to give a distinctly Victorian feel to the production.

In order to keep the sense of the erotic in the show, the first thing the audience sees as they enter the theatre is a proscenium arch lavishly encrusted with huge gold figures which, if scrutinized carefully, can be made out to be in various stages of ecstasy. This took two sculptors eight months to execute. Prince feels the time and money were well spent,

> since the images are insidiously shaping the spectators' attitudes from the very start. . . . And once we knew we were talking about eroticism, and we had the picture frame, we could begin to fill in the specifics, the fabrics, the patterns, the drapes, especially the drapes, since drapes have a lot of mystery about them. You can't go up and touch our props and our sets, but I think you can feel them. These solid elements give off an emotional, sensual texture.[17]

The effects also give off a strong sense of place, probably a direct result of Prince, Bjornson and Bridge's visiting the Paris Opéra. The use of the vast chandelier, aspects of Christine's dressing room, the great staircase, and the gigantic table in the manager's office, are all a result of choosing significant elements of the Paris Opéra and translating them to *Phantom*. For Bjornson, an opera singer's garb is a composite of costumes worn by Caruso. The dancers' appearance owes a great deal to Degas ballerinas. Bjornson drew on circus and comedia dell 'arte imagery to achieve a sense of the strange and sinister for chorus members. The costume which gave her the greatest creative satisfaction was that for the Phantom himself. "The half-mask was suggested by the curious visors worn by some scarred and blinded soldiers after World War I: plates colored by an artist to match the skin tone, with eyes actually painted on top."[18]

Early in their collaboration, Prince and Bjornson talked of filling the Phantom's cave-like basement space with opera memorabilia—costumes and props he had acquired on his trips upstairs to the opera house. Finally, they decided on "a suggestive simplicity: a cracked mirror, a dummy in the wedding dress prepared for Christine and, at the back, iron bars with a great, black vista beyond them, closing [Christina] in, a caged bird, a portcullis, that's the way you think when you're a designer," said Bjornson.[19]

Prince admired Bjornson's spareness, her sensitivity to light and shadow, and her eye for minutiae. He said, "She's a workaholic, and a perfectionist."[20] Bjornson found Prince a "refreshing change" from the kind of directors she knows best: those who tell her nothing, because their bias is intellectual and literary, and those who tell her everything, because they don't really trust her. "But [Prince] has a history-of-art background and a visual sense. He'll say, 'I see dark, and people coming out from nowhere, and shadows, and heavy drapes that drop and thud and pound.' He's a springboard for ideas."[21]

Andrew Bridge's lighting design was of major importance due to the emphasis placed on creating a sense of menace, secrecy and sexuality throughout the production. Audiences were supposed to wonder what was happening in the many shadows on stage. It was hoped they would feel a sense of disorientation. Above all, they were to be encouraged, in Prince's words, "to be contributors, to be collaborators, to use their imaginations to fill in the spaces we've deliberately left blank.[22] There is, therefore, a great deal of darkness around what are really simple and economical sets. Bridge uses only about 400 lighting fixtures, compared to the usual 700 or 800 in most Broadway shows. Additionally, the need to create the appearance of many candles aglow could not be filled with real candles because of fire laws in both London and New York. Bridge therefore designed tiny lamps whose tiny bulbs flicker inside a siloconget, giving off the impression of moving flame. To create the shimmer of light on water without using real flame, Bridge used motorized wheels and rotating disks. To achieve the flat amber look of the period on the opera house's professional presentations, the lighting designer used hidden lamps in the orchestra pit which reinforced the visible footlights. Bridge said, "What's been fun has been using modern technology to create an old-fashioned look."[23] Talking about his collaboration with Prince, Bridge said, "Well, he's always excited, always trying things out, like a kid with a new toy, always doing the unexpected. Most directors tell you, 'More light, more light.' Did you know he came up to me and said, 'I've never asked this of a lighting designer before, but can you make things darker?' I won't forget that."[24]

Gillian Lynne, choreographer for *Cats,* was signed to create the dance sequences for *Phantom.* For this show she created what she calls a Degas-style ballet class in the background for atmosphere and in counterpoint to another scene being played further downstage. For the "Hannibal" scene she did a tacky mock-*Aida.* Lynne says of her director,

> Hal is totally generous. He gave me the "Masquerade" scene at the beginning of the second act, and the Manager's scenes. Early on, I had said to my husband that those were the two scenes I would give my eyeteeth to do, but Hal would obviously do them because they are so fabulous. One day he just announced to the cast, "I've had some ideas about these scenes and I've told them to Gillian. I am handing them over to her. No fool I." At the same time, I didn't know it but he's not really interested in that kind of meticulous, detailed work. He's much more concerned with the overall sweep of the whole thing, the big picture.[25]

Judy Kaye, who was cast as Carlotta in the Broadway production of *Phantom,* explains how she feels Prince works with his collaborators:

> He relies on the participation of those people he hires . . . he trusts them . . . he hires people that he feels are the best and he lets them go . . . he lets them do their job and then he comes in and he edits.[26]

The London rehearsals began on 18 August 1986 and went very smoothly, according to Prince.

> We worked hard on the material prior to the rehearsals. . . . I kept flying to London to work with Andrew and with the lyricist and with the designer.

The Phantom of the Opera, 1988
David Romano sits on a mock elephant in an opera within the musical.
(Photo courtesy Clive Barda)

They came here and we exchanged trips across the ocean, frequently, probably a dozen trips. . . . And then when it was all ready, we did have a reading of it, somewhere halfway through the process, with actors singing it for us in Andrew's office— which is a big office. And we saw what was wrong with it, and what should be done and then went on to the next step. . . . We then went into rehearsals, which were 10 o'clock in the morning in a kind of recreation or community hall across the Thames in Lambeth. And there we rehearsed in an atmosphere that was lovely. I rehearsed every day from 10 to 1 or 2 p.m., staging things. By 1 or 2 I'd done what I'd done (almost everything is the way it was staged the first time), and then I would go home. It was beautiful weather. I'd walk around London, have a late lunch and then dinner with friends, go to theatre, and go back in the next morning. After four weeks of that we were in the theatre and then we previewed and it was a smash. . . . And it was really no more difficult or dangerous than that. . . . I think we energized each other, and we had a lot of respect for each other. And there was, you know, Cameron Mackintosh, the other producer, and there was none of the pressure of five million dollars, though God knows it was very expensive there. But England is healthy, shows open, they don't all get as good reviews and run as well as *Phantom*, but they run for a year or two—the way they used to here. . . . At the end of rehearsals, one of the cast on behalf of the whole company said they had a question that they all wanted to ask me. I said what is it. They asked what I do in the afternoon, after I leave rehearsal. I said I watch "Coronation Street," which was the truth. It's a soap opera . . . and everybody laughed a lot. But it's the truth. Well, you need that too when you're doing this kind of work.[27]

Sarah Brightman and Michael Crawford played the roles of Christine Daäe and the Phantom. Speaking of how he worked with Prince, Crawford said that the director at first gave him an outline of what he thought the character should be. Crawford explained that, because he works very much alone in the show,

I worked a lot of the time alone in rehearsal . . . and then obviously when it got to our [his and Brightman's] segments, I would then be in the rehearsal room and work with Hal and Sarah. . . . I would then sort of offer things that I thought of. What I liked was [Prince] allowed me the freedom to build up the characterization as I saw it and whenever it was off track he would put it right. I enjoy working in that kind of free way.[28]

Crawford said that Prince was a good editor, encouraging the actor to do more and go further emotionally. Crawford added, "I'm always slow in going for too much. I think Prince often said 'more, do more here, give more here,' because I'm often frightened, I guess, of making big mistakes. Therefore I always move very slowly rather than too quickly in my steps. . . . What Prince did in pushing me for more was to offer a kind of encouragement, like giving sugar lumps.''[29]

Crawford talked of how fast Prince moves during rehearsals. ''Under other circumstances,'' said Crawford, ''I might find that he moved too fast for me in the way he works . . . but it was good having the freedom that I had to develop the character. I did my work downstairs in the rehearsal room and so we worked fine together . . . and if you ever needed extra time for a problem, he'd find the time for you.''[30]

The Phantom of the Opera opened at Her Majesty's Theatre in London on 19 October 1986 and became a kind of theatrical phenomenon. Never before, said *Theatre Week* magazine, had a musical ''so completely captivated the imaginations of theatergoers.''[31] The musical's success in London's West End proved to be just the kind of major reversal of fortune that Prince needed after his series of successive Broadway flops. Jack Tinker in London's *Daily Mail* called *Phantom* ''a triumphant reworking of this vintage spine-tingling melodrama.''[32]

It wasn't long before the musical was being readied for a debut on Broadway. The advance excitement was high in New York, and before *Phantom* opened its first American engagement, $12 million worth of tickets had been sold to an eager audience more than willing to wait months to see the most anticipated musical in decades.

The Shubert Organization's venerable Majestic Theatre was chosen to house *Phantom,* mainly because its stage suited the production more than most others, but even so, it wasn't large enough. The basement was not deep enough for the huge machinery that operates the sets which appear and disappear through the floor of the stage. The producers and theatre owners therefore ripped up the stage, gutted the basement and backstage areas, developed a new fire curtain and used a neighboring theatre to physically support the back and roof of the musical's new home. The cost of adapting the Majestic for the *Phantom* was about $2 million. The need for space was a major consideration, since the production requires an enormous amount of room for its complicated machinery, sets and props. The Majestic's stage and roof were eventually held up by a steel grid which was built between the backs of the Majestic and its neighbor, the Broadhurst, only a few inches apart. A new stage floor was installed, with 97 specific holes and four trapdoors through which various set pieces, props and people travel up and down.

The costly renovation helped the Majestic appear to have been transformed into the nineteenth-century Paris Opéra. Even the outside of the theatre and the marquee were redesigned to be lit with gaslight in keeping with the Victorian motif. It is estimated that it takes about 200 people to carry the production off at each performance, including actors, musicians, a running crew, dressers, a full prop staff, carpentry staff, electrical department, cleaning staff, ushers and the doorman. When the Phantom's flames begin, they are carefully monitored, loaded and operated by a pyrotechnics expert and carry the approval of the New York City Fire Department.

Because it is such a technically complicated show, the play was rehearsed very carefully and slowly. There are radio-controlled items in the show, such as the boat that the Phantom and Christine glide along the subterranean lake in, and which works like a model car or airplane. An offstage operator controls its speed and direction as he does other special effects and props. There are many radio microphones which must be checked before each performance, as are the back-ups in case one mike breaks down.

Production stage manager Mitchell Lemsky sat with Prince during rehearsals so the director could explain any changes he wanted. During performances, Lemsky calls cues from the wings while watching the action on three video monitors. Because there is less space in the Majestic Theatre than there is at Her Majesty's, *Phantom* is more difficult to run in New York than in London. However, audiences in New York get a better view of the proceedings than their British counterparts.

After the New York opening, Prince continued to attend the show at least once a week and sometimes to keep an eye on the show's performance—human and mechanical. Michael Crawford said, "On the technical side, I used to sit and marvel at the way things would come together . . . as with any show . . . but he [Prince] is in particular command of the stage. . . . It was extremely impressive."[33]

The famous *Phantom* chandelier is commanded by the most advanced computer and back-up system ever used in a theatre. (The London production did not have this type of computerized equipment.) The chandelier and its operating paraphernalia were designed to the most precise specifications. It is run by two 10-horsepower motors, one of which brings it up over the heads of the audience, while the other brings it back to the stage for its spectacular fall. To protect the audience in case of any cable or mechanical failure, the complicated back-up system would be put into immediate operation.

One of the technical marvels of *Phantom* is the "travelator," which is suspended bridge-like between two towers on stage. As the Phantom spirits Christine to his lair, the bridge moves and tilts. A magical moment is their arrival at the underground lake. The gondola moves through mist created by dry ice, controlled by a stagehand operating his radio-control device. "This eternally anxious fellow must steer the boat through the one hundred candles that rise through underground traps."[34]

The drapes are another technical marvel, in that they swirl, leap, drop and fly in the many changes of scene. When not in view, the drapes are scooped up and held in huge plastic bags where they are kept as flat as possible since space backstage and in the flies is at a premium. With all these technical complexities, there is seldom a foul-up. One, however, did occur "when something got caught in the lighting board, which then went down. A flustered technician then cued the 'travelator," which moved into some scenery, trapping a bed onstage. The candles came up under the bed. A drape flew up revealing a set from a previous scene. The Phantom's throne and organ came on, crunching the candles while the boat got caught upstage. As this Rube Goldberg foul-up escalated, the stage manager had to decide instantly whether to stop the show. He decided not to. Michael and Sarah did their scene . . . dancing around all those trapped and crunched candles. It was brilliant. They got a standing ovation."[35]

The $8 million New York production of *The Phantom of the Opera,* which Mel Gussow in the *Times* referred to as a "phantasmagorical experience,"[36] opened on 27 January 1988 after a pre-opening period of unprecedented fanfare and hoopla in the media. Frank Rich, reviewing *Phantom* in the *New York Times,* called it

> a characteristic Lloyd Webber project—long on pop professionalism and melody, impoverished of artistic personality and passion—that the director Harold Prince, the designer Maria Bjornson and the mesmerizing actor Michael Crawford have elevated quite literally to the roof. . . . "The Phantom of the Opera" is as much a victory of dynamic stagecraft over musical kitsch as it is a triumph of merchandising über alles. . . . Mr. Crawford's moving portrayal of the hero notwithstanding, the show's most persuasive love story is Mr. Prince's and Ms. Bjornson's unabashed crush on the theatre itself, from footlights to dressing rooms, from flies to trap doors.[37]

Rich went on to call the show a gothic backstage melodrama, and suggested that it

> taps right into the obsessions of the designer and the director. At the Royal Shakespeare Company, Ms. Bjornson was a wizard of darkness, monochromatic palettes and mysterious grand staircases. Mr. Prince, a prince of darkness in his own right, is the master of the towering bridge ("Evita"), the labyrinthine inferno ("Sweeney Todd") and the musical-within-the-musical ("Follies"). In "Phantom," the creative personalities of these two artists merge with a literal lightning flash at the opening coup de theatre, in which the auditorium is transformed from gray decrepitude to the gold-and-crystal Second Empire glory of the Paris Opera House. Though the sequence retreads the famous Ziegfeld palace metamorphosis in "Follies," Ms. Bjornson's magical eye has allowed Mr. Prince to reinvent it, with electrifying showmanship.[38]

Rich did not like Sarah Brightman in the role of Christine, calling her "icily attractive and possessing a lush soprano by Broadway standards (at least amplified). . . . [She] reveals little competence as an actress."[39]

John Simon in *New York* magazine called *Phantom* a terrific technical achievement but felt the story as Richard Stilgoe and Andrew Lloyd Webber had adapted it "is hard to follow and harder to care about . . . lacking genuine emotion, sensitivity, soul."[40] He said that Prince's direction provided "stylishness and razzmatazz, ingenuity and wit."[41]

Clive Barnes in the *New York Post* pointed out, as did many other critics, how brilliant Michael Crawford was as the Phantom, saying of the actor, "His ultimate triumph is to humanize the Phantom—so that a story, and a show, that might have been coolly impersonal are warmed into life."[42] He went on to say of Crawford's performance that it "will rank in the annals of the musical for all time."[43]

Barnes termed Judy Kaye in her comic role as Carlotta Guidicelli as "coming dangerously close to stealing the show as a divine diva."[44] Some months after the show opened in New York, Kaye said of the experience of working with Prince:

> There are actors who are afraid of [Prince]. . . . He is not a director who spoonfeeds you . . . your character. . . . He hires you because he thinks you can do the job and he wants you to bring to the role all the possibilities that he thinks you possess. He wants you to participate and he does not coddle an actor. He doesn't give them strokes constantly. And there are a lot of actors,

The Phantom of the Opera, 1988
Michael Crawford as the Phantom in a scene from the hit musical.
(Photo courtesy Clive Barda)

dare I say most actors, who seem to need an awful lot of velvet glove treatment . . . constantly told that they're good and they're wonderful, and there are directors who do that—who do that very well. His point of view is for the whole. He's out there doing what I was always told a director is supposed to do which is to be the third eye—to be the eye of the audience. . . . With this show he set me free. He wanted me to take the ball and run with it as far as I could and I said "Well, listen, you may have to throw a net over me because I just will," and he said, "Great, I'll do that," and he edited me and he refocused the things that I was doing that perhaps he didn't agree with.[45]

Of Prince's work on *Phantom,* Barnes said that "more than in most musicals, the score and theme are here the thing; the director's job has been to visualize them, to give them theatrical form, and Prince has proved a wizard."[46] Summing up the general feeling around Broadway, Barnes called the show "a very palpable hit, and will be with us for years."[47]

The show's music did not share in the glowing reviews. Howard Kissel in the *Daily News* said, "To say the score is Lloyd Webber's best is not saying a great deal. His music always has a synthetic, borrowed quality to it. As you listen you find yourself wondering where you've heard it before. In this case you've heard a lot of it in Puccini, in the work of other Broadway composers and even the Beatles."[48] Kissel went on to say, "Much of the look of *Phantom* came from the thinking of its director, Harold Prince. It was Prince who told designer Maria Bjornson he had never done a show with curtains. The curtains she designed give *Phantom* a sumptuousness unlike any recent Broadway show."[49]

Few Broadway musicals have enjoyed the public excitement stirred up by Harold Prince's version of *The Phantom of the Opera,* with sold-out houses booked up to a year in advance. In June 1988, it walked off with seven Tony Awards out of the ten categories in which it was nominated. Not only was it voted the best musical of the 1987–88 Broadway season, but Michael Crawford won for best musical actor, Maria Bjornson was honored as best designer for both stage settings and costumes, Andrew Bridge was named for best lighting design and Judy Kaye was judged best featured actress in a musical. In addition to dominating the awards presentation, *Phantom of the Opera* put Hal Prince into a special niche in the Tony Awards history books, his citation as best director of the 1987–88 season marking his sixteenth Tony, a record unmatched by any other artist in Broadway history. Never one to appear to take awards very seriously in the past, Prince appeared sincerely moved as he made his acceptance speech. He talked of his devotion to his family, his wife Judy and his children Daisy and Charley, and expanded these warm feelings to what he called "the family of theatre." He then said, "Thirty-four years ago, I held the first of these [Tony statues] in my hands." He added that he hoped this "said something to newcomers."[50]

A TRIP TO PURCHASE:
Kiss of the Spider Woman

I don't want realism. I want magic! Yes, Yes, magic! I try to give that to people. I misrepresent things to them. I don't tell the truth, I tell what ought to be the truth. And if that is sinful, then let me be damned for it!—Don't turn the light on!

—Blanche DuBois in Tennessee Williams's *A Streetcar Named Desire*, quoted in *Kiss of the Spider Woman* program notes

The enormous success of *Phantom of the Opera* gave Harold Prince the psychological lift he needed. His renewed enthusiasm and energy were now focused on a number of diverse projects. With companies of *Phantom* opening all over the world, Prince found himself staging productions in Vienna, Hamburg, Chicago, Tokyo and other major cities. In addition, at the invitation of Beverly Sills, then general manager of the New York City Opera, he directed a new production of *Don Giovanni*, which opened the company's spring 1989 season. Prince then went on to direct a new production of *Faust* for the Metropolitan Opera in February 1990. Also, having optioned the novel *Kiss of the Spider Woman*, by Manuel Puig, he was planning to produce and direct a musical version of it with a score by John Kander and Fred Ebb and book by Terrence McNally.

The idea of doing a musical version of *Kiss of the Spider Woman* was Fred Ebb's, who had seen the movie version of the Puig novel and thought it was musical material. His partner John Kander thought so too, and they took the idea to Prince. "Hal is the person," said Ebb,

[who] I always think of in terms of knowing how to conceptualize a difficult piece, which I knew this would be. Our conversation during the phone call went this way: I said, "Hal, I just wanted to give you a title and you tell me what you think." Prince said, "OK, what is it?" and I said, *"Kiss of the Spider Woman."* Prince said, "I'll do it." It was exactly like that, and so Hal was involved from day one. I didn't bring him very much in terms of concept or notions of how this musical could be done. I just brought him the title and the idea. Then, under Hal's aegis, we began. Gradually, I began to have stronger notions of how it could be musicalized, but until Hal became a reality and connected with it, I didn't really give it a whole lot of thought. When we first started to musicalize it, I didn't bring Hal scenic ideas or songs or anything. I merely brought him a title and the notion of doing a musical with that theme.[1]

Terrence McNally had also read the novel and seen the film but hadn't initially thought of the material as a good bet for musicalization. Yet, when Fred Ebb approached him about doing the book for *Kiss of the Spider Woman,* McNally, like Prince, immediately said yes. McNally has said that he never re-read the novel or looked at the film again and that the dialogue in the libretto is his own.[2]

During the planning stages of *Kiss of the Spider Woman,* Prince was unable to say where the show would be presented. He hoped that by the time the material was ready there would be an institution capable of presenting full-size musicals away from the pressures of Broadway. Then the opportunity arose.

Martin J. Bell and Prince had first met in October 1986 at a meeting of The Producers' Group, where they found themselves talking about the plight of Broadway and, specifically, the musical theatre. Prince told Bell that in the current economic climate he could never have gotten *Cabaret* or *Follies* into production. He told Bell that in 1986 the people putting money into shows were usually lawyers, real estate owners or oil people who didn't generate projects themselves. According to Prince, these investors wanted to fund musicals that had already been accepted favorably by critics elsewhere (which usually means London). In other words, said Prince, they wanted a sure bet.

Both Prince and Bell felt the need to do something about this situation and decided to see if together they could come up with some kind of solution to the problem. Over the next three and a half years, they searched for a production site. One of the places considered was the Astoria movie studios in the New York City borough of Queens, across the East River from Manhattan. The space was fine and they felt they could raise the operating money but, ultimately, funds were insufficient to build a new facility within the old movie studio to house theatrical productions. Eventually, the theatre on the campus of the State University of New York (SUNY) at Purchase in Westchester County, just north of New York City, provided the best solution. It offered a beautiful complex of theatres and some of the most sophisticated theatre equipment available anywhere. Indeed, the lighting equipment at Purchase equalled that of any theatre on Broadway.

Prince unofficially joined forces with producer Bell in January of 1990 to launch this innovative multimillion-dollar musical theatre laboratory. The idea was to pay creators while they worked on their shows. The hits would pay for the flops, with the income reverting to the institution. The organization, named New Musicals, had already spent three years trying to raise money, enlist writers and work out arrangements with unions and suppliers. According to Prince, New Musicals was seen as filling a void in the American theatre—a place to do big, potentially expensive new American musicals at a sensible cost.

New Musicals hoped to schedule twelve original musical projects to be produced over a four-year period, with the first season to begin in May 1990. The first year's budget for four musicals was set at $9.5 million. The plan was to present limited runs of these musicals at Purchase, with an audience of seasonal subscribers to be developed through a major marketing campaign. The money thus generated would offset each production's expected $1.5 million budget. If a show proved to be a success, it might be transferred to Broadway or another venue, with New Musicals' in-house staff producing and managing the commercial production. Alternatively, a show might be picked up by another management for subsequent production.

For some time Prince had harbored a strong desire to work in the nurturing kind of environment offered by New Musicals rather than the traditional hot-house climate of Broadway. Even if he had great confidence in a property and was willing to risk the backers' $8 million, he felt that Broadway was no longer the Broadway where he had done most of his shows, the Broadway preceded by a lengthy stay in Boston or Philadelphia or New Haven, where he could shuffle a show's elements, fix the problems and bring a more-or-less "set" production into New York, ready for its first-night audience.

New Musicals, unlike the old Broadway, would be dedicated to creating, developing and providing a home for new American musicals. It would present full productions, with full sets, lighting, costumes and orchestrations of works in progress and open them to a paying public without the burden of reviews from professional newspaper and broadcast critics. New Musicals, however, was not created to be nonprofit. Its aim was to establish a relatively pressure-free yet fully equipped laboratory environment in which to develop pieces by fledgling as well as experienced musical theatre authors, composers, lyricists, directors and orchestrators, and then present full-scale productions of their works.

Harold Prince felt that this approach would give everyone a chance to work quietly on shows for eight weeks. If one out of eight shows became a substantial success, it would indemnify the others. Prince was not to be administratively involved, but did intend to use the program to develop all his future musical projects.

When Prince was asked whether he was concerned that New Musicals might become a clearing house for commercial producers to find commercial musicals, he said he was not. To the contrary, he hoped that it would happen because he feels that what Broadway now needs more than anything is commercial producers. Given the cost of producing today, Prince believes that investors need every encouragement to induce them to come back to Broadway. Prince has never taken the workshop route. He feels that workshops without scenery, costumes or orchestrations do not give producers a fair viewing. Although "small" seems better to many creators, Prince does not share that sentiment. He adds that a small environment may enhance material unrealistically. It takes a lot more talent for an Angela Lansbury to make contact with the audience from the cavernous stage of the Uris Theatre than for a lesser performer to do so in a postage stamp-sized environment. Prince finds it incredible that, in 1990, Stephen Sondheim's *Asssassins* was given only a three-piece instrumental accompaniment for its workshop production at Playwrights Horizons, an off-Broadway house. Prince said, "Can you imagine taking America's pre-eminent theatre composer-lyricist and saying the best we can give you is a drummer, a keyboardist and a bass fiddle?"[3]

Through all the initial planning for New Musicals, Prince had no idea of using it as a platform to launch *Kiss of the Spider Woman*, and when Martin Bell first suggested that Prince do *Spider Woman* at New Musicals, Prince felt that since he, Fred Ebb, John Kander and Terrence McNally were all successful theatre veterans they did not need to tap the resources of New Musicals and Prince turned Bell down. After all, New Musicals was to be primarily a vehicle for new composers, lyricists and librettists. Already slated for the first season were *The Secret Garden, My Favorite Year,* and *Fanny Hackabout Jones,* all with untried creators. (Although Marsha Norman, *Garden's* librettist, had won a Pulitzer Prize for her play *'night, Mother,* she had never before worked on a musical.) Bell told Prince that he feared he would be unable to raise the kind of money needed for the New Musicals project unless he had a show like *Kiss of the Spider Woman* to open the season. Prince in response worried that this would bring him and his collaborators right back into the "Broadway thing" that they had been trying to avoid. Finally, Bell took Prince aside and asked him what he had to lose. "I didn't realize it then," said Prince, "that what I could lose was my mind!" [4]

Like virtually every other Harold Prince show, *Kiss of the Spider Woman* would not be relaxation for the tired businessman. Its two leading characters—a political revolutionary and a homosexual window dresser bound together as cellmates in a Latin American prison—are hardly the heroes of popular light entertainment. The relationship of the two men develops within the stark reality of their prison cell. The revolutionary Valentin relies upon his ideological beliefs and macho self-image to sustain him through his captors' brutal attempts to break his spirit. The window dresser Molina resists authority by losing himself in a 1940's movie fantasy starring Rita Hayworth, recounting the fantasy to Valentin, with lavish production numbers depicting the fantasy in Molina's imagination. As the play progresses, Valentin and Molina's radically different approaches to life begin to blur and the audience comes to understand that they are not so different in their resistance to tyranny.

The job of turning such a dark tale into a viable musical was a daunting one and Prince and his collaborators worked on the show for about a year and a half before rehearsals began at the Michael Bennett Studios in Manhattan in the spring of 1990. The last two weeks of rehearsal, at the end of April, would be on stage at Purchase with the full set. The show was to run from 1 May to 24 June.

From the beginning, Prince worried that something was wrong with the balance of the show's elements. Perhaps the score wasn't gritty enough for the jail scenes or perhaps there were too many pastiche musical numbers. Still he hoped that the glamorous, quintessentially forties Hollywood movie, with its mythologized and innocent Rita Hayworth, could be used effectively in the production numbers, and would be seen by the audience as the defense mechanism it was—used by Molina, the window dresser, to protect himself against the horrible reality of his situation.

During rehearsals, the disproportionate ratio of pastiche musical numbers to serious prison material would continue to concern Prince. Did those numbers seem to be trying to take the audience's mind off the seriousness of the subject? He lost confidence that audiences would understand Molina's need to escape the reality of his prison cell, as *A Streetcar Named Desire*'s Blanch DuBois escaped the reality of her sordid life by misrepresenting herself to others—by keeping the lights turned low and creating the magic she thought people yearned for.

At the final rehearsal at the Bennett Studios before moving up to Purchase, Prince invited a few people in to see the show, including his family, office staff, designers and friends of the authors, all of whom reacted enthusiastically to *Spider Woman*, even though they had seen it performed without scenery, costumes or orchestrations. Prince decided he had been wrong to worry. In Purchase, however, once the scenery, costumes and orchestrations were in place, the imbalance surfaced again. Prince confesses to a surprise panic, the desire to "run and hide." He recalls thinking, "Oh, my God, what do I do now?"[5] But rehearsals progressed on schedule.

While the show was rehearsing, Prince was suddenly jolted by news of a serious illness in the family. It came as he was preparing for technical rehearsals at Purchase and cut seriously into the time he was able to devote to the show. He found himself traveling between the theatre and a hospital in New York, an hour and a half's drive each way. After the first public preview, he rehearsed changes in the script, or authorized them, but rarely stayed to see how they had worked out in performance, more often than not rushing off to the hospital in New York, calling the stage manager after each performance to find out the audience's reaction. Beverly Randolph, who stage managed many Prince shows, would reassure him that all was going well. Prince now feels that she was concerned for his personal problems and did not want to give him any more bad news. He calculated that he rehearsed the cast on an average of once a week and saw only about six full performances over the eight-week run.

An element vital to all the collaborators was the New Musicals policy of allowing no media reviews once their work had opened to the public. Writer John Harris, in a *TheatreWeek* article, quotes Martin Bell as saying that he had contacted the New York and tri-state press requesting that critics refrain from reviewing *Spider Woman* since it was not a finished product but a work in progress. According to Bell, "Each arts editor and critic agreed not to review the show except two: the *New York Times*, which said that it would make that decision at a later date, and Leida Snow, the theatre critic for 1010 WINS Radio, [who] similarly withheld her decision."[6]

Prince maintains that Bell assured him that there would be no reviews of *Spider Woman*. Bell recalled to Prince a luncheon he had had with Frank Rich, chief theatre critic of the *New York Times*, at which it was implied that there would be no problem. Bell told Prince that he had not asked the *Times* to put the promise in writing because calling the attention of the top brass to the matter might create a problem where none existed. "Had I known then what the outcome would be," says Prince, "I would have shopped around to do *Spider Woman* somewhere else; perhaps in London or Canada."[7]

On 16 May, Sheridan Morley surprised everyone by publishing a rave review of *Spider Woman* in the *International Herald Tribune*, calling it "the most important new musical of the season."[8] Morley also said that for a show of this importance to open 45 minutes away from Broadway rather than on Broadway was a sign of the changing times.[9]

A week later, on 24 May, Prince, Ebb, Kander, McNally and Bell converged on the *Times*, accompanied by Peter Stone, author and president of the Dramatists' Guild, playwright Treva Silverman, choreographer Susan Stroman, director Susan Schulman, author-director Julie Taymor and composers Mark St. Germaine, Lucy Simon and Elliot Goldenthals. The delegation met over an hour with assistant managing editor Warren Hoge and cultural editor Marvin Siegel, pleading that the *Times* not review the production at SUNY, explaining that Purchase provided their only chance to get full productions of their work and that while shows are still in constant evolution published reviews could create a destructive pressure and inhibit creative development.[10]

Despite the appeal, the *Times* opted to review *Kiss of the Spider Woman*. Hoge argued that *Spider Woman* was "a piece of theatre with some of the most distinguished names in the American theatre involved and it's being staged in our circulation area. If it were a show with a [later] Broadway opening date we wouldn't review it [at Purchase]. . . . We don't accept the notion that the act of reviewing is destructive and punitive."[11] Other reasons given for the *Times*'s decision were that New Musicals was a "for profit" enterprise and that Westchester County was a major *Times* market.[12]

New Musicals' rebuttal was that it could not produce full-scale musicals in a nonprofit environment; that it was saving millions of dollars via new contracts negotiated by the craft and performing unions and by avoiding out-of-town tryout expenses (cast, crew and artistic staff were commuting to Westchester for each performance); that it was still undecided whether *Spider Woman* would go to Broadway and that a *Times* review would be an unwanted variable in determining that fate.[13] Indeed, Bell went on to say that even a good review could injure the development of *Spider Woman*. If Rich liked the show, Bell felt it might impede the work-in-progress aspect of the situation and make the show appear ready for Broadway before the collaborators on the production felt that it was.[14]

After the *Times* announced its decision, other papers, including *Variety*, which had originally said it would respect the no-review policy New Musicals had requested, followed the leader and sent in their critics. On 29 May, Frank

Rich saw the twenty-seventh of the fifty-seven performances of *Spider Woman* given at Purchase.

Published on 1 June, Rich's review gave credit to Prince for having pushed Broadway a significant step forward in the past with his musical theatre concepts and for having, along with his collaborators Kander and Ebb, "far more radical ideas in mind in *Spider Woman*."[15] Rich said that this was the "first large-scale American musical told from an unapologetic and unsentimental gay point of view"[16] in that the narrative is seen through the eyes of Molina, a homosexual window dresser incarcerated in a Latin American prison. The show, he said, also "depicts torture with a grueling ferocity missing from Mr. Prince's *Evita*."[17] He added that *Spider Woman* wasn't "shy about taking chances."[18]

Negatively, Rich said he felt that the "fantasy film—here fittingly changed to an old movie musical—overwhelms the reality so completely that the compelling story of Molina and Valentin seems a mild, often incoherent intrusion."[19] Rich went on to say that "the glitzy routines of *Spider Woman* detract from, rather than enhance, the work's dramatization of fascist repression."[20]

Rich cited the choreography as "routine" and often guilty of defeating "even Kander and Ebb's better numbers."[21] He suggested that someone with the charisma of a Chita Rivera would have added a "dazzling musical-comedy presence"[22] to the star turns in the movie sequences, while he felt that Lauren Mitchell "had neither the personality nor the vocal authority for the task."[23] Nor did he like the casting of Kevin Gray as Valentin or John Rubinstein as Molina, charging the latter with pushing too hard.

Mentioning recent revivals of *Cabaret* and *Follies*, in which production numbers alternate with realistic book scenes to comment theatrically upon them, Rich felt that the production numbers seemed to "hold up better than the book scenes and *Spider Woman* shares that shortcoming."[24] Rich's final volley was targeted at Prince's direction: "Instead of concentrating on the performances crucial to this psychodrama, Mr. Prince seems fixated on the big production numbers and scenic effects, as if he felt obligated to warp his show to placate Broadway audiences' presumed insistence on spectacle even when he is ostensibly working away from the commercial dictates of Broadway. And the spectacle falls short."[25]

In what appeared to be an attempt to soften the blows he had just struck, Rich ended his review by observing,

> It's all frustrating because somewhere in *Kiss of the Spider Woman* is the compelling story its creators want to tell, which is nothing less than investi-

gation of what it means to be a man, in the highest moral sense, whatever one's sexual orientation. That story begins with two men in a tiny room, and if the creators of *Kiss of the Spider Woman* are to retrieve the intimate heart of their show, they may have to rescue it from the voluminous web in which it has so wastefully become ensnared.[26]

Prince remembers feeling beaten black and blue by the notice in the *Times*. Though Rich's criticism of the movie sequences came as no surprise, Prince was disturbed by the "viciousness" of the critic's attack on John Rubinstein and believes now, as then, that Rubinstein was wonderful in the role.[27]

Martin Bell said that Rich's review of the still-evolving *Spider Woman* was comparable to "sitting in John Updike's studio and reviewing the pages he throws out. The *Times* is destroying everything I've spent five years of my life trying to create."[28]

Fred Ebb feels that the *Times*'s decision to review was painful. He now says,

> We all felt the same as Hal did about reviewers coming in—a certain sense of betrayal that you feel as a creative person not being able to finish your work. I felt a little like a student preparing for an examination and being judged on his preparation rather than on the exam itself. I was disappointed that they came and a little hurt and disillusioned by it…but I find as time goes by I have really put the experience into some kind of perspective. In a way, I am grateful that it happened. I think we learned a great deal and I think we all profited in a painful sort of way from the experience.[29]

After the *Times* review of *Spider Woman* appeared, Clive Barnes, in the *Post*, wrote a column on how immoral it was for the rival newspaper to have reviewed *Spider Woman*. Then, in a paradoxical about-face, he went on to give the show its worst critique. Instead of scolding the *Times* staff for their action, Barnes appeared to have joined them.[30]

The *Daily News* critic also noted that he disapproved totally of reviewing the show, but his orders had been to see and write about *Spider Woman*. He said in his review that it was a work in progress and suggested that the collaborators continue working on it.[31]

Soon after *Spider Woman* closed in June 1990 at Purchase, the New Musicals project collapsed. Bell did not have the capital for additional productions, contradicting Prince's understanding of Bell's arrangement with his backers. Displaying characteristic grace, Prince says of New Musicals' sad demise, "I believe Marty's crime was too much idealism and optimism, too much wishful thinking at the wrong time. I understand wishful thinking.

There was a great deal of it in 1948 when I started. There's little room left for it today."[32]

One explanation of what happened to the funds that Bell had counted on is that Rocco Landesman, president of Jujamcyn Theatres, had put money into New Musicals but didn't like *Spider Woman*. Someone who worked at Jujamcyn (not Landesman) was finally responsible for the failure of the enterprise to secure funds enough to do its next production, telling Capital Cities/ABC (which had been generous to New Musicals) that *Spider Woman* was awful and, as a result, Jujamcyn was not going to invest in the other shows. Capital Cities/ABC, a large, publicly held corporation, decided that they could neither fight the bad publicity nor explain away the fact that Jujamcyn would not be contributing. And so they too decided not to invest in the remaining schedule.[33]

An article in the *Times* by Mervyn Rothstein listed among the investors in New Musicals Capital Cities/ABC, Columbia Artists Management, Jujamcyn Theatres, NAC Productions (a Los Angeles television producer) and a number of individuals. The article quotes Landesman of Jujamcyn as saying, "We're hoping that Marty [Bell] would make it go, but it became apparent as long as six to eight weeks ago that they weren't meeting their projection, especially as far as earned income."[34] Landesman went on to state that he and other investors had given money for the first year of a four-year commitment as well as 80 percent for the second year, but that the first year's money had been used to establish New Musicals and the 80 percent of the second year's money went for the first year of operation.[35]

Spokesmen for SUNY at Purchase reported that New Musicals had attracted more than 22,000 ticket buyers and brought in more than $600,000 with only two months' advance notice. It attracted more than 9,000 subscribers for its first season, though money had to be refunded to them as well as to single-ticket purchasers for the shows that were never to be presented. Bell is quoted as saying about New Musicals: "We failed, but I hope this does not discourage others from trying."[36]

Today Hal Prince is of the opinion that New Musicals should not have been launched with a show written by McNally, Kander and Ebb and directed by himself. Had it opened with *The Secret Garden,* more than likely the critics would have respected the no-review policy and stayed away. And many of the changes which were made after it received disappointing reviews on Broadway in 1991 could have been made at Purchase had it been presented there first.

After the Purchase disappointment, Judy Prince encouraged her husband and his collaborators to continue to work on *Spider Woman,* feeling that it was potentially too important a show to abandon. Prince has said that if it weren't for her, he might have walked away from what he considered, "the debris of it and gotten on with something else....My nature is: Okay, so it's a show. Goodbye. Don't carry around the black and blue marks of an earlier experience."[37] But *Spider Woman* was different. For one thing, Prince willingly admitted that the Purchase production was "wrongheaded" and that he was heavily responsible for making it so. Moreover, Prince and his collaborators had learned a great deal during the Purchase run. They knew, for example, that the important Rita Hayworth concept in the movie sequences hadn't worked and that the original book was too long. They also knew that they had failed to create the strong element of magical realism that they had sought. The next time around they were determined to get it right.

Grandchild of Kings

In 1992 Prince wrote *Grandchild of Kings*, a dramatization of Sean O'Casey's early life adapted from the first two volumes of O'Casey's autobiography. Having received permission to develop the work from Eileen O'Casey, the dramatist's 87-year-old widow, and his daughter, Shivaun, Prince had worked on the piece for two years, attempting to bring to the stage via dialogue and narration (99 percent of which is from O'Casey's original books), enlivened by song and dance, a boyhood in Dublin about a century ago.

As preparation for the production, the Irish Repertory Theatre Company arranged readings of the script in October 1991. Then, in the winter and spring of the following year, the work, now entitled *Grandchild of Kings*, was presented by that group, with the great Irish actress Pauline Flanagan playing O'Casey's mother. It ran at the Theatre for the New City on the Lower East Side, an intimate space with a capacity of 240. Eugene Lee designed the sets in the environmental mode he had used for *Candide*. The six-level space, full of ramps and stairways, enfolded the audience in a tumult that represented the streets, shops, hospitals, theatres and riverbanks of the young O'Casey's world.

In an interview in the *New York Times*, Prince explained why he was drawn to the autobiography: "I'm crazy about Dublin. If you went back 3,000 years in my ancestry you wouldn't find a drop of Irish blood in my veins, but I love the place." His wife, Judy, had given him the six volumes to read and he thought, "they would make wonderful theatre...[S]he said 'Why don't you try it? What can you lose?' "[38]

Prince directed a cast of 22 actors, most of whom played multiple parts, about 80 in all. Of this venture so far from the Broadway mainstream, Prince said, "This is the least-pressured, most joyful and satisfying theatre experience I can remember. It's wonderful that there aren't millions of dollars at stake. It's nice to stay up nights worrying about the material, and not about the investors who gave you $8 million to do your musical....I suppose a certain degree of adulthood has entered my life."[39]

After a couple of weeks of previews, the play officially opened on 16 February 1992, and in the *New York Times* Frank Rich immediately identified the roots from which the production sprang. He wrote, "The environmental staging, the use of a roving ensemble to conjure up the atmosphere of Victorian England and the relish in exposed stage machinery all echoed Mr. Prince's landmark productions of the 1970's: the arena-format revival of *Candide* and the original, proscenium-framed *Sweeney Todd*."[40] He continued that Prince "is certainly on top of his talent as a master of stage pictures"[41] and that replicating at least eleven productions of *Phantom* around the world "has in no way dulled his instinct for orchestrating performers, movement, sights and sounds into a vibrant theatrical landscape far removed from the opulence of West End and Broadway musical spectaculars."[42]

Though generous in his praise for the Eugene Lee stage designs and for the "teeming...background" Prince had created, Rich then commented, "The trouble with *Grandchild of Kings* is its foreground, which is pallid by comparison, and that failing is one of writing, not staging. The director has done his own adaptation...and he simply has not succeeded in transforming those books' prose into drama."[43] Rich found Prince's script "a diligent and intelligent exercise in excerptation" but complained that its episodes "are self-contained anecdotes given roughly equal weight" and that O'Casey's "emotional, political and artistic coming of age is always seen from the outside, not within...."[44] Rich concluded, "Like the young, vigorous and still artistically unformed O'Casey, [Prince] seems to be knocking loudly at a door that he has yet to walk through."[45]

But for Edith Oliver, writing in *The New Yorker*, Prince had indeed walked through the door, revealing "the richness of *Grandchild of Kings*. Every moment is alive with characters, with music and dancing, and with feelings that explode and vanish."[46] Of the acting she wrote, "Everyone in the cast is a deft performer..." and of the adaptor and director, "...the real triumph is Mr. Prince's. When I first heard of the project, I was concerned. The music will dilute those wonderful words, I thought. If O'Casey had wanted his memoirs to be dramatized, he'd have done it himself. No need to worry.

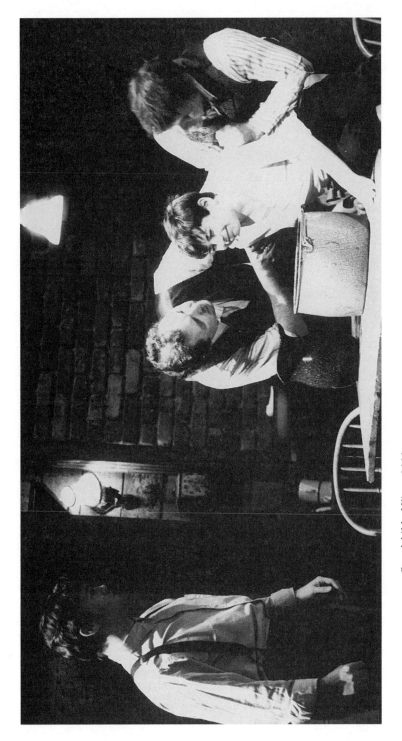

Grandchild of Kings, 1992
Adapted by Harold Prince from the first two volumes of Sean O'Casey's autobiography.
(Photo © Carol Rosegg. Reprinted by permission of the photographer)

Seldom can a writer as great as O'Casey have been treated with so much imagination and love."[47]

Grandchild was nominated by the Outer Critics Circle as Best Play of that season.

Kiss of the Spider Woman
REBORN

Spider Woman in Toronto

In 1988, not long before the Purchase production of *Spider Woman*, Harold Prince had begun a successful relationship with the Canadian producer Garth Drabinsky, the head of Live Entertainment (Livent) of Canada, Inc. Drabinsky had obtained the rights to do *Phantom of the Opera* in Canada and wanted Prince to repeat as director for the production in Toronto. Of his first meeting with Prince in September of 1988 in Prince's office, Drabinsky remembers,

> I've met plenty of icons before, but Hal is without question the most pleasant, least assuming icon I've ever met in show business. I walked into [his office] expecting a huge ego. After all, Hal Prince is the most important musical theatre creator of our lifetime and has been a Broadway producer and director for more than forty years....I found him sitting at his desk, glasses propped on his tanned, bald head, smiling....Later, I learned that this was how he always appeared—unshakable and in full control.[1]

In the summer of 1989, and about two months before their very successful Toronto opening of *Phantom*, Prince asked Drabinsky to participate in the Purchase production of *Kiss of the Spider Woman*. But the producer declined. In his book, *Closer to the Sun*, Drabinsky explained:

> Though I loved the notion of working with Hal again—clearly he and I were forging the early stages of a collaborative relationship—at that juncture it was

impossible for me to participate. I was still trying to buy back Cineplex Odeon and preoccupied with the opening [in Canada] of the Pantages [theatre] and *Phantom*. I just didn't have the time, or the mental energy, and declined.[22]

After seeing the *Kiss of the Spider Woman* production at Purchase, Drabinsky continued to resist involvement with the show. He, too, felt it needed further work, and he encouraged the collaborators to consider new scenery, lighting design and leading players and to work on the show's structural problems.

Prince, Kander, Ebb and McNally worked on revising *Spider Woman* during the summer of 1991. Armed with new lyrics and song ideas, John Kander spent July and August composing. As the revised piece took shape Prince became very enthusiastic. He considered it to be a totally new show since the book was about seventy to eighty percent different, and about half the music was new. As the members of the team worked, they recognized that they were giving the show an altered sensibility, one that pleased them all. Now the entire musical took place in the confined prison cell of the protagonists, with the movie escape sequences a series of disconnected events. Jerome Sirlin, known for his scenery projections for Philip Glass productions at the Brooklyn Academy of Music, designed a single unit set, revamping completely what had been done for Purchase. Florence Klotz's costumes were also reworked.

While preparing for the *Phantom* production in Vancouver in May 1991, Drabinsky and Prince took a trip over the mountains to Whistler, B.C. Somewhere above the Rockies Prince told the producer about the reworked book for *Spider Woman* and when they got back to their hotel, Prince gave Drabinsky the script, which he promptly read. Drabinsky recalled,

> I saw at once that they had solved the difficulties that had surfaced in Purchase and had met the challenges head on. As I read I felt flushed with possibilities. I believed the musical had the potential of being an artistic breakthrough, one that could push the theatrical envelope to a new dimension. I believed it could become the quintessential Hal Prince show. We went out for Chinese food to celebrate, and over the stir-fried chicken I agreed to produce *Kiss*. The one thing I remember we all agreed on was that we bring in Chita Rivera to play the title role.[3]

Prince now believes that Drabinsky's producing of *Spider Woman* was the best that anyone had done on a musical in years. He feels that Drabinsky coddled the work and that it was Drabinsky who salvaged it. Ironically,

Prince has said, "It's the one show that won't make him rich but he loves the piece and he's proud of it. I told him, 'You'll do a lot of giant mega-money-making shows, but you'll be known by anybody with any taste as the guy who salvaged *Spider Woman*.'"[4] Prince said this proudly as the show was about to celebrate its third anniversary on Broadway on 3 May 1995.

Once Drabinsky was on board, he suggested that the show be done in Canada and then come to New York. Prince agreed on Canada but said he didn't believe Broadway critics and audiences would accept the new production unless the memory of the negative Purchase reviews could be erased. What was needed, Prince felt, was critical acclaim in London: "Canada is Canada and London is London, so I wanted to go to London for six months."[5] Drabinsky worried that going to London for six months would be very costly. Prince agreed that it would be, but he was resolute in his conviction that it was important.

As agreed, when the new version of *Spider Woman* went into rehearsals in Toronto, Chita Rivera—who had enjoyed a rich and varied Broadway career highlighted by starring performances in *West Side Story, Bye Bye Birdie* and *Chicago*—was cast as the movie queen, the Spider Woman of Molina's imagination. She was playing a more "smoldering, enigmatic, almost Dietrich-like presence that defines a mood not present in the Purchase version."[6] Rivera had previously worked for Prince when she played Anita in his production of *West Side Story*, and later in the national company of *Zorba*, of which she had very fond memories.[7] She had first heard about *Spider Woman* through her friends, Kander and Ebb, during its Purchase incarnation. Rivera said, "Hal, John and Fred spoke to me about the role over the next few months. I subsequently rehearsed and performed in a reading in Toronto with Anthony Crivello and Richard Thomas. Freddy and John added several numbers for me to an already magnificent score."[8] During the rewriting, much attention was focused on clarifying Rivera's role as Aurora, the exotic temptress who dwells in Molina's subconscious.

Vincent Paterson, who had choreographed for Madonna, did the original hallucination dances in *Spider Woman*, which were inspired by the 1940's movies. However, Rob Marshall, who later choreographed the *Damn Yankees* revival, is credited with additional choreography.   Rivera said,

> Marshall choreographed new numbers for me with great style and excitement. *Spider Woman* was unusual and challenging because I play several roles, including the role of Molina's imaginary Spider Woman. The Spider Woman character consists of dreams and fragments; and it was a challenge to connect all of the fragments and make her whole, powerful and memorable.[9]

Asked to describe what she felt about the experience of being directed by Prince in *Spider Woman*, Rivera said, "Watching and listening to Hal, with his astounding energy and passion, is exciting. He draws you in, and you find that your journey is remarkable. You don't comprehend the many levels of his vision until you have been running for a while. Hal sees what no one else can see."[10] Prince said of his star in *Spider Woman*, "She's one of the few remaining musical comedy superstars. They don't exist that way any more. Chita sings as well as anybody around right now."[11]

Prince cast Brent Carver—whose distinguished twenty-year career in Canada spanned both classical and musical theatre—as Molina, and Anthony Crivello—who had appeared on Broadway in *Les Misérables* and as Che in *Evita*—as Valentin.

To crystallize the show's theme, Prince had both of them develop their characterizations in very specific ways. At the opening of the show, Prince wanted Valentin to irritate the audience with his didactic and humorless manner. Similarly, Molina had to make the audience uncomfortable with this manic, antic behavior. The characters of Molina and Valentin were then to evolve as the show progressed. Like peeling off layers of an onion, he wanted to reveal them as they grow and learn more about each other to be not at all what they appeared to be at first. Prince's goal was for the audience, by the end of the evening, to love them.[12]

Prince's interpretation of the Molina/Valentin relationship has a wider application than to just this prison encounter. In some ways, he says,

> I'm dealing with quite a different message than at Purchase. Then, I was thinking about an examination of escape. This time, I think it's about confinement and how to deal in close quarters with what appears to you to be your enemy. Two men are put in a cell eight by ten feet...in other words—an oversimplification if you will—like Serbs and Croats, and they're told, you can either annihilate each other or find out what's lovable and worthy of respect in each other and grow to live together. *Spider Woman* is about a man's journey to find himself.[13]

Prince sees *Spider Woman* fitting into the musical theatre concept he has always adhered to: material that would stimulate both him and the audience and that would make a show immediate in a large and important way. He says, "We are willing to equate entertainment with commitment to issues: to thinking."[14]

In addition to the two new male leads and the new leading lady in *Spider*

Woman, there were now two additional female roles, a prison warden, nine guards and other prisoners. The female chorus of dancers and singers of the original Purchase production were eliminated. Among the prisoners there would now be four dancers to back up Rivera.

The ending in the new production was entirely different than in the original version, which Prince thought was depressing. The new ending allowed audiences to leave feeling somewhat hopeful. Although Prince has never been personally committed to the idea of happy endings, he did feel that *Spider Woman* cried out for a final sense of renewal, and he went along with his instincts.

Spider Woman opened in Toronto on 14 June 1992, at the Bluma Appel Theatre. The revamped production received generally excellent reviews, which prompted Drabinsky to move ahead with the plan for a West End London production. There were a few dissenting voices, such as that of Karen Murray, whose review ran in the weekly *Variety* of 22 June 1992. She wrote,

> There's no disputing the power of the story. But Prince and his creative team haven't solved a number of problems. Molina's fantasies are acted out in numerous song-and-dance numbers, choreographed by Vincent Patterson [sic]. While they provide a strong contrast to the prison scenes, the sequences seem interminable, detracting from the strength of the story...In the final analysis, the elaborate staging proves much more provocative than the material.[15]

Despite the abundance of favorable reviews, Drabinsky thought that all the problems with the show had not been fully resolved: Paterson's choreography was not showing Rivera's talents to best advantage; the score needed boosting in the middle scenes; the book needed some clarification of characters and plot. While the show was getting standing ovations, Drabinsky said he couldn't entice many Canadians to come and see it. He "just couldn't pierce that national reticence....I concluded that Canadians still needed to read the critical endorsement of the foreign press before they would turn out."[16]

Prince, according to Drabinsky, was exhausted and left for a three-month summer vacation, saying that any changes the show needed could wait until the end of the Toronto engagement. Fred Ebb, who had been suffering angina pains throughout the Toronto rehearsal period, underwent quadruple bypass surgery within a few days of the opening. After his health was restored, he and Kander came up with a new song, "Where You Are," a show-stopping number that replaced the problematic "Don't Even Think About It."[17]

Moving to London

Prince returned during the final week of August 1992, at the end of the
Toronto run, to put the necessary changes into the show. It was at this point
that Rob Marshall added his new choreography for Rivera, "Where You Are"
was set in Act I, and another new number, "Russian Movie/Good Times," was
introduced at the top of Act II. The choreography and staging of the finale
were changed so that the *Spider Woman* and Molina now danced an increasingly tense tango of death, which, says Drabinsky, "culminates in Molina
bravely embracing her and seizing her kiss—literally and triumphantly
embracing death—to the cheers and bravos of the people in his life, members
of an audience viewing this ultimate movie fantasy of his in the moment
before his death."[18] All these improvements were to strengthen the show
immeasurably for the London opening.

A couple of weeks before *Kiss of the Spider Woman* arrived in London,
an IRA bombing campaign resulted in bombing incidents in locations near
the theatre. But any fear that theatre-goers might want to avoid the West End
proved groundless, as the previews enjoyed good sales. For this, Prince's first
musical in London since his hit *Phantom* had opened there, the favorable
advance word and press reports of the many celebrities who came to see the
production added to the excitement and anticipation by London audiences.[19]

The London opening of *Spider Woman* took place on 30 October 1992, at
the 300-seat Shaftesbury Theatre. With the stars of the Toronto production—
Chita Rivera, Brent Carver and Anthony Crivello—repeating their roles, the
London theatre press not only acclaimed the musical as a resounding success
but also treated it as an important theatrical breakthrough. Michael Coveney,
writing for *The London Observer*, called the show "a mature and deeply moving adaptation" of Manuel Puig's 1976 novel and Hector Banco's 1985 movie.
He continued,

> Some critics have found difficulty in reconciling the claims on our sensibili-
> ties of brutality and samba, defecation and camp but that acrid juxtaposition
> is exactly the point. Hence the butch prison officers, who double as chorus
> boys, and the idea that there is a precise connection between sexual and
> political loss of dignity. Harold Prince's brilliant production, a wholesale
> import from Toronto, bristles with these awkward but deliberate collisions in
> a presentation that is vivacious, fluent, muscular and, above all, impas-
> sioned.[20]

William Henry III, writing about the London production in *Time*, said that the show "is as much as anything a musical about the magic of musicals....The real star, as so often, is Prince, whose staging tricks are as spectacular as in his *Phantom of the Opera*. This time they serve a far better show."[21]

Sheridan Morley, the only reviewer to applaud the Purchase production of *Spider Woman*, continued to champion the revised piece at the Shaftesbury Theatre. He wrote, "If there is any justice, it should now go back to Broadway as a reminder of what was missed by American reviewers the first time around." Morely went on to say that this was a major score, "perhaps the best of Kander and Ebb since *Cabaret*, though closer in its dark tones to their less-known *Zorba*." Morley felt that the problem for Prince had always been to merge the life of the South American jail cell with that of the fantastic movie musicals wherein lie Molina's dreams and the chance of escape to another world.

> This is now solved thanks to the stunning back projected slides of Jerome Sirlin and a performance from Chita Rivera (in her first return to the West End musical stage in 30 years) who plays, or more accurately dances, the title role as a mix of Delores Del Rio and Louise Brooks....*Spider Woman* is that recession rarity: a challenging, dangerous and darkly adult musical. If it survives, it affirms the future of the stage musical as a serious form. If it goes down, stand by for a lot more revivals and songbook catalogue anthologies.[22]

Shortly after it opened, *Kiss of the Spider Woman* won the 1992 Evening Standard Award for best musical. The original cast album was released in England on First Night Records in February 1993 and in America in May on RCA Victor. Prince remains satisfied with his decision to do the musical in London between its runs in Toronto and New York. In London, it garnered the critical acclaim that helped underscore its transformation from the show that had first been done in Purchase.

Kiss of the Spider Woman on Broadway

The Broadway production of *Spider Woman* opened at New York's Broadhurst Theatre on 3 May 1993, with Rivera, Carver and Crivello again starring. The critics were almost unanimous in their approval of the production. This was a far cry from the initial reception in Purchase. Frank Rich, who had had so many reservations about the musical the first time around, felt differently

Kiss of the Spider Woman, New York, 1993
Prison scene. Brent Carver as Molina and Anthony Crivello as Valentin.
(Photo: Courtesy the Museum of the City of New York Theatre Collection, Gift of Mary Bryant)

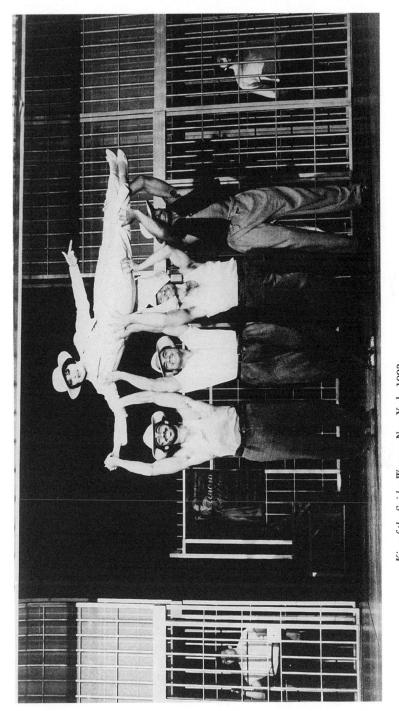

Kiss of the Spider Woman, New York, 1993
Chita Rivera as the Spider Woman of Molina's imagination.
(Photographer: Catherine Ashmore. Photo: Courtesy the Museum of the City of New York)

about the revised version. He wrote, *"Kiss of the Spider Woman* is a much improved version of the show Mr. Prince had first staged in Purchase, N.Y." He went on to say, however, that the musical did not "meet all the high goals it borrows from Manual Puig's novel. When it falls short, it pushes into pretentious overdrive (a 'morphine Tango' if you please) and turns the serious business of police-state torture into show-biz kitsch every bit as vacuous as the B-movie clichés parodied in its celluloid fantasies."[23] Rich did feel the production succeeded in giving Chita Rivera a glittering showcase and additionally succeeded in "using the elaborate machinery of a big Broadway musical to tell the story of an uncloseted, unhomogenized, unexceptional gay man who arrives at his own heroic definition of masculinity."[24] Rich found the depiction of Valentin, Molina's cellmate, as a cliché, "draining the heat from the show's central relationship and defusing its political content."[25] However, he felt Carver's Molina was far more honest than the Molina of the Oscar-winning William Hurt in the 1985 *Spider Woman* film.[26]

Despite some reservations about certain elements of the production (i.e., the choreography, music and lyrics), Rich continued,

> Mr. Prince's staging, by contrast, is almost always commanding....The evening's uncompromising darkness is not an affectation in this Broadway director's case, but the product of an entire career that began in earnest with *Cabaret*, the 1966 show that shares its historical atmosphere, show-biz framework and symbolic death figure with *Spider Woman*. For those who dote on Broadway musicals, Mr. Prince's new work would be worth seeing just for the Fellini-esque finale, a flashback to an old movie palace that is a variation on the famous "Loveland" sequence in his 1971 *Follies*. When he finally brings Mr. Carver into Ms. Rivera's arms to seal his fate with her long awaited kiss, you cannot help feeling the shiver of pure theater. Not because the kiss realizes the musical's lofty intentions, but because it consummates the showmanship of a director who wrote the book on how to spread a web of white heat through a Broadway house.[27]

Edwin Wilson wrote in *The Wall Street Journal* that Prince and his team "have achieved a frightening juxtaposition of the bitter reality of life in an excessively cruel prison and the escapism of fantasy and dreams. Prison life is made all too palpable...a serious musical with a capital 'S.' "[28]

Edith Oliver in *The New Yorker* found Mr. McNally's book often "witty or tender," Crivello's Valentin "extremely moving," Ms. Rivera "indefatigable," and wrote that Prince "never loses his magician's touch."[29]

Kiss of the Spider Woman was nominated for eleven Tony Awards as was its main competition, *Tommy*. Drabinsky has said that in the week before the

awards ceremony he had been hearing rumors that the industry was not prepared to give the best director award to Prince mainly because he had already
received nineteen Tonys during his career. Prince himself felt sure he would
not win. He assumed that the reminders in the press of all those Tonys he had
received were a way of saying, "He's had enough awards. Now let's encourage
the next generation of directors."[30] Drabinsky could not understand how the
voters could bypass Prince, who "had brilliantly reworked the piece over the
year between Purchase and Toronto, and who had directed three nominated
performances (Chita Rivera, Brent Carver and Anthony Crivello)."[31]

Spider Woman won seven Tony Awards, including best musical, and yet
Prince was denied the Tony for best director of a musical. The winner was
Des McAnuff for *Tommy*. Prince remained philosophical about being passed
over, saying he didn't mind and that it was a great evening for him because
the show and his collaborators had won. He said, "It's like that old thing...if
given a choice that I win or the show wins.... I was really thrilled for everyone else."[32]

Drabinsky, while planning his acceptance speech in the event that *Spider Woman* won the Tony for best musical, said he very much wanted to pay
tribute to Hal Prince in a way that all of America, Canada, and the industry
would hear. "I don't think this has been done nearly enough throughout Hal's
illustrious career. Our industry, as in all segments of the entertainment industry, has a shadow of envy and jealousy that creeps into everything. And here
was Hal, a man who had done more than anyone else, who reshaped musical
theatre as we know it, and I wanted to remind people of this."[33]

Prince still wonders why no one has pointed out that the SUNY Purchase
experiment actually did work after all: that it is possible to take a piece to a
place like Purchase, work on it for eight weeks, discover the problems and
then, at some later date, rework the show using the early experience to good
advantage. He seems disappointed that not one person in the press understood or expressed this. Prince feels that most of the critics treated *Spider
Woman* as if it had never been done prior to London and Broadway and that
no recognition needed to be paid to what had been learned at Purchase. But
Prince feels it is no loss to him:

> I'm 67 years old and we proved the point. But what about the next two musi-
> cals that were going to be done at SUNY? One was *The Secret Garden* and the
> other was *My Favorite Year*. They never had the benefit of an eight-week trial
> period which would have enabled them to first get it wrong and then work on
> it till they got it right. When they opened on Broadway, they were not ready.
> They were not as good as they could have been or even as good as they were

when they closed on Broadway after work on them had continued. If they had had the opportunity to try out their shows away from Broadway in Purchase, they could have then spent some time fixing the mistakes and tightening their shows as the collaborators on *Spider Woman* did before coming to Broadway where the reviewers are quick to make judgments. Once reviewed, it's too late to make those changes because the public has been informed of the flaws. And that is why *Spider Woman* is such a satisfying success.[34]

In July 1994, after playing the role of Aurora for two years, Chita Rivera was replaced by Vanessa Williams, who later relinquished the part to Maria Conchita Alonso. Rivera, however, reprised her role as the *Spider Woman* on the national tour. Three months after winning the Tony for Best Leading Actor in a Musical, Brent Carver, citing fatigue, returned home to Canada, replaced as Molina by Jeff Hyslop. Anthony Crivello eventually gave up the role of Valentin to Brian Mitchell. And after 16 previews and 906 regular performances, *Kiss of the Spider Woman* closed in New York on 2 July 1995.

Prince is enormously proud that he and his collaborators stuck with the show. The most important thing for him about its evolution and eventual success is what he feels it says about the quality of perseverance. Prince doubts that he would have been able to show such persistence ten or fifteen years earlier. He was then too impatient.[35]

RECREATING AN AMERICAN MASTERPIECE:
Show Boat

In 1927, Jerome Kern and Oscar Hammerstein II brought monumental innovation to the American musical theatre. Their masterpiece, *Show Boat*, opened on December 27th of that year. Based on Edna Ferber's novel of the same name, it was produced by the legendary Florenz Ziegfeld—of the famous Follies revues—at the Ziegfeld Theatre, with sets by Joseph Urban and a cast that included Helen Morgan, Howard Marsh, Charles Winninger, Edna May Oliver and Jules Bledsoe.

Show Boat is considered by most theatre historians to be the first great modern musical. Hammerstein's book merged the carefree naïveté of traditional Broadway musical comedy with serious contemporary themes, while Kern's score ranged from lighthearted, popular 32-bar songs to nineteenth-century operetta and grand opera and to the music of Dixieland and Mississippi Delta blues. "Undeniably, it is Jerome Kern's *Porgy and Bess*," says Harold Prince.[1]

The story begins on the *Cotton Blossom*, a riverboat that, like other floating theatres of the nineteenth and early twentieth centuries, offered entertainment to audiences in towns along the Mississippi. It centers on the romance between Gaylord Ravenal, a dashing riverboat gambler, and Magnolia, the daughter of the *Cotton Blossom*'s captain, Andy, and his wife, Parthy. The young couple's marriage is threatened by Ravenal's gambling and eventually, burdened with debt, he disappears. Magnolia, to support herself and her daughter, goes to Chicago and becomes a nightclub singer. Years later she returns to the *Cotton Blossom* where she is soon joined by the now-reformed Ravenal for a reunion at the final curtain. The book's secondary plot follows the misfortunes of the doomed Julie, a riverboat entertainer and Magnolia's closest friend. The victim of what we now call racism, Julie forced audiences to confront the subject of miscegenation for the first time in the context of a Broadway musical.

Garth Drabinsky was in London in 1990 when an Opera North production of *Show Boat* (in cooperation with the Royal Shakespeare Company) was playing at the London Palladium. Never having seen the show before, he attended a performance at his earliest opportunity. He remembers thinking that the production was unmemorable: he was sure that the physical aspects of the show could not possibly reflect or even compare to the scope of Ziegfeld's original epic. Nevertheless, he felt all the power of the piece, even after fifty years, and saw how the audience was moved by the show, which was playing to capacity crowds. The producer suspected that other than in its initial Broadway and London productions, and perhaps in a subsequent restaging in the thirties, *Show Boat* had never been graced with the budget and production values that would properly showcase its majestic score, its sweeping, multigenerational story, and its fascinating Mississippi River setting. Drabinsky then decided that if he could gather a dynamic, creative team of talents and acquire the world license needed to justify the enormous costs, *Show Boat* would be the ideal musical to open the new Main Stage Theatre at Canada's North York Performing Arts Centre (now called the Ford Centre for the Performing Arts).[2]

The producer recognized that the major ingredient needed for a project of this magnitude was a director who could bring to it unquestioned boldness and renewed vitality. "Naturally, for me there was only one man for the job," wrote Drabinsky, "and his name was Harold Prince."[3] Since Prince's direction of Drabinsky's Toronto production of *Phantom of the Opera*, the producer regarded their working collaboration as the "most satisfying creative association of my career."[4] He saw in Prince the dramaturgical skills that were essential to a revival of *Show Boat*. Because there was no one definitive script for the musical but rather a collection of librettos from the many and various stage and movie productions—as well as a mass of music, lyrics and dialogue—a director had to be able to pick and choose to come up with the most effective version for the nineties.

At the end of October 1990, after Drabinsky secured the rights to *Show Boat* from the Rodgers and Hammerstein Foundation, he arranged to meet with Prince at the director's Rockefeller Center office. Although he knew that Prince did not as a rule direct revivals (aside from his twenty-fifth anniversary re-creation of his own show *Cabaret*), Drabinsky would not allow that to stop him. "I told Prince, excitedly, 'I want you to direct a show for me. It's a revival.'⁵ Prince replied, 'If you're going to ask me to do *Carousel*, I pass.'"⁶ (Prince has explained that he could never figure out what to do about the problems of Act Two in *Carousel*. "It's a great show but when the show veers off somewhere in Act Two, I think to myself, what to do? what to do?...and I could never figure it out!"⁷)

After Drabinsky reassured Prince that it was not *Carousel* he had in mind but *Show Boat*, Prince stopped short and smiled. "Isn't that the funniest thing! I've been thinking about *Show Boat* for the past couple of years," he explained.⁸ For him, it had the best score ever written, with such memorable songs as "Can't Help Lovin' Dat Man," "Ol' Man River," "Why Do I Love You," and "Make Believe." Prince said, "It tells a wonderful story and it contains one of the best book scenes a director could ask for, which is the miscegenation scene where entertainer Julie is fired for being black and having a white husband. It's perfect and couldn't be improved upon today."⁹

He also confided that he had never seen a production of *Show Boat* that he had liked or that he felt had done justice to the musical. He thought the book—particularly the second act—needed a good deal of revision. He asked himself, "*Show Boat* is a great, great piece of material so...can you make it solve your problems with it? And that was the enticement in this particular case because I felt I knew what to do."¹⁰

Prince agreed to direct the show. His goal was to create a production with a realistic, gritty "documentary" feel, rather than a vacuous piece of pretty Hollywood make-believe. He wanted a *Show Boat* that took notice of the story's dramatically portrayed passage of four unsettling decades, from the post-Reconstruction Deep South of the 1880s to America's involvement in the First World War, and ending in the Jazz Age of the Roaring Twenties. To capture this sense of the movement of time, Prince would turn to modern technology—the latest developments in automation, computerization and lighting—to allow the show's twenty scenes to unfold with pace and fluidity. He told Drabinsky he wanted to recreate *Show Boat* in his own way, drawing from all the old librettos, even adding a new line or two if needed, and from the music of all the earlier versions, including the 1936 movie with Allan Jones and Irene Dunne. Eventually, Prince would restore six songs and change others to propel the action more effectively, and would rewrite some lines to enhance the realism of the moment.

The many sources Prince used included the original 1927 version of the show, the London script that followed, the 1936 film, and the 1946 Broadway revival, as well as John McGlinn's 1988 EMI-Angel recording, which consisted of the score of the 1927 production and the additional musical material written for *Show Boat* over the years, and which annotated every major production. Miles Kreuger's book, *Show Boat: The Story of a Classic American Musical,* a compendium of information on all the productions of *Show Boat,* also proved to be very helpful. Prince said, "Ironically, the original version of the play seemed to be more modern than the 1946 revival, which, while slick (in 1946 terms), lacked the sweep and historical punch of the original." [11] He also noted that some of the most beautiful songs written by Kern and Hammerstein were cut from the original show because they seemed too serious for the time, and he contemplated restoring them in his re-creation. [12]

As a nine-year-old boy, Bill Hammerstein sat with his father, Oscar Hammerstein II, at the opening night of the original *Show Boat* in 1927, and went on to watch many performances of the show from the wings of the theatre. Years later he was a stage manager of the last revival of *Show Boat* to be mounted before Jerome Kern died. His memories of the show, in Prince's view, are colored in that wonderfully rosy way one remembers endearing things of the past. And now Bill Hammerstein has become the keeper of his father's flame. As such, getting his approval for contemplated changes was high on Prince's agenda. For example, Prince wanted to restore the song "Mis'ry's Comin' Aroun' " in the show's first act, to which Hammerstein's reaction was, "Hal, they didn't do it in the first place because it's so depressing." Prince explained that the new version of the show was going to be unlike the old although it was not going to veer in any inappropriate directions. "I figured that "Mis'ry" would work," said Prince. [13] It is now Prince's favorite song in the show.

Hammerstein dealt very thoughtfully with each of Prince's suggested changes, even if at times he seemed to the director to be somewhat overprotective. But Prince and Hammerstein had been friends for forty years and, Prince observed, "I'm positive that if anyone else had directed the show they wouldn't have been permitted the leeway that I was permitted. What was really nice was that Bill Hammerstein, after the New York opening, said, 'Look, lest you think I'm not aware of it...I know that I was negative about a lot of things that I now like a lot.' " [14] Prince thanked him but in fact had never felt inhibited by Hammerstein's caution. Instead, he was very grateful for the freedom and enthusiasm that Bill Hammerstein and the Hammerstein Foundation had given him. He was totally sympathetic to the sense of responsibility they felt to Oscar Hammerstein II in allowing someone new to come in and do what he had done.

From the first, Prince wanted Susan Stroman to do the choreography for *Show Boat*. She had won many awards for her work on *Crazy for You* and had previously worked with Prince on his *Don Giovanni* production at the New York City Opera. She said that when the director called her to ask if she would be interested in working on his new production of *Show Boat* she was certain she had heard him wrong. "I thought I misunderstood the name of the show, because everybody else does Harold Prince revivals," she said.[15] Of Prince, Stroman said she felt an incredible desire to please him because, "Hal is walking history and he's a star in the theatre community. When Hal leaps up out of his chair everybody stops in his tracks."[16] Perhaps the high point of Stroman's choreography occurs in the second act of *Show Boat*, in which she creates a rapid montage of dance and mime to show the passage of time and the changing mores from the turn-of-the-century South to 1927 Chicago. Prince thought her achievement of this was brilliant.[17] Anna Kisselgoff, in the *New York Times*, observed, "She [Stroman] has come up with a swiftly paced urban ballet contrasting rich and poor. In her quicksilver vignettes, black street entertainers and musicians invent the Charleston, which is then co-opted by whites in the Roaring '20s."[18]

Florence Klotz was signed to do the costumes, a Herculean assignment. With nine principals in the show and a total of seventy-three in the cast (the largest cast on a Broadway stage since the original production in 1927), more than 500 costumes had to be created. Moreover, since the story of *Show Boat* takes place over a forty-year period and covers three generations, the costume design had to reflect dramatic changes in fashion and in the fortunes of the characters.

Eugene Lee was chosen to do the production design because, with his love of natural materials, Prince considered him the right person to create the look of Natchez, the *Cotton Blossom*, the Mississippi and its environs, circa 1887. Guided by photographs from the period 1884–1927, Lee used real materials, such as metal, wood pilings, clapboard, burlap, and muslin. His designs are less decorative than those of some past productions—less painted, less artificial—but, says Lee, "I have always found great beauty in texture and patina."[19] In the *New York Times* David Richards commented, "The sets are not just the stuff of the wide screen; they supplant one another cinematically, so that the dramatic action is rarely impeded."[20]

Lighting design for the show was by Richard Pilbrow and orchestrations were done by Robert Russel Bennett and William David Brohn. And, as customary in most Harold Prince shows, Ruth Mitchell was assistant to the director.

At the start, Prince wanted Robert Morse to play Cap'n Andy. While they had never worked together, Morse had played Prince many years earlier in a show called *Say, Darling*. When Prince first called him, the actor said that he could not talk to him at the moment because his wife was going to the hospital to have a baby; he promised to call back as soon as the baby was born. Actually, it was Prince who called back, four days later, to be told that Morse and his wife had had a girl. When Prince offered him the part of the captain, Morse responded, "Hal, I don't want to go back to Broadway. I just enjoyed a big success in *Tru* and I've just had a baby and I don't want to do that....If I can work for six months, I'd consider it."[21] Prince agreed. And so it was that Morse portrayed Cap'n Andy in Toronto but did not repeat the role in New York. Prince said while there were many theories about what had happened, the truth was not any more complicated than that: Morse just did not want to play Broadway.

Prince then chose one of his closest friends and long-term associates, John McMartin, to replace Morse as Cap'n Andy on Broadway. The two had already done five shows together and Prince was certain the actor would be superb in the role. Prince acknowledges that McMartin's portrayal differed from Morse's: "It has more energy." However, refusing to compare apples to oranges, Prince observed, "It worked out beautifully for everyone. Bobby didn't have to come to New York and I'm happy to be working with John again."[22]

McMartin recalls that he had seen the opening of *Show Boat* in Toronto and loved it, but it had never occurred to him that Prince might consider him for the part of the captain, since historically the role was always played by character actors. When Prince called him, said McMartin, "I told Hal that I really didn't think I was right for the role. It's funny that I tried to talk myself out of one of the best parts I've ever had. There's so much variety to it. You get to do everything....I had no idea there was this bag of goodies in that part....Now, I couldn't be happier. After Morse left, I played it for about five or six months in Toronto and then came down to join the cast in New York for the Broadway opening."[23]

McMartin said that Prince had not changed very much since they had worked together in the early days. "He's just as wonderfully crazed and wild when he's directing....I've learned not to subconsciously reject some piece of direction he may be giving me ...that I may not agree with, because somewhere down the line he's usually right."[24] In an interview with Joanne Kaufman, McMartin remarked about Prince, "Every time he starts a new project Hal's like a director reborn. It's like just before they opened King Tut's tomb when the professor was looking through the eyehole and somebody said, 'What do you see?' and the professor said 'I see wonderful things.' That's how I think of Hal at rehearsal: he sees wonderful things."[25]

McMartin continues:

> My biggest surprise was how he changed the production of *Kiss of the Spider Woman*. When I saw it in Purchase and then saw the reworked production, it was like two totally different shows. I didn't know how the same director can do that…have a totally different turn on [a show]….He never ceases to amaze me….When you see his direction you may think it's spontaneous or top of his head, but the truth is he's very meticulous in his detail and study. He gets the people he wants to work with and then there's a kind of shorthand of communication between them….He doesn't have to say much because subconsciously you're both on the same wavelength. He's never effusive about you or what you're doing, but he gives you great positive energy and you can always tell when he's pleased because his face lights up. It's almost childlike…he'll giggle and laugh….I always think that Hal would have been successful in any vocation he'd have chosen, but what a gift for us that it was theatre. Cap'n Andy says, "The lucky people get to do what they enjoy doing." I know that's where I'm at and I think that's where Hal is at also.[26]

When casting the role of Parthy, Prince said that Elaine Stritch was his first choice. "It's odd casting actors rather than comic performers, and I just love her."[27] His decision to have Parthy sing "Why Do I Love You?" to her newborn granddaughter, Kim, at the beginning of the second act was a problem for Bill Hammerstein. Originally it was a big chorus number set at the Chicago World's Fair. In later productions the song became a duet for lovers while the rest of the family also sang bits of it. Prince chose not to have the Chicago World's Fair scene open Act Two, believing the days when musicals had to open their second acts with big production numbers were gone. He wanted instead to get back to the book so that the arc of the second act is about family again—not only about the Captain's family, but also the *Show Boat* family and, in a larger sense, the family of man. The family includes Queenie, Joe, Julie, and the other characters. Further, with the birth of Kim, Magnolia's baby, Prince was able to focus on three generations, and he has Parthy first singing a kind of lullaby to her granddaughter and then later, toward the end of the act, Parthy doing a Charleston with Kim, now a grown-up flapper, to the same song. Jeremy Gerard, in *Variety*, agreed that it was "a nice touch and a gift to this great actress."[28] It was, however, a problem for some of the Toronto critics and, said Prince, "the hardest thing for Bill Hammerstein to swallow. But I did say to him—and I know it sounds arrogant as hell—while working on this show, the guide I'd always had in my head was, 'What would Oscar Hammerstein say now to what you're doing?' And each time I felt that he'd be happy. Because...he changed with the theatre customs of his day and so I felt if he were here now, he would understand it is important to change again."[29]

Prince completed casting the remaining leads with Lonette McKee as Julie, Rebecca Luker as Magnolia, Mark Jacoby as Gaylord Ravenal, Michel Bell as Joe, Dorothy Stanley as Ellie, Joel Blum as Frank, Gretha Boston as Queenie, and Tammy Amerson as the adult Kim.

In reworking the book of *Show Boat*, Prince tried to rid the libretto of all stereotypes and Uncle Tom-isms. "It wasn't something he necessarily did ...to be politically correct," said Dennis Kucherawy, then Vice President of Communications for Drabinsky's Livent Inc., "but as Prince said at a meeting held in Canada, 'I don't find stereotypes dramatically interesting.'"[30] Kucherawy also said that Prince brought considerable epic sweep to the second act by adding the two long montages that allow the audience to experience in a more dramatic way the lives of the main characters as they change with the passing of time. Throughout the show, Prince rethought the interpretation and placement of some of the more familiar songs, and when dialogue did not in his judgment provide proper motivation, he rewrote the script. For example, he added a line of his own as Julie's cue before she sings "Bill." After that song, he lifted a line for her from the 1936 film.

Before *Show Boat* opened in Toronto, the production ran into a maelstrom of trouble when a group calling itself The Coalition to Stop *Show Boat* protested that it was a racist play based on a racist novel. Six months before rehearsals were slated to begin, Prince, at Drabinsky's request, agreed to come up to Toronto to talk to the group.

Walking into the room in Drabinsky's office building for the meeting, he was confronted by representatives of thirty-five black organizations. Prince told them that his politics and his record spoke for themselves, and that the show he was planning to do would contain nothing to offend the black community. The group asked if they could read his script, but he turned them down. When they asked if they could assign someone to observe rehearsals, he again said no, he did not need any help on the show, "thank you." He felt that their requests smacked of censorship.

Prince remembers people got up and screamed that he should be ashamed of himself. They called Edna Ferber a bigot. Prince explained that nothing could be further from the truth. At worst, she had succumbed to certain stereotyping that is unacceptable today. And when they attacked Oscar

Hammerstein, Prince pointed out that Hammerstein's entire career reflected his commitment to anti-racist causes. Not only is the plot of *Show Boat* manifestation of that, but twenty years later he returned to an attack against prejudice in *South Pacific* and then again in *The King and I*. Prince read to the group the lyrics of "You've Got to Be Carefully Taught" from *South Pacific*.

Nevertheless, when *Show Boat* went into rehearsal in Toronto six months later, the coalition was there picketing and shouting in front of the theatre. For the seven weeks that Prince remained in Toronto, he struggled with the psychological pressure of trying to work on the show while knowing that this storm cloud hovered outside. On the first day of rehearsal, he spoke to the company for an hour about the issue, telling them how he felt about the protest and explaining what the show would be like. They seemed to understand, but were still to be tested. About three to four weeks into rehearsal, the protestors decided to picket the stage entrance during a weekend afternoon rehearsal, reasoning that the thirty-five blacks in the company would have to confront the picket line before and after the lunch break. Prince was in the theatre having his lunch (which he had had sent in) so he did not know that the picket line was out there. He came in after the lunch break, looked at the company and sensed that something had happened but didn't know what. Cast members then explained to the director that they had had to cross a picket line at the stage entrance. Things were very tense for the rest of the day. When Prince returned to his hotel, he told his wife Judy that he feared Monday was going to be hell because the cast had Sunday off to worry about whether they had a responsibility to the protesting community not to cross their picket line.

Indeed, when the cast arrived for rehearsal on Monday, they were uneasy and Prince tried to put their concerns to rest. He reaffirmed to them that he was essentially colorblind. He also pointed out that he had never understood why "African-American" was an appropriate description. He pointed out that over 100 years ago, his family had settled in America from Germany. Did that make him German-Jewish-American? Unless they were first-generation African-Americans, he confessed that he felt all these definitions to be counterproductive. "We are all Americans. It's as simple as that." At least to Prince.[31] From that day on, rehearsals went smoothly.

On the night of the first preview, the picket line stormed the theatre and the police had to be called. On opening night the picketers returned but a torrential rainstorm served to diffuse the disruption. The next morning, all of the newspaper reviews countered the claims of the protestors and the entire dispute faded away. Prince has since come to feel that the issue raised by the coalition was not as simple and misguided as it appeared to be, that it was complicated by political overtones that had little to do with his production of *Show Boat*, a show none of the protestors had ever seen or knew anything about. Harvard professor Henry Louis Gates, Jr., the distinguished American black historian and civil libertarian, called the production "a victory of tolerance and sensitivity." [32]

The Toronto premiere was both the first public performance of the Harold Prince version of *Show Boat* and the first show that Drabinsky and Prince had done together since winning the Tony for *Kiss of the Spider Woman*. Drabinsky was sure that the New York critics would want to come to Toronto to see the show on opening night and he proceeded to invite them all up to Canada. He also suspected that for Canadians it would be important to get the opinion of foreign critics before they would turn out to see the production. All the critics, including Frank Rich of the *New York Times,* were among the estimated 250 press people in the theatre for opening night—a very strong turnout.

Opening night was filled with tension. Bobby Morse seemed very edgy and skittish to the producer when he saw him backstage just prior to curtain time. But despite Morse's nervousness, the first act played well and the second went off even better, with Morse back in full control. By the final curtain, the response of the audience proclaimed that the show was an overwhelming success. According to Drabinsky, Prince was still not so sure. " 'Hal,' I said, 'relax, it's going to be gigantic.' " This seemed hilarious to the producer. "He's been through these scenes ten times more than I have, and I'm sitting there telling him to relax?" [33]

The reviews were mostly ecstatic. Some of the critics dealt with the political issues that had been raised by the now-silenced protestors. Most of them asked incredulously what all the fuss had been about, since the show in their view was positive about matters of race and in no way demeaned anyone or any group. In his book Drabinksy quotes *New Yorker* critic John Lahr:

> ...the black experience, in both its triumph and its tragedy, is at the heart of the show's perception of America....History is ambiguous, and so is the idealism of love and hate. *Show Boat* put that paradox center stage....Anyone with a demitasse for a hat can see the intention. Not, however, the Coalition, a politically correct sign of our winded times, which wants freedom for everything but thought....*Show Boat* still speaks to the informed heart of democracy....[34]

Jeremy Gerard in *Variety* called the show "a resplendent and powerful rethinking of *Show Boat*." [35] Frank Rich had some reservations about the

Show Boat, 1994. Wedding scene
John McMartin as Cap'n Andy; Rebecca Luker as Magnolia, and Mark Jacoby as Gaylord Ravenal.
(Photographer: Michael Cooper. Photo: Courtesy the Museum of the City of New York Theatre Collection)

acting in the show and observed, "What is missing from this show is emotional punch."[36] Commenting on the racial issues that had erupted in Toronto, he
wrote,

> To watch a drop that depicts a grim eternity of cotton fields be violently torn
> to the ground while a black chorus sings of plantation drudgery is to recall a
> similar eruption of underclass rage in *Sweeney Todd.* In fact, the anger this
> *Show Boat* directs against racism is far more caustic than the chants and
> signs of the polite, ill-informed local protestors who have accused the show
> of racism without bothering to see it.[37]

Rich went on to say of Prince,

> In today's American theatre, there may be no artist more indebted to *Show
> Boat* than Harold Prince, whose entire career, from the original production of
> *West Side Story* to the current *Kiss of the Spider Woman,* has been devoted to
> building on the serious musical that Kern and Hammerstein invented. So it
> is no surprise that Mr. Prince's staging of *Show Boat* here, as the opening
> attraction of the North York Performing Arts Center, is a seismic event in the
> American musical theatre.[38]

Show Boat opened on Broadway on 2 October 1994 at the Gershwin
Theatre. The top ticket price of $75, a new high for an open-ended Broadway
run, reflected the enormous cost of running the show—about $600,000 a
week. With its cast of seventy-three, lavish sets, costumes, wigs, etc., *Show
Boat* had the highest operating budget ever on Broadway. In its first week of
ticket sales, it broke all box office records, taking in $842,636, and in spite of
its mammoth operating costs, *Show Boat* recouped its investment by the week
ending 12 November 1995.[39]

The reviews were triumphant. Michael Walsh in *Time Magazine* first outlined what had been wrong with prior versions of the show: it had been the-
matically sprawling and too long; Julie and her husband virtually disappear
before intermission; "and in a dozen stage and film incarnations since its premiere the show has been hacked, squeezed, revised, prettified and bowdler-
ized nearly out of existence."[40] Walsh went on to observe,

> Now theatergoers at Harold Prince's wonderfully imaginative new Broadway
> production can ignore all of the above. Handsomely cast for both musical
> and dramatic effect, lavishly constructed by set designer Eugene Lee and
> cogently if somewhat briskly conducted by Jeffrey Huard, this *Show Boat* is a
> near perfect staging of the work that had announced to the world the maturity
> of American musical theater. The alleged racial bias in the plot, which

occasioned protests during the tryout of the Toronto production last year, is nowhere to be found here. To see *Show Boat* is to experience how potent the Broadway ideal can be in the hands of a master like Prince.[41]

Jack Kroll in *Newsweek* wrote, "So that's what a real show is. In case we had forgotten, Harold Prince's big, big-hearted production of *Show Boat* has arrived on Broadway to remind us....'Revival' is a meager word for Prince's production; it's a reincarnation." About the cast, he wrote, "Michel Bell delivers 'Ol' Man River' with a spine-tingling passion of resignation. Lonette McKee's rendition of "Bill" rekindles the torch in torch song....John McMartin's Cap'n Andy presides over the show's tragicomic revels like a hybrid of Puck and Uncle Sam...."[42]

Donald Lyons in the *Wall Street Journal* commented on Prince's "peerless feel for emotional coherence in the theatre. Mr. Prince has both rethought the drama and reimagined the spectacle of *Show Boat*. Real tears come here when strong performers are getting to us directly. It's not in these big, be-entertained-damn-you extravaganzas that Mr. Prince is really at his best; he is actually a closet sculptor of quietly beautiful emotional moments."[43]

Clive Barnes in the *New York Post* said that during the sixty-seven years of *Show Boat*'s life, it had been refurbished many times—and no version, he felt, could be called totally authentic. "But, " he wrote, "this new reading, which started in Toronto last year with virtually the same cast, is by far the most effective I have ever encountered on stage or screen." He also commented that "it is absolutely worth the $75 top ticket price."[44]

David Richards of the *New York Times* said, "A king-size budget and cast of more than 70 have allowed Mr. Prince, still the undisputed master of the Broadway musical, to pull together a sweeping panorama embracing four decades (1887–1927) of American history, fashion and mores. His acute social conscience has prompted him, whenever possible, to emphasize the racial rift that runs the length of the musical like a fault line in an earthquake zone. But his abiding sense of life's capricious ironies is what really darkens the glittering stage pictures....By making *Show Boat* less episodic, he invariably makes it a sadder, wiser musical."[45]

Prince says now that he could not have been happier with the reaction to *Show Boat*. He agrees with Frank Rich's comment in his Toronto review that, were it not for the original *Show Boat*, it is less likely that he would have ended up working in musical theatre. To *Show Boat* you can trace that first thread, the birth of the more thoughtful musical. For Prince, *West Side Story, Fiddler on the Roof, Cabaret,* his career with Sondheim and his many shows that followed all owe a debt to the courage that went into saying, "We're going to do this thing" (*Show Boat*) in 1927. Before that production, the texts of most musicals were absurd, and if the scores were often great, it was almost to make up for the "moronic" books. It is possible, he believes, to revive some of the great old shows, such as *Anything Goes* and the like, because their scores are worth reviving. "However, you really have to leave your brains outside," says Prince. "More importantly, they can be revived as museum pieces but you can't write them that way any more."[46]

Prince feels that *Show Boat* is more romantic than most of what he has done before. He explains: "It's really where my head is now. Before I was much more political. The state of the union used to drive me insane and I would ventilate on stage. But now I'm in another place and *Show Boat* reflects it....*Show Boat* is a love affair with the two things that I love most in the world—family and theatre. And what more does a guy like me want at this point in his life than to be directing something which addresses the two things that mean the most to me."[47]

Show Boat won five Tony Awards on 4 June 1995. Gretha Boston won for Best Featured Actress in a Musical, Florence Klotz won for costume design, Susan Stroman won for choreography. *Show Boat* won the Tony for Best Revival of a Musical, and the award was accepted by Garth Drabinsky. Harold Prince won his twentieth Tony for Best Director of a Musical. (Some years ago after winning his previous Tony award it was said to be his sixteenth. It was then learned that the count was incorrect and at that time he'd actually won his nineteenth award.) Additionally, the musical won five Drama Desk Awards, including Outstanding Musical Production, and four Outer Critics Circle Awards, including Outstanding Musical Revival.

The Petrified Prince

Within weeks of *Show Boat*'s opening in New York, Prince was preparing his production of *The Petrified Prince,* a musical based on a mid-1970's Ingmar Bergman script that Bergman had written and sold to Warner Brothers but that had never been made into a film. It was slated to open at Martinson Hall in the Public Theatre in New York. Prince, who had been working on the show for a couple of years, recalled:

> Warner Brothers hated it. One of their script readers, about twenty years ago, passed this judgment: "Someone had better tell Ingmar Bergman to retire...he's lost his touch." But when John Flaxman, who has his office down the hall from mine and is in the independent theatre, film, and TV business, asked me if I thought there was a musical in this, I did think so. At the time I thought it was a perfect project for New Musicals. Michael John LaChiusa, a young composer-librettist, wrote the music. While waiting for our show to be

produced, he made a successful debut with a new musical *Hello Again* at the Vivian Beaumont. The librettist, Edward Gallardo, is the author of a marvelous play, *Simpson Street,* which was presented originally by the Puerto Rican Traveling Theatre.[48]

Rob Marshall, who had last worked with Prince when he had been brought in to add some dance numbers in *Kiss of the Spider Woman,* was chosen to do the choreography, while James Youmans did the sets and Judith Dolan the costumes.

Prince described his vision of the setting of the play:

The proscenium encompassed a huge papier maché puppet stage, the sort of venue in which children would sit cross-legged in the Bois de Boulogne to watch Punch and Judy whack the hell out of each other with wooden sticks.[49]

Within the stage was another identical Punch and Judy stage containing a bed on which Punch (the old King) and Judy (the glamorous Queen) would be making loud scatological love, screaming four-letter words in each other's ears—"Do it to me! Yes, yes, yes!"—until the King collapsed on top of his Queen, dead of a heart attack. The rest of the evening consisted of her taking power and being venal, grasping, hysterical. Her son was heir apparent to the throne. The heroine: a simple-minded, pure and beautiful ex-courtesan.

In keeping with the Guignol puppets, Prince explored other traditional puppetry, including a Noah's Ark of animals, designed and executed by the Jim Henson team.

The show intended to be both outrageously funny and bitterly cynical; Bergman's source material was indisputably dark.

Garth Drabinsky invested in the production of *The Petrified Prince,* with its twenty-seven-member cast, thinking that he might take it to Broadway if the show fared well at the Public. Doing it as a workshop production allowed the various collaborators to see what they had accomplished to date, to determine what was and what was not working, and to measure audience reaction. They would then make the decision as to whether to continue working on the piece.

The show, explained Vincent Canby in the *New York Times,* is part operetta, part fairy tale and part satire about the kind of affairs of church and state that had not been relevant since the French Revolution.[50] The show's themes include murder, religious hypocrisy, political corruption, romance and self-awareness. The story takes place in 1807 in the mythical land of

Slavonia and deals with the emotional paralysis of the prince, Samson, a weak young man with a doting mother, Queen Katarina, the King's gold-digging wife, who rises to power by "literally screwing the king to death."[51] Katarina manipulates events in order to hold onto power via her son, who, literally petrified at the thought of taking the reins, can neither speak nor move. Eventually, through the love of the good-hearted Elise, he is cured.

Prince has said that the show is about emotional paralysis. "Most people are petrified in one aspect or another, probably their entire lives. That interested me."[52] The cast included Jane White, Marilyn Cooper, Mal Z. Lawrence, Candy Buckley as Katarina, Alexander Gaberman as Prince Samson, and Prince's daughter Daisy as the young romantic lead, Elise. It was LaChiusa who insisted that she be cast in the role. "Hal resisted," said LaChiusa, on the grounds of nepotism, "but I thought she had the right qualities."[53] Prince admits to great fatherly pride in his daughter and delights when he gets calls from his show business colleagues to praise Daisy's voice and her performances in various roles. (In May 1995 she was well received playing the ingenue part in *Pal Joey*, a revival mounted by Encores! Great American Musicals in Concert.)

George C. Wolfe, president of the New York Shakespeare Festival, put *The Petrified Prince* on the theatre's 1994–1995 schedule. He was anxious to get Michael John LaChiusa back working at the Public, and "the fact that Hal was attached made it more attractive," said Wolfe. Although Garth Drabinsky and John Flaxman helped underwrite the costs (and own the commercial rights to the music) and although no one knew whether the show would have a future life, Wolfe said, "I'd have produced the show without support...the primary thing here is to go into a room and work."[54] This clearly echoed Prince's long-held philosophy.

The show opened at the Public Theatre on 18 December 1994 after a few weeks of previews, and went on to play there until 15 January 1995.

Vincent Canby in the *New York Times* called it "a confusion of contradictory impulses, some of which have been dimly realized, and none of which have an easily recognized point." Although he felt nothing was working well in the show at this point, he did like James Youmans's lovely rust-red production design as well as Judith Dolan's costumes. But he warned audiences as they watched *The Petrified Prince* to remember that "you're looking over the shoulders of people at work."[55]

John Lahr in *The New Yorker* wrote, "Prince, an old pro, has marshaled the expert, moody lighting of Howell Binkley, the classy costuming of Judith Dolan and the shrewd choreography of Rob Marshall to great effect in a swift, slick, masterly display of showmanship." He also liked the "fine-voiced Daisy Prince," but felt the show was, "musically as flat as a Swedish pancake."[56]

Along with the reviewers, Prince agrees that there is work to be done on the piece. He has given it back to the authors to work out the problems that were uncovered in the workshop experience. He feels that *The Petrified Prince* as it was presented at the Public was hydra-headed. Much as the early version of *Kiss of the Spider Woman* at Purchase was two shows instead of one (a Hollywood musical and a jail story), here they had done a very dark, exotic, crazy, abstract Bergman screenplay with a romance. If they could have continued to work on the project, the problem would have been to decide whether to do the romance and forget the Bergman concept or do only the screenplay and let the chips fall where they may. Prince's hunch was to stay with Bergman's vision, although he suspects it would be easier to do the romance. "It would have been nice," he feels, "to have taken the project the next distance."[57]

Whistle Down the Wind

Andrew Lloyd Webber played a video workshop version of *Whistle Down the Wind* for Prince. He had presented it at his country home, Sydmonton, as part of an annual summer arts festival. Prince very much admired the score, which Lloyd Webber had written with an American pop songwriter, Jim Steinman.

Whistle Down the Wind, based on a film of the same name, concerns a group of farm children who befriend an escaped convict, mistaking him for a Jesus figure.

Prince and Lloyd Webber agreed to put it into rehearsal in the fall of 1996 and try it out in Washington, D.C. If it worked there, it would go back into rehearsal and come to New York later that spring.

But in Prince's words, "The less said, the better."[58] The work process, which had been so energizing and compatible on *Evita* and *Phantom* was completely lacking this time. Prince felt the show was well on its way to a successful New York opening, providing work was done. But it wasn't, and Prince chose to walk away.

Prince tends to place the blame for the atmosphere squarely on the enormous additional pressures faced by The Really Useful Group of planning a production originally for Broadway rather than the West End, where the atmosphere is undeniably more supportive.

Another staging of *Whistle Down the Wind* opened in London two seasons later and is still playing there. As of now, there is no plan for it to go to Broadway.

Parade

In 1994, Alfred Uhry, the Pulitzer-Prize-winning playwright and author of *Driving Miss Daisy* and *The Last Night of Ballyhoo,* suggested to Prince the idea of musicalizing the Leo Frank story, considered one of the first "Trials of the Century." In 1913, Frank—a twenty-nine-year-old New York Jew transplanted to Atlanta and married to a local socialite, Lucille Selig—was wrongfully accused and then convicted of killing a teenage girl, Mary Phagan, who was employed at the pencil factory managed by Frank. After being found guilty at trial he was sentenced to death by hanging. The death sentence was commuted to life imprisonment by the courageous governor of Georgia, John Slaton. However, two years later, Frank was taken from his cell in the state prison by a vigilante and hanged from a tree in Marietta, Georgia. The actual case generated such heated controversy in the United States that it resulted in the creation of the Anti-Defamation League and in the resuscitation of the Ku Klux Klan.

Born and raised in Atlanta, Uhry had a strong tie to this story. His mother's uncle was a German immigrant who had come to America and started a pencil factory, the National Pencil Company. It was he who had hired Leo Frank as his factory supervisor. Uhry's grandparents were in the same social group as the Franks and Lucille Frank was a friend of Uhry's grandmother. When Frank was accused of the crime, Uhry's two cousins became part of the Frank defense team.

Uhry knew Prince "in the way that we all know each other in the theatre."[1] Before the discussions about the Leo Frank project developed, Prince had asked Uhry to come to his office for a meeting about a musical that

Quincy Jones had proposed, based on the life of Sammy Davis. That project never materialized. The Leo Frank project did.

Of the project, Prince observed,

> The Leo Frank story is impossibly difficult when you first look at it. What I've learned over the years is that the impossibly difficult ideas can be the best. The challenge is to unlock them. It's the easy, can't-miss ideas that are always a problem for me. I mean, everybody's got a *Gone with the Wind* in his or her own head. But *Kiss of the Spider Woman*? *West Side Story*? Leo Frank? That's when they scratch their heads in surprise.[2]

Prince liked the story of *Parade*.

> Alfred and I, taking licenses with reality, created a story about two people living in a sterile, dreary, Victorian marriage arranged by their families. She, a Southern belle—accepting, grateful to be married to a hard-working, upstanding man. He, persnickety, anal, humorless, didactic, but, yes, upstanding and hard-working. One day he is accused of a murder he didn't commit. Because he's innocent, he doesn't defend himself, doesn't think he needs to. He's affronted and arrogant. It gets worse. The web gets tighter. And then both people undergo changes—giant changes. They reinvent themselves and they fall in love as they fight to prove his innocence. It all culminates with a conjugal visit in jail on the night before the vigilante took him away. Now, that's a good story. That's a good story....[3]

Initially, Stephen Sondheim had agreed to write the score, but because he had recently written *Passion*, he felt he wanted something less dark for his next project.

Prince then selected Jason Robert Brown, a 24-year-old composer, and arranged an introduction to Uhry. Prince's daughter Daisy had directed Brown's revue, *Songs for a New World* at Off-Broadway's WPA Theatre in the 1995–1996 season. Brown had also been the conductor of *The Petrified Prince*. However, he had not yet written a score for Broadway. Brown remembers that Prince gave him enormous amounts of research on the Frank story, suggesting that he write a couple of songs on spec. He did, and Brown and Uhry wrote a synopsis of the first three or four scenes at Uhry's Connecticut farm. The collaboration was cemented.

Although *Parade* is the first treatment of the Frank case to look into the musical possibilities of the story, the event inspired two unremarkable films and a 1998 docudrama on NBC, *The Murder of Mary Phagan*, with Jack Lemmon as the Georgia governor whose commutation of Frank's death sentence was regarded in the North as courageous and in the South as a betrayal.

Prince envisaged the production in a space similar to the one it eventually inhabited—the Vivian Beaumont Theatre at Lincoln Center.

The Beaumont's stage is equally divided—a proscenium space upstage of great depth and a thrust almost equally deep protruding into the auditorium and surrounded on three sides by audience.

The problem of melding the conventional stage with such a large apron is profound. Prince chose to present the real story in the style of a contemporary black-and-white documentary.

Taking its name from the Confederate Day Parade (the day on which Mary Phagan was murdered), the play moved deliberately in documentary fashion, starting with the parade itself and introducing the pertinent characters until the stage was filled with protagonists and antagonists.

Events followed inexorably until Leo Frank was hanged from a huge oak tree which had taken up the better part of the proscenium stage for the entire evening—an inert spectre—in the street, inside Leo's home, in the courtroom. Only at the hanging did it fulfill its function. A Broadway musical culminating in the hanging of its heroic principal player!

The rest of the surround consisted of rows of imposing windows—institutional?—and there were numerous traps on which a District Attorney, the Governor, newspaper reporters, jail guards, a prison bed, a visitor's table, or various streets in Atlanta were delivered, suddenly appearing and just as suddenly disappearing.

Riccardo Hernandez— who had designed *Bring in da Noise, Bring in da Funk*—was in charge of the *Parade* set, and Judith Dolan—who had won the Tony for the revival of *Candide* the year before—was the costume designer. Howell Binkley—who had won an Olivier award in London for *Kiss of the Spider Woman*—designed the lighting.

The dances for *Parade* were designed to function as source movement—pastiche activity to pastiche music. Real people behaving real-ly. This concept is difficult to achieve, but it is a speciality of choreographer Patricia Birch, four-time Tony nominee and Prince's collaborator on, among other projects, *A Little Night Music* and *Candide*.

Prince knew from the outset that he wanted Brent Carver for the role of Leo Frank:

> Brent's such a charismatic, complex person, on- and offstage. Enigmatic, the kind of personality you can't get a handle on—the danger in it creates such excitement on stage. On a personal note, you've got to admire a guy who wins a Tony Award (as Molina in *Kiss of the Spider Woman*), and, instead of going to Hollywood, goes home to Canada to play *Cyrano de Bergerac*.[4]

Carolee Carmello was cast to play Lucille Frank. Prince had seen her Off-Broadway in *john and jen* and was determined to work with her. She had also appeared in Lincoln Center Theatre's production of *Hello Again,* for which she had won an Obie Award.

Garth Drabinsky signed Livent Inc. on as producer and funded two readings and a staged workshop in Toronto.

The Lincoln Center Theatre, managed by Andre Bishop and Bernard Gersten, created a partnership with Drabinsky to present the musical now entitled *Parade* for the stage of the Beaumont Theatre. For his part, Prince said, "The Beaumont is this director's dream—original and evocative—just about perfect for *Parade.*"[5]

However, soon after Drabinsky joined the production team with Lincoln Center Theatre, the financial difficulties of Livent made the front pages of the *New York Times* and became a media nightmare. Accused of overextending the organization with its multiple companies of *Showboat* and *Ragtime,* Drabinsky was replaced and the company declared bankruptcy under Chapter 11. Three *Show Boat* companies in the United States and one in London closed, and Livent reneged on its obligations to Lincoln Center Theatre. This shortfall cut advertising at a critical time in the life of the fledgling show and eliminated the possibility of extending the run of the show to the time of the Tony Awards in June of 1999.

Of the Livent situation Prince has stated that he is one of the creditors, because of past-due royalties. But he does not blame Drabinsky, who he believes to be a showman with a true interest in the theatre. He does think that Drabinsky may have over-committed Livent's finances in his efforts to keep "too many balls in the air."[6]

Parade began previews at the Beaumont on 12 November 1998 and opened on 17 December. But Livent's over-publicized problems cast a pall over the show soon after its 17 December opening.

The press was sharply divided. Ben Brantley, in his *New York Times* review, observed: "One thing *Parade* cannot be accused of is fuzziness of focus....This musical provides a painstakingly rendered chart of the wheels of injustice. And it never lets up in its insistence on the innocence, on several levels, of its protagonist and the moral blindness and corruption of his persecutors."[7] But he discerned a flatness in the portrayal of Frank's character, and all in all, his review was disappointing. He did note that the courtroom fantasy interlude in which Frank becomes a leering, worldly figure provides "what is by far the best work of Mr. Carver and the choreographer Patricia Birch in

Parade, 1998. Courtroom scene
Brent Carver as Leo Frank, J. B. Adams as defense attorney Luther Rosser.
(Photo © Joan Marcus. Reprinted by permission of the photographer)

the show."[8] Also, he felt that Carolee Carmello gave a "stirringly heartfelt performance"[14] as Frank's wife. Brantley's reception was bad news for a serious musical.

On the other hand, David Patrick Stearns's review in *USA Today* was extremely positive, commenting that the show "boldly exploits the musical theatre medium to its fullest, fulfilling every promise implied by *West Side Story, Company,* and other ambitious musicals that have threatened to become Broadway anomalies."[10] Stearns praised Brown's score—which maintained the outline and echo of popular songs, church hymns and rags— noting that it was augmented "with a far richer emotional palette than could have been previously imagined."[11] He did feel, however, that in the first hour, the show seemed "chilly to a fault."[12] He went on to observe:

> The show's daringly gradual dramatic crescendo doesn't peak until well into Act II, when Frank's previously passive wife makes decisive moves to free her husband, launching an unorthodox love story that blossoms on separate sides of the jail bars. It climaxes in the ecstatic, wrenching duet 'All the Wasted Time,' a supremely powerful moment....Such moments are clearly the product of a careful five-year gestation, courtesy of the now-bankrupt Livent Inc., that allowed director Prince to do his best work, using Riccardo Hernandez's set design—often filling out crowd scenes with eerie-looking cardboard cutouts—with blazing theatricality. More important, the production captures a world in which extremes of cruelty and gentility are possible.[13]

Fintan O'Toole, reviewing for the *Daily News,* addressed the question of whether there are bad subjects for making a musical.

> The truth, of course, is that there are no bad subjects, only bad writers. In the right hands, the musical can be shaped to any story....*Parade,* in the steady and nimble hands of veteran director Harold Prince and playwright Alfred Uhry demonstrates this triumphantly....*Parade* looks death and injustice in the face, and chooses to affirm life and humanity.[14]

The *New York Post* reviewer, Donald Lyons, was more negative than positive, appreciating Brent Carver's performance as "the best male achievement in a musical since Michael Hayden in *Carousel,*"[15] but otherwise lukewarm to the production. He continued that *Parade* worked best and most powerfully "as an intimate study of a man, a woman and a marriage under nightmarish stress."[16]

John Simon—thought by many to be the most difficult of the critics today—gave the show a glowing critique in his *New York Magazine* review.

Now, why shouldn't what is rather too loosely called a "musical comedy" by some embrace a darker subject as long as it is handled with intelligence, skill, and, wherever possible, humor? This is not a monochromatically somber piece, but a suspenseful slice of unvarnished life, mixing anguish and grief with smiles and laughs, and graced with exceptional production values....*Parade* rates an A for courage and professionalism, and is superior, even as sheer entertainment, to the crudeness of a *Scarlet Pimpernel* and the ineptness of a *Footloose*.[17]

Simon applauded Uhry's book as consistently "apt and gripping. It gamely tackles a complex and sprawling subject, neither oversimplifying nor forfeiting cohesiveness. It enlightens without preachment, and lets the dramatic or ironic prose merge seamlessly with the musical numbers." He commended the sets by Riccardo Hernandez as "richly evocative and [find] the proper blend of realism and stylization, of solidity and fluidity, of *Here and Beyond*." Judith Dolan's costumes, he felt, "are suitably understated and nicely in period," and Howell Binkley's lighting "adds subtle ironies of its own."[18]

Simon was extremely enamored of the leads in *Parade*. He wrote, "Whoever plays Leo Frank faces the awesome task of having to be winning without obvious charm, manly despite his mousiness, and a star performer in a role that, except for length, has none of the splashy attributes of a star vehicle."[19]

I cannot think of anyone else nowadays able to carry this off with such shining modesty, such exemplary avoidance of mannerism, such unswerving conviction and convincingness as Brent Carver. He is matched every step of the way by the Lucille of Carolee Carmello. She plays a modern-day Joan of Arc without a scintilla of false—or even inapposite real—glamour , and infuses seeming ordinariness with enough lambent faith and dauntless determination to move a good-size mountain, if not budge human stupidity.[20]

Simon concluded his review:

If I mention no further names it is because they are too numerous and form an ensemble that should not be fractured. But glory be to the two guiding lights: Harold Prince (direction) and Patricia Birch (choreography). They have fused speech and song, movement and dance, incisive detail and all-encompassing panorama into as compact a whole as is dramatically possible. *Parade*, which could have been a millstone, emerges as a milestone.[21]

Despite controversy, the show was in financial difficulty from the beginning without the support of Livent. Although it was nominated for nine Tony Awards, the show closed on 28 February 1999.

Although the Tony Awards are synonymous with artistic excellence, they are also considered a critical marketing tool. Many wondered whether voters would give a Best Musical Tony to *Parade* which, having closed, was not in a position to reap the box office benefits. The voters did not.

Parade did win two Tony Awards: Alfred Uhry for the book, and Jason Robert Brown for the music and lyrics. In accepting his Tony, Uhry announced that a new production of *Parade* was scheduled to open in Atlanta on 12 June 2000, to be followed by an eleven-week tour. Hopefully, the tour could be extended to fill out the season. And perhaps—just perhaps—New York would get another chance to see *Parade*.

EPILOGUE

Dick Cavett: "What's important for success in the theatre?"
Harold Prince: Knowing your craft well, and luck…being in the right place at the right time.

—Interview, 19–20 March 1983

Harold Prince [reflecting on his comment above]: "How dishonest of me…downright coy! For consistent success, taste and talent don't hurt!

—Prince interview, 6 July 1999

He's the best director of musicals around by far. He has a sense of what the entire evening is about. He has a sense of the function of music in a show…knows what a musical number is about. He has a more acute ear than most producers. He takes it seriously and is more daring, imaginative and endlessly creative. He likes to take chances. He has a sense of dignity of the musical theatre and thinks it's the highest form of theatre and I happen to agree with him.…He's not condescending about musical theatre. He's an ideal collaborator. It's like collaborating with a writer…what spills out of Hal's mouth at a meeting could fill 67 songs and 87 scenes.

—Stephen Sondheim, Interview with the author, 20 July 1984

Hal Prince has been innovative, creative and daring both as producer and director. He has earned his reputation as a producer's producer and a director's director. During his four-and-one-half decades of work in the theatre he has been willing to take chances on shows considered risky in commercial theatre. Tackling topics and themes unusual for Broadway, Prince has inspired other producers and directors to move away from the cliché-ridden musical. Not all the shows he has produced and/or directed have been successful—either commercially or artistically—but this did not deter him. Over a forty-five-year career he has tried to present innovative shows that challenged as well as entertained audiences.

As a producer, Prince sought out new talent and gave this talent an opportunity to work on Broadway. He brought together composers and lyricists such as Kander and Ebb for *Flora, the Red Menace,* and Bock and Harnick for *Fiorello!* With *A Funny Thing Happened on the Way to the Forum,* Prince provided Stephen Sondheim with the first show for which Sondheim would create both music and lyrics. Recently, he retained this priority by introducing Jason Robert Brown on Broadway in *Parade.*

Boris Aronson had been an established set designer for years, but it was Prince who gave Aronson more freedom than he had been given by any other producer in such groundbreaking musicals as *Cabaret, Company* and *Follies.* Here the sets became important elements in the communication of themes.

Although Prince has employed such stars as Zero Mostel and Angela Lansbury, he has never produced shows as mere vehicles for stage luminaries. While other producers have tried to insure the success of their shows by casting big box office draws, Prince has carefully avoided this and hired only the performers he believed best suited for the roles.

An elusive element of Prince's success as producer and director is the atmosphere he creates among the artistic contributors to his productions. Over and over again, designers, actors, choreographers, songwriters and librettists have stated that Prince's enthusiasm and encouragement have led to the success of a production. The psychological reinforcement that Prince lends to a production team often makes the difference between success and failure. Stephen Sondheim has said that Prince's positive attitude and enthusiasm during *A Funny Thing Happened on the Way to the Forum* was the main reason that the production was kept alive. When difficulties paralyzed the collaborators' creative efforts, it was Prince who managed to move it along to its ultimate success. Sondheim said:

[Prince's] energy and enthusiasm are enormous and the driving force often—particularly when other people are getting discouraged. As a producer, I remember, on Forum, when we were all out of town, any other producer I think would have closed the show because we were getting such poor audience reaction. But not Hal. Even George Abbott wanted to close the show and Hal wouldn't do it. We brought Jerry Robbins in to restage some numbers and he saved it. Hal's enthusiasm is boundless even when he's privately discouraged. And he has a wonderful sense of family...a sense of responsibility to all the people in and around the show. He feels if he is going to be the captain of the ship he must be responsible to them. Therefore he does not do what a number of other directors do, which is to indulge himself in tantrums or even in gloom, except at home. The only person who knows how upset he is or [how] gloomy he gets is his wife. Occasionally me, simply because we're old friends. But rarely does he show anything except positive vibes, and that positive energy is—I wouldn't say it's unique in Hal—but there's more of it in Hal than anybody I've ever worked with.[1]

This quality of Prince's, described by his production colleagues as "enthusiasm," helps him to function as a creative catalyst. Just as a catalyst makes a chemical solution work, so Prince makes his mixture of production and performing ingredients "work" to bring out their best creative energies. The Broadway musical is, after all, a highly collaborative effort and the production team must work together to the same artistic end. As a director, Prince guides the production and helps create an atmosphere in which writer, composer, set designer and all the other creative elements blend their creative talents into one united concept.

Lisa Aronson has said of Prince's collaborators that "they were all strong people and an unusually gifted bunch and Hal was like the chief cook."[2] He has challenged people and then played the role of editor. She said of Prince's crew, "They're wonderful—all of them...tough—but all pros."[3] Prince has surrounded himself with a group of gifted and strong theatre artists, but he was the "unquestioned leader," says Ruth Mitchell, his associate producer.[4]

Because Prince excels in helping people to work well together, his colleagues have had the freedom to create their best. He differs from Jerome Robbins, for example, in this respect. Robbins can be difficult with his collaborators. Lisa Aronson said that Robbins's method of working "in some respects curtails the degree of creativity."[5] Choreographer Pat Birch agrees that Prince is not "restrictive."[6] He may ask for something specific from a collaborator, but if the collaborator comes back with something different and it works, it is accepted. Prince enjoys being surprised by his collaborator's ideas. Prince doesn't like "yes men." Lisa Aronson explained that her husband was a man who spoke his mind. Pat Birch said, "I'm not always an agree-er. And I think Hal likes that. I'm not a 'yes person.'"[7]

Prince and Sondheim, as well as the others, use metaphors for shows. They realize that a show may be about more than one thing and that different metaphors are not necessarily contradictory. A metaphor gives Prince a "handle" for his show. In addition, he seizes images and ideas from paintings. For instance, for *Cabaret* he studied George Grosz's German expressionist work; for *A Little Night Music,* he was inspired by Magritte's paintings. For *Company* he relied on Francis Bacon's work and for *Doll's Life* he looked at the paintings of Edvard Munch. Pat Birch said, "I think Hal is, number one, a conceptualist. He gets an image...a visual image. He works very much from visual images—paintings. He's one of the greatest concept men around."[8]

Stephen Sondheim agrees that Prince uses a visual approach to a show. "I don't think he can get a grasp on a show just from reading a script unless he gets a visual take. If he has a visual take then it makes him want to go ahead on a show whether it's a completed script or something that's merely an idea that he brings to a writer."[9]

Prince doesn't accentuate dance in his musicals, viewing shows differently from directors who are also choreographers. Prince explained, "I don't like mindless dancing. I like integrated musicals more. It seems a choreographer will lean too heavily on dance and not enough on character."[10] In an interview with critic Martin Gottfried, Prince discussed his collaboration with choreographers:

> I discuss with the choreographer my intention for the musical—my reason for doing it. Then, we talk about numbers. I certainly operate as an editor, as the final word. I must. I say this is good—that isn't. On the other hand, I can't move people's feet. I've staged numbers in the musicals I've done, but not anything that requires dancing. I'm a klutz and I know it. But I certainly have a sense of what I know is right in the overall concept of a musical.[11]

Prince maintains that his shows experience comparatively few traumatic episodes during rehearsals because the groundwork has been accomplished months before rehearsals begin. The major collaborators have been working at what the show should or should not be—how the story will be told, how the scenery will look, and how the people will move. Prince calls the latter the "motor" of the show. Prince feels that during this process each collaborator should be involved with the "total." This is not easy if each artist goes off on his own. The chance to meet together often, to toss ideas around, and to come up with mutually satisfying solutions makes for a unified production. If one person has a vision, he can try to convince his collaborators to support that vision. When rehearsals begin on a Prince show, the major decisions have thus been made and things progress fairly smoothly.

A second reason for the smooth rehearsal period is Prince's habit of reading and playing through the show in the months before rehearsals. He thinks that this is crucial. Sometimes actors do the reading, and at other times Prince does the parts himself. The songs are also played and sung, often by the composer and lyricist. The collaborators try to identify signals that may reveal a lack of variety or a relentless heaviness in the show. By listening to the piece over and over again, they can spot problems and try to remedy them before the short rehearsal period begins.

Rehearsals on a Prince show usually begin with a read-through in which the director explains the concept. The actual staging of the show begins immediately afterward—the blocking, the movement, the groupings of performers, character interpretation and the myriad of details that must coalesce to serve the overall concept of the show. Notes are given informally and publicly unless a special problem arises with an actor which may require privacy. Because so much of the show has been worked out beforehand and appears to have penetrated Prince's subconscious, he feels secure enough to let it appear as if the show is unfolding inspirationally—to have fun with it and keep it flexible enough to modify at any given moment.

Alexis Smith loved working with Prince on *Follies*. She said, "He knows exactly what he wants. There's no uncertainty and time-wasting." [12]

Visitors are permitted occasionally to rehearsals and run-throughs of Prince's shows, and he listens to their comments. However, he is selective. While open to suggestions, ultimately he listens to himself, holding off on any major changes until the cast is secure and able to adjust. And with regard to notes, Prince said, "If I've anything to say to the star, I say it in front of the entire company." [13]

John McMartin remembers that early in his career he auditioned for a Griffith-Prince show and was amazed that afterwards he received a written reply from Prince. McMartin said, "He is one of the few producer-directors who ever wrote a letter after he auditioned me saying, 'Thank you, you're just not right for this show, but perhaps we'll be able to use you in some future project.' I've never forgotten that." [14] Charlotte Moore remembers auditioning for Prince and Sondheim and other collaborators for one of their shows. Basically an actress, she was terrified at having to sing, and collapsed onto the floor weeping. After a momentary silence in the darkened theatre, Prince raced to the stage and knelt down, putting his arms around her and consoling her. He managed to calm a very frightened auditioner and Moore, too, has never forgotten.[15]

Prince has a concise answer for questions about how he directs. He says that it is necessary to learn the craft, believing strongly in the apprenticeship system, since that is the way he learned from George Abbott and Jerome Robbins. He respects technique and has no patience with self-indulgence or unpreparedness. Describing himself in the director's role, Prince says he is not a theorist. "I'm interested in round characters, honesty, and in avoiding business and lines that bring the cheap, easy laugh."[16] In addition, he never calls meetings at night: "Everything is too crazy. At night, everything in your brain turns to so much spaghetti. It's a simple lesson, but so few people learn it."[17]

"Prince has often played an important role in the shaping of the librettos of his shows," said Howard Haines, who was Prince's general manager.[18] Haines said that Prince sharpens and focuses the shape of a book and has a great sense of what to cut out if it appears to be extraneous to the piece or is what is generally considered as "filler." When asked to discuss the shows for which he had the most influence on the book, Prince said:

> The most common one, because perhaps I've read about it so much, is *Company*, because I'm the one who thought it should be a musical and I think George [Furth, the librettist] and Steve [Sondheim] thought I was nuts...and it's a terrific musical and its structure works well. It was just an idea—just an impulse ...but it worked. I certainly had a lot of input on *Pacific Overtures* and I had input on *Follies*. That's an interesting one because *Follies* was brought to me as *The Girls Upstairs* and it was then a very realistic musical. It was my notion to splinter time and to bring the young people on (the young alter egos of leading characters). And then the whole thing got abstracted with the whole Proustian thing. So I think I had a formidable impact there. Not so on *Sweeney* [*Todd*]. But a director's job varies entirely in relation to the need. I don't want to be an author unless I have to be an author. Sometimes it's a good idea. It's all about filling the needs of your collaborators.[19]

Since Prince has repeatedly expressed his debt to Meyerhold and Piscator as influences on his directing style, it is important to note that the Russian and German directors appear to be influential only in retrospect. Although Prince had become aware of certain facets of Meyerhold's work when he visited the Taganka Theatre, he didn't really know much about Meyerhold's particular style until people began to compare their work. John Dos Passos had written an article saying he had seen an extraordinary thing that a man named Meyerhold had done in a historical play in Moscow in the 1920s. It seems that the Russian director had amalgamated many theatrical styles such as French farce, English drawing room, American musical comedy, Italian opera and others. Ironically, that was Prince's original intention with *Pacific Overtures*. The concept was contained in his opening speech to the cast on the first day of rehearsals. At the time, Prince was unaware of Meyerhold's earlier attempts and has since commented on this phenomenon:

> I didn't know about the Dos Passos article until *Pacific Overtures* had already opened. So, there's some kind of symbiotic thing I feel about theatre that [Meyerhold] obviously felt about theatre. Josh Logan, after seeing something of mine, called me and said, "Years ago, I apprenticed to Stanislavsky in Moscow and I was living there for about a year. There was this Meyerhold man and I saw his work and I saw it in rehearsal. I saw what he was doing and I've just seen your work and that's what you're doing." So I was wildly complimented.
>
> It was strangely uncanny. Up till then, I hadn't seen photos of Meyerhold's work. Still, in *Evita*, I dreamed up five rocking chairs for six colonels to play musical chairs with. There's a photograph in Meyerhold's *D.E.* of six oligarchs in rocking chairs.[20]

Meyerhold's production of *The Inspector General* used tableaux of many people in a very small confined space, which was accomplished by putting a small space into a larger space—in other words, a stage within a stage. Prince did the same thing in *Evita* during the "Rainbow Tour": the entire company was placed onto a little vaudeville stage with newspapers, all posed, with the rest of the stage devoid of people.

After his shows open, director Prince visits them at least once a month to make sure that they have not become sloppy or lost pace. He will never come to a performance unannounced, however. This, he feels, is unfair to the actors. When he was a producer, he complained about directors who didn't come back to help retain a show's freshness. He will call additional rehearsals or redirect a part of the show if he finds it necessary. Stage managers as a rule, he finds, want to keep the show exactly the way it was set up. Prince feels you can't keep a long-running show fresh in this way. "When it's stale," he says, "you should say, 'Let's do it another way.' Going left instead of right can free you again. Making everyone adjust to the change freshens it all up."[21]

Most meaningful of all Prince's achievements as a director is how he has gradually changed the look, style and spirit of much of the American musical theatre. He has continued to experiment with both form and theme. When Rodgers and Hammerstein failed in a similar attempt with *Allegro*, they returned to the safer world of realism. Prince's shows have utilized such varied forms as pop art (*Superman*), surrealism (*Follies*), expressionism (*Cabaret* and *Kiss of the Spider Woman*), symbolism (*Evita*), Grand Guignol (*Sweeney Todd*), environmental theatre (*Candide*) and Japanese Kabuki (*Pacific Overtures*).

Realistic sets and painted drops have given way to abstract constructs and black velours. His theme-oriented and episodically structured shows such as *Company* have become an alternative to the romantic and lineally constructed musical plots of yesterday. He has also utilized cinematic techniques on stage. As a result of all this innovation, directors now may have a wider choice of stage techniques to test on audiences made somewhat more sophisticated by the theatrical chances taken by Hal Prince.

Michael Bennett, whose musicals have been popular with both critics and audiences, worked closely with Prince on two shows and was obviously influenced by that association. Frank Rich of the *New York Times* believes that Bennett's *A Chorus Line* borrows from *Follies*.[22] Bennett's *Dreamgirls* also consists of many elements in which Prince's influence can be noted. Bennett, in this latter musical, utilizes a group of revolving light towers to define his space. He uses no dialogue scenes or realistic sets. There are no dance numbers and Robin Wagner's set includes mobile, abstract units consisting of aluminum towers and bridges. Frank Rich explains that these abstract set pieces "keep coming together and falling apart to create explosive variations on a theme. Bennett used his special brand of cinematic stage effects (montage, dissolve, wipe), which seems to be Bennett acknowledging his historical debt to Prince."[23] Rich feels, however, that one thing wrong with today's musicals is their endless regurgitation of past ideas—many of them Prince's:

> In *Nine* like nearly every musical on Broadway, we find the other major form of déjà vu in the current musical theatre: the incessant recycling of directorial ideas. Mr. Tune [director Tommy Tune, who worked as an actor-dancer in Prince's *Baker Street*] has come up with many original sequences for this show, but nonetheless the most Felliniesque pageant he offers, the "Casanova" opera parody, is strongly reminiscent of the surreal (and brilliant) "Loveland" sequence of Mr. Prince's 1971 *Follies*. (In both shows a monochromatic set is suddenly filled with color, as a gaudy show-within-the-show drops down to resolve the story's emotional conflicts through fantasy.)[24]

There were other elements in Tune's *Nine* which showed Prince's influence on the young director. The musical has an episodic structure similar to *Company*, with an abstract constructivist set that is mostly a collection of large cubes.

Trevor Nunn, the English director, has also displayed in his work what appears to be a Prince influence. Frank Rich observed, "In *Cats* Nunn harks back to Prince's 1973 *Candide* just as his staging of *Nicholas Nickleby* owed something to both *Candide* and *Sweeney Todd*."[25] Rich is sorry that Prince's innovative stage techniques have now become merely imitative in others' hands. What were once exciting elements appear hackneyed today. Prince "did so much to destroy the clichés of musical staging that existed on Broadway when he began his career."[26]

Rich continues that he might feel better about the state of the musical theatre if a new *West Side Story* or *Fiddler on the Roof* or *Company* were waiting in the wings:

> It might be easier to tolerate an onslaught of video-arcade extravaganzas....What also gives one some hope for the musical is that Mr. Prince and Mr. Tune, like Mr. Bennett, do try to work with new performers and new writers in their shows....This is essential, because, without the push of superstar directors, producers are unlikely to gamble four million dollar budgets on the young, untried talents who might help recharge the writing of musicals.[27]

Prince, too, is seriously concerned about the plight of the American musical theatre. British critic Michael Billington has said, "Hal Prince is one of the few people who cares about the future of musicals."[28] The dilemma Prince has been facing in recent years is that of trying to avoid the Broadway trap of adding unneeded spectacle to concepts that don't call for it. Prince recalled what happened when he was directing *Merrily We Roll Along* as an example of how artistic aims are affected by Broadway economic factors. Having difficulty trying to visualize the show, he called in his staff and told them that he wanted to try something out on them:

> I said, "If I had my druthers, I would present it on a bare stage with no costumes whatsoever." "So do it," they all said. "Do it the way you want to do it." And I said, "Yes, but people are paying $35 to see a Broadway musical. And if they come into the theatre and there's nothing there, they're going to resent spending the money." Howard [Haines] said, "You must do what you see." But I didn't have the guts. Which means that the cost of things is beginning to influence my thinking creatively.[29]

In an interview with Prince in 1991, he explained that doing musicals on a small scale was not necessarily the better or even the right thing to do. Each musical needs the opportunity to be all that it aspires to be. One show might work best on a bare stage with neither props nor costumes, while another might demand an elaborate, expensive production. For example, speaking of *Show Boat,* Oscar Hammerstein said it was meant to be big. Prince kept it that way in 1994, with a cast of 71 and enormous stage sets.[30] Since economic pressures continue to escalate on Broadway, the opportunity to mount shows to maximum advantage may no longer exist. Prince finds that certain "agendas" prevail in New York that endanger the musical theatre art form. Theatre owners, he feels, have decided that in the interest of economy musicals can be done first on small stages and then expanded to meet the needs of larger Broadway houses. The producers either commit to a *Once on This Island,* which began Off Broadway and then moved to a small Broadway house, or they make a deal to bring over a "spectacular."

Prince worries that the *New York Times* has expressed its agenda. It seems to think that any show that starts in the nonprofit sector is motivated by greater idealism, hence, more art. Doggedly, Prince maintains, "The best of Broadway has always been the best there is. The trouble is how rarely we see the best anymore."[31]

Prince also takes exception to Pollyanna claims that Broadway is as healthy as ever. Not so, says Prince.

> Yes, there are these three megahits—*Phantom of the Opera, Les Misérables* and *Cats*—which will run forever. But to say that theatre business is robust is a misinterpretation. There were only six new musicals in the 1998–1999 season. And of those that remain on Broadway, how many will pay back their investment? What happens when you have a show that runs for two or three years and still doesn't return its investment? Where do you then go for the next investment? Also, you can't build up an advance sale in New York anymore.[32]

Prince, additionally, has strong feelings about the importance of the original direction of a new musical. He feels that along with the work of the writers, the direction of a new show becomes part of the script and that subsequent revivals of that show are based wholly or in part on the original director's conception. That the director is a crucial member of the collaborative team that creates a show is a fact rarely acknowledged when the show is revived. A theatre exhibit, devoted to the career of Harold Prince, opened at the Lincoln Center Library of the Performing Arts in April 1989. Upon entering, visitors were greeted by a Prince quote that stated his feelings on this subject:

> It makes me crazy that critics and theatre aficionados never acknowledge the fact that a show is originally directed the first time. The original director cut it, inspired rewrites, altered the cadence of sentences, chopped up a scene so that instead of it being one scene it's three scenes interpolated by a musical fragment, put a blackout right in the middle of a scene that never expected one and then brought the lights up again to shock the audience. That, in fact, becomes part of the finished script of a show. So directing a show for the first time and directing a revival of the show are two very different things.[33]

Having arrived at the year 2000, Hal Prince worries that Broadway actually has become the "fabulous invalid" it had been diagnosed as over and over again through the years. He wishes it were still a place where shows that are not blockbuster hits had a decent chance to run, but he suspects that this is unlikely. He regrets that Broadway has become predictable.[34]

Prince, however, sees a major problem in working away from New York—of creating shows in remote locations:

> For one thing, the current regional theatres are not equipped for more than chamber-size musicals. For another, so much of what has made musical theatre history was made on Broadway because the best people worked there and lived there. It was easier collecting them all in one place. In this respect London has an advantage over us. England is small and films are made where theatre is made and regional theatre is two hours away. There is a need for not-for-profit institutions in our country dedicated exclusively to full-size musical theatre.[35]

Although the huge success of *Phantom* has made Prince financially secure in his early seventies, he has no plans to retire and shows no signs of slowing down. Harry Haun noted that although Prince's energy and exuberance have always been legendary in the theatre circles—he has been known to "enter a room like a white tornado"—it appears he has mellowed.[36] He observed further that Prince now exudes a warmth and a sense of inner peace and contentment that was not necessarily lacking earlier but which may have been hidden by all the energy and verve.[37]

Prince does not have hobbies, although he has recently taken up skiing. Thanks to the insistence of his wife Judy, he manages to take breaks in his work for about six to eight weeks every winter and about three months in the summer. The Majorca home was sold some years ago, and the Princes vacation at their home in Florida or at their chalet in the French Alps with a view of Mont Blanc.

Although Prince's collaborators have often commented on and value his obvious enthusiasm, there is a dark side to the man as well, and he is fully aware of it. With a good deal of personal insight, he said some years ago: "I think the reason that I have so many positive thoughts is that I'm so goddamned frightened....I think that if I were to relinquish the battlements that surround me—that keep me positive—who knows what would happen? So I don't, and I never will. There's a degree of psychoanalysis beyond which I will not go."[38]

More than ever, he works for the pleasure of making theatre. No more, "Is the show going to be a hit at the box office?" And certainly no "Am I going to get hired next year?"[39] Despite the fact that Prince no longer produces the shows he directs, he retains the same level of authority on his shows as Steven Spielberg has on his films.

Prince's recent years have been personally satisfying. He was a John F. Kennedy Center for the Performing Arts honoree in 1994. The Kennedy Center honors artists who have made unique and valuable lifetime contributions to American culture through their work in the performing arts.

In May 1999, the board of the American Music Theater Festival, an organization that develops new musicals, opened a renovated movie house in downtown Philadelphia, naming it the Harold Prince Center for American Music Theater. Commenting on the plethora of honors and awards, Prince said, "It's an age thing. The trouble is, I'm too young for this!"[40]

One of the few sad notes in Prince's life during these recent years was the passing of his mentor, George Abbott, who died on 31 January 1995 at the age of 107, after sharing an office with Prince for nearly fifty years. In the last years of his life he lived in Miami, not far from Prince's home there. Prince, in a tribute in the *New York Times,* wrote, "There is no believing that George won't be available on the other end of the telephone, that I won't be receiving one of his inimitably brief but hilarious notes. How I will miss him."[41]

Six years ago, the Harold Prince Musical Theatre Program was established by the Directors Company of New York. The program aims to develop new musicals for the American stage by involving directors early in the collaborative process. The performance lab stage of the process, which takes place in New York City, is overseen by Prince and his associate Arthur Masella. Everyone working on the program is salaried except for Prince, who donates his time. Prince and Masella meet with the collaborating directors, writers and composers three times to observe and critique their work. Stephanie Coen wrote about this program in an article entitled "How to Make a Musical" (*American Theatre,* January 1996). She records that when Prince gives notes to the budding artists, "Swell" is high praise. One of his biggest criticisms is "That's not logical."[42]

Coen concludes that what Prince really cares about is the process. After watching him work with the collaborators, she noted that two things became especially clear: "His work will continue to be analyzed, admired—for its darkness, its abstraction....He is a master of physical space who simply knows where bodies belong on a stage, how they interact with space and light. And his dramaturgical sense—not only of what needs to happen in a scene but of what can happen in a scene—is unerring."[43]

As the year 2000 begins, Prince is planning a couple of new projects. He is in the early talking stages of a new musical, as yet untitled, with Stephen Sondheim and John Weidman. This will be the first time in nineteen years that Prince and Sondheim have worked together. Prince is also working on a new play by Carrie Hamilton and Carol Burnett.

At this stage in his life, Prince says he enjoys reflecting on how important his family—his wife and children—have been to him both personally and professionally. He rejoices that he is blessed with good health and his children are successful. Both children are now married; his son has presented him with a grandson, and his daughter has presented him with a granddaughter. Prince loves grandfatherdom. He feels his wife has been a strong intellectual influence and has helped him to find the courage to take chances in his work. He maintains that she also helps anchor him in times of distress:

> The woman I married is "that kind of smart," that has made me demand more of myself and be more serious than I might have been if I hadn't met her. You know, that fellow in *Say Darling* [a play in which he and other of his collaborators on *The Pajama Game* were satirized] is left way behind there somewhere. Obviously I was never a trivial fellow, but I was willing to accommodate the trappings of triviality. . . . The most interesting people I know happen to be my family. And there's a lot of impatience where I live for selling out. A lot of impatience for people not getting the most out of themselves.[44]

Summing up a career of box office successes and failures, critical successes that were box office failures, even a period when he felt he could do nothing to please either critics or audiences, Prince says

I've weathered it. I have found comfort in my family. That's where I've gone for protection and that's where I've rediscovered (or, more accurately, discovered for the first time) just how important they were. Once you know that, you never un-know that.[45]

APPENDIX

The following is a transcript of the keynote address by Harold Prince to the League of American Producers and Theatre Owners in New Orleans on 12 November 1999. It was followed by a question-and-answer session moderated by Rob Marx.

Keynote Address

There was a cartoon in *The New Yorker* four weeks ago that may be pertinent today. It showed a wife sitting on a couch in a room and her husband standing at the entrance. She is saying, "Do that thing where you leave." I hope you don't feel the same way in an hour and a half about me.

I am concerned, as clearly you are, about the paucity of creativity in the commercial theatre. It worries me because it is reaching epidemic proportions. It's not just our epidemic, but an epidemic in all forms of art, significantly influenced by corporate dictatorship. The theatre seems to me to have appropriated a concept of first to be second, or first to be third, or first to be fourth. What happened to first to be first? I note that in introducing me someone referring to audiences said, "What it is THEY want." I would propose that THEY do not always know what they want. The shows that established my reputation are those that nobody knew they wanted until they wanted them.

And don't fool yourselves, those of you who represent the road. You would really rather have a new equivalent *West Side Story* or *Fiddler on the Roof* than one of the McShows you are so busy trying to book. Everything is imitative, smaller, and a sense of occasion is lost.

I'm impatient with those who refer to some of my shows as "events." They're theatre and they tell a story, hopefully in a dynamic and engaging way. I am not a snob—well, I am a snob—but I'm not *that* kind of snob.

Arthur Miller was right at the Tony's this year—articulating the irony of picking up a Tony for a show he wrote in the forties, when you and I know that play, were it not a revival, would not be produced on Broadway today. It is doing a hundred plus percent each week and closes only because its star is leaving. Arthur Miller has another play coming in, *The Price,* which was produced in the early sixties. Were it a new play it would not be produced.

I don't accuse you of lacking the grit and imagination to be creative and courageous. I accuse you of not being creative and courageous. And that is very short-sighted because, God help us, the 1957 *West Side Story* still gets produced regularly, tours, and makes money. By not creating new plays and musicals, your are risking your economic futures. Where are the *Cabarets, Fiddlers, Evitas* that will replenish you in the years to come?

It's high time you started to think about the future of this art form. I have no problem calling ours the Theatre Industry. No problem calling it what it is. In fact, I'm not sure my friend Rob Marx is going to agree with me (I'm rather sure he isn't): as far as I'm concerned, the best of Broadway can be the best theatre there is.

The problem is there's less of the best of Broadway each year. In the name of commerce, worshipping the great God Mammon, venality, we're losing on all fronts.

What in the world have you actually accomplished? How many shows are paying off, showing a healthy profit and returning as part of the history of this art form? My wife keeps saying to me, "I don't know why you say that show ran for three years but didn't make any money. It ran three years!" Well, give a damn! The investors give a damn and you ought to give a damn.

We are losing our artists. We are losing our creative team. To television. To movies. And here's a surprising opinion, mine: I think a great deal on television is of a higher quality than we provide. Of course you have to be selective. There are a hundred channels and so much garbage. But there are some comedies to equal what was the bread and butter of every Broadway season. And there are real dramas, the kind that Sidney Kingsley and Lillian Hellman and Elmer Rice wrote. And they appear every week. And the quality of their writing is splendid. I know that it is easier to turn out a fragmented television hour once a week than a well-crafted play. But that doesn't matter. The writing on those shows is excellent and equaled by the quality of the acting.

You have displayed, many of you, an awful disregard for the artistic collaborators who presumably supply the foundation of the work you do.

In a moment of anger, which you are not going to see replayed today, I was heard to say to a small group of your members, "Why don't you raise the money and collaborate with the advertising agencies, forgetting the playwrights, the composers, the directors, the choreographers, the designers. They just get in your way."

For two seasons now, the Tony Awards have neglected to include those creators in its primetime ceremonies. What could be more metaphorically insulting?

The truth is, your futures lie with the playwrights, the designers, the directors, the composers, the choreographers and of course the actors.

Then we have the star system. How many stars do you really believe sell a show? I appreciate stars if they're appropriate to they roles they're playing. But you want the best person you can for each role and frequently that isn't a star. You can create a star, you know. It happens all the time.

We've all witnessed the disappearance of the mom-and-pop business in our country. The theatre is not a grocery store. It is the theatre and it needs mom-and-pop businesses. It needs young, energetic, creative producers with taste. And the people with the wherewithal, the money, the theatres who can so much better serve themselves if they create the next generation of producers.

It is much more difficult now than when I started. There's so much more money to raise, and this has caused a drain on really exuberant creative young people, who want to produce, because they can't act, because they can't direct, because they can't design, but love and want to work in the theatre.

Theatre used to have a lot more cachet than it does right now, but it has some cachet. I consider myself lucky because I'm available in my office to see young people who renew my confidence that there are those who would rather work in the theatre than television or movies. We have to hang on to them, nurture them. I have some ideas whereby they can creatively produce without undertaking the financial burdens, the amazing amount of time that goes into advertising, all the stuff which didn't bother me much 25 years ago.

In closing, something paradoxical: for about ten years as a young producer, I would call the press department. ("Press department," well, one person!). The going message was like this: "Ours is not the most anticipated show, not *Saratoga*, not *Breakfast at Tiffany's*, not *Dear World*, so we will not be buying publicity. One display ad, which should sell ten thousand dollars worth of tickets if we're lucky. And we're not doing any interviews. We're just going to come in and 'take this town by storm.' "

Times have changed.

The box office figures at the end of every season as published in the *New York Times* are ludicrously unimportant. Each year the gross box office take is better than the previous year's. But nobody bothers to mention that the price of the ticket probably went up and that a great many of the shows responsible for inflating the figures will close, never having returned their investments or profited their producers. You know better than to buy into such self-deception. And you cannot continue to live like that.

Question & Answer Session

Robert Marx: Could you, as an independent producer, start today and what are the factors contributing to the Griffith-Prince office being so successful right from the get-go?

Harold Prince: It didn't hurt that George Abbott was willing to direct our shows. But it didn't hurt that we had both been stage managers, so we knew a lot about the nuts and bolts of putting a show onstage, seeing what your money buys. I think that is critical. We knew what we bought. We had taste and gumption. You needed to know when to say "Yes" and more importantly, when to say "No." That requires taste, putting thumbs up or down on the purchase of scenery, costumes, contracting actors.

Also we determined that we would create a reputation if we paid shows off quicker than anyone else. That news would get around. *The Pajama Game* cost $160,000, and paid off in fourteen weeks, *Damn Yankees*, $162,000, paying off in twelve.

We raised $250,000 for each of those shows and when reviews and business were good on the road, we prepared checks and distributed $50,000 to arrive with the New York reviews the morning after the opening. That news got around!

How did we save so much money? Well, for one thing, we promoted everything. *The Pajama Game* was an easy one to promote because it took place in a factory, so all the fabrics, the pajamas, the sewing machines, all the gadgetry were free. But it wasn't easy to arrange. Not as easy as paying for it would have been.

We spent a substantial portion of our lives dealing with those hundred and seventy-two investors. Wrote them letters, spoke with them on the phone regularly and consciously infused them with an excitement about each project. So much so that they were willing to back the odd show that didn't stand a chance of returning its investment, simply because it was exciting and might make history. *Follies* would be one of those.

I'll tell you one thing we didn't do. We didn't let them read a script and they never shared with us what was wrong with the show and how to fix it.

I acknowledge that there's so much more stress and finesse raising money today.

I know you've scheduled a meeting later this week about international companies. It is thrilling that we can find ourselves with a dozen companies playing simultaneously all over the globe. But all of this is time consuming and producing has become a hydra-headed monster. It's possible that the same person can't do what I consider the creative part of producing as the one who raises the money, tends to complicated touring, and worries about advertising.

I have been wondering why some theatre owners or conglomerate chiefs don't establish a Freed Unit, emulating the MGM structure, wherein two, three or four young producer wannabees are underwritten. Their taste, enthusiasm, commitment, a sense of the history of the theatre, a desire to be with it for the long haul and empowerment to create material would generate material. Given seed money and a salary and line producers credit they would be launched.

Why has this been difficult to accept? Probably because the theatre has always been so seductive because having an opinion makes you an expert. When your car breaks down, do you pull up the hood and fix it or do you take it to someone who knows how? You own that car and you probably have more money than the guy who is going to fix it. What's the problem with admitting that you don't know how to create shows and enjoy the power of finding a person who can?

RM: And this is a road that can exist within today's commercial theatre?

HP: Oh, I think so, sure. Today's commercial theatre is the way it is, folks, because you made it that way. Not necessarily deliberately, but wanting to avoid the odd confrontation with unions. We had strikes. We sustained a nine-day Broadway blackout. And it affected the run of productions that season, cut them short. But facing that strike affected positively the future of the industry.

Today, you should be talking about the year 2020. Not the Millennium Year. That's tomorrow.

There will always be theatre but (and here's where I get redundant) quality is diminishing big time. And you are not creating literature to protect 2020.

RM: What is the best background, the best training for a commercial producer?

HP: Every element in theatre requires craft. Producing theatre is a craft as well. Part of today's epidemic is that everyone seeks the end result without the means to it. Do you remember in the old days when millionaires, raising their kids to take over, started them in the foundry, moved them laterally into the accounting office, building them slowly, giving them a foundation before they gave them the business?

I suppose it's worth pointing out to you that I don't lack self-confidence. A result of learning the nuts and bolts.

RM: I'm going to give you a couple of quotes from your book, *Contradictions.* "Clearly we were the wrong producers for *Tenderloin,* the whole notion of wrong and right producers has been discarded today, the personality of the producer's work, his identity is missing, and it seems to me therein lies one of the sicknesses of Broadway."

HP: I said that and I stand by it. (*Laughter.*) But there is another element: I have always been conscious of how necessary it is to be identified with your work. Producers are right to want to be recognized, to have someone say he or she produced that. Or, who produced that show? Personal identification.

And then there's the inevitability, the necessity of failure. But failure is unacceptable today because people who "fail" don't get the next chance.

I love to work, and sometimes just for the sake of working, I've worked. But I discern that each failure nurtures success. I can show you that *Zorba,* which did not make money, was instrumental in creating *Evita,* which did. In protecting the process you must protect failure.

RM: Here's one on the budget process. Quoting from *Contradictions:* "*Company* never played a sold out week. Often played to 60 percent capacity but it paid off and showed a profit and that is what the commercial theatre must ask of itself."

HP: Perhaps 60 percent is no longer realistic but 70 percent should be practical.

Steve Sondheim invented the game "Broadway"; in the Monopoly mode. It was about producing and as far as I know I'm the only one who ever won that game. To play it, you found a property, assigned the author, directors, a design team and then stars. Everyone always wanted to put Mary Martin, Ethel Merman, Alfred Drake and Ezio Pinza together on the stage. Steve constructed his game wisely so the tab to support all these actors, glamorous as that might be, made breaking even impossible. Letting everyone play the hare, I was the tortoise slowly winning every game because I played it with an eye on practical budgeting.

How much bang for the buck do you get if you have taste and how little if you don't! Each project's demands are different. I wouldn't do *The Phantom of the Opera* without the gilt and the crystal. Essentially, it's a simple black box production but expensively simple. Less is more only sometimes. More can be more.

RM: You said, "It occurs to me that I loved working on *Candide* in Brooklyn but I hated bringing it to Broadway. I must conclude from this that I'm growing older. The wear and tear on the nerves is more difficult to take." Is it possible that explains why so many theatre artists seem to retire in their forties or move away from directing or writing for the theatre into a more solitary creative experience? Or maybe, you simply didn't enjoy producing?

HP: Obviously I simply didn't enjoy producing. I wanted to focus on directing.

How fortunate I was to be born when I was, but twenty years earlier would have been better. There was more company then: thirty first-rate composers, lyricists, librettists, playwrights, directors, a couple of dozen producers, producing at least one play a season. There existed a community, interacting and supportive. There were so many plays opening each week that often you hoped to get the first-string critic at your opening night.

Prosperity made it easier to have a sense of community. With less envy—more community.

I was a 25-year-old trying to get a show on and during that period I met them all: Rogers and Hammerstein, Lerner and Lowe, Lindsay and Crouse, Moss Hart, Irving Berlin. Some even invested in my first show. I have kept letters from an astonishing number of luminous names from the 1940s and

1950s welcoming me to the theatre. Ten years later when I directed *She Loves Me*, the letters came again, welcoming me to directing.

I looked at your list of producers before I came here to speak and it is a very long list. If everyone was actively presenting new work, there would be just as much activity today as there was then. But there isn't, and can't be, given existing circumstances. So change existing circumstances. Easier said than done. But do-able.

RM: You started out as an independent producer, doing the work of other directors. You became a producer so that you could hire yourself and then the next face was Hal Prince's as producer, producing Hal Prince's productions. Then the producing ended, and you were a director working in the corporate environment. In that arc, across different generations in the theatre, how did that process change from work with the independent producer to the corporate environment?

HP: Some years ago I worked on a show that started out with one producer and ended up with eight. Eight, really is sixteen if they're married. (*Laughter.*) And if they are married, counting children, the figure is probably more like thirty-two. (*More laughter.*) During rehearsals one day, I was invited to the lounge in the theatre where the eight producers and some wives said that they would never bother me with all of their notes individually because I didn't deserve that. So they put everything on paper, handing me six single-spaced, typed pages of notes. No more of that for me! But I'm certain today, that scene is played over and over and over again.

As for working in the corporate environment, I suspect you're speaking of Garth Drabinsky. Well, he wasn't corporate and perhaps that was the cause for his downfall. Garth was an independent producer. At his best his was a mom-and-pop organization. Creative. Supportive. Enthusiastic. With an eye always on quality. His appetite, unfortunately, was too big; and his judgment compromised.

Many of you know the history of *Kiss of the Spider Woman*. It opened at SUNY Purchase and it was Marty Bell's ingenious invention to find a place where we could do new musicals, stay away from the press and get them right. But we weren't allowed to do that because we were "news." So *Kiss of the Spider Woman* was launched and then savaged by the press. Garth Drabinsky came along. Sure, it behooved him to do something dramatic, like taking a show that got terrible reviews and turning it into a Tony award winner. The point is that he did it.

RM: Is corporatization the seed of change in this industry?

HP: Yes. And it's very dangerous. We are treading on dangerous ground. I'll whisper it: Monopoly.

Do I think that what's happening to Microsoft will have any immediate resonance? Not for one second. Do I think it will have some resonance in the future when the pendulum swings the other way? When every newsboy isn't playing the market? Damn right. I don't even think so: I know so.

RM: In his introductory remarks, Alan Wasser mentioned that Disney is not a League member. Is that meaningful for the League?

HP: I wouldn't know. I am not a League member. I left years ago when I was still producing.

RM: Why did you decide to leave the League?

HP: I discerned that no organization could represent this mom-and-pop producer and conglomerate theatre owners because my priorities and theirs are so different. At that time I felt the League wasn't structured to address our different needs. I did not want to be where I was not equally represented. So I left.

RM: There has been considerable emphasis on the "branding" of Broadway as a marketing tool. How important is this? Is it a serious tool for the commercial theatre?

HP: I'm sorry. I didn't hear that word. Spell it.

RM: B-R-A-N-D-I-N-G.

FROM THE FLOOR: I think we should skip that question. *(Followed by audience disapproval and an explanation of "branding" by Marx.)*

HP: Well, it does sound like advertising speak to me. However, I do believe the best way to develop a reputation and an international audience is by playing in New York City and preferably on Broadway. It would be naïve to think that the imprimatur of Broadway is not a valuable one. Just as the "Tony" is a valuable identification.

Perhaps this is as good a time as any to point out that there are prevailing agendas in the press: That something not for profit is better BECAUSE it is not for profit. Not true. Not even remotely true. There are just so many first class artists and New York has the advantage of being home to the greatest pool of talent in the country. Putting together a consortium of the best is easier in New York. Outside of New York, there's likely to be dilution.

A word about the road, since so much of what I'm saying will be construed as negative or, more accurately, critical. The road has prospered. Not only at the box office but in terms of quality. In the fifties the road shows we sent out were largely a disgrace. For example, Gwen Verdon starred on Broadway in *Damn Yankees,* so when we sent out the tour, we found a girl who looked like Gwen Verdon, who had red hair, danced only adequately and didn't charm. Then we reproduced the sets, leaving out all the details—the patina, the brass work, the molding—slapping paint on canvas instead. Every time an actor entered the set, the walls shook.

Those days Claudia Cassidy wrote for the *Chicago Tribune.* She gave us hell every time we came to that city. So business suffered and such collective mediocrity almost destroyed the road.

Today, it is not uncommon to go out on the road and see a better production than the one you saw on Broadway.

RM: Today, how do you feed the road and what is the impact of so many revivals?

HP: You must replenish the road with new material and balance the menu with revivals. Revivals celebrate the history of theatre. However, recent revivals have taken a toll on me. I saw so many of the landmark musicals and so many of the less important entertainments when I was a kid and later when I went to college.

Too often lately, we've been fed McShow revivals and they have exacted a personal cost from me. You spend your life adoring a show and then find out it wasn't as good as you thought it was.

I think a revival is only justified if you meet the standard of the original or exceed it. And you can exceed it.

RM: I want to ask you something about mentoring. You've been phenomenal over so many years embracing so many young people. (Hal, in addition to his work on Broadway, is Mr. Good Citizen: working with the NEA in Washington, teaching seminars, interviewing aspirants.) Do you think that mentoring is going on in this business the way it should?

HP: I know it is not.

Steve Sondheim was Hammerstein's protégé. I was George Abbott's. That should support the notion of mentoring. George Abbott was able to be so generous, instrumental in the burgeoning careers of so many, because he was so secure.

I have interns, usually two per show. It's an exacting process, but I should point out that many of my most successful directing "graduates" failed to find careers in the theatre. One, Andy Cadiff, found fame and fortune directing "Home Improvement" and producing and directing "Spin City." One, making his mark in the theatre, is Mark Brokaw, who interned on *Kiss of the Spider Woman*. Another, Lonny Price, is directing the Broadway revival of *Finian's Rainbow,* and is artistic director of Musical Theater Works.

HP: Tell us how George Abbott and you worked together.

HP: George Abbott is a hard measuring rod for anybody else. He loved collaborating. A few years ago, he died at the age of 107, having directed his last hit at the age of 93, so we are discussing a phenomenon. But I will tell you, he knew, talented as he was, that he wasn't as contemporary as the young people coming up. So collaboration was self-serving as well as generous. He wanted a collaboration to be equal parts experience—his—and equal parts untested creativity.

I emulated that experience last season directing *Parade* with a book by an old pro, Alfred Uhry, and a score by Jason Robert Brown. Jason had never written a musical, only songs. In the four years it took us to get that show on a stage he learned how a song could serve the musical form.

So the journey was enormously valuable to me because his voice took me by surprise. We would tell him to write something and he would bring us something else. Something surprising, ingenious, something better. Something that expressed a contemporary vision. Thank God.

FROM THE FLOOR: I think your characterization of the theatre today is fair enough but I think you're ignoring a major change. I think there are people outside of Broadway who are doing great theatre.

HP: Of course there are. And without the regional and not-for-profit theatre we would have few original plays. However, it is dangerous to abrogate responsibility to another source.

You are the members of the League of American Producers and Theatre Owners and it all comes back to the same message: Are you solely about making money? If so, your short-sightedness will leave you bankrupt in twenty years. If, however, you invest in the future of the art form, paradoxically, you'll make a living and even, occasionally, a "killing."

NOTES

Note: NYPL Clipping Folder—article is from the Billy Rose Theatre Collection, New York Public Library at Lincoln Center; NYPL Critics' Reviews—article is from the New York Theatre Critics' Reviews, New York Public Library at Lincoln Center, by volume and page; interviews with individuals, unless otherwise noted, were conducted by the author.

Chapter 1

1. Harold Prince, *Contradictions: Notes on Twenty-Six Years in the Theatre* (New York: Dodd, Mead, 1974), p. 1.
2. Interview with Harold Prince, New York, 8 June 1988.
3. Alan Wallach, "Harold Prince," *Newsday,* 3 February 1980, p. 26.
4. Hubert Saal, "How to Play at Hal Prince," *Newsweek,* 26 July 1971, p. 70.
5. Wallach, "Harold Prince," p. 26.
6. Interview with Harold Prince, "Harold Prince: From Follies to Phantom," 26 June 1988, Arts and Entertainment Cable TV Network.
7. Ibid.
8. Prince, *Contradictions,* p. 3.
9. Ibid.
10. Ibid., p. 4.
11. Gary Paul Gates, "Broadway's Prince Charming," *Holiday,* April 1966, p. 102.
12. Interview with George Abbott, New York, 4 March 1983.
13. "Robert E. Griffith Obituary," *New York Herald Tribune,* 8 June 1961, NYPL Clipping Folder.
14. George Abbott, *Mister Abbott* (New York: Random House, 1963), p. 207.
15. Interview with Gwen Verdon, New York, 24 May 1983.
16. Abbott interview.
17. Ibid.

18. William Goldman, *The Season, A Candid Look at Broadway* (New York: Harcourt, Brace and World, 1969), p. 364.

19. Ibid., p. 364.

20. "From Follies to Phantom," A & E Cable TV Network.

21. Goldman, *The Season*, p. 364.

22. Ibid.

23. Interview with Ruth Mitchell, New York, 7 March 1983.

24. Goldman, *The Season*, p. 298.

Chapter 2

1. Interview with George Abbott, New York, 4 March 1983.

2. George Abbott, *Mister Abbott* (New York: Random House, 1963), p. 248.

3. Interview with Richard Adler, New York, 30 June 1983.

4. Harold Prince, *Contradictions: Notes on Twenty-Six Years in the Theatre* (New York: Dodd, Mead, 1974), p. 10.

5. Adler interview.

6. Ibid.

7. Walter Kerr, "Theatre," *New York Herald Tribune*, 14 May 1954, NYPL Critics' Reviews, vol. 15, p. 324.

8. Brooks Atkinson, "Theatre in Review," *New York Times*, 14 May 1954, NYPL Critics' Reviews, vol. 15, p. 325.

9. Prince, *Contradictions*, p. 12.

10. Ibid., p. 11.

11. Stanley Green, *The World of Musical Comedy* (New York: A. S. Barnes & Co., 1968), p. 37.

12. Abe Laufe, *Broadway's Greatest Musicals* (New York: Funk and Wagnalls, 1969), p. 32.

13. Interview with Gwen Verdon, New York, 24 May 1983.

14. *New York Times*, 24 November 1968, NYPL Clipping Folder.

15. Abbott interview.

16. Ethan Mordden, *Better Foot Forward, The History of American Musical Theatre* (New York: Grossman Publishers, 1976), p. 242.

17. Adler interview.

18. Verdon interview.

19. Ibid.

20. Ibid.

21. Ibid.

22. Ibid.

23. Walter Kerr, *New York Herald Tribune*, 6 May 1955, NYPL Clipping Folder.

24. John Chapman, *New York Daily News*, 6 May 1955, NYPL Clipping Folder.

25. Verdon interview.

26. Laufe, *Broadway's Greatest Musicals*, p. 191.

27. Adler interview.

28. Prince, *Contradictions*, p. 19.

29. Adler interview.

30. Gary Paul Gates, "Broadway's Prince Charming," *Holiday*, April 1966, p. 101.

31. Don Ross, "O'Neill Set to Music in Abbott's 'New Girl,'" *New York Herald Tribune*, 12 May 1957, section 4, p. 1.

32. Seymour Peck, "Anna Christie Sings," NYPL Clipping Folder.

33. Ibid.

34. Ibid.

35. Ibid.

36. Prince, *Contradictions*, p. 23.

37. Brooks Atkinson, "The Theatre: Singing Anna Christie," *New York Times*, 15 May 1957, NYPL Critics' Reviews, Vol. 18, p. 269.

38. Walter Kerr, "Theatre," *New York Herald Tribune*, 15 May 1957, NYPL Critics' Reviews, Vol. 18, p. 269.

39. Abbott, *Mister Abbott*, p. 254.

40. Prince, *Contradictions*, p. 26.

41. Ibid., p. 27.

42. Verdon interview.

43. Ibid.

44. Abbott, *Mister Abbott*, p. 254.

45. Verdon interview.

46. *Variety*, 13 February 1974, p. 70, NYPL Clipping Folder.

47. Hobe Morrison, *Variety*, 22 May 1957, p. 56, NYPL Clipping Folder.

48. John McClain, "New Girl in Town," *New York Journal American*, 15 May 1957, NYPL Clipping Folder.

Chapter 3

1. Gary Paul Gates, "Broadway's Prince Charming," *Holiday*, April 1966, p. 100.

2. Ibid.

3. Harold Prince, *Contradictions: Notes on Twenty-Six Years in the Theatre* (New York: Dodd, Mead, 1974), p. 32.

4. Hugh Fordin, *Getting to Know Him: Biography of Oscar Hammerstein II* (New York: Random House, 1977), p. 330.

5. Craig Zadan, *Sondheim & Co.* (New York: Da Capo, 1974), p. 16.

6. Ibid., p. 22.

7. Ibid., p. 16.

8. Ibid. p. 17.

9. Richard Watts, Jr., "Two on the Aisle: Romeo and Juliet in a Gang War," *New York Post*, 27 September 1957, NYPL Critics' Reviews, Vol. 18, p. 252.

10. Zadan, *Sondheim & Co.*, p. 19.

11. Interview with Harold Prince, *The South Bank Show*, 23 June 1978, London Weekend TV.

12. Martin Gottfried, *Broadway Musicals* (New York: Harry N. Abrams, 1979), p. 102.

13. Ibid.

14. Prince, *Contradictions*, p. 32.

15. Interview with Lonny Price, New York, 18 February 1982.

16. Watts, "Romeo and Juliet in a Gang War."

17. David Ewen, *New Complete Book of the American Musical Theatre* (New York: Holt, Rinehart & Winston, 1958), p. 560.

18. Zadan, *Sondheim & Co.*, p. 23.

19. Fordin, *Getting to Know Him*, p. 330.

20. Ibid.

21. Ibid.

22. Zadan, *Sondheim & Co.*, p. 23.

23. Ibid.

24. Prince, *Contradictions*, p. 37.

25. Zadan, *Sondheim & Co.*, p. 27.

26. John Chapman, " 'West Side Story': A Splendid and Super-Modern Musical Drama," *New York Daily News*, 27 September 1957, NYPI, Critics' Reviews, Vol. 18, p. 252.

27. Brooks Atkinson, "Theatre: The Jungles of the City," *New York Times*, 27 September 1957, NYPL Critics' Reviews, Vol. 18, p. 253.

28. Robert Coleman, " 'West Side Story': A Sensational Hit!," *New York Daily Mirror*, 27 September 1957, NYPL Critics' Reviews, Vol. 18, p. 254.

29. Zadan, *Sondheim & Co.*, p. 33.

30. Prince, *Contradictions*, p. 40.

31. Zadan, *Sondheim & Co.*, p. 31.

32. Gottfried, *Broadway Musicals*, p. 102.

33. Cecil Smith and Glenn Litton, *Musical Comedy in America* (New York: Theater Arts Books, 1981), p. 235.

Chapter 4

1. J. Waters, "Shows Out of Town," *Variety*, 17 September 1958, NYPL Clipping Folder.

2. Jerome Weidman, "Joining the Team," *Theatre Arts*, December 1959, p. 12.

3. Interview with Sheldon Harnick, New York, 4 February 1982.

4. Ibid.

5. Stanley Green, *The World of Musical Comedy* (New York: A. S. Barnes and Co., 1968), p. 363.

6. Sheldon Harnick, "What Comes First in a Musical? The Libretto," in *Playwrights, Lyricists, Composers on Theatre*, ed. Otis L. Guernsey, Jr. (New York: Dodd, Mead, 1964), p. 40.

7. Harold Prince, *Contradictions: Notes on Twenty-Six Years in the Theatre* (New York: Dodd, Mead, 1974), p. 52.

8. John Chapman, "Fiorello," *New York Daily News*, 24 November 1959, NYPL Critics' Reviews, Vol. 20, p. 220.

9. "Say, Darling, Look at Hal Prince Now," *New York Times*, 24 November 1968, section 2, p. D13.

10. Harnick interview.

11. Ibid.

12. Ibid.

13. Prince, *Contradictions*, p. 58.

14. Interview with Harold Prince, New York, 14 March 1983.

15. Ibid.

16. Interview with Aram Boyajian, New York, 30 May 1983.

17. Ibid.

18. Brooks Atkinson, "Fiorello," *New York Times*, 24 November 1959, NYPL Critics' Reviews, Vol. 20, p. 219.

19. Robert Coleman, " 'Fiorello': A Smashing Winner," *New York Daily Mirror*, 24 November 1959, NYPL Critics' Reviews, VoL 20, p. 222.

20. Richard Watts, Jr., "A Salute to the Little Flower, " *New York Post*, 24 November 1959, NYPL Critics' Reviews, Vol. 20, p. 221.

21. Gerald Bordman, *American Musical Theatre, A Chronicle* (New York: Oxford University Press, 1978), p. 615.

22. Interview with George Abbott, New York, 4 March 1983.

23. Prince, *Contradictions,* p. 59.

24. Ibid, p. 62.

25. Ibid. pp. 82-83.

26. Abbott interview.

27. Interview with Harold Prince, *The Dick Cavett Show*, videotape, 19-20 February 1980, Public Broadcasting Service, Channel 13, New York.

Chapter 5

1. Interview with Sheldon Harnick, New York, 4 February 1982.

2. Ibid.

3. Harold Prince, *Contradictions: Notes on Twenty-Six Years in the Theatre* (New York: Dodd, Mead, 1974), p. 68.

4. "Tenderloin," *New York Daily News*, I September 1960, NYPL Clipping Folder.

5. Richard Altman, with Mervyn Kaufman, *The Making of a Musical: "Fiddler on the Roof"*(New York: Oxford University Press, 1978), p. 26.

6. Stuart W. Little, "Theatre News," *New York Herald Tribune*, 16 August 1960, NYPL Clipping Folder.

7. Ethan Mordden, *Better Foot Forward, The History of American Musical Theatre* (New York: Grossman Publishers, 1976), p. 289.

8. Altman, *The Making of a Musical,* p. 28.

9. John McClain, "Musical Just Doesn't Sing," *New York Journal American,* 18 October 1960, NYPL Critics' Reviews, Vol. 21, p. 206.

10. John Chapman, "Tenderloin," *New York Daily News,* 18 October 1960, NYPL Critics' Reviews, Vol. 21, p. 208.

11. George Abbott, "A Call on Kuprin," NYPL Clipping Folder.

12. Jack Gaver, UPI "Newsfeature," NYPL Clipping Folder.

13. Henry T. Murdock, "Deluxe Melodrama Opens," *Philadelphia Inquirer,* 9 May 1961, NYPL Clipping Folder.

14. Gaver, UPI "Newsfeature."

15. Howard Taubman, " 'Call on Kuprin' Aims High, Hits Target," *New York Times,* 26 May 1961, NYPL Clipping Folder.

16. Prince, *Contradictions,* p. 72.

17. Ibid., p. 74.

18. Cecil Smith and Glenn Litton, *Musical Comedy in America* (New York: Theatre Arts Books, 1981), p. 282.

19. Prince, *Contradictions,* p. 73.

20. "They Might Be Giants, England," NYPL Clipping Folder.

21. Milton Shulman, "At the Theatre: An Attack Completely Out of Range," NYPL Clipping Folder.

22. Interview with George Abbott, New York, 4 March 1983.

23. Prince, *Contradictions,* p. 82.

24. Harnick interview.

25. Interview with Ruth Mitchell, New York, 7 March 1983.

Chapter 6

1. "Take Her, She's Mine," *Variety,* 6 December 1962, NYPL Clipping Folder.

2. Stuart W. Little, "Take Her, She's Mine," *New York Herald Tribune,* 31 October 1961, NYPL Clipping Folder.

3. Elinor Hughes, " 'Take Her, She's Mine,' Winner with Carney," *Boston Herald,* 6 December 1961, p. 28, NYPL Clipping Folder.

4. Ibid.

5. Harold Prince, *Contradictions: Notes on Twenty-Six Years in the Theatre* (New York: Dodd, Mead, 1974), p. 85.

6. John Chapman, " 'Take Her, She's Mine' Presents Art Carney as a Typical Father," *New York Daily News,* 22 December 1961, NYPL Critics' Reviews, Vol. 22, p. 149.

7. Prince, *Contradictions,* p. 86.

8. Gary Paul Gates, "Broadway's Prince Charming," *Holiday,* April 1966, p. 102.

9. Jerry Gaghan, "Out of Town Review [Philadelphia]," *Variety,* 17 January 1962, NYPL Clipping Folder.

10. Ibid.

11. Prince, *Contradictions,* p. 88.

12. Ibid.

13. Joseph Morgenstern, "Interview with Berman," *New York Herald Tribune*, 21 January 1962, NYPL Clipping Folder.

14. Thomas Buckley, "Prince vs. Prince," *New York Times*, 21 April 1963, p. 1.

15. Prince, *Contradictions*, p. 90.

16. Ibid.

17. Howard Taubman, "Theatre: 'A Family Affair,'"*New York Times*, 29 January 1962, NYPL Clipping Folder.

18. John Chapman, "'Family Affair' Bright and Funny," *New York Daily News*, 29 January 1962, NYPL Clipping Folder.

19. Walter Kerr, "'A Family Affair,'" *New York Herald Tribune*, 29 January 1962, NYPL Clipping Folder.

20. Interview with Richard Adler, New York, 30 June 1983.

21. Buckley, "Prince vs. Prince."

22. Burt Shevelove, "All About 'A Funny Thing Happened on the Way to the Forum,'" *Performing Arts: The Music Center Monthly 5,* no. 10 (October 1971): 31.

23. Ibid.

24. Ibid.

25. Ibid.

26. Craig Zadan, *Sondheim & Co.* (New York: Da Capo, 1974), p. 41.

27. "A Funny Thing Happened on the Way to the Forum," *New York Herald Tribune*, 10 May 1962, NYPL Clipping Foider.

28. Zadan, *Sondheim & Co.*, p. 73.

29. Prince, *Contradictions*, p. 8K

30. Zadan, *Sondheim & Co.*, p. 73.

31. Ibid., p. 75.

32. Ibid.

33. Ibid.

34. Martin Gottfried, *Broadway Musicals* (New York: Harry N. Abrams, 1979), p. 29.

35. Ibid.

36. Prince, *Contradictions*, p. 93.

37. Ibid.

38. Zadan, *Sondheim & Co.*, p. 84.

39. Abbott interview.

40. Sondheim interview, 30 August 1988.

41. Walter Kerr, "Friends, Romans, Vaudevillians," *New York Herald Tribune*, p. 1, NYPL Clipping Folder.

42. "Brendan Gill Interviews Harold Prince and Stephen Sondheim," videotape, 2 June 1975, Theatre on Film and Tape Project of the Lincoln Center Library.

43. Zadan, *Sondheim & Co.*, p. 79.

44. Ibid.

45. Ibid.

46. "Gill Interviews Prince and Sondheim."

47. Zadan, *Sondheim & Co.*, p. 77.

48. Hobe Morrison, "A Funny Thing," *Variety*, 10 May 1962, NYPL Clipping Folder.

49. Leonard Hoffman, "New York Play," *Hollywood Reporter*, 9 May 1962, p. 3.

50. Zadan, *Sondheim & Co.*, p. 80.

51. Prince, *Contradictions*, p. 94.

52. Richard L. Coe, "A Thin Night in Old Rome," *Washington Post*, 11 April 1962, NYPL Clipping Folder.

53. Zadan, *Sondheim & Co.*, p. 81.

54. Prince, *Contradictions*, p. 94.

55. Zadan, *Sondheim & Co.*, p. 81.

56. Sondheim interview, August 1988.

57. Howard Taubman, "Theatre: A Funny Thing Happened . . . ," *New York Times*, 9 May 1962, NYPL Clipping Folder.

58. Richard Watts, Jr., "Riotous Life of the Old Romans," *New York Post*, 9 May 1962, p.76.

59. Buckley, "Prince vs. Prince," p. 3.

60. Prince, *Contradictions*, p. 99.

61. Milt Freudenheim, "'She Loves Me' Has Pair Excited," *Miami Herald-Chicago Newswire*, NYPL Clipping Folder.

62. Ibid.

63. Ibid.

64. Leonard Harris, "'She Loves Me' Scribe Sticks His Neck Out," *New York World Telegram and Sun*, 20 April 1963, p. 10.

65. Interview with Sheldon Harnick, New York, 4 February 1982.

66. Ibid.

67. Interview with Joe Masteroff, New York, 14 June 1982.

68. Ibid.

69. Ibid.

70. Prince, *Contradictions*, p. 100.

71. Richard Watts, Jr., "Refreshing New Musical," *New York Post*, 24 April 1963, p. 66.

72. Harris, "'She Loves Me' Scribe," p. 10.

73. Howard Taubman, "Theatre: 'She Loves Me,' A Musical," *New York Times*, 24 April 1963, NYPL Clipping Folder.

74. Masteroff interview.

75. Prince, *Contradictions*, p. 100.

76. Masteroff interview.

77. Harnick interview.

78. Masteroff interview.

79. "On Craft," *New York Times*, NYPL Clipping Folder.

80. Prince, *Contradictions*, p. 101.

81. Harnick interview.

82. George Oppenheimer, "On Stage," *Newsday*, I May 1963, NYPL Clipping Folder.

83. Sandra Schmidt, "She Loves Me," *Village Voice*, 2 May 1963, p. 12, NYPL Clipping Folder.

84. Henry Hewes, "She Loves Me," *Saturday Review*, 11 May 1963, p. 26, NYPL Clipping Folder.

85. Ibid.

86. Harold Bone, "She Loves Me," *Variety*, 20 March 1963, NYPL Clipping Folder.

87. Ibid.

88. William Bender, "Musical of Gentle Love and Heady Perfume," *New York Herald Tribune*, 21 April 1963, NYPL Clipping Folder.

89. Prince, *Contradictions*, p. 102.

90. Ibid.

91. Buckley, "Prince vs. Prince," p. 3.

92. Walter Kerr, "She Loves Me," *New York Herald Tribune*, 24 April 1963, NYPL Clipping Folder.

93. Taubman, "Theatre: 'She Loves Me,' A Musical."

94. Martin Gottfried, "She Loves Me," *Women's Wear Daily*, 24 April 1963, NYPL Clipping Folder.

95. John Chapman, "She Loves Me," *New York Daily News*, 24 April 1963, NYPL Clipping Folder.

96. Watts, "Refreshing New Musical Comedy."

97. Henry Hewes, "She Loves Me."

98. Ibid.

99. Howard Taubman, "Discipline of Taste," *New York Times*, 5 May 1963, NYPL Clipping Folder.

100. Prince, *Contradictions*, p. 99.

101. Ibid.

102. Ibid.

103. Edward Sothern Hipp, "She Loves Me," *Newark Evening News*, 19 January 1964, NYPL Clipping Folder.

104. Ibid.

105. Prince, *Contradictions*, p. 102.

106. Ibid.

Chapter 7

1. John Chapman, "'Fiddler on the Roof' Great Musical; Zero Mostel Heads Superb Cast," *New York Daily News*, 23 September 1964, NYPL Theatre Critics' Reviews, Vol. 25, p. 217.

2. Richard Altman, with Mervyn Kaufman. *The Making of a Musical: "Fiddler on the Roof"* (New York: Crown Publishers, 1971), p. 20.

3. "Landmark Symposium: *Fiddler on the Roof*," *Dramatists Guild Quarterly 20*, no. 10 (Spring, 1983): 11.

4. Ibid.

5. David Ewen, *New Complete Book of the American Musical Theatre* (New York: Holt, Rinehart & Winston, 1958), p. 130.

6. Ibid.

7. Altman and Kaufman, *The Making of a Musical*, p. 21.

8. "Landmark Symposium: *Fiddler on the Roof*," p. 12.

9. Ibid.

10. Ibid., p. 14.

11. Altman and Kaufman, *The Making of a Musical*, p. 21.

12. Ibid., p. 22.

13. Ibid.

14. Ewen, *New Complete Book of the American Musical Theatre*, p. 130.

15. Altman and Kaufman, *The Making of a Musical*, p. 40.

16. "Landmark Symposium: *Fiddler on the Roof*," p. 17.

17. Ibid.

18. Altman and Kaufman, *The Making of a Musical*, p. 22.

19. Ibid., p. 23.

20. Ibid., p. 41.

21. Ibid., p. 97.

22. Ibid., p. 23.

23. Ewen, *New Complete Book of the American Musical Theatre*, p. 131.

24. Harold Prince, *Contradictions: Notes on Twenty-Six Years in the Theatre* (New York: Dodd, Mead, 1974), pp. 108-9.

25. Ibid., p. 106.

26. Ibid., p. 107.

27. Altman and Kaufman, *The Making of a Musical*, p. 47.

28. Ibid., p. 48.

29. Prince, *Contradictions*, p. 106.

30. Ewen, *New Complete Book of the American Musical Theatre*, p. 131.

31. Altman and Kaufman, *The Making of a Musical*, p. 63.

32. Howard Kissel, "Side by Side by Prince," *Horizon*, October 1981, p. 63.

33. "Landmark Symposium: *Fiddler on the Roof*," p. 25.

34. Altman and Kaufman, *The Making of a Musical*, p. 63.

35. Ibid.

36. "Landmark Symposium: *Fiddler on the Roof*," p. 22.

37. Ibid., p. 23.

38. Ibid.

39. Walter Kerr, "Fiddler on the Roof," *New York Herald Tribune*, 23 September 1964, NYPL Critics' Reviews, Vol. 25, p. 216.

40. Ibid.

41. Altman and Kaufman, *The Making of a Musical*, p. 107.

42. Howard Taubman, "Mostel as Tevye," *New York Times*, 23 September 1964, NYPL Critics' Reviews, Vol. 25, p. 216.

43. Richard Watts, Jr., "The Brilliance of Zero Mostel," *New York Post*, 23 September 1964, NYPL Critics' Reviews, Vol. 25, p. 215.

44. Prince, *Contradictions*, p. 109.

45. Kissel, "Side by Side by Prince," p. 63.

46. Martin Gottfried, *Broadway Musicals* (New York: Harry N. Abrams, 1979), p. 126.

47. "Fiddler on the Roof," *Newsweek*, 26 July 1971, p. 68, NYPL Clipping Folder.

48. Ibid.

Chapter 8

1. Interview with Jerome Coopersmith, New York, 24 February 1984.

2. Ibid.

3. Norman Nadel, "Irregulars Help Solve 'Baker Street' Problems," *New York World-Telegram and Sun*, 17 February 1965, NYPL Critics' Reviews, Vol. 26, p. 374.

4. Coopersmith interview.

5. Ibid.

6. Ibid.

7. Harold Prince: *Contradictions: Notes on Twenty-Six Years in the Theatre* (New York: Dodd, Mead, 1974), p. 113.

8. Ibid., p. 115.

9. Ibid., p. 114.

10. Coopersmith interview.

11. Elliot Norton, "Some Fun, Trouble Too, in 'Baker Street' Show," *Boston Record American*, 29 December 1964, NYPL Clipping Folder.

12. Coopersmith interview.

13. Norton Mockridge, "Baker Street," *New York World-Telegram and Sun*, NYPL Clipping Folder.

14. Coopersmith interview.

15. Harold Prince, letter to Oliver Smith, 29 July 1964.

16. Harold Prince, letter to Jerome Coopersmith, 21 August 1964.

17. Richard Watts, Jr., "Sherlock Holmes' Musical Career," *New York Post*, 17 February 1965, NYPL Critics' Reviews, Vol. 26, p. 376.

18. Harold Prince, letter to Jerome Coopersmith, 14 August 1964.

19. Ibid.

20. Interview with Lee Becker Theodore, New York, 23 February 1984.

21. Ibid.

22. Harold Prince, letter to Jerome Coopersmith, 2 September 1964.

23. Prince letter to Coopersmith, 21 August 1964.

24. Prince letter to Coopersmith, 2 September 1964.

25. Gary Paul Gates, "Broadway's Prince Charming," *Holiday*, April 1966, p. 107.

26. Prince, *Contradictions*, p. 115.

27. Coopersmith interview.

28. "My Fair Irene," *Saturday Review*, 6 March 1965, p. 22, NYPL Clipping Folder.

29. Walter Kerr, "Walter Kerr Reviews 'Baker Street,'" *New York Herald Tribune*, 17 February 1965, NYPL Critics' Reviews, Vol. 26, p. 377.

30. Howard Taubman, "Sherlock Holmes to Music," *New York Times*, 17 February 1965, NYPL Critics' Reviews, Vol. 26, p. 376.

31. Coopersmith interview.

32. John Chapman, " 'Baker Street' Is a Captivating Musical about Sherlock Holmes," *New York Daily News*, 17 February 1965, NYPL Critics' Reviews, Vol. 26, p. 375.

33. Taubman, "Sherlock Holmes to Music."

34. Watts, "Sherlock Holmes' Musical Career."

35. Kerr, "Walter Kerr Reviews 'Baker Street.'"

36. Chapman, "'Baker Street' Is a Captivating Musical."

37. Kerr, "Walter Kerr Reviews 'Baker Street.'

38. "Poor Bitos," *Variety*, 13 February 1974, p. 90, NYPL Clipping Folder.

39. John McClain, "Brilliantly Performed," *New York Journal American*, 16 November 1964, NYPL Critics' Reviews, Vol. 25, p. 147.

Chapter 9

1. Harold Prince, *Contradictions: Notes on Twenty-Six Years in the Theatre* (New York: Dodd, Mead, 1974), p. 118.

2. Ibid.

3. Interview with Lee Becker Theodore, New York, 23 February 1984.

4. Prince, *Contradictions*, p. 120.

5. "Flora Role Ended—But Her Melody Lingers On," *Diplomat*, September 1965, p. 6, NYPL Clipping Folder.

6. William Glover, "Liza Minnelli Determined to Make It on Her Own." *Lawton Constitution*, 7 June 1965, p. 28.

7. Stuart W. Little, "Flora, the Red Menace," *New York Herald Tribune*, 2 February 1965, NYPL Clipping Folder.

8. Interview with George Abbott, New York, 4 March 1983.

9. Theodore interview.

10. Gary Paul Gates, "Broadway's Prince Charming," *Holiday*, April 1966, p. 108.

11. Kevin Kelly, " 'Flora' Has the Stuff, But Needs Work," *Boston Globe*, 15 April 1965, p. 15.

12. Howard Taubman, "Flora, the Red Menace," *New York Times*, 12 May 1965, NYPL Critics' Reviews, Vol. 26, p. 330.

13. Walter Kerr, "Kerr Reviews 'Flora, the Red Menace,'" *New York Herald Tribune*, 12 May 1965, NYPL Critics' Reviews, Vol. 26, p. 331.

14. Ibid.

15. Prince, *Contradictions*, p. 118.

16. Ibid.

17. Interview with Fred Ebb, New York, I February 1982.

18. Interview with Lee Adams, New York, 8 March 1984.

19. Ibid.

20. Interview with Harold Prince, "The New York Harold," *Theatre One,* International Theatre Institute of the U.S. (New York: DBS Publications, 1969), p. 39.

21. Richard Watts, Jr., "There's No Denying It's Superman," *New York Post,* 30 March 1966, NYPL Critics' Reviews, Vol. 27, p. 311.

22. Norman Nadel, "The Theatre," *New York World-Telegram and Sun,* 30 March 1966, NYPL Critics' Reviews, Vol. 27, p. 312.

23. Adams interview.

24. Ibid.

25. Ibid.

26. Prince, *Contradictions,* p. 123.

27. Jerry Gaghan, "Shows Out of Town," *Variety,* 23 February 1966. NYPL Clipping Folder.

28. Walter Kerr, "A Self-Conscious Smirk on Superman's Face," *New York Herald Tribune,* 16 April 1966, NYPL Clipping Folder.

29. Richard Watts, Jr., "Through the Skies with Superman," *New York Post,* 17 April 1966, p. 6.

30. Adams interview.

31. Gaghan, "Shows Out of Town."

32. Adams interview.

33. Stanley Kauffmann, "'It's a Bird . . . It's a Plane . . . It's Superman,' It's a Musical and It's Here," *New York Times,* 30 March 1966, NYPL Critics' Reviews, Vol. 27, p.313.

34. Ibid.

35. Walter Kerr, "Superman," *New York Herald Tribune,* 17 April 1966, p. 32, NYPL Clipping Folder.

36. George Oppenheimer, "It's 'Superman' and He's in a Broadway Musical," *Newsday,* 31 March 1966, NYPL Clipping Folder.

37. "The Theatre," *Cue,* 9 April 1966, NYPL Clipping Folder.

38. Prince, *Contradictions,* p. 124.

39. Adams interview.

40. Ibid.

Chapter 10

1. Gerald Bordman, *American Musical Theatre, A Chronicle* (New York: Oxford University Press, 1978), p. 643.

2. Ibid.

3. Martin Gottfried, *Broadway Musicals* (New York: Harry N. Abrams, 1979), p. 29.

4. Ibid., p. 126.

5. "Landmark Symposium: *Cabaret,*" *Dramatists Guild Quarterly* 19 (Summer, 1982): 13.

6. Harold Prince, *Contradictions: Notes on Twenty-Six Years in the Theatre* (New York: Dodd, Mead, 1974), p. 126.

7. Interview with Harold Prince, "The New York Harold," *Theatre One*, International Theatre Institute of the U.S. (New York: DBS Publications, 1969), p. 38.

8. Interview with Joe Masteroff, New York, 14 June 1982.

9. Sandy Wilson, "Letter to Editor," *Dramatists Guild Quarterly 19* (Winter, 1983): 47.

10. "Landmark Symposium: *Cabaret*," p. 14.

11. Ibid.

12. Ibid., p. 15.

13. Ibid.

14. Prince *Contradictions*, p. 126.

15. Ibid., p. 27.

16. J. M. Flagler, "*Cabaret*," *Look*, November 1966, p. 72.

17. John Chapman, "*Cabaret*," *New York Daily News*, 21 November 1966, p. 64.

18. "Landmark Symposium: *Cabaret*," p. 17.

19. Masteroff interview.

20. "Landmark Symposium: *Cabaret*," p. 24.

21. Walter Kerr, "Cabaret," *New York Times*, 21 November 1966, p. 62.

22. Ibid.

23. Ibid.

24. Richard Watts, Jr., "The Innocence of Sally Bowles," *New York Post*, 21 November 1966,p. 54.

25. "Landmark Symposium: *Cabaret*," p. 18.

26. Ibid.

27. Chapman,"Cabaret."

28. "Landmark Symposium: *Cabaret*," p. 23.

29. Ibid.

30. Prince, *Contradictions*, p. 126.

31. "Garson Kanin Interviews Boris Aronson," videotape, 20 March 1975, Theatre on Film and Tape Project of the Lincoln Center Library.

32. Ibid.

33. Ibid.

34. Ibid.

35. Prince, *Contradictions*, p. 129.

36. Ibid., pp. 129-30.

37. Ibid., p. 130.

38. Allan Wallach, "Harold Prince," *Newsday*, 3 February 1980, NYPL Clipping Folder.

39. Howard Kissel, "Side by Side by Prince," *Horizon*, October 1981, p. 64.

40. Prince, *Contradictions*, pp. 131-32.

41. Ibid., p. 132.

42. "Garson Kanin Interviews Boris Aronson."

43. Kerr, "Cabaret."

44. "Landmark Symposium: *Cabaret*," p. 20.

45. Ibid.

46. Ibid.

47. Interview with Fred Ebb, New York, I February 1982.

48. "Landmark Symposium: *Cabaret*," p. 20.

49. Ibid.

50. Ibid.

51. Ibid., p. 24.

52. Ibid., p. 26.

53. Ebb interview.

54. "Landmark Symposium: *Cabaret*," p. 27.

55. Prince, *Contradictions*, p. 136.

56. "Landmark Symposium: *Cabaret*," p. 22.

57. Kerr, "Cabaret."

58. Watts, "The Innocence of Sally Bowles."

59. Norman Nadel, "Cabaret," *New York World Journal Tribune*, 21 November 1966, NYPL Clipping Folder.

60. Richard P. Cooke, "Cabaret," *Wall Street Journal*, 22 November 1966, NYPL Clipping Folder.

61. Whitney Bolton, "Cabaret," *New York Morning Telegraph*, 22 November 1966, NYPL Clipping Folder.

62. Gottfried, *Broadway Musicals*, p. 127.

63. Interview with Harold Prince, *The South Bank Show*, videotape, 23 June 1978, London Weekend TV.

64. David Ewen, *New Complete Book of the American Musical Theatre* (New York: Holt, Rinehart & Winston, 1958), p. 62.

65. Prince, *Contradictions*, p. 139.

66. Clive Barnes, "'Zorba' Is Here with Music," *New York Times*, 18 November 1968, NYPL Critics' Reviews, Vol. 29, p. 174.

67. Henry Hewes, "The Theatre," *Saturday Review*, 7 December 1968, p. 36.

68. Richard Watts, Jr., "The Musical Debut of 'Zorba,' " *New York Post*, 18 November 1968, NYPL Critics' Reviews, Vol. 29, p. 176.

69. Barnes, "'Zorba' Is Here with Music."

70. John Chapman, "Bernardi, Karnilova Are Superb in a Great Musical Play, 'Zorba,' " *New York Daily News*, 18 November 1968, NYPL Critics' Reviews, Vol. 29, p. 175.

71. Barnes, "'Zorba' Is Here with Music."

72. Prince, *Contradictions*, p. 139.

40. Prince, *Contradictions*, pp. 131-32.
41. Ibid., p. 132.
42. "Garson Kanin Interviews Boris Aronson."
43. Kerr, "Cabaret."
44. "Landmark Symposium: *Cabaret*," p. 20.
45. Ibid.
46. Ibid.
47. Interview with Fred Ebb, New York, 1 February 1982.
48. "Landmark Symposium: *Cabaret*," p. 20.
49. Ibid.
50. Ibid.
51. Ibid., p. 24.
52. Ibid., p. 26.
53. Ebb interview.
54. "Landmark Symposium: *Cabaret*," p. 27.
55. Prince, *Contradictions*, p. 136.
56. "Landmark Symposium: *Cabaret*," p. 22.
57. Kerr, "Cabaret."
58. Watts, "The Innocence of Sally Bowles."
59. Norman Nadel, "Cabaret," *New York World Journal Tribune*, 21 November 1966, NYPL Clipping Folder.
60. Richard P. Cooke, "Cabaret," *Wall Street Journal*, 22 November 1966, NYPL Clipping Folder.
61. Whitney Bolton, "Cabaret," *New York Morning Telegraph*, 22 November 1966, NYPL Clipping Folder.
62. Gottfried, Broadway Musicals, p. 127.
63. Interview with Harold Prince, *The South Bank Show*, videotape, 23 June 1978, London Weekend TV.
64. David Ewen, *New Complete Book of the American Musical Theatre* (New York: Holt, Rinehart & Winston, 1958), p. 62.
65. Prince, *Contradictions*, p. 139.
66. Clive Barnes, "'Zorba' Is Here with Music," *New York Times*, 18 November 1968, NYPL Critics' Reviews, Vol. 29, p. 174.
67. Henry Hewes, "The Theatre," *Saturday Review*, 7 December 1968, p. 36.
68. Richard Watts, Jr., "The Musical Debut of 'Zorba,' " *New York Post*, 18 November 1968, NYPL Critics' Reviews, Vol. 29, p. 176.
69. Barnes, "'Zorba' Is Here with Music."
70. John Chapman, "Bernardi, Karnilova Are Superb in a Great Musical Play, 'Zorba,'" *New York Daily News*, 18 November 1968, NYPL Critics' Reviews, Vol. 29, p. 175.
71. Barnes, "'Zorba' Is Here with Music."
72. Prince, *Contradictions*, p. 139.

73. Ibid., p. 141.

74. Ibid., p. 140.

75. Barnes, " 'Zorba' Is Here with Music."

76. Harold Bone, "Shows Out of Town," *Variety*, 9 October 1968, p. 67.

77. Barnes, " 'Zorba' Is Here with Music."

78. Richard P. Cooke, "Broadway Perks Up," *Wall Street Journal*, 18 November 1968, NYPL Clipping Folder.

79. Prince, *Contradictions*, p. 141.

80. Ibid., p. 140.

81. Ebb interview.

82. Prince, *Contradictions*, p. 142.

83. Frank Rich, " 'Zorba' and Quinn," *New York Times*, 17 October 1983, p. C15.

84. Ibid.

85. Whitney Bolton, "Closing of 'Zorba' Loss to Broadway," *New York Morning Telegraph*, 6 August 1969, NYPL Clipping Folder.

Chapter 11

1. Gottfried, *Broadway Musicals*, p. 32.

2. Craig Zadan, *Sondheim & Co.* (New York: Da Capo, 1974), p. 143.

3. Harold Prince, *Contradictions: Notes on Twenty-Six Years in the Theatre* (New York: Dodd, Mead, 1974), p. 143.

4. Ibid., p. 144.

5. Zadan, *Sondheim & Co.*, p. 129.

6. Mel Cussow, "Sondheim Scores with 'Company,' " *New York Times*, 28 April 1970, p. 50.

7. John Kane, " 'Company': A New Landmark?" *Plays and Players 9*, no. 5 (February 1972): 25.

8. Interview with Stephen Sondheim, New York, 20 July 1984.

9. "Brendan Gill Interviews Harold Prince and Stephen Sondheim," videotape, 2 June 1975, Theatre on Film and Tape Project of the Lincoln Center Library.

10. Louis Botto, " 'Company,' Broadway's Oddest Love/Hate Hit," *Look*, 8 September 1970, NYPL Clipping Folder.

11. "Stephen Sondheim," *Time*, 3 May 1971, p. 74, NYPL Clipping Folder.

12. Kane, " 'Company': A New Landmark?"

13. Stephen Sondheim, "The Musical Theatre: A Talk by Stephen Sondheim," *Dramatists Guild Quarterly 15*, no. 3 (Autumn, 1978): 13-21.

14. "Gill Interviews Prince and Sondheim."

15. Prince, *Contradictions*, p. 150.

16. Interview with Lisa Aronson, New York, 6 June 1984.

17. "On Collaboration Between Authors and Directors," *Dramatists Guild Quarterly 16*, no. 2 (Summer, 1979): 28.

18. Lisa Aronson interview.

19. Prince, *Contradictions*, p. 145.

20. "Garson Kanin Interviews Boris Aronson," videotape, 20 March 1975, Theatre on Film and Tape Project of the Lincoln Center Library.

21. Carson Kanin, *Boris Aronson: From His Theatre Work*, brocbure from exhibition, 31 March-15 August 1981 (New York: New York Public Library at Lincoln Center, 1981), p. 10.

22. Samuel Hirsch, "'Company' All Glitter, Cleverness," *Boston Herald Traveler*, 25 March 1970, p. 21.

23. Stanley Kauffmann, "Company," *New Republic*, 23 May 1970, p. 20.

24. Lisa Aronson interview.

25. Ibid.

26. Zadan, *Sondheim & Co.*, p.l35.

27. Lisa Aronson interview.

28. Zadan, *Sondheim & Co.*, p. 150.

29. Sondheim interview.

30. Zadan, *Sondheim & Co.*, p. 137.

31. Douglas Watt, "Musical Events," *New York Daily News*, 11 July 1970, p. 94.

32. Zadan, *Sondheim & Co.*, p. 141.

33. Ibid., p. 140.

34. Ibid.

35. Ibid., p. 141.

36. "Gill Interviews Prince and Sondheim.

37. Ibid.

38. Kevin Kelly, "You're in Brilliant 'Company,' " *Boston Globe*, 25 March 1970, NYPL Clipping Folder.

39. Ibid.

40. Guy Livingston, "Shows Out of Town," *Variety*, 8 April 1970, p. 120.

41. Botto, " 'Company,' Broadway's Oddest Love/Hate Hit."

42. Clive Barnes, " 'Company' Offers a Guide to New York's Marital Jungle," *New York Times*, 27 April 1970, p. 40.

43. Walter Kerr, "'Company' Original and Uncompromising," *New York Times*, 3 May 1970, p. Dl, NYPL Clipping Folder.

44. Ibid.

45. Ibid.

46. John J. O'Connor, "Company," *Wall Street Journal*, 28 April 1970, p. 21.

47. Richard Watts, Jr., "Lesson from the Married Set," *New York Post*, 27 April 1970, p. 45.

48. Henry Hewes, "The Theatre," *Saturday Review*, 9 May 1970, p. 4.

49. John Lahr, "On-Stage," *Village Voice*, 7 May 1970, p. 15.

50. Zadan, *Sondheim & Co.*, p. 143.

51. Robert Waterhouse, "Hal Prince and Boris Aronson Talk to Robert Waterhouse," *Plays and Players 19,* no. 6 (March, 1972): 16.

52. Zadan, *Sondheim & Co.,* p. 131.

53. Ibid., p. 143.

54. Ibid., p.144.

55. Prince, *Contradictions,* p. 157.

56. "Gill Interviews Prince and Sondheim."

57. Ibid.

58. Interview with George Abbott, New York, 4 March 1983.

59. Gottfried, *Broadway Musicals,* p. 127.

60. Zadan, *Sondheim & Co.,* p. 147.

61. "Prince and His Follies," **Look,** May 1971, NYPL Clipping Folder.

62. Cecil Smith and Glenn Litton, *Musical Comedy in America* (New York: Theatre Arts Books, 1981), p. 300.

63. Ibid.

64. Zadan, *Sondheim & Co.,* pp. 131-33.

65. Mel Gussow, "Prince Recalls the Evolution of 'Follies,' " *New York Times,* 9 April 1971, NYPL Clipping Folder.

66. Zadan, *Sondheim & Co.,* p. 133.

67. Ibid., p. 135.

68. Prince, *Contradictions,* p. 159.

69. Ibid.

70. Ibid., p. 160.

71. Ibid., p. 159.

72. Ibid., p. 160.

73. Ibid., p. 161.

74. Zadan, *Sondheim & Co.,* p. 152.

75. Gussow, "Prince Recalls the Evolution of 'Follies.' "

76. T. E. Kalem, "Theatre," *Time,* 12 April 1971, NYPL Clipping Folder.

77. Zadan, *Sondheim & Co.,* p. 153.

78. Ibid., pp. 152-53.

79. "The Once and Future Follies," *Time,* 3 May 1971, p. 71.

80. Ibid.

81. John Simon, "Follies," *New York,* 19 April 1971, p. 41.

82. Zadan, *Sondheim & Co.,* p. 155.

83. Martin Gottfried, "Flipping Over 'Follies,' " *New York Times,* 25 April 1971, section 2, p.l.

84. Zadan, *Sondheim & Co.,* p. 159.

85. Ibid.

86. Interview with Harold Prince, *The Dick Cavett Show,* videotape, 19-20 February 1980, Public Broadcasting Service, Channel 13, New York.

87. Zadan, *Sondheim & Co.*, p. 153.

88. Prince, *Contradictions*, p. 163.

89. Zadan, *Sondheim & Co.*, p. 153.

90. Ibid., p. 155.

91. Interview with John McMartin, New York, 10 June 1982.

92. Zadan, *Sondheim & Co.*, p. 157.

93. Kanin, **Boris Aronson: From His Theatre Work**, p. 15.

94. Prince, *Contradictions*, p. 164.

95. Hubert Saal, "How to Play at Hal Prince," *Newsweek*, 26 July 1971, p. 68.

96. Prince, *Contradictions*, p. 164.

97. Harold Clurman, "Theatre," *Nation*, 18 April 1971, NYPL Clipping Folder.

98. Sondheim interview.

99. Gussow, "Prince Recalls the Evolution of 'Follies.'"

100. "The Once and Future Follies."

101. Bendan Gill, "Casting Out Remorse," *New Yorker*, 10 April 1971, p. 67.

102. Clive Barnes, " 'Follies' Couples, Years Later," *New York Times*, 5 April 1971, p. 49.

103. Gottfried, "Flipping Over 'Follies.'"

104. Prince, *Contradictions*, p. 164.

105. Ibid., p. 165.

106. Ibid., p. 167.

107. McMartin interview.

108. Eugenia Shepard, "Flossie's Follies," *New York Times*, 30 March 1971, p. 39.

109. "Follies," *Variety*, 3 March 1971, p. 3, NYPL Clipping Folder.

110. Zadan, *Sondheim & Co.*, p. 159.

111. Prince, *Contradictions*, p. 168.

112. McMartin interview.

113. Ibid.

114. Kalem, "Theatre."

115. Douglas Watt, "Sondheim-Prince Team Scores for Second Time," *New York Daily News*, 11 April 1971, p. S3.

116. George Oppenheimer, " 'Follies,' A Cornucopia," *Newsday*, 5 April 1971, p. 32.

117. Barnes, " 'Follies' Couples, Years Later."

118. Walter Kerr, "Yes, Yes, Alexis! No, No, 'Follies,'" *New York Times*, April 1971, section 2, p. 1, NYPL Clipping Folder.

119. Jack Kroll, "Backstage in Arcadia," *Newsweek*, 12 April 1971, p. 121.

120. Ibid.

121. Gottfried, "Flipping Over 'Follies.'"

122. Ibid.

123. Ibid.

124. Sondheim interview, June 1988.

125. Saal, "How to Play at Hal Prince," p. 69.
126. Sondheim interview.
127. "Making a Business of Show Business," *Forbes*, I February 1972, p. 25.
128. Zadan, *Sondheim & Co.*, p. 169.
129. Ibid., p. 167.
130. Ibid., p. 169.
131. Interview with Harold Prince, New York, 8 June 1988.
132. Prince interview, 1983.

Chapter 12

1. Martin Cottfried, *Broadway Musicals* (New York: Harry N. Abrams, 1979), p. 126.
2. Ibid., p. 127.
3. Harold Prince, *Contradictions: Notes on Twenty-Six Years in the Theatre* (New York: Dodd, Mead, 1974), p. 131.
4. Ibid., p. 177.
5. Ibid., p. 172.
6. Craig Zadan, *Sondheim & Co.* (New York: Da Capo, 1974), p. 203.
7. Prince, *Contradictions*, p. 174.
8. Interview with Hugh Wheeler, New York, 24 June 1982.
9. Zadan, *Sondheim & Co.*, p. 203.
10. Wheeler interview.
11. Zadan, *Sondheim & Co.*, p. 203.
12. Prince, *Contradictions*, p. 174.
13. Zadan, *Sondheim & Co.*, p. 202.
14. Ibid.
15. Prince, *Contradictions*, p. 175.
16. Stephen Grover, "Behind the Scenes," *Wall Street Journal*, 7 February 1973, p. 19.
17. Zadan, *Sondheim & Co.*, p. 205.
18. Prince, *Contradictions*, p. 176.
19. Interview with Patricia Birch, New York, 15 June 1982.
20. Ibid.
21. Zadan, *Sondheim & Co.*, p. 206.
22. Birch interview.
23. Ibid.
24. Zadan, *Sondheim & Co.*, p. 206.
25. Ibid.
26. Grover, "Behind the Scenes."
27. Prince, *Contradictions*, p. 179.
28. Ibid.
29. Zadan, *Sondheim & Co.*, p. 212.

30. Robert Berkvist, "Miss Johns Hits a High Note," *New York Times*, 11 March 1973, p. D3.

31. Zadan, *Sondheim & Co.*, p. 209.

32. Prince, *Contradictions*, p. 180.

33. Zadan, *Sondheim & Co.*, p. 207.

34. Ibid.

35. Bonnie Jacobs, "A Little Night Music," *Boston After Dark*, 6 February 1973, p. 15, NYPL Clipping Folder.

36. Prince, *Contradictions*, p. 182.

37. Clive Barnes, "A Little Night Music," *New York Times*, 26 February 1973, NYPL Critics' Reviews, Vol. 34, p. 349.

38. Edwin Wilson, "A Musical Show with Elegance," *Wall Street Journal*, 27 February 1973, NYPL Critics' Reviews, Vol. 34, p. 350.

39. Douglas Watt, "'A Little Night Music': Operetta That's Exquisite but Fragile," *New York Daily News*, 26 February 1973, NYPL Critics' Reviews, Vol. 34, p. 348.

40. Martin Gottfried, "A Little Night Music," *Women's Wear Daily*, 26 February 1973, NYPL Critics' Reviews, Vol. 34, p. 349.

41. Ibid.

42. Ibid.

43. Zadan, *Sondheim & Co.*, p. 213.

44. Allan Wallach, "Harold Prince," *Newsday*, 3 February 1980, NYPL Clipping Folder.

45. Interview with Lisa Aronson, New York, 6 June 1984.

46. Prince, *Contradictions*, p. 178.

47. Robert Berkvist, " 'Candide,' or a Very Moving Story," *New York Times*, 24 February 1974, section 2, p. 1.

48. Prince, *Contradictions*, p. 191.

49. Ibid.

50. Ibid.

51. Ibid., p. 192.

52. Ibid.

53. Ibid., p. 194.

54. Ibid., p. 195.

55. Raymond Ericson, "Rare Bernstein," *New York Times*, 14 May 1975, p. 34.

56. Prince, *Contradictions*, p. 201.

57. Cecil Smith and Glenn Litton, *Musical Comedy in America* (New York: Theatre Arts Books, 1981), p. 331.

58. Ibid.

59. Prince, *Contradictions*, p. 197.

60. Berkvist, " 'Candide,' or a Very Moving Story."

61. Adler interview.

62. Birch interview.

63. Deborah Jowitt, "Candide," *New York Times,* 23 November 1975, p. A12.

64. Prince, *Contradictions,* p. 199.

65. Ibid., p. 206.

66. Ibid.

67. Geoffrey Holder, "Candide," *WNBC-TV News,* New York, 20 December 1973, NYPL Critics' Reviews, Vol. 34, p. 140.

68. Jack Kroll, "Voltaire in Brooklyn," *Newsweek,* 31 December 1973, NYPL Critics' Reviews, Vol. 34, p. 140.

69. George Oppenheimer, "Candide," *Newsday,* NYPL Clipping Folder.

70. Douglas Watt, "'Candide' Is Revived in Brooklyn," *New York Daily News,* 21 December 1973, NYPL Critics' Reviews, Vol. 34, p. 138.

71. Martin Gottfried, "Candide," *Women's Wear Daily,* 21 December 1973, NYPL Critics' Reviews, Vol. 34, p. 139.

72. Berkvist, " 'Candide,' or a Very Moving Story."

73. Prince, *Contradictions,* p. 213.

74. Ibid., p. 214.

75. Mel Gussow, "Prince Lays Part of 'Candide' Deficit to Cost of 'Musicians We Don't Need,'" *New York Times,* 23 September 1976, p. 29.

76. Ibid.

77. Ibid.

78. Mel Gussow, "Candide," *New York Times,* 23 October 1975, p. 29.

79. Ibid.

80. Richard Watts, Jr., "The World of Dr. Pangloss," *New York Post,* 13 March 1974, NYPL Critics' Reviews, Vol. 35, p. 337.

81. Martin Gottfried, " 'Candide' Moves to Broadway," *Women's Wear Daily,* 13 March 1974, NYPL Critics' Reviews, Vol. 35, p. 337.

82. Clive Barnes, "Superb 'Candide,' " *New York Times,* 13 March 1974, NYPL Critics' Reviews, Vol. 35, p. 338.

83. Douglas Watt, "A New B'way 'Candide,'" *New York Daily News,* 12 March 1974, NYPL Critics' Reviews, Vol. 35, p. 339.

84. Hobe Morrison, "'Candide' Still 310G in Red; Has Recouped 15G in 17 Months," *Variety,* 3 September 1975, p. 95.

85. Prince, *Contradictions,* p. 215.

86. Donal Henahan, "Bernstein's 'Candide' Is Back as a Winner," *New York Times,* 24 October 1982, section 2, p. H17.

87. Bernard Holland, "First 'Candide' of Year by City Troupe," *New York Times,* 17 October 1983, p. C22.

88. Donal Henahan, "The Return of Bernstein's 'Candide,'" *New York Times,* 20 July 1984, p. C3.

Chapter 13

1. Interview with John Weidman, New York, 16 April 1982. 2. Ibid.

2. Ibid.

3. Interview with Harold Prince, New York, 14 March 1983.

4. Interview with Stephen Sondheim, New York, 20 July 1984.

5. Prince interview, 1983.

6. Weidman interview.

7. "Milan Stitt Interviews Harold Prince and Stephen Sondheim," videotape, 1975, Writers Weekly.

8. Prince interview, 1983.

9. "'Overtures' Opens Doors for Orientals," *New York Times*, 3 March 1976, p. 24, NYPL Clipping Folder.

10. Ibid.

11. Prince interview, 1983.

12. Ibid.

13. "'Overtures' Opens Doors for Orientals."

14. Prince interview, 1983.

15. Robert Wahls, "Cheers for the Designer!," *New York Sunday News*, 25 January 1976, NYPL Clipping Folder.

16. T. E. Kalem, "The Theatre," *Time*, 26 January 1976, p. 46.

17. Prince interview, 1983.

18. "Pacific Overtures," *Theatre Crafts*, January-February 1976, p. 58, NYPL Clipping Folder.

19. "Japan via Florence," *Women's Wear Daily*, 9 January 1976, p. 15, NYPL Clipping Folder.

20. Stephen Sondheim, "The Musical Theatre: A Talk by Stephen Sondheim," *Dramatists Guild Quarterly* 15, no. 3 (Autumn 1978): 9.

21. R. S., "Pacific Overtures," *Cue*, 10 January 1976, p. 15, NYPL Clipping Folder.

22. Interview with Patricia Birch, New York, 15 June 1982.

23. Prince interview, 1983.

24. Weidman interview.

25. Prince interview, 1983.

26. Ibid.

27. Michael Feingold, "It's Some Musical But Noh Play," *Village Voice*, 26 January 1976, NYPL Clipping Folder.

28. Douglas Watt, " 'Pacific Overtures' Is a Pretty Bore," *New York Daily News*, 12 January 1976, p. 43.

29. Ibid.

30. Walter Kerr, "'Pacific Overtures' Is Neither East Nor West," *New York Times*, 18 January 1976, section 2, p. 2.

31. Hobe Morrison, "Pacific Overtures," *Variety*, 14 January 1976, p. 84.

32. Weidman interview.

33. Prince interview, 1983.

34. Clive Barnes, "'Pacific Overtures,' Musical about Japan," *New York Times*, 30 January 1976, p.39.

35. Craig Zadan, *Sondheim & Co.*, second ed. (New York: Harper & Row, 1986), p. 221.

36. Edwin Wilson, "An American Attempt at Kabuki Style," *Wall Street Journal,* 13 January 1976, NYPL Clipping Folder.

37. Martin Gottfried, "'Overtures'—A Remarkable Work of Theatre Art," *New York Post,* 12 January 1976, p. 18.

38. Howard Kissel, "Pacific Overtures," *Women's Wear Daily,* 12 January 1976, p. 28.

39. Interview with Harold Prince, *The Dick Cavett Show,* videotape, 19-20 February 1980, Public Broadcasting Service, Channel 13, New York.

40. Prince interview, 1983.

41. Weidman interview.

42. Martin Gottfried, *Broadway Musicals* (New York: Harry N. Abrams, 1979), p. 32.

43. Zadan, *Sondheim & Co.*, second ed., p. 226.

44. Ibid.

45. Ibid.

Chapter 14

1. Benedict Nightingale, "Mooney Tunes," *New Statesman,* 14 May 1976, p. 657.

2. Interview with Harold Prince, New York, 14 March 1983.

3. "Side by Side by Sondheim," *New York Post,* 23 April 1977, p. 17, NYPL Clipping Folder.

4. "Brit Cast in 'Sondheim' Revue Hears Alien Squawk from Equity," *Variety,* 2 March 1977, p. 71.

5. Alan Rich, "Side by Side," *New York,* 13 September 1976, p. 62, NYPL Clipping Folder.

6. "Side by Side," *New York Times,* 19 May 1977, p. C2, NYPL Clipping Folder.

7. Martin Gottfried, "Foggy Sondheim by British Cast," *New York Post,* 19 April 1977, NYPL Critics' Reviews, Vol. 38, p. 269.

8. Martin Gottfried, "Broadway Starts Singing Again," *New York Post,* 29 April 1977, p. 32.

9. Douglas Watt, "The Best of Sondheim," *New York Daily News,* 19 April 1977, NYPL Critics' Reviews, Vol. 38, p. 271.

10. Edwin Wilson, "A Workable Trio on Broadway," *Wall Street Journal,* 19 April 1977, NYPL Critics' Reviews, Vol. 38, p. 272.

11. Ibid.

12. Prince interview, 1983.

13. Ibid.

14. Ibid.

15. Ibid.

16. Robert Wahls, "Footlights," *New York Sunday News,* 25 September 1977, p. L9.

17. Prince interview, 1983.

18. Ibid.

19. Jonathan Takiff, "'Best Friends' Needs Help," *Philadelphia Daily News*, 12 October 1977, p. 28.

20. Harry Harris, "Shows Out of Town," *Variety*, 19 October 1977, p. 230.

21. Bob Sokolsky, "Ted Stuck with Bum Script," *Philadelphia Evening Bulletin*, 12 October 1977, p. 25.

22. Prince interview, 1983.

23. Richard Eder, "'Best Friends' Has Talking Oddities," *New York Times*, 26 October 1977, NYPL Critics' Reviews, Vol. 38, p. 161.

24. Martin Gottfried, "Good Knight, Sweet Prince, Some 'Friends' You've Got!," *New York Post*, 26 October 1977, NYPL Critics' Reviews, Vol. 38, p. 162.

25. Prince interview, 1983.

26. Ibid.

Chapter 15

1. Betty Comden and Adolph Green, "A New Head of Steam for the Old 'Twentieth Century,'" *New York Times*, 19 February 1978, section 2, p. 1.

2. Ibid.

3. Ibid., p. 6.

4. Ibid.

5. Ibid.

6. Interview with Harold Prince, New York, 14 March 1983.

7. Ibid.

8. Mel Gussow, "Broadway to Hear Sound of Musicals," *New York Times*, 11 January 1978, p. C15.

9. Comden and Green, "A New Head of Steam for the Old 'Twentieth Century,' " p. 6.

10. Patricia O'Hare, "Cullum: He Puts on a Good Act," *New York Daily News*, 24 February 1978, p. 5.

11. Comden and Green, "A New Head of Steam for the Old 'Twentieth Century,'" p. 6.

12. Prince interview, 1983.

13. Robert Berkvist, "Bound for Glory on the '20th Century,'" *New York Times*, 2 June 1978, p. C4.

14. Ibid.

15. Ibid.

16. Prince interview, 1983.

17. "Twentieth Century," *New York Post*, 25 April 1978, p. 10.

18. Prince interview, 1983.

19. Letitia Kent, "On Broadway, the Spectacle's the Thing," *New York Times*, 12 March 1978, p. Dl.

20. Richard Eder, "On the Twentieth Century," *New York Times*, 20 February 1978, NYPL Critics' Reviews, Vol. 39, p. 377.

21. Interview with Michael Billington, London, 19 March 1988.

22. Kent, "On Broadway, the Spectacle's the Thing."

23. F. Snyder, "Shows Out of Town (Boston)," *Variety,* 18 January 1978, p. 94.

24. Eder, "On the Twentieth Century."

25. Douglas Watt, "Twentieth Century Limited," *New York Daily News,* 20 February 1978, NYPL Critics' Reviews, Vol. 39, p. 376.

26. Howard Kissel, "On the Twentieth Century," *Women's Wear Daily,* 21 February 1978, NYPL Critics' Reviews, Vol. 39, p. 379.

27. *The South Bank Show,* Videotape, 1978, London Werkend TV.

28. "Review of Cast Album of 'On the 20th Century,'" *Variety,* 17 May 1978, p. 446.

29. Allan Wallach, "Harold Prince," *Newsday,* 3 February 1980, p. 25, NYPL Clipping Folder.

Chapter 16

1. Gerald McKnight, *Andrew Lloyd Webber: A Biography* (London: Granada, 1984), p. 149.

2. Ibid.

3. Ibid.

4. Ibid., p. 150.

5. Ibid., p. 165.

6. Ibid., p. 170.

7. Interview with Harold Prince, New York, 14 March 1983.

8. Ibid.

9. Ibid.

10. Robert Palmer, "Writing Musicals Attuned to Rock Era," *New York Times,* 10 February 1982, p. C21.

11. "Evita," *Hollywood Drama-Logue,* 2 January 1980, NYPL Clipping Folder.

12. Evita, record liner notes, MCA Records, 2-11007.

13. Stephanie Mardesich, "'Evita' in London," *Footlights,* December 1978, p. 28.

14. "Evita," *San Francisco Sunday Examiner and Chronicle,* p. 25, NYPL Clipping Folder.

15. John Corry, "Harold Prince: Craft Is the Key," *New York Times,* 20 January 1980, p. 6.

16. "Evita," *Hollywood Drama-Logue.*

17. "Evita," *San Francisco Sunday Examiner and Chronicle.*

18. Allan Wallach, "Harold Prince," *Newsday,* 3 February 1980, p. 19.

19. Ibid., p. 24.

20. Prince interview, 1983.

21. McKnight, *Andrew Lloyd Webber: A Biography,* p. 167.

22. Prince interview, 1983.

23. Derek Jewell, "Evita," [London] *Sunday Times,* 25 June 1978, NYPL Clipping Folder.

24. Ibid.

25. McKnight, *Andrew Lloyd Webber: A Biography,* p. 169.

26. Ibid.

27. Ibid., p. 176.

28. Ibid., p. 177.

29. Prince interview, 1983.

30. Ibid.

31. Ibid.

32. "Evita," *San Francisco Sunday Examiner and Chronicle.*

33. Interview with Kenneth W. Urmston, New York, 26 May 1982.

34. Prince interview, 1983.

35. Martin Gottfried, "Evita," *Cue,* 9 November 1979, p. 31.

36. Ibid., p. 32.

37. Ibid.

38. Mardesich, "'Evita' in London."

39. Gottfried, "Evita," **Cue.**

40. Walter Kerr, "'Evita,' A Musical Peron," *New York Times,* 26 September 1979, NYPL Critics' Reviews, Vol. 40, p. 149.

41. Ibid.

42. Edwin Wilson, "Dazzling Production of a Muddled Story," *Wall Street Journal,* 26 September 1979, NYPL Critics' Reviews, Vol. 40, p. 150.

43. Ibid.

44. Ibid.

45. Ibid.

46. Howard Kissel, "Evita," *Women's Wear Daily,* 26 September 1979, NYPL Critics' Reviews, Vol. 40, pp. 154-55.

47. Clive Barnes, "A Stunning Evita Seduces with Its Gloss," *New York Post,* 26 September 1979, NYPL Critics' Reviews, Vol. 40, p. 154.

48. Kissel, "Evita."

49. Jack Kroll, "Evita in Soft Focus," *Newsweek,* 8 October 1979, NYPL Critics' Reviews, Vol. 40, p.152.

50. Wilson, "Dazzling Production of a Muddled Story."

51. Kissel, "Evita."

52. Prince interview, 1983.

53. Wallach, "Harold Prince," p. 25.

54. "Evita," *Washington Star,* 11 December 1975, NYPL Clipping Folder.

Chapter 17

1. Daniel Gerould, *Melodrama* (New York: New York Literary Forum, 1980), p. 47.

2. Ibid.

3. Ibid., p. 8.

4. Ibid., pp. 9-10.

5. Ibid., p. 5.

6. "Sondheim Takes a Stab at Grand Guignol," *New York Times*, 25 February 1979, p. D5.

7. Interview with Harold Prince, New York, 14 March 1983.

8. "Sondheim Takes a Stab at Grand Guignol."

9. Gerould, Melodrama, p. 6.

10. Ibid., p. 7.

11. Ibid.

12. Ibid.

13. "On Collaboration between Authors and Directors," *Dramatists Guild Quarterly* 16, no. 2 (Summer, 1979): 14-34.

14. Ibid., p. 19.

15. Ibid., p. 28.

16. Ibid., p. 23.

17. Ibid.

18. Mel Gussow, "Sweeney Todd," *New York Times*, I February 1979, p. C15.

19. "On Collaboration between Authors and Directors," p. 19.

20. Ibid., p. 20.

21. Ibid., p. 18.

22. Interview with Stephen Sondheim, 31 August 1988.

23. "On Collaboration between Authors and Directors," p. 14.

24. Ibid., p. 15.

25. Gerould, *Melodrama*, p. 11.

26. "On Collaboration between Authors and Directors," p. 24.

27. Ibid., p. 25.

28. Howard Kissel, "Theatre," *Women's Wear Daily*, 2 March 1979, p. 10.

29. "On Collaboration between Authors and Directors," p. 29.

30. Gussow, "Sweeney Todd," p. C15.

31. Ibid.

32. Craig Zadan, *Sondheim & Co.*, second ed. (New York: Harper & Row, 1986), p. 254.

33. Arnold Aronson, "The Adventures of Eugene Lee," *American Theatre* 1, no. 8 (December 1984): 5.

34. Ibid.

35. Rex Reed, "'Sweeney' Soars," *New York Sunday News*, 4 March 1979, p. L7.

36. Harold Clurman, theatre criticism class, Hunter College, New York, March 1979.

37. Jack Kroll, "The Blood Runs Cold," *Newsweek*, 12 March 1979, p. 104.

38. Prince interview, 1983.

39. Ibid.

40. Ibid.

41. "On Collaboration between Authors and Directors," p. 17.

42. Ibid., p. 18.

43. Ibid., p. 27.

44. Ibid.

45. Prince interview, 1983.

46. "On Collaboration between Authors and Directors," p. 18.

47. Ibid., p. 19.

48. Kissel, "Theatre."

49. Edwin Wilson, "Sondheim Writes a Musical to Talk About," *Wall Street Journal*, 6 March 1979, p. 21.

50. Ibid.

51. Richard Eder, "Introducing 'Sweeney Todd,'" *New York Times*, 2 March 1979, p. C3.

52. Ibid.

53. Prince interview, 1983.

54. Michael Feingold, "Sweeney Todd," *Village Voice*, 12 March 1979, p. 85.

55. Julius Novick, "Sweeney Todd," *Village Voice*, 12 March 1979, p. 85.

56. Kroll, "The Blood Runs Cold."

57. Ibid.

58. Ibid.

59. Gussow, "Sweeney Todd."

60. John Simon, "A Little Knife Music," *New York*, 19 March 1979, p. 74.

61. Ibid.

62. Interview with Harold Prince, *The Dick Cavett Show*, videotape, 19-20 February 1980, Public Broadcasting Service, Channel 13, New York.

63. Interview with Michael Billington, London, 19 March 1988.

64. Prince interview, 1983.

65. Interview with Stephen Sondheim, New York, 20 July 1984.

66. Bernard Holland, "A Broadway Hit at City Opera," *New York Times*, 7 October 1984, p. 21.

Chapter 18

1. Judy Klemesrud, "Prince Wrestles with a New Show," *New York Times*, 15 November 1981, p. D5.

2. Ibid.

3. Ibid.

4. "Prince Gets 10% of 'Merrily' Net; Co-Producing with Marble Arch," *Variety*, 15 April 1981, p. 85.

5. Klemesrud, "Prince Wrestles with a New Show."

6. Ibid.

7. Interview with Lonny Price, New York, 18 February 1982.

8. Klemesrud, "Prince Wrestles with a New Show."

9. Carol Lawson, "Broadway," *New York Times,* 7 November 1980, p. C2.

10. John Corry, "Sondheim and Prince Team Up Again 'Merrily,'" *New York Times,* 3 September 1981, p. C17.

11. Ibid.

12. Ibid.

13. Price interview.

14. Linda Winer, " 'Merrily' Comes Tardily," *New York Daily News,* 13 November 1981, p. 3.

15. Ibid.

16. Ibid.

17. Price interview.

18. Ibid.

19. Ibid.

20. Ibid.

21. Ibid.

22. Klemesrud, "Prince Wrestles with a New Show."

23. Interview with Harold Prince, New York, 14 March 1983.

24. Stephen Holden, "Wit and Melody Enliven Two Musicals," *New York Times,* 11 April 1982, p. D25.

25. *Merrily We Roll Along,* record liner notes, composer's note.

26. Interview with Stephen Sondheim, New York, 20 July 1984.

27. Klemesrud, "Prince Wrestles with a New Show."

28. Ibid.

29. Price interview.

30. Ibid.

31. Frank Rich, "A New Sondheim 'Merrily We Roll Along,'" *New York Times,* 17 November 1981, p. 87.

32. Ibid.

33. Ibid.

34. John Simon, "Save Me from the Waltz," New York, 30 November 1981, p. 87.

35. Ibid.

36. Ibid.

37. T. E. Kalem, "Rue Tristesse," *Time,* 30 November 1981, p. 90.

38. Ibid.

39. Ibid.

40. Ibid.

41. Douglas Watt, " 'Merrily' Hits Every Bump on the Road," *New York Daily News,* 17 November 1981, p. 45.

42. Clive Barnes, " 'Rolling Along' Quite Nicely, Thank You," *New York Post,* 17 November 1981, p. 22R.

43. Ibid.

44. Ibid.

45. Prince interview.

46. Sondheim interview.

47. Interview with Lee Adams, New York, 8 March 1984.

48. Klemesrud, "Prince Wrestles with a New Show."

49. Hal Hinson, "Director Hal Prince Builds a Musical 'Doll's Life,'" *Los Angeles Herald Examiner,* 10 June 1982, p. Bl.

50. Ibid., p. B6.

51. Ibid.

52. Jeremy Gerard, "Hal Prince and Poetry of Abstraction," *Los Angeles Times,* 13 June 1982, p. 50.

53. Ibid.

54. Jeremy Gerard, "Will Ibsen's 'Doll' Come to Life on the Musical Stage?," *New York Times,* 19 September 1982, p. 8H.

55. Ibid.

56. Ibid.

57. Prince interview, 1983.

58. Gerard, "Will Ibsen's 'Doll' Come to Life on the Musical Stage?," p. 30H.

59. Ibid.

60. Ibid.

61. Michiko Kakutani, "Why a $4 Million Musical Lasted Only Four Days," *New York Times,* 27 September 1982, p. C11.

62. Eleanor Blau, "Prince Stars Unknown in Musical 'A Doll's Life,' " *New York Times,* 23 February 1982, p. C9.

63. Hinson, "Director Hal Prince Builds a Musical 'Doll's Life,'" p. B6.

64. Prince interview, 1983.

65. Hinson, "Director Hal Prince Builds a Musical 'Doll's Life,'" p. Bl.

66. Gerard, "Hal Prince and Poetry of Abstraction."

67. Ibid.

68. Ibid.

69. Ibid.

70. Ibid.

71. Gerard, "Will Ibsen's 'Doll' Come to Life on the Musical Stage?," p. 30H.

72. Ibid.

73. Dan Sullivan, " 'A Doll's Life': In This Case, It's Not All Bliss," *Los Angeles Times,* 17 June 1982, part Vl, p. 9.

74. Ibid.

75. Rick Talcove, "'A Doll's Life' Makes a Dead Musical," *Los Angeles Daily News,* 17 June 1982, section V, p. 4.

76. Ibid., section V, p. 1.

77. Bill Edwards, "A Doll's Life," *Daily Variety,* 17 June 1982, NYPL Clipping Folder.

78. Dan Sullivan, " 'A Doll's Life' Changes for the Better," *Los Angeles Times,* 18 July 1982, p. 51.

79. Kakutani, "Why a $4 Million Musical Lasted Only Four Days."

80. Ibid.

81. Frank Rich, "A Doll's Life," *New York Times,* 24 September 1982, NYPL Clipping Folder.

82. Douglas Watt, "'A Doll's' Lifelessness," *New York Daily News,* 24 September 1982, p. 3.

83. Clive Barnes, "Paper 'Doll's Life' Doesn't Cut It," *New York Post,* 24 September 1982, p. 110.

84. John Simon, "The Door Story," New York, 4 October 1982, p. 91.

85. Ibid.

86. Kakutani, "Why a $4 Million Musical Lasted Only Four Days."

87. Prince interview, 1983.

88. Kakutani, "Why a $4 Million Musical Lasted Only Four Days."

89. "Beverly Sills Interviews Harold Prince," videotape, 21 November 1979, Public Broadcasting Service, Channel 13, New York.

90. Prince interview, 1983.

91. Ibid.

92. Phil Cornell, "Passive 'Play Memory' Is Damaged by What It Leaves Out," [Princeton] *Courier-News,* 15 October 1983, p. B7.

93. Ibid.

94. Mel Gussow, "'Play Memory' Mines a Family Album," *New York Times,* 22 October 1983, p. 9.

95. Frank Rich, "Play Memory," *New York Times,* 27 April 1984, p. C3.

96. Ibid.

97. Carol Lawson, "Broadway," *New York Times,* 9 March 1984, p. C2.

98. Don Shewey, "Arthur Kopit: A Life on Broadway," *New York Times,* 29 April 1984, magazine section, p. 88.

99. Frank Rich, "New Kopit Play," *New York Times,* 7 May 1984, p. C15.

100. Frank Rich, "'Diamonds,' A Revue about Baseball," *New York Times,* 17 December 1984, p. C12.

101. Ibid.

102. Clive Barnes, "And It's 1, 2, 3, and You're Out—," *New York Post,* 17 December 1984, p. 61.

103. Douglas Watt, "Holy Cow! A Baseball Show That Scores," *New York Daily News,* 17 December 1984, p. 45.

104. Interview with Harold Prince, New York, 8 June 1988.

105. Jack Kroll, "A Bump for Every Grind," *Newsweek,* 29 April 1985, p. 65.

106. Prince interview, 1988.

107. *New York Times,* 14 April 1985, p. 6.

108. Kroll, "A Bump for Every Grind."

109. Interview with Harold Prince, New York photo session, 20 January 1985.

110. Kroll, "A Bump for Every Grind."

111. Ibid.

112. Douglas Watt, "A Grinding Halt," *New York Daily News,* 17 April 1985, p. 47.

113. Ibid.

114. Prince interview, June 1988.

115. Prince interview, June 1988.

116. Ibid.

117. William A. Henry III, "Where Are the Hit Musicals?," *Time,* 29 April 1985, p. 87.

118. Clive Barnes, "Too Many Bumps Spoil the Grind," *New York Post,* 17 April 1985, p. 85.

119. Ibid.

120. Ibid.

121. Frank Rich, " 'Grind' from Harold Prince," *New York Times,* 17 April 1985, p. C20.

122. Ibid.

123. Ibid.

124. Prince interview, June 1988.

125. Prince photo session interview, 1985.

126. Jeremy Gerard, "Prince Is Back on Broadway," *New York Times,* 1 October 1987, p. C21.

127. Prince interview, June 1988.

128. Joseph C. Koenenn, "Hal Prince's Triple Threat," New York *Newsday,* 30 August 1987, p. II/3.

129. Ibid.

130. Ibid., p. II/15.

131. Prince interview, June 1988.

132. Ibid.

133. Gerard, "Prince Is Back on Broadway."

134. Sylviane Gold, "Harold Prince, Triple Crown," *Elle,* October 1987, p. 162.

135. Ibid.

136. Kathy O' Steen, review of *Roza, Daily Variety,* 14 June 1987.

137. Tom Jacobs, review of *Roza, Los Angeles Daily News,* 14 June 1987.

138. Howard Kissel, "Not Worthy of a Prince," *New York Daily News,* 2 October 1987, NYPL Clipping Folder.

139. Clive Barnes, "'Roza' Role of a Lifetime," *New York Post,* 2 October 1987, NYPL Clipping Folder.

140. Ibid.

141. Kissel, "Not Worthy of a Prince."

142. Joel Siegel, review of *Roza,* WABC-TV News, Channel 7, New York, I October 1987.

143. Interview with Bob Gunton, New York, 6 June 1988.

144. Ibid.

145. Ibid.

146. Ibid.

147. Ibid.

148. Prince interview, June 1988.

Chapter 19

1. Interview with Harold Prince, New York, 8 June 1988.

2. Ibid.

3. Ibid.

4. Ibid.

5. Ibid.

6. Clive Barnes, "Grey Eclipses," *New York Post,* 23 October 1987, NYPL Clipping Folder.

7. Howard Kissel, "Rootin' Teuton," *New York Daily News,* 23 October 1987, NYPL Clipping Folder.

8. Frank Rich, " 'Cabaret' and Joel Grey Return," *New York Times,* 23 October 1987.

9. Kissel, "Rootin' Teuton."

10. Interview with Werner Klemperer, 7 July 1988.

Chapter 20

1. Cameron Mackintosh, "The Phantom's Trail," *The Phantom of the Opera* souvenir program, January 1988.

2. Interview with Harold Prince, New York, 8 June 1988.

3. Ibid.

4. Interview with Michael Billington, London, 19 March 1988.

5. "Recreating the Phantom," *The Phantom ofthe Opera* souvenir program, January 1988.

6. Ibid.

7. Ibid.

8. Ibid.

9. Jack Kroll, "The 'Phantom' Hits Broadway," *Newsweek,* 8 February 1988, p. 70.

10. Benedict Nightingale, "Conjuring Up an Eerie World for the Phantom," *New York Times,* 24 January 1988, section 2, p. 6.

11. Interview with Michael Crawford, New York, 5 June 1988.

12. Prince interview, June 1988.

13. Nightingale, "Conjuring Up an Eerie World for the Phantom," p. 1.

14. Billington interview.

15. Mackintosh, "The Phantom's Trail."

16. Nightingale, "Conjuring Up an Eerie World for the Phantom."

17. Ibid.

18. Ibid.

19. Ibid.

20. Ibid.

21. Ibid.

22. Ibid.

23. Ibid.

24. Ibid.

25. Robert Sandla, "On Her Toes: Gillian Lynne," *Theatre Week*, 1-7 February 1988, p.32.

26. Interview with Judy Kaye, New York, 23 June 1988.

27. Prince interview, June 1988.

28. Crawford interview.

29. Ibid.

30. Ibid.

31. "Entrance Lines," *Theatre Week*, 1-7 February 1988, p. 2.

32. *New York Times*, 14 October 1986, p. C13.

33. Crawford interview.

34. Jack Kroll, "The 'Phantom' Hits Broadway."

35. Ibid.

36. Mel Gussow, "The Phantom's Many Faces over the Years," *New York Times*, 3 January 1988.

37. Frank Rich, "Phantom of the Opera," *New York Times*, 27 January 1988, p. C19.

38. Ibid.

39. Ibid.

40. John Simon, "What Price Majesty?," *New York*, 8 February 1988, p. 89.

41. Ibid.

42. Clive Barnes, "Phabulous Phantom," *New York Post*, 27 January 1988, p. 28.

43. Ibid.

44. Ibid.

45. Kaye interview.

46. Barnes, "Phabulous Phantom."

47. Ibid.

48. Howard Kissel, "A Grand 'Opera,'" *New York Daily News*, 27 January 1988, p. 33.

49. Howard Kissel, "Curtain Calls," *New York Daily News*, S June 1988, p. 14.

50. Antoinette Perry (American Theatre Wing) Awards Ceremony, Uris Theatre, New York, 5 June 1988.

Chapter 21

1. Interview with Fred Ebb, New York, 14 October 1991.

2. Richard Seff, "This Kiss Could Be the Start of Something Big," *TheaterWeek*, 21 May 1990, p. 18.

3. Interview with Harold Prince, New York, 10 September 1991.

4. Ibid.

5. Ibid.

6. John Harris, "Will the Critics Kill *Kiss of the Spider Woman?*" *TheaterWeek*, 11 June 1990, p. 5.

7. Prince interview, 1991.

8. Harris, "Will the Critics Kill *Kiss of the Spider Woman?*" p. 5.

9. Ibid., p. 5.

10. Richard Hummler, "Times Spurns 'No Review' Policy of New Musicals," *Variety*, 30 May 1990, p. 61.

11. Ibid., p. 61; p. 65.

12. Harris, "Will the Critics Kill *Kiss of the Spider Woman?*" p. 5.

13. Ibid.

14. Ibid.

15. Frank Rich, "In a Jail Cell, 2 Men and a Movie Musical," *New York Times*, 1 June 1990, pp. B1–2.

16. Ibid.

17. Ibid.

18. Ibid.

19. Ibid.

20. Ibid.

21. Ibid.

22. Ibid.

23. Ibid.

24. Ibid.

25. Ibid.

26. Ibid.

27. Prince interview, 1991.

28. Harris, "Will the Critics Kill *Kiss of the Spider Woman?*" p. 5.

29. Ebb interview, 1991.

30. Clive Barnes, *New York Post*, 31 May 1990.

31. Don Nelson, *Daily News*, 1 June 1991.

32. Prince interview, 1991.

33. Ibid.

34. Mervyn Rothstein, "New Musicals Project Closes Down," *New York Times*, 31 July 1990, p. C 11.

35. Ibid.

36. Ibid.

37. Prince interview, 1991.

38. Glenn Collins, "Harold Prince Bound for Off Off Broadway, and Happy About It," *New York Times*, 13 February 1992, p. C 21.

39. Ibid.

40. Frank Rich, "Evoking the Youth of Sean O'Casey in Dublin," *New York Times*, 17 February 1992, p. C 13.

41. Ibid.

42. Ibid.

43. Ibid.

44. Ibid.

45. Ibid.

46. Edith Oliver, "Dubliners," *The New Yorker*, 24 February 1992, p. 82.

47. Ibid.

Chapter 22

1. Garth Drabinsky, with Marq de Villiers, *Closer to the Sun* (Toronto, Ontario: McClelland & Stewart, Inc., 1995), p. 388.

2. Ibid., p. 439.

3. Ibid., p. 449.

4. Interview with Harold Prince, New York, 1995.

5. Ibid.

6. Don Nelson, *Daily News*, 2 May 1993, p. 9.

7. Interview with Chita Rivera [faxed], 1 October 1995 .

8. Ibid.

9. Ibid.

10. Ibid.

11. Andrew Billen, *London Observer*, 11 October 1992, NYPL Clipping File.

12. Don Nelson, *Daily News*, 2 May 1993, p. 9.

13. Ibid.

14. Ibid.

15. Karen Murray, *Variety*, 22 June 1992, p. 50.

16. Garth Drabinsky, *Closer to the Sun*, p. 458.

17. Ibid., p. 459.

18. Ibid., pp. 459–60.

19. Interview with Dennis Kucherawy, New York City, 15 December 1995.

20. Michael Coveney, *London Observer*, NYPL Clipping File.

21. William Henry III, *Time*, 20 November 1992, NYPL Clipping File.

22. Sheridan Morley, *International Herald Tribune*, 28 October 1992.

23. Frank Rich, *New York Times*, 4 May 1993, NYPL Clipping File.

24. Ibid.
25. Ibid.
26. Ibid.
27. Ibid.
28. Edwin Wilson, *Wall Street Journal,* 5 May 1993, p. A 20.
29. Edith Oliver, "Escape Artists," *The New Yorker,* 24 May 1993, NYPL Clipping File.
30. Prince interview, 1995.
31. Garth Drabinsky, *Closer to the Sun,* pp. 465–66.
32. Prince interview, 1995.
33. Garth Drabinsky, *Closer to the Sun,* p. 467.
34. Prince interview, 1995.
35. Ibid.

Chapter 23

1. Harold Prince, "Director's Notes," *Playbill,* 1994, p. 35.
2. Garth Drabinsky, with Marq de Villiers, *Closer to the Sun* (Toronto, Ontario: McClelland & Stewart, Inc., 1995), p. 443.
3. Ibid., p. 444.
4. Ibid.
5. Ibid., p. 445
6. Ibid.
7. Prince interview, May 1995.
8. Ibid.
9. Barbara Eisenberg, "Prince at the Helm," *Los Angeles Times,* 9 October 1994, p. 75.
10. Prince interview, 1995.
11. Harold Prince, "Director's Notes," *Show Boat Souvenir Program,* 1994, p. 8.
12. Ibid.
13. Prince interview, 1995.
14. Ibid.
15. Barbara Eisenberg, "Prince at the Helm," p. 75.
16. Ibid.
17. Prince interview, 1995.
18. Anna Kisselgoff, "Broadway Dance: At Play with the Past," *New York Times,* 20 January 1995, p. C 5.
19. Eugene Lee, "Production Design," *Show Boat Souvenir Program,* 1994, p. 17.
20. David Richards, "Classic Musical with a Change in Focus," *New York Times,* 3 October 1994, NYPL Clipping File.
21. Robert Morse, quoted by Harold Prince, Prince interview, 1995.
22. Prince interview, 1995.
23. Telephone interview with John McMartin, New York, 20 October 1995.
24. Ibid.

25. Joanne Kaufman, "Another Opening, But Not Just Another 'Show Boat,' " *Wall Street Journal*, 29 September 1994, p. A 10.

26. McMartin interview, 1995.

27. Prince interview, 1995.

28. Jeremy Gerard, " 'Show Boat' Still Has Steam," *Variety*, 1 November 1994, NYPL Clipping File.

29. Prince interview, 1995.

30. Interview with Dennis Kucherawy, New York, 14 December 1995.

31. Prince interview, 1995.

32. Henry Louis Gates, Jr., quoted in Garth Drabinsky, *Closer to the Sun*, p. 479.

33. Garth Drabinsky, *Closer to the Sun*, p. 482.

34. John Lahr, quoted in Garth Drabinsky, *Closer to the Sun*, p. 483.

35. Jeremy Gerard, " 'Show Boat' Still Has Steam," NYPL Clipping File.

36. Frank Rich, "The Seminal American Musical Is Rebuilt from the Ground Up," *New York Times*, 20 October 1993, p. C 15.

37. Ibid.

38. Ibid.

39. Bruce Weber, New York Times, 1 November 1994, p. C 13.

40. Michael Walsh, "Just Keeps Rollin' Along," Time, 10 October 1994, p. 80.

41. Ibid.

42. Jack Kroll, " 'Show Boat'—It's Still Rolling Along," Newsweek, 10 October 1994, p. 77.

43. Donald Lyons, "Harold Prince Reinvents a '20's Classic," *Wall Street Journal*, 10 May 1994, NYPL Clipping File.

44. Clive Barnes, "Show-Stopper," *New York Post*, 3 October 1994, NYPL Clipping File.

45. David Richards, "Classic Musical with a Change in Focus," *New York Times*, 3 October 1994, NYPL Clipping File.

46. Prince interview, 1995.

47. Ibid.

48. Prince interview, 1991.

49. Prince interview, 1995.

50. Vincent Canby, "Out of Chaos a Show Is (Sometimes) Born," *New York Times*, 1 January 1995, p. H 5.

51. John Lahr, *The New Yorker*, 9 January 1995, p. 87.

52. William Harris, *New York Times*, 18 December 1994, p. 5.

53. Ibid.

54. Ibid.

55. Vincent Canby, "Out of Chaos a Show Is (Sometimes), Born," p. H 5.

56. John Lahr, *The New Yorker*, p. 87.

57. Prince interview, 1995.

58. Prince interview, New York City, June 1999.

Chapter 24

1. Alfred Uhry, interview with editors of the *Lincoln Center Theatre Review* (Fall 1998) p. 21.

2. Harold Prince, quoted in Jerry Tallmer, "Is There a Parade in Town?" *Playbill,* Vol. 98, No. 11 (November 1998), p. 12.

3. Harold Prince, interview with Andre Bishop, Artistic Director of the Lincoln Center Theatre, *Lincoln Center Theatre Review* (Fall 1998), p. 8.

4. Tallmer, "Is There a Parade in Town?" p. 12.

5. *Lincoln Center Theatre Review,* Fall 1998.

6. Interview with Harold Prince, New York, 7 June 1999.

7. Ben Brantley, "Martyr's Requiem Invokes Justice," *New York Times,* 18 December 1998, p. E1.

8. Ibid., p. E32.

9. Ibid.

10. David Patrick Stearns, "Parade Pointedly in Step with Today," *USA Today,* 18 December 1998, p. 4E.

11. Ibid.

12. Ibid.

13. Ibid.

14. Fintan O'Toole, "A Parade of Humanity," *New York Daily News,* 18 December 1998, p. 75.

15. Donald Lyons, "Carver, Carmello Lead a Wrenching Musical Parade," *New York Post,* 18 December 1998, p. 58.

16. Ibid.

17. John Simon, "Trial and Eros, Parade Is a Somber Show That Works," *New York Magazine,* 4 January 1999, NYPL Clipping File.

18. Ibid.

19. Ibid.

20. Ibid.

21. Ibid.

Epilogue

1. Interview with Stephen Sondheim, New York, 20 July 1984.

2. Interview with Lisa Aronson, New York, 6 June 1984.

3. Ibid.

4. Interview with Ruth Mitchell, New York, 7 March 1983.

5. Aronson interview, 1984.

6. Interview with Patricia Birch, New York, 15 June 1982.

7. Ibid.

8. Ibid.

9. Sondheim interview, 1984.

10. "Beverly Sills Interviews Harold Prince," videotape, 21 November 1979, Public Broadcasting Service, Channel 13, New York.

11. "A Conversation with Martin Gottfried," *Women's Wear Daily*, 17 April 1973, p. 7.

12. Louis Botto, "Prince and His *Follies*," *Look*, 18 May 1971, p. 38.

13. Thomas Buckley, "Prince vs. Prince," *New York Times*, 21 April 1963, p. 3.

14. Interview with John McMartin, New York, 10 June 1982.

15. Interview with Charlotte Moore, New York, 10 June 1982.

16. Buckley, "Prince vs. Prince."

17. John Corry, "Harold Prince: Craft Is the Key," *New York Times*, 20 January 1980.

18. Interview with Howard Haines, New York, 10 January 1982.

19. Interview with Harold Prince, New York, 14 March 1983.

20. Ibid.

21. "Beverly Sills Interviews Harold Prince."

22. Frank Rich, "What Ails Today's Musicals?," *New York Times*, 14 November 1982, section 2, pp. 1, 23.

23. Frank Rich, "Dreamgirls," *New York Times*, 21 December 1981, p. C11.

24. Ibid.

25. Ibid.

26. Rich, "What Ails Today's Musicals?"

27. Ibid.

28. Interview with Michael Billington, London, 19 March, 1988.

29. Prince interview, 1983.

30. Interview with Harold Prince, New York, 7 June 1999.

31. Prince interview, 10 September 1991.

32. Prince interview, June 1991.

33. Harold Prince statement, Harold Prince Exhibit, Lincoln Center Library of the Performing Arts, New York, April 1989.

34. Interview with Harold Prince, New York, 7 June 1999.

35. Ibid.

36. Harry Haun, "Can't Stop Lovin' That *Show Boat*," *Playbill*, Vol. 87, No. 5 (May 1987), pp. 10–14.

37. Ibid.

38. Prince interview, 1991.

39. Martin Gottfried, interview with Harold Prince, Metropolitan Museum of Art, Lecture Series, 3 May 1995.

40. Ibid.

41. Harold Prince, "Preferring the Truth, He Always Told It," *New York Times*, 12 February 1995, p. H8.

42. Stephanie Coen, "How to Make a Musical," *American Theatre* (January 1996), p. 27.

43. Ibid.

44. Prince interview, 1991.

45. Ibid.

BIBILIOGRAPHY

Print and Broadcast Reviews, Newspaper, Magazine and Journal Articles, Dissertations, Theses, Letters, Miscellaneous

(Note on abbreviations: NYPL Clipping Folder-article is from the Billy Rose Theatre Collection, New York Public Library at Lincoln Center; NYPL Critics' Reviews-article is from the New York Theatre Critics' Reviews, New York Public Library at Lincoln Center, by volume and page.)

Abbott, George. "A Call on Kuprin." NYPL Clipping Folder.

Aronson, Arnold. "The Adventures of Eugene Lee." *American Theatre* 1, no. 8 (December 1984): 4–9, 41.

Atkinson, Brooks. "Fiorello!" *New York Times*, 24 November 1959. NYPL Critics' Reviews, Vol. 20, p. 219.

___. "Theatre in Review." *New York Times*, 14 May 1954. NYPL Critics' Reviews, Vol. 15, p. 325.

___. "Theatre: The Jungles of the City." *New York Times*, 27 September 1957. NYPL Critics' Reviews, Vol. 18, p. 253.

___. "The Theatre: Singing Anna Christie." *New York Times*, 15 May 1957. NYPL Critics' Reviews, Vol. 18, p. 269.

Bahrenburg, Bruce. "The Sound of Sondheim." *Performing Arts: The Music Center Monthly* 5, no. 10 (October 1971): 33.

Barnes, Clive. "And It's 1, 2, 3, and You're Out." *New York Post*, 17 December 1984, p. 61.

___. " 'Company' Offers a Guide to New York's Marital Jungle." *New York Times*, 27 April 1970, p. 40.

___. " 'Follies' Couples, Years Later." *New York Times*, 5 April 1971, p. 49.

___. "Full Steam on 20th Century." *New York Post*, 20 February 1978. NYPL Critics' Reviews, Vol. 39, p. 380.

___. "Grey Eclipses." *New York Post*, 23 October 1987. NYPL Clipping Folder.

___. Review of "Kiss of the Spider Woman." *New York Post*, 31 May 1990. NYPL Clipping Folder.

___. "A Little Night Music." *New York Times,* 26 February 1973. NYPL Critics' Reviews, Vol. 34, p. 349.

___. " 'Pacific Overtures,' Musical about Japan." *New York Times,* 30 January 1976, p. 39.

___. "Paper 'Doll's Life' Doesn't Cut It." *New York Post,* 24 September 1982, pp. 51, 110.

___. "Phabulous Phantom." *New York Post,* 27 January 1988, p. 28.

___. "Rolling Along Quite Nicely, Thank You." *New York Post,* 17 November 1981, p. 22R.

___. " 'Roza' Role of a Lifetime." *New York Post,* 2 October 1987. NYPL Clipping Folder.

___. "Show-Stopper." *New York Post,* 3 October 1994. NYPL Clipping Folder.

___. " 'Side by Side by Sondheim' Is a Dream." *New York Times,* 19 April 1977. NYPL Critics' Reviews, Vol. 38, p. 269.

___. "A Stunning 'Evita' Seduces with Its Gloss." *New York Post,* 26 September 1979. NYPL Critics' Reviews, Vol. 40, p. 154.

___. "Superb 'Candide.' " *New York Times,* 13 March 1974. NYPL Critics' Reviews, Vol. 35, p. 338.

___. "Too Many Bumps Spoil the Grind." *New York Post,* 17 April 1985, p. 85.

___. " 'Zorba' Is Here with Music." *New York Times,* 18 November 1968. NYPL Critics' Reviews, Vol. 29, p. 174.

Bender, William. "Musical of Gentle Love and Heady Perfume." *New York Herald Tribune,* 21 April 1963. NYPL Clipping Folder.

Bennetts, Leslie. "Here Comes the Musical 'La Cage.' " *New York Times,* 21 August 1983, section 2, p. 4.

Berkvist, Robert. "Bound for Glory on the '20th Century.' " *New York Times,* 2 June 1978, p. C4.

___. " 'Candide,' or a Very Moving Story." *New York Times,* 24 February 1974, section 2, p. 1.

___. "Miss Johns Hits a High Note." *New York Times,* 11 March 1973, p. D3.

Billen, Andrew. Review of "Kiss of the Spider Woman." *London Observer,* 11 October 1992, NYPL Clipping Folder.

Bishop, Andre. "Interview with Harold Prince." *Lincoln Center Theatre Review* (Fall 1998), p. 8.

Blau, Eleanor. "Prince Stars Unknown in Musical 'A Doll's Life.' " *New York Times,* 23 February 1982, p. C9.

Bolton, Whitney. "Cabaret." *New York Morning Telegraph,* 22 November 1966. NYPL Clipping Folder.

___. "Closing of 'Zorba' Loss to Broadway." *New York Morning Telegraph,* 6 August 1969. NYPL Clipping Folder.

___. " 'Superman' Is Camp and Mostly WHAM!" *New York Morning Telegraph,* 31 March 1966. NYPL Clipping Folder.

Bone, Harold. "Flora, the Red Menace." *Variety,* 6 April 1965. NYPL Clipping Folder.

___. "She Loves Me." *Variety,* 20 March 1963. NYPL Clipping Folder.

___. "Shows Out of Town." *Variety,* 21 October 1959. NYPL Clipping Folder.

___. "Shows Out of Town: 'Tenderloin.' " *Variety,* 14 September 1960. NYPL Clipping Folder.

___. "Shows Out of Town." *Variety,* 3 April 1962, p. 86.

___. "Shows Out of Town." *Variety,* 9 October 1968, p. 67.

___. "Take Her, She's Mine." *Variety,* 29 November 1961. NYPL Clipping Folder.

Botto, Louis. " 'Company,' Broadway's Oddest Love/Hate Hit." *Look,* 8 September 1970. NYPL Clipping Folder.

___. "Prince and His Follies." *Look,* 18 May 1971, p. 38.

Brantley, Ben. "Martyr's Requiem Invokes Justice." *New York Times,* 18 December 1998, p. E1.

"Brit. Cast in 'Sondheim' Revue Hears Alien Squawk from Equity." *Variety,* 2 March 1977, p. 71.

"Broadway." *New York Times,* 3 June 1977, p. C2.

Buckley, Peter. "Prince of the Musical Theatre." *United Mainliner,* February 1982, pp. 43–71.

Buckley, Thomas. "Prince vs. Prince." *New York Times,* 21 April 1963, pp. 1, 3.

Bunce, Alan N. "Cabaret." *Christian Science Monitor,* 28 November 1966, p. 8.

"A Call on Kuprin." *Theatre Arts,* July 1961. NYPL Clipping Folder.

Canby, Vincent. "Out of Chaos a Show Is (Sometimes) Born." *New York Times,* 1 January 1995, p. H5.

___. "Screen: A Comic Parable." *New York Times,* 23 July 1970, p. 25.

Chapman, John. " 'Baker Street' Is a Captivating Musical about Sherlock Holmes." *New York Daily News,* 17 February 1965. NYPL Critics' Reviews, Vol. 26, p. 375.

___. "Bernardi, Karnilova Are Superb in a Great Musical Play, 'Zorba.' " *New York Daily News,* 18 November 1968. NYPL Critics' Reviews, Vol. 29, p. 175.

___. "Cabaret." *New York Daily News,* 21 November 1966, p. 64.

___. "Company." *New York Daily News,* 24 May 1970. NYPL Critics' Reviews, Vol. 31, p. 263.

___. " 'Family Affair' Bright and Funny." *New York Daily News,* 29 January 1962. NYPL Clipping Folder.

___. " 'Fiddler on the Roof Great Musical; Zero Mostel Heads Superb Cast." *New York Daily News,* 23 September 1964. NYPL Critics' Reviews, Vol. 25, p. 217.

___. "Fiorello!" *New York Daily News,* 24 November 1959. NYPL Critics' Reviews, Vol. 20, p. 220.

___. "Jean Anouilh, Donald Pleasence Make 'Poor Bitos' Good Theatre." *New York Daily News,* 16 November 1964. NYPL Critics' Reviews, Vol. 25, p. 147.

___. "Liza Minnelli Puts Needed Zing in Songs of 'Flora, Red Menace.' " *New York Daily News,* 12 May 1965. NYPL Critics' Reviews, Vol. 26, p. 330.

___. "New Girl in Town." *New York Daily News,* 15 May 1957. NYPL Critics' Reviews, Vol. 18, p. 268.

___. "She Loves Me." *New York Daily News,* 24 April 1963. NYPL Clipping Folder.

___. " 'Take Her, She's Mine' Presents Art Carney as a Typical Father." *New York Daily News,* 22 December 1961. NYPL Critics' Reviews, Vol. 22, p. 149.

___. "Tenderloin." *New York Daily News,* 18 October 1960. NYPL Critics' Reviews, Vol. 21, p. 208.

___. " 'West Side Story': A Splendid and Super-modern Musical Drama." *New York Daily News,* 27 September 1957. NYPL Critics' Reviews, Vol. 18, p. 252.

___. *New York Daily News,* 6 May 1955. NYPL Clipping Folder.

Clark, Herbert Whittaker. "Show-business." *Toronto Globe and Mail,* May 1957. NYPL Clipping Folder.

Clurman, Harold. "Theatre." *Nation,* 18 April 1971. NYPL Clipping Folder.

___. Theatre criticism class. Hunter College, New York, March 1979.

Coe, Richard L. "A Thin Night in Old Rome." *Washington Post*, 11 April 1962. NYPL Clipping Folder.

Coen, Stephanie, "How to Make a Musical." *American Theatre* (January 1996), p. 27.

Coleman, Robert. " 'Fiorello': A Smashing Winner." *New York Daily Mirror*, 24 November 1959. NYPL Critics' Reviews, Vol. 20, p. 222.

___. " 'West Side Story': A Sensational Hit!" *New York Daily Mirror*, 27 September 1957. NYPL Critics' Reviews, Vol. 18, p. 254.

Collins, Glenn. "Harold Prince Bound for Off Off Broadway, And Happy About It." *New York Times*, 13 February 1992, p. C21.

Collins, William B. "Sondheim's Magic of Night Music." *Philadelphia Inquirer*, 7 March 1974, p. 1H.

Comden, Betty. "How to Collaborate in a Collaborative Art." *Dramatists Guild Quarterly* 15, no. 4 (Winter 1979): 6–8.

Comden, Betty, and Green, Adolph. "A New Head of Steam for the Old 'Twentieth Century.' " *New York Times*, 19 February 1978, section 2, pp. 1, 6.

"A Conversation with Martin Gottfried." *Women's Wear Daily*, 17 April 1973, p. 7.

Cooke, Richard P. "Broadway Perks Up." *Wall Street Journal*, 18 November 1966. NYPL Clipping Folder.

___. "Cabaret." *Wall Street Journal*, 22 November 1966. NYPL Clipping Folder.

___. "Superior Confection." *Wall Street Journal*, 25 April 1963. NYPL Clipping Folder.

Cornell, Phil. "Passive 'Play Memory' Is Damaged by What It Leaves Out." *Princeton Courier-News*, 15 October 1983, p. B7.

Corry, John. "Harold Prince: Craft Is the Key." *New York Times*, 20 January 1980, pp. 1, 6.

___. "Sondheim and Prince Team Up Again 'Merrily.' " *New York Times*, 3 September 1981, p. C17.

Coveney, Michael. Review of "Kiss of the Spider Woman." *London Observer*. NYPL Clipping Folder.

Cushman, Robert. "Her Majesty's Company." *Plays and Players* 19, no. 6 (March 1972): 34.

Davidson, Ann M. "A Swim in the Sea." *Winter Park (Florida) Herald*, 8 May 1958, p. 2.

Drake, Sylvie. " 'Doll's Life': Questioning the Answers." *Los Angeles Times*, 18 July 1982, p. 51.

Eder, Richard. " 'Best Friends' Has Talking Oddities." *New York Times*, 26 October 1977. NYPL Critics' Reviews, Vol. 38, p. 161.

___. "Introducing 'Sweeney Todd.' " *New York Times*, 2 March 1979, p. C3.

___. "On the Twentieth Century." *New York Times*, 20 February 1978. NYPL Critics' Reviews, Vol. 39, p. 377.

Edwards, Bill. "A Doll's House." *Daily Variety*, 17 June 1982. NYPL Clipping Folder.

Eisenberg, Barbara. "Prince at the Helm." *Los Angeles Times*, 9 October 1994, p. 75.

"Entrance Lines." *Theatre Week*, 1-7 February 1988, p. 2.

Ericson, Raymond. "Rare Bernstein." *New York Times*, 14 May 1975, p. 34.

Evan, Ronald. "Cover Story." *Toronto Telegram*, April 1965, p. 22. NYPL Clipping Folder.

"Evita." *Hollywood Drama-Logue*, 2 January 1980. NYPL Clipping Folder.

"Evita." *San Francisco Sunday Examiner and Chronicle*, pp. 24–25. NYPL Clipping Folder.

"Evita." *Washington Star*, 11 December 1975. NYPL Clipping Folder.

Feingold, Michael. "It's Some Musical But Noh Play." *Village Voice*, 26 January 1976. NYPL Clipping Folder.

___. "Sweeney Todd." *Village Voice,* 12 March 1979, p. 85.

"Fiddler on the Roof." *Newsweek,* 26 July 1971, p. 68. NYPL Clipping Folder.

Flagler, J. M. "Cabaret." *Look,* November 1966, p. 72.

Flatley, Guy. "A Bio of Stephen Sondheim." *People,* 5 April 1976, p. 66.

"Flora, the Red Menace." *Dance Magazine,* July 1965, p. 23. NYPL Clipping Folder.

"Flora, the Red Menace." *Variety,* 3 February 1965. NYPL Clipping Folder.

"Flora Role Ended—But Her Melody Lingers On." *Diplomat,* September 1965, p. 6. NYPL Clipping Folder.

"Follies." *Variety,* 3 March 1971, p. 62. NYPL Clipping Folder.

Freedman, Samuel G. "After 50 Years, 'Porgy' Comes to the Met as a Certified Classic." *New York Times,* 3 February 1985, section 2, p. 1.

Freudenheim, Milt. " 'She Loves Me' Has Pair Excited." *Miami Herald-Chicago Newswire.* NYPL Clipping Folder.

F. R. J., "She Loves Me." *New Haven Journal Courier,* 19 March 1963. NYPL Clipping Folder.

Funke, Lewis. "A Happy Prince Heads Westward." *New York Times,* 10 April 1966. NYPL Clipping Folder.

___. *New York Times,* 6 May 1955. NYPL Clipping Folder.

"A Funny Thing Happened on the Way to the Forum." *New York Herald Tribune,* 10 May 1962. NYPL Clipping Folder.

Gaghan, Jerry. "Out of Town Review (Philadelphia)." *Variety,* 17 January 1962. NYPL Clipping Folder.

___. "She Loves Me." *Philadelphia Daily News,* 27 March 1963. NYPL Clipping Folder.

___. "Shows Out of Town." *Variety,* 23 February 1966. NYPL Clipping Folder.

___. " 'Superman' Lands for Stay at Shubert." *Philadelphia Daily News,* 16 February 1966, p. 32.

Gates, Gary Paul. "Broadway's Prince Charming." *Holiday,* April 1966, pp. 99–109.

Gaver, Jack. UPI "Newsfeature." NYPL Clipping Folder.

Gerard, Jeremy. "Calendar." *Los Angeles Times,* 13 June 1982, p. 50.

___. "Hal Prince and Poetry of Abstraction." *Los Angeles Times,* 13 June 1982, p. 50.

___. "Prince Is Back on Broadway." *New York Times,* 10 October 1987, p. C21.

___. " 'Show Boat' Still Has Steam." *Variety,* 1 November 1994. NYPL Clipping Folder.

___. "Will Ibsen's 'Doll' Come to Life on the Musical Stage?" *New York Times,* 19 September 1982, pp. 8H, 30H.

Gill, Brendan. "Casting Out Remorse." *New Yorker,* 10 April 1971, p. 67.

___. "The Theatre." *New Yorker,* 2 May 1970, p. 83.

___. "Zorba." *New Yorker,* 23 November 1968. NYPL Clipping Folder.

Giovannini, Joseph. "For Theatre Set Designers, All the Home's a Stage." *New York Times,* 24 February 1983, p. C6.

Glover, William. "Liza Minnelli Determined to Make It on Own." *Lawton Constitution,* 17 June 1965, p. 28.

Gold, Sylviane. "Harold Prince, Triple Crown." *Elle,* October 1977, p. 162.

Gottfried, Martin. "Broadway Starts Singing Again." *New York Post,* 29 April 1977, p. 32.

___. "Candide." *Women's Wear Daily,* 21 December 1973. NYPL Critics' Reviews, Vol. 34, p. 139.

___. " 'Candide' Moves to Broadway." *Women's Wear Daily,* 13 March 1974. NYPL Critics' Reviews, Vol. 35, p. 337.

___. "The Designing Director." *Cue,* 9 November 1979, p. 32.

___. "Evita." *Cue,* 9 November 1979, pp. 31–32.

___. "Flipping Over 'Follies.' " *New York Times,* 25 April 1971, section 2, p. 1.

___. "Foggy Sondheim by British Cast." *New York Post,* 19 April 1977. NYPL Critics' Reviews, Vol. 38, p. 269.

___. "Good Knight, Sweet Prince, Some 'Friends' You've Got!" *New York Post,* 26 October 1977. NYPL Critics' Reviews, Vol. 38, p. 162.

___. Interview with Harold Prince, Metropolitan Museum of Art, Lecture Series, 3 May 1995.

___. "A Little Night Music." *Women's Wear Daily,* 26 February 1973. NYPL Critics' Reviews, Vol. 34, p. 349.

___. " 'Overtures'—A Remarkable Work of Theater Art." *New York Post,* 12 January 1976, p. 18.

___. "She Loves Me." *Women's Wear Daily,* 24 April 1963. NYPL Clipping Folder.

___. "Theatre." *Women's Wear Daily,* 18 November 1968. NYPL Clipping Folder.

___. "Will Failure Spoil Harold Prince?" *New York Post,* 26 June 1976, pp. 2, 40.

[Griffith, Robert E.] "Robert E. Griffith, Obituary." *New York Herald Tribune,* 8 June 1961. NYPL Clipping Folder.

Grover, Stephen. "Behind the Scenes." *Wall Street Journal,* 7 February 1973, p. 19.

Guidry, Frederick H. " 'Red' Musical." *Christian Science Monitor,* 15 April 1965, p. 9. NYPL Clipping Folder.

Gussow, Mel. "Broadway to Hear Sound of Musicals." *New York Times,* 11 January 1978, p. C15.

___. "Candide." *New York Times,* 23 October 1975, p. 29.

___. " 'Company' Anew." *New York Times,* 29 July 1970. NYPL Clipping Folder.

___. "Harold Prince." *Newsweek,* 2 December 1968, p. 105.

___. "How 'Side by Side' Came to This Side." *New York Times,* 7 May 1977, p. 36.

___. "The Phantom's Many Faces Over the Years." *New York Times,* 31 January 1988. NYPL Clipping Folder.

___. " 'Play Memory' Mines a Family Album." *New York Times,* 22 October 1983, p. 9.

___. "Prince Lays Part of 'Candide' Deficit to Cost of 'Musicians We Don't Need.' " *New York Times,* 23 September 1976, p. 29.

___. "Prince Recalls the Evolution of 'Follies.' " *New York Times,* 9 April 1971. NYPL Clipping Folder.

___. "Sondheim Scores with 'Company.' " *New York Times,* 28 April 1970, p. 50.

___. "Sweeney Todd," *New York Times,* 1 February 1979, p. C15.

Harnick, Sheldon. "What Comes First in a Musical? The Libretto." In *Playwrights, Lyricists, Composers on Theatre,* pp. 38–51. Edited by Otis L. Guernsey, Jr. New York: Dodd, Mead, 1964.

Harris, John. "Will the Critics Kill 'Kiss of the Spider Woman'?" *TheaterWeek,* 11 June 1990, pp.5–6.

Harris, Leonard. " 'She Loves Me' Scribe Sticks His Neck Out." *New York World-Telegram and Sun,* 20 April 1963, p. 10.

Harris, William. [Article on "Petrified Prince."] *New York Times,* 18 December 1994, p. 5.

Haun, Harry. "Can't Stop Lovin' That Show Boat." *Playbill,* Vol. 87, no. 5 (May 1987), pp. 10–14.

___. " 'Kings': Fit for a Prince." *New York Daily News,* 2 February 1992, p. 9.

Henahan, Donal. "Bernstein's 'Candide' Is Back as a Winner." *New York Times*, 24 October 1982, section 2, p. H17.

Henry, William A. III. "The Return of Bernstein's 'Candide.' " *New York Times*, 20 July 1984, p. C3.

___. Review of "Kiss of the Spider Woman." *Time*, 20 November 1992. NYPL Clipping Folder.

___. "They Just Keep Rolling Along." *Time*, 2 September 1991, pp. 72–73.

___. "Where Are the Hit Musicals?" *Time*, 29 April 1985, p. 87.

Hewes, Henry. "She Loves Me." *Saturday Review*, 11 May 1963, p. 26. NYPL Clipping Folder.

___. "The Theater." *Saturday Review*, 7 December 1968, p. 36.

___. "The Theater." *Saturday Review*, 9 May 1970, p. 4.

___. "The Theater." *Saturday Review*, 1 May 1971, p. 16.

___. *Saturday Review*, June 1957, p. 22. NYPL Clipping Folder.

Hinson, Hal. "Director Hal Prince Builds a Musical 'Doll's Life.' " *Los Angeles Herald Examiner*, 10 June 1982, pp. B1, B6.

Hipp, Edward Sothern. "Cabaret." *Newark Evening News*, 21 November 1966. NYPL Clipping Folder.

___. "Grim Message Smothered in 'A Call on Kuprin.' " NYPL Clipping Folder.

___. "She Loves Me." *Newark Evening News*, 19 January 1964. NYPL Clipping Folder.

___. " 'She Loves Me' Darling Musical." *Newark Evening News*, 24 April 1963. NYPL Clipping Folder.

___. "Superman, Now a Musical Hero." *Newark Evening News*, 30 March 1966. NYPL Clipping Folder.

Hirsch, Samuel. " 'Company' All Glitter, Cleverness." *Boston Herald Traveler*, 25 March 1970, p. 21.

Hoffman, Leonard. "New York Play." *Hollywood Reporter*, 9 May 1962, p. 3.

Holden, Stephen. "Wit and Melody Enliven Two Musicals." *New York Times*, 11 April 1982, p. D25.

Holder, Geoffrey. "Candide." WNBC-TV News, 20 December 1973. NYPL Critics' Reviews, Vol. 34, p. 140.

Holland, Bernard. "A Broadway Hit at City Opera." *New York Times*, 7 October 1984, p. 21.

___. "First 'Candide' of Year by City Troupe." *New York Times*, 17 October 1983, p. C22.

Holmberg, Arthur. "His Plays Seek 'The Reality of the Mind.' " *New York Times*, 7 October 1984, section 2, p. 5.

Hughes, Elinor. "A Musical Adventure for Sherlock Holmes." *Boston Herald*, 19 December 1964. NYPL Clipping Folder.

___. " 'The Red Menace' Needs Some Work." *Boston Herald*, 18 April 1965, p. 18.

___. "Sherlock Holmes Set to Music with Elegance, Action and Fun." *Boston Herald*, 29 December 1964. NYPL Clipping Folder.

___. " 'Take Her, She's Mine' Winner with Carney." *Boston Herald*, 6 December 1961, p. 28. NYPL Clipping Folder.

___. "The Theatre: 'Tenderloin.' " *Boston Herald*, 21 September 1960. NYPL Clipping Folder.

Hummler, Richard. "Dr. Prince Opens Lab for Ailing Musical." *Variety*, 31 January 1990, p. 1.

___. "It's Taps for New Musicals After Only One Production." *Variety*, 1 August 1990, p. 2.

___. "New Musicals to Scale Down After 'Kiss' Ends on Sour Note; Second Production 'On Hold.' " *Variety,* 11 July 1990, p. 2.

___. "Times Spurns 'No Review' Policy of New Musicals." *Variety,* 30 May 1990, p. 61.

Jacobs, Bonnie. "A Little Night Music." *Boston After Dark,* 6 February 1973, p. 15. NYPL Clipping Folder.

Jacobs, Tom. Review of Roza. *Los Angeles Daily News,* 14 June 1987.

"Japan via Florence." *Women's Wear Daily,* 9 January 1976, p. 10. NYPL Clipping Folder.

Jewell, Derek. "Evita." (London) *Sunday Times,* 25 June 1978. NYPL Clipping Folder.

Johnson, Florence. "Flora, the Red Menace." *New Haven Register,* 6 April 1965. NYPL Clipping Folder.

Jowitt, Deborah. "Candide." *New York Times,* 23 November 1975, p. A12.

Kakutani, Michiko. "Why a $4 Million Musical Lasted Only Four Days." *New York Times,* 27 September 1982, p. C11.

Kalem, T. E. "Rue Tristesse." *Time,* 30 November 1981, p. 90.

___. "Salome's Revenge." *Time,* 10 December 1973. NYPL Critics' Reviews, Vol. 34, p. 164.

___. "String of Pearls." *Time,* 2 May 1977. NYPL Critics' Reviews, Vol. 38, p. 271.

___. "Theatre." *Time,* 12 April 1971, NYPL Clipping Folder.

___. "The Theatre." *Time,* 26 January 1976, p. 46.

___. "Valse Triste." *Time,* 12 March 1973, p. 86.

Kane, John. "Company: A New Landmark?" *Plays and Players* 9, no. 5 (February 1972): 25.

Kauffmann, Stanley. "Company." *New Republic,* 23 May 1970, p. 20.

___. " 'It's a Bird . . . It's a Plane . . . It's Superman,' It's a Musical and It's Here." *New York Times,* 30 March 1966.

NYPL Critics' Reviews, Vol. 27, p. 313.

Kaufman, Joanne. "Another Opening, But Not Just Another 'Show Boat.' " *Wall Street Journal,* 29 September 1994, p. A 10.

Kelly, Kevin, " 'Flora' Has the Stuff, But Needs Work." *Boston Globe,* 15 April 1965.

___. " 'Take Her, She's Mine' Opens at Shubert Theatre." *Boston Globe,* 6 December 1961. NYPL Clipping Folder.

___. "You're in Brilliant 'Company.' " *Boston Globe,* 25 March 1970. NYPL Clipping Folder.

Kent, Leticia. "On Broadway, the Spectacle's the Thing." *New York Times,* 12 March 1978, p. D1.

Kerr, Walter. "Cabaret." *New York Times,* 21 November 1966, p. 62.

___. "A Call on Kuprin." *New York Herald Tribune,* 26 May 1961. NYPL Clipping Folder.

___. " 'Company' Original and Uncompromising." *New York Times,* 3 May 1970. NYPL Clipping Folder.

___. " 'Evita,' A Musical Peron." *New York Times,* 26 September 1979. NYPL Critics' Reviews, Vol. 40, p. 149.

___. "A Family Affair." *New York Herald Tribune,* 29 January 1962. NYPL Clipping Folder.

___. "Fiddler on the Roof." *New York Herald Tribune,* 23 September 1964. NYPL Critics' Reviews, Vol. 25, p. 216.

___. "Fiorello!" *New York Herald Tribune,* 24 November 1959. NYPL Critics' Reviews, Vol. 20, p. 221.

___. "Friends, Romans, Vaudevillians." *New York Herald Tribune*, p. 1. NYPL Clipping Folder.

___. "A Funny Thing . . ." *New York Herald Tribune*, 9 May 1962. NYPL Clipping Folder.

___. "Kerr Reviews 'Flora, the Red Menace.' " *New York Herald Tribune*, 12 May 1965. NYPL Critics' Reviews, Vol. 26, p. 331.

___. "Kerr Reviews '. . . It's Superman.' " *New York Herald Tribune*, 30 March 1966. NYPL Critics' Reviews, Vol. 27, p. 310.

___. "A Libretto Has to Face the Music." *New York Times*, 13 December 1981, section 2, pp. D3, D6.

___. " 'Pacific Overtures' Is Neither East nor West." *New York Times*, 18 January 1976, section 2, p. 2.

___. "Poor Bitos." *New York Herald Tribune*, 16 November 1964. NYPL Critics' Reviews, Vol. 25, p. 148.

___. "A Self-Conscious Smirk on Superman's Face." *New York Herald Tribune*, 16 April 1966. NYPL Clipping Folder.

___. "She Loves Me." *New York Herald Tribune*, 24 April 1963. NYPL Clipping Folder.

___. "Superman." *New York Herald Tribune*, 17 April 1966, p. 32. NYPL Clipping Folder.

___. "Take Her, She's Mine." *New York Herald Tribune*, 22 December 1961. NYPL Critics' Reviews, Vol. 22, p. 149.

___. "Tenderloin." *New York Herald Tribune*, 18 October 1960. NYPL Critics' Reviews, Vol. 21, p. 206.

___. "Theatre." *New York Herald Tribune*, 14 May 1954. NYPL Critics' Reviews, Vol. 15, p. 324.

___. "Theatre." *New York Herald Tribune*, 15 May 1957. NYPL Critics' Reviews, Vol. 18, p. 270.

___. Walter Kerr Reviews "Baker Street." *New York Herald Tribune*, 17 February 1965. NYPL Critics' Reviews, Vol. 26, p. 377.

___. "West Side Story." *New York Herald Tribune*, 27 September 1957. NYPL Critics' Reviews, Vol. 18, p. 253.

___. "Yes, Yes, Alexis, No, No, 'Follies.' " *New York Times*, section 2, p. 1. NYPL Clipping Folder.

___. *New York Herald Tribune*, 6 May 1955. NYPL Clipping Folder.

"Kiss of the Spider Woman" Program, State University of New York, Purchase, NY Campus. May 1, 1990 June 24, 1990.

Kissel, Howard. "Curtain Calls." *New York Daily News*, 5 June 1988, p. 14.

___. "Evita." *Women's Wear Daily*, 26 September 1979. NYPL Critics' Reviews, Vol. 40, pp. 154–55.

___. "A Grand 'Opera.' " *New York Daily News*, 27 January 1988. NYPL Clipping Folder.

___. "Not Worthy of a Prince." *New York Daily News*, 2 October 1987. NYPL Clipping Folder.

___. "On the Twentieth Century." *Women's Wear Daily*, 21 February 1978. NYPL Critics' Reviews, Vol. 39, p. 379.

___. "Pacific Overtures." *Women's Wear Daily*, 12 January 1976, p. 28.

___. "Rottin' Teuton." *New York Daily News*, 23 October 1987. NYPL Clipping Folder.

___. "Side by Side by Prince." *Horizon*, October 1981, pp. 60–67.

___. "Theatre." *Women's Wear Daily*, 2 March 1979, p. 10.

Kisselgoff, Anna. "Broadway Dance: At Play with the Past." *New York Times*, 20 January 1995, p. C5.

Klein, Alvin. "She Loves Me." *New York Times,* 23 November 1980, Long Island section, p. 19

Klemesrud, Judy. "Prince Wrestles with a New Show." *New York Times,* 15 November 1981, p. D5.

Koenenn, Joseph C. "Hal Prince's Triple Threat." *New York Newsday,* 30 August 1987, p. II/3.

Kroll, Jack. "Backstage in Arcadia." *Newsweek,* 12 April 1971, p. 121.

___. "The Blood Runs Cold." *Newsweek,* 12 March 1979, pp. 101–104.

___. "A Bump for Every Grind." *Newsweek,* 29 April 1985, p. 65.

___. "Evita in Soft Focus." *Newsweek,* 8 October 1979. NYPL Critics' Reviews, Vol. 40, p. 152.

___. "Gotta Have Rodgers and Hart." *Newsweek,* 21 March 1983, p. 67.

___. " 'Show Boat'—It's Still Rolling Along." *Newsweek,* 10 October 1994, p. 77.

___. "The Sound of Music: Off- Off- Off-Broadway." *Newsweek,* 14 May 1990, p. 73.

___. "Voltaire in Brooklyn." *Newsweek,* 31 December 1973. NYPL Critics' Reviews, Vol. 34, p. 140.

Lahr, John. "On-Stage." *Village Voice,* 7 May 1970, p. 15.

___. Review of "Petrified Prince." *New Yorker,* 9 January 1995, p. 87.

"Landmark Symposium: Cabaret." *Dramatists Guild Quarterly* 19 (Summer 1982): 13–28.

"Landmark Symposium: Fiddler on the Roof." *Dramatists Guild Quarterly* 20 (Spring 1983): 10–29.

Laurents, Arthur. Quoted by Leslie Bennetts, "Here Comes the Musical 'La Cage.' " *New York Times,* 21 August 1983, section 2, p. 4.

Lawrence, Jerome, and Robert E. Lee. "A Call on Kuprin." NYPL Clipping Folder.

Lawson, Carol. "Broadway." *New York Times,* 7 November 1980, p. C2.

___. "Broadway." *New York Times,* 9 March 1984, p. C2.

Lee, Eugene. "Production Design." *Show Boat Souvenir Program,* 1994, p. 17.

Leeney, Robert J. "Musical for the Masses." *New Haven Journal-Courier,* 6 April 1965. NYPL Clipping Folder.

Little, Stuart W. "Flora, the Red Menace." *New York Herald Tribune,* 2 February 1965. NYPL Clipping Folder.

___. "Take Her, She's Mine." *New York Herald Tribune,* 31 October 1961. NYPL Clipping Folder.

___. "Theatre News." *New York Herald Tribune,* 16 August 1960. NYPL Clipping Folder.

___. "Theatre News." *New York Herald Tribune,* 10 March 1961. NYPL Clipping Folder.

___. "Theatre News: Russian-speaking Extras Join 'Kuprin' Rehearsals." *New York Herald Tribune,* 25 April 1961. NYPL Clipping Folder.

Livingston, Guy. "Shows Out of Town." *Variety,* 8 April 1970, p. 120.

Lockridge, Richard. "The Bandwagon." *New York Sun,* 4 June 1931. Collection of Newspaper Clippings of Dramatic Criticisms, 1930–1931, A-C. New York Public Library at Lincoln Center.

Loney, Glenn. "The Best of All Possible Shows." *After Dark,* March 1974, pp. 38–39.

___. "Prince of the Golden West." *Opera News,* October 1978, pp. 34–37.

Lyons, Donald. "Carver, Carmello Lead a Wrenching Musical Parade." *New York Post,* 18 December 1998, p. 58.

___. "Harold Prince Reinvents a '20's Classic." *Wall Street Journal,* 10 May 1994. NYPL Clipping Folder.

Maddocks, Melvin. "Take Her, She's Mine." *Christian Science Monitor,* 6 December 1961. NYPL Clipping Folder.

"Making a Business of Show Business." *Forbes,* 1 February 1972, pp. 20–26.

Maloney, Alta. " 'Flora, the Red Menace' at Colonial." *Boston Traveler,* 15 April 1965, p. 39.

Mann, Martin. "The Musicals of Frank Loesser." Ph.D. dissertation, City University of New York Graduate School, 1974.

Mardesich, Stephanie. " 'Evita' in London." *Footlights,* December 1978, pp. 27–30.

McClain, John. "Alas, Poor Holmes." *New York Journal-American,* 21 February 1965. NYPL Clipping Folder.

___. "Art Carney Dominates in an Ingratiating Play." *New York Journal-American,* 22 December 1961. NYPL Critics' Reviews, Vol. 22, p. 150.

___. "Brilliantly Performed." *New York Journal-American,* 16 November 1964. NYPL Critics' Reviews, Vol. 25, p. 147.

___. "Flora-Honest Musical." *New York Journal-American,* 16 May 1964. NYPL Critics' Reviews, Vol. 26, p. 329.

___. "Liza Minnelli, Big New Star." *New York Journal-American,* 16 May 1965. NYPL Clipping Folder.

___. "Music Magnificent in Overwhelming Hit." *New York Journal-American,* 27 September 1957. NYPL Critics' Reviews, Vol. 18, p. 254.

___. "New Girl in Town." *New York Journal-American,* 15 May 1957. NYPL Critics' Reviews, Vol. 18, p. 269.

___. "Superman." *New York Journal-American,* 30 March 1966. NYPL Critics' Reviews, Vol. 27, p. 311.

___. "Suspenseful Melodrama." *New York Journal-American,* 26 May 1961. NYPL Clipping Folder.

___. *New York Journal-American,* 15 May 1957. NYPL Clipping Folder.

Mockridge, Norton. "Baker Street." *New York World-Telegram and Sun.* NYPL Clipping Folder.

Morgenstern, Joseph. "Interview with Berman." *New York Herald Tribune,* 21 January 1962. NYPL Clipping Folder.

Morley, Sheridan. Review of "Kiss of the Spider Woman." *International Herald Tribune,* 28 October 1992.

Morrison, Hobe. " 'Candide' Still 310G in Red; Has Recouped 15G in 17 Months." *Variety,* 3 September 1975, p. 95.

___. "A Funny Thing." *Variety,* 10 May 1962. NYPL Clipping Folder.

___. "Pacific Overtures." *Variety,* 14 January 1976, p. 84.

___. "She Loves Me." *Variety,* 1 May 1963, p. 86. NYPL Clipping Folder.

___. *Variety,* 22 May 1957, p. 56. NYPL Clipping Folder.

___. *Variety.* NYPL Clipping Folder.

Morse, T. K. "Reds at the Colonial." *Boston Patriot Ledger,* 15 April 1965, p. 32.

Murdoch, Blake. "A Call on Kuprin." *Variety,* 10 May 1961. NYPL Clipping Folder.

Murdock, Henry T. "De Luxe Melodrama Opens." *Philadelphia Inquirer,* 9 May 1961. NYPL Clipping Folder.

___. "She Loves Me." *Philadelphia Inquirer,* 27 March 1963. NYPL Clipping Folder.

Murray, Karen. Review of "Kiss of the Spider Woman." *Variety,* 22 June 1992.

"My Fair Irene." *Saturday Review,* 6 March 1965, p. 22. NYPL Clipping Folder.

Nadel, Norman. "Cabaret." *New York World Journal Tribune,* 21 November 1966. NYPL Clipping Folder.

___. " 'Family Affair' at Billy Rose." *New York World-Telegram*, 29 January 1962. NYPL Clipping Folder.

___. " 'Fiddler on Roof' Is Humorous, Tender Musical." *New York World-Telegram*, 23 September 1964. NYPL Critics' Reviews, Vol. 25, p. 214.

___. "Irregulars Help Solve 'Baker Street' Problems." *New York World-Telegram and Sun*, 17 February 1965. NYPL Critics' Reviews, Vol. 26, p. 374.

___. "A Happy Moment on Broadway." *New York World-Telegram and Sun*, 26 May 1965, p. 26.

___. " 'She Loves Me' Opens at O'Neill Theater." *New York World-Telegram and Sun*, 24 April 1963. NYPL Clipping Folder.

___. "The Theater." *New York World-Telegram and Sun*, 30 March 1966. NYPL Critics' Reviews, Vol. 27, p. 312.

Nelson, Don. "A Showcase Attuned to New Musicals." *New York Daily News*, 31 January 1990, p. 31.

___. Review of "Kiss of the Spider Woman." *New York Daily News*, 1 June 1990.

___. Review of "Kiss of the Spider Woman." *New York Daily News*, 2 May, 1993, p. 2.

Nelson, Margery. "Family Affair." *Backstage*. NYPL Clipping Folder.

"The New York Harold." Interview with Harold Prince. *Theatre One*. International Theatre Institute of the U.S. New York: DBS Publications, 1969.

New York Times, 24 November 1968. NYPL Clipping Folder.

New York Times, 14 April 1985, p. 14.

Newsweek, 26 July 1971, p. 68. NYPL Clipping Folder.

Nightingale, Benedict. "Mooney Tunes." *New Statesman*, 14 May 1976, p. 657.

Nordell, Roderick. "Prince's New 'Company' and Its Concept." *Christian Science Monitor*, 26 March 1970. NYPL Clipping Folder.

Norton, Elliot. " 'Girl' Leaves Town Pruned, Polished." *Boston Record*, 2 May 1957. NYPL Clipping Folder.

___. "Some Fun, Trouble, Too, in 'Baker Street' Show." *Boston Record American*, 29 December 1964. NYPL Clipping Folder.

Novick, Julius. "Sweeney Todd." *Village Voice*, 12 March 1979, p. 85.

O'Connor, Jim. *New York Journal-American*, 12 December 1961. Quoted by Prince, *Contradictions*, p. 56.

O'Connor, John J. "Company." *Wall Street Journal*, 28 April 1970, p. 21.

O'Haire, Patricia. "Cullum: He Puts on a Good Act." *New York Daily News*, 24 February 1978, p. 5.

Oliver, Edith. "Escape Artists." *New Yorker*, 24 May 1993. NYPL Clipping Folder.

___. "The Theatre: 'Dubliners.' " *New Yorker*, 24 February 1992, p. 82.

"On Collaboration between Authors and Directors," *Dramatists Guild Quarterly* 16, no. 2 (Summer 1979): 14–34.

"On Craft." *New York Times*. NYPL Clipping Folder.

"The Once and Future Follies." *Time*, 3 May 1971, pp. 71–72.

Oppenheimer, George. "Cabaret." *Newsday*, 21 November 1966. NYPL Clipping Folder.

___. "Candide." *Newsday*. NYPL Clipping Folder.

___. " 'Follies,' A Cornucopia." *Newsday*, 5 April 1971, p. 32.

___. "I Come to Praise." *Newsday*, 16 May 1962. NYPL Clipping Folder.

___. "It's 'Superman' and He's in a Broadway Musical." *Newsday*, 31 March 1966. NYPL Clipping Folder.

____. "On Stage." *Newsday,* 1 May 1963. NYPL Clipping Folder.

____. "Pacific Overtures." *Newsday,* 18 January 1976. NYPL Clipping Folder.

O'Steen, Kathy. Review of Roza. *Daily Variety,* 14 June 1987.

O'Toole, Fintan. "A Parade of Humanity." *New York Daily News,* 18 December 1998, p. 75.

" 'Overtures' Opens Door for Orientals." *New York Times,* 3 March 1976, p. 24. NYPL Clipping Folder.

"Pacific Overtures." *Theatre Crafts* (January–February 1976): 58. NYPL Clipping Folder.

Palmer, Robert. "Writing Musicals Attuned to Rock Era." *New York Times,* 10 February 1982, p. C21.

Peck, Seymour. "Anna Christie Sings." NYPL Clipping Folder.

Popkin, Henry. "The Theatre." *Wall Street Journal,* 7 April 1971. NYPL Clipping Folder.

Piro, Joseph M. "Kabuki Meets Broadway: Crafting the Oriental Musical Pacific Overtures." M. A. Thesis, Queens College (City University of New York), 1978.

"Poor Bitos." *Variety,* 13 February 1974, p. 90. NYPL Clipping Folder.

Prideaux, Tom. "Hiring Hamlet to Promote Holmes." *Life,* 2 April 1965, p. 138.

"Prince Gets 10% of 'Merrily' Net; Co-Producing with Marble Arch." *Variety,* 15 April 1981, p. 85.

Prince, Harold. "Director's Notes." *Playbill,* 1994, p. 35.

____. "Director's Notes." *Show Boat Souvenir Program,* 1994. p. 8.

____. Letter to Oliver Smith, 29 July 1964.

____. Letter to Jerome Coopersmith, 14 August 1964.

____. Letter to Jerome Coopersmith, 21 August 1964.

____. Letter to Jerome Coopersmith, 2 September 1964.

____. "Places I Love." Interview, *Travel and Leisure,* March 1982, p. 202.

____. "Preferring the Truth, He Always Told It." *New York Times,* 12 February 1995, p. H8.

____. "Prince on 'Company.' " *New York Sunday News,* 20 June 1976.

____. Statement displayed at entrance to Harold Prince exhibit, Lincoln Center Library of the Performing Arts, April 1989.

Reed, Rex. " 'Sweeney' Soars." *New York Sunday News,* 4 March 1979, p. L7.

"Review of Cast Album of 'On the 20th Century.' " *Variety,* 17 May 1978, p. 446.

Rich, Alan. "Candide." *New York Magazine,* 21 October 1974, p. 100. NYPL Clipping Folder.

____. "How the East Was Won." *New York Magazine,* 26 January 1976, p. 54.

____. "Side by Side." *New York Magazine,* 13 September 1976, p. 62. NYPL Clipping Folder.

Rich, Frank. " 'Cabaret' and Joel Grey Return." *New York Times,* 23 October 1987. NYPL Clipping Folder.

____. "A Doll's Life." *New York Times,* 24 September 1982. NYPL Clipping Folder.

____. " 'Diamonds,' A Revue about Baseball." *New York Times,* 17 December 1984, p. C12.

____. "Dreamgirls." *New York Times,* 21 December 1981, p. C11.

____. "Evoking the Youth of Sean O'Casey in Dublin." *New York Times,* 17 February 1992, pp. C13, C16.

____. " 'Grind' from Harold Prince." *New York Times,* 17 April 1985, p. C20.

____. "In a Prison Cell, 2 Men and a Movie Musical." *New York Times,* 1 June 1990, p. Bl, B2.

____. "London's 'Starlight Express.' " *New York Times,* 25 July 1984, p. C17.

___. "New Kopit Play." *New York Times,* 7 May 1984, p. C15.

___. "A New Sondheim, 'Merrily We Roll Along.' " *New York Times,* 17 November 1981, p. C9.

___. "Phantom of the Opera." *New York Times,* 27 January 1988, p. C19.

___. "Play Memory." *New York Times,* 27 April 1984, p. C3.

___. Review of "Kiss of the Spider Woman." *New York Times,* 4 May 1993. NYPL Clipping Folder.

___. "The Seminal American Musical is Rebuilt from the Ground Up." *New York Times,* 20 October 1993, p. C15.

___. "Should We Expect Magic to Happen When a Theatre's Lights Darken?" *New York Times,* 10 December 1981, p. C21.

___. "What Ails Today's Musicals?" *New York Times,* 14 November 1982, section 2, pp. 1, 23, 25.

___. " 'Zorba' and Quinn." *New York Times,* 17 October 1983, p. C15.

Richards, David. "Classic Musical with a Change in Focus." *New York Times,* 3 October 1994. NYPL Clipping Folder.

Rockwell, John. "Will 'Candide' Thrive in the Opera House?" *New York Times,* 10 October 1982, section 2, p. H19.

Ross, Don. "O'Neill Set to Music in Abbott's 'New Girl.' " *New York Herald Tribune,* 12 May 1957, section 4, p. 1.

R. S. "Pacific Overtures." *Cue,* 10 January 1976, p. 15. NYPL Clipping Folder.

Rothstein, Mervyn. "New Musicals Project Closes Down." *New York Times,* 31 July 1990, p. C11.

___. "Off Broadway (Way, Way Off), A Tuneful 'Spider Woman' Is On." *New York Times,* 26 April 1990, p. C17.

Saal, Hubert. "How to Play at Hal Prince." *Newsweek,* 26 July 1971, pp. 68–70.

Sandla, Robert. "On Her Toes: Gillian Lynne." *TheaterWeek,* 1–7 February 1988, p. 32.

"Say, Darling, Look at Hal Prince Now." *New York Times,* 24 November 1968, section 2, p. D13.

Schier, Ernest. "She Loves Me." *Philadelphia Evening Bulletin,* 27 March 1963, p. 30. NYPL Clipping Folder.

Schmidt, Sandra. "She Loves Me." *Village Voice,* 2 May 1963, p. 12. NYPL Clipping Folder.

Seff, Richard. "This 'Kiss' Could Be the Start of Something Big." *TheaterWeek,* 21 May 1990, pp. 17–20.

Sheppard, Eugenia "Flossie's Follies." *New York Post,* 30 March 1971, p. 39.

Shevelove, Burt. "All About 'A Funny Thing Happened on the Way to the Forum.' " *Performing Arts: The Music Center Monthly* 5, no. 10 (October 1971): 31.

Shewey, Don. "Arthur Kopit: A Life on Broadway." *New York Times,* 29 April 1983, magazine section, pp. 88, 105.

Shulman, Milton. "At the Theatre: An Attack Completely Out of Range." NYPL Clipping Folder.

"Side by Side." *New York Times,* 19 May 1977, p. C2. NYPL Clipping Folder.

"Side by Side by Sondheim." *New York Post,* 23 April 1977, p. 17. NYPL Clipping Folder.

Siegel, Joel. Review of *Roza.* WABC-TV News, Channel 7, New York, 1 October 1987.

Simon, John. "The Door Story." *New York Magazine,* 4 October 1982, pp. 91–92.

___. "Follies." *New York Magazine,* 19 April 1971, p. 41.

___. "A Little Knife Music." *New York Magazine,* 19 March 1979, p. 74.

___. "Save Me from the Waltz." *New York Magazine,* 30 November 1981, p. 87.

___. "Theatre." *Theatre Arts,* July 1962, pp. 66–67.

___. "Trial and Eros, Parade is a Somber Show That Works." *New York Magazine,* 4 January 1999. NYPL Clipping Folder.

___. "What Price Majesty?" *New York Magazine,* 2 February 1988.

___. "When Greek Meets Shriek." *New York Magazine,* 9 December 1968. NYPL Clipping Folder.

Sloan, Ronna Elaine. "Bob Fosse: An Analytic-Critical Study." Ph.D. dissertation, City University of New York, Graduate School, 1983.

Snyder, F. "Shows Out of Town (Boston)." *Variety,* 18 January 1978, p. 94.

Sokolsky, Bob. "Ted Stuck with Bum Script." *Philadelphia Evening Bulletin,* 12 October 1977, p. 25.

Sondheim, Stephen. "The Echo Song." Copyright 1971 by Stephen Sondheim. Burthen Music Co.

___. "The Future of American Musical Comedy." *Stereo Review,* July 1971, p. 74.

___. Introduction to *Getting to Know Him: Biography of Oscar Hammerstein II,* by Hugh Fordin. New York: Random House, 1977.

___. "The Musical Theatre: A Talk by Stephen Sondheim." *Dramatists Guild Quarterly* 15, no. 3 (Autumn 1978): 13–21.

___. "Theatre Lyrics." In *Playwrights, Lyricists, Composers on Theatre,* pp. 61–102 . Edited by Otis L. Guernsey, Jr. New York: Dodd, Mead, 1964.

"Sondheim Takes a Stab at Grand Guignol." *New York Times,* 25 February 1979, p. D5.

Stearns, David Patrick. "Parade Pointedly in Step with Today." *USA Today,* 18 December 1998, p. 4E.

"Stephen Sondheim." *Time,* 3 May 1971, p. 74. NYPL Clipping Folder.

Sterritt, David. " 'Company': Amusing, Inventive, Hummable." *Boston After Dark,* 1 April 1970, p. 4.

Sullivan, Dan. " 'A Doll's Life': In This Case, It's Not All Bliss." *Los Angeles Times,* 17 June 1982, part IV, pp. 1, 9.

___. " 'Doll's Life" Changes for the Better." *Los Angeles Times,* 18 July 1982, pp. 46, 51.

"Sweeney Todd." *Variety,* 19 March 1980, p. 1.

"A Swim in the Sea." *Variety,* 30 July 1958. NYPL Clipping Folder.

"A Swim in the Sea." *Variety,* 2 October 1958. NYPL Clipping Folder.

"Take Her, She's Mine." *Variety,* 6 December 1962. NYPL Clipping Folder.

Takiff, Jonathan. " 'Best Friends' Needs Help." *Philadelphia Daily News,* 12 October 1977, p. 28.

Talcove, Rick. " 'A Doll's Life' Makes a Dead Musical." *Los Angeles Daily News,* 17 June 1982, section V, pp. 1, 4.

Tallmer, Jerry. " 'Candide' Rejiggered." *New York Post,* 21 December 1973. NYPL Critics' Reviews, Vol. 34, p. 138.

___. "Comedy Tonight." *Village Voice,* 17 May 1962. NYPL Clipping Folder.

___. "Is There a Parade in Town?" *Playbill* 98, no. 11 (November 1998), p. 12.

Taubman, Howard. "A Call on Kuprin." *New York Times,* 26 May 1961. NYPL Clipping Folder.

___. " 'Call on Kuprin' Aims High, Hits Target." *New York Times,* 26 May 1961. NYPL Clipping Folder.

___. "Discipline of Taste.' *New York Times,* 5 May 1963. NYPL Clipping Folder.

___. "Flora, the Red Menace." *New York Times,* 12 May 1965. NYPL Critics' Reviews, Vol. 26, p. 330.

___. "Jean Anouilh's 'Poor Bitos' Opens." *New York Times,* 16 November 1964. NYPL Critics' Reviews, Vol. 25, p. 148.

___. "Mostel as Tevye." *New York Times,* 23 September 1964. NYPL Critics' Reviews, Vol. 25, p. 216.

___. "People in Russia." *New York Times.* NYPL Clipping Folder.

___. "Sherlock Holmes to Music." *New York Times,* 17 February 1965. NYPL Critics' Reviews, Vol. 26, p. 376.

___. "Theatre: 'Family Affair.' " *New York Times,* 29 January 1962. NYPL Clipping Folder.

___. "Theatre: 'A Funny Thing Happened...' " *New York Times,* 9 May 1962. NYPL Clipping Folder.

___. "Theatre: 'She Loves Me,' A Musical." *New York Times,* 24 April 1963. NYPL Clipping Folder.

___. "The Theatre: Virtue vs. Vice to Music." *New York Times,* 18 October 1960. NYPL Critics' Reviews, Vol. 21, p. 205.

___. "Theatre: Young in Heart." *New York Times,* 22 December 1961. NYPL Critics' Reviews, Vol. 22, p. 150.

"Tenderloin." *New York Daily News,* 1 September 1960. NYPL Clipping Folder.

"Tenderloin." *Variety,* 20 April 1960. NYPL Clipping Folder.

"The Theatre." *Cue,* 9 April 1966. NYPL Clipping Folder.

"They Might Be Giants, A." NYPL Clipping Folder.

"They Might Be Giants, B." NYPL Clipping Folder.

"They Might Be Giants, C." NYPL Clipping Folder.

"They Might Be Giants, England." NYPL Clipping Folder.

Today Show, with Mike Jensen. 18 January 1985. WNBC-TV.

"Twentieth Century." *New York Post,* 25 April 1978, p. 10.

Uhry, Alfred. "Interview." *Lincoln Center Theatre Review* (Fall 1998), p. 21.

Variety, 13 February 1974, p. 90. NYPL Clipping Folder.

Wahls, Robert. "Cheers for the Designer!" *New York Sunday News,* 25 January 1976. NYPL Clipping Folder.

___. "Footlights." *New York Sunday News,* 25 September 1977, p. L9.

Wallach, Allan. "Harold Prince." *Newsday,* 3 February 1980, pp. 18, 25. NYPL Clipping Folder.

Walsh, Michael. "Just Keeps Rollin' Along." *Time,* 10 October 1994, p. 80.

Waterhouse, Robert. "Hal Prince and Boris Aronson Talk to Robert Waterhouse." *Plays and Players* 19, no. 6 (March 1972): 16.

Waters, J. "Shows Out of Town." *Variety,* 17 September 1956. NYPL Clipping Folder.

Watt, Douglas. "The Best of Sondheim." *New York Daily News,* 19 April 1977. NYPL Critics' Reviews, Vol. 38, p. 27E

___. " 'Candide' Is Revived in Brooklyn." *New York Daily News,* 21 December 1973. NYPL Critics' Reviews, Vol. 34, p. 138.

___. "A Doll's Lifelessness." *New York Daily News,* 24 September 1982, pp. 3–4.

___. "A Grinding Halt." *New York Daily News,* 17 April 1985, p. 47.

___. "Holy Cow! A Baseball Show That Scores." *New York Daily News,* 17 December 984, p. 45.

___. " 'A Little Night Music': Operetta That's Exquisite but Fragile." *New York Daily News,* 26 February 1973. NYPL Critics' Reviews, Vol. 34, p. 348.

___. " 'Merrily' Hits Every Bump on Road." *New York Daily News,* 17 November 1981, pp. 45, 47.

___. "Musical Events." *New York Daily News,* 11 July 1970, p. 94.

___. "Musical Events." *New Yorker,* 18 September 1978, p. 148.

___. "The Musical 'Superman' Shows Early Hardening of Arteries." *New York Daily News,* 30 March 1966. NYPL Critics' Reviews, Vol. 27, p. 312.

___. "A New B'way. 'Candide.' " *New York Daily News,* 12 March 1974. NYPL Critics' Reviews, Vol. 35, p. 339.

___. " 'Pacific Overtures' Is a Pretty Bore." *New York Daily News,* 12 January 1976, p. 43.

___. "Sondheim-Prince Team Scores for Second Time." *New York Daily News,* 11 April 1971, p. S3.

___. "Twentieth Century Limited." *New York Daily News,* 20 February 1978. NYPL Critics' Reviews, Vol. 39, p. 376.

Watts, Richard, Jr. "The Brilliance of Zero Mostel." *New York Post,* 23 September 1964. NYPL Critics' Reviews, Vol. 25, p. 215.

___. "Comedy of the College Generation." *New York Post,* 22 December 1961. NYPL Critics' Reviews, Vol. 22, p. 148.

___. "An Effective Cold War Melodrama." *New York Post,* 26 May 1961. NYPL Clipping Folder.

___. "Happy Evening in Sweden." *New York Post,* 26 February 1973. NYPL Critics' Reviews, Vol. 34, p. 348.

___. "The Innocence of Sally Bowles." *New York Post,* 21 November 1966, p. 54.

___. "Lesson from the Married Set." *New York Post,* 27 April 1970, p. 45.

___. "Musical Comedy about a Wedding." *New York Post,* 29 January 1962. NYPL Clipping Folder.

___. "The Musical Debut of 'Zorba.' " *New York Post,* 18 November 1968. NYPL Critics' Reviews, Vol. 29, p. 176.

___. "Refreshing New Musical Comedy." *New York Post,* 24 April 1963, p. 66.

___. "Review." *New York Post,* 14 May 1954. NYPL Critics' Reviews, Vol. 15, p. 326.

___. "Riotous Life of the Old Romans." *New York Post,* 9 May 1962, p. 76.

___. "A Salute to the Little Flower." *New York Post,* 24 November 1959. NYPL Critics' Reviews, Vol. 20, p. 221.

___. "Sherlock Holmes' Musical Career." *New York Post,* 17 February 1965. NYPL Critics' Reviews, Vol. 26, p. 376.

___. "There's No Denying It's Superman." *New York Post,* 30 March 1966. NYPL Critics' Reviews, Vol. 27, p. 312.

___. "Through the Skies with Superman." *New York Post,* 17 April 1966, p. 6.

___. "Two on the Aisle: Another Triumph for Gwen Verdon." *New York Post,* 15 May 1957, p. 268.

___. "Two on the Aisle: Romeo and Juliet in a Gang War." *New York Post,* 27 September 1957. NYPL Critics' Reviews, Vol. 18, p. 252.

___. "When Everything Goes Right." *New York Post,* 5 April 1971. NYPL Critics' Reviews, Vol. 32, p. 309.

___. "The World of Dr. Pangloss." *New York Post,* 13 March 1974. NYPL Critics' Reviews, Vol. 35, p. 337.

Weber, Bruce. Review of "Show Boat." *New York Times,* 1 November 1994, p. C13.

Weidman, Jerome. "Joining the Team." *Theatre Arts,* December 1959, p. 12.

Wilson, Ed. "Frustration on Two Stages." *Brooklyn Eagle,* 30 September 1960. NYPL Clipping Folder.

Wilson, Edwin. "Alternating Fun and Blood Lust." *Wall Street Journal,* 10 December 1973. NYPL Critics' Reviews, Vol. 34, p. 164.

___. "An American Attempt at Kabuki Style." *Wall Street Journal,* 13 January 1976. NYPL Clipping Folder.

___. "Dazzling Production of a Muddled Story." *Wall Street Journal,* 26 September 1979. NYPL Critics' Reviews, Vol. 40, p. 150.

___. "A Lavish Musical Loses Track of Itself." *Wall Street Journal,* 22 February 1973. NYPL Critics' Reviews, Vol. 39, p. 378.

___. "A Musical Show with Elegance." *Wall Street Journal,* 27 February 1973. NYPL Critics' Reviews, Vol. 34, p. 350.

___. Review of "Kiss of the Spider Woman." *Wall Street Journal,* 5 May 1993, p. A 20.

___. "Sondheim Writes a Musical to Talk About." *Wall Street Journal,* 6 March 1979, p. 21.

___. "A Workable Trio on Broadway." *Wall Street Journal,* 19 April 1977. NYPL Critics' Reviews, Vol. 38, p. 272.

Wilson, John S. "A Fired-Up 'Zorba.' " *New York Times,* 15 December 1968, p. 12H.

___. "Liza Minnelli and 'Flora.' " *New York Times,* 25 May 1965. NYPL Clipping Folder.

Wilson, Sandy. "Letter to Editor." *Dramatists Guild Quarterly* 19 (Winter 1983): 47.

Winer, Linda. " 'Merrily' Comes Tardily." *New York Daily News,* 13 November 1981, p. 3.

___. "Stephen Sondheim." *USA Today,* 29 October 1984, p. 30.

Witchell, Alex. "New Musicals Project Puts 2nd Production on Hold." *New York Times,* 10 July 1990, p. C13.

Zolotow, Sam. "Superman Toils for Musical Role." *New York Times,* 17 November 1965. NYPL Clipping Folder.

Books

Abbott, George. *Mister Abbott.* New York: Random House, 1963.

Altman, Richard, with Mervyn Kaufman. *The Making of a Musical: "Fiddler on the Roof."* New York: Crown Publishers, 1971.

Atkinson, Brooks. *Broadway.* New York: Macmillan, 1970.

Bordman, Gerald. *American Musical Theatre, A Chronicle.* New York: Oxford University Press, 1978.

___. *American Operetta; From "H. M. S. Pinafore" to "Sweeney Todd."* New York: Oxford University Press, 1981.

Drabinsky, Garth, with Marq de Villiers. *Closer to the Sun.* Toronto, Ontario: McClelland & Stewart, Inc., 1995.

Engel, Lehman. *The American Musical Theatre.* A CBS Legacy Collection Book. New York: Macmillan, 1967.

___. *The Critics.* New York: Macmillan, 1976.

___. *This Bright Day: An Autobiography.* New York: Macmillan, 1974.

___. *Words with Music: The Broadway Musical Libretto.* New York: Schirmer Books, 1972.

Ewen, David. *New Complete Book of the American Musical Theatre.* New York: Holt, Rinehart & Winston, 1958.

Fordin, Hugh. *Getting to Know Him: Biography of Oscar Hammerstein II.* Introduction by Stephen Sondheim. New York: Random House, 1977.

Frankel, Tobia. *The Russian Artist.* New York: Macmillan, 1972.

Gerould, Daniel. *Melodrama.* New York: New York Literary Forum, 1980.

Goldman, William. *The Season, A Candid Look at Broadway.* New York: Harcourt, Brace and World, 1969.

Gottfried, Martin. *Broadway Musicals.* New York: Harry N. Abrams, 1979.

Green, Stanley. *Encyclopedia of the Musical Theatre.* New York: Dodd, Mead, 1976.

___. *Ring Bells! Sing Songs!: Broadway Musicals of the 1930's.* New York: Galahad Books, 1971.

___. *The Rodgers and Hammerstein Story.* New York: J. Day Co., 1963; reprinted, New York: DaCapo Paperback, 1980.

___. *The World of Musical Comedy.* New York: A. S. Barnes and Co., 1968.

Guernsey, Otis L., Jr., ed. *Playwrights, Lyricists, Composers on Theatre.* New York: Dodd, Mead, 1964.

Jackson, Arthur. *The Best Musicals from "Show Boat" to "Sweeney Todd."* New York: Crown Publishers, 1977.

Kanin, Garson. *Boris Aronson: From His Theatre Work.* Brochure from exhibition, 31 March–15 August 1981. New York: New York Public Library at Lincoln Center, 1981.

Kislan, Richard. *The Musical: A Look at the American Musical Theatre.* Englewood Cliffs N.J.: Prentice Hall, 1980.

Kreuger, Miles. *"Show Boat'. The Story of a Classic American Musical.* New York: Oxford University Press, 1977.

Laufe, Abe. *Broadway's Greatest Musicals.* New York: Funk & Wagnalls, 1969.

McKnight, Gerald. *Andrew Lloyd Webber: A Biography.* London: Granada, 1984.

Mordden, Ethan. *Better Foot Forward, the History of American Musical Theatre.* New York: Grossman Publishers, 1976.

___. *Broadway Babies: The People Who Made the American Musical.* New York: Oxford University Press, 1983.

Mostel, Kate, and Madeline Gilford. *170 Years of Show Business (with Jack Gilford and Zero Mostel).* New York: Random House, 1978.

Perry, George. *The Complete Phantom of the Opera.* New York: Henry Holt & Co., 1987.

Prince, Harold. *Contradictions: Notes on Twenty-Six Years in the Theatre.* New York: Dodd, Mead, 1974.

Rich, Frank, with Lisa Aronson. *The Theatre Art of Boris Aronson.* New York: Alfred A. Knopf, 1987.

Richards, Stanley, ed. *Great Musicals of the American Theatre.* Radnor, Pa.: Chilton Book Co., 1976.

___, ed. *Ten Great Musicals of the American Theatre.* Radnor, Pa.: Chilton Book Co., 1973.

Simon, John. *Uneasy Stages: A Chronicle of the New York Theatre, 1963–1973.* New York: Random House, 1973.

Smith, Cecil, and Glenn Litton. *Musical Comedy in America.* New York: Theatre Arts Books, 1981.

Zadan, Craig. *Sondheim & Co.* New York: Da Capo, 1974.

___. *Sondheim & Co.,* 2nd ed. New York: Harper & Row, 1986.

Interviews

(Note: All interviews conducted by the author in New York City and London.)

Abbott, George. Producer, Director, Librettist. 4 March 1983.

Adams, Lee. Lyricist. 8 March 1984.

Adler, Richard. Lyricist. 30 June 1983.

Aronson, Lisa (Mrs. Boris Aronson). Set Design Assistant. 6 June 1984.

Billington, Michael. Critic for *The Guardian* (England), 19 March 1988.

Birch, Patricia. Choreographer. 15 June 1982.

Boyajian, Aram. Film Editor, Film Producer. 30 May 1983.

Colton, Chevi. Actress. 22 August 1983.

Coopersmith, Jerome. Librettist. 24 February 1984.

Crawford, Michael. Actor. 5 June 1988.

Ebb, Fred. Lyricist. 1 February 1982; 14 October 1991.

Gordon, Mel. Professor of Theatre, New York University. 9 June 1983.

Gunton, Bob. Actor. 6 June 1988.

Haines, Howard. General Manager and Associate Producer to Harold Prince. 10 January 1982.

Harnick, Sheldon. Lyricist. 4 February 1982.

Kaye, Judy. Actress. 23 June 1988.

Klemperer, Werner. Actor. 7 July 1988.

Kucherawy, Dennis. Former Vice President of Livent, Inc. 14 December 1995.

Masteroff, Joe. Librettist. 14 June 1982.

McKenzie, Julia. Actress, Singer. 10 October 1983.

McMartin, John. Actor. 10 June 1982; 20 October 1995 (telephone interview).

Mitchell, Ruth. Associate Producer to Harold Prince. 7 March 1983.

Moore, Charlotte. Actress. 10 June 1982.

Prince, Harold. Producer, Director. 14 March 1983 (interview); 20 January 1985 (photo session); 8 June 1988; August 1988; 10 September 1991; May 1995; 7 June 1999; 23 March 2000.

Price, Lonny. Actor. 18 February 1982.

Rivera, Chita. Actress. [Faxed] 1 October 1995.

Sondheim, Stephen. Composer. Lyricist. 20 July 1984; June 1988; 31 August 1988.

Theodore, Lee Becker. Choreographer. 23 February 1984.

Urmston, Kenneth W. Assistant Stage Manager and Dance Captain. 26 May 1982.

Verdon, Gwen. Actress, Singer, Dancer. 24 May 1983.

Weidman, John. Librettist. 16 April 1982.

Wheeler, Hugh. Librettist. 24 January 1982.

Wolf, David. Playwright. 15 July 1988.

Record Liner Notes

Cabaret. Record liner notes by Charles Burr. Columbia KOS 3040.

Candide. Record liner notes by William Evans. Columbia S2X 32923.

Company. Record liner notes by Charles Burr. Columbia OS-3550.

Damn Yankees. RCA Victor LOC-1021.

A Doll's Life. Original Cast Records, 1982, OC 8241.

Evita. MCA Records 2-11007.

Fiddler on the Roof. RCA Victor LSO-1093.

Fiorello! Record liner notes by Miles Kreuger. Capitol WAO 1321.

Flora, the Red Menace. Record liner notes by Mort Goode. RCA Red Seal CBLl-2760.

Follies. Capitol SO-761.

A Little Night Music. Record liner notes by William Evans. Columbia JS 32265.

Merrily We Roll Along. Record liner notes by Robert Kimball. Composer's note by Stephen Sondheim. RCA Red Seal CBLl-4197.

Pacific Overtures. Record liner notes by William Evans. RCA Red Seal ARL 1-1367.

The Pajama Game. Record liner notes by Mort Goode. Columbia S 32606.

She Loves Me. Record liner notes by James T. Maher. MGM E 41180C-2.

Sweeney Todd. Record liner notes by Robert Kimball. RCA Red Seal CBL 2-3397.

West Side Story. Record liner notes by George Dale. Columbia OL 5230.

Zorba. Record liner notes by Stanley Green. Capitol SO-118.

Videotapes

(Note: Taped for the Theatre on Film and Tape Project of the Lincoln Center Library, unless otherwise noted.)

"Beverly Sills Interviews Harold Prince." 21 November 1979. PBS, Channel 13, New York.

"Brendan Gill Interviews Harold Prince and Stephen Sondheim." 2 June 1975.

Company. Complete show.

The Dick Cavett Show, with Harold Prince. 19 February 1980; 20 February 1980. PBS, Channel 13, New York.

"Garson Kanin Interviews Boris Aronson." 20 March 1975.

"Harold Prince: From Follies to Phantom." Interview with Harold Prince. 26 June 1988. Arts & Entertainment Cable TV Network.

"Milan Stitt Interviews Harold Prince and Stephen Sondheim." 1975. Writers Weekly.

Pacific Overtures. Complete show.

The South Bank Show, London Weekend, with Harold Prince. 23 lune 1978.

Sweeney Todd. Complete show.

INDEX